My Thoughts

Charles-Louis de Secondat,
Baron of La Brède and of Montesquieu

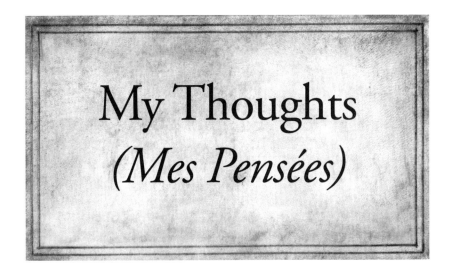

My Thoughts
(Mes Pensées)

Charles-Louis de Secondat, Baron of La Brède and of

MONTESQUIEU

TRANSLATED, EDITED, AND WITH
AN INTRODUCTION BY

Henry C. Clark

LIBERTY FUND

INDIANAPOLIS

This book is published by Liberty Fund, Inc., a foundation established to encourage study of the ideal of a society of free and responsible individuals.

The cuneiform inscription that serves as our logo and as the design motif for our endpapers is the earliest-known written appearance of the word "freedom" (*amagi*), or "liberty." It is taken from a clay document written about 2300 B.C. in the Sumerian city-state of Lagash.

Library of Congress Cataloging-in-Publication Data

Montesquieu, Charles de Secondat, baron de, 1689–1755.
    [Mes pensées. English]
My thoughts / Charles-Louis de Secondat, Baron of la Brède and of Montesquieu; translated, edited and with an introduction by Henry C. Clark.
        p.   cm.
Includes bibliographical references (p.) and index.
ISBN 978-0-86597-824-9 (hardcover: alk. paper)
—ISBN 978-0-86597-825-6 (pbk.:
alk. paper)
    1. Montesquieu, Charles de Secondat, baron de, 1689–1755—Notebooks, sketchbooks, etc.   I. Clark, Henry C.   II. Title.
PQ2011.A2C58 2012
848'.509—dc23   2012016646

Liberty Fund, Inc.
8335 Allison Pointe Trail, Suite 300
Indianapolis, Indiana 46250-1684

Contents

Introduction

CHARLES-LOUIS DE SECONDAT, Baron of La Brède and of Montesquieu (1689–1755), was born into a noble family in southwestern France. After an early education at home and with the village schoolmaster, he was sent away to Juilly, an Oratorian school in Meaux, just outside of Paris, at the age of eleven. Returning to Bordeaux for legal studies, he seems again to have been in Paris for four years, from 1709 until 1713, to gain legal experience. In 1713, at the death of his father, he went back to Bordeaux and in 1715 married the well-to-do Huguenot Jeanne de Lartigue, with whom he would have a son, Jean-Baptiste (1716), and two daughters, Marie-Catherine (1717) and Marie-Josèphe-Denise (1727). When his uncle (also named Jean-Baptiste) died in 1716, Montesquieu inherited most of his fortune, including his office as president in the Parlement of Bordeaux, a magistracy possessing both judicial and administrative authority.

At about the same time (April 1716), he became a member of the provincial Academy of Bordeaux, where he conducted and observed scientific experiments, read and discussed essays on history and philosophy, and generally became an active member of the region's intellectual life. In 1721 he published anonymously in Amsterdam the first of the three major works by which he is known today. He called *Persian Letters* "a sort of novel" and once described its principle of coherence as "a secret and, in some respects, hitherto unknown chain."[1] Using the literary device of the guileless foreign visitors, Montesquieu presented a wide-ranging and candid discussion of religion, politics, economics, history, manners, and morals. While the narrative structure did much to shape the French Enlightenment method of indirection that would later be developed by Voltaire and Diderot, *Persian Letters* was anchored by the story of Roxana, the Persian wife who struggles with the conflict between her desire to love her despotic and self-deluded master, Usbek, and her natural liberty.

---

1. *The Persian Letters,* trans. George R. Healy (Indianapolis: Hackett, 1999), 4.

The spectacular success of this work—it went through several printings in its first year—made its author a sought-after companion in the salons of Paris, where he spent much time in the 1720s. He had the unusual experience of being elected to the French Academy (1727) mainly on the strength of a work that many found both light and of dubious orthodoxy. At the end of the decade, he traveled throughout Europe, including to Holland, Italy, Switzerland, Germany, Hungary, Austria, and, notably, to England, where he spent a year and a half, becoming friends with Alexander Pope, the Tory leader Viscount Bolingbroke, and many others. It was then (1729–31) that he read the English political press, attended debates in Parliament, and otherwise became more familiar with the English political and constitutional system that he would one day do so much to define.

It was also now that Montesquieu seems to have conceived the idea of writing what would become the second of his major works, namely, the *Considerations on the Causes of the Greatness of the Romans and Their Decline.* Published anonymously in Amsterdam in 1734 and revised for a 1748 edition, *Considerations* was one of the most influential interpretive studies of Roman history. The book is less a narrative history than an attempt, not unlike Machiavelli's *Discourses on Livy,* to isolate analytically the factors conducive to Roman success and failure. Montesquieu saw Rome as an agrarian power, not a commercial one, and laid great emphasis upon conquest as the leitmotif of Roman experience. His explanation for Roman decline went beyond the standard narrative of the corruption of moral and civic virtue by Oriental luxury. Instead he provided the kind of deliberately complex, multilayered analysis—embracing laws, institutions, manners, and morals, even the intellectual influences of Epicureanism and Christianity—that he would develop further in *The Spirit of the Laws* (1748). It seems that Montesquieu conceived of his famous chapter on the English constitution (*Laws,* 11.6) as a twenty-fifth and final chapter in the *Considerations*—an idea he abandoned, apparently, when he witnessed the censorship in 1733 of Voltaire's *Philosophical Letters,* a work that criticized France by praising England. That chapter was going to underscore the fundamental difference Montesquieu saw between ancient and modern liberty. Where ancient liberty in its Roman guise hinged upon virtue and conquest, modern liberty rested more on commerce, communication, information, and the arts of peace. The contrast between conquest and commerce, like that between ancients and moderns, would become a recurrent theme in his writings.

The Spirit of the Laws turned the author from a moderately important figure into one of the founders of modern thought. Exercising an influence often described as diffuse rather than focused, Montesquieu's magnum opus has been detected at the birth of sociology, comparative legal studies, and, indeed, any social science involving the cross-cultural analysis of some or all of the factors isolated by the author at the beginning of his study—namely, the "physical aspect of the country," the "way of life of the people," the "degree of liberty that the constitution can sustain," the people's "religion," "inclinations," "wealth," "number," "commerce," and "mores and manners," and the relationships among the laws themselves.[2]

One of the most important avenues of his influence concerned constitutional theory; the principles of checks-and-balances and separation of powers are the best-known examples. According to one study, the American founders turned to Montesquieu more often than to any other source—four times as frequently as the second-most-cited figure (John Locke). But at the local level, too, his influence in areas such as criminal-justice reform was pervasive and fundamental. In France as well as in America, Montesquieu's work had a more authoritative status in constitutional discussion throughout 1789 than that of Voltaire, Rousseau, Mably, or any other important figure.[3] More broadly, he had a formative influence on the Scottish Enlightenment through his friendship with David Hume and in the writings of Adam Smith, Adam Ferguson, and others. Even in China, he was one of a handful of Western figures—along with Mill, Spencer, Thomas Huxley, Jevons, and Adam Smith—who were translated into Chinese by Yan Fu in the first decade of the twentieth century in hopes of liberalizing and modernizing that vast country. In sum, there is no disputing Montesquieu's central and durable place in enlightenment thought.

The work translated here, which Montesquieu called *Mes Pensées*, is a

2. *The Spirit of the Laws*, ed. Anne Cohler, Basia Miller, and Harold Stone (Cambridge: Cambridge University Press, 1989), I.3, 9.

3. For the American scene, see Donald S. Lutz, "The Relative Importance of European Writers in Late Eighteenth-Century American Political Thought," *American Political Science Review* 189 (1984): 189–97. For the French situation, see Renato Galliani, "La Fortune de Montesquieu en 1789: un sondage" [Montesquieu's fortunes in 1789: a poll], in *Etudes sur Montesquieu*, ed. R. Galliani and F. Loirette (Paris: Lettres modernes, 1981), 31–47.

long series of handwritten notes that the author began compiling in bound notebooks around 1720—either in his own hand or with the help of private secretaries—and assiduously maintained until his death, with the idea of eventually working most of them into published form (*pensée* 1). Some contemporaries knew he was keeping such a collection, and a few of the entries found their way into print during the eighteenth century. But generally this treasure trove did not come to light until the twentieth century (see "A Note on the Text"). The *pensées* shed much light on the Montesquieu corpus. Sometimes they enable students of Montesquieu to trace the development of specific ideas over time. At other times, they directly illuminate the meaning of his published texts. And although some of the material will seem either familiar to those knowledgeable about his career or extraneous to the substance of his thought, the overall effect of the *pensées* is to offer a cornucopia of thought-provoking reflections on every conceivable topic.

Montesquieu warns at the beginning of the collection that he will not "answer for all the thoughts that are here" (*pensée* 3). This necessary precaution imposes a certain interpretive restraint, reminding us of the unfinished state of many of the entries and of the seriousness with which the author took the publication process. But the disclaimer also has varying applicability. Some of the items ended up being incorporated verbatim into his published works, especially *Laws*. Others are referred to elsewhere in the collection, indicating at least a certain level of authorial satisfaction. At the other end of the spectrum, some entries are signaled by Montesquieu himself for their inadequacy, with deletions or marginal notes of rejection. Between these two poles, there are some *pensées* that are reasonably straightforward and others so obscure and so lacking in context that it is difficult to know what to do with them. Specialists have struggled to find an adequate characterization of the project as a whole, describing it variously as an "intellectual laboratory," a "writing crossroads," or a "portfolio of portfolios."[4] The reader can expect to find in this volume tools and materials in every stage of the production process.

In *pensée* 1525, Montesquieu offers another observation that affects the way the reader approaches the collection. Discussing the art of printing

---

4. The preface and essays by Carole Dornier and Carole Volpilhac-Auger in *Revue Montesquieu* 7 (2003–4) offer these characterizations.

and its effect on the writing of history, he observes that "princes have made of this art the principal object of their administration; the censors they have set up direct all pens. In the past, one could speak the truth but did not speak it; today, one would like to speak it but cannot." Throughout his career, Montesquieu had his own encounters with the French censorship apparatus, and one value of the *pensées* is the opportunity to sample some of the author's more unvarnished thinking, especially on topics such as religion and current politics where the censors would have been particularly vigilant.

Montesquieu was a fussy editor of his own writings, one who left far more unfinished works than finished. Indeed it is difficult not to detect a note of personal defensiveness in *pensée* 1950, where he states that "An author who writes much regards himself as a giant and views those who write little as pygmies." Montesquieu wrote much, but he published little—only a handful of substantial titles in his lifetime. In *pensée* 1631a, at the beginning of the third and final manuscript notebook of the *pensées,* he summarizes some of the wide variety of abortive projects covered in that notebook alone.

One of these unpublished works is a *History of Jealousy,* a work that evidently would have combined his interests as an observer of manners and morals with the critical approach to history that he would make famous in *Laws.* In this case, only deleted fragments are left to us (see especially *pensées* 483–509). In *Treatise on Duties,* on the other hand, what we seem to have are mostly polished sections of a work that Montesquieu abandoned before seeing it through to the press (see especially *pensées* 1251–61, 1263, and 1265–80). Of avowedly Ciceronian inspiration, the work resembles the *De Officiis* in its application of moral principles to the civic world. But it also provides suggestive reflections on the differences between ancients and moderns.

As a historian Montesquieu wanted to go far beyond his Roman foray in *Considerations.* In the very long *pensée* 1302, he provides an outline for a sweeping history of France. In other entries he occasionally elaborates on some of the historical questions preoccupying his contemporaries. In *pensée* 1184, for example, he comments on Boulainvilliers's own history of France, and in *pensée* 1962 he offers an extended critique of Voltaire's use of historical evidence in the contemporary controversy over Richelieu's *Political Testament.*

Montesquieu had planned a separate study of the long and important reign of Louis XIV (*pensée* 1306), who occupied the throne during all of his own formative years (he was twenty-six when the Sun King died). But of equal interest, perhaps, is his ill-fated history of the rather neglected French king Louis XI (r. 1461–83), to whom he appears to have attributed special significance. The remarkable story of how that manuscript seems to have been lost is told at *pensée* 1302, note 14, below. But in *pensée* 1302 itself, he begins his lengthy account of the Spider King's reign with a ringing remark, "The death of Charles VII [in 1461] was the last day of French liberty." Such a comment, so tantalizing for understanding Montesquieu's view of liberty and of France, foreshadows Tocqueville's later reflection that the middle of the fifteenth century saw "the period of transition from feudal freedom to absolute government."[5]

Montesquieu's general definitions of liberty are well known from books 11 and 12 of *The Spirit of the Laws,* but the *pensées* offer revealing insights into their evolution. For the concept of liberty is one of those that can be traced throughout the present volume. From his rather wry and skeptical treatment in *pensée* 32, an early entry, through his piecemeal development of the metaphor of the fish caught in the fishnet (*pensées* 434, 597, 828, 874, and 943), through his entry at *pensée* 751 entitled "Liberty"—which may be an early source of his famous definition of English constitutional liberty— Montesquieu's engagement with the contested and ill-defined concept of liberty was variegated and persistent. Sometimes he found a clever salon-like witticism or a lapidary formula to express his views, as at *pensées* 577, 783, 784, and 1574. But in *pensée* 884, entitled "Political Liberty," he expressly distinguishes his view from that of the "orators and poets," indicating a preference for the more analytical approach for which he is known. In *pensée* 907, indeed, he refers to his evolving ideas as "my system on liberty." He also offers interesting perspectives on the origins, consequences, or prospects for liberty throughout the volume—for example, in *pensées* 1630, 1735, and 1780, and in his important letter to the Englishman William Domville on the prospects for English liberty at *pensée* 1960.

More specifically redolent of Tocqueville's later enterprise is Montesquieu's discussion of the office of intendant, the royal agent given broad

---

5. See Alexis de Tocqueville, *The Old Regime and the Revolution,* ed. and intro. François Furet and Françoise Mélonio, trans. Alan S. Kahan (Chicago: University of Chicago Press, 1998, 2001), 1:368.

powers to implement the king's will at the local level. Tocqueville would make the intendant a focal point of his sustained critique of centralization in the Old Regime French monarchy. Montesquieu, who never discusses the intendant in his published works and mentions that figure only in passing in his correspondence (usually with reference to specific individuals), presents some more-pointed general remarks about them here (at *pensées* 977, 1353, 1572, 1835, 1840, 1846, 1898, 2066, and 2099).

Relatedly, the question of whether Montesquieu had a normative preference for republics or monarchies has occurred to many readers of *The Persian Letters,* the *Considerations,* and *The Spirit of the Laws,* and the *pensées* again provide numerous insights on this question—see *pensées* 769, 1208, 1494, 1760, 1854, and 1891 for some examples. After the upheavals of the Napoleonic wars, Madame de Staël would look back upon the eighteenth century and cite with approval what she called the "science of liberty" that it had developed; the present volume shows perhaps the leading "scientist of liberty" at work in his workshop.[6]

Other frequent topics of Montesquieu's attention are economics and finance. Although he died just a couple of years before political economy was launched with the emergence of the Physiocrats, his numerous treatments in *Persian Letters* and *Considerations,* and especially his chapters 20–23 in *The Spirit of the Laws,* had a powerful influence on economic and financial discussion throughout the century. In the *pensées,* his remarks are sometimes in the vein of observations about current events (for example, *pensées* 17, 153, 169, and 249), sometimes they have a more normative or theoretical bent (see *pensées* 45, 146, 161, 178, and 246 for some samples), and on still other occasions he makes broad historical observations informed by his economic views (*pensées* 77, 86, 113, and 245 for a few examples). Montesquieu saw the "spirit of commerce" as distinctive of modernity and of modern liberty, an approach illuminated at numerous points in the *pensées.*

Mes Pensées also contains candid observations on topics such as life at court, the reign of Louis XIV and of the Regency after his death, or the place of women in modern societies. The art of the aphorist was highly valued in the social circles that Montesquieu frequented, especially in Paris,

---

6. See Germaine de Staël, *Considerations on the Principal Events of the French Revolution,* ed. and trans. Aurelian Craiutu (Indianapolis: Liberty Fund, 2008), 682.

and his attempt to cultivate that art is on prominent display throughout the collection. Moral-psychological topics such as happiness, jealousy, vengeance, boredom, and courtship are frequent preoccupations. One moment he is offering alternative Persian letters; another, he is providing further ruminations about the challenge posed by Hobbes's and Spinoza's moral anthropology. And throughout, he presents wide-ranging strategic reflections on European power politics, past and present.

One of the noteworthy topics on which he expresses unusually frank views is religion, especially in its political dimension. The role of the Jesuits as royal advisors and mobilizers of Catholic opinion, to take one prominent example, was a durable feature of French life from the Counter-Reformation into the eighteenth century. The Society of Jesus became increasingly controversial as the century wore on, however, until they were expelled from one Catholic realm after another (Portugal, France, Spain, Naples, the Duchy of Parma, Austria, the Kingdom of the Two Sicilies) in the two decades after Montesquieu's death. His comments on the Jesuits can be traced in this volume (see, for example, *pensées* 11, 55, 104, 180, 293, 394, 395, 453, 482, 544, 581, 715, 728, 730, 1038, 1223, 1301, 1302 n. 52, and 1959). Readers can also follow his thoughts about the bull *Unigenitus,* a papal edict of 1713 that began as a declaration of heresy against certain French Jansenists (that is, austere Augustinian critics of Jesuit laxity and royal pomp) but soon triggered a recurring dispute involving the Church hierarchy, the Jansenist-led parlementary magistrates, and the Crown. This imbroglio lasted through Montesquieu's lifetime and beyond (see especially *pensées* 55, 215, 273, 426, 437, 764, 914, 1226, 2158, 2164, and 2247).

As is often the case with compendia of this sort, however, the true pleasure of reading it is the pleasure of discovery. Not unlike the more famous eponymous work by the seventeenth-century mathematician and religious thinker Blaise Pascal (1623–62), which Montesquieu owned, Montesquieu's *Mes Pensées* often features paradoxical or unexpected observations about the condition of man in the world and in society that provide rich food for thought—not only for the author, as was its intention, but now for the reader as well. The Baron of La Brède was an inveterate observer of all around him, and this volume presents an essential window onto his energetic and creative mind, one of the formative minds of the eighteenth century and of the modern world.

A Note on the Text

THE PENSÉES, a set of three bound handwritten notebooks, were not published in the author's lifetime. Thus, except for those individual entries that were eventually published—often appearing in the notebooks with indications that they had already been "put in the *Romans*" or "put in the *Laws*"—we have no conclusive knowledge of the author's intentions at a given point in the text. Nor do we know exactly when they were written. The reader can assume that the *pensées* appear in at least roughly chronological order, beginning in the early 1720s and continuing to the end of the author's life. On occasion, Montesquieu dates an entry himself (see *pensées* 17, 141, 873, 1226, 1962, 1965, 1967, 2048, 2158, and 2164), which usefully lights the reader's way, although it does not resolve all dating problems (cf. *pensées* 17 and 141, for example).

In addition to the chronological uncertainties, there are at least three other features of the manuscript with which any editor has to contend. First, for more than three decades the text underwent significant revisions under several pens. Although much progress has been made in identifying or at least distinguishing among the different hands, and even situating them approximately in time, there are still many passages of unidentified hand and uncertain purpose.

Second, a few of the manuscript markings are ambiguous. What strikes one reader as a deletion might strike another as an intercalation. In rather more cases, what seems to one reader like a later addition might seem to another like part of the original text. Montesquieu was fastidious about expressing his published thoughts with precision, and this disposition accounts for his notebooks' being festooned with editorial markings. Although the meaning of most of the entries is clear enough, there are many points of doubt throughout.

Third, there are numerous errors in the manuscript, ensuring that fidelity to the text will sometimes conflict with fidelity to the author's intentions. These errors span the spectrum from incorrect spelling (less fixed in the eighteenth century than now), to mangled syntax, to missing or repeated words. In most cases, the probable intention is discernible; in a few cases, there is more than one plausible interpretation. But this Liberty Fund volume does not pretend to be a critical edition. Instead, the preference here has been to err on the side of readability by selecting the most probable rendering, indicating possible alternatives only where there was a material difference in meaning between them. Likewise, punctuation has been modernized, although the reader will find some terms capitalized that would not be in a modern text.

The base text for this edition is *Montesquieu: Pensées, Le Spicilège,* edited by Louis Desgraves for the Robert Laffont press in 1991. His edition has the virtues of being the most recent available and of containing the lifetime's knowledge of one of the world's leading Montesquieu specialists. A number of adjustments have been made to the Desgraves text for the present edition. First, whereas Desgraves used square brackets to indicate both deletions from and later additions to Montesquieu's text, signaling only the deletions in his notes, the present edition uses square brackets for deletions and curly brackets for additions. Second, Montesquieu frequently began an entry one way, crossed it out, and started over. Whereas Desgraves reproduced most of these cross-outs where legible (indicating them with the phrase "first version"), the present edition, again for readability's sake, reproduces only those cross-outs that represent a substantive change. In those cases, I insert punctuation suitable to the final text likely intended by Montesquieu. Finally, the present edition incorporates textual corrections contained in the transcription work supervised by Carole Dornier.

As for the footnotes, the 155 pages of endnotes contained in the 1991 Desgraves edition, which are often adapted and elaborated from Henri Barckhausen's notes in the original 1899–1901 edition,[1] furnish an invaluable resource for students of Montesquieu and form the base text for the notes contained here. Again, however, several adaptations have been made in the presentation of those notes. While maintaining all of Desgraves's references to Montesquieu's published works to which a given entry is related, I have condensed significantly the quotations Desgraves used to illustrate such relationships. I have streamlined the primary and secondary literature

---

1. *Pensées et fragments inédits de Montesquieu,* ed. Henri Barckhausen, published by Baron Gaston de Montesquieu (Bordeaux: Gounouilhou, 1899–1901), 1:510–38 and 2:535–82.

referred to in Desgraves's notes and have added cross-references for the reader's convenience. I have contributed some identifying or illustrative notes where it seemed appropriate and have added notes concerning points of translation as well. Whenever a new note appears, for whatever reason, it has been distinguished from the Desgraves notes by use of the present editor's initials (HC). In addition, I have translated foreign-language titles of works that Montesquieu refers to in text or in notes where cognates did not make the translation obvious.

There is a select bibliography at the end of this volume. The most common abbreviations used in the notes are as follows:

Adam	Montesquieu. *Lettres persanes* [Persian letters]. Edited by Antoine Adam. Geneva: Droz, 1954.
Allen	Montesquieu. *The Personal and the Political: Three Fables by Montesquieu.* Translation and commentary by W. B. Allen. Lanham, Md.: University Press of America, 2008.
Brèthe	Montesquieu. *De l'Esprit des lois.* Edited by Jean Brèthe de La Gressaye. 4 vols. Paris: Belles Lettres, 1950–61.
Catalog	Louis Desgraves, ed. *Catalogue de la bibliothèque de Montesquieu* [Catalogue of Montesquieu's library]. Geneva: Droz, 1954.
Considerations	Montesquieu. *Considerations on the Causes of the Greatness of the Romans and Their Decline.* Translated by David Lowenthal. Indianapolis: Hackett, 1999.
DAF	*Dictionnaire de l'Académie Française* [Dictionary of the French Academy]. 1694, 1762, 1798, and 1835 editions.
Derathé	Montesquieu. *De l'Esprit des lois.* Edited by Robert Derathé. 2 vols. Paris: Garnier Frères, 1973. A notes and variants edition.
Dodds	Muriel Dodds. *Les Récits de voyages, sources de "l'Esprit des lois" de Montesquieu.* Paris: Champion, 1929.
Encyclopédie	*Encyclopédie, ou Dictionnaire raisonné des sciences, des arts et des métiers, par une Société des gens de*

lettres [Encyclopedia, or critical dictionary of the sciences, arts and trades, by a Society of men of letters]. Edited by Denis Diderot and Jean Le Rond d'Alembert. 17 vols. Paris: Briasson et al., 1751–67.

Furetière   Antoine Furetière. *Dictionnaire universel contenant generalement tous les mots françois tant vieux que modernes et les Termes de toutes les sciences et des arts* [Universal dictionary, containing generally all French words, old and new, and terms from all the sciences and arts]. 3 vols. The Hague: Leers, 1690.

Laws   Montesquieu. *The Spirit of the Laws.* Translated and edited by Anne Cohler, Basia Miller, and Harold Stone. Cambridge: Cambridge University Press, 1989.

OC   Montesquieu. *Œuvres complètes de Montesquieu.* Edited by André Masson. 3 vols. Paris: Nagel, 1950–55.

OC Volt   Montesquieu. *Œuvres complètes de Montesquieu.* Edited by Jean Ehrard, Catherine Volpilhac-Auger et al. 22 vols. Oxford: Voltaire Foundation and Société Montesquieu, 1998–2010.

PL   Montesquieu. *The Persian Letters.* Translated by George R. Healy. Indianapolis: Hackett, 1999. Letter numbers in roman, pages in arabic.

Shackleton   Robert Shackleton. "La Genèse de *l'Esprit des lois*" [The genesis of *The Spirit of the Laws*]. *Revue d'Histoire Littéraire de la France* 52 (1952): 425–38. Reprinted in *Essays on Montesquieu and on the Enlightenment,* edited by David Gilson and Martin Smith, 49–63. Oxford: Voltaire Foundation, 1988.

Spicilège   Montesquieu. *Le Spicilège.* In *Pensées, Le Spicilège,* edited by Louis Desgraves. Paris: Robert Laffont, 1991. Numbered by entry, not by page.

Vernière   Montesquieu. *Lettres Persanes.* Edited by Paul Vernière. Paris: Garnier Frères, 1960.

although at one point (*pensée* 1546), in discussing the Venetian republic, Montesquieu expressly equates the "state" with the collectivity of
subjects, so "state" does not mark a distinction between government
and governed as clearly as it might later on. Often, too, the term has
a social meaning, in which case it has been translated as "status" or
"condition."

fable. Normally translated as "myth" except when the context suggests
"fable."

génie. Since "genius" often has a strong, almost transcendent inflection in
modern usage that it lacked in the eighteenth century, I have only rarely
resorted to it, instead preferring terms like "talent" or "character" that
retain the more mundanely descriptive function of the original (despite
its etymology).

les grands. Ambiguous because *grand* can mean both "large" and qualita-
tively "great." I have reluctantly adopted the term "grandees" for most
instances despite its slightly archaic flavor, though on occasion I have
gone with "the great nobles" or even "the great" where the context
dictated.

honnête. Can mean "honest," "honorable," or even "good," depending on
the context.

industrie. Generally a moral rather than strictly economic category in this
period, meaning "dexterity," "ingenuity," "industriousness," "resourcefulness," and the like. On rare occasions (*pensées* 181 and 639, for example), Montesquieu applies the term specifically to artisans, but even
then it is not clear that this moral dimension is entirely absent. Rarely
does it apply to manufacturing as a sector (see *pensées* 281, 291, 323, 1650,
1801, and 1960 for possible or partial exceptions), and never to factory
industry.

liberté. Generally I have used "liberty," except where the specific context
seemed to make "freedom" more advisable.

mœurs. Notorious for its coverage of the English terms "manners," "customs," and "morals," this word has been translated "mores"—which
evokes them all—unless the context clearly indicates a more conclusive
alternative.

pays; patrie. Pays is a general term that can refer to any distinct territory,
whether city or region or province or nation. *Patrie* can also refer to
these geographically diverse entities in the eighteenth century, but since

it always means "natal land," it puts the emphasis on the human dimension rather than on the merely physical, a fact that would become clearer in the generations after Montesquieu's death, when patriotism would emerge with emotive force. In Montesquieu's text, "country" is often the best translation for either *pays* or *patrie.* To preserve the distinction between them, however, I have capitalized Country to indicate *patrie,* and have left it uncapitalized where the term was *pays.* (See *pensées* 1158, 1260, and 1645 for cases where Montesquieu uses both terms nearby in the same entry.)

police. This distinctively eighteenth-century term can have either an administrative or a cultural significance. Administratively, it can mean "administration" or even "government" if it refers to an entire state, or to "regulations" if it refers to a specific institution within a state. Culturally, it can mark off the broader difference between civilized and precivilized societies; on a few occasions (*pensées* 108 and 1532), the context has made "law and order" seem like the best option, but generally I have translated the term in its cultural dimension simply as "civilization."

société. On a few occasions, this word may be translated as "society," indicating the sum of individuals living in a certain place, as in modern usage. But usually what Montesquieu means is better captured by such terms as "association," "human intercourse," or even "company," as in "the company of our friends."

A Note on Currency

AT A NUMBER OF POINTS in his *Pensées,* Montesquieu discusses monetary values (see, for example, *pensées* 17, 181, 214, 245, 250, 274, 317, 386, 530, 650, 661, 801, 1188, 1302, 1320, 1339, 1452, 1485, 1489, 1639, 1641, 1645, 1649, 1651, 1708, 1826, 1877, 1962, 2168, 2174, 2232, and 2258). Although it is famously difficult to perform cost-of-living conversions across the centuries, and although the currencies themselves were remarkably variable through time and place, it will at least convey a sense of Montesquieu's orders of magnitude to know that an *écu*—translated as "silver crown" for recent periods, "gold crown" for earlier ones—was equal to 3 French pounds, a gold louis was worth 24 pounds, a French pound (or *franc,* an older term still used for accounting purposes in Montesquieu's time) was equal to 20 *sols,* or *sous,* and a sol was equal to 12 *deniers* (from L., *denarius*). For the English equivalents, 1 pound sterling was 20 shillings, and 1 shilling equaled 12 pence; one guinea was 21 shillings. The rough Dutch equivalent to a French pound was the guilder.

Historians have attempted to measure cost of living by developing rough calculations of, for example, the income of day laborers. An English laborer in the middle of the eighteenth century might earn roughly 20 pence per day, or 20–30 pounds sterling per year. In France, a Parisian construction worker in Montesquieu's time was making about 15–20 sous per day, or a very few hundred French pounds per year, and a Dutch apprentice might earn a similar number of guilders per year.[1]

1. See Jan de Vries, *The Economy of Europe in an Age of Crisis, 1600–1750* (Cambridge: Cambridge University Press, 1976), 186.

Acknowledgments

I BEGAN THIS PROJECT AS a visiting scholar at Liberty Fund in India-napolis in 2005–6. Without the generosity of that foundation, and the congenial surroundings they supplied, this volume would not have been conceived, much less executed. In particular, Emilio Pacheco deserves my heartfelt gratitude for supporting this undertaking from the beginning.

Professor Catherine Volpilhac-Auger, President of the Société Montes-quieu, was unfailingly helpful whenever I approached her with general questions about this enterprise. Professor Carole Dornier, who has been supervising a new transcription of the *Pensées,* has been a frequent source of encouragement and illumination, generously and promptly respond-ing to many inquiries over the years of our correspondence. The changes I have made to the Desgraves edition of the text (*Montesquieu: Pensées, Le Spicilège,* edited by Louis Desgraves, [Paris: Éditions Robert Laffont, S.A., 1991]) draw heavily upon her efforts.

My institutional debts begin with my former employer Canisius Col-lege, for a sabbatical and for generous release time during the drafting and completion of the volume. In 2009–10 I was a visiting scholar at the Clem-son Institute for the Study of Capitalism; the institute (under its director, C. Bradley Thompson), as well as the Clemson Department of History, afforded me a most welcome venue for the final work on this edition.

The interlibrary loan services and technical support staffs of Canisius College, Dartmouth College, Liberty Fund, and Clemson University, as well as the rare book librarians at the Rauner Library of Dartmouth Col-lege, have lent their assistance from start to finish.

A number of individuals have contributed their time and expertise to the translation itself along the way. Christine Henderson spent many hours offering her sound advice early on. Once a draft was complete, Alan Ka-han reviewed a substantial portion of the manuscript, answering numerous questions and providing many useful recommendations. David Carrithers brought his unrivaled knowledge of Montesquieu to the task of reviewing a later draft sample, supplying pages of helpful suggestions and corrections. Laure Marcellesi and Marie-Paule Tranvouez patiently clarified some fine points of French usage.

In translating the Italian passages, I am indebted to Nancy Canepa and Graziella Parati for their helpful advice. The much more abundant Latin passages fall in two categories. Many consist of quotations from classical texts now available in modern editions. Unless otherwise indicated, all translations of these are taken with permission from the Loeb Classical Library®, a registered trademark of the President and Fellows of Harvard College. Many others are nonclassical sources, such as book titles, common phrases, medieval law codes, or Montesquieu's own compositions. Kathy Alvis has reviewed all Latin quotations and kindly offered her suggestions. Tom Banchich and Kathryn Williams of the Canisius College Department of Classics have also helpfully responded to particular inquiries.

Many other people have made useful suggestions or answered queries concerning the text or translation, including Keith Michael Baker, Holly Brewer, Paul Carrese, Aurelian Craiutu, Paul Rahe, Stuart Warner, Catherine Larrère, and perhaps others to whom I apologize for forgetting. Despite these numerous helping hands, the responsibility for all translations—from whatever language—and for all editorial decisions remains my own.

As to the volume itself, my sincerest thanks go to Colleen Watson, Patti Ordower, and Madelaine Cooke for their admirable patience and professionalism in preparing the text, and to Kate Mertes for her usual thorough work on the index.

Finally, my wife, Kathleen Wine, has been a constant companion and consultant throughout this long-gestating enterprise, at a time when many other distractions beckoned, and has put her mark upon the translation in innumerable ways. It is a pleasure to dedicate this volume to her.

My Thoughts

[1] SOME DETACHED REFLECTIONS OR THOUGHTS THAT I HAVE NOT PUT IN MY WORKS.

[2] These are ideas that I have not delved into deeply, and that I am putting aside in order to think about them as the occasion allows.

[3] I will be very careful not to answer for all the thoughts that are here. I have put most of them here only because I have not had time to reflect on them, but I will think about them when I make use of them.

[4] Devotion arises from a desire to play some role in the world, whatever the cost.[1]

[5] My son,[1] you have enough good fortune not to have to either blush or swell with pride because of your birth.[2]

{My birth is proportionate to my fortune[3] in such a way that I would be disturbed if one or the other were greater.}

You will be a man of the robe[4] or the sword. Since you will be responsible for your status, it is up to you to choose. In the robe, you will find more independence and freedom; in the sword camp, grander hopes.

You are permitted to want to rise to the more eminent posts, because every citizen is permitted to want to be in a position to render greater services to his Country. Moreover, noble ambition is a sentiment useful to society when it is well directed.

[It is a great workman who has made our being and has given our souls certain tendencies and certain penchants.]

[4]
1. On devotion, see *pensées* 445, 594, 1140, and 1405.

[5]
1. Jean-Baptiste de Secondat (February 10, 1716–June 17, 1795), Montesquieu's only son. He was a man of neither robe (i.e., the magistracy) nor sword nobility. Raised in Paris, he engaged in scientific research at the Jesuit *collège* (secondary school) of Louis-le-Grand. On August 30, 1740, he married Marie-Thérèse de Mons in Bordeaux.

2. By his father, Jacques de Secondat, and his paternal uncle, Jean-Baptiste de Secondat, Montesquieu belonged to a family of sword and of robe; by his mother, Marie-Françoise de Pesnel, he descended from the noble house of La Lande, which from the end of the eleventh century was established on the territory of La Brède.

3. See *pensée* 1183 for a reworking of this thought.

4. *Robe*, magistracy, legal profession, so called because of the long gown worn by its members; often contrasted with *épée*, or sword, as being two types of nobility. See also *pensée* 30.—HC

Just as the physical world continues to exist only because each part of matter tends to move away from the center, so too the political world is maintained by that restless inner desire possessed by everyone to leave the situation in which he is placed.[5] It is in vain that an austere morality would efface the features that the greatest of all workmen has imprinted on our souls. It is up to morality, which would work on man's heart, to regulate his sentiments, not destroy them.

[6] Our moral authors are almost all extremists; they speak to the pure understanding, not to that soul which in its unity is newly modified by means of the senses and the imagination.

[7] It is always adventurers who do great things, not the sovereigns of great empires.

[8] The invention of the postal service has created politics; we don't politick with the Mughal.[1]

[9] Does this art of politics make our histories more splendid than those of the Greeks and Romans?

[10] There are few events in the world that do not depend on so many circumstances that it would take a worldly eternity for them to occur a second time.

[11] If the Jesuits had come before Luther and Calvin, they would have been masters of the world.

[12] Perhaps one could say that the reason why most peoples give themselves such an ancient lineage is that, the creation being incomprehensible to human understanding, they think the world itself has existed forever.

[13] Nice book by one André cited by Athenaeus:[1] *De Iis quae falso creduntur* [*On those things that are wrongly believed*].[2]

---

5. First version: "by a certain tendency to leave the situation in which he is placed."

[8]
1. See also *pensées* 145 and 2207. "Politicking" (*politiquer*) means to engage in conversation over politics; the term was colloquial in Montesquieu's time and soon passed out of use.—HC

[13]
1. Athenaeus of Naucratis, Greek grammarian and rhetorician (fl. A.D. 200), author of a work in thirty books, the *Banquet of the Learned*, of which Montesquieu possessed the 1657 Latin edition (*Catalogue*, 1821). In the *Catalogue*, the notice is followed by this autographed note from Montesquieu: "The author is bad, but his work is precious—because of the innumerable particular facts one finds only there, the knowledge he gives us of the private life of the Greeks, and the fragments of the works of poets that we no longer have. When will we have the translation, the restorations and the notes of M. Adam?" In the *Spicilège*, 561, Montesquieu notes: "finish reading Athenaeus."
2. In the 1612 Lyon edition of Athenaeus, VII, 90, p. 312, one reads: "*Andreas libro De iis qui falso*

[**14**] When one wants to abase a general, one says that he is lucky. But it is fine that his good fortune makes the public fortune.

[**15**] A courtier is like those plants made for creeping, which attach themselves to everything they find.

[**16**] What an obscure mystery is generation! The microscope, which revealed larvae in the seed of fertile animals but not in infertile ones like the mule, gave currency to the notion of the larvae, which has its difficulties. For (1) the larva must carry its placenta with it, for if the placenta were in the egg, how would one conceive of the larva attaching itself to this [umbilical] cord, which would pierce it in the navel in order to establish a vascular continuity; (2) it is difficult to conceive of how it is—given a million larvae, two tubes, and two ovaries—that children are not normally born as twins: thus, it must be that in each female, there is always only one egg fit to be fertilized. {*Journal des Savants,* March 21, 1690, there are many curious things on these matters.}[1]

It is very difficult to say why mules do not procreate and why a mare which has conceived from a donkey can no longer conceive from a horse. {Countess Borromée[2] had a mule that procreated.}

[**17**] England is in virtually the most flourishing condition it could be in. Yet she owes fifty-three to fifty-four million sterling, that is to say, as much as she could owe at the height of her greatness without losing her credit. Thus, this high point of greatness has become a necessary condition for her; she cannot fall from it without being ruined.

---

creduntur, eos mentiri scribit qui aiunt Muraenam in lutulentam maris oram progredientem cum vipera misceri, quae in coenosio non versatur, sed nemorum solitudinem amat." [Andreas, in his book *On those things that are wrongly believed,* writes that those men lie who say that the eel, in approaching the muddy shore of the sea, mates with the snake, which does not live in a muddy place but loves the solitude of the woods.]

[16]
1. The book reviewed in the *Journal of the Learned* is *Introduction à la philosophie des Anciens. Par un amateur de la vérité* [Introduction to the philosophy of the ancients. By a truth lover] (Paris: Thiboust, 1689).

2. Clélia del Grillo of Geno (1684–1777) married Count Jean Benoît Borromée in 1707. Montesquieu met her in Milan in September 1728; he had been recommended to her by abbé Conti. Montesquieu wrote to Conti on September 29, 1728 (*OC*, 3:914), "Countess Borromée greeted me as if I had descended from Mount Parnassus. . . . I am astonished by her prodigious erudition." See also the *Voyages* (*OC*, 2:1025). At home, she had founded the Academia di "Vigilanti," and her palace had become the gathering place for the learned, and the center of the rebellion against Austria in favor of restoring the Spanish regime in Milan. She lent Montesquieu books on architecture and other subjects (*OC*, 3:918).

As for France, she owes much, but only as much as comports with the decadence she has reached, so that all the probabilities are in favor of France in this regard, just as they are all against England.

England needs to dominate in order to sustain herself {and maintain the established government}; France, on the contrary, needs only a middling condition.

English commerce must be more odious to France than that of any other power. For if the other powers extend their trade far and enrich themselves, we profit from their opulence, since they engage in much trade with us; whereas England, hardly trading with us at all, acquires wealth that is entirely lost to us. We run the risk without ever being able to enjoy the profit.

The present rivalries between Austria and Spain, on the one hand, and England on the other, can in this regard become advantageous to France, if it could thereby ensue that the prohibitions against the transport of English merchandise to Spain and the lands of the Emperor[1] were to last beyond the peace. {It was impossible for that to last.}[2] This is because the English would then find themselves deprived of two great markets: the Imperial lands and Spain; thus, she would lose much more than she would gain by the preservation of Gibraltar and the ruin of the Ostend Company.[3]

This May 7, 1727.[4]

[18] We seek out the authors of the ancient fables. They were the nursemaids of ancient times and the old men who amused their grandchildren by the fire. It is like those stories that everyone knows, even though they don't deserve to be known by anyone, the beauty of the better ones not being so well grasped by ignorant folk. The fewer books there were, the more of these sorts of traditions there were. A Locman, a Pilpai, an Aesop[1] compiled them. They may even have added some reflections, for I know of

[17]
1. Charles VI (Vienna, 1685–1740), German emperor from 1711 to 1740.
2. This note seems to date from sometime between 1743 and 1746.—HC
3. In 1722 Emperor Charles VI granted a monopoly for the East Indies trade to the Ostend Company, with assets of six million guilders. England and the United Provinces obtained from Charles VI the suspension of the privilege in 1727, and its abolition in 1731.
4. This *pensée* may shed light on the last paragraph of *Laws,* 22.17, and on 22.18.

[18]
1. Locman was the presumed author of a collection of Arab fables a millennium or so before Christ; Pilpai, or Bidpai, was the supposed author of ancient Hindu fables; Aesop, the author of Greek fables in the sixth or seventh century B.C.

nothing in the world on which a tolerably moral man cannot make some speculations.

It does the fables too much honor to think that the Orientals invented them to speak truths to princes indirectly. For if they could have a specific construction, nothing would be gained, because in that case, an indirect truth is no less offensive than a direct one, and often even more so. For then, there are two offenses: the offense itself, and the offender's idea that he could find a man stupid enough to endure it without noticing.

But if these truths were merely general, it would still have been useless to take an allegorical detour. For I don't know if there has ever been a prince in the world who has been offended by a treatise on morality.

[19] How many abuses are there, which have been introduced as such and tolerated as such, and which are found afterward to have been very useful, even more useful than the most reasonable laws! For example, there is scarcely a sensible man in France who does not rail against the venality of offices, and who is not scandalized by it.[1] And yet, if you pay close attention to the indolence of neighboring countries, where all the offices are given out, and if you compare it with our activity and resourcefulness, you will see that it is extremely useful to encourage in citizens the desire to make a fortune, and that nothing contributes more in this regard than making them see that wealth opens the path to honors. In all governments, there have been complaints that people of merit attained honors less often than others. There are many reasons for this, and especially one that is quite natural: it is because there are many people who lack merit, and few who have it. Often, there is even great difficulty in distinguishing between them without being mistaken. That being the case, it is always better that rich people, who have much to lose and who, moreover, have been able to have a better education, assume public office.

[20] How imperious is chance! And how shortsighted are the politicians! Who would have said to the Huguenots, when they saw Henry IV on the steps of the throne, that they were ruined? Who would have said to Charlemagne, when he elevated the power of the Popes against that of the

[19]
1. For Montesquieu's apparent support for the venality of offices, see *Laws,* 5.19. In a long letter to Montesquieu on April 10, 1749 (*OC,* 3:1218), David Hume found still other reasons to approve of the system of venality. See *The Letters of David Hume,* ed. J. Y. T. Greig (Oxford: Clarendon Press, 1932), 1:134–35.

Greek emperors—the sole enemies that he had to fear—that he was going to humiliate all his successors?[1]

[21] The Epicurean sect[1] contributed much to the establishment of Christianity. For in revealing the stupidity of paganism and the artifices of the priests, it left without religion people accustomed to having a rite. Although the Christians were their mortal enemies (witness Lucian,[2] an Epicurean or nearly so who cruelly insulted the Christians), nonetheless, they both were treated by the pagan priests as enemies, as unholy, as atheists. They made only this distinction: they did not persecute the Epicureans, since the latter did not break statues and had only contempt and not hatred for the dominant religion.

Thus, when the Christians attacked pagan errors, it was a great advantage for them to speak the language of the Epicurean sect, and when they established their dogmas, it was also a great advantage to speak the Platonists' language. But it was gratuitous for us to have taken up Aristotle's jargon,[3] and I don't know that we have ever gained anything by it.

[22] The idea of false miracles[1] comes from our pride, which makes us believe that we are an object important enough for the supreme being to overturn all of nature on our behalf; which makes us view our nation, our city, or our army as more dear to the divinity. Thus, we want God to be a partisan being, who is constantly declaring himself for one creature against another and enjoys this sort of warfare. We want him to enter into our quarrels as passionately as we do, and at every moment to do things even the smallest of which would paralyze all of nature. If Joshua,[2] who wanted to pursue the fugitives, had demanded that God truly stop the sun, he would have been asking to be annihilated himself; for if the sun stops

---

[20]
  1. Henry IV, King of France (r. 1589–1610); Charlemagne, King of the Franks (r. 768–814) and Emperor of the West (800–814).

[21]
  1. Epicurus, Greek philosopher (341–270 B.C.).
  2. Lucian of Samosata, Greek satirical writer (ca. 120–ca. 192); Montesquieu possessed the 1563 Basel edition in Latin, in four volumes (*Catalogue*, 1907).
  3. Plato (428–348 B.C.) and Aristotle (384–322 B.C.), Greek philosophers.

[22]
  1. For Montesquieu's attitude toward miracles, see what he says on the liquefaction of Saint Januarius's blood in the *Voyages* (*OC*, 2:1159–60, 1162).
  2. See Joshua 10:12–13.

in reality {This example is poorly chosen, for one can scarcely interpret Scripture here except literally}, and not in the manner usually interpreted, then there is no more movement, no more vortices, no more sun, no more earth, no more men, no more Jews, no more Joshua.

[23] The gods are equally charged with the care of all men; they return the great nobles to equality through misfortune.

[24] When Commodus[1] made his horse consul, he committed a great offense against himself: he removed the sense of illusion from office, including his own.

[25] The vast number of things that a legislator decrees or prohibits makes the people more unhappy, not more reasonable.[1] There are a few good things, a few bad things, and an enormous number of indifferent ones.

[26] The Romans killed themselves only to avoid a greater evil, but the English kill themselves for no other reason than their own sorrow.

The Romans were bound to kill themselves more easily[1] than the English because of a religion that left them scarcely any sense of accountability.

The English are rich, they are free, but they are tormented by their minds.[2] They despise or are disgusted by everything. They are really quite unhappy, with so many reasons not to be.

[27] Christian humility is no less a dogma of philosophy than of religion. It does not signify that a virtuous man must think himself a worse man than a thief does, or that a man of talent must believe that he has none, since this is a judgment impossible for the mind to form. It consists

[24]
1. Lucius Aurelius Commodus, son of Marcus Aurelius, Roman emperor (r. 180–92).

[25]
1. See *Laws*, 29.16, 616.

[26]
1. See *Considerations*, XII, 117. In *L'Homme moral opposé à l'homme physique de M. R****: *Lettres philosophiques où l'on refute le déisme du jour* [The Moral man opposed to the physical man, by M. R***: Philosophical letters in which the deism of the day is refuted] (Toulouse, 1757), seventeenth letter, p. 102, Fr. Louis-Bertrand Castel, who had advised Montesquieu at the time of the printing of the *Considerations*, writes: "The sole article on suicide slipped, I don't know how, into the second or third edition. The author clung to that Anglo-Roman item. The true magistrates, and the author himself, without my getting involved in it, had it removed." In a copy in the Bordeaux Municipal Library (Amsterdam: J. Desbordes, 1734), bearing the ex libris of his friend President Jean Barbot, the passages relating to suicide have been deleted (pp. 130–31). See also *Laws*, 14.12, 241–42, and see *pensées* 310, 681, and 1570.
2. "Put that" (M.); cf. *Laws*, 19.27.

in making us visualize the reality of our vices and the imperfections of our virtues.[1]

[28] Those who devote themselves to disgraced grandees in the hope that the return of the latters' fortunes will make their own are engaging in an extraordinary self-deception. For they will be forgotten by them as soon as they are restored to favor. A man who emerges from disgrace is charmed to find people everywhere who yearn for his friendship. He devotes himself to these new friends, who give him a livelier image of his grandeur. Just as what amused him in his disgrace no longer amuses him, he classes you with the things that are no longer amusing. He has changed, and you, who have not changed, inspire aversion. However, there is injustice on your part in wanting a heart that everyone seeks to fill to be as much yours as it was {in solitude}. Amidst the noise of great fortune, he returns to his old friends, as he would return to solitude. It seems they remind him of his humiliation. If you make him aware that you sense his change, he looks upon you as he would an inconvenient creditor. He will soon come to dispute the debt, and the more he removes his friendship, the less he will believe he owes you. [There you have the source of most men's ingratitude.]

[29] The natural purpose[1] of vengeance is to reduce a man to the feeling of wishing he had not offended us. Vengeance does not lead to this goal, but instead makes it so that the man would be happy if he could offend us again. Forgiveness would lead a man to repentance much more surely.

There is still another pleasure, which is the honor we think we obtain from the advantage we have gotten over our enemy.

The Italian who makes his enemy commit a mortal sin before killing him loves the vengeance for itself and independent of the point of honor; he wants him to repent for all eternity at having offended him.

Nothing diminishes great men more than the attention they give to certain personal conduct. I know of two who have been entirely unmoved by these things: Caesar and the last Duke of Orleans.[2] When the latter en-

[27]
1. See *pensée* 469.
[29]
1. First version: "The true purpose."
2. Philippe, Duke of Orléans (1674–1723), regent after the death of Louis XIV. See Jacques Solé, "Montesquieu et la Régence," in *La Régence* (Centre aixois d'Études et de Recherches sur le XVIIIe siècle; Paris, 1970), 125–30.

tered government, he rewarded his friends and relieved his enemies of their just fears; they found themselves at peace in the shadow of his authority.

[30] Happiness[1] or unhappiness consists in a certain arrangement of organs, either favorable or unfavorable.

With a favorable arrangement, accidents such as wealth, honor, health, or illness either increase or decrease happiness. On the other hand, with an unfavorable arrangement, the accidents increase or decrease unhappiness.

When we speak of happiness or unhappiness, we are always mistaken, for we judge conditions and not persons. A condition is never an unhappy one when it pleases, and when we say that a man in a certain situation is unhappy, this means only that we would be unhappy if we, with the organs that we have, were in his place.

Let us therefore cut from the ranks of the unhappy all those who are not at Court, even though a courtier regards them as the most unfortunate members of the human Species. {It is said that everyone thinks himself unhappy. It seems to me, on the contrary, that everyone thinks himself happy. The courtier thinks it is he alone who lives.} Let us cut out all those who live in the provinces, even though those who live in the capital regard them as vegetating beings. Let us cut out the philosophers, even though they do not live in the bustle of the world, and the worldly, even though they do not live in retreat.

Let us likewise remove from the number of the happy the great nobles, even though they are adorned with titles; state financiers, even though they are rich; men of the robe,[2] even though they are proud; men of war, even though they often talk about themselves; young people, even though they are thought to enjoy good fortune; women, even though they are flirted with; finally Churchmen, even though they are able to acquire reputation by their obstinacy and dignities by their ignorance. The true delights are not always in the hearts of kings, but they can easily be there.

What I say can scarcely be disputed. And yet, if it is true, then what will become of all those moral reflections, ancient and modern? We have scarcely ever more grossly deceived ourselves than when we have wanted to reduce men's feelings to a system; and undoubtedly the worst copy of man is the one found in books, which are a pile of general propositions, almost

[30]
1. Other pieces of the "Reflections on Happiness" are found in *pensées* 69, 658, 819, 978, and 1181.
2. On *robe,* see *pensée* 5.—HC

always false. {Look at the galley slaves, all cheerful and gay; after that, go seek a blue ribbon[3] for your happiness.}

An unhappy author, who does not feel fit for pleasure, who is overwhelmed with sadness and distaste, who lacks the fortune to enjoy the conveniences of life (or the wit to enjoy the conveniences of his fortune), has nonetheless the vanity to claim to be happy and gets lost in words: sovereign good, childhood prejudices, dominion over the passions.

There are two types of unhappy people.

One type has a certain lassitude of soul, which nothing can excite. The soul lacks the strength to desire anything, and everything that touches it excites only vague feelings. The owner of this soul is always in a state of languor; life is a burden to him; all its moments weigh upon him. He does not love life, but he does fear death.

The other type of unhappy people, the opposite of the former, are those who impatiently desire everything they cannot have and who pine away in the hope of some good that is always receding.

I am speaking here only of a frenzy of the soul and not a simple movement. Thus, a man is not unhappy because he has ambition {Somewhere in this volume I have written down how much pleasure ambition brings.}, but because he is devoured by it. And even such a man almost always has his organs so constructed that he would be unhappy in any case, even if, by some chance, ambition—that is, the desire to do great things—had not entered into his head.

But the simple desire to make a fortune, far from making us unhappy, is, on the contrary, a game that delights us with a thousand hopes. A thousand routes seem to lead us there, and scarcely is one closed off before another seems to open up.

There are also two types of happy people.

One type is strongly excited by objects that are accessible to their soul and that they can easily acquire {hunting, gambling that one can afford}. They desire strongly, they hope, they enjoy, and soon they begin to desire again.

Others have their machinery constructed in such a way that it is being constantly but mildly put in motion. It is maintained, not agitated; a reading or a conversation is enough for them.

3. The reference is to the ribbon attached to the cross of the order of the Holy Spirit.—HC

It seems to me that nature has labored for the ungrateful. We are happy, but our speech is such that it seems we have no inkling of it. Still, we find pleasures everywhere; they are attached to our being, whereas pains are merely accidents. Objects seem to be everywhere prepared for our pleasures; when sleep calls, the darkness pleases us, and when we awaken, the daylight delights us. Nature is adorned with a thousand colors; our ears are gratified by sounds, dishes possess pleasurable tastes. And as if this were not enough existential happiness, our machinery also has to need constant restoration for our pleasures.

Our soul, which has the faculty of receiving through the organs both pleasant and painful feelings, has the resourcefulness to procure the former and discard the latter. And in this, art constantly supplies the defects of nature. Thus, we constantly correct external objects; we subtract from them what might harm us, and add what can make them agreeable.

There is more. Sensual pains necessarily lead us back to pleasures. I challenge you to cause a hermit to fast without simultaneously giving him a new taste for his vegetables. It is in fact only sharp pains that can injure us. Moderate pains are very close to pleasures; at least they do not take away that of existing. As for mental pains, they cannot be compared with the satisfactions that our perpetual vanity gives us; there are very few quarter-hours when we are not in some way self-contented. Vanity is a mirror that always reflects to our advantage; it diminishes our faults and enhances our virtues; it is a sixth sense of the soul, which at every moment gives it new satisfactions. The agreeable passions serve us with much greater exactness than the sad ones. If we fear things that will not happen, we hope for a far greater number that will not happen. Thus, these are so many happy quarter-hours gained. Yesterday a woman hoped she would find herself a lover. If she does not succeed, she hopes that another one she saw will take his place, and thus she spends her life hoping. Since we spend more of our lives in hope than in possession, our hopes are multiplied quite differently from our fears. All this is a matter of calculation, and it is thus easy to see how far what is for us outstrips what is against.

[31] If pain distracts us from pleasure, doesn't pleasure distract us from pain? The slightest object acting on our senses is capable of eliminating the most all-consuming thoughts of ambition.

{Men ought to be persuaded of the happiness they are overlooking at the very moment they are enjoying it.[1] I have seen the galleys of Livorno and of Venice;[2] I have not seen a single sad man there—seek now, if you would be happy, to wear your scrap of blue ribbon[3] like your colors.}

[32] The sole advantage that a free people has over another is the security each individual possesses that a single individual's whim will not take away his property or his life.[1] A subject people who had that security, whether well- or ill-founded, would be as happy as a free people—mores being equal, because mores contribute even more to the happiness of a people than laws.

This security of one's condition is[2] not greater in England than in France, and it was scarcely greater in certain ancient Greek republics which, as Thucydides says,[3] were divided into two factions. Since liberty[4] often generates two factions in a state, the superior faction mercilessly exploits its advantages. A dominant faction is not less terrible than a wrathful prince. How many individuals have we seen lose their lives or their property during the recent disturbances in England! It is useless to say that one needs only to remain neutral. For who can be sane when the whole world is mad? Not to mention that the moderate man is hated by both parties. Moreover, in free states, the common people are normally insolent. It is useless; there is scarcely an hour in the day when an honorable man doesn't have some business with the lower classes, and however high up a nobleman may be, one always ends up in that situation. As for the rest of it, I count for very little the happiness of arguing furiously over affairs of state and never uttering a hundred words without pronouncing the word *liberty*, or the privilege of hating half the citizenry.

[33] Who are the happy people? The gods know, for they see the hearts of philosophers, kings, and shepherds.

[34] The Athenians subjected defeated peoples to their dominion, the

[31]
1. See *pensée 708*.
2. See *Voyages* (*OC*, 2:985).
3. For the blue ribbon, see the note at *pensée 30*.

[32]
1. "[Put in my Moral thoughts]" (M.); see *pensée 57*.
2. First version: "is much less in England than in France, and it was likewise less in the ancient Greek and Italian republics, because liberty, to speak only of England, making"
3. Thucydides (ca. 460–ca. 395 B.C.), Greek historian, author of the *History of the Peloponnesian War*, which Montesquieu possessed in three Latin editions (*Catalogue*, 2798–99).
4. See *Laws*, 11.4.

Lacedemonians gave them their laws and their liberty. The latter acted like Hercules and Theseus,[1] the former like Philip and Alexander afterward.[2] [The people of Athens were greater, the people of Lacedemon more magnanimous.] Marvelous thing! There was no more ambition in Sparta than in Capua, Croton, or Sybaris.

[35] THEOLOGIANS. They love a new article of belief more than a million Christians; provided they gain an article for the profession of faith, they are not bothered by the loss of some of the faithful.

A tyrant had an iron bed where he measured everyone.[1] He arranged to cut off the feet of those who were taller, and stretch out those who were shorter. But these go further: to torment more, sometimes they extend the bed, sometimes they shorten it.

[36] THE CARTHAGINIANS, THEIR GOOD FORTUNE AND THEIR SUDDEN HUMILIATION.[1] Great wealth, but no military virtue; bad armies, which, however, they easily rebuilt.

Their weakness arose from the fact that their great strengths were not in the center of their power. Internal vice.

1. The cities of Africa were not enclosed by walls.

2. They had none-too-friendly neighbors who abandoned them when they could do so without peril. And then, enemies within and without, combined, put them within a hair's breadth of their ruin.

3. Their constant imprudence: they would send half an army into exile; they would punish their generals for their misfortunes, so they were thinking more about defending themselves against the citizenry than against the enemy.

4. Their disastrous divisions.

5. Bad administration.

6. The mania for distant conquests: Carthage would think about conquering Sicily, Italy, and Sardinia, while paying a tax to the Africans.

[34]
1. Hercules (Heracles in Greek), a Roman demigod celebrated for his twelve labors; Theseus, Attic hero, son of Aegeus or of Poseidon and Aethra.
2. Philip II, king of Macedon (r. 356–336 B.C.), and his son Alexander III the Great (r. 336–323 B.C.).

[35]
1. The tyrant Procrustes was killed by Theseus after the iron-bed torture had been inflicted on him.

[36]
1. "I have put this in the *Considerations on the Roman Republic*" (M.); cf. *Considerations,* IV.

Thus, all those who landed in Africa drove them to despair: Agathocles, Regulus, and Scipio.[2]

African heat. Harsh domination. Carthaginians hated as foreigners.

[37] The Greeks had a great talent for making themselves look good. There was nothing really remarkable in the war against Xerxes.[1] That prince has a boat bridge built across the Hellespont;[2] not a very difficult thing. He has his army cross. The Lacedemonians seize the passage at Thermopylae, where manpower could be advantageous only in the long run. The Lacedemonians are exterminated; the remaining Greek troops are defeated and retreat. Xerxes comes along, conquers virtually all of Greece. All his gains evaporate in the battle he loses at sea, where there was little inequality. He was going to die of hunger, no longer being master of the sea. He retreats with the greater part of his army and leaves Mardonius[3] to preserve his conquests. The battle is joined. It is contested. The Persians are defeated and expelled from Greece.

Speechifying apart, there you have the bottom line of Greek history, which amounts to a war like countless others, from which one can conclude only that a maritime power is hardly ever destroyed except by another and superior maritime power, and that it is highly reckless to expose a land army against it if you are not absolute master of the sea.

As for the history of Alexander,[4] although the conquest is true, there is hardly a sensible man who does not see it in virtually all its circumstances as grossly false.

Those who had the mania for getting their princes to imitate Hercules and Bacchus[5] imagined adventures to match. But the world of Alexander's time was not like it was in the time of Hercules.

[38] The peoples of that American continent between Spanish and English country give us an idea of what the first men were like, before agriculture and the establishment of large societies.

---

2. Agathocles, tyrant of Syracuse (ca. 361–289 B.C.); Marcus Atilius Regulus, Roman politician and general who died at Carthage ca. 250 B.C.; Scipio Africanus (235–183 B.C.).

[37]
1. Xerxes I, Achmaenid king of Persia (r. 486–465 B.C.).
2. The Hellespont is the present Dardanelles Straits.
3. Mardonius, Persian general who died at the battle of Plataea in 479 B.C.
4. See the portrait of Alexander in *Laws*, 10.14 and 21.8; by "the history of Alexander," Montesquieu may be referring to Quintus Curtius's flawed first-century work *Historiae Alexandri Magni*, which Montesquieu owned in a 1545 Basel edition (*Catalogue*, 2772).—HC
5. Bacchus, Latin form of Dionysus, god of the vine and of wine.

Hunting peoples are generally man-eaters. They are often exposed to hunger. Moreover, since they live only on meat, they have no more horror of a man they have taken than of an animal they have killed.

[39] Who would have said that the styloceratohyoidian[1] was a little muscle that serves only (tenth)[2] to move a tiny bone? Doesn't such a grand and Greek name seem to promise an agent that would move our entire machinery? And I am convinced that, as for the omphalomesenteric[3] vessels, a simple little monosyllable would have honorably fulfilled all the functions of this magnificent term.

[40] Those who perfect their souls by the virtues and knowledge they acquire resemble those men from the myth who lost all their mortality by feeding on ambrosia. But those who base the excellence of their being only on external qualities are like those Titans[1] who thought they were gods because they had large bodies.

[41] Here, it seems to me, is how time was shortened and how the difference in calculation between the Septuagint[1] and the Hebrew text was introduced.

During the advent of Jesus Christ and long after, there was a tradition that the world must have existed for only six thousand years. When Jesus Christ came into the world, it was reckoned that the end of the world was near; that is, that the six thousand years were already well advanced. That is what made St. Paul[2] talk about the consummation of the ages, the last times. St. Barnabus[3] follows the same idea in the epistle attributed to him. According to Tertullian,[4] public prayers were performed in order to push

[39]
1. The styloceratohyoidian muscle extends from the apophysis (swelling or bony protuberance) to the large horn of the hyoid (bone at the base of the tongue).
2. It is not clear what the word "tenth" is doing in this sentence.—HC
3. Name given to two arteries and a vein through which circulation occurs from the embryo to the umbilical vesicle.

[40]
1. Titans are the generic name for the six sons of Ouranos and Gaia.

[41]
1. The Septuagint are the Greek translations of the Hebrew Bible done in Alexandria in the third and second centuries before Christ; said to be the work of seventy-two rabbis, six from each tribe of Israel, brought together by Ptolemy II Philadelphus. Isolated for seventy-two days on the island of Pharos, they are said to have arrived at a translation identical to the Law.
2. Paul, I Corinthians 1:8, and 7:29.
3. Saint Barnabas, Jewish native of Cyprus, one of the first converts to Christianity, is the author of an *Epistola Catholica* [Catholic letters].
4. Quintus Septimius Florens Tertullianus (Carthage, ca. 155–220), apologist and theologian.

back this end of the World: "*Oramus etiam pro Imperatoribus, pro statu saeculi, pro rerum quiete, pro mora finis.*"[5]

In the third century, as this end was not arriving and as no one wanted it to arrive so soon, they counted only fifty-five hundred years; that was the chronicle of Julius Africanus.[6]

In the fifth century, it was necessary to push back again, since no one wanted to see this end of the World, so they counted no more than fifty-two hundred years.

Writing in the year 320, Lactantius,[7] following the calculation of Julius Africanus and based on the idea that the world was to exist for only six thousand years, says that the world is going to last for only two hundred more years.

Finally, as the prescribed time passed by, it was necessary to push back again and posit only four thousand years to the advent of Jesus Christ. Toward the end of the seventh century, one finds in the Talmud[8] the tradition of the house of Elie,[9] which maintains that the World is to last six thousand years: two thousand years of futility, two thousand years under the Law, and two thousand years under the Messiah, which affords plenty of time before the six thousand years are over.

It is thus clear that, to the extent that time added up after Jesus Christ, time had to diminish before Jesus Christ. Notice that the cuts were made quite easily, because they were made on empty times. Notice also how well fitted this division of the World's duration is between two thousand years and two thousand years.

Nota that it was reading the extract from the *Defense of the Antiquity of Time*, from the *Bibliothèque universelle* [Universal library] (page 104, volume XXIV, February 1693),[10] that gave me the occasion to bring forth this idea. {See my remark with an asterisk on the shortening of time. It is (I think) on the occasion of the Persian or Arab chronology, where they put

---

5. "Let us pray also for the emperors, for the state of the world, for the peace of the empire, for the delay of the end [of time]." See Tertullian, *Apology*, 39.2.

6. Sextus Julius Africanus is the author of a *Chorography*; cf. *Spicilège*, 312.

7. Caecilius Firmianus, called Lactantius (ca. 260–ca. 335), Christian apologist. Montesquieu possessed a 1535 Latin edition of his *Divine Institutions* (*Catalogue*, 357).

8. The Talmud spans a period of eight centuries, from the third century B.C. to the end of the fifth century A.D.

9. Elie, Biblical prophet (ca. 873–853 B.C.).

10. By Paul Pezron (Paris, 1691). By this author, Montesquieu possessed (*Catalogue*, 2654) a work on the same subject published in 1687.

(I think) Abraham and then David. Thus, see either the extract from the Koran, or from Chardin, or from Hyde.[11] See also my extract from Justinus (book 36, p. 65).[12] The story of Joseph is recounted there with tolerable accuracy. He says Moses was his son, proof that ignorance of history has rather the effect of shortening time than of lengthening it.}

[42] SPANISH WOMEN. The Spanish country is hot, but the women are ugly. The climate[1] is made in favor of women, but the women are made against the climate.

[43] Isn't it something, the things that make the most personal distinctions among us! The loosening of two or three fibers would have turned Mme de Mazarin into a very unappealing woman.[1]

[44] See the *Journal des Savants* XXXIII of the year 1720, in-4°, page 516,[1] where there is a description of the different beds and levels of earth found in the territory of Modena,[2] up to seven or eight of them, including a city at fourteen feet, and at fifty feet an underground river whose noise you can hear. When they dig down to the sand bed, a little too far down, they often penetrate the sand, and, to the great danger of the workmen, they fill the excavation and go right to the roofs of the neighboring houses. I believe it could be the case that this underground river, swelled by some accident, may have produced some openings from time to time by which the waters have passed, become elevated, covered the countryside, and suc-

11. The extracts from Montesquieu's reading on the Koran, as well as this one from Chardin, are lost. Jean Chardin (1643–1713) had long traveled in Persia and wrote works about his travels published in 1687 and 1711 (*Catalogue*, 2738–39) that were important sources for Montesquieu's *Persian Letters*. The Orientalist Thomas Hyde (1636–1703) is the author of the first study of the Zoroastrian religion, *Historiae religionis veterum Persarum eorumque magorum . . . Zoroastris vita . . .* (Oxonii, 1700); Montesquieu made some extracts that have been lost.

12. M. Junianus Justinus, also known as Justin, Latin historian from the second, third, perhaps even fourth century, author of an abridged *Universal History* of Pompeius Trogus in a 1640 edition (*Catalogue*, 2845); Montesquieu's extracts are lost.

[42]
1. See *pensée* 268; on climate more generally, see *Laws*, bks. 14–17.

[43]
1. Hortense Mancini, Duchess of Mazarin (1643–99), niece of Cardinal Mazarin, wife of Armand-Charles de La Porte de La Meilleraye, Duke of Mazarin (1631–1713).

[44]
1. The August 19, 1720, issue, pp. 513–20, reviews *Viaggi per l'Italia, Francia e Germania di Niccolo Madrisio* [Niccolo Madrisio's voyages through Italy, France and Germany]. 2 vols. Venice: Hertz, 1718.

2. See *Spicilège*, 15, on the Fountains of Modena.

cessively created new levels—the waters receding or the passage becoming blocked up, once the cause of these swelling underground waters ceased. {No. The terrain has become packed together. See my itinerary on Viterbo or afterward.[3] See my extract on this: Bernardino Ramazzini, *De fontium mutinensium admiranda scaturigine.*}[4]

[45] Wealth consists in real estate or in movable property.[1] Real estate is ordinarily possessed by natives, since every State has laws that deter foreigners from the acquisition of its land. Thus, this sort of wealth belongs to every individual State. As for movable property—such as money, paper instruments, bills of exchange, or shares in companies, any kind of merchandise—they are common to the whole world, which, in this respect, counts for a single State, of which the other States are members. The State that possesses the most of this movable property in the world is the richest; Holland and England have an immense quantity of it. Each State acquires it by its commodities, its workers' labor, its ingenuity, its discoveries—even by chance—and the avarice of nations competes for the furniture of the world. There may be found a State so unfortunate as to be deprived not only of all the assets of other States, but also of practically all its own, so that the owners of its real estate would be nothing but colonies of foreigners. This State will be poor, lacking everything and deprived of all means of acquisition. It can happen sometimes that States where commerce flourishes see their money disappear for a certain time. But it returns immediately because the countries that have taken it at a certain rate of interest owe it and are obliged to return it. But in the countries we are talking about, the money never returns, because those who take it owe them nothing.

[46] It should not be surprising that all false religions have always had something childish[1] or absurd about them. There is this difference between

<hr />

3. See *Voyages* (*OC,* 2:1093) for his description.
4. The work of Bernardino Ramazzini (1663–1714), Italian physician, had been published in 1692; Montesquieu's extract is lost. The work, whose title may be translated *On the amazing bubbling waters of the springs of Mutina* (ancient Modena), was never translated into French or English.

[45]
1. "Put in the *Laws*" (M.). This *pensée* is in fact the source of *Laws,* 20.23, where Montesquieu adds the examples of Poland and Japan.

[46]
1. First version: "low."

religions and human sciences, that religions come from the people first-hand and pass from there to the enlightened, {who systematize them}, whereas the sciences are born among the enlightened, whence they can be spread among the people.

[47] BORING. There are quite a few types. Some are so uniform in their conversation that nothing ever comes of it. Others are so lazy that they let everything drop; in vain do you exhaust yourself trying to revive the conversation; you toss out some topics to them, they abandon them all. Others make us go into the void, *trahunt per inania.*[1]

[48] In Rome, everyone was permitted to accuse those suspected of intending to stifle the liberty of the Republic.[1] But since all those accusations produced only debates, they only added to the divisions and armed the leading families against each other. The remedies against nascent factions were very long, since they had recourse only to speeches. In Venice,[2] on the other hand, the Council of Ten[3] stifles not only factions but unrest. It is highly prudent of the Venetians never to combine honors and power in the same person.

[49] {By an overly long war, Hannibal[1] accustomed the Romans to war. He pressed too hard to attack Saguntium, he should have shored up his power in Spain beforehand.[2]

Rome, which alone was at war constantly, defeated all the republics, one after the other. She then defeated the kings by means of kings: Philip with the help of Attalus,[3] and Antiochus[4] with the help of Attalus and Philip.}

[47]
1. "Drag us through the emptiness."

[48]
1. ["I've put this in what I wrote on the Roman Republic"] (M.); cf. *Considerations*, IX, 93.

2. This one may have been written during Montesquieu's trip to Venice, between August 16 and September 13, 1728; cf. *Voyages* (*OC*, 2:977–1016).

3. On the Council of Ten, see *Voyages* (*OC*, 2:980): "The formidable Council of Ten is not the formidable Council of Ten . . . Its laws are no longer observed, for if a disgruntled man who finds himself in office has them executed, the relative of the victim or the victim himself who is elected after him avenges himself immediately. The problem is thus in the constant change in offices that are voted on every sixteen months."

[49]
1. Hannibal (ca. 247–183 B.C.), Carthaginian general and political leader.
2. Hannibal's siege of Saguntium (219 B.C.) precipitated the Second Punic War.
3. Attalus, King of Pergamum (241–197 B.C.).
4. Antiochus III the Great (ca. 242–187 B.C.).

[**50**] PLAGIARIST. One can make that objection with very little ingenuity.

Thanks to petty talents, there are no more original authors. There is no one up until Descartes[1] who did not derive his entire philosophy from the Ancients. They find the doctrine of the circulation of the blood in Hippocrates,[2] [and, if the differential and integral calculus were not saved by their sublimity from the pettiness of these people, they would find it in its entirety in Euclid].[3] And what would become of commentators without this privilege? They could not say: "Horace[4] said this . . . —This passage is related to another by Theocritus,[5] where it is said . . . : I am committed to finding in Cardano[6] the thoughts of whatever author, even the least subtle." To those authors who have seemed original in several places in their works, one owes the justice of acknowledging that they have not stooped so low as to descend to the condition of copyists.

[**51**] There are three tribunals that are almost never in agreement: that of the laws, that of honor, and that of religion.

[**52**] SINGULAR PEOPLE. There are people so bizarre that they are the grotesque figures of our species.

{Their minds generally diverge from all minds.}

As soon as a man thinks and has a character, they say: "He's a singular man."

Most people resemble each other in that they do not think: eternal echos, who have never said anything but have always repeated; crude artisans of others' ideas.

Singularity has to consist in a fine manner of thinking that has eluded others, for a man who can distinguish himself only by a special footwear would be a fool in any country.

The thoughts and actions of a singular man are so particular to him that another man could not employ them without betraying and diminishing himself.

[50]
1. René Descartes, French philosopher (1596–1650).
2. Hippocrates (ca. 460–ca. 377 B.C.), Greek physician.
3. Euclid, Greek mathematician, third century B.C.
4. Quintus Horatius Flaccus (65–8 B.C.), Latin poet.
5. Theocritus (ca. 312–ca. 250 B.C.), Greek poet, author of *Idylls.*
6. Gerolamo Cardano (1501–76), physician, mathematician, and philosopher; see *Catalogue,* 1418–20, for Montesquieu's possessions. Here he refers to *De Subtilitate* [On subtlety].

[53] LAZINESS. "Valet of the Society!—Say, what do you have better to do?" I should rather excuse the laziness of monks[1] who are occupied only with eternity. But that which has no purpose serves only to make a man unhappy.

[54] The obsession with astrology is a pompous extravagance. We think our actions are important enough to merit being written in the great book of Heaven. And there is no one, down to the poorest artisan, who does not believe that the immense and luminous bodies that roll overhead are made only to announce to the World the hour when he will emerge from his shop—or again, that in an hour, he will emerge from his shop.

[55] The Jesuits and Jansenists are going to carry their quarrels all the way to China.[1]

[56] In France, it is not noble names but well-known ones that give luster: a celebrated prostitute or a celebrated player[1] honors her house by placing it among the ranks of the well known.

[57] If the immortality of the soul[1] were an error, I would be very upset not to believe it. I do not understand how atheists think. I admit that I am not as humble as the atheists. But for me, I do not want to swap and will not go on to swap the idea of my immortality for that of a day's felicity. I am very charmed to believe myself immortal like God himself. Independent of revealed truths, metaphysical ideas give me a very strong expectation of my eternal happiness, which I would not want to renounce.

[58] Whatever I said about happiness[1] being founded on our machinery, I do not on that account say that our soul cannot also contribute to our

[53]
1. On this theme, see *Laws,* especially 14.7. When he was criticized for his views on monasticism by the University of Paris Faculty of Theology, and in a report to Rome's Congregation of the Index, Montesquieu defended himself, but by indicating that his views "did not include the transcendence of the Church, which must enjoy, relative to the civil power, all the freedom necessary for the accomplishment of its supernatural mission." See Brèthe, 2:401 n. 25. *Laws* was placed on the Index early in 1752.

[55]
1. On this dispute and on the Jesuit initiative in China, see Derathé, 2:526 n. 18.

[56]
1. *Joueuse* indicates a female player, without indicating what is being played.—HC

[57]
1. "I've put this in my *Pensées morales*" (M.); cf. *pensées* 220–24.

[58]
1. See *pensée* 30.

happiness by the habit that it takes on. The reason is that since most sorrows are greatly amplified by the imagination (which appears very clearly in women and children, who despair over the least pains and the least sorrows), they are also greatly amplified by fear of the aftereffects. Now one can accustom one's soul to examine things as they are. One cannot vanquish one's imagination—that is impossible—but one can diminish its fitfulness. One of the most effective reflections for hardening ourselves against our misfortunes is reflection on the immensity of things and the pettiness of the sphere we inhabit. Since these are things that philosophy proves to us by the senses themselves, we are much more affected by them than when they are proven to us by theological and moral reasoning, which reach only pure mind.

[59] It is not two hundred years since French women made the decision to wear petticoats; they soon got rid of that obstacle.

[60] As soon as polygyny is prohibited and monogamous divorce[1] is also prohibited,[2] it is absolutely necessary to prohibit concubinage. For who would want to get married if concubinage has been permitted?[3]

[61] We never reflect disagreeably upon ourselves without vanity immediately creating some distraction: we immediately look at ourselves from a different angle. [And we seek to compensate ourselves in some respect.]

[62] [Envy is normally more sensitive to glory than to shame. That is because vanity inflates things in the one, but in the other it diminishes them.]

[63] Modesty is fitting for everyone, but you have to know how to master it and never lose it. {Every man must be polite, but he must also be free.}[1]

[64] Theologians maintain that there is no one whose atheism is a matter of feeling. But can one judge what happens in the hearts of all men? The existence of God is not a clearer truth than these: man is composed of two substances; the soul is spiritual. And yet, there are whole nations that

[60]
1. See *Laws*, 26.13, 506.
2. First version: "prohibited among the Christians, religion had to prohibit concubinage."
3. "Put in the *Laws*" (M.); cf. 23.6, 430.

[63]
1. See *pensée* 74.

doubt these two truths. This is because our inner feeling is not theirs, and education has destroyed it. It is true that there are clear truths, but there are blind people. There are natural feelings, but there are people who do not feel.

[**65**] Saint-Evremond[1] speaks in French the way Saint Augustine[2] used to speak in Latin. In reading them, one gets exhausted seeing the words always clashing, and finding their minds always enclosed within the boundaries of an antithesis.

[**66**] The Pythagoreans always hid behind their master. "*Ipse dixit*," they said. But *Ipse dixit* is always a nonsense.[1]

[**67**] If there was no time before the Creation, it would necessarily follow that the world is as old as God and is coeternal with him.[1]

[**68**] We have no tragic author who imparts greater movements to the soul than Crébillon;[1] who tears us more from ourselves; or who fills us more with the vapor of the god who agitates it. He makes you enter into the transports of the Bacchae. You cannot judge his work, because he begins by disturbing the reflecting part of the soul. [He is the true tragic author of our time, because he excites (the only one who knows how to excite) the true passion of tragedy, which is terror.]

[**69**] To be always forming new desires and satisfying them as they are formed is the height of felicity. The soul does not linger enough on its anxieties to become overly sensitive to them, nor on its satisfactions to lose its taste for them. Its movements are as mild as its rest is animated, which prevents it from falling into that languor that drains us and seems to presage our annihilation.

[**70**] Most men who are called *fools* are so only relatively.

[65]
1. Charles de Marguetel de Saint-Denis de Saint-Evremond (1610–1703), Epicurean writer and conversationalist.
2. Saint Augustine, bishop of Hippo (354–430).

[66]
1. Disciples of Pythagoras, Greek philosopher and mathematician, sixth century B.C.; *Ipse dixit* means "he himself said."

[67]
1. See *pensées* 12 and 41.

[68]
1. Prosper Jolyot de Crébillon (1674–1762), French playwright; Montesquieu possessed the 1713 edition of his *Œuvres* (*Catalogue*, 2024); see *pensées* 1198 and 1215.

[**71**] The world is full of men like Janus in the myth, who was depicted with two faces.[1]

[**72**] The Stoics believed that the world was going to perish by fire. Thus, minds were prepared to hear that prophecy of Jesus Christ, who predicted that the end of the world would arrive in this fashion.

[**73**] The miser loves money for itself, not because of the utility he derives from it. That is called *appetere malum quia malum.*[1]

[**74**] [One can be polite in society while preserving one's freedom.][1]

[**75**] When Elizabeth provided judges to Mary Stuart, she weakened in English minds the idea of sovereign grandeur.

{It is probable that Cromwell[1] would never have imagined having the head cut off the one, if the head had not already been cut off the other.}

[**76**] One can say that everything is animated; everything is organized. The slightest blade of grass makes millions of brains see. Everything is constantly dying and being reborn. So many animals that have been recognized only by chance[1] must give rise to conjectures about others. Matter, which has experienced a general movement by which the order of the heavens has formed, must have specific movements that lead it to organization.

Organization, whether in plants or animals, can scarcely be other than the movement of liquids in tubes. Circulating liquids can easily form some tubes, or stretch out other ones. That is how trees arise from cuttings. They come from seedlings only by analogy with the cuttings,[2] the seedling being merely a part of the wood. {Reserving thought to man, it is difficult to deny feeling to everything that exists.}

[71]
1. Janus was a Roman god represented with two opposing faces.

[73]
1. "Seeking evil for evil's sake."

[74]
1. See *pensée* 63 .

[75]
1. Elizabeth, queen of England (1558–1603); Mary Stuart (1542–86), daughter of James V of Scotland, who had married Francis II of France in 1558; and Oliver Cromwell (1599–1658), whose Parliamentary colleagues voted to condemn Charles I to death in January 1649.

[76]
1. See *Essai d'observations sur l'histoire naturelle* [Experimental observations on natural history] in *OC,* 3:100.
2. See ibid., 107.

With regard to animals, circulation from mother to child occurs quite naturally in a body such as that of the mother, where all the liquids are in movement; everything found there is permeated by them.

[77] It is surprising that men had not invented bills of exchange until so recently, even though there is nothing in the world so useful. It is likewise with the postal service.[1] By the invention of bills of exchange, the Jews have assured themselves of permanent refuge{; they have stabilized their uncertain status}. For any prince who would like to get rid of them will not, for all that, be of a disposition to get rid of their money.[2]

Besides that, we have the invention of linen; plus, many specific remedies. But we also have many diseases that did not exist before.

[78] Father Calmet[1] doubts the existence of Sanchuniathon,[2] but the reasons he adduces are pathetic.

1. He says that Porphyry,[3] great enemy of the Christians, postulated him in order to adapt to the pagans everything that Moses attributes to the Jews. It is true that everything that comes from Porphyry's pen must be suspect. But if one pays attention to Sanchuniathon's account, one will find it so different, and conforming in such small and inessential circumstances, that one cannot use such conformity to reject an author venerable for his antiquity—and the only one who presents to us all the authors of Phoenician history.

2. If such a factor of conformity holds water, it would also be necessary to reject Pherecydes,[4] who begins his book like that of Moses. It would be necessary to reject Aesop, from whom Saint Paul copies a thought; that other author from whom Saint Paul has taken *"Cretenses semper mendaces, ventres pigri."*[5] It would be necessary to reject the entire Platonic

---

[77]

1. On bills of exchange, see *Considerations,* XXI, 199; *Laws,* 21.20, 389, and 22.10; and Derathé, 2:510 n. 38. On the postal service, see *pensées* 8 and 2207.

2. See *pensée* 280.

[78]

1. Dom Augustine Calmet (1672–1757), author of an early eighteenth-century Biblical commentary (*Catalogue,* 7).

2. Sanchuniathon, Phoenician historian, said to have furnished Philo of Byblos the material for his Phoenician history; his history was translated into Greek in the second century.

3. Porphyry, Neoplatonic philosopher (234–ca. 305), editor of Plotinus's *Enneads.*

4. Greek philosopher of the sixth century B.C. Author of a *Theogony,* according to which the world is formed of recesses in which the great gods were seated.

5. "The Cretans—always liars, indolent bellies."

sect, which spoke like Saint John. We must put to trial the Bishop of
Avranches,[6] who maintained that the patriarchs were no different from the
heroes of Antiquity. We must thunder against Father Thomassin[7] as a man
who wants to degrade the Jews' legislator, and we must regard these two
great men as new Porphyries.

Was it not merely these sorts of advantage that Porphyry had over
the Jews?

At least this was not how Apion[8] reasoned. He went straight to the target: he told them that in the beginning, they were a multitude of lepers;
that Moses was a priest of Heliopolis; that he gave them a law out of hatred
for the Egyptians, whom they had served. Then he denied, attenuated, or
whimsically explicated all the miracles of the Ancient Law. There you have
all his blows, and not those deflected blows that are so many lost blows.

[79] BIRD FLIGHT. Here, there are three things to consider: the weight
of their bodies, the extension of their wings, and the strength of the muscle
that pushes the air. Different observations are necessary for different birds:
given an adequate number of wings for flight, see if the extension (or diameter) of the wing is proportional to the weight, and what relationship there
is with the strength; for the stronger the muscle is, the more quickly it can
act upon the air. Now it is this speed that creates the force; witness the sheet
of paper that a bullet pierces without making it move. Besides this, there
is also habit, for birds that are not accustomed to flying can no longer fly.

Now what prevents men (I believe) from managing to fly is:

1. Their great weight, which would require a wing of excessive extension
that would be too difficult to move without accident;

2. The movement of the shoulder that must supplement that of the
wing's muscle, which is so strong in birds, would be too weak in man;
not to mention that the movement has to start from the center of gravity,
which cannot occur in man. To make up for that, the wings would have
to stretch along the whole body; and even so, you would have to imagine
some machine by which the strength of the shoulder's movement might
be enhanced.

6. Pierre-Daniel Huet (1630–1721), bishop of Avranches in 1692.

7. Louis de Thomassin, of the Oratory (1619–95), author of a *Traité sur l'ancienne et nouvelle discipline dans l'Eglise* [Treatise on past and present discipline in the Church] (1672).

8. Apion, Greek grammarian and scholar (first century); hostile to Philo and to the Jews, according
to Flavius Josephus's *Against Apion*.

3. The danger.

Even if the necessities were in place for flying, one would still not succeed on that account; every man can swim, but very few know how to do so, and thus to reduce to act what they have in potential. In this case, you would have to be suspended on a rope along your whole body and put yourself in motion to move the wings. Thus the Romans, before putting a fleet out to sea, instructed their future sailors by making them perform the maneuver on land. The birds in our barnyards do not fly (I believe) most of the time because they are not accustomed to flying.

One could give strength to arm movement by making a sort of lever, applying the fulcrum to the middle of the arm. The long arm would be from the arm to the fulcrum; the short one, from the fulcrum to the point where the wing was attached.

One could provide a feather tunic constructed in such a way that in beating the wing to ascend, the feathers would become attached to the body, after which, they would stand on end.

You would have to choose young children: more boldness, less weight; more docile, and with practice, the arm muscles would strengthen.

They would begin by letting themselves fall from a spot not very high up, onto a spot covered with straw or cushioning.

I think that their feet would have to fall under their stomachs, and that you would have to give them a sort of tail. The same action that makes the wings move could make this tail move.

The fulcrum would be applied to an iron belt, very thin and light.

You would have to compare the wings of several birds with their weight. You would see what remains, with respect to muscle strength.

You would have to see the clarifications you could get from Borelli's treatise, *De Motu Animalium* [On animal motion].[1] {There is a book on bird flight, in-folio. Must look at it.}

[80] To pacify all religious disputes in France, you would have to prohibit monks from receiving any novice who had not taken his philosophy and theology in the universities, and prevent them from having courses in these sciences in their own institutions. Otherwise, the disputes will last forever. Each order will form a sect apart, and a very unified sect. Monks

[79]
1. Giovanni Alfonso Borelli (1608–79); Montesquieu had the Lyon 1710 edition (*Catalogue,* 1411).

have always been great squabblers. *Pace vestra liceat dixisse: "Primi omnium Ecclesiam perdidistis."*[1] In the earliest ages of the Church, when monks still worked with their hands, didn't the monks of Scythia put everything in tumult?[2] They had to have this proposition passed: "One of the Trinity has been crucified." *Idem* {p. 56}, the monks cause dispute over the three chapters. Each order has a library of its authors, and individuals study only in that library.

[81] I believe that what especially causes the declination of the ecliptic is a certain conjunction of the Earth—aside from differences in weight, the northern side weighing more toward the Sun than the southern. That indeed seems to be the case, in that the largest seas are found on the southern side. Thus, the earth is deeper there, and, in addition, my sense is that water weighs less than earth. On this, must look at *History of the works of the learned,* February 1692, article 10: *Essay on the new system of the world.*[1]

[82] It is difficult to understand by reason alone the eternity of the punishments of the damned,[1] for punishments and rewards can be established only in relation to the future. A man is punished today so that he will not err tomorrow, so that others will not err as well. But when the blessed are no longer free to sin, nor the damned to do good, what good are punishments and rewards?

[83] The ecstasies with which Muslim men look at courtesans and dancers make it quite clear that the gravity of marriage bores them.

[84] Precepts must not be made that cannot be commonly followed: abstinence from women by Christians, from wine by Muslims. When you have breached the barriers, you become emboldened, and you indulge yourself everything else.

[80]
1. "With your permission I must tell you the truth, that 'you teachers more than anyone have been the ruin of the Church.'" Montesquieu was probably adapting Petronius, *Satiricon,* 2, where the ruined subject is "true eloquence" rather than "the Church."—HC
2. "See p. 48, *Histoire des ouvrages des savants* [History of the works of the learned], October 1691, extract from vol. 5 of Dupin's *Bibliothèque ecclésiastique* [Ecclesiastical library]." (M.).

[81]
1. The *Histoire des ouvrages des savants* (February 1692), art. xiv, 263–69, reviews a 1691 *Essai d'un nouveau système du monde.*

[82]
1. Montesquieu is said to have composed in his youth, around 1711, an essay *Against the eternal damnation of the pagans* (*OC,* 3:6), whose text is lost. See also *pensées* 591 and 629.

For this reason, one must make laws only on important things, for whoever has violated a useless law will diminish the respect for those laws that are necessary to society; and as soon as he has ceased to be faithful, by violating one point, he follows his convenience and violates all others that get in his way.

[85] Just as there should be no childish religious precepts, there should also be no laws that are useless, or on frivolous things.

[86] Our eau-de-vie, which is a new invention by the Europeans, has destroyed an enormous number of Caribbeans; likewise, since they have been drinking it, they do not live as long. And I am not surprised, given that they are not prepared by the prior usage of wine for the drunkenness caused by eau-de-vie, that it should have such strange effects on them.

We have also brought the Caribbeans the Siamese disease.

I believe that we have also brought them the smallpox (as to America), which had been brought to us by the Arabs.[1]

These countries have brought us yaws, which is transmitted (some say) by the sting of certain flies on a spot where the skin has peeled, which communicates through the blood, or (as an English author says) by a snake bite.

Mortal diseases are therefore not the most catastrophic ones. If flies had carried only the plague, those who had it would be dead, but the contagion would have ceased; instead, it has become endless.

With the wealth of all climes, we have the diseases of all climes.

[87] When you look at ancient statues, you find a quite remarkable difference between the Ancients' faces and ours, and it is impossible for it to be otherwise, since each nation has, so to speak, its own color{, height} and physiognomy. But since the Greeks and Romans, nations have become so dislocated, everything has become so displaced, that all the ancient peoples' physiognomies have been lost and new ones have been formed, so there is no longer any Greek or Roman face in the world.

Our imaginations are extremely deceptive. Since we know that the Romans were a victorious people and master of others, we imagine they were a people of large stature; a small woman will never evoke in us the image of

[86]
1. See *PL,* CV, 175; see also *pensée* 1813.

a Roman woman. And yet, in the ancient statues that are not inflated, the eyes always find a certain compression, and in fact we must be larger than they, because since that time, the peoples of the North have inundated Europe.

{Vegetius[1] says in plain language that the Romans cannot compete in size with the Gauls.}

However little our trade with the West Indies were to grow—that is, if the Spanish were to lift the prohibition they have imposed, on pain of death, against all Europeans approaching the Indies—the white color would run the risk of being lost to the world, and there would remain only the image of our beauties of today.

A proof of this is that in the West Indies, where the three colors—black, white, and that of the faces of America—have mingled, there are no longer any whites properly speaking, and out of two hundred faces, no two are the same color.

The Turkish nation and the Persian are made by art—by the males of these nations and the women of Circassia, Georgia, and Mingrelia.

If a more distant nation than the Tartars had conquered China, farewell to the Chinese faces, and if the yellow peoples of Asia spread into Europe, what would become of us?

And what do we know about the changes that would have occurred in our species as a whole, not only in appearance but also in reasoning, if care had not been taken to kill all the monsters?

[Today's sculptors should therefore not take a Greek statue as their model, nor judge Greek statues by our modern appearances.]

As for the mind, I would not want to say that there could not be a certain mélange of nations, such that the most inventive nation possible—in relation to the bodily organs—might be formed.

[88] As for differences in constitution, as soon as we talk about them, we latch onto spices, as if they were the sole cause of the malady or a new cause.

The Ancients had their spices, their relishes, just like us; these things stimulated their appetites, just like ours.

[87]
1. Flavius Vegetius Renatus, late fourth, early fifth century; Montesquieu owned a 1553 edition of *De re militari* [Military institutions] (*Catalogue,* 1742).

[89] There's an author[1] who has written a treatise on diseases of the arts; I would like to write one on diseases of religions.

[90] I would not dare say that the oak trees of the past were not taller than those at present, and likewise with other plants. The earth is being used up, by virtue of being cultivated. We see it in our Antilles islands, where the land is already tired of producing. Perhaps the only reason Asian land is more fertile than that of Europe is because it has not been exhausted by continual cultivation. It is happening in all the world's changes, which we do not perceive because we are not in touch with the two extremities.

[91] [At every moment, new species of animals are being formed, and I believe that some are being destroyed at every moment as well.]

[92] In their apologies, the earliest Fathers did less to prove Christianity than to destroy Paganism, and they did well to go at it in that way, since nothing is better suited to make people embrace a new religion than an understanding of the absurdity of the old one. This is because most men, not wanting to live without religion, return to the one that remains.

Two other things solidified the establishment of Christianity: the length of Constantine's reign, the brevity of Julian's.[1]

The Pagans were ill-equipped to contest the miracles of Scripture: the miracles of the Platonists were countless, and [almost] all the philosophers' sects were oriented toward the most childish credulity.

It is true that the Christians' apologies were scarcely seen by the Pagans. The contemptuous terms the former used when speaking about them would have been imprudent if their works had been seen by the Pagans. {The Christians' apologies were written to persuade Christians themselves.}

Eusebius, in his *Evangelical Demonstration,* is (it seems to me) the first to lay out the system of our religion in its full light.[2]

[89]
1. Bernardini Ramazzini, whose *Opera omnia medica et physiologica* [Complete medical and physiological works] (Geneva, 1717) Montesquieu possessed (*Catalogue,* 1184).

[92]
1. Constantine, emperor (r. 306–37); Julian the Apostate (r. 361–63), whom Montesquieu praises in *Considerations,* XVII, 161, and *Laws,* 24.10; see also Montaigne's *Essays,* II, 19, and *pensée* 98.
2. Eusebius (ca. 265–340), bishop of Caesarea, was involved in conflicts between orthodoxy and Arianism. Montesquieu owned several Latin editions of his *Works* (*Catalogue,* 329–32).

[93] An ungrateful Country constantly tells its learned men that they are useless citizens, and while it enjoys the fruits of their long labors, it asks them what they have done with them.

[94] One takes pity seeing Hannibal—returned from Trebia, from Cannae, and from Trasimene—go and administer Carthage![1]

[95] I had put in my *Dialogue of Sulla:*[1]

"I soon had present actions for myself, whereas Marius[2] had only the always faint memory of past things. I walked in his steps, and as soon as he stopped, he found me in front of him."

[96] If the gods were as depicted, they ought[1] to blush at their whimsy.

[97] Bad faith of the French, since they have so many judges to repress it.

[98] Julian was not an apostate, since he was never properly a Christian; for you cannot be a Christian without renouncing Paganism, whereas you can be pagan without renouncing Christianity, since Paganism adopts all sects, even the intolerant ones. That is why Constantine's change did not produce a revolution in the Empire.

In the time of Constantine, his children, and even Julian, Christianity was not very widespread. Paganism flourished as before under Constantine, and it was destroyed only under Theodosius.[1]

It is probable that Julian would have been fatal to Christianity upon his return from Persia, but his death, bolstered by the prejudice about divine punishment, was a very favorable blow, because it struck wavering minds.

[94]
1. Hannibal defeated the Romans at Trebia in 218 B.C., and again, under Flaminius, at Trasimene in 217; he fought Varro in the battle of Cannae in 216.

[95]
1. This dialogue, published in *Mercure de France* in February 1745, is said to have been read by Montesquieu at the Club de l'Entresol in the 1720s and found in the papers of its host, abbé Alary. See Depping, *Introduction aux Œuvres de Montesquieu* (Paris: Belin, 1817), 1:xx; Lanier, "Le Club de l'Entresol (1723–31)," in *Mémoires de l'Académie d'Amiens*, 3rd series, 6 (1880), 46ff. For an English version and commentary, see *The Personal and the Political: Three Fables by Montesquieu*, trans. William B. Allen (Lanham, Md.: University Press of America, 2008).
2. Caius Marius (157–86 B.C.).

[96]
1. First version: "men ought."

[98]
1. Theodosius the Great, emperor from 379 to 395.

One cannot marvel enough at the moderation of that emperor toward the seditious speech the Christian clergy engaged in against him, even in his presence; never has the crime of *lèse-majesté* been carried further than it was against him.

[99] In Alexander's time, the world situation was such that everything that was not Greek was barely noticed, and there was no world but his empire.

I find nothing so splendid[1] as the world's confusion and consternation after his death. The whole world looks at itself in profound silence. The rapidity of his conquests had outrun all laws. The world could have been subjected to the conquerors; wonder kept it faithful. The world had been seen as conquest, but not succession. All the captains found themselves equally incapable of obeying and commanding. Alexander dies, and he is perhaps the only prince whose place could not be filled. Both the man and the king were lacking. The legitimate succession was despised, and it was impossible to agree even on a usurper.

That great machine, deprived of his intelligence, became dismembered. All his captains parceled out his authority; out of respect, no one dared succeed to his title. The word *King* seemed to be buried with him—not, as has sometimes happened, out of hatred, but out of respect for the one who had borne it.

The captive nations forgot their chains and mourned him; it seems they believed their captivity began only on that day, after having lost that man whom alone it was not shameful to obey.

[100] From time to time there are inundations of peoples in the world who impose their morals and customs everywhere. The inundation of the Muslims brought despotism, that of the Northern peoples brought government by nobles. It has taken nine hundred years to abolish this latter government and to establish in each state the government of one. Things will continue like that, and it seems we will move along from age to age to the final degree of obedience, until some accident changes the arrangement of brains and makes men as indocile as they were in the past. Behold how there has always been a constant ebb and flow of empire and liberty.[1]

[99]
1. See *Laws*, 10.14, 150.

[100]
1. See *PL*, CXXXVI, 231.

[101] In our current taste for collections and libraries,[1] there ought to be some industrious writer who wants to make a catalogue of all the lost books cited by ancient authors. It ought to be a man free of cares and even of amusements. Some idea ought to be given of these works and of the life and character of the author—as much as possible given the fragments that remain and the passages cited by other authors who have escaped the ravages of time and the zeal of emerging religions. It seems we owe this tribute to the memory of so many learned men. Very many great men are known by their actions and not their works. Few people know that Sulla wrote *Commentaries* and that Pyrrhus wrote *Military Institutions*{, and Hannibal some *Histories*}.

This work would not be as immense as it appears at first. One would find fertile sources in Athenaeus, in Plutarch, in Photius, and in some other ancient authors.[2] One could even limit oneself and treat only poets, philosophers, or historians.

I would also like someone to work on a catalogue of the arts, sciences, and inventions that have been lost, giving as precise an idea of them as possible, the reasons why people lost their taste for them or why they have remained neglected, and finally, how they have been replaced.

I would also like someone to write about the diseases that no longer exist and those that are new, the reasons for the end of the former and the birth of the latter.

{I would also like someone to collect all the quotations from Saint Augustine, the lost authors and others, etc.}

[102] These animals that we call *mythical,* because we no longer find them on earth, even though they have been precisely described by ancient authors—could they not have existed and their species disappeared? For I am convinced that species undergo extraordinary change and variation, that some are lost and new ones formed. The earth is changing so markedly

[101]

1. Libraries with specialized lists drawn up by cultivated persons who have read, annotated, and often summarized the texts whose titles they assemble. See the Benedictine *Histoire littéraire de la France* (begun in 1733) and the work of abbé Claude-Pierre Goujet (1723–46) for examples; also Louise-Noëlle Malclès, *Manuel de bibliographie* (Paris, 1969), 25–26.

2. Lucius Cornelius Sulla (138–78 B.C.), Roman general and political leader; Pyrrhus (ca. 318–272 B.C.), king of Argos; Plutarch (ca. 46/49–124), Greek biographer, moralist, and author of *Parallel Lives,* of which Montesquieu owned several editions (*Catalogue,* 2790–97) as well as the *Moral Works* (*Moralia*); Photius (ca. 820–ca. 895), Byzantine theologian, patriarch of Constantinople.

every day that it will give constant employment to natural philosophers and naturalists. {*Idem,* illnesses to physicians.} What am I saying? It will always dishonor them. Pliny and all the ancient natural philosophers will be convicted of fraud, however true they were in their own time.[1] There is no one today who, looking at the river Jordan, does not regard everything said about it by the sacred authors as a pompous form of expression. A fountain today has a certain property; it is impossible, in the movement of all its elements, for it to maintain that property without variation. Now the more or the less would suffice to change everything. The authors who describe Gaul to us could not have erred to the point of being mistaken on a thing so general and well known. Look, however, at how Justin describes it! We constantly accuse the Ancients of betraying the truth. Why do we pretend they love it less than we do? On the contrary, they would have loved it more, because their philosophy had morals as its object more than ours does. That admirable work by the gentlemen of the Academy[2] that we regard as the natural truth will someday be subject to the criticisms of future moderns; they will be unable to stand reading descriptions they find inconsistent with what they see. [*Nota* that I have heard of a voyage by Addison where he sought—by things the poets celebrated and by what those things are at present—to reveal how dangerous it would be to believe them.[3] But what he attributes to poetic lies could well be attributed, perhaps, to real changes.]

[**103**] {I have seen Lake Regillus, which is no larger than a hand.}[1]

[**104**] If the books written against the Jesuits endure into a distant future and survive the Jesuits themselves, won't those who read them think that the Jesuits were assassins, men blackened with crime, and won't they be surprised that they could have been allowed to live? They surely will not imagine that they are pretty much like other religious, like other ecclesiastics, like other men. "If those people still existed," they would say, "I would not want to find myself on a highway with them."

[102]
1. Caius Plinius Secundus, Pliny the Elder (23–79).
2. *History of the royal academy of sciences* (1703ff.); *Catalogue*, 2566.
3. Joseph Addison, whose travel account of Italy was translated into French in 1722; Montesquieu made extracts of it in *Geographica* II (*OC,* 2:923–24) without personal annotations, adding only: "I have not finished reading this book."

[103]
1. See *Voyages* (*OC,* 2:1147) for the same remark.

{I don't know that Bayle hasn't said something like that.}[1]

[105] An original work almost always causes five or six hundred others to be constructed; these latter use the former rather like geometers use their formulae.

[106] When a man lacks a quality that he cannot have, vanity compensates and makes him imagine that he has it. Thus, an ugly woman believes she is beautiful; a fool believes he is smart. When a man feels that he lacks a quality that he could have, he compensates by jealousy.[1] Thus, one is jealous of the rich and the great.

{The true reason is that it is not possible for vanity to deceive itself on wealth and greatness.}[2]

[107] Giving pleasure in a vain and frivolous conversation is today the only merit. For this, the magistrate abandons the study of his laws. The doctor would think himself discredited by the study of medicine. We flee as something pernicious any study that might take away from the frivolity.

To laugh about nothing and carry some frivolous thing from one house to another is called the *science of society*, and one would fear losing it if one applied oneself to another science.

Eliminate from the constant conversations the detail of some pregnancy or some childbirth; that of some women who were at the Races or the Opera that day; some news item brought from Versailles, that the Prince did that day what he does every day {of his life}; some change in the interests of fifty-odd women of a certain air, who take on, barter with each other, and give back to each other fifty-odd men, also of a certain air—you have nothing left.

I remember that I once had the curiosity to count how many times I would hear told a little story that certainly did not merit being told or retained for the three weeks that it occupied the polite world. I heard it told two hundred twenty-five times, which made me very happy.

[104]

1. Pierre Bayle (1647–1706), Huguenot exile and leader of the "republic of letters" through his journalistic and editing enterprises. For an attack on his "paradox," see *Laws*, 24.2; see also *pensées* 1096 and 1946 and Robert Shackleton, "Bayle and Montesquieu," in *Pierre Bayle: Le Philosophe de Rotterdam* (Amsterdam, 1959), 142–49.

[106]

1. See *pensées* 483, 1622, and 1726.

2. "The great" (*les grands*) and "greatness" (*les grandeurs*) in these last two sentences probably refer to the honors and dignities of the social elite.

[**108**] {Out of several ideas that I had, here are those that did not make it into my work on *Taste and the works of the Mind.*}[1] We owe to the rustic life that man led in early times that joyful air diffused throughout all the myths. And also those happy descriptions, those naïve adventures, those agreeable divinities, that spectacle of a condition different enough from ours for us to desire it, but not far enough removed to shock our sense of verisimilitude; finally, that mixture of passions and tranquillity. Our imagination laughs at Diana, Pan, Apollo, the Nymphs, the woods, the fields, the fountains.[2] If the earliest men had lived as we do in the cities, the poets would have been able to describe to us only what we see every day with anxiety, or what we feel with distaste. Everything would reek of avarice, ambition, and the tormenting passions. All that would matter is [the rules of law and order, the cares and in the end] all the fatiguing detail of social life.

The poets who describe the rustic life for us speak to us of the golden age, for which they are nostalgic; that is to say, they speak to us of a time even more happy and tranquil.

[**109**] There has hardly ever been a legislator who, to make his laws or his religion respectable, has not resorted to mystery. The Egyptians, who are the authors of all sanctity, used to hide their ritual with very great care.

It was prohibited among the Greeks to unveil the ceremonies of Ceres, and the Romans regarded it as an inexpiable sacrilege to reveal the mysteries of that Greek divinity and those of the Egyptian divinities.[1]

There was another type of mystery, which consisted in hiding the name of the divinity being worshipped. It was prohibited to the Jews, on pain of death, to pronounce the name of God, and it was prohibited to the Romans, on the same punishment, to pronounce that of the gods of their city {and even the true name of the city}.

The reason for this prohibition was not, however, the same for the two

---

[108]

1. The *Essay on taste* [*Essai sur le goût dans les choses de la nature et de l'art*] was published in Diderot's *Encyclopédie* (7:762–67); there is also a 1967 Geneva edition by Charles-Jacques Beyer.

2. Diana, Roman goddess identified with the Greek Artemis; Pan, god of Arcadian shepherds; Apollo, son of Zeus, Greek god of light.

[109]

1. Ceres, divinity of fertility.

nations: a religious fear held back the Jews, but a political fear held back the Romans.

The Jews regarded the name as the principal attribute of the thing. Thus God, who always acted in conformity with the ideas that that people should have, took particular care to impose a name on things as he created them, and to change the names of the patriarchs as they changed their situation and their fortune.

But the Romans feared that if foreigners knew the names of their city gods, they might call them forth and thereby deprive the Romans of their support and their presence.

There is a sort of religious mystery that consists in attributing to certain places a sanctity that must exclude the profane.

Christians also have their mysteries, which do not consist, like those of the Ancients, in certain hidden ceremonies, but in a blind submission of reason to certain revealed truths.

Here would be a question: to know whether the mysteries of the Ancients, which consisted in hiding ritual, were more striking than those of the Christians, which consisted in hiding dogma.

Be that as it may, all religions have had their mysteries, and it seems that otherwise, there would be no religion.

[110] I admit my taste for the Ancients. That Antiquity enchants me, and I am always led to say with Pliny: "It is to Athens that you are going. Respect their gods."[1]

[111] I like to see the quarrels of the Ancients and the Moderns; this makes me see that there are good works among the Ancients and the Moderns.

[112] In the system of the Jews, there is a great deal of aptitude for the sublime, since they had the habit of attributing all their thoughts and actions to the particular inspirations of the divinity, which gave them a very great agent. But although God thus appears to act as a corporeal being as much as in the pagan system, he nonetheless appears to be agitated only by certain passions, which eliminates not only graciousness but also variety from the sublime. And besides, a lone agent cannot offer variety; he leaves the imagination with a surprising void, instead of that plenum formed by the innumerable pagan divinities.

[110]
1. The passage is from Pliny the Younger, *Letter to Maximus,* VIII.24.

The Christian system (I use this term, improper though it is), in giving us healthier ideas of the divinity, seems to give us a greater agent. But since this agent neither permits nor experiences any passion, the sublime must inevitably atrophy. Moreover, the mysteries are sublime rather for reason than for the senses, and it is with the senses and the imagination that works of the mind are concerned.

But what seals the loss of the sublime among us and prevents us from amazing and being amazed is this new philosophy that speaks to us only of general laws, and eliminates from our minds all particular thoughts of the divinity. Reducing everything to the communication of motion, it speaks only of pure understanding, clear ideas, reason, principles, consequences. This philosophy, which has extended down even to that sex that seems to have been made only for the imagination, diminishes the taste one naturally has for poetry. It would be too bad if a certain people were to become infatuated with the system of Spinoza; for aside from the fact that there would be no sublime in the agent, there would be none even in actions.[1]

[113] Frightful diseases, unknown to our forefathers, have attacked human nature right down to the source of life and pleasure.[1] We have seen the great families of Spain, which had survived so many centuries, almost all perish in our time; devastation that war has not caused, and that must be attributed solely to an evil that is too common to be shameful, but that is nothing less than disastrous.[2]

Pleasure and health have become almost incompatible. The pains of love, so rhapsodized by the ancient poets, are no longer the rigors or the inconstancy of a mistress. Time has given birth to other dangers, and the Apollo of our day is less the god of verse than of medicine.

[114] Homer was a theologian only to be a poet.

---

[112]
1. Baruch Spinoza (1632–77), author of *Tractatus theologico-politicus* (1670) and *Ethics* (1677). Montesquieu attacks his putatively fatalistic philosophy in *Laws*, 1.1. After he was accused by the Jansenist *Nouvelles ecclésiastiques* of being a Spinozist, Montesquieu defended himself vigorously in *Défense*, pt. I, 1. See Paul Vernière, *Spinoza et la pensée française avant la Révolution* (Paris: Presses Universitaires de France, 1954), 2:446–66.

[113]
1. "I've put this in my *Différence des génies*" (M.); that is, the *Essai sur les causes qui peuvent affecter les esprits et les caractères,* doubtless before 1742; see *OC,* 3:397ff.
2. See *Laws,* 14.11, 241.

[115] The divine work of this age, *Telemachus,*[1] in which Homer seems to come alive, is irrefutable proof of the excellence of that ancient poet.

I am not among those who regard Homer as the father and master of all the sciences.[2] This accolade is ridiculous for any author, but it is absurd for a poet.

[116] M. de La Motte is an enchanter who seduces us by force of charms and spells.[1] But one must beware of the art he employs. He has brought to the dispute that divine genius, those happy talents that are so well known in this age, but that posterity will know better still.

Mme Dacier, on the other hand, has joined to all of Homer's defects all those of her mind, all those of her studies, and I even dare say all those of her sex, like those superstitious priestesses who dishonored the god they revered, and who diminished the religion by dint of augmenting the worship.[2]

I am not saying that Mme Dacier does not merit that fine place she has been accorded in the Republic of Letters, and that she seems to have obtained in spite of Destiny itself, which had brought her forth to make the happiness of some Modern rather than for the glory of the Ancients. Everyone has felt the skill and even the fire of her translations. But she ended her life in an age in which the sovereign merit is to think precisely, and which, while admiring a fine translation of the *Iliad,* is not less impressed by bad reasoning on the *Iliad.*

Thus, one could say of this war what is said about the war between Pyrrhus and the Romans: that the Epirotes did not defeat the Romans, but the consul was defeated by the king of the Epirotes.

[115]
1. Fénelon's *Télémaque* (1699) was one of the most widely reprinted and influential works of the eighteenth century.
2. The reference is to Mme Dacier (1654–1720) and her side in the quarrel of the Ancients and Moderns. She translated the *Iliad* in 1699 and the *Odyssey* in 1709 (*Catalogue,* 2059–60).

[116]
1. Antoine Houdar de La Motte (1672–1731) sided with the Moderns in publishing a translation of the *Iliad* in French verse with a Discourse on Homer (Paris, 1714; *Catalogue,* 2058). In *Persian Letters,* Montesquieu sided strongly with the Moderns, whose leaders, La Motte and Fontenelle, deliberately applied Cartesianism to literary criticism. Thus, in the Discourse, La Motte sees in Homer "a pleasure consisting in illusion and bias founded on the authority of the suffrage; all this is not reason, and yet it belongs to reason alone to appreciate everything." For all this, see Vernière, 290 n. 1; see also *pensées* 872 and 1881.
2. In 1714 Mme Dacier criticized La Motte's Discourse in *Des causes de la corruption du goût* [On the causes of the corruption of taste].

[**117**] I admit that one of the things that has most charmed me in the works of the Ancients is that they capture the grand and the simple at the same time; whereas it almost always happens that our Moderns, in seeking the grand, lose the simple, or in seeking the simple, lose the grand. It seems to me that in the former, I see vast and beautiful landscapes with their simplicity, and in the latter, the gardens of a rich man with their thickets and parterres.

I urge you to look at most of the works of the Italians and the Spanish. If they lean toward the grand, they go beyond nature instead of depicting it. If they lean toward the simple, it is clear that it has not presented itself to them, but that they have sought it out, and that they have so much wit only because they lack genius.

[**118**] Of all the genres of poetry, the one where our Moderns have equaled the Ancients, to my taste, is the play. I believe I have discovered the reason. It's that the pagan system counts for much less in it. That sort of work is by its nature movement itself. Everything, so to speak, is on fire. There is neither narrative nor anything historical that needs extraneous assistance; all is action. You see everything; you hear nothing. The presence of the gods would be too jarring and too unrealistic. It is rather a spectacle of the human heart than of human actions. Thus, it has less need of the wondrous.

I am not saying, however, that the pagan system does not have a lot of influence here, for very often the spirit and nearly all the main or subsidiary ideas are derived from it. Witness the beginning of *The Death of Pompey*,[1] where neither gods nor goddesses enter as actors:

> Fate hath declar'd herself, and we may see
> Th' Intrigue of the great Rivals Destiny:
> That quarrel which did all the Gods divide,
> Pharsalia hath the Honour to decide.

and this other passage where Cornelius says, etc.

[**119**] Our Moderns are inventors of a certain genre of spectacle which, made solely to ravish the senses and enchant the imagination, has needed

---

[118]
1. Pierre Corneille (1644), 1.1.1–4. The translation comes from *Pompey: A Tragoedy*, trans. Katherine Philips (Dublin: John Crooke, 1663).

those alien expedients that tragedy rejects. In that spectacle, made to be admired but not examined, such happy use has been made of the resources of myth, ancient and modern, that reason has protested in vain, and those who have failed at simple tragedy, where nothing helped them agitate the heart, have excelled in this new spectacle, where everything seemed to come to their aid. Such has been the success that the mind itself has gained by it. For everything that we have of the greatest delicacy and exquisiteness, everything that the heart has that is most tender, is found in the operas {of Quinault, Fontenelle, La Motte, Danchet, Roy,[1] etc.}.

[**120**] One sees nothing so pitiful as the poetry of five or six centuries ago. And yet, everything should have contributed to give us good works. The number of poets was countless. The nobility made a profession of the poet's craft. Fortunes were made from poetry around women and princes. Europe could not have lacked for genius. Emulation existed, too. And yet, one sees only miserable works, written by people whose only ideas are taken from Holy Scripture. {The extravagant interpretations of many monks in the reading of Scripture brought forth quite a few bad profane works. All etymologies were taken from the Hebrew, and all histories were related to those of the Holy books.} But as soon as people began to read the Ancients, after losing a century in translating and commenting on them, they saw the authors appear, and (what seems to me the glory of the Ancients) they could compare them to the Moderns.

[**121**] With the Ancients, we must not analyze things in detail in a way that they are no longer able to support. This is all the more true with regard to the poets, who describe mores and customs, and whose beautiful turns, even the least refined, mostly depend upon circumstances that are forgotten or that no longer move us. They are like those ancient palaces whose marble is under grass but which still let us see all the grandeur and magnificence of the design.

[**122**] We criticize the Ancients for having always elevated heroes' bodily strength. But in works made to stimulate wonder, we, whose new methods of combat have rendered bodily strength useless, still represent heroes who

[119]

1. Philippe Quinault (1635–88); Antoine Danchet (1671–1748), author of tragedies and operas; Pierre-Charles Roy (1683–1764), poet and dramatic author; and Bernard Le Bovier de Fontenelle (1657–1757), whom Montesquieu got to know during his first trip to Paris in 1714–15. See Louis Desgraves, "Montesquieu et Fontenelle," in *Actes du colloque Fontenelle* (Paris, 1989), 307–15.

kill everyone and overturn everything that stands in their way. Sometimes it's giants, sometimes lions, sometimes floods. And to show the marvelous, we always return to that bodily strength that our mores, not nature, make us regard as contemptible.

[123] I am inclined to believe that epithets should be frequent in poetry. They always add something; they are the colors, the images of objects.

The style of *Telemachus* is enchanting, though as full of epithets as that of Homer.[1]

[124] The Greeks who violated a cadaver were perhaps following nature in doing so. A certain ceremonial politeness, misplaced when religion is not its source, has made us weep at the death of our enemy, by which we are delighted within our souls; for otherwise, we would not have killed him, etc.

[125] I do not know if the Ancients had better minds; but by the passage of time, it has happened that we sometimes have better works.

[126] But to judge Homer's beautiful turns, one must put oneself in the Greeks' camp, not a French army.

[127] We can enjoy seeing the mores of a barbarous people represented, provided we find passions that are pleasing and moving. [And although the Slavs have not mastered, as we have, the way of acting most destructive of the human species, this matters not: it is enough that their passions move us.] We like to see the same passions on a new subject. We much prefer to hear the vizier Acomat speak of his manner of loving, than Bajazet as a naturalized Frenchman.[1]

[128] One cannot be sufficiently astonished at how slowly the French arrived at *Venceslas* and *Le Cid,* and at how rapidly the Greeks passed from the bad to the excellent. I believe we were damaged by the ideas of Holy Scripture, which we always wanted to carry over into poetry.

[129] Sophocles, Euripides, and Aeschylus at the outset carried the genius of invention to the point where we have changed nothing since then in the rules they left us, which they could only have done through a perfect knowledge of nature and the passions.

[123]
1. See *pensée* 115.

[127]
1. Acomat, lively character in Racine's *Bajazet* (1672); Bajazet is merely an instrument in his hands.

[**130**] Those who have scant knowledge of Antiquity see Homer's defects arising with the times that succeeded him.

[**131**] [My whole life, I have had a decided taste for the works of the Ancients.] Having read many critiques of the Ancients in our time, I have admired many of these critiques; but I have still admired the Ancients. I have studied my taste and examined whether it was not one of those sick tastes on which you should base nothing substantive. But the more I examined it, the more I found that I was right to think the way I felt.

[**132**] What Homer added to the system of myths in Hesiod's *Theogony* ought to be looked at.

[**133**] The gods' adulteries were not a sign of their imperfection; they were a sign of their power{, and talking about their adulteries honored them}. {The reason for this could be given, derived from the nature of the subject.}

[**134**] Wouldn't the poets' epithets come from the superstition of the Pagans, who believed that the gods wanted to be called by a certain name and liked to be considered under certain attributes? The poets therefore had to adjust to this. Heroes were treated like gods.

[**135**] There are none who are more in need of avoiding dishonor than those who have made a reputation for themselves in the world by their knowledge, their wit, or some talent. For if, in spite of what they have in their favor, their bad qualities have broken through, if they have caused the public that had been seduced to turn against them, these bad qualities must be very great, and the contempt they have obtained must be entirely just, since it is only after lengthy wavering that the people have bestowed it on them.

[**136**] It has been said that a body cannot entirely lose its motion; since it is always sharing it, there always remains some for itself. I find this very reasonable, for a body that encounters another communicates its motion, as if it were merely the same body. Thus, it always keeps some in proportion to its mass. In addition, it seems to me that if a body were ever at rest, it would be impossible for it to move except by the action of an infinite cause, since there is an infinite distance from rest to motion.[1]

[136]
1. See Montesquieu's *Discourse* on this subject read to the Bordeaux Academy on May 1, 1720 (*OC*, 3:89–93).

[137] It seems to me that we in Europe are not in a position to make appropriate observations about the plague.[1] That disease, transplanted here, is not manifested with natural symptoms. It varies more according to the diversity of climate, not to mention that we cannot make continual observations, since the disease is not continuous, as whole centuries go by in between outbreaks; besides which, the observers are so disturbed by fear that they are not in a condition to make any observations.

But very precise, very enlightened, very well-paid observers ought to be sent to places where this disease is epidemic and occurs every year, like Egypt and several parts of Asia. We should look into what are its causes, what seasons are favorable or unfavorable, the winds, the rains, the nature of the climate, the ages and temperaments of those who are more exposed, what remedies, preventatives, cures, varieties there are; getting observations from many places, many times, using some insight that certain countries can give us. Egypt, among others, is subject to the plague every year, and it stops as soon as a certain rain that they call the *drop* has fallen. We should examine the nature of this *drop* and see if, along with a bedpan, we couldn't produce in the bedrooms of the stricken an artificial *drop,* in the way that all natural phenomena have been imitated: since M. Lémery has made earthquakes, bombs, etc.[2] Remedies have been found in the home of the smallpox that were not in our climes, and one could cite plenty of similar examples.

[138] When we say that nature is so provident that she always makes us find particular remedies in the places afflicted with certain diseases (because, absent that, men would not have been able to survive there), we must beware that we are reasoning *a priori,* even though we would perhaps do better simply to relate these remedies to different combinations. On earth, there are certain locations that are uninhabitable; others that are habitable without any drawback; others, finally, that would not be habitable because of certain drawbacks, if some remedies for these drawbacks had not been encountered. Thus, it is not, I believe, true that, through

[137]

1. Perhaps a reference to the plague in Marseilles in 1720, which he discusses in his correspondence. See also *Laws,* 14.11, 241.

2. Lémery (1645–1715), pharmacist and chemist, author of a *Cours de Chimie* (*Catalogue,* 1340) and a *Pharmacopée universelle* (*Catalogue,* 1305).

special providence, remedies have been established in certain locations to render them habitable; it must instead be said that the remedies having been found, the locations have been rendered habitable.

[**139**] According to Justin, I, page 232, 1.23, the Sabis is a river that runs into the Danube. I have not found it in Baudran, nor in Stephanus of Byzantium, Holstenius, Moréri, Bayle, or Corneille.[1]

[**140**] It would be difficult[1] to find in history two princes who more strongly resembled each other than the King of Sweden, Charles XII,[2] and the last duke of Burgundy:[3] same courage, same self-importance, same ambition, same boldness, same success, same misfortunes, same designs executed in the flower of youth and at a time when other princes are still being governed by their regent. Charles XII undertook to dethrone King Augustus, just as the Charolais undertook to dethrone Louis XI, and when he was covered with glory, he went and lost his entire army before Poltava, just as the other one lost his before Morat.[4]

[**141**] On December 22, 1722. There is appearing here a play called *La Fagonnade.*[1] A violent tax has given the author the fire and brimstone of Rousseau.[2]

Racine's poem on *Grace* is infinitely admired and disdained here.

[**139**]
    1. Justin (Marcus Junianius, third century?), *Epitome of the Philippic History of Pompeius, Trogus,* XXXII, 3; Michel-Antoine Baudrand (1633–1700), a geographer whose 1682 work Montesquieu owned (*Catalogue,* 2452); Stephanus of Byzantium, Greek geographer from the sixth century, author of *Ethnica,* a geographical lexicon (see *Catalogue,* 2645, for Montesquieu's holdings); Lucas Holstein, author of a 1684 commentary on Stephanus which Montesquieu owned (*Catalogue,* 2625). The Sabis is today's Sambre River.

[**140**]
    1. "I've put this in the *Journal*" (M.), that is, the *Reflections on the character of some princes;* cf. *OC,* 3:538.
    2. Charles XII, king of Sweden (r. 1697–1718); see *Laws,* 10.13.
    3. Charles the Bold (1433–77).
    4. King Augustus II of Poland (1697–1733); Louis XI, king of France from 1461 to 1483; Charles XII was defeated at Poltava in the Ukraine in 1709 by Peter the Great; Charles the Bold was beaten at Morat by the Swiss on June 22, 1476.

[**141**]
    1. Louis Fagon (1680–1744) was the younger son of Louis XIV's physician and held a number of positions in the royal finances. In his *Sottisier* (literally, collection of howlers), Montesquieu's friend President Jean Barbot transcribed a "Satire against M. Fagon, Counsellor of State, otherwise known as the Fagonnade."
    2. Jean-Baptiste Rousseau (1671–1741), the poet and not the Genevan *philosophe.*

[**142**] Contradiction of Marsham,[1] who bases his book on a passage by the ancient author Syncellus,[2] and who, a page later, says that Syncellus is a man without credibility and without judgment.[3]

[**143**] I heard the first performance of the tragedy *Inès* by M. de La Motte;[1] I clearly saw that it succeeded only by virtue of being beautiful, and that it pleased the spectators in spite of themselves. [One may say that the grandeur of tragedy, the sublime, the beautiful prevail throughout.] There is a second act that, to my taste, is above all the others. [I found in it a hidden and learned art, one that does not reveal itself at first showing.] I was more touched the last times than the first. There was a children's scene in the fifth act that seemed ridiculous to many people, and the audience was divided; some laughed, others cried. I am convinced that that scene would be surprising to a people whose mores were less corrupt than ours. We have achieved a too-unfortunate refinement.

Everything that has some connection with the education of children, with the natural sentiments, seems to us something low and vulgar. Our mores are such that a father and mother no longer raise their children, no longer see them, no longer nurture them. We are no longer moved to pity at their sight; they are objects concealed from all eyes; a woman would no longer be sophisticated if she appeared to concern herself with them. By what means can minds prepared in this way savor a scene of that sort? Racine, who would have been able to do this with more impunity, did not risk it and did not dare show Astyanax.[2] Little Regulus used to be enjoyable because mores were not so perverted; at present, we would no longer put up with him. There is a surprising injustice in men's judgments: we accuse our forefathers of having little intelligence because they wept on seeing little Regulus; we think they were weeping because they lacked common sense. No! They had as much intelligence as we do, neither more

[142]
1. "Examine this" (M.). Thomas Marsham (1602–83), author of works on chronology (see *Catalogue,* 2692).
2. George the Monk, Byzantine chronicler, who was *syncellus,* that is, private secretary, of Tarasius, patriarch of Constantinople; he died in 806. The reference would be to his work *Chronographica.*
3. "This article is not by me" (M.).

[143]
1. The first staging of *Inès de Castro* was April 6, 1723; see *Mercure de France* for April 1723, p. 777.
2. Astyanax, son of Hector and Andromache.

nor less, but their mores were different, their hearts differently arranged. That is why they wept, and we do not. The same can be said about virtually all tragedies.

[**144**] Against the supposed constancy of the martyrs, some have pointed to what happened to the Jews during their prosperity. Each good fortune brought a fall along with it. But since they were the most wretched people in the world, they were as firm as they were inconstant.

Progress of Lutheranism and Calvinism despite the Inquisition.[1]

[**145**] State ministers can know from the currency exchange a neighboring State's secret movements,[1] because a great military enterprise cannot be launched without money, and thus without a big change in exchange rates.

[**146**] There have been States which, to keep a foreign commodity at a low price, have raised the export tariff. That does no good, because the merchant impeded by this can bring in little. He does not want to be impeded. And even though he does not profit at all from permission to export the commodity (disdaining a small profit), he nonetheless wants to have this capacity, in order to save on the transport risks.

[**147**] By Justinian's laws, it appears that in the earliest ages, simple fornication was not regarded as illicit.[1] Justinian, who had taken it so much to heart to abrogate all laws contrary to Christianity, made one, the third in the Code,[2] *Communia de Manumissionibus* [General Rules of Manumissions], by which an unmarried man who has taken one of his slaves as a concubine and dies, leaves this concubine free: "*Ipsi etenim domino damus licentiam ancilla sua uti,*"[3] which would not be the same, he says, if he had

---

[144]

1. For Montesquieu's criticism of the Inquisition, see *PL,* XXIX, 53–54; *Spicilège,* 472, 610, and 779; and *Laws,* 25.13 and 26.11–12.

[145]

1. "I've put this in my *Romans*" (M.); see *Considerations,* XXI, 199, and *Laws,* 22.10 and 22.13, as well as Derathé, 2:514 n. 11.

[147]

1. Justinian I, Eastern Roman Emperor (r. 527–65). Under his authority, Tribonian and Theophilus arranged the laws promulgated since Hadrian (117–38) into the *Justinian Code* (528–29 and 534); he had the *Novella* and the *Digest* or *Pandect* edited, and he published the *Institutes,* the basis of the *Corpus juris civilis;* Montesquieu owned several editions of the *Institutes,* in Latin and in French (*Catalogue,* 710, 716). See also S. P. Scott, ed., *The Civil Law,* 17 vols. (Cincinnati: Central Trust, 1932).

2. *Justinian's Code,* VII.15. (See the *Digest,* XL.1, in Scott, 9:45ff.—HC)

3. "We grant permission to the master, during his lifetime, to make use of his female slaves."

a wife: "*Hominibus etenim uxores habentibus concubinas habere nec antiqua jura nec nostra concedunt.*"[4] *Antiqua,* that's the pagan religion; *nostra,* that's the Christian.

[**148**] "*Obedite principibus etiam dyscolis!*"[1] and certainly a Christian revolting against an Emperor because he was an idolater was doing wrong, because the constitution of the State was such that the empire was supposed to be in the hands of idolatrous princes.

[**149**] What La Bruyère[1] said—"A man has invented a story; by virtue of retelling it, he ends up persuading himself that it is true"—is very well put. It is because he remembers retelling it better than he remembers inventing it. If this is true, what must be the power of childhood prejudices!

[**150**] If thieves who do not kill were not punished by death, they still would not kill, certain thereby of avoiding the gibbet.

[**151**] The English have the convenience of disseminating all sorts of pamphlets by means of their foot post. {That is why people have not wanted to establish it in Paris.} The Queen[1] testified to the 1713 Parliament that she would like a law to be established to repress the pamphlet mania. Parliament refused; one member said this would make the government too powerful.

[**152**] It is not in France's interest to make an offensive and defensive alliance with England. The assistance of France is prompt, but that of England is long and uncertain because of the deliberations. It is true that France is more exposed than England, and thus more often needs assistance.[1]

[**153**] England has no regular tariff schedule with other nations; their schedule changes, so to speak, with each Parliament. To unload a landed property, they impose very large fees.

4. "For neither the ancient laws nor our own permit men possessing wives to keep concubines."

[148]
1. The precise text is: *Servi, subditi estote . . . dominis . . . etiam dyscolis.* "Servants, be submissive to your masters, even when out of temper." 1 Peter 2:18.

[149]
1. Jean de La Bruyère (1645–96); Montesquieu owned his *Characters* in the 1714 edition and his *Sequel* to it in the 1700 edition (*Catalogue,* 660–61).

[151]
1. Anne Stuart, second daughter of James II, queen of England (r. 1702–14).

[152]
1. The reference may be to the Anglo-French alliance of 1716, which lasted until 1731.—HC

The import tariff on foreign wheat falls in proportion to the rise in the wheat price there.[1]

[154] England and Holland have made very bad use of their credit. Those same establishments and companies that have made their power will one day destroy it. This is because men abuse everything. It is only a hundred years since these companies were established, and already their debts are immense and are increasing every day.[1] In a country where there is credit, all the projects that enter the head of a state minister are implemented; in other countries, they stay put.

[155] [Our refugees[1] are all Whigs, and if the English throne is ever overturned, it will be by those people, as it was in Charles I's time[2] by the French refugees of that time.]

[156] Substance, accident, individual, genus, species, are merely a manner of conceiving things according to the different relationships they have with each other. For example, roundness, which is a bodily accident, becomes the essence of a circle, and redness, which serves as the color of a physical circle, becomes the essence of a red circle. *Idem,* for the idea of genus, which is nothing in itself, being only that of an individual insofar as I do not determine it, and which I keep in mind without applying it to one subject rather than another; the idea of the infinite, in which Father Malebranche[1] finds so much reality that he believes particular ideas come from it, making a kind of arithmetical subtraction (if I dare use this term) from it, whereas it is only by adding ceaselessly to the end without finding any limit that I form the idea of the infinite. It is thus that I think of an extension that I am always adding to, of a being whose perfections I limit so little that I could always add new ones in my mind. But I have no

[153]
1. See *Laws,* 22.18, most of which is drawn from the *pensées.*

[154]
1. "Put in my *Laws*" (M.); see *Laws,* 21.22, 22.18, and especially 22.10 on privileged and colonial companies, and Derathé's discussion in 2:503 n. 15.

[155]
1. The Jacobites or loyalists of the ousted Stuart King James.
2. Charles I, second son of James I; until his execution, king of England, Scotland, and Ireland (1625–49).

[156]
1. Nicolas de Malebranche (1638–1715) of the Oratory. Montesquieu owned several books from his library.

idea of matter or a being to which I would be unable to add anything, any more than I do a time or a number. It is quite true that God has been for all eternity, for there is no entity that can be made from nothing, so there has been infinite duration. But for all that, I have no idea of such duration, and I only see it from the consequences I derive from certain principles.

[157] When Father Malebranche says, "We do not see objects in themselves, for those who are sleeping see them without being present; nor in ourselves, for we have the idea of the Infinite; we therefore see them in God," one can respond that we see objects as we feel pain: all of this is in ourselves. We even feel our soul, which reflects upon itself and perceives that it is thinking without doubt within itself. Notice that Father Malebranche's argument proves nothing more than that we do not know how we perceive objects.

[158] A prince could conduct a fine experiment. Raise three or four children like animals, with some goats or some deaf and mute nurses. They would fashion a language together. Examine this language. Look at nature in itself, disengaged from the prejudices of education. Learn from them, after their instruction, what they were thinking about; exercise their minds, by giving them everything necessary for invention; finally, write up the history.

[159] A prince, in the middle of a circle of courtiers, becomes a courtier himself as soon as another prince more prestigious than himself appears; the second will experience the fate of the first if a third and greater one happens on the scene. The worshippers change the object of their cult. If the king appears, he will absorb all honors; the courtiers will forget those they have just given, and the princes, the adoration they have received.

Women who change clothes four times a day resemble actresses who, after playing the role of empress in one play, run off and undress to play that of chambermaid in a second one.

[160] Government by nobles, when nobility is hereditary and not the reward for virtue, is as defective as monarchical government. Republican government in which the public funds are diverted in favor of private individuals is also defective like monarchy, for economy is the advantage of republican government.[1]

The estates of France being divided into three bodies assembled in three

[160]
1. "I've put in the *Romans* what concerns republican government in this remark" (M.); see *Considerations* VIII.

chambers, jealousy was sown among them. What the Clergy wanted, the People or the Nobles did not want. {The Nobles and Clergy ought to have formed one chamber.}

[**161**] Gold, easier of transport, is more disadvantageous to a State than silver.

[**162**] A prince who pardons his subjects[1] always imagines he is engaging in an act of clemency, whereas he is very often engaging in an act of justice. When he punishes, on the contrary, he believes he is engaging in an act of justice, but often he is engaging in an act of tyranny.[2]

[**163**] Observations are the history of natural science, and systems are its myth.

[**164**] STUPIDITY: CRUDE FOLKS. One can compare men of this sort to peoples that the Ancients imagined being in the unknown zones. "*Intra, [si] credere libet*, says Pomponius Mela in speaking of Africa, *vix jam homines, magisque semiferi.—Blemmyis capita absunt; vultus in pectore est. Satyris praeter effigiem nil humani. Gamphasantes, sine lectis et sine sedibus, vagi, habent potius terras quam habitent.*"[1]

[**165**] RABELAIS. Every time I have read Rabelais,[1] he has bored me; I have never managed to enjoy him. Every time I have heard him cited, he has pleased me [which has made me think that he is good in himself, and I find him bad only because I do not understand him.] {I have since read him with pleasure.}

[**166**] I have never seen a book so far below its reputation as Father Quesnel's *Moral Reflections;*[1] never so many base thoughts, never so many childish ideas.

[**162**]
    1. "I've put this in the *Journal*" (M.).
    2. See *pensée* 1986.—HC

[**164**]
    1. Pomponius Mela, first-century Latin geographer; Montesquieu owned two editions of *De orbis situ*, the 1540 and 1582 (*Catalogue*, 2629–30). "In the interior, if one is to believe it, now scarcely men and more half-animal, the Blemmyes lack heads, the face is in the chest, except for the likeness to Satyrs not at all human. The Gamphasantes, without beds, without homes, wandering, occupy the earth rather than dwell on it." See I.4 and I.8.

[**165**]
    1. François Rabelais (1494–1553), author of *Gargantua and Pantagruel*.

[**166**]
    1. Pasquier Quesnel (1634–1719) of the Oratory passed for the leader of the Jansenists; his 1671 work was condemned by the Papal letter of Clement XI (July 13, 1708). Montesquieu had the 1693 edition (*Catalogue*, 35).

[**167**] When it is said that the Egyptians took up the Hebrews' customs, it is as if one were telling me that the French have taken from the Irish {Jacobites} their manner of speaking and getting dressed.

[**168**] *"Dixit insipiens in corde suo: 'Non est Deus.'"*[1] That does not apply to atheists except in a broad sense; it means in the literal sense: *"Non est Jehovah!"* What is spoken of here is nations who disdained the God of Israel, and who said he was an imaginary god. The Chaldeans were not prone to atheism; in no passage in Scripture is it a question of this enormous outrage.

[**169**] I am convinced that the Spanish prohibition against foreigners engaging in the Indies trade is highly detrimental to their power.[1]

If they could engage in it themselves, and if foreigners did not engage in it in their name, their policy would be good; but this prohibition is laughable.

Moreover,[2] the same foreigners engage in this trade through their interloping merchant vessels, which destroy the Cadiz trade;[3] not to mention that smuggling is always ruinous to the nation against which it is practiced, because it ruins their customs revenue.[4] So that the victimized nation pays dearly for merchandise and gets no profit from its customs.

Free trade would lead all European nations to harm each other. The abundance of commodities they would send would keep them cheap, that is, would raise the price of gold, and silver, and the rest of the country's merchandise.

The king of Spain would have his free fifth and some immense sums in customs from the country's other commodities.

His expenses against freebooters would cease, and it would be left to the other nations of Europe to incur them, in whole or in part.

Spain would not face the burden of populating all those vast continents alone.

At his whim, the king would impose duties on European and American

---

[**168**]
1. Psalm 14:1: "The fool says in his heart, 'There is no God.'"

[**169**]
1. "This idea might be right. However, I have my doubts; perhaps it is better for Spain to leave things as they are" (M.). See *Laws*, 21.23, 396–97.
2. First version: "It is harmful in that foreigners are doing it. These same foreigners must not engage in this trade."
3. See *Laws*, 19.10, 313, and *Considerations on the wealth of Spain* (*OC*, 3:137–55).
4. First version: "because to make it work, you have to sell at a high price."

merchandise, and the more inhabitants there were, the greater the duties would be.

They could be well protected against the betrayals and encroachments of foreigners, and even their trading posts would be secure against possible insults and vexations.

The king of Spain could farm out his customs to private companies, and all European nations would become his vassal-states.

It would be easy to prevent foreign religions from corrupting the purity of the dominant religion.

The Spanish are so well established, since the long possession they have had, that a few foreign or naturalized merchants are not to be feared.

In a word, when a nation cannot engage in a particular trade alone, it must allow others to do so to its greatest advantage.

What at first led them to this prohibition was that the Spanish were afraid of being disrupted in their conquests. Thus, they prohibited foreigners from traveling there on pain of death.

[170] [Notice that the good faith of the Spanish has ruined their trade and transferred it to foreigners who engage in it without any fear under the name of a Spaniard.]

[171] [I like the quarrels over the works of the Ancients and Moderns; they prove that there are excellent authors among the Ancients and Moderns.[1]]

[172] The mathematician[1] goes only from the true to the true or from the false to the true by *ab absurdo* arguments. They do not know that middle which is the probable, the more or less probable. In this respect, there is not more or less in mathematics.

[173] XENOCRATES AT PHERAE.[1]

{You want me to talk to you about Pisistratus.}

---

[171]
1. See *pensée* 131.

[172]
1. "I've put this in the *Bibliothèque*" (M.).

[173]
1. This letter is the first version of the *Lettres de Xénocrate à Phérès;* Pisistratus represents the regent. See also *pensée* 800. These *Lettres* (*OC,* 3:129–35) were composed in 1723 at the time of the regent's death; see Denis R. Landry, "A Note on the Date of Composition of Montesquieu's *Pensée* 173 and *Lettres de Xénocrate à Phérès,*" in *Les Bonnes Feuilles* (1972), 15–18.

Of all the great men who have appeared on earth, there are hardly any more singular than Pisistratus.[2]

He was born with a superior talent, and yet he was subject to the influence of all other talents.

He has no vanity, and he has a sovereign contempt for all men.

Those who have deceived him have so discredited men in his mind that he no longer believes in honorable people.

He has few vices that come from a bad nature; not all of his virtues come from a good one.

[He accords to virtue only what he grants to the importunity of vicious people.] With him, the whole privilege of virtue is that it does no harm.

He well knows that he is above other men; but he does not feel it enough. That is why there is no one of talent who is unable to discover the art of leading him.

He is not familiar with that infinite distance between the honorable and the wicked man, and all the different degrees between these two extremities.

He has an ease in manners and command that charms all who obey him.

No one has carried domination so far, but he has not made it felt in proportion to its weight.

He sees men as individuals differently from the way he sees them in the midst of company.

He has an indifference toward events that is fitting only in those not brought forth by Heaven to determine them.

He does the work of the politicians without even trying; he encounters everything they had reflected on, and his witticisms are as sensible as their meditations.

He makes of his mind what others make of their senses. He governs all of Greece without seeming to, without even thinking about doing so, and everyone follows the order of his designs as if following the torrent of his power.

He succeeds much less in governing the interior of his realm, and while he treats with kings from a position of superiority, he is the eternal dupe of his courtiers.

In governing the interior, he always wants to go from good to better; he is always more struck by the malady than by the risks in fixing it.

---

2. "Put in the *Bibliothèque*" (M.).

He corrects where toleration is called for. He imagines that the people, who think with such slowness, will follow the rapidity of his genius, and that they will open their eyes in an instant, to regard as abuses things that time, example, and reason itself have made them regard as laws.

With that sublime mind that produces great men and great crimes, Pisistratus would be a wicked man if his heart did not make up for his lack of principles. But his heart so dominates him that he knows neither how to refuse nor punish. Incapable of falling into any difficulties while doing ill, he falls into them constantly while doing good.

When he rose to the government of Sicyon,[3] he pardoned the offenses that had been committed against him; he even pardoned (which is harder) those that were still being committed against him. You had to work at it to exhaust his clemency. But at that point, he struck promptly and boldly, and surprised both those who had offended him and those who feared to see him offend with impunity.

In the early years, Pisistratus loved. He found a tender heart and pleasures that Love reserves for true lovers.[4] Afterward, he ran from object to object, and achieved possession without relish. He exhausted his senses in restoring what he lost, and he so used up the motive force of his passions that he became almost incapable of what is falsely called *enjoying.*[5] Finally, he threw himself into debauchery, and he brought some charm to it. But whatever one may say about it, debauchery does not become refined. His mistresses became no more than witnesses to a life not free but licentious. But in his debauches, Pisistratus lost his reason, never his secret.

The gods, irritated at Sicyon, sent Pisistratus a dream one night: he thought he was master of all the world's treasures, but this dream was the cause of public poverty.

A man of obscure birth[6] was received into Pisistratus's house. At first he was regarded with disdain, but afterward, without passing through esteem, he obtained trust. Proud of possessing his secret, he dared ask for the sovereign priestly ministry, and he obtained it. Soon Pisistratus, tired

3. Sicyon, ancient Peloponnesian city near Corinth; here an allegory of France.
4. Anne Larcher, Countess of Argenson (1706–54), the regent's mistress.
5. The French word *jouir* here has a sexual connotation.—HC
6. Guillaume, abbé, then Cardinal Dubois (1656–1723), prime minister in 1722.

of command, placed sovereign power in those hands. The traitor prepared the cruelest acts of ingratitude against him. But Venus sent him a disease that made all his plans fade away.

Pisistratus was fortunate to have reigned at a time when obedience obviated the necessity of command, so to speak; for if he had reigned in times of disorder or confusion, the arrangement of his mind was such that he would never have dared enough, and he would have undertaken too much.

I certainly believe that Pisistratus fears the immortal gods; but it seems that he has no great regard for their ministers' interests, and that he is too impressed by this principle: that Religion is made for men, not men for Religion.

Pisistratus refused few women of the court of Sicyon, but not a single one of them could boast that he had any esteem for her.

The king of Sicyon had conquered a neighboring prince's states and left him only his capital. He sent Pisistratus to besiege it.[7] The prince, reduced to despair and believing that not to exist or not to command was all the same to him, made some incredible efforts. Aid arrived. The Sicyonians let it pass. Pisistratus had all the conquests abandoned. He could have preserved them. But everyone defended Pisistratus's honor: the soldiers agreed that he had not lacked resolution; the captains, that it was not he who had lacked leadership.

In unsuccessful affairs, a general is blamed for all the failures of the army and Court. Here the Court and the army blamed themselves for the entire failure, in order to absolve the general.

Pisistratus knew not the art of humiliation, but he knew the art of reversal.

Pisistratus was less touched by the good and the beautiful than by the extraordinary and the marvelous.

He had a brave heart and a timid mind.

He was more flattered for his talents than his virtues.

Pisistratus's timidity came as much from laziness toward action, and from the pain of doing harm, as from any weakness of soul.[8]

7. In 1706, the Duke of Orléans had been sent to Piedmont to end the siege of Turin during the War of the Spanish Succession; Prince Eugene obliged him to retreat.
8. First version: "serious self-examination."

When it came to vices, finally, his mind was everything and his heart nothing.

Pisistratus is the only man I have known who has been uselessly cured of prejudices.

Pisistratus's unhappiness was a sick taste, which led him to present himself as being worse than he was. He had a certain hypocrisy with regard to vices, which made him affect to appear to have them, as proof of his freedom and independence.

[**174**] Slavery is contrary to natural right,[1] by which all men are born free and independent.

There are only two sorts of dependence that are not contrary to it: that of children toward their fathers; that of citizens toward magistrates. This is because, since anarchy is contrary to natural right (the human species being unable to exist with it), the power of magistrates, which is opposed to anarchy, must be consistent with it.

As for the right of masters, it is not legitimate, because it cannot have had a legitimate cause.

The Romans admitted three means of establishing servitude, all of them equally unjust.

The first, when a free man sold himself. But who does not see that a civil contract cannot violate natural right, by which men are as essentially free as they are reasonable? {Moreover, there cannot be a price attached. The slave was sold; all his goods passed to the master, and thus the reward for his money. Thus, the master gave nothing and the slave received nothing. Thus, no price. Moreover, a man can only contract as a citizen. Now a slave is not a citizen. Nature has made him a citizen; he cannot contract, for no longer being a citizen.}[2]

The second, when a man was taken in war; for since the victor was free to kill him, they said, he was also free to make him a slave. But it is false to say that it is permissible, even in war, to kill except in case of necessity; but as soon as one man makes a slave of another, it cannot be said that he was under a necessity to kill him, since he did not do it.[3]

[174]
1. On slavery, see *Laws*, bk. 15. See also Derathé, 1.504 n. 1, and Julien K. Lafontant, *Montesquieu et le problème de l'esclavage dans "l'Esprit des lois"* [Montesquieu and the problem of slavery in the *Spirit of the Laws*] (Sherbrook, 1979); Montesquieu did not make the point about natural right in *Laws*, 15.1.
2. See *Laws*, 15.2.
3. "Put in the *Laws*" (M.).

The entire right that war can give over captives is that of being so assured of their persons that they can no longer harm the victor.[4]

{We regard as assassinations the murders committed in cold blood by soldiers after the heat of action.}

The third means was birth. This one falls with the other two; for if a man could not sell himself, still less could he sell his unborn son.[5] If a prisoner of war cannot be reduced to slavery, still less his children. {Civil law, which has allowed men the division of property, could not rank among the property a portion of the men who were to make this division.}

The reason why a criminal's death is a licit thing is that the law that punishes him has been passed in his favor. A murderer, for example, has profited from the law that condemns him; it has preserved his life at every moment. He thus cannot complain about it.[6] It is not at all the same with the slave; the law of his slavery has never been of any use to him. It is against him in all cases without ever being for him, which is against the fundamental principle of all societies.

If it were said that it could be useful to him because the master has given him food, slavery would thereby have to be limited to persons incapable of earning a living.[7] But those sorts of slaves are not at all wanted.

A slave can thus make himself free; it is permissible for him to flee.[8] Since he is no part of the society, the civil laws do not concern him.

The civil laws form chains in vain; natural law will always break them.

This right of life and death, this right to seize all the goods that a slave may acquire, these rights so barbarous and so odious are not necessary for the preservation of the human race; they are therefore unjust.

To condemn to slavery a man born of a certain woman is a thing as unjust as the Egyptians' law that condemned to death all red-haired men;[9] unjust, in that it was unfavorable to a certain number of men, without being able to be useful to them.

And how could they think of taking from a father the property of his children and from the children the property of their father?

---

4. This is in *Laws*, 15.2, except for the words "the victor."
5. "Put in the *Laws*" (M.), 15.2.
6. "Put in the *Laws*" (M.), 15.2.
7. "Put in the *Laws*" (M.), 15.2.
8. "Put in the *Laws*" (M.), 15.2.
9. "Put in the *Laws*" (M.), 15.5.

Spartacus's war was the most legitimate ever waged.[10]

Woe betide those who make laws that can be violated without crime!

[175] In the *New Account of the French Islands in America*,[1] it is seen that Louis XIII[2] was extremely pained at establishing the slavery laws for the negroes of America, and that it was only on the expectation of their conversion that he consented.

[176] {Slavery, establishment of a right that renders a man so much the property of another man that the latter is the absolute master of his life and goods.}[1]

[177] No one is ignorant of the power of the ancient kings of Sicily over land and sea; rivals or allies of the Carthaginians or Romans, often victors of one or the other. That island itself had in its midst several great powers, a very sizeable number of large cities which governed themselves by their laws, equally capable of making war and sustaining it.

When Sicily became a Roman province, it was, with Egypt, the granary of Rome and Italy, and, consequently, one of the principal parts of the Empire.

Alien causes must therefore have put this fine country in its condition of decadence. I believe its origins must be sought nowhere else than in the causes I am going to provide: the absence of its sovereigns, who always removed gold and silver from the country; the depopulation occurring because of the large number of priests and monks—which is felt more in the southern countries, which are always being depopulated more than those of the North, because people live much less long there. [Here you have what should be done to obviate these problems.]

Don Carlos would attract a large Sicilian party if he employed their revenues in maintaining a fleet, and thereby, he would be highly respected on the coasts of the Archipelago, Asia, Barbary, Italy, Spain, and even by the English and the Dutch, who would need him for their trade.[1] He could hold the Turk in check by sea. The taxes would not leave Sicily and would

---

10. Spartacus, leader of rebel slaves, died in 71 B.C.; cf. *Laws*, 15.13.

[175]

1. See P. Jean-Baptiste Labat, O.P., *Nouveau voyage aux iles de l'Amérique avec des figures* (Paris, 1722), 4:114 (in *Catalogue*, 2746).

2. Louis XIII, King of France (r. 1610–43); cf. *Laws*, 15.4, and *PL*, LXXV, 129.

[176]

1. "Put in the *Laws*" (M.), 16.1.

[177]

1. Don Carlos (1716–88), son of Philip V, King of Spain, and Elizabeth Farnese.

be consumed there, and the country would be in a better position to bear its tax burden. Fewer land troops would be needed in Sicily, since the fleet would guard the coasts. The king of Naples can scarcely use the land troops he has in Sicily, where they are hemmed in, so to speak. To put Sicily in a position to maintain this fleet, he has means at hand that other sovereigns do not. Since he exercises pontifical power in Sicily, he could at will reduce the number of monks, cut back on their property and use it to increase public revenue. A pretext suffices for these sorts of things. He could oblige the ecclesiastics either to farm their uncultivated lands or rent them out. He should conduct himself in such a way as to display plenty of respect for the indifferent superstitions, while destroying the harmful ones. The infirm among the royal troops could be placed in Sicily—they would serve to guard it—and the revenues from the main benefices applied to them. There should be laws favoring marriage, and an exacting rigor in administration. Jews and foreigners should be sought out and favored. The silks that arrive there should be employed in manufactures. Cultivation could be encouraged in two ways: (1) by favoring the export of Sicilian grain and finding an outlet to sell it to the Dutch, the Marseillais, and even in the Archipelago, where it is sometimes lacking; (2) by maintaining a slightly elevated price of wheat, which could be done very easily. Now, nothing does more to bolster the master's and the settler's enthusiasm for work than the hope of a reasonable price for his wheat. There is always a natural relationship between the price of the earth's bounty and the wage given to the people who work it: if the crops are worth little, they are given little; if they are worth much, they are given much. Now it is clear that in this latter case, they are in a better position to pay taxes. The result of the policy of the Italian princes, who always maintain wheat at a very low price, is poverty for the master and idleness for the settler.

[178] The more populous a country is, the more it is in a position to furnish wheat to foreigners.

[179] In the five years of his pontificate, Sixtus V—by his good government, the moral austerity he established, the destruction of bandits, the constant protection given to the laws—saw himself in a position to effect immense projects in Rome, to amass great treasure and to make the Spanish jealous.[1]

[179]
1. Felix Peretti, Pope Sixtus V (1585–90). Montesquieu owned (*Catalogue,* 265) *La Vie du pape Sixte cinquième, traduit de l'italien de Gregorio Leti,* 3rd ed. (Paris, 1699).

[**180**] The Romans had rigorous laws against those who remained celibate. All ancient peoples were horrified by sterility. It would be easy to prevent celibacy among the secular clergy by establishing the Roman laws.

In Bordeaux in 1622, out of sixty students of the Jesuits, there were thirty who entered the monastery.

Since all big changes are dangerous in a State, monasticism should be not destroyed but limited.[1] All it would take for this is to reestablish the law of Majorian and the novella of Leo.[2] I am not even sure that Louis XIV didn't issue a law to prevent the taking of vows before age twenty-five. Innocent X destroyed all the little monasteries of his State:[3] he got rid of fifteen hundred of them, and he had resolved to press all Christian princes to do the same thing. Fathers and mothers should be encouraged to raise their children. Small secondary schools should be destroyed, and the ones in the big cities promoted. Just as it is important for people of a certain status to be raised to be conversant with the world of letters, it is pernicious to orient the common people in that direction. Small benefices should be consolidated, which would reduce the number of benefice holders.

Paternal education would prevent many a vice. It would also make people pay more attention to marrying off and getting rid of their daughters. Prohibit the keeping of unmarried domestics over the age of twenty-five. Prevent the Parlements from annulling marriages so easily, the jurisprudence being such that most marriages last only because they have not been attacked. Thus, those that have been annulled should be celebrated anew. Give privileges to those who have a number of children, and certain honors to the same. Solidify uncertain ranks by the number of children. A special preference in all wills to whoever has the most children. A magistracy in every city hall to whoever has the most children. Make those who live in celibacy pay for twelve children.

Prevent the spread of venereal disease by establishing a kind of quarantine and inspection of those coming from the Indies.

In countries where there are slaves, they should be able to expect liberty by the number of their children.

<hr>

[180]

1. Also on this theme, see *Laws,* 22.29.

2. In 458, Leo and Majorian, emperors of the East and West, prohibited girls from entering the religious life before the age of forty.

3. Pope Innocent X (1644–55).

Giving the three-children privilege to those who did not have them, as the Romans did, should be guarded against, unless they lost them at war.[4]

The number of celibate people multiplies proportionally the number of prostitutes, and just as monks are rewarded by nuns, the celibate are rewarded by prostitutes.

General rule: it is only marriages that populate.

Females of animals have a fairly constant fertility, so that one can fairly well estimate how many little ones a female will produce throughout her whole life. But in the human species, passion, fantasy, caprice, the troubles of pregnancy and of an overly large family, the fear of losing one's charms, all hinder the multiplication of the species.

Thus, you cannot expend too much effort in taking stock on the matter of fertility.

If an emerging people multiplies rapidly, this is not, as one author has said, because they did not check each other as they will later on, when they harm each other like trees, for this explanation leaves us with the whole problem. It is instead that the advantages of celibacy and small family size, which are enjoyed in a nation experiencing its full grandeur, are a very big inconvenience in an emerging nation.

[181] Most people complain about the great property possessed by the Church. As for myself, I believe that the main problem is not there, but in the great number of those who share it.[1]

Here's how.

There is scarcely any little town that does not have one or two little ecclesiastical chapters, in which there are anywhere from ten to twenty or thirty positions of very small income, and which consequently can only be desired by the dregs of society. They become objects of ambition for the principal artisans and farmers, who attempt to get their children to study in order to obtain them, so that all these positions steal so many good subjects away from industry and agriculture. {These sorts of people are obliged to go live among artisans, where they could not live a very ecclesiastical life.}

4. This law, passed by Augustus, remained on the books until the sixth century. The first to receive such a special exemption was Augustus's own wife Livia.—HC

[181]
1. See *Laws*, 14.7.

If these positions were more prestigious, they would concern the nobility, which is the only lazy body in the Realm, and the only one that needs alien property to support itself.

There is nothing so ridiculous as committing a man, for fifty silver crowns, to a breviary and eternal continence.

People of this stamp—without education, without letters, without respect—are the shame of the Church and the constant subject of worldly mockery.

It would be easy to remedy this problem by consolidations or eliminations, and you would fashion benefices that could be possessed with some dignity.

There wouldn't even be need for foreign authority; that of the king and the diocesan bishop would suffice for this.

[182] Pope Innocent X destroyed all the little monasteries of the ecclesiastical State, and had their houses and properties sold. He abolished around a thousand {five hundred}, and if he had not been prevented by death, he would have invited all Catholic princes to do likewise in their States.

It is well known that the little monasteries serve only to support the relaxation of monastic discipline.

They also support the prodigious number of monks who, spread out to the tiniest hick town,[1] have relatives everywhere, and who, looking in every child for the first inkling of sorrow or caprice or devotion, grab them immediately.

The properties of these little monasteries could be joined to other monasteries or to benefices, and in this case, one could favor many royally nominated benefices which, by the passage of time, have lost their properties and preserved virtually nothing but their name.

If they were joined to other monasteries, there should be no fear of their becoming too rich; for *primo*, the objection cannot concern mendicants, and monks who are paid rent would be in a better position to bear the State's taxes.

Moreover, since they would have several distant properties, they would

[182]

1. *Bicoque;* the pejorative usually refers to military defenselessness, though Montesquieu does not seem to use it that way here.—HC.

be inclined to let them out for rent, which would be a very big benefit to the State.

{One might allow only one house per order in the same city. (See extract from the *Journal des Savants,* 1689, a council that prohibits increasing the number of monks.)}[2]

[183] One of the greatest abuses in the realm is the establishment of mini–high schools[1] in the small towns, where even artisans send all their children in order to teach them a few Latin words.

Far from being favorable to knowledge, this supports ignorance. For just as it is useful for there to be good academies in the main cities, where a certain youth may be instructed in the humanities, so too is it dangerous to put up with these mini–high schools in small towns, where artisans and petty traders are alienated from their status, without being put on track to fulfill another one very well.

[184] Machiavelli says it is dangerous to make big changes in a State, because you attract the enmity of all those to whom they are harmful, and the good is not felt by those to whom it is useful.[1]

I have still another reason to offer: by eliminating the respect one ought to have for the established things, they serve as an example and authorize the fantasy of someone who wants to overturn everything. [And indeed, there are plenty of things that do not last, because they have not been attacked like the great properties of . . .]

[185] Here are the laws that I would think most appropriate to make a republic or colony flourish.[1]

All property will be divided equally among the male [and female] chil-

---

2. The book reviewed there is Michel du Perray, *Traité des portions congrues,* 2 vols. (Paris, 1682).

[183]

1. The word is *demi-collège,* which I have not found in the dictionaries.—HC

[184]

1. Niccolò Machiavelli (1469–1527), *Discourses,* I.16. Montesquieu owned several of his works (*Catalogue,* 2399–2405). See André Bertière, "Montesquieu lecteur de Machiavel," in *Actes du Congrès Montesquieu réuni à Bordeaux du 23 au 26 mai 1955 pour commémorer le deuxième centenaire de la mort de Montesquieu* [Acts of the Montesquieu Congress convened in Bordeaux from May 23 to May 26, 1955, to commemorate the bicentennial of Montesquieu's death] (Bordeaux, 1956), 141–58; R. Shackleton, "Montesquieu et Machiavel," in *Comparative Literature Studies* (1964), 1–13.

[185]

1. This *pensée* is largely taken up in *Laws,* 23.21.

dren, without the fathers and mothers being able to favor the male child
they think worthiest with more than a third of their estate.

{Daughters will take a third less of the inheritance than the males.}

[Not daughters but male consanguineous cousins will succeed to the
inheritance; daughters will have only the daily necessities.]

In the division of property at succession,[2] no distinction among property
types will be allowed[3]—mobile and immobile, proper, acquisitions made
during and outside of marriage, property that the husband does (through
the dowry arrangement) and does not control, noble or commoner.

After one of the marriage partners is deceased,[4] the enjoyment of his
or her goods passes to the survivor—except, however, the third of the deceased's inheritance, the enjoyment of which passes to the children.

[Where there are no children, each spouse will be able to dispose of
half as he or she wishes, but the other half will belong to the nearest male
relations.]

During marriage, the entire estate will be considered to belong to the
husband as far as its use is concerned, and he will be able to dispose of it
freely; all right of legal initiative will be in his hands.

In the event of dissipation and prodigality, the wife will ask for separation and will obtain a third of the {remaining} property for herself, another
third for her children, and the final third will remain for the husband's
subsistence, under a guardian's authority.

Those who have no children will be unable to make a will. {Their estate
will pass to the nearest relative, the males being preferred;} but they will be
able to make whatever donation they want to living persons, provided they
immediately divest themselves of its use, and provided they dispose of no
more than half their estate. {Contradiction with what I have said hereafter,
that one cannot receive by will.}

What children acquire by their industry or through donations from
strangers or collateral relations will belong to them both as property and
in usufruct, and they will be considered free of paternal authority on this
count. If said children die without issue, the father and mother, not the
brothers, will inherit. Girls at the age of twenty and boys at the age of

---

2. On wills, see *Laws*, 27; on the right of primogeniture, see *PL*, CXIX, 200.

3. On the division of goods, see *Laws*, 6.1, 72–73.

4. What follows in the first version is: "two thirds of the property will be considered to belong to
the husband or his heirs, the third to the wife or her heirs."

twenty-five will be able to marry without the consent of their fathers, and in this case alone, if they acquire property, the fathers may not inherit it.

There will be no regard to the right of representation, nor of *retrait lignager;*[5] substitutions and *fidéicommis*[6] will not take place.

Unmarried males will be unable to give and receive in wills {from the age of twenty-five}.

Unmarried persons will succeed, however, to their father and mother like the other children; will not be able to possess any judicial office, or be witnesses in a civil case. All places of honor will be indicated in churches and other locations according to the number of children.

Wherever there is competition for [offices and] privileges or honors, the decision will be by the number of children—except, however, for military awards and honors.

Those with seven children alive or having died in war will be exempt from every type of tax; those with six will only pay half.

All ordinary privileges, such as exemption from guardianship and from the burden of billeting war personnel, will be accorded those with five children.

Finally, the city dweller who has the most children will enjoy the honors and privileges of magistrates—not, however, the functions. And in case of a tie, whoever had a child that year will be preferred.

Disparity of social condition will not be sufficient reason to annul a promise of marriage. Abduction by seduction will not be a capital crime, but will be followed by marriage.

Every unmarried daughter living outside the company of her father and mother, grandfather or grandmother, without their express permission authorized by the magistrate, will be punished as a woman of bad morals.

Every girl of bad morals will be sheltered in a workhouse and will not leave until someone presents himself to marry her.

All women who keep places of debauchery will be punished in such a way as to prevent recidivism.

A man under forty will not be able to marry a woman over fifty.

[Disparity of social condition will not be sufficient reason to annul a promise of marriage, any more than the bad morals of one of the parties.]

---

5. The right of relatives to reclaim sold property back for the family.—HC
6. The conditional use of property by an heir.—HC

The entire Republic will be divided into families.

It will be prohibited to keep any unmarried domestic, unless he is at least twenty-five—except, however, for girls.

Substantial property, an amount to be fixed by Law, will be necessary to attain judicial office.

In trial sentencing, neither counsel nor a lawyer nor a prosecutor will be used. There will be no writing, unless the judge orders it for his instruction. The counsel of a friend, however, may be used.

You will grab the attention of your party {before two witnesses} to lead him before the judges, and he will be obliged to follow orders, under stiff penalty.

There will be only one level of jurisdiction, and up to five judges will always be judging.

No regular returns[7] will be possible on properties that cannot be indemnified; no debts that cannot be liquidated by consignment.

There will be no real takings, but on a creditor's demand, the judge will condemn the debtor to convey a sales contract to his creditor for the assets that are most agreeable to said creditor. All this, for the settling of the debt and subject to the advice of experts.

There will be no privileged creditors. There will be debtors' prison for debts above one hundred pounds.

Judges will be able to release a prisoner after a certain time, when his good faith and insolvency are well known.

All sorts of contractual restitutions, such as damages for more than half in the sale, more than a quarter in the distribution, will not be allowed.

Personal fraud will not be subject to restitution, but it will be pursued as a criminal matter.

Minors and the children of families will be compelled to pay their debts, except when usurers are being punished.

Those named guardian by the father will accept the guardianship on pain of infamy. Their governance will end at the age of fourteen. Within three months thereafter, they will render their accounts before experts commissioned by the judge. They will be held only for fraud or for negligence that approaches fraud. If receipts exceed expenses, they will not be

---

7. The *Encyclopédie*, 14:116, cited by Derathé, 1:451, defines *rentes constituées* as returns "constituted by a sum of money whose principal is alienated."

obliged, if they do not want to, to place the money in an interest-bearing investment. They will farm out the fixed property, unless, on the advice of the parents, they agree to the contrary.

No one will be able to sell his fixed property before the age of twenty, without the permission of the parents and the judge.

One may lend at interest in any way one wants, provided the interest does not exceed a fifteenth of the principal.

Criminal laws will be so fashioned that, on the one hand, punishment can be achieved, and on the other, people will be safe from the ambushes of slanderers.

All benefices will be for cure of souls, and there cannot be more ecclesiastics than benefices. Said ecclesiastics will be maintained appropriately, and will occupy themselves in service, not contemplation.[8]

[186] THE KNIGHTS TEMPLAR. Their condemnation proves nothing; neither do the trials in which a prince left.[1]

The Jews accused of the fire in Rome—falsely, but condemned.[2]

The affair of the nuns of Loudun.[3]

Our earliest Christians condemned for ridiculous crimes. If we had legal procedures, we would see witnesses, confessions, accused, etc.

The Knights Templar had been virtually condemned before being accused; at least their destruction had been decided.

Saint Bartholomew's![4] Didn't the king send out letters everywhere in which he said the Huguenots meant to kill him? Didn't he even go to court and have some Huguenots hung by the Parlement of Paris? And yet, who doesn't know what it was all about, and that their destruction had been decided long beforehand?

[187] Notice that after civil wars, the most calamitous that States face, they suddenly are in the highest echelon of their power.[1]

---

8. See *pensées* 233, 236, and 274.

[186]
1. The Templars were condemned by Philip the Fair in 1314.
2. In the time of Titus (r. 79–81) and Hadrian (r. 117–38).
3. That is, involving claims of demonic possession, in 1634. See *pensée* 293.—HC
4. The St. Bartholomew's Day massacre, August 24, 1572.—HC

[187]
1. "I've put this in my *Considerations on Spain*" (M.); in fact, it is the *Considerations on Rome*, XI, 107.

We have seen it three times: in France, under Charles VII, under Henry IV, Louis XIII, and Louis XIV; we have seen it in England, under Cromwell and under Henry VIII; in Rome, after the wars of Sulla and those of Caesar's faction.[2] This is because, in civil war, the whole people is at war, and when, with the return to peace, the arts begin again to flourish and forces are again combined, this State has a very great advantage over the state that has only bourgeois.[3]

Every State has to think of making soldiers, and the one that has the most is the strongest.

[**188**] Chimerical plan for a perpetual peace in Europe, attributed to Henry IV: good for arming Europe against Spain, but bad if viewed in itself; the first barbarians would have subjugated Europe.

[**189**] In his *Ecclesiastical Annals,* Father Lecointe maintains, against all the ancients, that the assembly of the Franks did not send away to the Pope to consult him on the deposition of the last king of the first dynasty.[1] The Oratorian Father Châlons,[2] in a *History of France* whose extract is in the eighteenth *Journal des Savants* (1720),[3] says there is no evidence the Pope wanted to commit such a great injustice. That's charming: he will not acknowledge that the Pope could do something that he admits all lords have done.

[**190**] I can't understand French historians.

Look at how Father Alexandre cast doubt on the most certain facts of French history, in order to diminish the Pope's authority.[1] How can the testimony of all contemporary historians be contradicted? Can it be denied that there was a lot of blindness in those days regarding the Pope's authority? What good does it do to deny one of these individual facts? Isn't the

2. Charles VII, king of France (r. 1422–61); Henry IV, king of France (r. 1589–1610); Louis XIV, king of France (r. 1643–1715); Henry VIII, king of England (1509–47).
3. "Put this in the *Romans,* up to the cross-out" (M.).

[189]
1. Fr. Charles Le Cointe (1611–81), whose eight-volume work in Latin came out in 1665–83. See the criticism in *Laws,* 31.16, 695.
2. Vincent Chalons (1620–94), whose *Histoire de France* came out in three volumes in 1720.
3. See the issue of July 22, 1720, 437–41.

[190]
1. Fr. Noël Alexandre (1639–1724), *Selecta historiae ecclesiaticae* [Selections in ecclesiastical history] (1676–86).

whole historical record a monument to the blindness of our forefathers in this regard? For myself, I would rather not write history than write it for the purpose of following the prejudices and passions of the times.

Here, someone makes the Capetians descend from the Merovingians; there, someone else has it that the name *very Christian* has always been applied to the {French} princes.

They don't form a system after reading history; they begin with the system and then search for proofs. And there are so many facts over a long history, so many different ways of thinking about it, its origins are ordinarily so obscure, that one always finds materials to validate all sorts of opinions.

[191] THE MAID OF ORLEANS. The English took her for a sorceress; the French, for a prophetess and envoy of God. She was neither. Look at the same *Journal,* where one seems inclined to believe that it was a deception, and look at the historical reasons given there.[1] On an event of this nature, however little the story may lend itself to a similar explanation, one must embrace it, because reason and philosophy teach us to doubt something so offensive to both of them. The witchcraft prejudice is no more, and that of the possessed barely survives. Look at the story of Jacques Cœur in the history of France; he was Charles VII's treasurer.[2]

If the story of the Maid is a myth, what can one say about all the miracles that all the monarchies have claimed, as if God governed a realm with a special providence, different from that with which he governs its neighbors?

[192] The Chinese annals[1] observe that in 1196 B.C. the Barbarians of the North spread into the oriental islands because of their great number.

[193] Look at how much danger conquests bring: Roman soldiers were rebellious and insolent from the time of the victory over Perseus.[1]

[191]
1. *Journal des savants* (1720), 438–39.
2. Jacques Cœur (ca. 1395–1456).

[192]
1. Montesquieu perhaps is referring to Fr. Martino Martini's *Sinicae historiae* (Amsterdam, 1659; *Catalogue,* 3154).

[193]
1. Perseus, last king of Macedon (r. 179–168 B.C.), defeated by Aemilius Paullus at Pydna on June 22, 168.

[194] ROMAN REPUBLIC, SULLA.[1] Caesar's victory had the same effect with respect to the Roman Republic as the victory of Marius over
Sulla would have had, if he had won.[2] And if Pompey had come out on
top, perhaps he would have restored liberty to his country, as Sulla did.
For whoever supports the people, being from the people himself, has
interests that are more tangled up than the nobleman who supports the
noble party.

All the ancient republics perished by the people, who authorized one
man against the senate.

Two {chance} causes of the fall of the Roman Republic: the rendering of
accounts that Cato arranged for the Knights; the division of fields to the
soldiers.[3]

{Cause of the fall of the Empire: the seat transferred by Constantine to
Byzantium.}

[195] One must not be surprised by the change in spirit among the
Romans after Caesar.[1] They were the same as they were in the time of the
Gracchi,[2] the Mariuses, the Catilines;[3] not to mention that this change is
no greater than the one we have seen in our France from century to century, especially the transition from Charles VII to Louis XI.[4]

[196] You ask me why the English, who have much imagination, invent little, and the Germans, who have little imagination, invent much.[1]

There are things invented by chance, and in this connection, it cannot
be asked why one nation invents more than another; thus, the Germans
cannot be either blamed for, or credited with, the invention of gunpowder
and other things of that sort.

Moreover, imagination is good for inventing systems, and on that score,
the English have provided their share more than any other nation; but

[194]
1. See the *Dialogue de Sylla et d'Eucrate,* in Allen, 98–109.
2. "Put in the *Journal*" (M.).
3. Marcus Porcius Cato, called Cato the Elder (234–149 B.C.).

[195]
1. "Put this in the *Roman Republic*" (M.), *Considerations,* XII.
2. Members of the Gracchus family, from a plebeian branch of the Sempronian tribe.
3. Lucius Sergius Catiline, Roman politician (108–62 B.C.).
4. On this transition, see *pensée* 1302, section on Louis XI.—HC

[196]
1. See the letter by Jean-Jacques Bel to Montesquieu, ca. 1730, in *OC,* 3:941, for a discussion of the
English and the Germans, and of the process of invention.

most discoveries in natural science are only the result of long and arduous labor, of which the Germans are more capable than other nations.

You see clearly that a thousand German chemists who experiment constantly and never get sidetracked will more easily discover the effects of combining certain elements in chemistry than a thousand Englishmen who study some chemical element, but who spend three-quarters of their time discoursing about religion and government.

[197] CHARLEMAGNE. His injustice in plundering the Lombards and supporting the Popes' usurpation.

The Popes support the Carlian House in its usurpation, and the Carlians support the Popes in theirs.

The Merovingians were excluded without cause.

Charlemagne raised the Popes' power because his authority was founded on that power. I have heard this observation made: that the reason why he gave lands to the Holy See was that they were borderlands of the two empires and served as a barrier between the Empires of the Occident and the Orient. Now, he was not afraid that the Emperor of the Orient and the Pope, who harbored a mortal hatred for each other, would ever reach an accommodation.

[198] In my extract of the *Works of the Learned,* November 1690, page 114,[1] you will see the horrible persecutions in Sweden and discover the character of those times, and of Charlemagne's reign.

[199] Here is my reason to prove that the first dynasty was hereditary: it is that long line of kings, all without power and authority. The French must therefore have had a respect for the family of Merovech nearly equal to that of the Turks for the blood of Othman, which presupposes a hereditary and not an elective crown. And if it were elective, how would they have elected all those idiots?[1]

[200] Marks of indifference should not affect us,[1] but marks of contempt certainly should.

[201] Men never appear more extravagant than when they disdain, or

[198]
1. The reference is to Claude Ornhialms's history of Sweden in Latin (1689); Montesquieu's extract is lost.

[199]
1. The references are to Merovée, king of the Salian Franks (r. ca. 447–58) and founder of the Merovingian dynasty, and to Othman (or Osman, 1258?–1326), founder of the Ottoman Empire.

[200]
1. First version: "have never touched me"

when they admire; it seems there is no middle between the excellent and the detestable.

[202] Metaphysics has two very seductive things.

It accords with laziness; one studies it everywhere: in one's bed, on a walk, etc.

Moreover, metaphysics treats only big things; big interests are always being negotiated in it. The scientist, the logician, the orator are concerned only with small subjects, but the metaphysician invades all of nature, governs it at will, makes and unmakes gods, gives and takes intelligence, puts man in the condition of the beasts or removes him from it. All the notions it offers are interesting, because present and future tranquillity are at stake.

[203] I am more moved when I see a beautiful painting by Raphael that represents a nude woman in the bath than if I saw Venus emerge from a wave.[1] This is because the painting represents only women's beauty, and nothing that can reveal her defects. Everything pleasing is seen, and nothing that can diminish one's interest. In the painting, moreover, the imagination always has something to do; this is a painter who always represents the beautiful side.

Why does *Aloisia* charm us so much in Latin and so little in French?[2] It is because French represents things to the Frenchman as they are. It gives him an exact idea, which is so clear that he cannot add accessories to it. In the Latin, which we do not understand perfectly, the imagination adds to the true idea an accessory idea, which is always more agreeable. That is why translations do not please us as much as the originals, even though in reality they are equally beautiful, since each language has its equally perfect expressions.

[204] Constantine made a mistake in consenting that the ecclesiastical jurisdiction that the Christians had established among themselves from the time of the pagan Emperors be authorized.[1]

[203]
1. Raphael (1483–1520). See *Voyages* (*OC*, 2:1090, 1115ff., and passim), as well as Montesquieu's letter to Mme de Lambert (December 26, 1728) for his comments on Raphael. He was initiated into the history of painting on his trip to Italy by Hildebrand Jacob (1693–1739); see *Spicilège*, 461, and J. Ehrard, *Montesquieu critique de l'art* (Paris, 1965).
2. *Aloisia*, by Nicolas Chorier (1612–92), is an erotic work in dialogue written in Latin and presented by the author as a Latin version (written by the Dutch scholar Johannes Meursius) of a Spanish text by Luisa Sigea, from Toledo. See also Corrado Rosso, "Montesquieu et l'humanisme latin," in *Cahiers de l'Association internationale des études françaises* 35 (1983): 243.

[204]
1. On Constantine, see *Laws*, 23.21, 448.

The Christians could hardly go plead their trial cases before the Pagans, for they would have conveyed a bad idea of the charity prevailing among them.

[205] Marriages between relatives to the first and second degree are prohibited in virtually all religions. And although there used to be peoples {(there still are: the Tartars and other peoples, the Huns, etc.)}[1] where it was permissible for fathers to marry their children, I don't know that there are any like that in the world today. At least they are so obscure that they are not worth being cited.[2]

And yet, considering these marriages in themselves, they are no less licit than others, for they are not contrary to natural law, like the sin of Onan[3] and of cities that perished by the flame. Nor, by their nature, are they contrary to civil and political law, like arson, robbery, and murder. They even offend against divine law only in the sense that it prohibits them, and not in themselves, like impiety and blasphemy. So all that can be said about them is that they are prohibited because they are prohibited.

It seems that this prohibition is quite ancient, indeed that it is as ancient as can be, that is, that it comes from the earliest patriarchs, and that it has avoided our natural inconstancy.

This appears clearly in the fact that, if these marriages were legitimate among some of the earliest peoples, it was only by the abolition of the ancient custom, because we see the marriage of one's sisters introduced by Cambyses, that of mothers and their children by Semiramis.[4]

Now, in considering the mores of the earliest times, we will easily dis-

---

[205]

1. Montesquieu showed a lively interest in the Tartars after reading Juan de Palafo y Mendoza (1600–1659) and Pètis de La Croix, *Histoire du grand Gengiskhan* (1710). Fr. Castel, *L'Homme moral opposé à l'homme physique*, 125, reports: "I recall going one day to see the celebrated president Montesquieu, at the beginning of our friendship, over thirty years ago [ca. 1725]. I found him in a certain creative frenzy, all excited at the discovery he had just made (he said) of a uniquely conquering people in the world—it was the Tartars. At that moment, Mr. Montesquieu was at the eighteenth conquering breakthrough that this people had made in our triple continent—European, Asiatic, African. What caused his enthusiasm and made for the author's specific and proper discovery was that, strictly speaking, he claimed that this people alone, at the exclusion of all others—Greek, Roman, Mede, or Persian—was created by nature and given by God himself, with the specific and characteristic quality of a conquering people." See also *PL,* LXXXI.

2. "I have treated the subject better in my *Laws*"; cf. 26.14.

3. Genesis 38:9–10.—HC

4. Cambyses II, king of Persia (r. 529–521 B.C.), and Semiramis, legendary queen of Assyria and Babylonia.

cover the reasons for a repugnance that has since passed into the force of law.

In these earliest ages, there was no other authority than that of fathers. That was the plenitude of power: father, magistrate, monarch signified the same thing.

In the earliest times, we do not find that men exercise the same dominion over their wives as over their children. On the contrary, the first marriages give us the idea of a perfect equality and a union as sweet as it was natural. It was only with the despotic empires that the enslavement of women was established. Princes, always unjust, began by abusing that sex, and found subjects entirely disposed to imitate them. In free countries, you never saw these disproportions.

It is clear that such a difference must have generated a repugnance for marriages among relations. How would a daughter have married her father? As a daughter, she would have owed him unbounded respect; as wife, there would have been equality between them. These two conditions would therefore have been incompatible.

Once this repugnance was established, it soon spread to marriages of brothers and sisters. For since the first type of marriage inspired horror because of the consanguinity, it is clear that a lesser proximity was bound to evoke less horror, but still some.

Once this was engraved in men's minds, God wanted to conform to it, and he made it a fundamental point of his law. For when God gave laws to men, he had only one thing in view, which was to have a faithful people, the natural source of all precepts.

Of these precepts, there are two types: those concerning the relationship that men have among themselves, which I will call moral precepts; and others concerning the relationship they have with him, which I will call sacred precepts.

There are again two sorts of moral precepts: those which have some relation to the preservation of society, as almost all do; and others, which are founded only on the ease of execution. The prohibition against marriage between relations may be placed among these latter.

Likewise, there are two sorts of sacred precepts: some are entirely founded on an eternal reason, such as loving and worshipping God; others are purely arbitrary and are rather a sign of the religion than the religion itself, and these are the ceremonial ones.

The foundation of religion is to love God and worship him, and the ceremonies are designed merely to express this sentiment. But they must signify what they are supposed to signify, and God rejects those that cannot signify a true worship, and that are bad as signs because they are bad in reality: such was the case with those that made him the author of the most infamous prostitutions.

[206] ON THE ETERNITY OF THE WORLD. Lucretius's argument[1] against the eternity of the world proves too much:

> *Praeterea, si nulla fuit genitalis origo*
> *Terrai et Caeli, semperque aeterna fuere*
> *Cur supre bellum Thebanum et funera Trojae*
> *Non alias alii quoque res cecinere poetae?*
> *Quo tot facta virum toties cecidere? Nec usquam*
> *Aeternis famae monumentis insita florent?*
> *Verum (ut opinor) habet novitatem summa, recensque*
> *Natura est Mundi, neque pridem exordia cepit.*[2]

I say it proves too much. We know nothing before the Olympiads, that is to say before two thousand five or six hundred years. All the rest is myth and obscurity. We are certain, however, that the world has lasted for at least six thousand years. We therefore have three thousand five hundred years of the world's existence, at least, for which the history is lacking.

For Lucretius's argument to be valid, we would have to have a quite precise and continuous history from the epoch of the world's birth.

Now one could say: "The world must not have begun beforehand, since we have no memory of anything preceding it."

But here, there is a previous era that is certain, of which we have no memory, and for the knowledge of which we need revelation.

His other proof:

[206]

1. Titus Lucretius Carus (98–55 B.C.), whose *De rerum natura* Montesquieu owned in a French edition (*Catalogue*, 1491). See also his letter to Dodart in October 1725 (*OC*, 3:814).

2. Lucretius, *De rerum natura*, V.324–31: "Besides, if there has been no first birth-time for earth and heaven, and they have been always everlasting, why have not other poets also sung other things beyond the Theban War and the ruin of Troy? Into what place have so many deeds of men so often fallen, and nowhere flower implanted in eternal monuments of fame? But, as I think, the world is young and new, and it is not long since its beginning."

Quare etiam quaedam nunc artes expoliuntur,
Nunc etiam augescunt; nunc addita navigiis sunt
Multa: . . .[3]

is worth no more; for it would have to be proven beforehand that there has
never on earth occurred a catastrophe similar to the one the Greeks speak
of in their Deluge, and Moses in his Genesis. For if one or a very small
number of men were left in a large country in which communication was
difficult, all the arts would necessarily decline and be forgotten—even if
they were the most knowledgeable men in the nation, since one or two men
know only a few of the arts and are even less able to practice them; even if
they knew the art, they would neglect it. Moreover, poverty—necessarily
attached to a small number of men—will cause all the arts to be forgotten,
except those that can procure the most indispensable necessities. {More-
over, virtually all the arts are connected; a needle is the result of many arts.}
Do not imagine that a Noah or a Deucalion thought about the printing
press and exerted themselves in making distance glasses or microscopes, or
that they put money in use. Unable to construct a ship, would they have
remembered or even bothered with the compass?

Imagine a pastor among his flock; how many arts does he know something about? A peasant in an unfrequented place—how many ideas does
he have? The entire people would thus have to start with this small number
of ideas. And before they made the least progress, how much time would
pass! For most of the arts concern a great people, not just a certain number
of men. Before they made good laws, before they had the imagination to
make a State flourish, how much time would flow by?

It is certain that the origin of the world is proven only by the sacred
Books, because, as for historical proofs, they are all against the accepted
system. The unanimous agreement of all historians in favor of a more distant antiquity forms a demonstration of this sort. To say that all peoples
have pushed back their origins out of vanity is to be unreasonable, since
vanity has little to do with this. Don't we have a writer of our history who
has cut back our earliest kings? It's Father Daniel.[4]

---

3. Lucretius, *De rerum natura*, V.332–34: "Therefore even now some arts are being perfected, some
also are in growth; today many improvements have been made in ships . . ."

4. Fr. Gabriel Daniel (1649–1728), *Histoire de France depuis l'établissement de la monarchie française
dans les Gaules* [History of France since the establishment of the French monarchy in Gaul], 3 vols.
(Paris, 1713).

It seems the theory of the indestructible world also presupposes that it had no beginning. The theory of the world's destruction by fire, which is the ancient philosophers' theory and which is orthodox among us, involves only a disturbance of order—which, by the laws of motion, must necessarily lead to another orderly arrangement. Our whole theology—the resurrection of bodies, destruction by fire—all this merely presupposes a new orderly arrangement. And assuming that matter in motion is unacceptable, the world must last eternally. Lucretius reasons unphilosophically when he says that the destruction we see in parts of the world implies total destruction, since each thing is being reordered to the extent that any other thing is disordered. A vortex, for example, cannot be destroyed without growing larger or forming another, nor a planet without forming other small ones or moving closer to or further from its sun.

Most of the reasoning of the Ancients is not precise, which arises from the fact that they did not have the ideas about the universe that the discoveries of our time have provided. They paid attention almost exclusively to the vast expanse of the earth, which they considered almost by itself to be the universe, and they easily imagined that it could perish. Here's how they reasoned, and rightly—especially Lucretius and the Epicureans, who thought the stars had only their apparent size: "If you admit," they said, "that peoples have perished, great cities have been destroyed, rivers have formed and covered the countrysides, you must also admit that it is very easy for heaven and earth to be dissolved, if the causes became greater."

> *Quod si forte fuisse antehac eadem omnia credis*
> *Sed periisse hominum torrenti saecla vapore,*
> *Aut cecidisse urbeis magno vexamine mundi,*
> *Aut ex imbribus assiduis exisse rapaceis*
> *Per terras amneis, atque oppida cooperuisse:*
> *Tanto quippe magis victus fateare necesse est,*
> *Exitium quoque terrai caelique futurum.*
> *Nam cum res tantis morbis tantisque periclis*
> *Tentarentur, ibi si tristior incubuisset*
> *Causa; darent late cladem, magnasque ruinas.*[5]

5. Lucretius, *De rerum natura*, V.338–47: "But if by any chance you believe that all these things have been the same before, but that the generations of men have perished in scorching heat, or that their cities have been cast down by some great upheaval of the world, or that after incessant rains rivers have issued out to sweep over the earth and overwhelm their towns, so much the more you must own yourself worsted, and agree that destruction will come to earth and sky. For when things were assailed

[207] One cannot think without indignation about the cruelties the Spanish inflicted upon the Indians, and when forced to write on this subject, one cannot avoid assuming a pompously polemical style.[1]

Bartolomé de Las Casas, eyewitness to all these barbarities, writes a horrific account.[2] The hyperboles used by the rabbis to describe the seizure of Bethar do not convey ideas as frightful as does the naïvete of this author. Hadrian punished the rebels.[3] Here free peoples are exterminated. Peoples as populous as those of Europe disappear from the earth. The Spanish, in discovering the Indies, have at the same time revealed the height of cruelty.

It is fortunate that the ignorance publicly professed by the Infidels hides our histories from them. They would find the wherewithal there to defend themselves and to attack. If they judged our religion by the destruction of the Indians, Saint Bartholomew's[4] and five or six other equally clear markers, how could one answer them? For in the final analysis, the history of a Christian people must be the practical morality of Christianity. *The Persian Letters* brought out the vanity contained in the pretexts that forced the Spanish to arrive at this extremity:[5] unique method of self-preservation which the Machiavellians therefore cannot call *cruel.* It has been proven by the opposite conduct of the Portuguese, who have been expelled from practically everywhere.[6] But the crime loses nothing of its enormity by the utility derived from it. It is true that actions are always judged by the outcome, but in morality, this judgment by men is itself a deplorable abuse.

If politics was the motive, religion was the pretext. It has been a long time since a poet complained that religion had fathered the worst evils,

---

by so great afflictions and so great dangers, if then a more serious cause had come upon them, there would have been widespread destruction and a mighty fall."

[207]

1. See *Laws* 10.4, 142, and 15.4, 249. According to Dodds, 121, Montesquieu drew on Garcilaso de La Vega y Vegas (1495–1559), whose *Histoire des guerres civiles des Espagnols* (1658 ed.) and *Commentaire royal* (1633 ed.) he owned (*Catalogue*, 3173–74), for his discussion the Indians in Mexico and Peru.

2. Las Casas (1474–1563), would-be reformer, bishop of Chiapa in Mexico, author of the *Brief Relation of the Indies.*

3. In 130, Hadrian founded a colony in Jerusalem that took the name of Aelia Capitolina. A revolt of the Jews followed (132); they were dispersed and crushed at Bitar in 134–35.

4. On the St. Bartholomew's day massacre of 1572, see *pensée* 186.

5. See *PL*, CXXI, 204. Vernière, 257 n. 1, wonders whether *The Persian Letters* is being used in this case for the *Traité des devoirs* [Treatise on duty].

6. For the Portuguese, see *PL*, CXXI, 205.

and it must indeed be true in the pagan religion, since it is not even always false in that of Jesus Christ.

What kind of abuse is it to make God serve the interests of one's passions and crimes! Is there a more mortal offense than the one committed under the pretext of honor?

[208] How do we know that there have not been several worlds in succession before this one? This hypothesis would explain quite naturally the origin of good and bad angels. It would be appropriate to add to each world a universal judgment. The destruction of these worlds would be not annihilations but disturbances.

[209] Some years after the Spanish had discovered the New World, one of their storm-tossed ships capsized on the coast of an unknown island. This island was deserted. The inhabitants had abandoned it because the air was so bad that people did not live for more than thirty years there. The terrain was marshy but very fertile. The island was filled with goats[1] so full of milk that they vied with each other to let themselves be milked, and this milk was always the diet of our Spaniard. What was hardest for him was that he was naked, having discarded his clothes when he saved himself by swimming.

He had been on this island for more than six months when, one day as he was on the beach, he saw a young twelve-year-old girl bathing; she was the only person on the island. She had been left behind (I don't know how) when the inhabitants abandoned it. At first, they were both surprised, but they soon sensed that they were not enemies. As the Spaniard approached, the young American girl also approached, for she had not learned to be ignorant of what it is impossible not to know. They loved each other and gave each other a mutual pledge that they could not violate.[2] They had four children.[3] The father died, and the mother only survived him by a few days, leaving four inhabitants on the island, of whom the oldest was not yet four years old. The goats, accustomed to come nurse the little children, still continued to come, and still took care of them.

[209]
1. First version: "cows"
2. "This was a natural prayer" (M.).
3. First version of what follows: "They had five children. And when the father died, the oldest was only four or five, and the mother survived only a few months, leaving a small people whose oldest was only three and a half. The goats, accustomed to come and nurse the little children, still continued"

When they had reached the age of twelve, they began to feel the designs of nature. The island was soon repopulated, so that in eighty years' time, in the space of seven generations, a nation was made that had no idea that there might be other men or another people on earth. They made themselves a language.

A vessel[4] having shipwrecked near the island, two men who had saved themselves by swimming came ashore. The inhabitants welcomed them with humanity and gave them milk, which was the only food they had yet imagined.

When they had learned the country's language, they saw an entirely new people . . .

One of the islanders asked the old stranger how old he was. He answered: "I am ninety years old." "What do you mean by a year?" replied the islander. "I call a year," said the stranger, "twelve lunar revolutions." "And by this reckoning, how old are you in lunar revolutions?" "Let me think a little. I would be a thousand eighty." "Can one lie like that?" said the islander. "You would be older than our earliest forefathers!" "If you don't believe me," said the stranger, "perhaps you will believe this young man, who came with me and is from the same city where I had my birth." "What?" said the islander, "are there then other cities than ours?" "Yes," said the young stranger. "The city we are from is almost half the size of your island. Don't think my compatriot wants to impose on you. He was the same age as my father, who, if he were alive today, would be no less than a thousand eighty in lunar revolutions."

The whole people began to laugh. "Don't be surprised at that!" resumed the young man. "We live a long time in our family. I've heard from my father that my grandfather died after ninety times twelve moons. My great grandfather was seventy." "Gods! What lies!" cried the islander. "I am the son of Heptalip. His father was named *Berzici,* who was the son of Agapé, who lived for only fifteen years. Agapé's father was Narnacun, who was born from a goat, as well as Neptata, his wife and sister, from whom you are descended just as we are." (Note that the story must be told by the youngest stranger from the island. Note that in the Indies women conceive at eight years of age. {Perhaps I could weave this into a longer novel.})

---

4. "This is what I've gathered from what I could learn of the country, and from the history of a lost ship in those times, near a Mexican island still remembered in Mexico, where some of the people from the vessel took refuge in a rowboat; and that island has not been discovered since" (M.).

[**210**] LACEDEMONIANS. There is nothing that resists people who observe the laws out of passion, who support a State out of passion and not with that cold indifference that one most often has for the society one is in. *Idem,* most of the Greek republics and the earliest Romans.[1]

[**211**] Greek philosophy amounted to very little. They spoiled the whole world—not only their contemporaries, but also their successors. Look at the pathetic precepts of the Pythagoreans, which were to be hidden from the people: don't sit on the horse's measuring cup; don't cut the fire with the sword; don't look behind you when you go outside; make even-numbered sacrifices to the heavenly gods and odd-numbered ones to the worldly gods, and other childishness. {All this was only enigmas; we do not have enough monuments of their philosophy. Diogenes Laertius was a bad author. Aristotle's works are corrupted. We no longer understand the ancient systems. Plato's is so fine that it is practically our own. We do not know Heraclitus's system any better than we would Newton's by reading *Newton's Weight and Void.* Cicero has given us only metaphysics and morals, and what he has given us is perfectly good.[1] What Lucretius has given us of Epicurus is very fine; he was lacking only a knowledge of astronomy. As for geometry, they got quite far along.}

Tatianus Assyrius,[2] in a *Discourse against the Greeks,* proves they did not invent the arts and sciences, but got them from the Barbarians.[3]

[**212**] What brought the Greeks to the world's attention was a crisis that occurred within the Greek body, which a hundred petty tyrants were gov-

[210]

1. "I'll put it in the *Romans.*" {I've put it there"} (M.); cf. *Considerations,* IV, 45–46.

[211]

1. Diogenes Laertius, early third century, author of *Lives, doctrines and maxims of illustrious philosophers,* of which Montesquieu owned two editions (*Catalogue,* 1142–43); on Isaac Newton (1642–1727), there is Montesquieu's still-unpublished "Mémoire concernant quelques explications et propriétés de la refraction pour servir d'intelligence de l'extrait de *L'Optique* de M. Newton que M. le P[resident] de Montesquieu a commencé à lire à l'Académie" [Memoir concerning some explanations and properties of refraction to serve in understanding the extract from Newton's *Optics* that P(resident) Montesquieu began to read at the Academy] (of Bordeaux).

2. Tatian (120–73), disciple of Saint Justin, wrote ca. 170 an apologia for the Christians, entitled *Discours aux grecs* (*Catalogue,* 1686).

3. "Theodoret, *de curatione Graecorum affectuum,* 497, Sirmond edition; Joseph, *contre Appion Alexandrin.* Ought to read Sigonius, *De republica Atheniensium.* I have it. It is entitled *De antiquo jure civium romanorum*" (M.). The reference is to Theodoret (ca. 393–457), bishop of Cyrus and author of *Remedy for the diseases of the Greeks* (*Catalogue,* 90); Jacques Sirmond (1559–1651), industrious Jesuit scholar and editor of early Fathers (*Catalogue,* 138, 211, 214, 266, and 380); and Carlo Sigonio, *On the Athenian Republic* (Bologna, 1564; *Catalogue,* 1966–67, 2873–74, and 3074).—HC

erning. All these monarchies were set up as republics. In these new times, the liberty frenzy[1] gave them a love of Country, a heroic courage, a hatred of kings that made them do the greatest things. Their power and glory attracted foreigners to them, and consequently the arts. Their situation on the sea brought trade their way.

[213] A person of my acquaintance said:[1]

"I am going to do a pretty foolish thing: here is my self-portrait.

"I know myself well enough.

"I have hardly ever experienced sorrow, and boredom even less.

"My bodily machinery is so fortunately constructed that all objects strike me forcefully enough so they can give me pleasure, but not enough to give me pain.

"I have enough ambition to take part in the things of this life, but not enough for the post that nature has placed me in to be distasteful to me.

"When I taste a pleasure, I am affected by it, and I am always surprised at having sought it out with such indifference.[2]

"In my youth, I was happy enough to attach myself to women who I thought loved me. As soon as I ceased to believe it, I would suddenly detach myself from them.

"Study has always been for me the sovereign remedy against life's unpleasantness, since I have never experienced any sorrow that an hour's reading did not eliminate.

"In the course of my life, I have never found folks who were generally despised except those living in bad company.

"I wake up in the morning with a secret joy; I see the light with a kind of rapture. The whole rest of the day I am happy.

"I pass the night without waking up, and in the evening when I go to bed, a kind of torpor prevents me from engaging in reflection.

"I am almost as happy with fools as with smart people, and there are few men so boring that they have not amused me very often; there is nothing so amusing as a ridiculous man.

[212]
1. First version: "the hatred of kings, the frenzy."

[213]
1. First version: "I must give thanks to my good genie for being born lucky."
2. Erased: "I am delighted to obtain the public's esteem, but I am aware that in certain ways I would console myself for its loss."

"I have no aversion to making inner sport of the men I see, which does not prevent them from doing the same to me in their turn.

"When first looking at most grandees, I have had a childish fear. As soon as I have gotten to know them, I have made the transition to contempt with almost no middle ground.

"I have often enough liked to pay banal compliments to women and to render them services that cost as little.

"I have had a natural love for the well-being and honor of my Country, but little for what is called its glory. I have always felt a secret joy when a statute or ordinance has been passed that tends toward the common good.

"{When I have travelled[3] in foreign countries, I have become attached to them as to my own; I have shared in their fortunes and would have wished a prosperous condition for them.}

"I have often thought I detected *esprit* in people who passed for not having any.

"I have not been sorry to pass for being distracted: this has made me risk many a nonchalance that would otherwise have made things awkward for me.

"In conversation and at the table, I have always been delighted to find a man who was willing to take the trouble to shine: a man of this sort always presents his flank; all others are uptight.

"Nothing amuses me more than to see a boring raconteur tell his minutely detailed story, without quarter; I am attentive not to the story but to the manner of telling it.

"For most people, I would rather approve of them than listen to them.

"I have never been willing to put up with a witty man taking it into his head to mock me two days in a row.

"I have loved my family enough to do what tended toward the good in the essential things, but have emancipated myself from the little details.

"Although my name is neither good nor bad, having hardly three hundred fifty years of proven nobility, nonetheless I am very attached to it, and I would be one to make legal substitutions.[4]

"When I confide in someone, I do so without reserve, but I confide in few persons.

---

3. See *PL,* LXVII, III, for the same thought.
4. That is, in bequests.—HC

"What has always given me a rather bad opinion of myself is that there are few stations in the Republic for which I might have been truly well-suited.

"As for my occupation as president, I had a very correct heart, I understood the questions in themselves well enough, but as for the legal procedure,[5] I understood nothing. I applied myself to it, however. But what disgusted me the most was that I would see idiots with the very talent that eluded me, so to speak.

"My machinery is so arranged that I need to collect myself in any subject matter that is at all elaborate. Otherwise, my ideas become confused, and if I sense people are listening, it then seems that the whole question vanishes before me. Many traces are revived at once, and it thereby happens that no trace is revived.

"As for discursive conversations, where the topics are constantly being cut off, I do pretty well in them.

"I have never seen tears flow without being moved.

"Because I do not know how to hate, I forgive easily. It seems to me that hatred is depressing. When someone wants to make up with me, I have felt my vanity flattered, and have ceased to regard as an enemy a man rendering me the service of giving me a good opinion of myself.

"On my property, with my liegemen, I have never been willing to bear being embittered on someone's account. When someone has said to me: 'If you knew what people were saying!' 'I don't want to know,' I've replied. If what they were telling me was false, I did not want to run the risk of believing it. If it was true, I did not want to take the trouble of hating a scoundrel.

"At the age of thirty-five, I still loved.

"{It is as impossible for me to go to someone's home with a view to my self-interest as it is to fly in the air.}

"When I have been in society, I have loved it as if I could not stand retreat into the country. When I have been on my property,[6] I have no longer thought about society.

"I am (I believe) practically the only book author who has ever labored under a constant fear of getting a reputation as a know-it-all.[7] Those who

5. First version: "as for the hassle of legal procedure."
6. First version: "in retreat"
7. *Bel esprit;* see translator's note.—HC

have known me know that in my conversation, I did not try too hard to appear like one, and that I had tolerable skill at assuming the language of those with whom I was living.

"I have very often had the misfortune of conceiving a dislike for the people whose good will I had most desired. As for my friends, with one exception, I have always preserved them from this.

"*I have always had the principle of never having another do what I could do by myself.* This is what has led me to make my fortune by the means I had at hand—moderation and frugality—and not by alien means, always low or unjust.

"I have lived with my children as if with my friends.

"When I have been expected to shine in conversation, I never have. I have preferred to have a witty man assist me rather than fools approve of me.

"There is no one I have despised more than the little know-it-alls {and the grandees of no integrity}.

"I have never been tempted to compose a song verse against anyone, whoever it might be.

"I have not appeared to be a spender, but I have not been a miser. And I can't think of anything feasible that I have not done to make some money.[8]

"What has hurt me a lot is that I have always overly despised those I did not esteem."

[214]   The good of the Church is an equivocal term.[1] In the past, it expressed holiness of manners. Today, it signifies nothing but the prosperity of certain people and the increase in their privileges or revenue.

To do something for the good of the Church is not to do something for the Kingdom of God and that society of the faithful of which Jesus Christ is the head, but to do something opposed to the interests of laymen.

When someone has wanted to attach the goods of the Church to certain associations of the poor, such as at the Invalides[2]—that is, to people

---

8. "I have not neglected (I believe) to enhance my property; I have made big improvements to my lands. But I felt it was rather for the sake of a certain image of skillfulness that this gave me, than with the idea of becoming richer" (M.). See also *pensées* 973, 1003, and 1236.

[214]
1. On Church property, see *pensées* 181, 273, and 1077, and the more discreet *Laws* 25.5, a chapter that was not censured. See Brèthe, 3:435 n. 23, and *Laws*, 31.10.
2. A hospital for military veterans in Paris.—HC

who, aside from their poverty and their wounds, also possess a shame that prevents them from asking for support for their daily lives—the Church has been opposed and has regarded this as a profanation. And people have yielded and have believed its outcries legitimate—proof positive that the goods of the Church are regarded not as the goods of the poor but as those of a certain association of people dressed in black who do not marry.

When our kings have sworn their oath at their consecration, do not imagine that the Church, which has demanded it, has made them swear to see that the laws of the Realm are observed, to govern their subjects well, to be fathers of their people. No! They have been made to swear only that they will preserve the privileges of the Church of Reims.[3]

When the Estates have been held, do not imagine that the Clergy have asked for a reduction in taxes and relief for the people. They did not think about an evil that they did not feel, but asked only for some extension of their jurisdiction or privileges. {The reception of the Council of Trent, which is favorable to them.}

They did not dream of a reformation of morals. It is a fact that when the other orders spoke of it, they cried out that it belonged only to them to meddle in their affairs—wanting always to be the reformers, in order never to be the reformed.

Everyone is so convinced that the ecclesiastics' great wealth is an abuse that if I presumed to prove it here, I would pass for an imbecile. But such is the force of prejudice that it endures even after having been destroyed. And whoever tells you that the ecclesiastics' great wealth is the most violent abuse will be the first to tell you that religion prevents you from touching it and from (as they say) putting your hand on the thurible,[4] as if to reduce their revenue was to usurp their functions.

I urge you to make three reflections here:

The first is that, whatever tax is imposed on the Clergy, this cannot be pernicious to the State; whereas if the cultivator is overcharged with the *taille* or the bourgeois with tolls, the entire State will necessarily be turned upside down. If a peasant is taxed in such a way that the *taille* exhausts his revenue, or that this revenue is so meager that it is not worth the trouble to make the expenses and payments for the cultivation, he will leave his

---

3. The royal coronation took place at Reims.—HC
4. Idiom for "encroaching on Church prerogatives."—HC

land uncultivated or will do only the work necessary to live. Again, if you overburden merchandise with entry tolls, there will be no consumption. But as for the Church, it can be taxed with impunity because, since virtually its entire revenue consists in land rents and tithes, there is no danger of their abandoning them, however small the profit from collecting them might be.

The second reflection is that Church wealth is contrary to the interests of the Churchmen themselves, because it makes them the slaves of princes and magistrates. Ecclesiastics can undertake nothing, for fear of the seizure of their temporal goods, and bishops can no longer say: "One must obey God rather than men." {And even if the faith were in peril, perhaps there would be some who would hardly bother about an article of faith or discipline that would deprive them of fifty thousand pounds in land rent. In the Parlement, Henry IV used to put it very well to all the great League blowhards: "All I have to do is give them a benefice to make them shut up."}[5]

This gives birth to my third reflection, which is that the Pope also has no stake in protecting the Church's wealth, since it works against him and prevents him from being able to dispose of bishops at will: witness the affairs of Sicily under Clement XI and of Venice further back.[6]

Furthermore, the Pope is {almost} without interests {today}, for he derives nothing from benefices and monasteries, except for some provisions in the former, which do not amount to much. In France, he no longer has promissory notes to give out, tenths[7] to raise, the right of spoils, and other rights which in the past it would have been in his interest to uphold, and for which Rome in the past published its bull *In Cena Domini*.[8]

There is more. All this wealth always puts it in danger of losing ground. It puts Catholicity in danger, by facilitating the means by which princes interest all the most respectable families of their States in its destruction, and attach them to schism and heresy as strongly as to their fortune—as the example of the Protestant princes has made clear enough. In France itself, we see in Mézeray that, if the Huguenots had been exempted from

---

5. The reference is to Henry IV (r. 1589–1610) and the Catholic League, an organization active in opposing Protestant influence in France during the wars of religion.—HC

6. Pope Clement XI (1700–1721).—HC

7. That is, *décimes,* levies for specific Church projects such as a crusade.—HC

8. *On the Lord's Supper.* This bull covered a wide array of offenses and was issued periodically from 1363 until its abolition owing to states' opposition by Pope Clement XIV in 1770.—HC

the payment of tithe during the reigns of Henry II's children, everyone would have been Huguenot.[9]

Thus, the device of the inverted torch suits the Church very well: "What nourishes me kills me."[10] It groans under the weight of gold.

The first Christians were almost all poor, the poor being attracted to a religion that honored poverty and sanctified that state.

I would much rather there be no poor people in a State than to see so many houses set aside to provide for them.

When the Church is rich, the government has a stake in its disorders; witness what is said in the *Life* of Abelard.

It is a matter of indifference to the people whether clergy or laity judge certain cases, and yet the disputes on this head are the most disputed things. It is not a matter of indifference to the people that ecclesiastics abound in wealth, but no one gets upset about this. {Cardinal Richelieu, who sought all sorts of renown, who had plenty to expiate in the eyes of Rome through his concord with the Protestants, who had to manage a devout prince, began the reforms.}

[215] LIBERTIES OF THE GALLICAN CHURCH. They should much rather be called the servitude of the Gallican Church, since they serve only to maintain the King's authority against ecclesiastical jurisdiction and take away the Pope's power to maintain it, since they remove the ecclesiastics' right over magistrates and kings themselves, as members of the faithful.

These liberties are not Church liberties in the normal sense—that is, the liberties of ecclesiastics—for they are almost always contrary to the privileges that they claim to have. They are the liberties of the people of France, who have the right to uphold the independence of her laws.

It should not be said that they are everything brought forth by the ancient canons, for France would be in a sad state if she were obliged to accept as law the collections made of these.

These liberties are founded only on the law of nations, by which a nation that is governed by its laws and has not been subjugated is not subject

---

9. François-Eudes de Mézeray (1610–83), *Histoire de France* (1643–51) and *Abrégé chronologique* [Chronological digest] (1643–51; *Catalogue,* 3012) both in three volumes. Henry II was French king from 1547 to 1559.

10. Thanatos, demon of death, carried an inverted torch. "Quod me nutrit me destruit," or "Qui me alit, me extinguit," seem to be Latin proverbs popular in the sixteenth century; see Shakespeare, *Pericles,* II.ii.33.—HC

in temporal matters to a foreign power; and in spiritual matters, they are founded on divine law, by which the Council is above the Pope {and on Reason, which also says this}, since there is no body that does not have more authority united than divided.

[216] It is credible that syphilis came to us from the Indies, and that it was unknown to the Ancients. Mézeray (chapter 8) says the French got it from the Neapolitans, who got it from the Spanish returning from the Indies. Those who have confused this disease with leprosy are unaware that there are countries where these two diseases are both known. There are people who claim it came from the Caribs, who ate men.

The *Novus Orbis*[1] says that in 1506 syphilis ravaged the land of Calcutta,[2] that this previously unknown disease had been brought there by the Portuguese seventeen years before, which squares with the discovery of the Indies in 1493. {On the last Scottish campaign, some officers who had taken refuge in the mountains brought syphilis there, where it had never been.[3] The men fell apart; surgeons from Edinburgh or London had to be sent.} If it be objected that there have been no more lepers since smallpox has been known, this comes from the fact that there are no more crusades; men no longer descend in massed formation on the Holy Land, where that disease is common. What makes one lean toward the opposite view is that Suetonius, in the *Life of Tiberius,* gives him all the symptoms of that disease: pimples, rash on the forehead, insomnia.[4]

[217] SHOWS. I remember that, leaving a play entitled *Aesop at Court,*[1] I left so deeply touched by the desire to be a better man that I am not aware of ever having formed a stronger resolution; quite different from that ancient who used to say that he never left a play as virtuous as when he had entered.

{That is because it is no longer the same thing.}

[218] SECONDARY SCHOOLS. The education received in secondary

[216]
1. *New World,* published in Basel in 1532 (*Catalogue,* 2637).
2. Calicut, on the Malabar coast, the first Indian port visited by the Portuguese; see *PL,* CXIII, 189, and *Laws,* 14.11, 241.
3. Since this sentence was inserted by secretary E (1734–39), the reference is probably to the Jacobite Rising of 1715.
4. Suetonius (ca. 70–128), author of the *Lives of the Twelve Caesars* (*Catalogue,* 2875–79).

[217]
1. Comedy by Edmé Boursault (1638–1701), staged for the first time in 1701, after the author's death.

schools is low.[1] I can say nothing worse about it than that the best you take away from it is a spirit of phony devotion. A hundred petty betrayals that a man is made to commit every day against his comrades, the treacheries inspired in him, can well serve to maintain a certain external order in these houses, but they ruin the hearts of all the individuals.

[219] It is not accepted that a knave might become a good man, but it is well accepted that a good man might become a knave.

[220–224] SOME FRAGMENTS THAT DID NOT MAKE IT INTO MY "MORAL THOUGHTS."

[220] Human actions are the subject of duties.[1] It's reason that is the source of duties, and this makes us fit to perform them. It would debase this reason to say that it has been given to us merely for the preservation of our being, for the animals preserve theirs just as we do. Often, indeed, they preserve theirs better, since instinct, which leaves them all the passions necessary for the preservation of their life, almost always deprives them of those that might destroy it; whereas our reason not only gives us destructive passions, but often makes us engage in a very bad use of those meant to preserve us.

Just as there are forces in us that annihilate the citizen's spirit by leading us to evil, there are also those that slow it down by distracting us from doing good. Among them are those that inspire a kind of quietism, which takes a man away from his family and Country.

The means of perfecting the virtue of justice is to make such a habit of it

[218]

1. From October 1700 to September 11, 1705, Montesquieu studied at the Oratorian *collège*, or secondary school, at Juilly, where the modern instruction, steeped in Cartesianism, gave an important place to geography, national history, and mathematics.

[220]

1. "I've put virtually all this in what I presented to the Academy on *Duties*." (M.) After the publication of the *Persian Letters* (1721), Montesquieu devoted part of his intellectual activity to the drafting of a *Treatise on duties* whose genesis he gives in a letter to Fitz-James, October 8, 1750 (*OC,* 3:1327): "About thirty years ago I devised the plan of writing a work on duties. The treatise on *Duties* [*de Officiis*] by Cicero had enchanted me, and I took it as a model, and since you know that Cicero copied Panaetius, so to speak, who was a Stoic, and since the Stoics were those who best treated this matter of duties, I read the main Stoic books, and among others, the moral reflections of Marcus-Antoninus, which seems to me the masterpiece of antiquity." The *Treatise on duties* was not completed; Montesquieu read fragments at the Bordeaux Academy on May 1, 1725, extracts of which were published in the *Bibliothèque française* VI (March 1726): 238–43 (*OC,* 3:158–62). The manuscript is lost; it figures, however, in the "Catalogue of manuscripts sent to my cousin in England," in 1818, with the following notice: "Another notebook entitled *Treatise on duties,* corrected copy." Robert Shackleton gives a reconstruction in "La genese de l'*Esprit des lois*," in *Revue d'Histoire Littéraire de la France* (1952), 433ff. *Pensée* 220 belongs to chapters 7 and 8 of the *Treatise,* "Habit of justice"; cf. also *pensée* 1008.

that it is observed even in the smallest things, and that one bends to it even in one's manner of thinking. Here is a single example. It is quite indifferent to the society in which we live that a man who lives in Stockholm or Leipzig makes epigrams well or poorly, or is a good or bad scientist. However, if we bring our judgment to bear on it, we must seek to judge justly, in order to prepare ourselves to do likewise on a more important occasion.

We all have machines that subject us constantly to the laws of habit. Our machine accustoms our soul to think in a certain fashion, or it accustoms it to think in a different fashion. It is here that science could find place in the study of morals, by making us see how far the dispositions toward human vices and virtues depend on bodily mechanics.

[**221**] It is love of Country that has given Greek and Roman history that nobility that ours does not have. It is the continual spring of all their actions, and one feels pleasure in finding it everywhere, that virtue dear to all those who have a heart.

When one thinks about the pettiness of our motives, the baseness of our means, the avarice with which we seek out vile rewards, the ambition—so different from love of glory—one is astonished at the difference in the spectacles, and it seems that, ever since those two great peoples ceased to exist, men have lost a few inches in stature.[1]

[**222**] Of all the sayings of the Ancients, I don't know any that indicate more barbarism than a saying by Sulla.

He was presented with a fisherman from the city of ***, who was bringing him a fish.

"After all I've done," he said, "is there still a man left in the city of ***?"

That sinister man marveled that his cruelty could have some limits.

[**223**] If science had no other inventions but gunpowder, one would do quite well to banish it like magic.[1]

[**224**] This principle of Hobbes is quite false:[1] that since the people

[**221**]
1. See *Laws*, 3.5, 25.

[**223**]
1. See *PL*, CV, 175.

[**224**]
1. For Montesquieu's refutation of Hobbes's political theory, see *Laws*, 1.2. Montesquieu owned his *Opera philosophica* (Amsterdam, 1668) and two French translations of *De cive* [On the citizen], including that of Sorbière coming from the Oratorian library of Paris (*Catalogue*, 1473, 2393–94). See Simone Goyard-Fabre, *Montesquieu, adversaire de Hobbes* (Paris, 1980).

have authorized the prince, the prince's deeds are the people's deeds, and consequently, the people cannot complain about the prince nor demand any account of his actions, because the people cannot complain about the people. Thus, Hobbes has forgotten his principle of natural law: *Pacta esse servanda*.[2] The people have authorized the prince under conditions; they have established him under a convention. He must observe it, and the prince represents the people only as the people have wanted or are reputed to have wanted him to represent them. {Besides, it is false that the delegate has as much power as the one who delegates, and no longer depends upon the latter.}

[225] Regulus's deed has been so strongly praised that we can scarcely praise that of Francis I. A prisoner of Charles V, ceding Burgundy for his ransom, he excused himself as soon as he was free on the grounds that Burgundy did not want to change masters.[1] But he did not return to Madrid as Regulus did to Carthage.

[226] Our duchy of Guyenne has been the occasion for two deeds of great integrity: Louis the Bold and St. Louis both handed it over—the one to Eleanor, the other to the English.[1] {But Louis the Bold was forced to; Eleanor's subjects would never have obeyed him.}

[227] Consecration of the crocodiles[1] in Egypt. —Prohibition against sailing on the rivers in Persia. —Destruction of houses touched by an Infidel in some parts of the Indies.

[228] It is essential not to inspire men with too much contempt for death; they would thereby elude the legislator.

[229] A religion that offered sure rewards in the afterlife would see its faithful disappear by the thousands.

[230] The dogma of the soul's immortality inclines us toward glory, whereas the contrary belief weakens our desire for it.

2. "Contracts are binding."

[225]
1. Marcus Atilius Regulus, Roman general imprisoned by the Carthaginians in 256 B.C. and sent to Rome to treat on the ransom of prisoners and on peace, on the promise that he would return in case of failure; he dissuaded his fellow citizens from negotiating and returned to Carthage, where he was put to death. Francis I (1515–47) was imprisoned by Charles V (1519–56) after the battle of Pavia (February 24, 1525).

[226]
1. Louis VII the Bold (r. 1137–80), Eleanor of Aquitaine (1122–1204), and Louis IX (r. 1226–70).

[227]
1. First version: "animals."

[**231**] The dogma of the soul's immortality—that so blessed dogma—seems as if it was bound to produce only feelings of gratitude for a Creator who had made our being as durable as his own, feelings of trust toward such a great benefactor, feelings of equity, of justice toward men fated for eternity like us and with us. But superstition,[1] which exaggerates everything—far from having derived such natural consequences from it—has, one may say, used it to ravage the human species. Go to Egypt and look at those barbarous monuments to the dogma of immortality, which cost so much labor, were the source of so many vexations, and made princes so odious to peoples. Go see the kings' sepulchres in Persia, whose upkeep could furnish the subsistence of many cities. Go to the Indies and watch this dogma give birth to that of the transmigration of souls. Look at the men, after suffering hunger from having to live on vegetables, suffer again from the cold, not daring to burn any wood, which might serve as a refuge for some insect; the women forced to burn themselves after their husband's death;[2] the treasures everywhere buried and returned superstitiously to the earth, whence they have been gotten.

Look throughout Asia at that countless number of dervishes[3] and fakirs who, with their pompous and austere penances, turn toward them the entire devotion of the people, whom they astonish; so that instead of candor, good faith, and virtue, which religion ought to inspire, all duties are limited to honoring or enriching them.[4]

But this is not all that superstition has taken from the dogma of immortality. We have seen men devote their entire persons, and princes receive from their subjects that horrible tribute of their frenzy. We have seen ill or elderly fathers killed or eaten by their children's frightful compassion.

[**232**] The Hebrews must have been far removed from the Egyptians not to have picked up from them the dogma of the soul's immortality. It is because the Hebrews did not, strictly speaking, go down amongst the Egyptians, but amongst the shepherds, from Avaris[1] to Cethron.

{A proof that the Hebrews went down not amongst the Egyptians but

[**231**]
1. First version: "devotion."
2. On human sacrifices to follow the dead into the afterlife, see *Laws*, 24.21.
3. See *Laws*, 14.7, for a climatic analysis of monasticism.
4. First version: honoring "these wretches" or "these wretched ones . . ."—HC

[**232**]
1. Egyptian city, presently San el-Hagar.

amongst the people of Cethron is that they did not pick up from them the dogma of the soul's immortality. But how did they get so many other things from the Egyptians? It is because the people of Cethron had superstitions that they picked up, and besides, the Hebrews were so ignorant, so crude, and so poor that they took up nothing but their own superstitions.}

[233] Only marriages propagate. They are discouraged in France, *primo*, in that the laws give such great nuptial advantages to women that everyone is afraid to get married—so you see yourself ruined if you survive your wife, or your children ruined if you do not survive her. It is the men who need to be encouraged toward marriage, not the girls, because the latter's situation adequately inclines them to marry, since honor permits them to taste the pleasures of life only by starting with marriage.

Fathers are equally inclined to bring an end to their daughters' perilous condition.[1]

Wise laws ought to encourage second marriages; ours discourage them. There is also among us this unfortunate fact that the condition of the unmarried is more favorable; they enjoy all the laws' favor, without having the burdens of the Republic. Marriage, moreover, is unfavorable in that it determines ranks and puts limits on social condition.

[234] What I have said on world depopulation requires some modification with regard to China, which seems to be a special case [although they kill their children]. {The population of China: (1) there are no eunuchs, as there are in the rest of Asia; (2) the Chinese propagate because of religion, in order to give their ancestors people who can worship them. Look at what I have collected from M. Fouquet on China.[1]

Rice, cause of the population of China and of other countries where it appears.}

It must be that the nature of that country's climate encourages generation,[2] to which one may add the general abundance of all things necessary for life,[3] the impotence of the Chinese to wage a war against their

---

[233]
1. See *Laws*, 23.21 and 23.9; according to Derathé, 2:519 n. 9, the text of this *pensée* is taken up in the manuscript of *Laws*, V, fol. 58, in a deleted passage.

[234]
1. Montesquieu had met in Rome (*Voyages, OC*, 2:1191; *Spicilège*, 481, 483–84, and 508) Fr. Fouquet—Jesuit, bishop *in partibus* of Eleutheropolis, who had lived in China from 1699 to 1720.
2. See *Laws*, 8.21, 127–28, on this theme.
3. First version: "the mildness and justice of the government."

neighbors, except the Tartars, since their country is entirely separate from the others. That country must not be as populous at present as the ancient accounts say, because of the Tartar wars and the introduction of the sect of Foë, etc.[4]

The marvel of the Chinese empire's duration vanishes when approached closely. This is no more the same empire than the Persian is the same as that of Cyrus, or the government of Europe is the same as in Caesar's time. China being separated from other nations, it has always been regarded as a special empire, whatever revolution it has endured.

[235] Whatever one may say, the Chinese were barbarous people; they ate human flesh, etc.

[{This item is (I believe) false, even though reported by the *Relation*[1] of the two Arab travelers.}]

[236] What sustained the Huguenot party in the civil war that took place under Charles IX[1] in Poitou and in provinces beyond the Loire was the sale of ecclesiastical properties by the Huguenot chieftains. The Huguenots from these areas boldly employed what they had, because of the good market and the expectation they were given that neither the King's authority nor the Catholic religion would ever return to these areas.

[237] I will not write a dedicatory epistle:[1] those who profess to speak the truth must not expect protection on earth.

I am undertaking a long-term work; the history of the society is more fruitful of great events than that of the most warlike nations. A great company is found there, in a continual war against a world of enemies, attacking and defending itself with the same courage. Always persevering in good times and bad, it profits from the former by its dexterity and remedies the latter by its constancy. It is under the banner of religion that they fight for purely human interests, and work to destroy each other. The

---

4. Foë, Chinese name for Buddha.

[235]
1. Abbé Eugène Renaudot (1646–1720), *Anciennes relations des Indes et de la Chine de deux voyageurs mahométans . . .* [Ancient accounts of the Indies and China by two Mohammedan travelers] (Paris, 1718; *Catalogue,* 3151). Montesquieu made extracts in the *Geographica* (*OC,* 2:926).

[236]
1. Charles IX, king of France (1560–74).

[237]
1. It is not known what work Montesquieu is referring to here.

princes brought to the scene, far from pacifying the disorder, exacerbate it, and instead of comporting themselves as mediators, they themselves become factional leaders.

[238] {In the meeting that took place July 13, 1727, at the home of Prince Eugene of Savoy on the subject of the obligatory act signed by . . .}[1]

[239] Since Louis XIV, there have been nothing but great wars—half of Europe against half of Europe. The allies of Hanover[1] have 585,000 men; those of Vienna,[2] 555,000.

[240] Scripture says that Tubalcain invented ironworks.[1] It is not the invention of ironworks that is remarkable, nor that of smelting or cutting, etc.; it is extracting it from the earth. How was it conceived that this earth, whose surface shows us no metals, contained them in its bowels? How could it be conceived that the inner earth—metallic—contained substances of a different nature from the ordinary earth? It seems to me that many centuries were needed for that.

[241] What accounts for most of man's contradictions is that physical logic and moral logic are almost never in agreement. Moral logic should lead a young man to avarice, but physical logic turns him away from it. Moral logic should lead an old man to prodigality; physical logic leads him to avarice. Moral logic gives an old man strength and constancy; physical logic deprives him of it. Moral logic gives an old man contempt for life; physical logic makes it more precious to him. Moral logic should give life great value to a young man; physical logic diminishes it. Moral logic makes us regard the pains of the afterlife as very near; physical logic, by attaching us to all that is present, distances us from them.[1]

[238]
1. François-Eugène de Savoie, called Prince Eugene (1663–1736), son of Eugene-Maurice, Duke of Savoy-Carigna, and of Olympia Mancini. Louis XIV having refused him permission to pursue a military career, he went into the service of the Emperor, at the age of twenty; he distinguished himself against the Turks and won several battles over French armies. Montesquieu made his acquaintance in the course of his travels.

[239]
1. France, Great Britain, and Holland assembled in the Triple Alliance (1716) for the maintenance of the treaties of Utrecht.
2. Austria and Spain.

[240]
1. Genesis 4:22: "Zillah bore Tubal-cain; he was the forger of all instruments of bronze and iron."

[241]
1. Montesquieu developed these ideas in *Essay on the causes that can influence minds and characters* [l'Essai sur les causes qui peuvent affecter les esprits et les caractères], before 1742.

[**242**] What makes a good actor is not making the appropriate facial movements at the time the lines are being recited; it's making them appear beforehand; for most of the time the recited lines are merely the effect of some new passion that has been produced in the soul. This passion must therefore be made to appear. This is where Baron[1] always excels.

[**243**] The greatest project ever conceived[1] is the foundation of Alexandria by Alexander after the destruction of Tyre.[2] By it, he opened trade with the two seas, weakened that of the Carthaginians, and opened up, so to speak, the Orient. One has only to see what the Ptolemies,[3] the richest kings in the world, made of this: Egypt, the finest kingdom in the world by its situation, its fertility, the number of its inhabitants.

[A king of France (or of Spain), with thirty thousand men and a well-stocked fleet, would conquer all of Egypt and would have the finest kingdom in the world for trade and the finest establishment for his youngest brother. Free exercise of all sorts of religion everywhere. No allies, but surprise. No people of established fortune. Egypt still conquered by main force. Nonetheless, it is easy to defend, except for the seacoast.]

[**244**] A great minister who would like to restore Spain, ruined by the monks,[1] ought to increase their honors and decrease little by little their number and their authority.

[**245**] In the preface to the *Dictionary of Commerce*,[1] it is said that the customs of Alexandria rose to more than thirty million pounds per year in the Ptolemies' time, a prodigious sum!

[**246**] Right of escheat and shipwreck,[1] ridiculous right, of little use to the prince, extremely harmful in that it discourages foreigners from

---

[242]
1. Michel Boyron, called Baron (1653–1729), playwright and actor.

[243]
1. "Put, more or less, in the *Romans*" (M.), *Considerations*, IV, 47.
2. Alexandria was founded in 332 B.C. by Dinocrates on orders from Alexander; Tyre had been conquered by Alexander in 332.
3. The name of fifteen Macedonian sovereigns who reigned in Egypt from 323 to 30 B.C.

[244]
1. First version: "to reduce the bad effects of the monks in Spain."

[245]
1. Savary des Bruslons, *Dictionnaire universel de commerce,* 2 vols. (Paris, 1723), 1:iv.

[246]
1. Under the *droit d'aubaine,* the goods of someone who dies in a country where he is not naturalized belong to the authorities. See *Laws,* 21.7.

coming and establishing themselves. "God bless our coasts," they say in countries where the right of shipwreck is established.

Letters of reprieve, pernicious.[2]

[247] The not-doing, says Montaigne,[1] is more difficult than the doing; few treaties, no commitment.

[248] A prime minister should not displace the ministers he inherits; the follies they commit are not on his account, but those of the people he puts in certainly are.

[249] The Electorate of Saxony[1] is a very small State. And yet, whether from trade or from the silver mines, it yields very substantial revenues. It used to be the trading post of all the neighboring States. But merchandise has now been so burdened with tolls that far fewer people pass by Saxony. It is a surprising thing what the king of Sweden drew from there in one year: it reached more than one hundred million, French currency. Its mines[2] still produce silver, which remains in the country.

[250] POLAND. The King does not get six hundred thousand silver crowns of his revenue in Poland.[1] Nothing is so easy for the Prince as to acquire great credit in Poland; he gives out all sorts of favors in every village. There are the same officials as in the kingdom. The King gives out all that. The realm is divided among many great lords who come carrying the list of offices for the King to fill. If the King lets this list go for even two weeks without responding, you'll see even the man with the greatest credit sink into nothingness. Whence the baseness of the Great toward those who have some credit at Court.

[251] GREEK AUTHORS. They had less wit than the Roman authors.

2. The "lettres de répi" were delays granted by the sovereign to debtors.—HC

[247]
1. See Montaigne, *Essays*, III, 10.

[249]
1. Dresden was the capital of the Electorate of Saxony.
2. On his trip to Hungary, Montesquieu visited the mines of Kremnitz, Schemitz, and Neu-Sohl—today Kremnica, Stiavnica, and Bystrica in the Slovak Republic. On his return, he used his notes to compose his *Mémoires sur les mines*. The first was read at the Academy of Bordeaux on August 25, 1731; the other three were read at the December 2 meeting. In 1751, Montesquieu drafted a new *Mémoire sur les mines du Harz*, in which he inserted the text of the second and third memoirs from 1731; see *OC*, 3:435–67.

[250]
1. Augustus II (r. 1697–1733), elector of Saxony who lavished attention on its capital city of Dresden and also became king of Poland.

Plutarch, almost the only one. He also had profited from the Latins. The Greeks did not know the epigram, nor the Latins until Martial;[1] the Greek epigrams were scarcely more than inscriptions, and they were not familiar with *acute dictum*.[2] It seems to me that the Greeks were bold in style, timid in thought. M. says he is surprised the English so admire the Ancients, since there is no one who imitates them so little and is further removed from them. I said to an Englishman who was showing me something fairly delicate: "How have you folks been able to say such nice things in such a barbarous language?" In the time of Francis I, it was the learned who made an author's reputation; today, it is the women. Ronsard proves this.[3] He cannot be read any more, even though no one had a higher reputation. And what ruins him personally is that authors further back than he are still admired.

[252] All European States spend their capital; revenues are not enough. Public credit, well established in certain countries, ruins them because, since the funds are always present, States have been ever more inclined to undertake things. The constant bankruptcies of the government of this realm have ruined many families, but they have brought relief to the rest, who were paying all they were able to for current expenses. Europe is ruining itself and will ruin itself more and more unless by common consent it reduces the number of troops, which would amount to the same thing. The only means I can think of for cutting the debt, and the least onerous, would be for each individual's royal assets to be cut in proportion to his other remaining assets. Because a man who has twenty thousand pounds in real estate rent and two thousand pounds in royal assets would gain from the loss of his two thousand pounds in paper returns, since by this arrangement, his lands would get relief, and {thereby}, those who should most be spared are those who have all their income tied up in the State.[1]

[253] One ought not make proposals in countries where, once the people have been persuaded, it still remains to persuade the Minister—who always rejects the proposal because it is not his own.

[251]
1. Marcus Valerius Martialis, Latin poet (ca. 40–ca. 104).
2. Sharp speaking.—HC
3. Pierre Ronsard (1524–85), leading Renaissance poet.

[252]
1. See *Laws,* 22.17 and 22.18, and *Mémoire sur les dettes de l'Etat* [Memoir on state debts], which Montesquieu sent to the regent in 1715 (*OC,* 3:23–31).

[254] In England, there are investments in land and investments in companies. There are forty million acres in that realm. Whatever the Nation owes, it must be paid—by the owners of land investments, by the owners of company investments, by the very creditors of the State, who are obliged to pay themselves; and finally, by the workers and artisans.[1] But since these latter still have their subsistence, if they pay taxes to the State concurrently with the other citizens, they are then compensated by a premium from the other citizens, in the form of an increase in the price of the things their industry produces relative to the tax on them. Thus, only the first three types of individuals should be counted as paying State debts. And what we have said of the artisans could also, for the most part, be said of the merchants and others who live by their own resourcefulness.

[255] In Europe's current condition, State creditors and debtors are in a perpetual war. Investors in real estate and in the companies are at war against the State creditors, and the State creditors are also at war against themselves,[1] because they must pay themselves a part of what the State paid them and what the State paid out of the taxes it levied on them.

[256] There must be proportionality between the State as creditor and the State as debtor,[1] for the State can be a creditor indefinitely, but it can be a debtor to only a certain level; if this level is surpassed, the status of creditor vanishes.[2]

[257] Every individual in the Kingdom should cede to the State a tenth of his capital, and should make this payment in whatever assets it may be—whether in a quittance, or in company assets, or in money, or in lands sold for the State's profit.[1] That way, there will not be a single individual who pays a cent, since one pays only what one would have been obliged

[254]
    1. "Put in my *Laws,* book XXV" (M.). This note, and those that follow, suggest that Montesquieu changed the order and the numbering of the books of *The Spirit of the Laws,* since public debts are actually treated in 22.17 and 22.18.

[255]
    1. "Put in the *Laws, ibidem*" (M.), 22.18.

[256]
    1. "Put *ibidem*" (M.), *Laws,* 22.18.
    2. This *pensée* is reproduced in *Laws,* 22.18; see also the letter from Montesquieu to X, June 24, 1726 (*OC,* 3:837).

[257]
    1. "Put in the *Laws,* book XXV" (M.); see 22.18.

to pay anyway. The creditor loses nothing; the only cutback he faces is what the taxes would have obliged him to pay himself. But State funds will be much relieved, and Brittany as creditor will be superior to Brittany as debtor.

[**258**] A lottery,[1] with money shares and paper tickets. A gain of one-fifth. The tickets given out in payment, then retaken as tickets in a new lottery.[2]

[**259**] Our situation is vastly more fortunate than England's. With the tax of four shillings per pound sterling on land, she raises only six million sterling, but she owes three in interest.

{She pays no more than one shilling per pound. As of this November 7, 1733, she owes only 51 million pounds sterling, at 3 percent. Some of these accounts, too, are coming to term. Thus, she owes only a million and a half plus 30,000 pounds sterling, which is only a quarter of what she raises.

She does not owe that in 1734, but no more than 48 million plus.}

We, who owe barely 46 million, French currency (before the reduction of lifetime annuities, after all, we owed only 52 in money rent, French currency),[1] assuming the pound sterling equal to 20 pounds in France, we owe only 2,000,300 pounds sterling in rent, and we raise 10; for our revenues amount to 200 million in our currency. Half the English revenues are therefore earmarked, and only 23/103 of the French, which is only about 1/5 to 1/4.

[**260**] By the union with Scotland,[1] English power has been extraordinarily enhanced. For the government used to have to send over money to get what it wanted passed in Parliament, and nothing or almost nothing was brought back to England. Today Scotland, which used to owe nothing, has entered into the debts of the Nation; she pays in proportion. [Her trade is not enhanced, as used to be said; it has instead been destroyed.]

[258]
1. See *Spicilège*, 237.
2. First version: "Without counting that the Portuguese who have very large ports in the East Indies that could very well be useful to our commerce."

[259]
1. The royal declaration of June 15, 1726, had fixed the value of the currency; see also the letter from Berthelot de Duchy to Montesquieu, June 29, 1726 (*OC*, 3:839), and from Lamoignon de Courson to Montesquieu, July 1726 (*OC*, 3:845).

[260]
1. May 1, 1707.

Everyone leaves the realm to go to England: the rich, [the *beaux esprits*], the younger sons of households; no more Parliament in Edinburgh. Taxes carry off all the money.

{It is true that Scotland has been cultivated and has dedicated herself to trade. The peasants have abandoned arms for work. Thus, she has not become impoverished; on the contrary, she has become wealthier in spite of the abovementioned disadvantages.}

[**261**] England has paid little or nothing of her debts since the treaty of Utrecht.[1] It is difficult for her to pay: (1) because of the wars that the contested succession brings her, and those which the Empire's affairs will always bring her, and which she will no longer be able to avoid getting involved in {and those which Gibraltar will bring her. It is in France's interest that the English keep Gibraltar, which will always keep them embroiled.} Lord Oxford's plan[2] a good one: to place the States of Germany on another head. The fortunes of princes who have acquired new States have always been baleful to one or another of these States. Didn't Aragon lose much by the succession to Castile? Flanders, by the succession to both of them? These are new means placed in princes' hands to overturn those new States.

[**262**] Horrible blunder by Spain and Portugal—which, on the pretext of a useless war with the Turks, deprive themselves of the trade of the *Echelles du levant*,[1] which they could have much more easily than other nations, since they have the silver bullion which is indispensable for that trade and which the Dutch and other nations seek out from them or from the Genoese. There is no Dutch vessel en route to the Levant, for example, that does not stop at Cadiz or Livorno to take on some piastras that the Genoese furnish them. Moreover, the cloth that the English bring to the Levant is {almost} all of pure Spanish wool, and the rest of their trade, except for their fish {and a few other items}, is practically all in knitted fabric. They could transport cochineal, wood from Brazil, indigo (especially to Smyrna), vermilion to Egypt.[2]

[261]

1. The peace of Utrecht signed in 1713 between France, England, and Holland ended the War of the Spanish Succession; England's acquisition of Gibraltar was one of the provisions.

2. Robert Harley, count of Oxford (1661–1724); cf. *Spicilège*, 434, 449.

[262]

1. The Echelles du Levant (Ports of Levant) were trading posts set up by Christian nations in Islamic territory from the seventeenth to the early twentieth centuries.

2. "See the page vis-à-vis" (M.), *pensée* 264.

[**262a**] [Every day, cheating goes on by means of those who ought to prevent it. All sorts of prohibited things are done easily. The only remedy for this is to use a valet whose practice is to send swindlers on assignment and bear their burdens . . . and a man . . .][1]

[**263**] A monastic convent placed in Bagnères or Barèges[1] would do quite well in a period ignorant of science and religion. What sources of wealth! Besides, what kind of virtue would it be, joined to the power of nature and of trust?

[**264**] LEVANTINE TRADE FOR SPAIN. They would receive: waxes from Barbary, Smyrna, Constantinople, Alexandria, Satalie,[1] and would impose a heavy tariff on all merchandise to enter Spain from the Levant in foreign ships; the wheat brought from the nearby coasts of Smyrna and even from some islands of the Archipelago; if they set up manufactures, some first-hand mohair from Angora and some cotton from Aleppo and other ports.

In addition, they would directly draw all sorts of cotton cloths from Aleppo, some admirable mixed-fabrics from Alexandretta,[2] and finally {a part} of that boundless merchandise that comes into Europe from Cairo and Alexandria. Nothing has done more harm to Spain than this interdiction of mutual trade between her States and the Sultan's, because it so reduced her shipping as to transfer naval power to the heretical nations of Europe, which has so alienated the kingdom of God and so weakened Catholics' power. Spain's situation makes this trade natural, and now that she is deprived of parts detached from her domination, she will be detached so to speak from the rest of the world, if shipping and trade do not bring her back into it.

Moreover, Spain could conduct the Levantine trade by means of a company established in Barcelona or some other Mediterranean port, where the King himself could take part.[3] And the convoys he would offer, as the Dutch are obliged to do because of the Barbary pirates, would increase shipping commensurately.

[262a]
1. These ellipses indicate undecipherable text.

[263]
1. Bagnères-de-Bigorre et Barèges (Upper-Pyrenees).

[264]
1. Antalya in modern Turkey.—HC
2. Modern Iskenderun.—HC
3. See *Considérations sur les richesses de l'Espagne* (*OC*, 3:139–55).

If the King of Spain established cloth manufacturing, it would be much more suitable for the Levant than for America, because the Levant needs cloth that is much nicer and much finer—that is to say, of pure Spanish wool. {Spain also profits from trade with England, which consumes some of her commodities that others would not consume.}{Much coarse cloth is also needed.}

[265] It seems the pagans must have regarded the worship of only one god as a greater crime than the Christians regard that of[1] worshipping many, because whoever worships many does not destroy the true god's divinity completely, but among the pagans, a man who worshipped only one god insulted all the others.

[266] A Jewish city should be built on the Spanish frontier, in a place fit for trade, like Saint-Jean-de-Luz or Ciboure.[1] They would swarm in there and manage to bring all the wealth they have into that realm. Just give them the same privileges they have in Livorno, or even more if you want.

[267] [We have the air of being happy but we are not; it is a false air.]

[268] ON PORTUGAL. [I should be quite happy here; all I find is people uglier than I am.] —The climate is made in favor of women, but the women seem to be made against the climate.[1] [For me, with new tendencies to become libertine, I have almost become a *dévot*.[2]] Nothing about a Portuguese woman inspires detachment. The Angels rejoice when a Frenchman is near a Po(rtuguese) woman. They have remedies for preserving their beauty that Ovid did not prescribe, and that Love never approved. Behold the fair sex! {You can judge the other one.} [If you have been marked by grace, come here.] The only real preachers for women are ugly men [and we excel here in this method of conversion—a devout woman is happy, Madam, in this country. No occasion to flee, no revolt to fear. One must be saved in spite of oneself. Come here then, but if you come here, things would soon change for me and I would lose all the advantages you may see in me. I would soon complain of being so attracted to you].

[265]
1. First version: "than we would regard the idolatry of."

[266]
1. Saint-Jean-de-Luz and Ciboure (Atlantic Pyrenees).

[268]
1. See *pensée* 42.—HC
2. A staunch and practicing religious believer.—HC

[**269**] The reason why the British, French, and other merchants have lost the years 1723 to 1730 in the Brazilian trade is that Spain forbade the transport of piastras from Potosì to Buenos Aires. Now, merchandise used to be sent into Brazil to make it pass through Buenos Aires into America. But since the merchandise fetched no money—since Spain had arranged to have some merchants hanged who, contrary to the ordinances, had sent some piastras by the continent instead of sending them by Panama and Portobello[1]—the European merchants who have had merchandise in Buenos Aires have found the country devoid of money.

[**270**] I am firmly convinced that the Emperor could run the East Indies trade through Trieste[1] at much less expense than the other nations of Europe. He would have to have from the Turk—through exchange, purchase or some other way—Ercokko {or Quaquen},[2] which he conquered from the Abyssinians, or some other fortified place on the Red Sea, to be the center of his trade between the Orient and the Occident. If not, Suez would suffice, because the Emperor, by virtue of his forces in the Occident, is in a position to make himself respected in the Orient and to obtain the best capitulations of any prince in Europe. Even the Treaty of Passarowitz brings him a fair amount of benefit.[3] The only thing needed would be to stipulate a reduction {or abolition} of tariffs on merchandise that is not consumed in Turkey and that passes duty-free into Trieste, Naples, Sicily, Italy.

The Emperor would have to attempt to sign a trade treaty with the Abyssinians' emperor, and open up, so to speak, an entrée into that great empire, with which other nations trade only in an indirect manner. For it is difficult to make big profits in the trade conducted in competition with the English and Dutch.[4]

What made the route around the Cape of Good Hope seem more advantageous is that at that time, a single nation (the Venetian) was engaging in that trade. {Which meant that she sold at the price she wanted}, she

[269]
1. Portobello, important Caribbean port in the colonial era, in the present republic of Panama.

[270]
1. See *Voyages* (*OC*, 2:982): "The Emperor wants a port: Trieste is worthless."
2. Quaquen, Sudanese port on an islet of the Red Sea.
3. The Treaty of Passarowitz (today Pozarevac in Serbia), signed July 21, 1718, between the emperor Charles VI, Turkey, and Venice, recognized the Banat of Timisoara—from Wallachia to Oltenia, and part of Serbia including Belgrade; cf. *Laws*, 21.9, 371–72.
4. On Dutch commerce, see *Voyages* (*OC*, 2:1291) and *Laws*, 20.6.

did not buy first hand, she suffered countless outrages by the Turks, much more barbarous and much less timid than today.

It cannot be the ease and convenience of transport that has ruined the Indies trade through Egypt, or the difficulty of the isthmus of Suez. That distance is so short that it could not have made such a prodigious difference—all the more so since merchandise is still transported from the Indies to Aleppo[5] via Basra, which is a prodigious distance by land. The Spice Islands, the tribute the Portuguese exacted from the Indian princes, the arbitrary conditions they imposed on trade with the Indians, the nearly universal exclusion of the Indians from shipping, the duties they levied when shipping, the immense profits from the Japan trade, the spices that took the place of money {for the purchases they made in the Indies}, which cost them little, which they sold at the price they wanted—these things brought an absolute collapse in the Indies trade through Egypt. And since the Dutch have inherited the maxims and the power of the Portuguese, this is what still gives them {and will give them} commercial superiority over other nations, whether they conduct this trade by {way of} Egypt or by the Cape of Good Hope.

Since the Dutch are obliged to maintain a large number of fortresses and many forces by land and sea, their Indies trade is far from being as lucrative as it might be; all the more so in that, to ruin other nations' trade, they often sustain deliberate losses, so that neither they nor others get all the advantage they could from their trade. Notwithstanding, the Dutch make very big profits, and other nations make a great deal as well.

Some believe they can assure us that the expense would be much less by Egypt than by the Cape of Good Hope—insofar as the African route is long, the trade winds halt your course, and a long voyage kills sailors.

Still, trade at Trieste is far more advantageous than at Ostende, through the ease of distributing returns in Italy and in the Hereditary Countries.

Merchandise could easily be transported from the Austrian lands to Alexandria or even Trieste.

Perhaps an emporium beyond the straits of Bab el Mandeb would be needed for depositing merchandise when the straits are difficult to pass.

In the emporium chosen either on this side or the other side of the straits, there would always be small vessels busily going from the Red Sea

5. First version: "from the Orient to Smyrna."

to the Indies and returning from the Indies to the Red Sea, and also going from the emporium to Suez and from Suez to the emporium.

{I do not say that this would be impossible for some other power, but it is for the Emperor, for whom Trieste is absolutely useless. There are neither men nor merchandise in Trieste, nor anywhere in that territory, and an immense journey by land would be needed to send out commodities and bring back others.}

[**271**] What gives strength to the military forces of France[1] is that they communicate so well that it seems they are brought together into one point.[2] The army of Flanders is right next to that of the Rhine; that of the Rhine, next to that of Dauphiné; that of Dauphiné, next to that of Roussillon; that of Roussillon, next to that of Guyenne—the only places by which the realm (in any case defended by mountains, large rivers, or the sea) can be attacked by land. These armies can be transported, in whole or in part, from one of those places to a neighboring one in a week's time, and orders are sent in one day or in a day or two. In short, you could, if you needed to, combine all your armies in three weeks' time. You thus have your forces everywhere, so to speak, and you are not afraid of any enterprises that need more than a fortnight or three weeks to be executed. And virtually all great enterprises need much more time.[3]

It is the moderate size of the French realm that gives it these advantages, a size proportioned both to the speed that nature has given men to be transported from one place to another, and to the length of time necessary for the execution of men's ordinary enterprises. Thus, if a power that had defeated[4] the army of Flanders were going on to besiege Paris, first, the remainder of the army would reassemble easily because the retreats would be close by, and because that night or the next day a new corps would be formed, whereas it is impossible for an army that is dispersed and has no retreat within a hundred leagues ever to reassemble, or at least for a very long time; (2) a portion of our troops would receive orders to come to the aid of Paris in one, two or three days. They would arrive—some one week, and some a fortnight afterward.[5] The enemy, embroiled in a large siege,

[**271**]

1. This *pensée* is a draft of *Laws*, 9.6, 135, first three paragraphs. See also *pensée* 561.
2. "[Put this in the *Romans*]" (M.).
3. "[In the *Romans*]" (M.).
4. First version: "had destroyed"
5. "[Put that in the *Romans*]" (M.).

occupied moreover with the difficulties of provisioning their army in enemy territory and bringing in everything demanded by a large enterprise,
would perforce endure great battles and all the endless obstacles put in the
way of their designs—cutting off their supply lines, burning all their boats,
depriving them of communication by river.

Let us now examine a great and vast realm. Let us take that of Persia.
This is a realm of such prodigious extent that it takes two or three months
for its troops to be able to communicate with each other. Notice too that
you do not force troops to march for three months, as you do for a week or
two. {It is only a gambler who has his money two hundred leagues away.}[6]
Let us suppose the army of Kandahar is dispersed. A part of the victorious
army advances with great progress, finds no resistance, goes and captures
some advantageous posts in the capital city, and fills all with consternation.
The victor has arrived before Ispahan {and is preparing the siege there},[7]
by the time the governors of the frontier provinces are alerted to send
assistance. These governors, who see that a revolution is imminent, that
the capital and also the Prince will be taken before they can arrive, speed
up and bring about the revolution by not obeying and by thinking of
their private interests. People accustomed to obeying because punishment
is extremely near no longer obey when they see it is extremely far. The
Empire is dissolved, the capital is taken, and the conqueror contests the
provinces with the governors. It is in this fashion that the Empire of China
has been destroyed several times by bandit chieftains and several times by
the Tartars.

In a word, for a state to be in a condition of permanence, there must
be a correspondence between the speed with which an enterprise can be
executed against it, and the speed with which the enterprise can be rendered vain.

Notice that the princes of large States[8] usually have few neighboring
countries that can be the object of their ambition. If there had been any,
they would have been swallowed up in the rapidity of the conquest. Thus,
they are usually vast deserts, seas or mountains—territories, in short,
whose poverty brings them disdain. Thus, a vast State founded by arms is
no longer sustained by arms, but lapses into a profound peace. And just as,

6. See *pensée* 630.
7. "[In the *Romans]*" (M.).
8. Cf. *Considerations*, XVI, 153.

whenever there is disorder and confusion somewhere, one cannot imagine how peace can return, so too, when full peace and obedience reign, one cannot imagine how it might come to an end. Such a government thus inevitably neglects the troops and the military, because it thinks it has nothing to hope for and nothing to fear {from enemies. The military can only be against the State. Thus, the Prince seeks rather to weaken it.} It is therefore prey to the first accident.[9]

[272] Father Buffier has defined beauty: the assemblage of that which is most common.[1] When his definition is explained, it is excellent, because it accounts for something very obscure, because it is a matter of taste.

Father Buffier says that beautiful eyes are those of which there is the greatest number of the same kind; likewise the mouth, the nose, etc. It is not that there isn't a much greater number of ugly noses than beautiful noses, but that the ugly ones are of different kinds, and each kind of ugly one is much less numerous than the kind of beautiful ones. It is as if, in a crowd of a hundred men, there are ten men dressed in green, and the ninety left are each dressed in a different color; it is the green that dominates.

In short, it seems to me that deformity has no bounds. The grotesques of Callot can be varied indefinitely.[2] But regularity of features is within certain limits.

This principle of Father Buffier is excellent for explaining how a French beauty is hideous in China, and a Chinese hideous in France.

In a word, it is excellent {perhaps} for explaining all the beauties of taste {even in the works of the mind}. But this will require some thought.

[273] There is a danger that Papal authority might someday be undermined by the Jansenists.[1] The acts of persecution against them in France have led some of them to opt to move to Holland,[2] where they have

---

9. For this last paragraph, see *pensée* 688.—HC

[272]
1. Fr. Claude Buffier, S.J. (1661–1737), *Traité des premières vérités et de la source de nos jugements* [Treatise on first truths, and on the source of our judgments] (Paris, 1724).
2. Jacques Callot (1592–1635), French engraver noted for his illustrations of the Thirty Years' War (1618–48).

[273]
1. Cf. the *Mémoire sur la Constitution Unigenitus* (*OC*, 3:469ff.). See also *pensées* 426, 914, 1226, 2158, and 2164.
2. On the Jansenists of Holland, cf. *Voyages* (*OC*, 2:1292).

adopted principles contrary to an authority that was constantly condemning them. Now, it is impossible that the Jansenists of France and Holland
are not communicating with each other a great deal. Since the Jesuits—by
their credit, their ingenuity, their arduous labors—are still arming that
power against them, it is scarcely possible for them to free themselves from
the Jesuits except by undermining that power. And if a Prince ever gets it
into his head to plunder the Church of its property, there can be no doubt
that the Jansenist party, out of vengeance against the Court of Rome, will
be for him. And if he employs these properties for the subjects' relief, there
can be no doubt that the people will be for him, too.

The bishops will be urged not to create any more ecclesiastics until those
already created, seculars as well as regulars, are provided with benefices.
And if they were to create one, he will be exiled outside the Kingdom.
Idem, for the monks, besides which, the prior who receives a novice will
also be exiled with him.

Although I do not in any way approve of such an enterprise, here is how
I imagine it will be executed, if it ever is. All the abbeys, monasteries, prio-
ries, chapels, cathedral churches, and nonepiscopal canon chapters will
be abolished, and only the bishoprics and pastoral offices, hospitals,[3] and
universities will be kept. Everyone will be left with the peaceful possession
of his goods, but as a benefice becomes vacant it will be abolished, and the
goods attached to it, even the houses, will be sold for the State's profit. The
monks and religious will also remain in the possession of their goods, but
as they die, those who have not made a vow of stability[4] will be transferred
from urban convents into rural convents, and the empty convents and
goods attached to them will be sold for the State's profit. As for the monks
who have made a vow of stability, the portion belonging to the deceased
will accrue to the State and will be sold in due course.

The bishops will be urged not to create any more ecclesiastics until those
already created, seculars as well as regulars, are provided with benefices.
And if they were to create one, he will be exiled outside the Kingdom.
Idem, for the monks, besides which, the prior who receives a novice will
also be exiled with him.

The sale of vacant properties will be made to the highest bidder, and in
contracts or official royal papers. Said properties will be subject to taxes and
charges of the localities where they are situated, and what these properties
had paid when they were ecclesiastical will be cut from the charges on the
clergy. Every year a calculation will be made of the amortized royal bonds,

---

3. *Hôpitaux,* houses for the sick and the poor.—HC
4. A vow to remain all one's life in the same religious establishment.—HC

and some onerous tax will be lightened proportionally; for example, the salt tax could be abolished.

It will be essential to be on guard against changing anything in the religion, and especially against deviating from what has been defined by the holy Council of Trent. That is why I imagine that such a prince, if he is wise, will not permit monks to break their vows or leave their cloisters.

[**274**] Here are the principal operations that I have in mind to make the Kingdom flourish and restore its finances.[1]

I estimate that forty-seven million are due in payments of all kinds.

I would begin, first of all, by relieving myself of around seven million by cutting out one sou per pound on everything the State pays out and draws from the royal treasury, with the exception of soldiers' pay.

Next, I should think the present goal ought to be to relieve the subjects rather than to pay off the capital debt, because once prosperity is restored, it would be easy to pay.

In the event that the proposal on Church properties were to be implemented, the salt tax would be abolished, and the King would be content with a 20 percent tax on the salt that comes from the salt mines and marshes, to be distributed throughout the Realm.

As pensions fall vacant (they amount to 5 million), I would restore only half of them. *Idem,* princes' pensions.

As governorships fall vacant, they would be abolished, and only the commanders would remain.

A quarter of the royally ordained salaries of all the officers of justice, administration, and finance would be cut. Naturally, those presently in office will sustain no cuts during their lifetimes.

Every year there would be an exclusive lottery, in order to reduce the capital owed.

The Louvre, three royal houses, and three captains' lodgings: reduction of expenses on this item.

Reduction in the number of ambassadors and in the amount in foreign subsidies, inasmuch as the great princes ought rather to receive from the petty ones, for their protection, than give to them.

[274]
1. See the *Mémoire sur les dettes de l'Etat* [Memoir on state debts] (*OC,* 3:23ff.).

At each change in ownership, the perpetual annuities would be reduced by one-thirtieth[2] from father to son and one-tenth in collateral cases.

{Besides this, the holders of royal debt would pay an annual tax that would reduce the value of their holdings by three percent.}

Add to this what is inevitably gained on the death of lifetime annuity owners.

A triple head tax would be imposed on all unmarried lay persons in the realm.

Those provinces subject to the salt tax, which alone would be relieved,[3] ought to contribute to relieving the burden of the other provinces—and on a prorated basis.

When, by these arrangements, the King has recovered what he will have lost by the abolition of the salt tax, it will be necessary to think of other projects.

Eliminate tariffs between provinces reputed and not reputed to be foreign—and this, with the King bearing one-quarter of the loss, the other three-quarters being made up by a 5 percent increase in tariffs at the entry into, and exit from, the Realm. The charges on tariff collection eliminated, along with the vexations by the officials, will be a gain for the people.

To recover the loss that the King would incur in taking on himself a quarter of this cutback, a recoinage would be called for, of such minor scope as not to deter anyone from bringing the coin in. It could be, for example, at a profit of four or five percent. Which profit would be employed in paying 80 million in cash that the King owes the Indies Company in return for 100 million in State notes at 4 percent, which the Company took so that the King might take back his tobacco concession. Which payment would be made by the King in four years, in such a way that the King would recover a quarter of the concession in the first year[4] (20 million paid), half in the second year, until the payment and reversion are complete.

It should be noted that, in the said period of time, a second recoinage could be done, in order to contribute to the payment of the said 80 million.

2. First version: "one-twentieth."
3. That is, by its proposed abolition.—HC
4. First version: "every year."

These operations must be undertaken only little by little, one after the other—while waiting, through the passage of time, for the King to gain what we have said he was going to gain.

Once the above-mentioned operations have been done, it would be time to think of reducing the registration fees, by following pretty closely the model implemented in Paris: increasing the stamped paper and imposing a light tax [one-time only] on notaries and on cities, a tax payable only in royal notes and for only three years. Cities would be permitted to borrow, or to sell their domain lands for this. A sale of certain onerous taxes to the subjects could be offered, all in royal notes. [Some commercial establishment would have to be set up.]

All these things ought to be implemented slowly and with prudence, taking care not to put the King in arrears on his revenue, and not eliminating the means to be able to collaborate in making commerce and the arts flourish, and in making public reparations.

Inasmuch as the Royal domains are always poorly managed, a State law ought to ensure that they are sold irrevocably and in perpetuity—and this, for the good of the State (with the exception of the forests). Which sale will be made at 3 1/3 percent in royal notes, at the rate of 5 percent. And as for simple mortgages, they would be sold in perpetuity, by the proprietors paying appropriate charges in royal notes: an equitable adjustment that could be done in such a way that the King gains a third by it.

The King would sell his right of escheat to his subjects, as well as his right over bastards; he would join the Admiralty to the Crown during a vacancy, and would sell its duties and charges in royal notes and currency. In cases where he did not want to unduly humble the house that possesses it, he could leave them the title, while attaching to it the office and functions of Secretary of State for the Navy.

Once these things are done, and receipts are again squaring with expenses, the taille and *taillon*[5] would be abolished, and only the head tax would be left, so there would only be one type of tax of this nature. But the head tax would be increased, once and for all, by half (more or less), to whatever the sum of the eliminated taille may have covered. Thereby,

---

5. The *taillon* was a taille (income tax) for upkeep of the royal military police, until the eighteenth century, when the two became indistinguishable.—HC

the tax would be borne more equally by rich and poor alike, and the countryside, which is the source of the Kingdom's wealth, would get more relief. And there would be this law that whoever finds himself taxed beyond a fifth of his income could relinquish said fifth to the tax collectors. Of course, if he were of bad faith and brought to justice, he would be condemned to pay four times as much.[6]

Any man convicted of embezzlement in the management of public revenues, punished by death.

No death penalties other than hanging or beheading.[7]

Once this is done, a recoinage of 50 million would be undertaken at State profit to amortize 3 million in payments, by means of which the King would relieve his subjects of 4 million in taxes.[8] By this means, a way would be sought of setting up a fiscal administration that is less onerous to the subject, and if this were possible, these taxes would remain, converted to a toll.

To achieve this goal {and compensate the King for the loss of a million}, all taxes on the Jews that have been given to private individuals will be eliminated, and broader privileges would be sold to them, in exchange for a sum payable in royal assets for three years {all of it valued at one million in revenue}; so they would come into the enjoyment of a third of these privileges during each of the said years.

Once these things are done over the space of twelve or fifteen years, no further change in the finances would be made, except for the lotteries, to achieve the reduction[9] in payments backed by the city of Paris. Let the annual gain be merely 100,000 silver crowns. The people would contribute to it willingly, if they saw fidelity in it, and if they saw a tax reduction at year's end equal to the State's gains. And to encourage these lotteries, all sorts of games of chance would have to be eliminated under dire penalties, and these lotteries made a sort of game {or else revalue the currency by a seventh; taxes by a tenth; abolish the salt tax}.

[275] I said: "We don't know how to go about doing a great deed. If our interest is involved, we say it's self-love; if it is not involved, we say it's fanaticism."

---

6. First version: "condemned to the galleys for two years."

7. Breaking on the wheel, drawing and quartering, and burning at the stake are among the methods Montesquieu implicitly excludes here. Hanging and beheading were seen as more dignified.—HC

8. Literally, *aides,* excise taxes.

9. First version: "the extinction"

[**276**] There is a falsity about women. This comes from their dependence; as dependence increases, falsity increases. It is like the royal tolls: the more you raise them, the more you increase smuggling.

[**277**] It is said the king of France is rich. He is not. His expenses exceed his revenues. It is only the kings of Asia, whose revenues exceed their expenses and who put the surplus in their treasury every year, who are rich.

[**278**] FUNDAMENTAL PRINCIPLES OF POLITICS.

First Principle.[1] The legislator must not compromise his laws. He must prohibit only things that can be prohibited. Thus, women must have their affairs, and theologians must debate.

Second Principle.

[**279**] Louis XIV had a soul larger than his intellect. Mme de Maintenon[1] constantly humbled that soul to make it do her bidding.

[**280**] [Since the invention of bills of exchange, the Jews have assured themselves of fixed refuge, for any prince who would really like to get rid of them is not, for all that, of a disposition to get rid of their money.[1]]

[**281**] It is impossible for a nation built on industry not to fall from time to time,[1] for the very prosperity it has enjoyed is harmful afterward, and produces decline. Thus, a State's flourishing trade in manufactures causes the workers to become more expensive, spend more and consume more. Merchandise becomes more expensive, and other nations can offer it at a better price.

[**282**] We have left to princes the gratifications of command, in order to have those of obedience. They were to have the grandeur and perils for themselves; we, the moderation, security, and repose. But there is a constant effort to worsen our deal: our smallness is left to us, but they want to take our tranquillity from us.

[**283**] The manner in which women are treated in France, where a young

---

[278]
  1. First version: "Since the object of the legislator is to prevent only things that can happen, he must not compromise"

[279]
  1. Françoise d'Aubigné, Marquise de Maintenon (1635–1719), morganatic wife of Louis XIV.

[280]
  1. See *pensée* 77.

[281]
  1. "Put in the *Universal Monarchy*" (M.), II.

woman of eighteen, as pretty as Love itself, is despised by her husband in his demeanor—this is a debauchery of the mind, not a vice of the heart.

[284] It is said that the Turks are wrong, that women must be managed, not tyrannized. Myself, I say they must either command or obey.

[285] Transpositions, permitted in poetry, often give it an advantage over prose, because the important word for the thought is put in the most striking place, and the whole sentence can turn on this word.

Thus, in the lines:

> Et vous, d'un vain devoir imaginaires lois,
> Ne faites point entendre une inutile voix.
> Sans vous, chez les mortels, tout était légitime.
> C'est vous qui, du néant, avez tiré le crime.

> (And you, fanciful laws of an idle duty,
> Don't make us a useless voice to hear.
> Without you, all was licit among mortals.
> It's you who, from the void, made crime appear.)

The impression would have been less striking if it had said: "Sans vous tout aurait été légitime chez les mortels: c'est vous qui avez tiré le crime du néant." (Without you everything would have been licit among mortals; it is you who have made crime appear from the void.)

[286] There are as many vices that arise from too little self-esteem as from too much.

[287] It is impossible, almost, to fashion good new tragedies, because almost all the good situations have been taken by the early authors. It is a vein of gold that is exhausted for us. There will come a people who will be for us what we are for the Greeks and Romans. A new language, new mores, new circumstances, will produce a new body of tragedies. The authors will take what we have already taken, from nature or from our own authors, and soon they will be exhausted as we have become exhausted. There are only about thirty or so good characters, marked characters. They have been taken: *the Doctor, the Marquis, the Gambler, the Coquette, the Jealous man, the Miser, the Misanthropist, the Bourgeois*. A new nation is needed to create new plays, to mix their own mores with men's characters. Thus, it is easy to see the advantage the earliest authors of our dramatic

pieces have over those who work in our time. They have had the grand features, the marked features for themselves. All that is left for us is refined characters, those who elude common minds—that is, almost all minds. Thus, Destouches's plays {and Marivaux's} are more labored in their high quality than Molière's.[1]

[288] Curiosity, source of the pleasure one finds in works of the mind. Hobbes says curiosity is peculiar to man, on which he is mistaken; every animal has it within the sphere of its acquaintance.

[289] Test weight[1] by means of magnetite carried to the top of a tower or down below. Or from a mountain or a quarry. {See if it weighs less up high than down below.}

[290] QUIETISTS.[1] It is impossible to have any sense and not see that love of self and love of union are the same thing; a lover who wants to die for his mistress does so only because he loves himself, because he imagines that he will taste the pleasure of knowing that he has done such great things for her. His brain is modified not by the idea of death, but by the pleasure of the love he has for his mistress.

[291] It is unfitting for M. Ramsay, Fréret,[1] and their ilk to make up their system {of the idea of the three states of man among all peoples}: felicity and innocence, degradation and corruption after the fall, and restoration.

[287]
1. Philippe Nericault, called Destouches (1680–1754); Pierre Carlet de Chamblain de Marivaux (1688–1763); Jean-Baptiste Poquelin, called Molière (1622–73), playwrights.

[289]
1. At its meeting of May 1, 1719, the Academy of Bordeaux had chosen, as the topic of its prize for 1720, the cause of weight. In the absence of the sitting director, Jean-François Melon, inspector of the tax farms, Montesquieu made the speech reporting the prize in his place at the public assembly of May 1, 1720; cf. *Discours sur la cause de la pesanteur des corps* [Discourse on the cause of bodily weight] (*OC*, 3:89–93).

[290]
1. See *Spicilège*, 121.

[291]
1. Chevalier Andrew Michael Ramsay (1686–1743), follower of Socinianism, was converted by Fénelon around 1709; propagator in France of Freemasonry, which he wanted to reconcile with monarchy and Catholicism. Montesquieu doubtless refers to his 1719 *Essai de politique;* Nicolas Fréret (1688–1749), ex-student of Fr. Desmolets, had been elected to the Bordeaux Academy in November 1715. Erudite, he worked on ancient history, chronology, and archeology and was interested in the history of China. It is doubtless through him that Montesquieu made the acquaintance of the Chinese Arcadio Hoange; see André Masson, "Un chinois inspirateur des *Lettres persanes*," in *Revue des Deux Mondes* (May 15, 1951): 348–54; Danielle Elisseef-Poisle, *Nicolas Fréret* (Paris: Collège de France, 1978).

For *primo,* the ancient philosophers are quite unknown, and although they speak the same terms, they do not have the same ideas. Greek philosophy is quite unknown to us: we have scarcely more than a few fragments of Diogenes Laertius {none-too-accurate author}. Aristotle and Plato are the only two originals who remain; Plato speaks almost exclusively in sayings, and Aristotle is very obscure. What we know of the systems of these philosophers is enough to make us see that we do not have them. Thus, when a philosopher tells us that the origin of things is water, we see clearly that we have only a saying, and are ignorant of the meaning. But if we know almost nothing about Greek philosophy, how ignorant are we of that of the Egyptians, the Persians, and the Chaldeans? If we know only a tenth of Greek philosophy, we know only one two-hundredth of the Egyptian, and a thousandth of the Persian and Chaldean. Thus, one cannot form a common system from these three religions. I would add that the idea of the three conditions is not even found in Greek philosophy, which is the best known. The Greek idea of the golden age, which supposedly corresponds to the state of innocence among the Hebrews and Christians, does not come from the same source: it came to the Greeks only from pastoral life, which was innocent and tranquil, and which men abandoned to go live in the cities—which was followed by commerce, industry, the arts, business, and, consequently, by crimes, which engendered the iron age. {Abbé Mongaut[2] believes that} the idea of the four ages of the world comes from the four ages of the life of man. Thus, if the only philosophy that is at all well known eludes system, what is to be said about that of other peoples?

[292] I saw in Prideaux that the reason why Cyrus sent the Jews back home was that Babylon was a newly conquered city, that the Jews were in and around Babylon, and that he wanted to weaken it. If that were true, then it would be the case that Providence disposed things in such a way that Cyrus's policy was obliged to follow it.[1]

[293] I have heard that in the story of the possessed of Loudun, one finds a very subtle devil. Expulsed by the force of the exorcisms, he took refuge from one place to another, going from the concupiscible to the

---

2. First version: "A man of wit derives."—HC. Abbé Nicolas-Hubert de Mongault (1674–1746), member of the French Academy and of the Academy of Inscriptions.

[292]

1. Humphrey Prideaux (1648–1724); Montesquieu owned a 1718–19 English edition of his *History of the Jews* in three volumes, and a 1728 French translation in six volumes (*Catalogue,* 3189–90).

irascible faculties. Finally, not knowing where to go, he went and jumped into the mouth of the exorcist, a Jesuit who described the ravages that devil committed in his body.[1] Though the ravages were frightful, his soul was always in a state of tranquillity from which, as if from a haven, it viewed the ravages of his senses.

[**294**] It was for very good reason that the Popes made such efforts to establish priestly celibacy.[1] Without it, their power would never have reached so high and would never have lasted if every priest had been attached to a family, or if they themselves had been so attached. Then monasticism arrived, even more attached to the Popes than the earlier clergy had been. What distinguishes our priests is opposition to the lay state, in which they are entirely different from the pagan priests.

[**295**] I found this exposition in Chardin, concerning the peculiar dethronement of the last king of Persia.[1] Besieged in Ispahan by Mir-Mahmoud,[2] he left his palace and went on foot dressed in mourning on a kind of procession through the streets of Ispahan; then he went to Mahmoud's camp and placed the crown on his head, ceding him the realm, on condition that he save his life and spare his wives. It is because the Persians believe that the last imam will return, and when he does, the king will be obliged to cede him the crown and assume a private life. Apparently the Persians thought Mahmoud was the last imam. It is a fact, however, that Mahmoud was not of the same sect.

[**296**] A State dedicated only to agriculture {must be subjected to an equal distribution of land, as in the ancient republics, or else it} cannot be populated; this is because, if each family cultivates a field that yields more wheat than necessary for its subsistence, all the cultivators in general will have more wheat than they need. {This is the condition of Spain and Portugal, because of their particular situations, but not the ancient republics of Rome or Lacedemon.} Thus, to engage them to cultivate the

[293]
    1. Fr. Jean-Joseph Surin (1600–1665) had been sent as an exorcist to Loudun in 1634 (on this episode, see *pensée* 186); see the 1966 edition of his correspondence, edited by Michel de Certeau.
[294]
    1. See *Laws*, 23.21, 449, and 25.4, 483.
[295]
    1. Hussein I, shah of Persia (r. 1694–1722).
    2. Mir-Mahmoud, Afghan sovereign of Persia (r. 1722–25).

following year, they must no longer have useless wheat. The wheat would therefore have to be consumed by lazy people. Now lazy people will lack the wherewithal to pay for it; thus, it must be the artisans. {Besides, for a man to cultivate beyond the necessities, he needs to be given an incentive to possess the surplus. Now, it is only the artisans who provide it.}[1]

[297] The number of Catholic feast days causes them to work a seventh[1] less than the Protestants;[2] that is, Catholic manufacturers make a seventh less merchandise than Protestant manufacturers, and in that way, with the same number of workers, England sells a seventh more products than France.

[298] San Pietro, portitore del Paradiso. Cerbero dagli Antichi, era creduto esser alla porta del Inferno.[1]

[299] IDEAS THAT DID NOT MAKE IT INTO MY "ACADEMY DECLAMATION."

If I did not have some hope of one day resembling the great man[1] that I am succeeding, I would have to commence, in receiving the honor you have done me, by blushing; consenting in advance to such a debasement, I would have to act like those children who are overwhelmed by their father's glory. No, no! However distant he has been, it is up to me to follow him, and one must not attribute to pride what has become a necessity.

Gentlemen, I dare say nothing to you of the choice you have made. There is vanity in speaking of oneself, even when one is speaking with modesty; it is a method of attracting the attention of others. One reveals all one's self-love when one appears so ingenious in hiding it; (or else) and

[296]
1. See also *PL,* CVI, 178, on this theme.

[297]
1. First version: "sixth."
2. See *Laws,* 24.23, for an explanation of the difference in number of feast days.

[298]
1. "Saint Peter, Heaven's gatekeeper. Cerberus was believed by the Ancients to be at the gateway to Hell."

[299]
1. Louis-Silvestre de Sacy (1654–1727), translator of Pliny the Younger and Cicero, author of essays on friendship (1703) and on glory (1715), known as the "oracle" of the salon of Mme de Lambert, which Montesquieu frequented. He was replaced in the French Academy by Montesquieu; cf. *Discours prononcé le 24 janvier 1728, par M. le président de Montesquieu.* See also *pensée* 1259.

to tell you that I did not merit your endorsement would be to demand it from you again, at a time when I no longer have any reason to fear your rejection.

You have lost a fellow member: his talent, his virtues, even your regrets have made him renowned . . . [He believed that having written on morality, it would be inexcusable if he abandoned his own maxims; that he had to be more demanding than another regarding his duties; that there were no exemptions for him, because he had laid down the rules; that it would be ridiculous for him not to have the strength to do the things of which he had believed all men capable; that he was his own deserter; and that in every deed he had to blush simultaneously at what he had done and what he had said . . .

No wonder that such a man should have well fulfilled the Academy's designs, for you want Virtue always to accompany those who stride toward glory, and the finest genius would be unworthy of You, if he were merely a fine genius. Whatever talents he may have, you would have believed that nature had made of him but a poor gift, suited only to provide strength or a wider stage for his vices.

Your founders . . . , they wanted to march toward posterity, but they wanted to march there with you, all covered with your laurels and with theirs.[2]]

Since the gods do not receive incense indiscriminately from all mortals, it seems that these great men have sought only your praise and that, wearied by public acclaim, they wanted to silence the multitude, in order to hear only you . . .

Séguier[3] . . . He knew that fidelity[4] is found between liberty and servitude, and that true dominion is never exercised except on a contented people.

Louis XV . . . You depict this charming physiognomy, which strikes all who view him, and which he alone does not see. You rank secrecy among the virtues of his childhood. You follow him in that youth that is amiable, but exempt from the passion that most often blinds kings. By the just accolades that you bestow on him, do not cease to encourage him to surpass

2. Montesquieu added in the margin: "All this is put down, except this phrase: 'that he was his own deserter'"; this text, however, differs markedly from that of the *Discours.*

3. Pierre Séguier (1588–1672), chancellor of France and protector of the French Academy.

4. First version: "felicity."—HC

himself. Let whatever you say, whatever you admire, aim always at the public felicity. It would be dangerous to speak to him about the victories he might win. One ought to be fearful of exciting this young lion; he would be rendered terrible. If he heard the sound of trumpets, everything the wise man near him might do to pacify him would be useless; he would feel only his strength and would follow only his courage.

Depict the Prince's love for his people, and the People's love for such a good prince. Happy subject to treat! You will make future kings aware that between those who command and those who obey, there are stronger ties than terror and fear. You will be the benefactors of the human race. Your writings will be admired for their genius, and cherished for their utility. Those who praise a wicked prince cover themselves with all the vices of which they approve. As for you, Gentlemen, you will praise Louis, and you will find your glory therein.

Or again:[5] Begin to give them the idea of a splendid reign. Let it be sacred and venerable for them. Give the gift of a model to future kings. They will perhaps imitate it. You will be the benefactors of the human race. Your writings will be admired for their genius and cherished for their utility. That is how an illustrious Greek instructed kings, not by precepts but by the simple exposition of the life of Cyrus. The philosophers of the Orient instructed by myths and allegories. You will instruct by the truth of history. It is the mark of virtue to make itself loved as soon as it is revealed. Cicero used to say to his brother: "Can it be that you do not know how to make yourself loved in your governance after reading the *Life of Agesilaus?*"

He has all the virtues that adorn men, along with all the ones that embellish kings. Each day reveals new perfections within him, and with such an interest in resembling himself, he is always better than himself.

Richelieu: under his ministry, the great Nobles, sometimes distinguished by command, were always equal in obedience . . .

In giving me his[6] position, it seems you have compared me to him. Pardon me, Gentlemen, for this reflection. I fear there is considerable vanity in having made it . . .

M. de Sacy often abandoned the serious work in his study for *belles-lettres*. This was, so to speak, the sole debauchery he allowed himself. The

---

5. "Turn a page" (M.). The section that follows, up to "End," below, was apparently meant to be read together, in contrast to the order that appears in the Desgraves edition.—HC

6. Sacy's.

public lost nothing by it; he carried over from his study those graces that invite reading . . .

I sought out only your mind, your talents, your immortal writings, and despairing of ever being able to resemble you, I believed that it mattered little for me to be closer to you.

END

Most authors write to make themselves admired. It seems that M. de Sacy wrote only to make himself loved . . .

They have established you to be the depositories of their glory, to be jealous of it as they were themselves, to transmit to all times deeds which, during their lives, renown had transmitted to all places . . .

You have lost an illustrious fellow member, and I must not seek to console you for it. Sorrows are a species of pain that is dear to us. We love to feel it; we do not want to lose it; we are touched by everything that enhances it. It seems it must take the place within us of the very subjects that produced it.

He was far removed from those authorial jealousies that prevent so many well-adorned minds[7] from enjoying their reputation, and that one often disguises from oneself—sometimes under the name of *emulation,* sometimes under that of *equity.* He did not feel the pangs of envy, and he never placed that weight upon his heart. He would have preferred everyone to feel all that he felt and to know all that he knew.

This was a man who will always be praised, less for the interest of his glory than for the honor of virtue; a man who, to the qualities that confer a great reputation, joins also that sort of merit that does not make a fuss, and all those virtues that are so easily neglected—perhaps because they are necessary, and because they are the virtues of man, not of the illustrious man.

This was one of those accomplished men—infinitely more rare than those commonly called *extraordinary men,* than those who, with external aid and often with some vices, find the path of glory . . .

You will describe, at first, the happiness of peoples: this happiness so often promised, always hoped for; today tasted and felt.

7. *Beaux esprits;* see translator's note.—HC

You are, Gentlemen, like those children, whose illustrious fathers have left them a great name to uphold, and who, if they were to debase their inheritance, would be disgraced again by their ancestors' very splendor . . .

The illustrious Richelieu[8] was your protector only by preserving the right to be your rival. He held indiscriminately all the routes that could lead to glory. He followed avidly the careers of your poets and your orators. Superiority of mind was not enough for him; he also sought out superiority of talent. He was indignant at second place, in whatever sphere he found it. He was the first to recognize that *Le Cid* should not unsettle his disposition, and that first place in French poetry could still be disputed.

If you were to cover him with a thousand new accolades, you could not add a single day to the eternity that he will have in the memories of men . . .

An illustrious man merits all your regrets; you have sustained a loss that you have not yet repaired . . .

Everything, even my Country, seemed destined to distance me from the position you have accorded me . . .

[300] Let us not look for marvels in Antiquity.[1] Those of Babylon and those other cities that contained a world of inhabitants: that world was a single city within a State. They employed art and an immense labor to make walls that could resist scaling. That city made up the State's strength; everything else was nothing. This is why you see expeditions among the Ancients but never wars,[2] and it was impossible for a prince who had lost several battles not to see his country invaded. The marvel is France, Flanders, Holland, etc. Under Louis XIII and Louis XIV, we have seen things that are found only in our history: under Louis XIII, the Spanish, during twenty or twenty-five campaigns, almost all of them unsuccessful—without losing, however, more than a small part of a small territory under attack. Louis XIV, in the last war, overwhelmed by the cruellest scourges a prince can receive: Hochstädt, Turin, Ramillies, Barcelona, Oudenarde, Lille[3]—bearing the wrath and the constant superiority

8. Armand-Jean du Plessis, Cardinal de Richelieu (1585–1642).

[300]
1. "[I've put this in the *Romans*]" (M.).
2. See *pensée* 750.—HC
3. The battle of Hochstädt was lost August 18, 1704, by Tallart and Marsin against the Anglo-Austrian troops of Marlborough and Prince Eugene; the siege of Turin occurred in 1706; on May 23,

of the enemy, while losing practically nothing of his grandeur. This is what is not found among the Ancients, and there is nothing remotely comparable to it among them except the Peloponnesian War; and again, that war lasted as long as it did only because victory was divided for a very long time; as soon as it was determined against one side, the latter was suddenly annihilated.

The cities of Asia could be much larger, *primo,* because much less is necessary for the subsistence of the Asiatics than of the Europeans. For what may prevent the growth of cities is the necessity of provisioning the people; it is the mortalities, the plagues, etc.; it is the difficulty of communications, the nearly inevitable expense of transport from one area to another.

I find more to marvel at in the king of France having two hundred well-fortified places on the frontiers of his State, and having them in three rows, than in the king of Babylon having one place in the center, in which he employed all his power.

[301] Here is how I would pay off all the capital on the bonds the King owes and abolish the taille throughout the realm, leaving the head tax.[1]

I assume that the bonds amount to 48 million, and the tailles likewise.[2]

Of these 48 million, there are about 11 or so that are lifetime annuities only.

Useless monasteries would be abolished—that is to say, all of them—and their houses and estates would be sold off as perpetual annuities.

The King's profits from perpetual annuities would serve to increase the fund for the creation of lifetime annuities.

All duplicate entries throughout the realm, all nonmilitary pensions, not renewed[3] as they become vacant; all this to increase the fund for lifetime annuities.

In a word, the 48 million would still be paid. Everything that reduces the perpetuals would increase the lifetimes. With the perpetual annuities

---

1706, Marlborough defeated Marshal Villeroy at Ramillies; on July 11, 1708, Vendôme was defeated at Oudenarde by Prince Eugene; Bouffler surrendered at Lille, then under siege by Prince Eugene, on October 28, 1708.

[301]
1. On Montesquieu's financial ideas, cf. *Mémoire sur les dettes de l'Etat* (*OC,* 3:23ff.), and *pensée* 274.
2. First version: "at a fortieth."
3. First version: "abolished" instead of "not renewed"

coming to an end, the tailles would be reduced in proportion as the life-time annuities expired, up to their abolition.

Or again, I would make some cuts in certain areas that are not absolutely necessary, such as several Court expenses, and for nineteen years. I would abolish for nineteen years, for example, the registers of officeholders, a third of the pensions, and on this basis I would create lifetime annuities. For example, if the cut[4] were two million, I would create as many lifetime annuities as would be liquidated by a million in perpetual annuities. I would reduce by a million the excise tax and the salt tax. *Idem,* in the other areas. And since, at the end of nineteen years, there would remain some portion of the lifetime annuities, I would leave the old lifetime annuities in place, and not replace them with anything the last three years, so that those who survive the nineteen years have a certain fund.

[302] [An atheist: *Bacchatur vatis magnum si pectore possit excurisse deum.*][1]

[303] Sire,[1] the French Academy would seem obliged to speak to kings, her protectors, only with that eloquence that {is the purpose of its estab-lishment}. {Permit us, Sire, to make your Majesty a party to our fears. Everyone was afraid of losing a King . . . , or a generous friend, or a tender father.} But she will appear to your Majesty more simple and more naïve. She comes to speak to you in the language of all your subjects. She loves you. The mind has nothing to say when the heart can speak so well. She makes bold to say that she is untouched by the brilliance and the majesty that surround you. Nothing shows her her king except your very person. Glory, grandeur, majesty—she finds everything there.

{We cannot forebear making your Majesty a party to the fears that we have had. We were trembling for the days of a king, a citizen, a friend, a father. For Sire, among so many royal virtues, we were especially struck by those . . . }{Excuse us, Sire, if, among so many royal virtues, we cannot

---

4. First version: "the abolition"

[302]

1. "[See if this application isn't in Bayle]" (M.). In the *Catalogue,* Montesquieu applies this citation not to atheists but to Jews: "*Judaici, impii et antichristiani*"; the citation comes from Virgil, *Aeneid,* VI.78–79: "[The prophetess] . . . storms wildly in the cavern, if so she may shake the mighty god from off her breast."

[303]

1. This speech was doubtless addressed by Montesquieu to the king, in the aftermath of his restoration.

forebear singling out those which would have distinguished you from all Frenchmen, if you had been born to private life.}

{Each was afraid of losing the head of his family. It seemed that throughout the realm you no longer had subjects; you had only friends. Our principal desire is to live to see the great things for which heaven has preserved you.}

[304] I find that most people labor to make a great fortune only to despair, once they have made it, that they are not of illustrious birth.

[305] Never has a religious visionary had more common sense than Father Malebranche.

[306] It is dangerous to rescue from humiliation those whom unanimous consent has condemned to it.

[307] TALKERS. Certain occupations make men talkers.[1] Thus, the Persians call courtiers *dellal,* or big talkers.

People who have little to do are very big talkers. The less one thinks, the more one talks. Thus, women talk more than men, by dint of idleness. They have nothing to think about. A nation in which women set the tone is more talkative. Thus, the Greek nation, more talkative than the Turkish [the French, than the Italian].

All people whose occupation is to persuade others are big talkers, because their interest is to prevent you from thinking, and to occupy your soul with their reasonings. Another matter is those people who seek less to persuade you than to persuade themselves.

[308] FRIENDS. Your friends snipe at you {by choice} so that they will avoid being criticized for lack of subtlety in their discernment, and for not having been the first to see the faults you have.

There are also friends who, in the accidents that befall you or in the mistakes you have made, show a false pity, so that by dint of being sorry for you, they exaggerate your mistake.

Moreover, to make clear that they have more wisdom than you, they make you seem either opinionated or incorrigible by the fine things they say about their own foresight, or by the prudent things they pretend to have said to you.

If you are on the receiving end of a good joke, you can be sure that it is

[307]
1. "I've inserted in the *Différence des génies*" (M.). See *OC,* 3:426, as well as *pensées* 113, 423, 1191–92, 2035, and 2265.

one of your friends who has done it to you; someone else would not have taken the trouble or picked up on it.

Friendship is a contract by which we engage[1] to render small services to someone, so that he will render large ones to us.

[309] Praise is speech by which one seeks to display one's wit or one's good nature {or else it is an attack on someone to confound him or make him show his effrontery}.

Raillery[1] is speech in favor of one's wit against one's good nature {only pleasantry is tolerable}.[2]

[310] VOLUNTARY DEATH. Given the manner in which the English think about death, if the laws or religion came to favor it, it would wreak frightful havoc in England.[1]

[311] Nothing is extraordinary when one is prepared. We are astonished that Nero took up acting, but not that Louis XIV danced a ballet.[1] This is because dancing came from tournaments, I believe, and had a fine pedigree.

[312] The excellence of this realm of France consists especially in the great number of commodities suitable for abroad that grow here, as can be seen by the single example of the drugs appropriate for dying; France produces them in greater quantity than any country in the world; as . . .

Which is even more significant if you look at what our colonies produce or could produce;[1] they could cultivate all the drugs brought to us by most of the countries of the world. Cayenne is {roughly} at the fifth degree of northern latitude; Santo Domingo, at the fifteenth; our other islands, between the two; the island of Bourbon, at roughly the twenty-third degree of southern latitude. It cannot be doubted that in climates so similar to those of the East Indies, you could obtain most of the drugs that come here, as has already been experienced in coffee.[2] A large part of the Mississippi has the

[308]
1. First version: "by which I engage"

[309]
1. First version: "Criticism"
2. See *pensée* 510.

[310]
1. On suicide, see *pensée* 26 n. 1.

[311]
1. Lucius Domitius Claudius Nero, Roman emperor, 54–68.

[312]
1. See *Laws*, 21.21, 392.
2. Cf. *pensée* 342 for Cayenne coffee.—HC

same climate as a very large part of China. {Canada has part of the climate of Northern Europe.} Our northern and southern France produce different drugs according to their climate. In such different countries, I do not doubt that one could attempt the cultivation of most of the world's drugs and plants, and it has often happened that seeds or plants brought from elsewhere have fared better than in the countries from which they came. With a good knowledge of climate and of the nature of the territories where certain plants are cultivated, one could therefore easily multiply the commodities of our trade, and conduct trials and experiments on similar lands.

[313] [It would be very much in the Duke of Savoy's interest to exchange his Sardinia[1] for the Mediterranean Riviera of the State of Genoa; the Genoese as well. They would put the center of their power in Bonifacio, at the tip of the island of Corsica, which almost touches Sardinia, and would create a great maritime power there.

Primo, it is in the King of Sardinia's interest[2] not to divide his forces; the more he can be attacked in a large number of places, the weaker he is.

It would be exceedingly convenient for him to have the Mediterranean Riviera. By means of Savona, he could conduct the same trade as Genoa, and Genoa would fall almost to nothing. But she would be compensated by this new power. If the States of Sardinia and Corsica became powerful, this would be in the interest of the prince who possessed Savoy and Piedmont, since the least powerful princes maintain themselves best only when power in Europe is most divided.

He should not be afraid of losing the title of *King,* having already that of *King of Cyprus,*[3] which was already giving him honors within Europe; and there is no doubt that, in increasing his power, he will find his honors disputed.]

[314] Sardinia will always be a poor realm in the hands of a prince for whom she is a mere tool; in case of war, occupied or defended with a large reduction of forces.[1]

[313]

1. On Sardinia, see *Voyages* (*OC*, 2:1039).

2. Victor-Amadeus II (1665–1732), who exchanged Sicily for Sardinia in 1720.

3. Charles I, duke of Savoy, had taken the title of king of Cyprus in 1482, and transmitted it to his successors.

[314]

1. "Titus-Livy (book X, decade iv) says: 'In Sardinia, many battles were waged against the Ilienses, peoples who even today have not been either defeated or subjugated all over.' What has caused the misery of that realm is that it has virtually always depended on a foreign power" (M.). Montesquieu's translation is an approximation of Livy, *History of Rome*, XL.xxxiv.13.

On the other hand, what advantages have the Venetians derived from their Morea?

[315] Charles-Emmanuel took the Mediterranean Riviera.[1]

[316] I would like to pass this law in Spain:

Those who have been convicts are prohibited from engaging in farming or the liberal arts; but we permit them to live on alms.

Any man who calls another *lazy* or *idler* will be condemned to a fine and subjected to criminal prosecution.

[317] On commodities, customs are better than taxes.[1] A shoemaker from whom you demand two silver crowns in taxes will dispute it as much as he can; but if you make him pay twenty-five pounds in customs for a hogshead of wine, he will pay it without noticing, and gaily.

[318] A prince thinks he will be made greater by a neighboring State's ruin.[1] On the contrary! Things in Europe are such that States depend on each other. France needs the opulence of Poland and Muscovy,[2] just as Guyenne needs Brittany, and Brittany, Anjou. Europe is one State composed of many provinces.

[319] On women's birthmarks, two impossibilities: that all bodies are so formed that they will never have certain marks; the other, that these marks do not resemble something.[1]

[320] [In 1714, there appeared a book entitled *The Witnessing of the Truth*.[1] The author maintains that in the councils, bishops are merely witnesses to their church's faith.

It is like the French Academy, which does not . . .]

[321] One indication that the English nation is mad is that the English perform only great deeds but not middling ones; only those who perform the great and the lesser are prudent.

[315]
1. Charles-Emmanuel, king of Sardinia, 1730–33.

[317]
1. Cf. *Laws*, 13.14.

[318]
1. "I've put this in the *Journal*" (M.); cf. *Réflexions sur la monarchie universelle en Europe*, XVIII (*OC*, 3:378; *OC* Volt, 2:360).
2. See *Laws*, 19.14, 316.

[319]
1. *Taches des envies;* literally, "marks of desire," referring to the popular belief that a birthmark resembled something the mother had craved during pregnancy.—HC

[320]
1. By Fr. Vivien de La Borde, of the Oratory (1714).

[322] There is no pace better for health than that of a horse. Thus, whoever invented the iron coach has rendered a great disservice to the public. {A horse's every step causes a heartbeat in the diaphragm, and in one league, there are roughly four thousand heartbeats more than one would have had.}

[323] Spain is bound to perish, because she is composed of excessively honorable men. The integrity of the Spanish has transferred all trade to foreigners, who would not have taken part in it if they had not found people in whom they could invest unlimited confidence.[1]

If, on the one hand, virtue ruins the Spanish, then honor, which makes them ashamed of commerce and industry, ruins them no less.[2]

[324] We have some authors of the ancient history of France who are favorable to the Burgundians; others, to the Austrasians.[1]

Today, now that these different interests have ceased, this partiality scarcely makes itself felt.

An author ceases to be partial by virtue of being ancient, and we must well believe that past writers were like the above-mentioned ones.

[325] Roman curse: *Ultimus suorum moriatur!*[1] A terrible punishment to have no children to be your heirs; to give you the honors of the sepulcher. It was a way of thinking quite favorable to the propagation of the species!

[326] *Facienda erit extractio extractorum nominata "Ridicula."*[1]

[327] In my stay in Italy,[1] I was very much converted to Italian music.[2] It seems to me that in French music, the instruments accompany the voice,

[323]
1. See *Laws*, 19.10, and *pensée* 169.
2. See *pensée* 1979.—HC

[324]
1. "See what is said in the extract from the Academy of Belles-Lettres, on the works of Fredegarius" (M.). Fredegarius is the presumed author of a chronicle of the Merovingians.

[325]
1. "May he die the last of his own people."

[326]
1. "An extract of extracts called 'jokes' ought to be made."

[327]
1. This begins a long autobiographical sequence, starting from the conclusion of his European travels in 1731. Inspection of the secretarial hands allows the entries from *pensées* 327 to 760 to be situated in the period 1731–34.—HC
2. For his earlier, perhaps less serious appreciation of Italian music, see Montesquieu's letters to Bonneval and to Conti on September 29, 1728 (*OC*, 3:913–14).

but in the Italian, they take it and lift it up. Italian music is more supple than the French, which seems stiff. It is like a more agile wrestler. {The one enters the ear, the other moves it.}

[328] *Flavus capillus, flava coma;*[1] it is the blond, not the redhead. Red hair is hated because it is regarded as a sign of other natural defects. {David is praised, *quia erat rufus.*[2] In warm countries, there is little blond hair.}

[329] It is surprising that the Romans, who had glass, did not employ it in windows, but instead used transparent stones, which certainly do not create such a good effect.

[330–338] SOME FRAGMENTS THAT DID NOT MAKE IT INTO MY "DIALOGUES."

[330] Flora said: "My conduct has been very disorderly. Most women do not want my company. I have only one remedy: to make myself a goddess. Men bestow worship more easily than esteem."

[331] "All the other gods have temples, but I have none. —Love, I say, all hearts are your temples. Go into the temple of Cephisia. Make your presence felt there. You will be worshipped there by all mortals."

[332] The other day, Venus was getting dressed. The Graces wanted to put her sash on her. "Leave it, leave it," she told them. "Today, I am seeing only my husband. This is enough beauty for him. I reserve my charms for the god of War."

[333] "Divine Apollo, how is it that all the Nymphs flee from you? You are young, you have blond hair, and your face is very handsome. Do you want me to tell you? You are much criticized among them. They believe you don't think about a word of what you are saying. I am only a poor shepherd, but Cephisia does not flee from me. When I am around her,[1] I keep quiet, I sigh, I gaze, I wander, I burn, I embrace her. {I swoon, I expire.}"

[334] ["I cannot understand, Mercury, how you, who have given laws and mores to savage men, are such a big thief." —M[ercury]: "You think then, do you, that it is for your good that I have placed you in society, {have made you work in the mines} . . ."]

[328]
1. "Golden tresses, blonde hair."
2. "Because he was ruddy."

[333]
1. First version: "When I want to express my love"

[335] "Yes, Cloris, you can love me. —Alas! I no longer know what I'm allowed. The pleasure I feel in loving makes me suspect that I must not love. How is it that I can't tell you this without blushing?"

[336] "Ulysses, you have turned down immortality in order to see your wife again, and see whether she has been having forty good years. I would not have suspected that of you, for you have searched throughout your whole life for the very shadow of immortality, which is glory. —Eumaeus![1] Are we reasoning? All we are doing is feeling . . ."

[337] Procrustes: "I am continuing my reform. You know that all the men I catch, I place them stretched out on my bed. Those who are too short are extended, and those who are too tall have their legs trimmed. Look! I intend that all men be made like me. But they are so stubborn, they all want to keep their height . . ."

[338] "Cruel Myrrhine, because you are followed by thirty thousand women foot soldiers and ten thousand women cavalry, you want to reduce Africa to servitude."[1] Myrrhine: "I want to emancipate my sex from the tyranny it is in. You place us under honor's laws only to be able to dishonor us when you please. You're irritated if we refuse you, and you despise us if we don't. When you tell us you love us, that means that you wish to plunge us into the greatest dangers, without sharing them."

[339] I said I wanted to see Hungary, because all European States used to be the way Hungary is at present, and I wanted to see our forefathers' mores.

[340] CAUSE OF DUTCH POWER.[1] It is the lowest country on all sides, so that a very large number of rivers flow into it, such as the Scheldt, which receives the Lys and others; the Meuse, which receives the Sambre and others; the Rhine, which receives the Main, the Mosel, the Lippe, and others; and finally, the Ems {flows there}, of which Holland is mistress by way of Emden. Moreover, she is mistress of all the navigation of these rivers and streams, by means of fortresses she has possessed by treaty, and those

[336]
1. Eumaeus, Odysseus's swineherd and the first person to meet him on his return to Ithaca.—HC

[338]
1. In Aristophanes' play *Lysistrata,* Myrrhine refuses sexual satisfaction to her husband Kinesias after seducing him.

[340]
1. On Holland, see also *Voyages* (*OC,* 2:1289–1301).

she has had demolished: Dunkirk[2] is demolished; on the sea, Nieuport is worthless and obstructs Ostend's trade. She has a garrison in Meenen, on the Lys. She has the Scheldt by means of Tournai, the Barrière fortress, and Dendermonde, where she has half the garrison by treaty. She has eliminated the port of Anvers on the Scheldt and has obstructed it still more by the territories whose transfer she has arranged in the Lower Scheldt, by the treaty of Barrière.[3] She has a garrison in Namur, at the confluence of the Sambre and the Meuse. On the Meuse, she has had the fortresses of Huy and Liège razed. She has Maastricht, Steenvoort, and Venlo. The Rhine is divided in Holland, and she has the Ems by way of Emden.

[341] State debts[1] could be paid off by setting up a sinking fund, which would be: one sou per pound {held back} on all debts; 6 deniers per pound, on everything the King pays, and double that at each transfer of ownership; 3 deniers per pound on any increase in the King's levy, which would make a fund of at least 6 million. Let the King add the excess of the gold mark[2] for the upkeep of the Order,[3] and a third of all the royal favors he distributes, up to the point where the redemption fund is 8 million. Let the redemption[4] take place every year, in proportion to the fund in the Bureau: either in cash, retaining five percent, or a bond from the managers {negotiable}, payable in a year. Let shares as well as contracts be purchased, to the King's profit. Let the King resell the shares he buys; he would have the sole dividend from the trade. Let half the interest from the repurchased assets accrue to the fund, and the other half serve to reduce taxes proportionately each year; this would barely reduce {taxes} except at the end of the operation.

[342] If things continue, nations will be trading with themselves virtually alone. Each nation that has establishments in America trades there alone. Efforts are being made to attract into these establishments what is procured from foreign countries. Thus, the English want to get from their

---

2. In 1713, at the Treaty of Utrecht, England had imposed upon a reluctant France the dismantling of Dunkirk's fortifications and the filling in of its port, which was assured on site by an English representative until 1783.

3. Also known as the Treaty of Anvers (November 15, 1715).

[341]

1. See *pensées* 252, 274, and 301.

2. *Marc d'or;* officeholder's fee.—HC

3. First version: "charity"—HC

4. First version: "payment"—HC

North American[1] colonies what is useful for their navy. We want to import silks from the Mississippi, coffee from Cayenne and even from Bourbon Island. We have placed or found cassia in the Antilles islands. And in fact, having territories in practically all climes, there are few products that we could not bring here.[2]

[343] Even though nations that do not have manufactures are establishing them, it seems to me that this ought not to alarm those that have them. The former are powerless to dress themselves; they must act like the Hungarians, who wear the same outfit for fifteen years.[1] And with them, the establishment of manufactures merely puts them in a better position to buy from those nations they cannot imitate—whether because they do not have the same industry or because they lack something in the nature of their soil.

[344] People say: "A league with the Italian princes!" But how to ally yourself with nothing? This is a league on paper. Only the King of Sardinia has preserved his military power, and he will lose it again if Italy's neutrality and our distaste for conquests there last for long.

{Since this comment, our last war in Italy has put the King of Sardinia in position to maintain his military power more than ever.} {That was the war of 1733. That of 1741 has made the whole comment absurd.[1] One more try, and we will make him master of Italy, and he will be our equal.}

[345] Those Dutch, French, and English fish—what a terrible indictment they are against Italy and Spain! Those nations would find it in their interest to change their manner of abstinence. [They could engage in fishing themselves, especially in the Papal States . . .]

[346] There was no one who should not have thought that Charles V was going to dominate everyone, and the Popes were so convinced of it that out of fear of his power, they lost England. France, which had to resist him, had neither the authority at home nor the power abroad that she has

[342]
1. First version: "South American."
2. Cf. *pensée* 312.—HC

[343]
1. "Put in the first book *Sur le Commerce*" (M.), *Laws,* 20.23.

[344]
1. The references are to the campaign of Villars in Italy, and the alliance with Frederick II, respectively.

at present. She possessed less of: Calais, part of Flanders, Hainault, Artois, Cambrésis, the principality of Sedan, part of Luxembourg, Lorraine,[1] the Three Bishoprics, Alsace, Strasbourg, Franche-Comté, Bresse, Bugey, Valromey and Gex, Roussillon, Béarn and Lower Navarre, and her establishments in the Indies. She resisted him, nonetheless. This is because Charles's power was too divided.

[347] Only the conquests we have made step-by-step remain to us. But we have always been unsuccessful in the distant enterprises. It is hard to keep track of how many times we have conquered and lost the Milanese territory, the Kingdom of Naples, and other Italian States. We are difficult to defeat on our frontiers, but *cavendum a nimia ambitione.*[1] It is impossible for us to leave our Country for long. The idea of a stay in Paris immediately assaults the minds of our young people.[2] After the battle of Turin,[3] didn't the impatience to return—I don't say of our dandies but of our generals—make us retreat to France and lose Italy?[4]

[348] The manners and mental characteristics of different people, guided by the influence of the same court and the same capital, I call the *genius of a nation.*[1]

[349] No one wants to die. Every man is strictly speaking a sequence of ideas that one does not want to interrupt.

[350] If I knew something that would be useful to my nation and ruinous to another nation, I would not bring it before my prince, because I am a man before being a Frenchman; or again, because I am necessarily a man but am only a Frenchman by chance.[1]

[351] I miss that last branch of the House of Austria, which since Ferdinand[1] has produced such good princes.

[346]
1. First version: "part of Lorraine"

[347]
1. "Beware of excessive ambition."—HC
2. First version: "lords."
3. During the War of the Spanish Succession, in 1706. See also *pensée* 380.
4. See *pensée* 354.—HC

[348]
1. "Put in the *Génies*" (M.); cf. *Essai sur les causes qui peuvent affecter les esprits et les caractères* [Essay on the causes that can affect minds and characters] (*OC,* 3:397–430).

[350]
1. See *pensée* 741, where Montesquieu amplifies upon this text.

[351]
1. Ferdinand I, Emperor of Germany (1558–64), brother of Charles V.

[352] If the Low Countries are worth one in the hands of the Emperor, they would be worth a hundred in the hands of France.[1]

[353] The Emperor would be one of the world's great princes if the Low Countries were ruined by an earthquake. That is his weakness, the Low Countries.[1]

[354] French indiscretion, in the insults made to the honor of Italian husbands, has lost them the Kingdom of Naples, that of Sicily, the Milanese territory, and some of those states several times. They butchered them in Sicily; they revolted elsewhere; and at a time when those people were most tired of the French, the French were no less tired of them, owing to the mania for returning to France.[1]

[355] The true power of a prince consists solely in the difficulty of attacking him. Thus, it is far from being the case that a Duke of Savoy is as powerful with Sardinia as without Sardinia, because he can be taken from this weak side at the outset, and if he fortifies it—whether during peace or war—he weakens his states.

[356–358] THOUGHTS THAT DID NOT MAKE IT INTO MY "DIALOGUE OF XANTHIPPUS."[1]

[356] In truth, Gylippus,[1] if the gods had placed me on earth only to lead a voluptuous life, I should think they would have given me a great and immortal soul in vain. To enjoy the pleasures of the senses is something all men are capable of,[2] and if the gods have made us only for that, they have made a work more perfect than they intended; they have accomplished more than they have undertaken.[3]

---

[352]
1. The Republic of the United Provinces had been constituted at Utrecht in 1579 by the Protestant provinces that separated from the Spanish and Catholic Low Countries, under the impulse of William of Orange, stadholder of the province of Holland.

[353]
1. Cf. *Voyages* (*OC,* 2:1167) for a similar thought.

[354]
1. See *pensée* 347.

[356–358]
1. Xanthippus, Lacedemonian general who, heading the Carthaginian army during the First Punic War, in 255 B.C., defeated the Romans and took prisoner the consul Regulus.

[356]
1. Montesquieu had at first given the name of Gylippus to Xanthippus's interlocutor.
2. In *Lysimachus,* we read: "which all men are easily capable of"; see Allen, 76–77.
3. "This article is in the dialogue of Lysimachus" (M.).

[357] Sparta: a nation that not only despises but detests the soft pleasures, where people and kings alike know how to command and obey, where the least of the citizenry are what philosophers alone are elsewhere.

[358] I love only my Country; I fear only the gods; I hope only for virtue.

[359] FRAGMENTS OF A TRAGEDY[1] THAT I WROTE IN HIGH SCHOOL, AND THAT I TOSSED IN THE FIRE.

The subject was taken from *Cleopatra*,[2] {the name}, *Britomartis*

> (Pompey says to me)
> "I fly where the fate of the whole world calls me;
> But I leave you a son, the fruit of our amours,
> The image of a husband who adores you always."
> He left, and soon the civil discords
> Laid waste the fields, overturned the towns,
> And in Pharsalus, at last, Caesar, victorious,
> Saw blush the mortals—whimsies of the Gods.

> {Dream:}
> One night when I was in that tranquil state
> Where one's mind—more free, less weighted down—
> Is not to sense's empire subordinate

> {Britomartis says:}
> I've chased a thousand times my liberty;
> But failing to squelch the consuming fire
> I can't stop loving what I raptly admire.

> The blood whence you came,
> All kings, all hearts that give unto you your due,
> And Divinity, in its work's prevailing hue.

> But far from snuffing out a flame so fine,
> My efforts merely grant it endless time.

[359]
1. On this tragedy, see Jean Tarraube, *Montesquieu: auteur dramatique* (Paris: Lettres modernes, 1982).
2. Gautier de Costes, sieur de La Calprenède (1609–69), author of the swashbuckling novel *Cleopatra* (1647–58) in twelve volumes (*Catalogue*, 2234).

Alas! They had to hide from my view
The celestial attractions that belong to you.
Such is the art they have to charm us;
To commence to see you is to commence to love.
One moment saw rise an everlasting flame;
Each instant that follows shows you off again.
It brings to my eyes a thousand new allures.
In just one of your charms, I see all amours.
If a crime it be, to love you and adore,
I will each day be criminal, and every day still more.
But why in fact would my love be so at odds?
Worship does not at all insult the gods.

Ah! Don't blame me for my furious arms;
My entire crime was not knowing such charms.
Why hid you the shine of your ocular rings?
I'd have ceded, Madame, to such gods, to such kings.
I'd have borrowed from them such a thunderous crash,
I'd have borrowed from them these fate-directed shafts.
And to march o'er your steps, and to fight by your laws,
I'd have known how to live by such gods, by such kings.

Let resentment fall, along with your chains,
And in rank supreme, where the gods make your reigns,
Follow them, Madame, and pardon my pains.

   (Tigranes says:)
My tiniest passion is all violent,
It's the frightening storm of a soul turbulent:
Reason sees nothing in this foggy gloom.

A lover more gracious who lifted my chains,
In this messy mélange of pleasures and pains,
Just now underneath, just now more above,
Would then taste the pleasure of lover and loved.

   (Elise says:)
In the state I'm now in, alas! what can I say
And why should I bother, and why should I bay?

If Mars and his wrath would send terror to me
Or some stronger god who would reign over me,
I feel all moved, and maybe, Phoedimus,[3]
The emotion itself may indeed be a crime.

When a heart, to abhor, all constricts self and sinks,
It finds that amour is more near than one thinks.

Love claiming its rights over each living thing,
On both heaven and earth it alone is the king.
I have no more enemy, when I have no more equal.

  (Elise to Tigranes:)
No! You alone bring forth by big test:
My heart, full of you, is closed to the rest.
If only you knew how I do you detest.

I heeded you not when your name led the race
Do you think I'll hear better with you mired in disgrace?

I'm not at all sure, in the frenzy I feel,
If you'll see my love first or my temerity.

You knew how to win me after so much combat,
In one word, I love you, and won't blush for that.
The time to feel shame was when my insensate soul
Dared to conceive of the first idea bold.
The time to feel shame was when the cruel poison
Left in my mind a small speck of reason.
Now beaten down and now filled with glee,
I was clinging still then to my urge to be free.
But while making no unneeded efforts today
I dare say I love, send my blushes away.

  (Phraates, from Britomartis:)
Just one of his looks casts me down all nonplussed.
I just cannot bear his so arrogant line.

---

3. Phoedimus, a character in Ovid's *Metamorphoses*?—HC

The star of his birth has e'en more force than mine.
At the baleful recital of his deeds and his times,
I imagine him armed to avenge all my crimes,
And this terrible hero, all a haze in my head,
Shows virtues and enemies equally bred.

   (Tigranes says:)
      Gods! . . .
It's you who have settled the staff in my hand
Just to make of a king the entirely last man.
I accuse only you of a design so sinister,
And Britomartis, in brief, was merely the minister.
You'll have no more rights to mistreat such a wretch.
I return you now till the day you have said.

   (Britomartis says:)
      A great heart . . .
Does not want to escape fate's decree.
And always, impassive, he awaits his demise.
Upon Heaven's word, he accepts where it lies.

   (Tigranes speaks:)
What's this! Is it true? What sweetness for me!
The gods are appeased, Madame, if you'd agree.

   (Elise says:)
Death is a cruel torment
Which leaves but a single moment
To worship Britomartis.

   (Phraates says:)
When bathing myself in the blood of my kin,
The gods, the just gods, just did not rein me in.
In the deepest aplomb, they allowed me to reign,
Such a great criminal thereby saved himself pain.
Even those who had blood that was spilled by my crimes
Served as victims to me to appease Heaven's times:
This Heav'n, which now dared no more thunder below,
Seemed to fear a mere mortal who such fear did not know.

But ever since losing my first impudence,
Arbatus, I've wished to step back with some sense,
And ever since virtue appeared to my eyes,
And I gave up on crime and respected the Skies,
Then my cursed innocence, since that unlucky date,
Has done nothing but rain on me vengeance and hate.
Always unhappy, no surcease as a prey,
The deity weighs on me up to this day.

[360] It is said that in Venice, since the settlement with Paul V,[1] ecclesiastics can no longer make new acquisitions, but are obliged to take their
money to a bank, where they are paid interest, so they pay for the interest
on old capital with the aid of the new. I would like to see much the same
happen in France for new acquisitions; let the clergy be obliged to sell half
of their capital in contracts on City Hall. It is good that the clergy has its
capital in money,[2] for it is constantly increasing in Europe. It is good for
this capital to be in the Prince's hands.

[361] Cardinal Corsini[1] has said that the invention of wigs ruined
Venice because the old men, no longer having white hair, are no longer
ashamed to make love. I would add that, in the Council, there was no
longer any distinction made between the advice of the old men and that
of the young.

[362] Buying peace: what a bad business that is! You buy it because you
have already bought it. The Duke of Savoy was sought out by both parties
in the last war,[1] because he had put France to the trouble of giving him a
good thrashing in the previous one.

[363] A man wanted to write the history of bad deeds by cardinals.

[364] Maxims of State need to be changed every twenty years because
the world changes. The dukes of Tuscany had played a big role due to the
credit they had in Rome in Henry IV's time, when Rome was the center of

[360]
1. The settlement occurred in 1607; Paul V was Pope from 1605 to 1621.
2. See *Laws*, 25.5.

[361]
1. First version: "A man." Cardinal Laurent Corsini (1652–1740), elected pope in 1730 under the
name of Clement XII. Montesquieu had known him in Rome; cf. *Voyages* (*OC,* 2:1122 and 1191).

[362]
1. War of the Spanish Succession, 1701–14.

everything. (They could do this easily because they always had a cardinal from their house as protector of some great crown, and always gave out pensions to the officers of the Roman court.) They continued to play such a role under Cosimo III, at a time when the Court of Rome no longer had any power. Charles II's will and testament is the only big affair in which Rome has had a part, and in fact, I am not even sure about that.[1]

[365] The Ancients made the main attribute of the gods immortality. They did not say the good gods, or the powerful gods, but the immortal gods. This is because they regarded that quality as the distinctive quality.

[366] It is within the past fifty years that in Spain, when a man had his right arm bled, his left arm was bled as well, to keep the equilibrium. It is only within the past few years that cinchona bark has been used in Italy; at present, mercury and emetic are very frightening there. {Fashions arrive slowly in medicine.}

Our forefathers—who took daily ablutions and caustics in health; who in sickness kept their fever until it left them; who burdened themselves with as many medicinal juleps as the apothecaries gave out to them; who kept a lint bandage[1] on wounds for six months—would be quite surprised if they saw the expeditious method of our medicine and surgery.

[367] In the past, the apothecary's fees were one of the big expenses; for the family's care, you gave as much to the apothecary as you give nowadays to a purveyor.

[368] One will therefore never want to calculate, and yet I want to; I want to weigh in the balance the old medicine and the new.

I want to take the most famous princes and private individuals from the major countries, from century to century,[1] and see: with what medicine did they live the longest; what did the new discoveries, the specific new remedies, do; what effect did the old diseases have, the new diseases. It is certain that in the old days, they {almost} all died of an unknown

[364]
1. Cosimo III, duke of Tuscany (r. 1670–1723); Charles II, king of Spain (r. 1665–1700), son of Philip IV and Marie-Anne of Austria; without issue, he designated as his successor Philip of Anjou, grandson of Louis XIV, which led to the War of the Spanish Succession.

[366]
1. The lint bandage (*tente*) was a bundle of shredded linen elongated and deep-set in the wound.

[368]
1. First version: "I want to take the princes from the time of the first race, the princes from the time of the second, those from the time of the third—to take, I say, all."

disease—from a tumor, said the people, and the historians followed them; for the people always claim that princes die in some extraordinary way. And since princes love to live as much in one era as in another, we must believe that they have always defended themselves against poison with the same care.

All princes who died violently should be excluded from my calculation. They should, however, be mentioned.

This calculation should be made for every country: begin with France. And I think one should take up whole social conditions, because there, certainly, there is no choice involved. Thus, you would take all kings, all chancellors, all first presidents, all archbishops of Paris and other dioceses; all queens, who are less exposed than kings; all dukes and duchesses of Lorraine, all dukes and duchesses of Savoy; lists of other princes or lords who come after. And get the results from this.[2]

[369] There is no authority that has fewer limits than that of a prince who inherits a Republic after defeating it.[1] For he inherits a power that has no limits, namely, that of the people or the republic; for the people have not had to {nor been able to} limit its {own} power. Thus, the kings of Denmark, the dukes of Tuscany (who cannot properly be called princes) have a power that is limited by no tribunal.

[370] An aristocratic State cannot be called free.[1]

[371] When there are factions in a republic, the weakest party is no more cast down than the strongest; it is the republic that is cast down.[1]

[372] The English Republic[1] lasted for only a short interval, namely, between the defeat of the King's party and the beginning of Cromwell's military power. During Cromwell, it was tyranny. After him, up to the restoration, part tyranny, part anarchy.

2. "For this, see Moréri, Father Petau" (M.); Fr. Denis Petau, S.J. (1583–1652) is the author of, among other things, *Rationarium temporum* [An account of time] (the 1703 edition is in the *Catalogue*, 2705) and *Pierre de touche chronologique* [Chronological touchstone] (1636; *Catalogue*, 2706).

[369]
1. "I've put this in the *Roman Republic*" (M.); cf. *Considerations*, XV, 138.

[370]
1. See *Laws*, 2.3.

[371]
1. See *Laws*, 2.3, 16.

[372]
1. That is, after the execution of Charles I in 1649; see *Laws*, 3.3, 22.

[373] An Englishman {historian} has said of Henry VIII what we could well apply to Louis XI, that if the memory of the Dionysiuses, the Neros, the Caligulas were lost, this reign would bring back an idea of it.[1] Henry VIII hanged the Catholics, who did not believe him to be head of the Church; he burned the Protestants, who were far removed from the opinion of the Catholics. Under Louis XI, no lord was sure of being alive the next day.

[374] One sign that intolerance is a dogma of the Jewish religion is that in Japan, where there are, I believe, seventy sects, there is no dispute for preeminence among them, even though the Dairo is the head of a sect and is esteemed by the Emperor more than the Pope is by our kings.[1]

I am not aware that there are disputes between different sects in China. {Father Du Halde reports an erudite work against the sectarians of Buddha.}[2] There are quite a few against the Christians, because we begin by saying: "All religions are bad except ours."

[375] I said, "I do not believe, like Louis XIV, that France is Europe, but the leading power of Europe."

[376] An Englishman, a Frenchman, an Italian: three *esprits*.

[377] Somewhere I have treated the prohibition against marriage between children and parents and have derived its origin and cause from the fact that f***ing[1] is an act of intimacy.[2]

[378] I would have done well at fulfilling the pagan religion: it was just a matter of bending the knee before some statue. But with us, not f***ing[1] is a frightful matter.

[373]

1. Dionysius the Elder, tyrant of Syracuse (430–367 B.C.); Caligula, Roman emperor, r. 37–41.

[374]

1. Montesquieu drew most of his information on Japan from the 1727 English version of Engelbert Kaempfer, *History of Japan* (*Catalogue*, 3213); cf. Dodds, 99–100.

2. Fr. Jean-Baptiste du Halde, S.J. (1674–1731) had been assigned to edit the collection of *Lettres édifiantes* and had received abundant documentation, of which a part was used in his *Description géographique, historique, chronologique, politique et économique de la Chine et de la Tartarie chinoise* (1735); Montesquieu used Barbot's copy and made extracts in the *Geographica* (*OC*, 2:943–51).

[377]

1. The term (*foutre*) is abbreviated in the manuscript.—HC

2. See *pensée* 205, and *Laws*, 26.14, title and first lines.

[378]

1. Here, *foutre* is spelled out in the manuscript; the reference would seem to be to the strictures against onanism.—HC

[379] The wars of the Low Countries did not move along quickly, because they were wars involving the slowest nations in the world: the Spanish and the Dutch.[1]

[380] I want to make a list and see how many times the French have been expelled from Italy, how many times they have been expelled because of their indiscretions with women. In my Pufendorf extract,[1] I calculated that they have been expelled nine times—almost always because of their indiscretion—not to mention their retreat to France after the battle of Turin, which occurred only by their impatience.[2]

I also want to see how many times the Popes have excommunicated the Emperors, and how many times they have caused Italy and Germany to revolt.

[381] In my travels, I always found the leagues near big cities to be shorter than in the country,[1] and I would reflect that the reason for this was that leagues around the big cities are determined by people who are always bored, namely, the great lords who go to their estates or their neighbors'; whereas in the country they are determined by people who never get bored, namely, the peasantry.

[382] Villages are closer to each other near the big cities. Now, we do not like fractions. If there are three-quarters of a league, we say one league. {False}

[383] General B. was telling me[1] that there had been some thought of putting him at the service of Denmark, as commanding general. I told him: "You would have done badly. I imagine that troops who have always been defeated have an internal defect (I don't know what), which produces this effect, so that whoever commands them always loses his reputation. The Danish have some Germans, but these Germans, back home, are always defeated." "You're right," he said, "and I think this defect comes from

[379]
1. The reference is to the wars of Dutch independence, 1568–1648.—HC

[380]
1. This extract is lost.
2. See also *pensée* 347.

[381]
1. Cf. *Voyages* (*OC*, 2:1235).

[383]
1. Claude-Alexandre, Count of Bonneval (1675–1747), whom Montesquieu met in Italy; cf. *Voyages* (*OC*, 2:1016).

the fact that with the general, there is always a Court commissary who has charge of the army provisions and who has more credit than the general, so it is his ignorance and greed that guide the army."

Likewise, the Saxons have always been defeated by another internal defect: namely, that the peasants of Saxony, all rich, do not want to get themselves killed once they become soldiers.

[384] There is a certain noble pride that suits those who have great talent.[1]

[385] Magliabecchi did not like to go see the late Grand-Duke, when the latter summoned him.[1] He found his company too painful. When strangers spoke well of him to the Grand-Duke, the latter would say: "E vero; ma non lo posso praticare."[2]

[386] In Italy, there is always a certain king of France who has wanted to heap gold on one of their paintings, and a certain *signor inglese*[1] who has wanted to buy their gallery for twenty, twenty-five, fifty thousand silver crowns! After that, you cannot offer little for them, or make a low estimate. I have never been able to meet this *certo signor inglese, ch'era pieno di denaro.*[2]

[387] When I see Rome, I am always surprised that Christian priests have managed the creation of the world's most delectable city, and have done what Mohammed's religion has not been able to in Constantinople or any other city—even though the latter religion is founded on pleasure, and the former on opposition to the senses.[1]

The Roman priests have managed to make devotion itself delectable through the constant music that is found in the churches and that is excellent {all the artistic masterpieces that are in the churches}. They have established the best operas, and they profit from them. One lives there

---

[384]
1. See *pensée* 1075 and the beginning of *pensée* 1256.—HC

[385]
1. Antonio Magliabecchi (1633–1714), the duke of Tuscany's librarian.
2. "It's true, but I can't get to know him."—HC

[386]
1. "English lord."—HC
2. "Certain English lord, who will pay big money."—HC

[387]
1. Montesquieu traveled in Rome from January 19 to April 18, 1729, then from May 6 to July 4; cf. *Voyages* (*OC,* 2:1092ff.).

with a liberty in the love affairs of one or the other sex that the magistrates do not permit elsewhere.

As for the government, it is as mild as it can be.

[388] {I cannot get used to the voices of the castrati.}[1] The reason (I think) is that, if a castrato sings well, that does not surprise me, because he is made for that, independent of his talent, and I am no more surprised by it than when I see a bull that has horns or an ass with big ears. Moreover, it seems to me that all the castrati's voices are the same. These castrati, I think, first arrived in Venice through the trade that city had with Constantinople. They came from the Greek Emperors, who made much use of them in their palace service, so much so that they sometimes became army generals.

[389] In Rome, there is good reason to establish a severe inquisition against those who are so unfortunate as to speak or write against religion; for in other countries, this is impiety, but in Rome, it is impiety plus rebellion.

[390] All unhappy people have recourse to God, often from human perspectives. The man who is led to the scaffold wants there to be a God so that He will take vengeance upon his enemies. Louis XI wants God to convey to Mr. Good Fellow the power to cure him.[1] Our unhappiness makes us seek out this powerful being; happiness makes us flee him or fear him. We are curious to know his nature because we have an interest in knowing it, just as subjects seek to know what their king is like, and domestics seek to know their master.

[391] This great power that God has placed in the hands of the King, my master, does not make him more fearsome to his neighbors. It is a pledge from Heaven for the peace and liberty of Europe. And just as the weakest princes muster the courage to extend their power, the great ones do likewise to moderate their own.

[392] A libertine could say that men made a bad deal in renouncing paganism, since paganism encouraged the passions and imparted to religion a laughing countenance.[1]

[388]

1. On the castrati, see Montesquieu's comment in *Voyages* (*OC,* 2:1110).

[390]

1. The reference is to St. Francis of Paula, or Paola (1416–1507), summoned by a guilt-ridden Louis XI (1461–83) to his deathbed; called *Le Bon Homme* (good fellow) at Court.—HC

[392]

1. See *pensée* 420.—HC

[393] Maybe¹ it's that there are good French poets, but that French poetry is bad.

[394] I was very surprised in my travels to find Jesuits governing Venice¹ and entirely lacking credibility in Vienna.

[395] I fear the Jesuits. If I offend some grandee, he will forget about me, I will forget about him; I will go to another province, another realm. But if I offend Jesuits in Rome, I will find them in Paris; they will surround me everywhere. The custom they have of constantly writing each other extends their enmities. {An enemy of the Jesuits is like an enemy of the Inquisition: he finds his intimate circle everywhere.}¹

[396] Horace and Aristotle already told us about the virtues of their forefathers and the vices of their times, and authors down through the centuries have spoken in like manner. If they had told the truth, men would nowadays be bears. It seems to me that what makes all men reason this way is that we have seen our fathers and our masters correcting us, and we believe them exempt from the faults for which they were correcting us.

This is not all. Men have such a bad opinion of themselves that they have believed that not only their minds and souls have degenerated but also their bodies, and that they have become smaller; and not only themselves but the animals; the earth, less fertile; themselves, less perfect. This was the opinion of the Stoics, Egyptians. (See my extract from Coringius, *De Habitu Corporum Germanorum*.)¹ Saint Cyprian,² who reasoned very badly, instructed a heretic that there is no longer as much rain in winter, as much warmth in summer, there is less marble in the mountains, less gold and silver, less harmony in friendships, fewer farmers in the fields, and other nonsense.

[393]
1. First version: "I find"

[394]
1. See *Voyages* (*OC*, 2:993); also Paul Bastid, "Montesquieu et les Jésuites," in *Actes du Congrès Montesquieu réuni à Bordeaux du 23 au 26 mai 1955 pour commémorer le deuxième centenaire de la mort de Montesquieu* [Acts of the Montesquieu Congress convened in Bordeaux from May 23 to May 26, 1955, to commemorate the bicentennial of Montesquieu's death] (Bordeaux, 1956), 305–25.

[395]
1. See *pensée* 482.

[396]
1. *On the bodily condition of the Germans, ancient and modern* (1652). Hermann Conring (1606–81) taught physics, philosophy, medicine, and law at Hemstädt; Montesquieu made an extract of this work, now lost, and owned a copy of his 1654 *De Imperii Germanici Republica acroamata* [On the German imperial state] (*Catalogue*, 3108); cf. *pensée* 1918 and *Spicilège*, 562.
2. Saint Cyprian (early third century to 258), father of the early Latin Church.

{Moreover, men are found to be depicted in splendid colors in the histories, but the men we see are not like that; and there are certain faults that need to be seen in order to be grasped, such as the habitual ones.}

[397] I have put in my *Spicilegium*[1] some remarks on painting, sculpture, and architecture that I picked up from certain conversations with M. Jacob.[2] Here are the observations I have made since then, which did not make it into my various works.

[398] In the Florentine school of painters,[1] I found a forcefulness of design that I had not felt elsewhere. They put the body in quite unusual postures, but there is never anything awkward about it. Sometimes the shading is a bit dry, but the design is so well pronounced that it always brings you up short. The Florentines do not put the body in darkness; they do not affect false shadows; they make it appear in sunlight. Whatever their shading, you are moved by the boldness of their brush. Look at the figures from the back, from the side, in profile, head turned, lowered, the body bent. Everything you see seems to make you see everything that is hidden. The body is always in a precise equipoise, placed just as it should be.

[399] The sculptor—who has none of the expedients of the painter, is supported neither by color nor by the advantage of elaborate arrangement, nor by the sense of surprise evoked by the art of making bodies emerge and flee from a flat surface—has only the expedient of putting fire {and motion} into his works, by putting his figures in fine postures and giving their heads graceful airs. Thus, when he has put proportion into his figures, when his drapery is fine, he has done nothing if he does not put them in action, if the position is hard or stiff; for sculpture is naturally cold.[1]

Symmetry in the postures is unacceptable here (I have spoken of it in *Taste*). But overly contrasting contrasts often are as well, such as when one

[397]
1. *Spicilège*, 461.
2. Montesquieu had met the Englishman Hildebrand Jacob, who initiated him into the history of art, in Vienna; cf. *Voyages* (*OC*, 2:977).

[398]
1. Montesquieu traveled in Florence from December 1, 1728, to January 15, 1729; see *Voyages* (*OC*, 2:1077–92 and 1313–56).

[399]
1. "I've used this in my work on the Beautiful" (M.); cf. *Essai sur le goût dans les choses de la nature et de l'art* [Essay on taste], published in the *Encyclopédie*, 7:762–67.

arm is seen doing exactly what the other is doing, and when one sees that a real effort has been made to make one precisely like the other.

In a statue, the flanks must not be equally pushed in and, as the Italians say, *pari à pari;* one should be going in and the other out.

A shadow that falls on a statue{'s limb}, or some object that is applied to it, such as a shepherd's stick on a saint's arm, can reduce the appearance of these parts of the body.

The eyes in the creases must be narrower, less rounded, and more un-refined than the rest of the creases. Likewise, the crease or the part of the crease that is down below must be more unrefined and less rounded than the one above.

Bas-reliefs are a large part of the difficulty in painting: the figures have to be made to flee; the distances must be perceived; elaborate arrangements must be made.

One reason why our sculptors do not make draperies as well as the Ancients is that the Carrara marble used today is harder than that of the Ancients. It is like a flintlock. It is even harder than it was forty years ago. The quarries have crumbled; the veins have been lost. Thus, the marble resists the workers.

Our monks and saints sometimes have impossibly graceless outfits.

[**400**] Foggini was lame and deformed,[1] which accounts for his works not having all the perfection one might desire; for when making a statue, one must not always be seated in one place. It must be seen from all sides—near, far, up, down, in all directions. Paintings are seen from only one point of view, but statues are seen from many, which is what makes it difficult for sculptors.

[**401**] You cannot find a painting by Il Domenichino, Il Guido, or Car-racha that is badly designed. {They are like Rousseau, who could never versify badly.}[1] You can scarcely find a painting from the School of Venice in which there is not something to criticize from a design point of view.

[400]
   1. Giambattista Foggini (1652–1737), architect and sculptor, student of Hercules Ferrata in Rome; he was known in France in the eighteenth century, under the name of Fog, for his reproductions of ancient statues; Montesquieu mentions him several times in his *Voyages;* e.g., *OC,* 2:131.58.

[401]
   1. Domenico Zampieri, called *Il Domenichino* (1581–1641), cf. *Voyages* (*OC,* 2:1096 and 1129); René Guido, called *Le Guide* (1575–1642), cf. *Voyages* (*OC,* 2:1096 and passim); the Carrachas were a family of Italian painters; the Rousseau referred to is Jean-Baptiste, the poet.

[402] I clearly see four sorts of contour: that of women, which are plump, fleshy, and not strongly marked; that of noble men, which are similar to those of women and are like those of the *Apollo:* large, rounded, little marked; that of powerful men, like that of the *Hercules,*[1] which are marked, but fleshy, large, rounded, and dominant over lesser ones; that of old men, which are marked, dry and pointed. That of rustic men—which are fleshy but coarse, confused, uncertain, numerous, and which are all equal in having nothing—is the contour of working men. On the one hand, the gross essence of their diet makes them fat, but on the other hand, fatigue and labor make creases throughout their bodies. Thus, their hands and faces are seen to be wrinkled, marked, divided into little parts; *idem* for the rest of their bodies. *The Little Faun*[2] from the gallery of Florence gives a good idea of this latter contour.

[403] When you arrange a building in rustic[1] form, it is essential that there be a kind of deterioration about it, so that the stones at the bottom have more mass than the ones above, and the interspaces between the bosses are always less. In fact, if it is not that way, it should appear that way, because what is higher up has to be seen from a narrower angle. A fine example of this deterioration is seen in the Strozzi Palace[2] in Florence, which is rustic on all floors.

And if only the first is rustic, the second must be Doric with as few ornaments as possible, for the eye cannot pass from the grossness of rustic to the gentleness of the Ionic or the Corinthian.

[404] When a window is placed too high, the cantilever in the projecting part can be made to protrude a great deal, which will make it appear lower. When a pedestal is too low, it must be kept free of ornament and all of a piece to make it appear higher. When a street is too narrow, the projecting parts must not be large, for they could not be seen. When a church is narrow, projecting parts must not be placed on the column pedestals along the wall—like tori, reglets, and others. {Thus, when one face of a building is on a broad street and the other on a narrow street, the cornice on the narrow street must be reduced proportionally.}

---

[402]
1. On *Apollo* and *Hercules,* see *Voyages* (*OC,* 2:1325 and 1321, respectively).
2. On *The Little Faun,* see *Voyages* (*OC,* 2:1318 and 1326).

[403]
1. *Rustique,* or "Tuscan."—HC
2. See *Voyages* (*OC,* 2:1101).

[405] Look at what I have said in my work on *Taste* about chiaroscuro in painting, sculpture, architecture.

[406] What makes most Italian churches seem large is their darkness; for in the light, their borders are more visible. It is said that this makes for more meditation and respect. The painted windows also eliminate the daylight. It is not worth the trouble to stop for them, since they are poorly painted; the Italians have never succeeded in that art like the French. {That is because it is older than the renewal of painting in Italy.}

[407] Climbing up with a scale and a string with a plumb at the end of it, one makes all the measurements in architecture: not only height but protuberance, which requires close attention. For if painting, which is mere imitation, is so concerned with making bodies advance and retreat, how about architecture?

[408] Joy itself is fatiguing in the long run; it employs too much spirit. And it must not be imagined that people who are always at table and playing games are getting more pleasure than others. They are there because they cannot be elsewhere, and they become bored there in order to become less bored somewhere else.

These are people who have demanded incompatible things of their bodily machinery: constant pleasures and forceful pleasures. Viewing life as enjoyment, they have believed that each moment was irretrievable, and have wanted each instant to pay returns.

But by virtue of giving their fibers big stimuli, they have rendered them sluggish and eliminated any recourse to moderate stimuli.

[409] The true does not always have verisimilitude; here is an example. When Dionysius-the-Tyrant, Phalaris[1] [, Nero] and Caligula inflicted all their barbarisms, it was thought at first that those folks believed they were doing ill, and you would pass for crazy if you said today that they believed they were doing good. But what will be said one day about a category of men who are every day inflicting exactly the same cruelties as those folks, and who believe they are doing good? That's the Inquisitors from Spain and Portugal.

[410] The terms beautiful, good, noble, great, perfect are attributes of objects that are relative to the beings who consider them.

It is essential to put this principle in one's head: it is a sponge for handling most prejudices. It is the scourge of all ancient philosophy, Aris-

[409]
1. Phalaris, tyrant of Agrigento (ca. 570–554 B.C.).

totle's science, Plato's metaphysics. And if one reads the latter philosopher's dialogues, one finds that they are but a tissue of sophistries made out of ignorance of this principle. {Father Malebranche has fallen into countless sophistries by his ignorance of it.}

[411] In the *Regenskii Exercitationes Sex,* p. 85, a rabbi advises lunch for thirteen reasons. It is not difficult to imagine the best one.[1]

[412] Many people in France, especially M. de La Motte, maintain that there is no harmony. I prove that there is, just as Diogenes proved to Zeno that there was motion by walking around the room.[1]

[413] We always want to fix the manifestations of God's power. We fix it to a land; we fix it to a people, a city, a temple, . . . It is everywhere.

[414] Pagan temples were small. They had hardly any common worship; everyone offered his sacrifices and prayers as an individual. No sermons to listen to. Few common sacrifices.

[415] The French language consists entirely of iambs—that is, everything is separated into intervals of two syllables, in which the first is short, the second long. The Italian language, on the contrary, consists entirely of trochees, and is cut into intervals of two syllables, one long, one short. This makes for two totally different declamatory styles, which can scarcely be understood if one is ignorant of the reason for it. Since the Italian recitative is a higher declamation, we Frenchmen can no more bear it than we can the Italian declamation itself. Now, whatever produces such a different declamation must also produce very different music. Italian music emphasizes the penultimate syllable; French the last one.

The English and Germans {and Teutonic natives} form neither trochees nor iambs; they form dactyls. Lord Cārtĕrĕt; dĕr, dĕn Vătĕr; and since the dactyl is closer to the trochee than to the iamb (for the last syllable is short in each), these languages[1] are better able to bear Italian than French music.

---

[411]
  1. Perhaps the twelfth-century Regensburg Rabbi Petahya ben Yaaqov's *Peregrinatio R. Petachiae Ratisbonensis* [The journey of R[abbi] Petahya of Ratisbon (Regensburg)], included in the Hebraist J. Wagenseil's *Exercitationes sex varii argumenti* [Six exercises on various proofs] (Altdorf, 1697), which contained Hebrew text and Latin translation in parallel columns. Rabbi Petahya (or Petachia) traveled throughout Eastern Europe and the Middle East.—HC

[412]
  1. Diogenes the Cynic (ca. 412–323 B.C.) and Zeno of Citium (335–264 B.C.) were Greek philosophers.

[415]
  1. First version: "nations"

Each music is therefore excellent; that is, it is as excellent as each language can support. It just seems to me that our declamation is better, but our music less good. The difference between these two styles of music must be sought in these principles. {Examine whether this difference in declamation does not arise from the fact that one of these two languages has more vowels than the other, or from some other reason. It is an arbitrary matter that one turns on trochees, the other on iambs.}

Italian declamation is weak and cannot be good in tragedy, because it is impossible to pronounce a word with emphasis, because one always ends with a short syllable.

I do not yet know why verse {rhyme} is unbearable in an Italian comedy or tragedy, as I am told.

The advantage of our iambs over the Italian trochees is that iambs strike the organs better. The long syllable that finishes the word seems to add something to it; the short one that finishes it seems to take something away. When we want to move a body, we shake it and always reserve the big striking action for the end. It is the same with the movements of the soul. Thus, the Ancients put iambs in verses that were to be declaimed, in order to strike the ear constantly. And in examining Italian declamation, it is clear that the Italians do well to stick to the Polichinelles and the Harlequins; this is because they cannot do better. The tragic needs strength, and Italian pronunciation does not have this strength. The cadence in dance and music is to fall suddenly in order to shake the soul. All Latin verses ended their rests and the last foot with a long syllable; a short one was a license. There you have, I believe, why a French play cannot be well translated into Italian as well as an English play can. It is because English always has dactyls and ends with short syllables like the Italian. It is also true that there is another reason, which is that the French language is purer and simpler, and the Italian is loftier and more elevated. This means that what is grand for us is common for them, and what is for us common is for them insipid.

Articles, with which our language is replete, prevent our verse from being as concise as Latin verse. That elongates the words, even though the sense is the same. The Greeks also had articles, but they trimmed them when they wanted to. These articles are barren. Moreover, it is only the transpositions of the genitive and dative that are permitted in French. We always have our caesura in the same place, but the Italians put it after the first, second, or third foot; witness the first three lines of Tasso.

[416] The main difference between the pagan system and our own is that we believe that intelligent beings of an inferior order were created, and the pagans, who did not have the idea of creation, believed them to be engendered.

[417] Paganism had to be. Let us say there are some Mexicans or Peruvians[1] imbued with the Christian religion who go a hundred years without books and preachers; they would soon be idolaters. For we are inclined to fix our ideas of greatness, superiority, wonder on some particular object; besides which, obsequiousness would bring about the same result.

[418][1]

[419] Notice that all countries that have been heavily populated are very unhealthy; thus, the territory of Rome has become very unhealthy, Egypt[1] has become very unhealthy. Apparently men's great projects, the ones which penetrate the earth—canals, cellars, underground shelters—take in water which stagnates there. The country is destroyed little by little, and the destruction is increased by the negligent maintenance of the old canals. Thus, Egypt has that plague every year.

[420] M. Pascal's famous argument is very good for giving us fear, but not for giving us faith. Epicurus made gods, so as not to be treated like Socrates.[1] He wanted, he said, to deliver men from the yoke of religion, but pagan religion was not a yoke.[2]

[421] Is it not true that the author of nature views differently Dionysius-the-Tyrant, who pillaged temples, and Antoninus and Trajan,[1] those pious princes who were so zealous for paganism? Thus, if the Christian religion were false, it should still be protected, because we would please the divinity more than if we were to violate it.

[417]
1. First version: "Indians"

[418]
1. This number was omitted by Barckhausen in numbering the manuscript.

[419]
1. See *Laws*, 14.11, and *pensées* 137 and 113.

[420]
1. That is, sentenced to death for teaching impiety to the young.—HC
2. Blaise Pascal (1623–62), French mathematician and philosopher; Socrates (470–399 B.C.); see *pensée* 392.

[421]
1. Antoninus Pius (138–61) and Trajan (98–117) were Roman emperors.

[422] Those who say there are no punishments or rewards in the after-life are not saying it on behalf of the good, for they are depriving them of rewards.[1] They are thus establishing their system on behalf of the bad, whom they are relieving of punishment. This argument, which Cardinal de Polignac put in his *Lucrèce,* would be stronger in the law of nature or in a religion that only recognized equity, than in a law which, acknowledging a revelation, damns those who do not believe, and in which Hell and Heaven are distributed between believers and nonbelievers.[2]

[423] In all nations, the first authors have always been much admired, because for a while, they were superior to all who were reading them.[1]

[424] Just as Tasso imitated Virgil and Virgil Homer, Homer may have imitated someone else.[1] It is true that Antiquity is silent in this regard. Some have nonetheless said that he merely collected the myths of his time.

[425] Sheep do not cry when they are fleeced, because in their machinery, crying is not the expression of pain.

[426] Tranquil people who love peace never act in an affair—like, for example, that of the Constitution[1]—as effectively as those who love war. For they bring to it the tranquillity that has given them their character, whereas those who love war bring the vivacity that has given them that

[422]

1. See *Laws,* 25.2, 480.

2. Cardinal Melchior de Polignac (1661–1741), who received the cardinal's hat May 18, 1712, was *chargé d'affaires* for France in Rome from August 1724 to March 1732. Montesquieu was intimately connected with him in Rome (*Voyages* [*OC* passim]) and attended the reading of the first canto of the *Anti-Lucrèce* on June 4, 1728; the latter was only published in 1747.

[423]

1. "I've put this in the *Discours sur la différence des Génies*" [Discourse on the difference between Talents] (M.); cf. *OC,* 3:422.

[424]

1. Torquato Tasso (1544–95) completed the epic poem *Gerusalemme liberata* [Jerusalem delivered] in 1580.

[426]

1. By the bull *Unigenitus,* Clement IX on September 8, 1713, condemned a hundred and one propositions extracted from the *Réflexions sur le Nouveau Testament* [Reflections on the New Testament] by Fr. Quesnel. The bull was registered by the Parlement of Paris on February 15, 1714, under pressure from Louis XIV and despite the views of Chancellor d'Aguesseau and Cardinal Noailles, Archbishop of Paris. After the death of Louis XIV, the cardinal took the direction of the Council of conscience and the quarrel revived: the Sorbonne declared the bull "registered but not accepted"; four bishops asked the pope for a future council. By a declaration of October 7, 1717, the regent imposed silence and a cessation of publications on the matter. Montesquieu returns to the subject below at *pensées* 914, 1170, 1226, and 2247; cf. also *pensée* 273.

character. A man therefore who is only guided by reason is always cold compared with one who is led by zeal, and one man of faction will make more noise than a hundred prudent men. I will always remember a good one told by an Englishman {I think it was Lord Falkland},[2] during the long dispute in the English Parliament under Charles I: namely, whether bishops should be abolished or not. Those defending the Church were prudent and moderate people who left when the dinner hour arrived; the others stayed behind. One man said that those who loved the bishops loved them less than their dinner, and those who hated them hated them more than the devil.

[427] An ass, pressed to flee the enemy, said: "I know what I can carry; I'm not going to be made to carry more."

The ass, in dialogue with the horse, which wants to persuade him to come into the stable: "Does one *baudoisine*[1] there?" he says. "Shut up!" says the horse, "the stableboy would take a fork."

Those asses have often said some very good things [they're folks with good sense].

[428] Great maxim for France to compel England always to have a land army. That costs her a lot of money, ties her up because of the distrust she has toward that army, and reduces proportionally the funds available for the navy.

[429] It seems to me that the places that have been very populous in the past and that no longer are, such as the Roman Campagna {and the Kingdom of Naples}, Egypt, have become unhealthy—unstable weather in the one, plague in the other.[1]

[430] No religious figures in public affairs! If they are good churchmen, they have a poor understanding of worldly affairs. If they understand worldly affairs, they are bad churchmen.[1]

---

2. Lucius Cary, Second Viscount Falkland (1610–43), died at the battle of Newbury.

[427]

1. *Baudet*, slang for *âne*, or "ass," and connotes a stupid man; the verb *baudouiner* is what *baudets* do when they "work toward the preservation of the species" (Furetière)—that is, copulate. Montesquieu may also have La Fontaine's fable on the ass and the horse as a point of reference here.—HC

[429]

1. See *pensée* 419.

[430]

1. See *pensée* 540.

[**431**] In a letter, Saint Cyril speaks of the Ephesian people's acclaim when they learned that the council had declared the Virgin to be mother of God.[1] "All the people," he says, "were at the gates. Everyone, upon seeing us, went out in front of us, thanked us, congratulated us, blessed us, . . ." The people are always delighted to enhance the cult and are always led toward these sorts of devotion, and if left alone, they would always go further.

[**432**] Cardinal de Polignac said that the only happy people are princes who die a violent death—they follow their fantasies, think about nothing. But prudent princes, who spend their life in foresight, live a long time and unhappily.

Mme de Montespan said that the King was always talking politics with her.[1]

[**433**] It is a surprising thing how all histories of the Orient always smack of servitude. When the old emperor of China became drunk, the man he had gotten drunk with was suddenly possessed of the thought that in his drunken state, the King had condemned him to death, which made him never get drunk again.

[**434**] Admirable idea of the Chinese, who compare God's justice to a net so big that the fish that wander into it think they are free, but actually they are caught.[1] Sinners, likewise, think they will not be punished by God; but they are in the net.

[**435**] When I act {in the ordinary actions of my life}, I always act from a motive that is efficacious, because I act; this does not eliminate my freedom, because I was able to not act. It is the same with works that need grace. I act in the same manner, I act freely, I act efficaciously, but with a grace—that is, by a motive that comes to me from the other world. For if I had had no knowledge of revealed truths, I would not have resolved to do good. {This is from Cardinal Polignac.}

[431]
1. Saint Cyril (ca. 376–444), patriarch of Alexandria, *Epistles*, 24ff.; the Council of Ephesus called by Theodosius II in 431 backed Cyril against Nestorius in a doctrinal dispute. See *pensée* 443, and *Laws*, 25.2, 480.

[432]
1. Françoise Athénaïs de Rochechouart de Mortemart, marquise de Montespan (1640–1707), mistress of Louis XIV. The verb Montesquieu uses is *politiquer;* on which, see *pensée* 8.—HC

[434]
1. For this image, see *pensées* 597, 828, 874, and 943.

[436] Fr. Malebranche compares the God and man of the Thomists to a sculptor who has made statues that lower their heads when he pulls a little brass wire and commands them to lower their heads when he pulls the wire. When he has not pulled the wire, since they do not lower their heads, he whacks them with a sword—except for one, to display his goodness, which salutes him because he pulls the wire . . .

[437] It was enough to condemn Calvin because his principles destroy freedom, and Pelagius because his destroy grace, without going off to look for sufficient grace or congruent grace to explain why.[1] It is enough to say: "It is certain from Scripture that God issues me some commandments. I am therefore free: for it would be ridiculous for him to issue me commandments if I were not free." {Polignac}

[438] The Romans who built temples to patrician Modesty and plebeian Modesty could not imagine their wives' modesty as a Goddess. They therefore were only honoring Providence insofar as it gives women the virtue of modesty.[1] {Polignac}

[439] There are orders {of religious} that do penance; others that practice a trade.

[440] Happiness of the Romans, who never had but a single war, and whose enemies never formed a league, so they oppressed them one after the other. They became more proud as they became less successful. Thus, Tacitus says it was possible to prevail over them in a battle, but never in a war: "*Facile superari posse praelio, bello numquam.*"[1]

[441] It seems to me that what made Rome populous in a neighborhood that had not been beforehand is that, upon the return of the Avignon Popes,[1] they went and lodged at the Vatican, and not at the Lateran Palace.

[442] There is no profession that custom cannot bring into credit and encourage all manner of people to embrace. Witness that of the gladiators,

[437]
  1. Pelagius (360–ca. 422), whose doctrine on grace was condemned by Saint Augustine, did not agree that Adam's disobedience had baleful consequences for posterity.

[438]
  1. First version: "chastity."—HC

[440]
  1. Montesquieu himself translates this passage in the text; see also *Considerations,* VI.

[441]
  1. The reference is to the period after 1305–78, during which the papacy had been lodged in Avignon in southern France.—HC

who brought people down into the arena by the thousands, even senators, even emperors; witness Commodus, who called himself in an inscription *Sovereign Prince of Gladiators,* and who, say the authors, had killed ten thousand with his left hand. An infamous profession, set aside at first for criminals or slaves, then debtors, then citizens, then senators, emperors.[1]

[**443**] Constantine spoke at the Council of Nicaea for Jesus Christ's divinity.[1] That emperor was like the Jews, who wanted to have a king, as the Nations did;[2] as for himself, he wanted to have a God, like the Nations. When it was a question of declaring whether the Virgin was mother of God, the people of Ephesus hastened to support this declaration; this brought him more pleasure. Divine truths have always encountered something like seeds in people's minds that have made them germinate and led them to believe them.

[**444**] I wrote to a young man: "You are entering the world and I am leaving it. Everything gives you hope and me regret."

[**445**] Why is it that most kings are devout?[1] It is usually from a misunderstanding. Devotion allows them politics, and politics allows them all the vices: avarice, pride, thirst for others' goods, ambition, vengeance. What does it cost them to be devout? They would be bloody fools to mess with Heaven over nothing, to vainly renounce the pleasure of hoping. Besides, they bring gravity to most of their actions. Now, to conduct oneself in a church with gravity, that is being devout. (Write a treatise on the vices of princes.)

[**446**] A civil history of the kingdom of France, as Giannone has written the *Civil History of the Kingdom of Naples.*[1]

[**447**] The Papal States would perish if they were not attached to an eternal asset, which cannot be used up, for whoever is sovereign pope is so only on borrowed authority, and those who have the properties will again only enjoy them on borrowed authority.

[442]
1. See *pensée* 566.—HC

[443]
1. See *pensée* 431.
2. The reference is to 1 Samuel 8; see also the story of the Troglodytes in *PL,* XI–XIV.—HC

[445]
1. "I've put this in the *Journal*" (M.); cf. *pensée* 1007.

[446]
1. Pietro Giannone (1676–1748), *Storia civile del regno di Napoli* (1723); see also *pensée* 1690 on him.

[448] To respond to libertines who doubt the Gospels' authenticity, I say: Origen must indeed have believed them true, since he castrated himself over a passage he read.¹

[449] There are no people who are better orators for persuading us than those we esteem.

[450] [There are two or three arguments that corner atheists, to which it is impossible to respond well; but they make their best effort to elude them: (1) that of the pers . . .]

[451] I am not surprised to see the ambitious give themselves an air of modesty and renounce ambition as one would a shameful vice. Whoever revealed all his ambition would amaze all who would like to serve him. Besides, since no one is assured of success on the path of fortune, one prepares the expedient of making others believe one has disdained it.

[452] A young man¹ who is incapable of either proving or destroying his religion by his reasoning takes on the air of ridiculing it. I say he takes on an air, because the ridicule seems to presuppose that he has reasoned, examined, judged; in a word, that he is sure of his success.

[453] Send a Jesuit and a Jacobin¹ into a newly discovered realm: in a year, you will learn that the Jesuit is at Court, and the Jacobin with the rabble.

[454] All men are beasts; princes are unattached beasts. {Cher.}

[455] We private men are surprised at the ardor with which ministers seek out affairs, and the grandees the Court. We do not know the gratifications they taste. {Cher.}

[456] Women are often¹ avaricious out of vanity, and to make others see that someone is spending money on them.

[457] Unfortunate people should be pitied, even those who have deserved it, even if only because they have deserved it.

---

[448]
1. Origen (ca. 184–ca. 255), master of the catechetical school of Alexandria; excommunicated in 230, he retired to Caesarea. The reference is to Matthew 19:12.

[452]
1. First version: "An atheist"

[453]
1. "Jacobin" means Dominican here.

[456]
1. First version: "sometimes"

Misfortunes are new chains for well-made hearts.

[458] The heroism professed by Morality touches but few people. It is the heroism that destroys Morality that impresses us and makes us marvel.

[459] I knew an ecclesiastic who made himself esteemed because he was fat. He projected a serious air that was spread throughout all the dimensions of his body, and he spoke so little that it took him practically all day to utter three silly remarks.

[460] A thing is not just because it is the law, but it should be the law because it is just.[1]

[461] The most that can be said about an individual who does something impolite is that he does not know how to live, but a judge who lacks consideration can make himself fearsome, can raise doubts about his integrity and impartiality.

[462] I think we need to be zealous for others' salvation, but this should not make us any less zealous for our own. Now, it is truer that murder, assassination, torture, and persecution are prohibited than that they are allowed for the conversion of others and the glory of Religion (which does not need glory).

[463] There is no State that is so dangerous, and that so threatens other States with conquest, as a State that is in civil war.[1] This is because all the people—nobles, bourgeois, yeomen—become soldiers. Moreover, great men are made then because in the confusion, those who have merit come to the fore; whereas when the State is at peace, men are chosen, and chosen badly.

The Romans after the civil wars of Marius and Sulla, of Caesar and Pompey; the English after the civil wars under Cromwell; the French after the civil wars under Henry IV, after the civil wars under Louis XIII, after the civil wars under Louis XIV; the Germans against the Turks, after the civil wars in Germany; the Spanish under Philip V[2] in Sicily, after the civil

[460]
1. See *Laws,* 1.1, 4, for this text.

[463]
1. "I've put this in the *Considerations on the Roman Republic*" (M.), XI, 107; see *pensée* 187.
2. Philip V (1683–1746), son of Louis, dauphin of France, and of Marie-Anne of Bavaria, recognized king of Spain, November 16, 1701; married to Marie-Louise-Gabrielle of Savoy on September 11, 1701, later to Elizabeth Farnese.

wars for the succession. {If, therefore, the State is not destroyed, which easily happens, it becomes stronger. It is destroyed by partition or by a neighbor's usurpation.}

[464] It is the desire to please that gives cohesion to society, and such has been the good fortune of the human species that this self-love, which should have dissolved society, instead fortifies it and renders it unshakeable.

[465] With regard to fashions, reasonable people should be the last to change, but they should not keep others waiting.

[466] Nations that live in slavery, where men are like beasts, whose lot is only obedience and instinct.

[467] ENVY. Wherever I find it, I take pleasure in driving it to despair. In the presence of an envious man, I always praise those who make him turn green . . . What baseness to feel deflated by the happiness of others and to be burdened by their good fortune!

[468] Fear of the punishments of the afterlife is not as constraining a motive as fear of the punishments of this life, because men are impressed by evils not in proportion to their size, but in proportion to how far removed they are in time, so that a small present pleasure affects us more than a large distant pain. Witness women, who do not make a big deal of the pains of childbirth at the moment they are going about causing them, because childbirth is a distant thing, {Pleasure acts nearby; pain affects at a distance.} so it is a very fortuitous part of nature that so much time is needed from conception to childbirth. Now those who see the evils as closely as the pleasure, such as those who are afraid of venereal diseases, usually abstain from the pleasure.

Mohammed offers two motives for observing the Law: fear of the pains of this life, and of the other.

[469] Aristotle says that vengeance is a just thing, founded on this principle: that it is necessary to render each his due.[1]

And this is the only means nature has given us of arresting the evil inclinations of others; it is the sole coercive power that we had in that state of nature. {Each person had a magistracy that he exercised out of vengeance.}

[469]
1. See *pensées* 27 and 29; perhaps the reference is to Aristotle, *Rhetoric*, 2.2.1 (1378a).—HC

Thus, Aristotle would have reasoned well if he had not spoken of the civil state. Since vengeance needs measures, and since an offended heart or a man in a state of passion is scarcely in a position to see justly the punishment that the offender merits, the civil state has seen the establishment of men who have taken on themselves all the passions of others, and have exercised their rights in cold blood.

If the magistrates do not avenge you, you must not on that account take revenge yourself, because it is assumed they think you ought not to take revenge.

Thus, when the Christian religion prohibited vengeance, it did nothing more than maintain the tribunals' power. But if there were no laws, vengeance would be permitted—not the feeling that makes taking an eye for an eye enjoyable, but an exercise of justice and punishment.

Thus, in countries where there are no tribunals for women, children, slaves, or subjects, private individuals exercise their vengeance like magistrates.

And there are even occasions when pardoning is contrary to duty. Thus, the law says to prosecute the father's assassin. It even obliges disinherited children and {encourages} slaves to do this.

It is the same for the father who does not pardon a son who has merited disinheritance. The father is acting like a judge.

[470] ECCLESIASTICAL JURISDICTION. I am not obsessed about the privileges of the ecclesiastics,[1] but I would like injustices against them to be avoided. I would prefer that the boundaries of their jurisdiction be marked out once and for all, but that they be reciprocal, and that Févret's hypotheses[2] and the private decrees not have legal force against them. Otherwise, this jurisdiction is sure to be wiped out, since new decrees are constantly chipping away at it. And it is certain that, if discernment is not lacking in the judges, it will at least be lacking in the compilers. The poor Church-court judge[3] almost never knows where to turn; whatever side he pronounces on, there is an abuse.

The Courts,[4] which are also absorbing seigneurial justice, have not

[470]

1. See *Laws,* 2.4, 18.

2. Charles Févret (1589–1661), author of the Gallican work *Traité de l'abus* [Treatise on abuses] (1653), often reedited.

3. *Official,* a judge delegated by an ecclesiastical authority to exercise jurisdiction in his or its name.

4. "Put this item in the treatise on the *Laws*" (M.); cf. *Laws,* 2.4, 18.

wanted an exact definition of royal cases. And at the time of the new ordinance,[5] the functionaries had this tag line added to the enumeration of royal cases: "those which royal judges have, from all time, judged," and were not ashamed {virtually} to acknowledge that this was in order to plunder the other judges more easily.

[471] By the fanciful distinction between the tithe's *pétitoire* and its *possessoire,* ecclesiastics have entirely lost the understanding of this matter.[1]

[472] Against the writers of anonymous letters[1] (such as Father Tournemine, who wrote to Cardinal Fleury against me when I was nominated to the French Academy),[2] I say, "The Tartars are obliged to put their names on their arrows, so it is known whom the shot is coming from."

In the siege of a city, Philip of Macedon was hit by an arrow. On the arrow, it read: "Aster sends this mortal shaft to Philip."[3]

[473] I said: "It is good fortune to be of great birth; it is not ill fortune to be of mediocre birth; merit is consolation for everything."

[474] The French labor to amass and spend suddenly. "It seems," I said, "that they have one greedy hand and the other prodigal." {They are at the same time Milanese and Florentines.}[1]

[475] I do not espouse opinions, except those in Euclid's books.[1]

[476] DETHRONEMENT. A sin which, as soon as it is committed, becomes a just matter.

---

5. The ordinance of 1667 on civil procedure. The manuscript of *Laws* clarifies (fol. 38): "In France, during the time of the ordinance of 1667, no one wanted to define royal cases with precision. The motives behind this are found in the official legislative history of this ordinance." See Brèthe, 1:247 n. 35, for the citation that follows.

[471]
1. *Petitoire,* a legal demand to have a real right over immobile property recognized in its proper extent; *possessoires* concern actual possession. On the tithe, see *Laws,* 31.12.

[472]
1. "Put this in my *Spanish Journal*" (M.).
2. Fr. René-Joseph de Tournemine, S.J. (1661–1739), director of the *Journal de Trévoux,* had approached Cardinal Fleury with a cabal to prevent the election of Montesquieu to the French Academy; André-Hercule, Cardinal Fleury (1654–1743), ex-tutor of Louis XV, minister of State, raised to the Cardinalate, August 15, 1726.
3. See *Laws,* 12.24.

[474]
1. See *pensée* 1164.—HC

[475]
1. See *pensée* 820.

[477] I heard someone say to Cardinal Imperiali:[1] "There is no man that Fortune does not come to visit once in his life. But when she finds that he is not ready to receive her, she enters by the door and goes out the window."

[478] Regarding the horrors and tyrannies of the Turks, the Persians, and the Roman Emperors,[1] I said it is remarkable that the Christian religion, which was created only to make us happy in the next life, also makes us happy in this one. A king is no longer afraid that his brother will steal his crown; the brother does not even think about it. This arises from the fact that subjects in general have become more obedient and princes less cruel.

[479] We trust in an honorable man as we trust in a rich banker.

[480] "There is in Europe," I said, "too much intolerance and too much tolerance: Spain, England."

[481] We argue about dogma but do not practice morality. That is because it is difficult to practice morality, but very easy to argue about dogma.

[482] The Jesuits, I am afraid of them. It is a corps that envelops me and finds me everywhere. If I offend a great lord, I leave and do not encounter him anymore. But the Jesuits are like the intimate circle of the Inquisition.[1]

The princes who make them their confessors do very badly. For this spreads a spirit of servitude throughout the nation and makes me honor a Jesuit priest in the provinces as a courtier honors the confessor.

Moreover, since corps have particular interests, confession—where they always treat matters between the Prince and themselves—provides them the expedient of being secret informers and ruining whomever they want, without his being able to defend himself.

[483] I had written a work entitled *History of Jealousy;* I have changed it into another: *Reflections on Jealousy.*[1]

[477]
1. Giuseppe Renato Imperiali (1651–1737), cardinal in 1690. Montesquieu met him in Italy; cf. *Voyages* (*OC,* 2:1183–84).

[478]
1. "I've put this in the *Journal*" (M.); cf. *Laws,* 24.3, 461.

[482]
1. "Put above" (M.); cf. *pensée* 395.

[483]
1. The fragments extend from 484 to 509; other fragments of *L'Histoire de la jalousie* are preserved at *pensées* 719, 1622, and 1726.

Here are the fragments that did not make it into the new project:

[484] I am very pleased, my dear ***, to dedicate this little work to you, so that if chance should make it pass into posterity, it will be the eternal monument of a friendship that is no less precious to me than glory.[1]

[485] In honor of Isis, Egyptian wives had all the authority in the family,[1] the public positions, the external affairs; the husband had the domestic details.[2]

In the marriage agreement, the husband promised to be submissive to his wife.

In the fragments of Nymphodorus[3] (*Rerum Barbar.*, book XIII), we find that Sesostris introduced this custom to demoralize the Egyptians. But those are not the real characteristics of that prince, who exuded only war and granted the soldiers so many privileges.

[486] The Scythians[1] were a people composed of many others; they were rather a name for barbarism than for a nation.

[487] It could well be that the cult of Semiramis was the reason for the obscurity of the effeminate reigns that followed.[1] History has had nothing to say about them. Sardanapalus's end made people speak of his life.[2] That life seems to have been entirely dedicated to the goddess. Arbaces the Mede,[3] the only one who saw him, found him amidst his wives, dressed like them (a religious act),[4] distributing wool to them, and performing his task as they were.

[488] History makes mention of four colonies that came from Egypt

[484]
1. See *pensées* 770, 1655, and 1820 for similar language.—HC

[485]
1. First version: "in the house."
2. "Pomponius Mela, Herodotus" (M.); cf. Pomponius Mela, *De Orbis situ,* I.9. (*Catalogue,* 2629–30), and Herodotus's *Histories* II.35, which Montesquieu owned in several Latin and French editions (*Catalogue,* 2781–84); see *Laws,* 26.14, 508. Isis was an Egyptian divinity.
3. Nymphodorus of Syracuse, third-century Greek chronicler.

[486]
1. Inhabitants of Scythia, ancient country of northeastern Europe, between the Danube and the Don.

[487]
1. Semiramis, legendary queen of Assyria and Babylonia, to whom the foundation of Babylon and the suspended gardens are attributed.
2. Sardanapalus, legendary king of Nineveh (ninth century B.C.).
3. Arbaces, legendary prince of Media, said to have revolted against Sardanapalus.
4. "Note that the men dressed up as women in honor of the Syrian Goddess" (M.).

to set up in Greece. One, led by Danaüs, founded the kingdom of Argos. Another, mingling Egyptian and Phoenician peoples, had Cadmus as its head, who, originally from Egyptian Thebes, founded Boeotian Thebes. Cecrops and Erechtheus, who were both kings of Athens, were the leaders of two others.[1] Thus, the Egyptians said that the political governance of Athens was similar to theirs.

[489] Before Cecrops, marriages were unknown among the Athenians. That prince, who reduced to formalities what nature alone had regulated before him, wanted men to marry only one woman. Those who have said that Socrates had two have been criticized by sensible authors.

[490] The Greek people were a composite of Egyptians, Phoenicians, and earth children, that is, of men who had escaped the great catastrophe that afflicted Greece—whether they had been born there, or came from the North.

[491] Solon raised a temple to a common Venus, which he did not allow to run short of priestesses.[1] When the Greeks wanted to implore Venus for protection, they did so through the agency of the courtesans. During the Persian war, the Corinthian courtesans assembled and prayed for the salvation of Greece. When the People asked her for some indulgence, they immediately promised to bring some new courtesans into her temple.

Thus, it should not be surprising that those sorts of women were so highly honored among the Greeks. They played a role in the world; they had gods and altars.

It could be said of them what a Roman orator said about a Vestal: "You should not disdain the one who sways the gods for you, who preserves the eternal flame and applies herself night and day for the Empire's salvation."

[488]
1. The references here are to Danaüs, king of Egypt and then of Argos (a Greek city in the northeast of the Peloponnese), father of the Danaids; Cecrops, pelagic hero, said to be the first African king; and Erechtheus, Athenian hero whose myth is linked to the city's origins. Cadmos was the Phoenician founder of Thebes in Boeotia, who, conforming to the Delphic oracle, followed a wandering cow which stopped, exhausted, on the site of the future Thebes. There he killed a dragon, whose teeth he sowed, on Athena's orders. Some armed men were born, who all killed themselves except five; the latter helped him build Thebes.

[491]
1. Solon, Athenian statesman, considered among the Seven Sages of Greece (ca. 640–558 B.C.); cf. *Laws*, 21.7, 363.

Thus, some great figures[2] have employed their pen in writing about the lives of Athenian courtesans—their character, that of their lovers, their repartee, the features of their minds and their faces, the luster and decline of a profession that is never the last to be embraced.

[492] The Lydians introduced the practice of women's eunuchism.[1] History notes that this was not out of jealousy, but so that the serving women might be fresher and keep their youth longer.

It is not well known whether the operation was the same as is still done in some countries, or whether it was a veritable extirpation. What argues for the latter opinion is the motive for this practice. There are two opposite causes that spoil women's beauty: pregnancies and weary virginity. Now it is only a complete extirpation that can simultaneously remedy both of these disadvantages.

[493] Candaulus was not subject to that jealousy that makes one fear all the witnesses to one's happiness.[1] Intoxicated by the Queen's charms, he thought he would enjoy them less if someone else did not envy them.

[494] The Lydian kings down to Gyges were of the Heraclid race.[1]

[495] The Greek colonies submitted to Croesus, and contested their liberty only when the Persians, a barbarous people, wanted to become their masters.[1]

History says there was no difference between Lydian and Greek customs, except that {all} the Lydian girls prostituted themselves, a thing the Greek girls did not do.

2. "Antiphanes, Apollodorus, Aristophanes, Ammonius, Gorgias" (M.). Apollodorus of Athens, scholar of the second century B.C. and author of a *Bibliotheces* (*Catalogue*, 2225, for the 1661 edition); Ammonius, a Greek philosopher of the late second and early third century A.D. and founder of the Neoplatonic school; Gorgias, Greek philosopher and orator (ca. 487–ca. 380 B.C.).

[492]
1. Lydia in Asia Minor, bounded by the Aegean Sea on the west and situated between Mysia and Caria, with the Maeander River as the southern frontier.

[493]
1. Candaulus, legendary king of Lydia (r. 731–713 B.C.), victim of his favorite, Gyges.

[494]
1. "See Herodotus, book I, 7" (M.). Gyges, king of Lydia (687–652 B.C.). According to legend, he possessed a ring that could make him invisible. He deposed Candaulus and perished defending his realm against the Cimmerii and the Lydians.

[495]
1. Croesus, last king of Lydia (ca. 560–546 B.C.), Alyattes's son and successor; he owed his riches, it was said, to the exploitation of the golden sands of the Pactolus. After subduing Asia Minor, he was defeated by Cyrus at Thymbrus and imprisoned in Sardis, his capital.

In Lydia, there was an immense work made almost wholly by the hands and the money of these girls.

[496] The peoples of Africa bordering upon Egypt had the same customs as the Egyptians.[1]

The Greeks built Cyrene[2] in Libya.

[497] When Dido[1] had arrived in Cyprus, the grand-priest of the island joined her, on condition that he have the same dignity. Since they lacked women, they took some of those girls who were prostituting themselves on the beach in honor of Venus. This should not have shocked them, since the women of their country prostituted themselves in honor of the Syrian goddess. {This clearly proves that syphilis was unknown.}

[498] As for the other coastal peoples, the authors spoke of the Nazamons, among whom the husband carried home on his wedding day all the gifts that his wife had received from her lovers, and the Gyndames, whose women wore fringes around themselves where they made knots to indicate their love affairs; those most heavily loaded with these knots boasted of having a greater share of public esteem.

As for the peoples of the interior, they were so barbarous that they had no laws. Men but not citizens, they breathed the air but were not alive.[1] Most of them did not know marriage, and found children only by resemblance.

[499] Besides the good treatment that the Romans were obliged to accord the Sabine women[1] whom they had abducted, the Roman women, who had manifested zeal for the public good in difficult times, received new marks of esteem.

Such an engaging sex is always picking up new advantages. They rendered their husbands less hard to please every day and made them agree to

[496]
1. "See Herodotus, book IV, 168" (M.).
2. Cyrene was founded in 631 B.C. by Dorian colonists from Thera, modern Santorini.

[497]
1. Dido, daughter of Mutto, king of Tyre, and sister of Pygmalion. When her husband, Sychaeus, had been killed by Pygmalion, she fled and went off to found Carthage.

[498]
1. See *pensée* 1555 for this remark.—HC

[499]
1. After the foundation of Rome, Romulus organized games to attract women from neighboring cities; during the festival, the Romans abducted women of Sabine origin.

things to which other peoples were not accustomed. An old censor waxed indignant at seeing a people who commanded all men being entirely dominated by women.

Jealousy was so little known among the Romans that the surviving authors hardly ever speak of this passion. And the abuse went so far that the public authority was obliged to punish husbands for their excessive indulgence toward their wives. And the Roman Emperors, in their continual abuse of power, disdained to make use of it to keep their own wives within the bounds of fidelity. They were almost always content to repudiate them, and often they pushed patience further. We see a long train of empresses who dishonor the imperial bed in a reprehensible manner; several were even public courtesans such as Messalina, Claudius's wife, and Julia, Severus's wife.[2] The name of Julia became proverbial as a name for debauchery and prostitution.

It is not that attempts were not frequently made to correct the dissipation, especially when the Republic was governed by prudent people. Under Caesar, Augustus, Tiberius, laws were made which, on the pretext of maintaining the Roman matron's dignity, were a bit inhibiting.[3] But when the mores and character of a nation are fixed at a certain point, what is necessary to change them is not laws but a revolution.[4]

It is in vain that Livia seeks to correct the mores of her age by means of her own;[5] Rome sees only Julia's debaucheries, and that is the sole example she follows.

When Caesar's law punished matrons' adultery, they eluded the punishment by making themselves public courtesans. But Tiberius's law chased them from this shameful shelter.

But to what lengths would they not carry their impudence? Not only did they attend public spectacles,[6] even those where naked men were seen in combat;[7] they dared to engage in combat themselves, and go into the arena with the athletes and gladiators. They even appeared all naked in

2. Messalina (d. 48), celebrated for her debaucheries; Emperor Claudius (r. 41–54); Julia (ca. 158–217), second wife of Septimus Severus, emperor (r. 193–211).

3. Augustus, emperor (r. 27 B.C.–A.D. 14); Tiberius, emperor (r. 14–37).

4. See *PL,* CXXIX, 217.

5. Livia (ca. 55 B.C.–A.D. 29), wife of Augustus, mother of Tiberius and Drusus.

6. "Suetonius, *In Augusto*" (M.), XLIV.

7. "Suetonius, *In Domitiano*" (M.), IV.

the public baths, and soon were reduced to being ashamed of covering themselves up. When some of them did so, you can see in the poets what humiliating conclusions were drawn from that modesty.

Trajan was obliged to pass a law prohibiting them from bathing with men. He obliged them in spite of themselves to hide those charms which, if modesty would not keep them secret, prudence alone would conceal from the eyes, the better to reveal them to the imagination.

[500] At the time when the Roman Empire was in its grandeur, there emerged another destined to mortify it: the Parthians. {They made Crassus perish and covered Marc Antony with shame; they insulted Tiberius.[1] In short, the Carthaginians, Mithridates, and they themselves were the Romans' only real enemies.}[2]

[501] If someone wanted to marry a Sace girl, he was obliged to engage her in combat, and if he was defeated, she carried him off as a prisoner.

[502] CHRISTIAN RELIGION. Paganism exhausted itself in vain trying to destroy it. Superior to princely talent, to magistrates' severity, to priestly jealousy, to popular superstition, it made itself dominant.

[503] The Christian prophets, who were put on display in humiliation, established equality everywhere. Mohammed, who lived in glory, established subordination everywhere.

Once Mohammed's religion was carried to Asia, Africa, and Europe, the prisons were created. Half the world disappeared; all you saw anymore was iron bars and bolts. Everything in the world was covered in black, and the fair sex, buried along with its charms, everywhere wept for its liberty.

[504] To assure themselves of their wives, the Italians in the past found means that had eluded the Asiatic imagination: they armed them with spikes and grates and did with them what those ancient poets used to do who, to make their heroes more courageous, made them invulnerable.

[505] Eunuchs are not permitted to approach women—unless, in addition to the capacity to procreate, they have also been denied even its appearance. No foothold is afforded to an imagination that is always straining. There are even countries where the wretches fabricated in this way still cause anxiety. No scalpel can bring reassurance. Four eunuchs carry in a

[500]

1. Marcus Licinius Crassus (114–53 B.C.); Antony (83–30 B.C.).

2. "I've put this in the *Treatise on the Romans*" (M.), *Considerations*, VII; Mithridates VI Eupator, the Great, king of Pontus (r. ca. 120–63 B.C.).

well-closed sedan the queen of Tonkin, and she is seen only by her ladies-in-waiting and her king.

[506] We have a certain fear of ridicule which the jokers of all nations have heaped onto the accidents of marriage. Everyone is always happy to bring up a passion which, when evoked in one man, has its effect on all others.[1]

[507] Speak about vengeance, and you will touch only the one who is steeped in an affront he has received. Everyone else will be like ice. But speak about love, and you will find all hearts open and all ears attentive.

[508] Religion has almost always decided the rights of the two sexes and the fate of marriages, and modesty has quite naturally made religion get involved in these things.[1] Since certain causes and certain acts have been hidden, people have been inclined to regard them as impure and illicit; since they were necessary, however, religion had to be called in to legitimize them in one case and reprove of them in another.

[509] Love wants to receive as much as it gives; it is the most personal of all interests. It is there that one compares, that one counts, that vanity mistrusts and is never adequately reassured.

For being loved, love gives us a title that our vanity wants to enforce with rigor, and the least lovable men always label as ingratitude one's indifference toward their passion. If, in the uncertainty or fear of being unloved, we come to suspect someone of being loved, we feel a pain called jealousy. It is much more natural for us to relate the contempt that one shows toward us to the injustice of a rival than to our own defects. For our vanity always serves well enough to make us believe that we would have been loved if another had not acted against us. We hate a man who takes what we believe is our due; in love, we imagine that the claim alone confers a legitimate title.

[510–513] FRAGMENTS THAT DID NOT MAKE IT INTO MY WORK ON "CRITICISM."[1]

---

[506]
1. See also *pensée* 719.—HC

[508]
1. "Put in the *Laws*" (M.), 26.13, 505.

[510–513]
1. All that is left of this lost work is these four fragments and *pensée* 1006.

[510] Works lacking in talent prove only the memory or patience of the author.

[511] Critics have the advantage of choosing their enemy, attacking the weak point, ignoring the strong, and, through contradiction, making at least problematic what the other had advanced as certain. [The works of our finest talents are like the children of the Amazons, destined to be maimed suddenly after their birth.][1]

They are like bad generals who, unable to conquer a country, poison the waters.

[512] The joke that is not grasped rebounds onto the one who tells it.[1]

[513] There is a prevailing disgust for new works, which comes from the fact that, for most people, there are already only too many good works; they are stocked up. There is so little reading that in this area, receipts are well above expenses.

[514] In England, there is plenty of useless money.

[515] The epoch of the Reformation is put down to doctor Luther, but its coming was inevitable. If it had not been Luther, it would have been another. The sciences and letters brought from Greece had already opened eyes about abuses.[1] Such a cause had to produce some effect. Proof of this: the Councils of Constance and of Basel had introduced a sort of reformation.[2]

[516] In a short life of St. Giovanni Nepomuceno,[1] written in a blue book,[2] it is said that when a woman had scorned that saint's cult, he took his revenge against her in that, in leaving the Church, a wind arose that affected only that lady, and the wind lifted her skirts so that it revealed her a——— to the whole assembly.

[511]
1. Cf. *Spicilège*, 241; *PL*, XXXVIII, 66.

[512]
1. See *pensée* 309.

[515]
1. For "abuses," the first version was: "the Roman court's debaucheries."
2. The Council of Constance (1414–18) condemned Jan Hus to death and ended the Great Schism; the Council of Basel (1431–37), transferred to Ferrara in 1438–39 by Eugenius IV, then to Florence from 1439 to 1442, somewhat curtailed the powers of the papacy.

[516]
1. John Nepomucene (ca. 1330–ca. 1393).
2. The *livres bleus* were cheap, pocket-sized publications for popular consumption.—HC

[517] TO SARRAU OF PICHON.[1] You are not, as you say, a simple farmer in the Republic of Sciences (observer), unless this is like bygone days, when kings were farmers and shepherds.

[518] A secretary of Prince Louis of Baden did not take money, but he sold lazy old saddle horses to all who needed him.[1]

[519] I said: "The Catholic Religion will destroy the Protestant Religion, and then the Catholics will become Protestants."

[520] One must clearly distinguish when an author has meant to speak a truth,[1] and when he has meant to utter a witticism. For example, when Saint Augustine said: "*Qui te creavit sine te, non te salvabit sine te,*"[2] it is clear that the author meant to create an antithesis.

[521] Princes must travel very young, so they can be teachable; but we must travel at a ripe age, so we can be in a better position to be instructed. {Private individuals, just the reverse.}

[522] The Popes' good fortune was that the Kingdom of Italy was attached to the Empire, and that the Emperors went to reside in the Kingdom of Germany. Thus, the Emperors being Germans, the Popes had the opportunity to take up the defense of Italy against the invasion of the Germans.[1]

[523] Since the Quadruple Alliance, the great European princes have acted like the Romans: they dispose of the small princely States from the standpoint of their interests, not justice.[1]

---

[517]
1. Isaac de Sarrau de Boynet, lord of Pichon (ca. 1685–1772), eldest son of Isaac de Sarrau, Reformed minister. His musical events were the origin of the Academy of Bordeaux; cf. Montesquieu's "Résomption de la dissertation de M. de Sarrau sur les coquillages de Sainte-Croix-du-Mont" [Summary of M. de Sarrau's essay on the shellfish of Sainte-Croix-du-Mont] in *OC,* 3:85.

[518]
1. Louis Guillaume, Margrave of Baden (1655–1707).

[520]
1. First version: "a fine idea."
2. "He who made you without you does not save you without you," where Montesquieu changes Augustine's "justify" to "save." See sermon 169.13 in Augustine, *Sermons on the New Testament, 148–183,* pt. 3, vol. 5 of *The Works of Saint Augustine: A Translation for the Twenty-first Century,* ed. John E. Rotelle, trans. Edmund Hill (New Rochelle: New City Press, 1992).—HC

[522]
1. "Put in the *Universal monarchy*" (M.), XII, in *OC,* 3:371; *OC* Volt, 2:351.

[523]
1. The Quadruple Alliance was formed in 1718 between France, England, the United Provinces, and the Empire to maintain the treaties of Utrecht.

[524–526] SOME FRAGMENTS THAT DID NOT MAKE IT INTO THE
"SPANISH LIBRARY" ARTICLE ON PRINCES.[1]

[524] An individual who respects the laws that threaten him can, without morality and as if in spite of himself, be a good citizen; but a prince without morality is always a monster.

[525] An individual criminal has this advantage over a prince who has performed a bad deed, that it took him a sort of courage to endanger himself by violating the laws that threatened him.

[526] The author says, "Such a prince had better hope that his subjects are more honorable than he is, for if that were not the case, his state would immediately be overturned."

[527] Since, in England, the {income from} real estate depends on the number of sheep whose wool the farmer can sell, they see the prosperity of their commerce by the high price offered their lease.

[528] It is not surprising that London is growing: it is the capital of the three kingdoms and of all the English establishments in the two Indies.

[529] In his book *On the Nature of the Gods,* Cicero says, "If one saw houses in Brittany, would one not say that there were men? And if one found a clock, would one not say there were skilled workers there? Thus, when one sees this order in the world . . ."[1] What is funny is that today, it is from that barbarous Brittany that the best watches in the world are coming. (Pembroke)[2]

[530] Holland is remarkable in having only a single specie for payment, fixed in trade, namely, silver specie. When you want gold, you go to the Jews, who speculate in it. Whereas in England, where the price of the guinea has been set at twenty-one shillings {in silver}, the guinea is worth more or less depending on whether the Spanish fleets arrive or not, so that a man is free to pay you in gold or silver, and always pays you in whatever is worth less. *Idem,* in France.[1] But if you proceeded as in Holland, where

[524–526]

1. The reference is to the *Reflections on the character of some princes* (*OC,* 3:537–51), of uncertain date; other fragments are preserved below at *pensées* 540, 601, 628, 640, 1253, 1631, and 1983–2003.

[529]

1. Cicero, *De natura deorum,* II, 35.

2. Thomas Herbert, eighth Count of Pembroke (1656–1733), lord of the Admiralty in 1690, plenipotentiary at the Congress of Ryswick in 1697; man of science, he presided over the Royal Society in 1689–90. Montesquieu must have known him in England; cf. *OC,* 3:277, and *Spicilège,* 628.

[530]

1. For Montesquieu on monometallism, see *Laws,* 22.9.

you can only pay in silver, there would be no need to fix the proportion, because it would fix itself of its own accord. This was apparently Law's idea in proscribing gold.[2]

[531] I would not want people to go preach to the Chinese; since it is necessary to make them see the falseness of their religion, they would be bad citizens before one could make them Christians.[1]

[532] The mourning rituals introduced in all nations make it quite clear that we always assume that men seek to make themselves loved.

[533] What an idea for a dying prince, to think that his misery is going to constitute the public felicity.

This idea brings tyrants such despair that many of them, in order to prevent the day of their death from being a day of joy, have decreed that a portion of their people be exterminated on that day, to prevent the rest from rejoicing.

[534] Generally, princes are badly raised because those who are entrusted with their education are themselves intoxicated by their grandeur. Thus, they make princes feel what they feel themselves. When one says to a prince that he should be humane, one proves it with the worst reason, namely, that it is useful to him to make himself loved. So if it happens, which is not rare, that they disdain a man enough not to take the trouble to please him, they are no longer humane. Thus, one must at the same time bring them back to the great principles of religion, society, natural equality, the accident of greatness, and the commitment they are engaged in to make men happy.

[535] It is good for you to know, O Princes, that in the conflicts that those who exercise your authority have with your subjects, they are usually wrong. Far from thinking of attacking those who have your power in their hands, the people—who are naturally timorous, and with reason—actually have trouble bringing themselves to complain.[1]

---

2. For Montesquieu's critique of Law's financial policy, see *PL*, XLV, CXXXVIII, CXLII, and *Laws*, 2.4, 19; 22.6, 22.9, and 29.6. Montesquieu met Law in Venice, *Voyages* (*OC*, 2:1004–7), where Law gave him a memoir he had written in 1715 on French trade and the means to restore it; preserved in the municipal library of Chartres, this manuscript was destroyed in 1940. See also *pensées* 1017, 1610, and 2143.

[531]
1. See *Laws*, 19.17 and 19.18.

[535]
1. Cf. *Laws*, 11.4.

[536] When a prince elevates some dishonorable man, he seems to be showing him to the people to encourage them to resemble him.

[537] Men's corruption is such that it is prodigiously increased by the hope or fear one can imagine on the prince's part. Thus, the condemnation of the criminal is not always proof of the crime of the accused, and in this respect, they cannot have their consciences at peace if they do not allow the justice of the established tribunals to act, without providing for special tribunals.

[538] The word *justice* is often quite equivocal. Louis XIII was given the name *the Just* because he witnessed with aplomb his minister's acts of vengeance; he was severe, not just.[1]

[539] There is a kind of prince who would consider himself reduced to nothing if he did not have advisors around him deliberating at all times.

[540] M. Zamega[1] asks if a prince should put his state affairs in the hands of those who govern his conscience. "No! No!" he says, "for those who have a worldly spirit are entirely incapable of governing his conscience, and those who do not have this spirit are incapable of governing his state." He even says this would make his director of conscience useless, for he is put there to warn him about the mistakes he is making. But how will he warn him about those mistakes he would cause him to make? A prince is not all square with God by relying upon his director for the obligations God has imposed upon him. For he is not discharging his duties, and he is preventing the other from discharging his own. "In a word," he says, "of all those who approach his person, the one who directs his conscience is the one who should have the most credit, and the one who should have the least."

M. Zamega also wonders if the Prince should consult his director on the choice of persons that he should elevate to honors. He again answers more affirmatively than not. This can be subject to countless drawbacks. Since the choice of some necessarily entails the exclusion of others, and since you do not exclude anyone without giving the reason, it happens that each

[538]
1. According to Shackleton, 434, this *pensée* belongs to the *Traité des devoirs,* ch. 9: "Equivoque de la justice."

[540]
1. "Put this in the *Princes*" (M.); cf. *pensées* 524–26n. See *pensées* 1993 and 2002 for more information on Montesquieu's intentions for M. Zamega.

individual would be judged in a secret tribunal, without having any way of justifying himself.

He does not even believe that the Prince should bestow credit on those who are attached to a particular monastic body, and he gives very sensible reasons for this, including among others: this afflicts a nation and brings a spirit of servitude to it that is entirely contrary to the Prince's interests. For just as whoever he seeks in a corporate body to vest his trust in is respected at Court, those who are from the same body are equally respected in town and country. Thus, since the lowest henchman from this body is an important figure, each one finds a thousand favorites hounding him instead of one, and all you see on all sides are masters.

The sovereign's trust: The exercise of sovereign power must be communicated to as many people as necessary, but to as few as possible. Princely authority must be communicated to as many people as necessary, through the laws, but to as few as possible. The Prince must share it with those he has chosen,[2] but in such a manner that it not pass into other hands.

[541] Someone was saying to me that despotic princes should be better because, since men belong to them, they should be afraid of losing them. I respond that the loss is trivial compared to the satisfaction of following his passions. Besides, the comforts of despotism make the Prince throw himself into pleasure, not governing but leaving all the governing to his ministers. But men do not belong to the minister.

[542] States are governed by five different things: religion, general government maxims, individual laws, mores, and manners.[1] These things all have a mutual relationship with each other. If you change one, the others follow only slowly, which brings a kind of dissonance throughout.

[543] The Christian Religion weakened the Empire—first as not being tolerated, then as not being tolerant. When a state is plagued by religious disputes, it happens that the Prince's providence is entirely occupied with these disputes and neglects the other less essential points. It happens[1] that

2. First version: "his ministers"; the paragraph as a whole contains numerous confusing revisions.—HC

[542]
1. "Put in the *Laws*" (M.); cf. 19.4. According to Robert Shackleton (*Montesquieu: A Critical Biography* [London: Oxford University Press, 1960], 316), the *Laws* version of this text was written between 1740 and 1743; *pensée* 542 was written between 1731 and 1733, and *pensée* 584, between 1733 and 1738. For a commentary on the variations among these three texts, see Derathé, 1:523 n. 6.

[543]
1. "[Put in the *Romans*]" (M.); cf. *Considerations*, XIX, 175.

a great many people are disgusted by the government. Although the ill will of a sector of the citizenry appears impotent, because they do not make a flashy impact, they nonetheless have their silent effects, which occur in the shadows and over time; whence arise great revolutions. It happens that it is neither personal merit that garners offices nor incapacity that takes them away, but alien qualities such as the advantage of being from a certain faction or the misfortune of being from another one.[2]

[544] Who would have guessed that the Jesuits—so blackened with accusations against our kings, so often accused and even condemned—would come to govern France with a dominance unprecedented up to that time?

[545] Roman historians constantly observed that the Northern peoples, who were practically invincible in their own country, were very far from it in warmer countries.[1] They never stop making this remark about the Gauls, the Germans, the Suebi, the Alamanni. This is why Marius only wanted to fight the Cimbrians and Teutons in the most scorching times and places. And on these matters, there are no historians who can help us form more solid conjectures, because the Romans were at war constantly for eight hundred years, successively with all the world's peoples.

This has not stopped the Northern peoples from always subjugating the Southern peoples, because they are eternal, invincible peoples— mainly because they are not worth the trouble of being defeated—who take the Southern empires in the period of their decadence, and precipitate their fall.

[546] That Aristotle was Alexander's tutor, or that Plato was at the court of Syracuse—this counts for nothing toward their glory. [Although in the past, this might perhaps have contributed more to their reputation than their philosophy.][1] Their philosophical reputations have absorbed everything. Who knows Rubens by his negotiations?[2]

[547] It is good that there are goods and evils in the world; otherwise, one would despair at quitting life.

---

2. See *pensée* 690, third and fourth paragraphs.—HC

[545]
1. On the Northern peoples, see *Laws,* 14.2.

[546]
1. "Delete what is between the two lines" (M.).

2. The painter Peter-Paul Rubens (1577–1640); from 1627 to 1630, as councilor for the infanta Isabella, he was involved in the great events agitating Europe; he negotiated the peace between Spain and England.

[548] Letter from Iris.

You have found a new means to be assured of my faithfulness;
I am no longer fit for anyone.
You have rendered me incapable of serving others' pleasure.
Love, to give you a happy retreat,
Increased my capacity.
It says to you: Dear abbot, I know that I'm adding
To your immensity.

When you were quite ready to leave me, I fixed up
My coiffure and rose up.
Dear abbot, such long arms
Must vanquish the world.
Your stiffness enchains
Hearts eluding your charms.

I've felt just for you a marvelous flame.
I never have loved as I do at this hour.
Priapus himself was my last silly fling,
But you were my first real amour.

Your inflexible firmness
Makes great your domain
Your inflexible firmness
Makes it majestic.

[549] Nothing would be more capable of bringing the Cardinal[1] that immortality which is so fitting for his name, his virtues, and his talent, than a reform in the laws of the realm.

By some imperceptible changes in jurisprudence, quite a few trials could be eliminated.

The lawyers, delighted to see the fate of all individuals in their hands, will not go along with such a plan; all experts[2] are suspect.

[549]
1. Cardinal Fleury; see *pensée* 472 n. 2.
2. *Gens de métier,* or "experts," a term normally used for the manual trades in this period but which Montesquieu seems to use figuratively here for lawyers.—HC

M. Law wanted to cut the number of judges, but it is the trials that need to be cut.

Just as the multiplicity of treaties among princes only multiplies the occasions and pretexts for war,[3] so too, in civil life, the multiplicity of laws merely gives birth to disputes among individuals.

[550] It takes only one gallant woman[1] in a family to make the family known and place it among the first rank of families.

There are some illustrious families that are scarcely known because for two or three centuries, there has not been one woman who has distinguished herself.

[551] Although the Christian religion has not produced many virtuous princes, it has nonetheless tempered human nature. It has done away with the Tiberiuses, the Caligulas, the Neros, the Domitians, the Commoduses, and the Heliogabaluses.[1]

[552] In commercial cities such as the imperial cities and the Dutch cities, people are accustomed to put a price on everything; they rent out all their actions; they traffic in the moral virtues; and the things demanded by humanity, they sell for money.[1]

[553] It seems to me that the origin of allodial freehold in France comes from the fact that there were many Gauls who could not be made serfs—whether because of their birth, their employment, their credit, or even the service they had rendered in disposing the people to submit to the conquerors.[1] Nor did people want them to have fiefs,[2] that is, to bear arms and serve in war, for every fief involved that. Thus, the allodial freehold was invented.

---

3. See *pensée* 742; see also *PL,* LXVIII, 119.

[550]
1. *Femme galante* may mean a woman of easy virtue, or one who is respectably polite and enterprising.—HC

[551]
1. All Roman emperors; Domitian and Heliogabalus reigned 81–96 and 218–22, respectively.

[552]
1. "See the passage by Ammianus Marcellinus" (M.). Ammianus Marcellinus was a Latin historian, born in Antioch ca. 340, a continuator of Tacitus who wrote a history from Nerva's death to Valens's death in thirty-one books, of which the first thirteen are lost (*Catalogue,* 2812).

[553]
1. On the origins of the allodial freehold, see *Laws,* 30.17, 641.
2. First version: "to be noble."

[**554**] The inflated and pompous style is so far the easiest, that if you see a nation emerge from barbarism, such as the Portuguese for example, you will see that at first their style favors the sublime; afterward they descend to the naturalistic. The problem with the naturalistic is that it borders on the vulgar. But there is an enormous distance between the sublime and the naturalistic, and between the sublime and gibberish.[1]

[**555**] [Even if France had won the battle of Hochstädt, this would not have made her the universal monarchy.][1]

[**556**] Whoever believes that he needs to be involved in important affairs to have some merit in the world, and that he no longer counts for anything when he can no longer hide behind the figure of a public man, has precious little vanity.

[**557**] France, which considered herself mistress of all Europe because she had had some great successes, initiated the War of the Spanish Succession.[1] She was already exhausted. She fielded more troops than she could handle. She extended her forces, occupied Italy on one side, pressed into Spain and toward the Danube. The {old} troops, defeated or killed, were replaced by new troops, by peasants. People think these were French troops; not at all: these armies were different from the ones that prevailed in previous wars. Never full battalions, while the enemy's always were. And impoverished officers, too. When the officers are rich, they can aid an ailing soldier; he has a wagon, a horse, he puts the ailing soldier in it. When an officer has been on foot, and upon his arrival you tell him to join an expedition, he has no more good will. The soldiers die off. The great secret is to have troops that do not perish. When a soldier is ailing, when he stays in a bush, he dies, he deserts. In the last war, the stronger enemy battalions always outflanked ours. If you had set out a rope for a tug-of-war, one enemy battalion would have pulled two of ours.

[**558**] By their enthusiasm alone, the Jews defended themselves better

---

[554]
  1. First version: "an enormous distance between the naturalistic and the sublime, and a marked difference between the sublime and gibberish." See also *pensée* 599.

[555]
  1. See *pensée* 562.

[557]
  1. During this war (1701–14), France fought Austria, England, and the United Provinces.

against the Romans than all the other peoples who were absorbed into that empire.

[559] The title *Unitary,* which the Caliphs gave their soldiers, did much to enhance their zeal.

[560] Enthusiasm is quite the thing! When the Jews were guided by it, they destroyed all the Syrian armies with a handful of men. But after such brilliant successes, when they had made themselves masters of Jerusalem[1] and created a principality, giving sovereignty to Simon, then under his successor Hyrcanus, Antiochus Sidetes[2] {much weaker than his predecessors} took hold of Judea, besieged Jerusalem, and was on the verge of taking it, so they were obliged to pay him tribute and give him five hundred talents. This is because by then, they were no longer defending anything but the prince's interests.

[561] France's strength consists in the fact that the capital is closest to the weakest border.[1] That makes her pay more attention to that which demands more, and enables her to send aid there more easily.

[562] I say it is not true that, if we had won the battle of Hochstädt, we would have been masters of Europe.[1] Our frontier was becoming too extended. The Germans would have awakened and, instead of selling some troops, would have made it their own affair.[2]

[563] LYSIMACHUS. As far as I have trusted the gods in my adversity, just so far do I fear them in my good fortune.[1]

[564] FROM A "DIALOGUE BETWEEN VULCAN AND VENUS." I don't

[560]

1. In 142 B.C.

2. The reference is to Simon Maccabee, the ethnarch and High Priest of the Jews from 142 to 135 B.C.; John Hyrcanus, his son and successor as ethnarch and High Priest from 134 to 104 B.C.; and Antiochus VII, called Sidetes, king of Syria from 133 to 130 B.C.

[561]

1. "Put in the *Universal monarchy*" (M.), 20 (*OC,* 3:379; *OC*Volt, 2:361). See also *pensée* 271.

[562]

1. Often known as the Battle of Blenheim, the second and more decisive Battle of Hochstädt was won by the Duke of Marlborough and the Grand Alliance on August 13, 1704. See also *pensée* 726.—HC

2. "Put in the *Romans*" (M.); cf. *pensée* 555.

[563]

1. This sentence does not seem to have been taken up in the *Lysimachus;* on which, see also *pensées* 1666 and 2161. See also Allen, 76–81.

know what pains me more, that I'm an a—— or that everybody knows it. In truth, I think it's that I'm an a——, because when I called the gods to see Mars and Venus in my grasp, I was charmed. They were quite confused . . . But I don't want to let my wife go running around anymore in Cyprus, Paphos, Cythera . . . I have no use for that troop of Nymphs, Loves, and Graces, and that coquettish paraphernalia that's always following them. Let the whole world talk as much as they want about Vulcan's jealousy. Wouldn't the whole world talk anyway about Venus's betrayals? I feel good thinking about the disgraces I'm going to avoid. [But here Venus appears.—My wife, you know that duty binds us?

Venus:

Yeah, so it binds us!

Vulcan:

But I claim you are mine.

Venus:

Hey, I'm here! Get drunk on my favors. Be my husband, since you want it so much. Levy Hymen's taxes.

Vulcan:

But you have no love for me.

Venus:

Hey, if I have no love, then no need for you to stand on ceremony. That way, you'll make up for my offense in the contempt I show you.

Vulcan:

But I'll know how to guide you.

Venus:

The good favors I've always had for you, you owe them solely to your sweet humor and remarkable indulgence; otherwise, I'd have played many a dirty trick on you.

Vulcan:

Oh, my wife! Let's not start in on those discussions; let's not talk about what's been done.

Venus:

Vulcan, I've always served you well; I've artfully managed the tenderness I'm capable of toward you. And if I'd wanted to listen to your sorrows, you'd have seemed to me a hundred times more lame and deformed than you are.]

[565] [Here is what religious zeal is based on: When I debate someone

about an opinion, I feel I can be mistaken, as he can.[1] Thus, I am not stubborn or extremely obstinate. But when I belong to a religion, by the very fact that I believe it to be good, I believe the others to be bad. I cannot bear that others do not see what I see clearly. And a man that you want to preach to, and who sees that you are wrong, is likewise indignant that you want to make him exchange the truth for an error.]

[566] Custom can bring credit to anything: at first, gladiators were slaves condemned to death, then they were knights, then senators, then women, then emperors.[1]

[567].[1]

[568] Europe, which has created the commerce of the other three parts of the world, has been the tyrant of these other three parts. France, England, and Holland, which have created Europe's commerce, have been the three tyrants of Europe and the world, but this will not last. That is why the three powers made such a prodigious effort in the last war.[1]

[569] {Almost} all princes treat public affairs like Caligula treated his. During the diplomatic mission of Philo,[1] who was admitted into his audience, the Emperor—passing through a gallery, his rash young followers with him—said to Philo: "Is it true that you don't eat pig?" "Ha ha ha!" said the Emperor in passing, and his courtiers likewise.

[570].[1]

[571] It is said that to get the natives to fight, some missionaries told them that Jesus Christ was French, that the English had crucified him.

[572–580] USELESS FRAGMENTS FROM THE WORK ON THE ROMANS.

[572] However much the Romans may have enjoyed recounting their

[565]
1. "Put in the *Romans*" (M.).

[566]
1. See *pensée* 442.—HC

[567]
1. Passage deleted and textually recopied, *pensée* 572.

[568]
1. The War of the Spanish Succession (1701–14).—HC

[569]
1. Philo of Alexandria, Jewish philosopher (40 B.C.–A.D. 40); Montesquieu owned a 1612 French translation of his works (*Catalogue*, 367).

[570]
1. In numbering the manuscript of the *Pensées,* Barckhausen omitted 570.

war with the Gauls, they nonetheless made that shameful treaty whereby they engaged thenceforward to use iron only for tilling the soil. And Brennus, despite the defeat they talk about so much, nonetheless pursued his course and his robberies.[1]

[573] Philip and Perseus were frightened rather than defeated.[1] The Egyptian kings appeared only as supplicants. All the other kings bowed down their heads. Those of Pergamum and Bithynia boasted of their servitude.

[574] There is no reason to have started a {kind of} new epoch at Nerva, and to have counted twelve Caesars up to him, as if they had formed but one family that became defunct with Domitian.[1] It seems probable that, since Suetonius wrote the life of these twelve Caesars, and since we have from Tacitus practically nothing but the history of these twelve emperors, the custom arose of putting them together and of counting, so to speak, a new dynasty with Nerva.

[575] The ancients, who had a religion that made them worship the ancient heroes as gods who had come to reveal themselves to men, had very mistaken ideas about genuine glory and virtue. Since Hercules and Theseus and others had been placed in the ranks of the gods because of their military deeds, this caused those who imitated them to be regarded as virtuous men, of a nature more excellent than other men.

Alexander was being perfectly logical in his vanity when he called himself son of Jupiter, like Hercules and Bacchus. He did not believe that, having done the same things they did, he was merely a man for having done them after they did. Instead, it was supposed to be said that there was a time when Hercules and Bacchus were merely Alexanders, or that Alexander was another Hercules and Bacchus.

Thus, men conquered without motive, without utility. They laid waste the earth to exercise their virtue and show the excellence of their being. Since we have begun to weigh the value of things a little better, heroes have been covered in ridicule, so much so that whoever wanted to defend them would be even a thousand times more ridiculous.

[572]
    1. Brennus, leader of the Celtic Senones, sacked Rome ca. 390 B.C.
[573]
    1. Perseus, last king of Macedonia (179–168 B.C.), son and successor of Philip V. He was defeated at Pydna by Lucius Aemilius Paullus (168 B.C.) and died captive in Italy.
[574]
    1. Marcus Cocceius Nerva (r. 96–98); Titus Flavius Domitianus (r. 81–96).

[576] MARCUS AURELIUS.[1] Never has a philosopher better conveyed to men the gratifications of virtue and the dignity of their being. The heart is touched, the soul enlarged, the mind is elevated.

[577] Liberty is obtained only by brilliant strokes, but it is lost by an imperceptible force.[1]

[578] [The truth of the matter is that the king of England is more absolute than . . .][1]

[579] Bad territories are generally free; this is because they do not provide the prince enough to enable him to become their master.[1]

[580] Perseus was a man in whose hands a great enterprise could never succeed. He had a stupid avarice that made him view the preservation of his treasures as independent from that of his realm. For him, whatever might cost him money was not a means of defending himself. As soon as he enjoyed the least success, he deceived his allies. At the least reversal, he fell into a consternation that caused him to lose his sense. All he had to do was keep the routes into Macedonia closed; in his panic, he opened them. In a word, this prince—who was always occupied in discussing petty interests, who regarded cunning as the sole royal virtue—loved great affairs with a total incapacity to succeed in them.

If he had had some personal qualities, he was in circumstances where the Greek peoples were beginning to see that the Romans were talking to them about liberty only to become their masters. The Rhodians were no longer willing to act except as mediators.

[581] To indicate a great deception, the English say: "That is Jesuitically false, *jesuiticaly false*."[1]

[582] The old men who have studied in their youth need only to remember, not learn. That is very fortunate!

[576]
1. Marcus Aurelius Antoninus, Roman emperor (r. 162–180) whom Montesquieu admired; cf. his letter to Fitz-James on October 8, 1750 (*OC*, 3:1327), and *Considerations*, XVI, 145.

[577]
1. "Put, I believe, in the *Romans*" (M.).

[578]
1. The incomplete and deleted text of this *pensée* is found again at *pensée* 1992, which is one of the fragments on the *Prince* jotted down much later.

[579]
1. Cf. *Laws,* 18.1.—HC

[581]
1. The italicized words are written in English.—HC

[583] In Burnet's *History,* I found that Henry VIII, in a law he passed, ordered all his subjects to believe that . . .[1] Nero's life does not reveal a tyrant as cruel as that of Henry VIII. [In that entire reign, too, not one subject is seen performing a noble deed.] Under the forms of justice, the people were governed in the most unjust fashion.

[584] I think it was in Charles II's time that a man was brought to trial for saying that the king of England does not cure those with scrofula.[1]

[585] These two lines were written for Conti;[1] I apply them to Montaigne:

> His fancy and his judgment such;
> Each to the other seems too much.[2]

[586] It seems to me that the Spanish and Italian ecclesiastics who build up the ignorance of the lay people are like the Tartars who gouge out the eyes of their slaves so they can better churn their milk.[1]

[587] Take note that most things that give us pleasure are unreasonable.

[588] A modesty capital yields a very large interest.

[589] I said: "Even though the Parlements of France do not have much authority, this does not keep them from doing good.[1] Neither the ministry nor the prince want to be disapproved by them, because they are respected. Kings are like the Ocean,[2] whose impetuosity is often curbed, sometimes by the grasses, sometimes by the stones."

[583]
1. Gilbert Burnet (1643–1715), Anglican bishop of Salisbury, violently opposed to Catholicism, author of a *History of the Reformation of the Church of England,* of which Montesquieu owned the French translation of 1686 (*Catalogue,* 3195). See *Laws,* 12.10.

[584]
1. Charles II, King of England (1660–85); French kings continued to perform the curative ceremony of the "royal touch" for this disease until Louis XVI in 1775.—HC

[585]
1. Abbé Antonio Conti (1677–1749) had traveled to Paris from 1718 to 1726 and had met Montesquieu there; Montesquieu encountered him in Italy, *Voyages* (*OC,* 2:1007 and 1016), then maintained a correspondence with him.
2. These two lines appear in English in the manuscript.—HC

[586]
1. "Put in the *Romans*" (M.), XXII, 205.

[589]
1. See *Laws,* 2.4, 19.
2. See *Laws,* 2.4, 18, for a similar image.

[590] Most princes, all things considered, are more honorable men than we are.[1] Perhaps in the sphere entrusted to us we abuse power more than they do. There is scarcely a single one of them who does not want to be loved, but they cannot {easily} succeed.

[591] There is no nation that needs religion more than the English;[1] whoever is not afraid of being hanged has to be afraid of being damned.

[592] In Holland every {service} is for sale.[1] I said: "A Dutchman can die at the age of eighty without ever doing a good deed."

[593] I said: "There are no petty sums when it comes to avarice. Didn't {the Duke of} Marlborough ask for a shilling he had won, to pay (so he said) his porters, and then go off on foot? Pultney was a witness.[1] In the end, he complained even about his avarice."

[594] Devotion is a belief that one is worth more than another person.[1]

[595] I said: "I wish to have simple manners, to receive as few services as I can and make as much of them as possible."

[596] I said: "Despotic government constrains the talents of subjects and great men, just as the power[1] of men constrains the talents of women."

[597] In a well-ordered monarchy, the subjects are like fish[1] in a big net: they think they are free, and yet they are caught.

[598] I said that someone ought to write a Byzantine history, instead of the collection of so many volumes in-folio of detestable authors that we have on it.[1]

---

[590]
1. Cf. *Notes sur l'Angleterre* (*OC,* 3:286) for a similar thought.

[591]
1. Cf. *Notes sur l'Angleterre* (*OC,* 3:292) as well.

[592]
1. See *Voyages* (OC, 2:1290) for a similar observation, and cf. *Laws,* 20.2, 338–39.

[593]
1. John Churchill, first duke of Marlborough (1650–1722), military commander, and William Pultney, first count of Bath (1684–1764), English politician. The reference seems to be to sedan porters.

[594]
1. See *pensée* 4.

[596]
1. First version: "the domination"; the French is *pouvoir.*

[597]
1. See *pensées* 434n, 828, 874, and 943.

[598]
1. For Montesquieu's holdings in Byzantine history, see *Catalogue,* 3114–22.

[599] Here are the verses composed in Moscow on the death of Peter II.

Clauditur in Jano sic vita janua Petro.
Mors aperit limen, quando paratur hymen.[1]

You see that rhymed verse is always found when people are beginning to emerge from the earliest barbarism.

[600] The reason why fools succeed {usually} in their enterprises is that, since they never know or see when they are being importunate, they never stop. Now, there is no man foolish enough not to know how to say: "Give me that."

[601] [In ordinary debates, since each man feels he might be mistaken, stubbornness and obstinacy are not extreme. But in religious ones, since it is in the nature of the subject that everyone is sure that his is true and others' are false, he is indignant at all those who, instead of changing themselves, are bent on making him change.][1]

[602] In the earliest times, *heretic* merely meant whoever had a private, particular opinion. But in the bitterness of debate, the word *heretic* signified all the most horrible things in the world and the most monstrous things in hell. But with the establishment of Lutheranism and Calvinism, since these religions have been tolerated in some countries and have been tolerant in others, men have been content to hate each other a great deal, without hating each other to the point of madness.[1]

[603] Since a particular form of government gives a certain orientation, a certain disposition to minds, you change the former without the latter following you, and you combine the new government with the old manner of thinking, which produces very bad effects.

[604] Tigranes, King of Armenia, as weak as he was presumptuous.[1]

[599]
1. "For Peter, the door is closed in January, as is life. Death opens the doorway just as the marriage song is being prepared." Peter II Alexeyevitch, Russian emperor (1727–30), died at the moment he was going to be married. See also *pensée 554*.

[601]
1. "Put in the *Romans*" (M.), XXII, 208; see also *pensée 565*.

[602]
1. See *Laws*, 12.5 and 25.12.

[604]
1. Tigranes the Great, of the Arsacid dynasty (95–54 or 55 B.C.).

He had himself served by kings because he was not merely a man. He undertook the war against the Romans, and he did not even have the sense to worry that he might not win. He put to death anyone who came to tell him that the Romans dared to advance. A single day—what am I saying? one moment—defeated him, and his loss of heart completed his ruin.

[605] The Romans were thinking they were in a state of grandeur where they no longer had anything to hope or fear, when they now saw themselves in danger of perishing. The Cimbri and the Teutons appeared in an instant—unknown enemies who astonished by their number, their ferocity, their war cries; who, like Hannibal, attacked Rome in Italy; and who came to destroy or be destroyed. Marius had the good fortune to exterminate them, delaying by several centuries the great revolution that the nations of the North were to bring about.[1]

[606] [The constant disputes[1] over the primacy of the patriarchate completely indisposed the Popes against the Greek emperors. And Charlemagne—who {had just founded a new empire, and} had become a neighbor in Italy to the Eastern Emperor—seeing that he could not fail to become embroiled with a prince who would be equally jealous of his dignity and his power, thought he could do no better than to put the Pope, the Greeks' irreconcilable enemy, between the two of them.[2] Thus, he gave him some lands that might put him in a position to attack and defend himself. But in the event, this barrier was just as fatal to the empire he had just founded.

{False notion: the schism only arose after Charlemagne.}]

[607] Plutarch always charms {me}; he has a way of connecting circumstances to persons that always gives pleasure. In the *Life of Brutus,* when he describes the accidents that befell the conspirators, the objects of their fright at the moment of execution, one pities the poor conspirators.[1] Then one pities Caesar.

{At first, one trembles for the conspirators; then one trembles for Caesar.}

[605]
1. See *Considerations,* II, 35, for more on Marius.

[606]
1. Between Rome and Constantinople.
2. "[This idea is not (I believe) new]" (M.).

[607]
1. See Plutarch, *Life of Brutus,* XIV–XVII; cf. also *pensée* 698.

[608] I said: "One proof of men's inconstancy is the institution of marriage that had to be set up."[1]

[609] I said: "I speak of the different peoples of Europe as I speak of the different peoples of Madagascar."

[610] {In *The Princes,*}[1] I said of kings:
"Love for the successor is nothing else but hatred of the predecessor."

[611] The Spanish ought to have pulled out as many Indians for Spain as they sent Spaniards to the Indies.[1]

[612] For all their vanity, the disproportions among men are quite meager. Some have gout, others the stone. Some are dying, the others are going to die. They have the same soul for eternity, and these are only different for a short while—that is, for as long as they are joined to a body.[1]

[613] It seems that plant seeds are analogous to animal eggs: their seminal spirit is in the earth. It is uncertain whether the virgin lands that produce plants have the seminal spirit within them, or whether the air is filled with it.[1]

[614] Never has a prince done harsher penance for his vices than Henry III.[1]

[615] CATHERINE DE MEDICI.[1] She was always surrounded by astrologers, soothsayers, and all those sorts of people who [only ever] follow weak souls.

[608]
1. See *Laws,* 23.21, 450.

[610]
1. See *Reflections on the character of some princes* (*OC,* 3:537ff.).

[611]
1. See *PL,* CXXI, 204.

[612]
1. See also *pensée* 2071.—HC

[613]
1. See *Essai d'observations sur l'histoire naturelle* [Experimental observations on natural history], read at the Academy of Bordeaux on November 16, 1719, and November 20, 1721 (*OC,* 3:99–118).

[614]
1. On Henry III, King of France (1574–89), see *Reflections on the character of some princes* (*OC,* 3:545–46); the "vices" include Henry III's reported homosexuality.

[615]
1. Catherine de' Medici (1519–89), married in 1533 to the future King Henry II; see *Reflections on the character of some princes* (*OC,* 3:548).

[616] [DUKE OF GUISE'S ASSASSINATION. Whatever the circumstances the King found himself in, it is impossible to approve of what he did. One must either condemn that act or, for the sake of virtue's honor, withhold judgment. But as for Loignac and his Forty-Five, they will be covered with eternal infamy.][1]

[617] Philip II's desire to see his daughter on the French throne, and Louis XIV's to see his grandson on the Spanish throne, equally weakened their respective powers.[1]

[618] Never did the gates of Hell open more widely than when the most wicked of men was seen on the Holy See, a thing less attributable to the perversity of those who elected him than to a secret judgment of God upon the faithful (Alexander VI).[1]

[619] CHANCELLOR DE L'HÔPITAL.[1] His death can be ranked as a public calamity.

[620] The King of Spain was Catholic in good faith, that is, with a religiosity that well accommodated his ambition.

[621] Catherine[1] {a woman in the study as in the ruelles[2]} brought together the old Huguenots and many Catholics, and presumed through a declamation by Pibrac,[3] drawn from the examples of the Persians, Turks, and Muscovites, to demonstrate submission—examples, in my opinion, quite incapable of seducing men who have arms at hand. It is like that proconsul who brought all the philosophers to the square in Athens to make them agree.

---

[616]
1. The third Duke of Guise, leader of the Catholic party, assassinated on King Henry III's orders in 1588; Loignac, the king's chief agent in the assassination; see also the novel by Alexander Dumas, *Les Quarante-cinq* [The forty-five guardsmen].—HC

[617]
1. The reference is to Philip II, King of Spain (1556–98); his daughter, the Infanta Isabella Claire Eugenia; and Louis XIV's grandson, the Duke of Anjou, who became King of Spain in 1700; see *Reflections on the character of some princes* (*OC*, 3:540).

[618]
1. Alexander VI Borgia, pope from 1492 to 1503.

[619]
1. Michel de l'Hôpital (ca. 1504–73), chancellor (1560–68), known for a policy of religious tolerance.

[621]
1. Catherine de' Medici.
2. Literally, the space between a bed and the wall in a bedroom.—HC
3. Guy du Faur, lord of Pibrac (1529–84).

[**622**]   Catherine, woman who was the comet of France. Fortunate France, if that marriage had merely degraded the majesty of her kings!

[**623**]   Sixtus V[1] had made the greatest fortune that even a monk born to thirst for that condition could make. He was among those that Fortune sometimes elevates to inflame the hopes of those who worship her. Few popes who preceded him and none who have followed him have brought pride in supreme rank any further. In the disorder and confusion of things, he dared to see that religion had to be restored, but the Spanish—who were protecting it—abased.

[**624**]   One must choose as ministers those who have the most public esteem; then, one no longer stands surety for one's choice.

[**625**]   Jacobites, ridiculed at present in England.[1] That is because the doctrine of passive obedience has become so. In fact, it is unimaginable that it had so much credit. But what can't the clergy cause to be persuasive and supported?

[**626**]   It's a cruel business, the history of Henry VIII. Not an honorable man in his entire reign. {Perhaps Cranmer and certainly More must be excepted.}[1] Here is where we see that tyrants who mean to use the laws are as tyrannical as those who trample on them. That king had his parliament do things that he would never have dared undertake himself. What laws he had passed—a law that obliged a girl whom a king would marry to declare it if she was not a virgin, on penalty of treason. *Idem,* for mothers and relatives {who knew about it} to make a similar declaration, on pain of *misprision* and treason.[2] No one dared to inform him of his impending death, for fear of being punished by the statute passed against those predicting the king's death—which had become treason.[3]

---

[623]

1. Pope Sixtus V (1585–90); see *Reflections on the character of some princes* (*OC,* 3:541) and *pensée* 1633.

[625]

1. The Jacobites were English legitimists who, after the Revolution of 1688, supported the cause of James II, exiled in France, against William of Orange, and later the last Stuarts against the house of Hanover. Through Marshal Berwick, Montesquieu was connected with the Jacobites exiled in France.

[626]

1. Thomas Cranmer (1489–1556), first Anglican Archbishop of Canterbury, executed by Mary I in 1556; Thomas More (1478–1535), leading humanist, author of *Utopia* and chancellor under Henry VIII, who had him executed in 1535.

2. See *Laws,* 26.3, 496; see also *pensée* 583n; Montesquieu puts "misprision" in English.

3. "See the two kings Philip III and IV in the extract from Sidney: what's said about them" (M.). The reference is to Algernon Sidney, *Discourses Concerning Government* (1698).

In 1539 under that reign, there began to be trials—and condemnations—without hearings. Perhaps this originated in more barbarous times, like (I believe) the bills of attainder.

[**627**] The French lords did not usurp royal authority; they could not usurp from the kings what the kings did not have. They merely continued certain offices in their families, as would happen in Poland if the palatinates became hereditary; the king would lose no other right than that of naming the palatine. As for the fiefs, they belonged to them under the conditions that the laws established, that is, as long as they could perform the service.[1]

[**628**] When you are prodigal with honors, you gain nothing,[1] because all you do is ensure that a greater number of men are worthy of them, so that the more you reward people, the more it happens that others deserve to be rewarded. Five or six other persons are worthy of an honor you have granted to two or three; five or six hundred are worthy of an honor you have granted to a hundred, and so forth.

[**629**] The religion that condemned a man for going hunting would make hunters who would otherwise have been honorable men no longer take the trouble to be.

[**630**] The monarch of a large empire is a prince who has his ready cash three hundred leagues from him.[1]

[**631**] In love affairs, I have always thought that he who was the most gullible[1] plays the finest role.

[**632**] {In Rome, I said to} Cardinal Alberoni {that he} had restored Spain with these two words: *Yes* and *no.*[1] When he had uttered one of these words, and he would utter them up front, they were irrevocable. {There was} no more slowness.

[**627**]
1. On fiefs, see especially *Laws,* 18.22 and 31.33.

[**628**]
1. "Put in the *Prince*" (M.). *See Reflections on the character of some princes, OC,* 3:537–51.

[**630**]
1. See *pensée* 271.

[**631**]
1. First version: "the most foolish."

[**632**]
1. Jules Alberoni (1664–1752), prime minister and Spanish grandee, disgraced for his foreign policy failure on December 5, 1719. Montesquieu met him; see *Voyages* (*OC,* 2:1100 and 1125–27).

[**633**] In most authors, I see the writing man; in Montaigne, the thinking man.

[**634**] Though one should love one's Country, it is as ridiculous to talk about it with prejudice as about one's wife, one's birth, or one's property. How foolish vanity is everywhere![1]

[**635**] The slow passions do not reason anymore than the raging ones. Does avarice calculate? Examples: the King of Prussia,[1] Louis XIII, Lord Marlborough.

[**636**] Avarice grows stronger with age. {This is because we always want to enjoy.} Now, in youth we can enjoy by dissipating, but in old age, we can enjoy only by preserving.

[**637**] Expense is a comparison between the money we spend (or the price of what we would like to imagine having) {for our pleasure} and the thing we are spending on. Now in old age, few things bring us pleasure by themselves.

[**638**] In poor nations, the poorest are the most powerful. In rich nations, the richest are the most powerful.

[**639**] It is no longer possible today for a small power to stop a large one; States are more disproportioned than they were in the past.[1] In most of the little republics of Greece and Italy, or rather of Europe in the past, there was a division of land: each citizen, equally rich, had an equal and dominant interest in defending his Country, and his life was a small matter when he compared it with the loss of his liberty, his family, and his possessions. That is what made an entire nation [of soldiers] fit for war, as well as a disciplined army.

But when the division was no longer equal, the number of citizens fell immediately; a twentieth or a thirtieth of the people had everything, and the rest nothing. Whence the arts, as much to satisfy the luxury of the rich as to be a situation for maintaining the poor. Whence two things: bad soldiers (for artisans do not have a Country, properly speaking, but enjoy

[634]
1. See *pensée* 946; *Country* here (*patrie*) may mean nation or natal region.—HC

[635]
1. The reference is probably to Frederick William I (r. 1713–40), father of Frederick II, the Great (1740–86).

[639]
1. "Put in the *Romans*" (M.), III, 39.

their industry everywhere, since they have hands everywhere); and again, few soldiers (for the yield from these landed estates, which had fed only soldiers, must also feed the entire retinue of the rich and a certain number of artisans, without which the State would perish). And it is something experienced [by us] today that a State that has a million subjects can only maintain ten thousand by vexing the people a great deal. In Lacedemon, Lycurgus had established —— portions,[2] from which he drew as many citizens. The law having allowed purchase, there were no more than seven hundred citizens. See Plutarch, *Life of Cleomenes.*[3]

[640] FRAGMENTS THAT DID NOT MAKE IT INTO THE "LETTERS FROM KANTI."[1]

Power does not belong to me: I have only its use, and only for a moment.[2]

If any being could abuse its power, it would be heaven, which, being eternal, sees all creatures pass before it. But it conducts itself with as much order and regularity as if its power were dependent.

Show my justice only with my mercy. Do as heaven does, which unleashes its thunder on one criminal only to alert many.

[641] HISTORY OF CHARLES XII.[1] There is an admirable fragment, written as vividly as anything in there, namely, Schulenburg's retreat.[2] Sometimes the author lacks sense, as when he says that Patkul was surprised when he was informed that he was going to be put on the wheel— this man who had been courageous in battle.[3] As if death and the manner of death were not two different things.

---

2. According to Plutarch's *Life of Lycurgus,* Lycurgus established thirty-nine thousand portions; Montesquieu left blank the space for the number.

3. Plutarch, *Life of Agis and Cleomenes,* V.

[640]

1. This fragment is the sole passage preserved from the *Letters from Kanti.*

2. "Put in the *Prince.* I believe I'll delete it" (M.).

[641]

1. The first edition of Voltaire's *History of Charles XII* appeared in 1731. Charles XII was king of Sweden from 1697 to 1718.

2. See Voltaire's *History,* III. According to Claude Lauriol, *Un correspondant de Montesquieu: La Beaumelle,* p. 17 n. 24, the reference is to Count Werner Schulenburg (1679–1755), whom Montesquieu had met when he was occupying the post of envoy for the king of Denmark at the court of France.

3. Johann Reinhold Patkul (1660–1707), governor of Livonia; he battled Charles XII, who had him tortured to death.

[642] When, in a kingdom, there is more advantage in paying one's social respects than in doing one's duty, all is lost.

[643] TORTURE. Each province[1] has established special torments for torture, and it is a painful spectacle to run through one's mind the fecundity of inventions in this regard, most of them absurd.[2] In some places, a criminal is stretched out on a wheel, as Procrustes used to do.[3] It was established that there would be twelve turns for ordinary torture, twenty-four for the extraordinary. It is easy to see that they wanted to double the punishment, but they have more than quadrupled it, since the thirteenth turn was doubtless the cruellest.

I have noticed that nine out of ten persons condemned to torture are made to undergo it. If so many innocents have been condemned to such a great punishment, what cruelty! If so many criminals have escaped death, what injustice!

But, someone will say, a practice authorized by so many laws cannot be rejected. But by the same reasoning, trial by hot iron, by cold water, by duels ought not to have been abolished, nor the absurd and infamous practice of trying married couples for their sexual potency. All thin people or people who have lungs made in such a way as to keep them afloat should also be punished as witches.

Menochius (book 1, question 89) treats the indications for torture.[4] He has some absurd ones, such as those derived from bad physiognomy, *ex nomine turpi*,[5] from the fact that the accused has made the blood of a cadaver flow.

Torture comes from slavery: *servi torquebantur in caput dominorum*,[6] and this is not surprising. They would be whipped and tormented on that occasion as they were on every other, and for the least fault. Since they were not citizens, they were not treated as men. {This was not more extraordinary than the law that put to death all the slaves of a man who had been assassinated, even though the guilty party was known.}

[643]
1. Montesquieu seems to have ecclesiastical "provinces" in mind.—HC
2. For Montesquieu's critique of torture, see *Laws,* 6.17, 92–93.
3. On Procrustes, the mythic brigand, see *pensées* 35 and 337.
4. Jacopo Menochio (1532–1607), author of a 1588 *Commentaria* (*Catalogue,* 969).
5. "From a shameful name"
6. "The slaves were being tortured on the masters' authority."

[644] The celebrated author of *Portrait of the Inconstancy of Demons and Witches*,[1] who has a man who was saying he had been at the witches' sabbat stay up all night, when he had not budged from his bed! He says the Devil had put an imaginary body in his place. The force of prejudice prevented that judge from submitting to the sole proof that the accused could have of their innocence.

[645] In the last war, we saw a power whose principal force consists in her credit and her trade use those two advantages to send into combat against us as many men as she could buy.[1] Tranquil within, but lacking a single fortified city to defend herself, she made fictive wealth real against us, and became a tranquil spectator of her mercenaries, whom she lost[2] without regret and replaced without difficulty. Whereas out of a spirit of whimsy, we awaited the blows in order to receive them and fielded great armies only to see our fortresses taken and our garrisons demoralized, and to languish in a defensive war of which we are not capable. The thing to do would have been to go to that nation, to try constantly to cross the sea, and to drench her natal land with her blood and our own. To make war on her would have been to defeat her; to place her in danger would have been, for us, to conquer her. We would have been making her lose the credit that was so fatal to us, and casting suspicions on the credit of another maritime power. We would have compelled her to recall her Hannibal with his old army, or make peace, or halt before us.

The sole great enterprise that we undertook abroad was fatal to our cause. We went and awakened the jealousy, the fear and the hatred of a nation that was merely an instrument of that war. Slow and almost immobile by herself, receiving all her movement from elsewhere, this nation was like Antaeus,[3] who constantly rediscovered the strength he had lost.

[646] Death for a Roman and death for a Christian are two different things.

[644]
1. Pierre de Lancre, councilor in the Parlement of Bordeaux (1560–ca. 1630), author of a 1612 work (*Catalogue*, 2597) on witchcraft, and participant in the witchhunt in the Basque country.

[645]
1. The reference is to England in the War of the Spanish Succession (1701–14).
2. *Perdait* can also mean "ruined."—HC
3. Antaeus, son of Poseidon and Gaia; he recovered his strength each time he touched the soil.

[647] The invention of money contributed much to the making of great empires.[1] Thus, all those empires in which there is no money are savage, for the prince cannot surpass other men enough in wealth to make himself obeyed, nor buy enough men to overwhelm everyone else. Every man has few needs and satisfies them easily and equally. Equality is therefore forced upon them. Thus, savage and Tartar chieftains are never despotic.

[648] Throughout the various changes of religion in England, the ecclesiastics of the various parties burned each other in turn.

[649] It is surprising that in the Catholic Church, where the marriage of priests has been prohibited so they will not meddle in worldly affairs, they meddle more than in England and other Protestant countries, where marriage has been permitted to them.[1]

[650] The power that the various European countries had in the past must not be judged by what they have today. It was not only a kingdom's extent and wealth that made its power, but rather the size of the princely domain.[1] The kings of England, who had very large revenues, did very big things, but the kings of France, who had greater vassals, were less aided than obstructed by them for a long time.

When armies conquered, the lands were parceled out between them and the chieftains. But the older the conquest, the more it happened that kings could be dispossessed by rewards or usurpations. And since the Normans were the last conquerors, King William[2]—who preserved all of his ancient domain, along with what he had by the new apportionment—was the richest prince in Europe.

[651] Henry VIII, contradictory man. He had the Catholics hanged and the Protestants[1] burned. He demanded subsidies from his parliament for war; then he demanded them for peace, which, he said, had cost him more than the most onerous war. He had his marriage with Anne Boleyn

[647]
1. See *Laws*, 22.1, for this theme.

[649]
1. "Put this in the *Romans*" (M.), XXII, 206.

[650]
1. "Put this in the *Universal monarchy*" (M.), XI (*OC*, 3:370; *OC*Volt, 2:350).
2. William I the Conqueror (ca. 1027–87). "His revenues rose to 1061 pounds sterling per day (*Oderici Vitalis liber I*), which in today's measurement comes to 4 or 5 million sterling per year" (M.).

[651]
1. First version: "non-Catholics"

declared null, and at the same time had her condemned for adultery. The whole rest of his life is of the same stamp. {He made Cromwell peer and Knight of the Garter, then had his head cut off for that.}²

[652] An honorable man is a man who orders his life by the principles of his duty. If Cato were born in a monarchy¹ established by Law, he would have been as faithful to his prince as he was to the Republic.

[653] We have discovered a large-scale new world and a small-scale new world, through the telescope and the microscope. We have the printing press to preserve these discoveries, the compass to publicize and disseminate them.

[654] For a long time, I have sought the reason why the Roman soldiers who worked on so many projects, who were so burdened that Marius's soldiers were called mules, did not die when they were made to work—as ours do, as we have seen in the [indecipherable] camp and elsewhere.¹

I think the reason that the Roman soldiers did not die during the work projects is because they worked all the time, whereas ours are do-nothings who never move the soil; for we use sappers or local peasants for that.

Look at what a Roman soldier's duties were.

[655] I said: "If there were no king in England, the English would be less free."¹ This is proven by Holland, where the people have become more enslaved since there is no longer a stadholder;² all the magistrates {of each city}, petty tyrants.

[656] In England, I saw a dog playing cards and answering questions put to it by assembling the letters and arranging the names asked of it— and, so to speak, writing. When I had discovered the signs that this art

---

2. On Henry VIII, see *De la Politique* (*OC*, 3:166); the other references are to Anne Boleyn, queen of England (r. 1533–36), and Thomas Cromwell, count of Essex (ca. 1485–1540) and powerful royal administrator under Henry VIII.

[652]
1. First version: "under a despotic government"

[654]
1. "I've put this in the *Romans*" (M.), II, 34.

[655]
1. See *Notes sur l'Angleterre* (*OC*, 3:292) for a significant elaboration.

2. See *Voyages* (*OC*, 2:1299). There were two periods when no stadholder was in power: 1651–72 and 1702–47. The stadholder began as a provincial functionary, lieutenant of the king of Spain in his province. But the princes of Orange, stadholders of the province of Holland, managed after the secession of 1579 to get themselves recognized as stadholder of all the other provinces, and to preserve this function hereditarily, thus making of the republic a sort of monarchy. See Brèthe, 2:315 n. 7.

depended on, without intending to I became upset; which makes me see clearly how much men love the marvelous.

{The letters were tossed on the ground; the man was talking constantly, and when the dog had its nose on the required letter, he stopped talking.}

[657] England is like the sea, which is agitated by winds that are made not for submerging but for leading to port.

[658] Each man must procure throughout life as many happy moments as possible. For this, one must not flee the affairs of life, for they are often necessary for its pleasures, but one must ensure that they are ancillary to these pleasures, and not vice versa. And one must not get it into one's head to enjoy constant pleasure; this is impossible. But the more one can . . . Thus, when the Sultan is tired of his wives, he must go out of his seraglio. When one has no appetite, one must leave the table and go hunting.

[659] AVARICE. There are often misers who are not bothered by whole-sale expense. It is only retail expense that troubles them. This is because they are creating a work that engages them: forming a gross sum out of petty ones. I compare them to that folly of Marc Antony's soldiers in the Parthian expedition who ate a grass whose effect was to make them arrange all the stones in a pile, after which, they didn't care about it.

[660] I do not like petty honors; beforehand, it was not known what you deserved, but these define you and determine precisely what is done on your behalf.

[661] What I dislike at Versailles is an impotent desire, which you see everywhere, to do great things. I always think of donna Olympia, who said to Maldachini, who was doing what he could: "*Animo! Maldachini. Io ti faro cardinale.*"[1] It seems to me that the late King said to Mansard:[2] "Courage, Mansard! I'm going to give you a hundred thousand pounds in income." As for him, he made his efforts; he put on a wing, then a wing, then another. But if he had put them on all the way to Paris, he still would have made a small thing.

[662] The Queen of England[1] did me the honor of telling me that she thanked God that the English kings' power was limited by law. I said

[661]

1. "Courage, Maldachini! I'm going to make you a cardinal."

2. Jules Hardouin Mansart (1646–1708); the "late king" is Louis XIV.

[662]

1. Caroline of Ansbach (1683–1737), wife of George II. See *pensées* 762 and 1003.

to her: "Madam, Your Majesty is saying something here so splendid that there is not a decent man anywhere who would not give his right arm for all the world's kings to think the same way."

[663] COMMENTATORS. Some have pruned the authors, like the Jesuits. Others have added to them, like Nodot in his *Petronius*.[1]

[664] I believe the inventors of engraving plates paved the way for the invention of printing, or that printing made people think of engravings.

[665] In my travel journal, I have noted the gourmandise or rather the gluttony of the ancient Romans and their surprising sobriety today.[1] I did not indicate the reason, but I believe I have found it: it is the Ancients' frequent use of baths.

In the *Edifying Letters*,[2] volume II (Father Antoine Sepp's letter to Father Guillaume Stinglhaim, on Paraguay), it is said: "The rivers are necessary for Indian habitations, because these peoples, being of a markedly warm temperament, need to bathe several times a day. I have even been surprised to see," he adds, "that when they have eaten too much, a bath was the only remedy that cured them of their indigestion."

You will note that the Romans always bathed before dinner. This appears in Plutarch, I think in the *Life of Cato*. See my Plutarch extract, where I think I put down some passages on this.[3] *Idem*, ancient Greeks.

I believe, moreover, that in the populated countryside around Rome, the air may have become heavier and consequently have less resilience to it.

All one can point to in response is the Turks, who bathe much and eat little. But they smoke constantly, which takes away their appetite.

[666] The same missionary, Antoine Sepp, discovered a stone called *itacura,* strewn with black marks, which separate in the fire and make a very good iron, which he needed for building.

[663]

1. François Nodot, army commissar and author of a translation of Petronius (1693–94; *Catalogue,* 2139), in which he inserted some supposed unedited fragments. See *Spicilège,* 99 n. 2.

[665]

1. In December 1732, Montesquieu had his *Réflexions sur la sobriété des habitants de Rome comparée à l'intempérance des anciens Romains* read at the Bordeaux Academy (*OC,* 3:357–60).

2. The *Lettres édifiantes et curieuses écrites des Missions étrangères par quelques missionnaires de la Compagnie de Jésus* [Edifying and curious letters written from foreign Missions by some missionaries of the Company of Jesus] came out in Paris in thirty-four collections from 1717 to 1776; this one is borrowed from vol. II, p. 414.

3. This extract is lost.

[**667**] The *Maxims* of M. de La Rochefoucauld are the proverbs of the witty.[1]

[**668**] We love our grandchildren better[1] than our sons. This is because we know almost precisely the help we get from our son, the fortune and merit that he has, but we have hopes and sweet illusions for our grandson.

[**669**] Three incredible things among the incredible things:[1] the pure mechanism of animals, passive obedience, Papal infallibility.

[**670**] With despotic monarchs, law is merely the Prince's momentary will.[1]

[**671**] Despotism collapses of its own weight.[1]

[**672**] {Someone said that} medicine changes with cuisine.

[**673–678**] LEFTOVER FROM MY WORK ON THE ROMANS.[1]

[**673**] When one sees a prince whose life is full of splendid deeds tarnished by the historians, it is a sure sign that he found himself in circumstances that made more of an impression on their way of thinking than all his virtues could do. And when another one, despite his vices, is elevated to statuesque levels, it is certain that he found himself in circumstances that flattered the historians' prejudice more than his faults offended their reason.

[**674**][1]

[**675**] The elephants employed in Asian and African armies were good only the first time against a nation; they inspired terror at the outset, but soon a way was found of making them rage against their own army.

[667]
1. François VI, duke of La Rochefoucauld (1613–80); first edition 1665.

[668]
1. First version: "Grandparents love their little ones better"

[669]
1. First version: "There are three things that those who uphold them do not believe."

[670]
1. See *Laws*, 2.1 and 2.4, 18.

[671]
1. See *Laws*, 8.10, and *pensée* 885.

[673–678]
1. These entries were therefore written after 1734, when *Considerations* was published.

[674]
1. Deleted and recopied at *pensée* 713.

[676] The Romans had the good fortune to find a machine that gave them great facility in hooking up with enemy vessels, so that their soldiers, who were better than the Carthaginians', engaged in combat at the outset. And it happened that, although they had no knowledge of maneuver, the coasts, the seasons, or the weather patterns, they ended up having the advantage and the honor, so much so that the consul Lutatius's victory ended the First Punic War.

[677] Dio[1] says that Augustus wanted to have himself called Romulus, but when he learned that the people were afraid that he wanted to make himself king, he desisted.[2]

The earliest Romans did not want a king because they could not put up with a king's power. The Romans of that time did not want a king in order not to put up with his manners. For although Caesar, the Triumvirs, Augustus were real kings, they had kept all the trappings of equality, and their private life contained a kind of opposition to the royal pomp of that time. And if they did not want a king, this meant that they wanted to keep their manners and not pick up those of the African and Asian peoples.[3]

{Florentine simplicity of manners.[4]

Misfortune of Alexander for wanting to make himself worshipped by the Macedonians.

Princes who have changed the form of the State, who have made themselves masters and want to prevent the people from perceiving it, must keep the Republic's simplicity of manners as much as they can, because nothing is more capable of making people think that the State has not changed or has changed little, since they still see the trappings of the republican State. And this is what the grand dukes of Florence did wondrously well; they took over domination, but preserved the Republic's simplicity.}

[678] Augustus set up[1] a five percent income tax. That caused mur-

[677]

1. Montesquieu owned a 1592 edition of Dio Cassius's *Romanorum historiarum* [Roman History] (*Catalogue*, 2828) and used it in the *Considerations* for the imperial period.

2. "Put in the book on the *Laws*" (M.), 19.3.

3. Joseph Dedieu, *Montesquieu et la tradition politique anglaise: les sources anglaises de "l'Esprit des lois"* (Paris: Lecoffre, 1909), 297–98, sees here an echo of a passage in Thomas Gordon's *Discourses upon Tacitus II* (1737), disc. IX, sect. III.

4. On this theme, see *Voyages* (*OC*, 2:1076) and Montesquieu's letter to Mme de Lambert on December 26, 1728 (*OC*, 3:926).

[678]

1. "Put in the *Laws*" (M.), 13.12, though the fact is not mentioned there.

muring among the people and the Senate. He told them to look for some other, less onerous way of raising money. They were confounded, and it was necessary in the end to return to the five percent. It would be easy for princes to rescue their subjects from the despair in which the very name of certain taxes plunges them. The natural weakness of the people and the ignorance in which they are kept make them so sick that there is an inhumanity in not wanting to cure them.

[**679**] [Antoninus Pius having a good heart that led him to the good, an enlightened mind that showed him the best.]

[**680**] Mithridates alone, with great talent and an even greater soul, suspended the fortunes of the Romans.[1] He grew old in his hatred, his thirst for revenge, and his ardor for victory. He was indignant at the blows he received, like a lion looking at his wounds. Always present or ready to reappear, never vanquished except when on the point of vanquishing, constantly constructing new power, he went to look for nations to lead them into combat again. He made them emerge from their deserts and showed them the Romans. He died a king, betrayed by an army that was frightened by the grandeur of his designs and the perils he had conceived.

[**681**] If Charles I, if James II, had lived within a religion that permitted them to kill themselves, would they have accepted so many outrages from Fortune? What a death for the one, and what a life for the other![1]

[**682**] The ancient Romans had five meals. The fifth {took place during the night,}[1] was called *comissatio*. Not everyone had it.

Today in Rome, a dignity that is obtained only in old age inspires in the leaders, and thus in everyone, a general sobriety.[2]

[**683**] The ancient physicians said that the sick never rebelled so much

[680]
1. "Put, for the most part, in the *Romans*" (M.), VII.

[681]
1. "Put in the work on the *Romans*" (M.), XI; this observation was deleted from the third printing onward of the *princeps* edition of *Considerations*.

[682]
1. "I took this fact from the *Ouvrages des Savants* [Works of the learned] 1688–89, art. 12" (M.). *Comissatio* is a late-night revel.
2. See *Réflexions sur la sobriété des habitants de Rome* [Reflections on the sobriety of the inhabitants of Rome] (*OC,* 3:358) and *pensée* 665.

as when they prohibited them from using the baths: "*Artemidorus ait balneum nihil aliud suo aevo fuisse quam transitum ad coenam.*"[1] (Lipsius)

[684] Often a particular taste is evidence of a general taste; the Muses are sisters who touch one another and live in company.

[685] The French are wrong to mix together what the English call *wit, humor, sense, understanding.*[1]

[686] Believe me, *esprit*[1] is often present where it does not shine, and {like those artificial stones} it often seems to shine where it is not present.

[687] It is not surprising to find so much antipathy toward those who have too much self-esteem, because there is not {much} difference between greatly esteeming oneself and greatly disdaining others.

[688] [An empire founded by arms needs to be supported by arms.[1] But just as, when a State is in trouble and confusion, we do not imagine how it can escape, so too, when it is at peace and its power is respected, it does not enter our minds how that can change. Thus, it inevitably neglects the military, from which it thinks it has nothing to hope and much to fear. It even seeks to weaken it, and thereby becomes prey to the first accident.][2]

[689] When one has as a neighbor a State that is in decline, one should take great care to do nothing to hasten its ruin, because this is the most fortunate situation to be in. There is nothing more convenient for a prince than to be near another who receives in his stead all the blows and outrages of fortune.[1]

[690] When a State is wracked by religious disputes, it inevitably hap-

[683]
1. "Artemidorus says that in his time, the bath was nothing more than a transit to the meal," *Oneirocritica* [Interpretation of dreams], 1.66, *De Balneo* [On the baths]. Artemidorus of Ephesus was a Greek writer of the second century. Justus Lipsius (1547–1606) was a humanist whose *De Constantia* (On constancy] did much to shape late Renaissance Neostoicism.

[685]
1. The italicized words appear in English in Montesquieu's manuscript.—HC

[686]
1. Montesquieu seems to suggest that *esprit* is the word that Frenchmen use to cover the four English words cited in *pensée* 685.—HC

[688]
1. "Put in the *Romans*" (M.), XVIII, 171.
2. See the last paragraph of *pensée* 271.

[689]
1. See *Laws*, 9.10, for this text.

pens that the Prince is entirely occupied by them, which makes him subordinate all other points to these, as being less essential.

It happens that, since the Prince almost always becomes an interested party, these disputes fix upon him at the same moment the love and respect of one portion of his subjects and the hatred and contempt of the other.

It happens that, just as the Prince is no longer judged according to his vices or virtues, so too the Prince no longer judges his subjects except by extraneous qualities; that it is no longer personal merit that confers place, nor incapacity that takes it away, but the advantage of being from a certain faction or the misfortune of being from another.

It happens that countless people are disgusted at the government. Now, although the ill will of a part of the citizenry seems impotent because it does not make a flashy impact, this does not stop it from having silent effects that are produced in the shadows and over time; whence arise great revolutions.[1]

It happens that foreign countries are full of citizens expelled from their homeland who reveal its secrets, communicate its advantages, exaggerate its strictness, desire its humiliation—in a word, who seek to make people feel sorry for them in all sorts of ways.

The prudent men who might be able to remedy the evil—being, by their very moderation, soon wearied by contention—bring the indolence of their characters into their actions, whereas the others bring all the activity of their own characters.

To remedy the evil, it is useless to work on the theologians' minds, but not on the people's; since the latter enter passively into the quarrel, they are more capable of being cured.

The attention {paid} to this problem increases it immeasurably, by making people think it is greater than in fact it is; the present questions become frivolous after a while, whereas religion, as a heavenly matter, frees itself from them and still endures.

The theologians have to be reduced to defending their opinions solely through love of truth, by which means they will never go very far.

If you want to accommodate the parties, you give them credibility, by

[690]
1. See also *pensée* 543.

indicating that their manner of thinking is very important—decisive for the State's tranquillity and the Prince's security.

By a contradiction that is natural to the human mind, two parties that you want to unite become, by that fact alone, more inclined toward mutual contention.

We always want to have recourse to the Prince's authority, because we love to give luster to quarrels.

One should not be surprised that many people love these disputes, because they embroil in public affairs all kinds of people whose status, birth, and profession had excluded them.

The people scarcely enter into these contests except for the role that the Prince wants them to take, and at once, everyone becomes a spectator to see what will be the role of such a large actor.

At that time, the Prince puts his subjects in a position to offer him the only resistance they are capable of, which is to follow their opinions.

[691] Those who have read only Holy Scripture constantly derive the origins of all peoples from the Hebrew.

[692] When I read the *Letters of the Kn[ight] of H[e]r . . .* ,[1] I am enraged to see such a great man write like that.

[693] It cannot be said that something has not been done because it is bizarre. Didn't Sejanus used to make sacrifices to himself?[1]

[694] On their rings, the Romans would have figures engraved that they believed had certain special virtues. If they wanted to make themselves loved, they put the Graces there; to make themselves feared, a Gorgon.[1] To shelter themselves from accidents, they wore the figure of the Emperor. Thus, they took one of the great examples on earth of Fortune's inconstancy, and made it a model or even a cause of its immutability.[2]

[695] The Asians regard female chastity as mere powerlessness to falter.

[692]
1. This was a youthful work of Fontenelle, published in 1683, which narrates the adventures of a knight whose gallantry is most often highly stylized and sometimes also ingenious.

[693]
1. Lucius Aelius Sejanus, favorite and minister to Tiberius (ca. 18 B.C.–A.D. 31).

[694]
1. The Gorgons were mythic pre-Olympian monsters.
2. "Look into what I have put in my account of Italy" (M.); cf. *Voyages* (*OC,* 2:1112–13).

[696] Fear adds to our pains, just as desires add to our pleasures.

[697] [It used to be said[1] {of Caligula} that there has never been a better slave or a more wicked master. This is natural; the same mental disposition that makes us impressed by the unlimited power of whoever commands also makes us impressed by it when we ourselves command.]

[698] Two masterpieces: Caesar's death in Plutarch, Nero's in Suetonius. In the first, you begin by pitying the conspirators, whom you see in danger, and then Caesar, whom you see assassinated. In Nero's, you are surprised to see him obliged by degrees to kill himself without any constraining cause, and yet, in such a way that he cannot avoid it.[1]

[699] What made the Goths who invaded the Roman Empire establish republican government is that they were not aware of the idea of any other.[1] And if, by chance, a prince had taken it into his head in those days to talk about unlimited authority and despotic power, he would have made his whole army laugh, and he would have been viewed as insane.

[700] What produces grievous divisions in the world is sovereign authority, on the one hand, and the force of desperation, on the other.

[701] The king of Prussia, who absolutely wants to resemble the king of Sweden,[1] is like the kings who succeeded Alexander {whom Plutarch talks about, *Life of Pyrrhus*}, who sought to imitate him in his clothes, his guards, his way of tilting his neck, and his manner of speaking pompously, but did not imitate him in his impetuosity and his movement in battle.

[702] The English are not like Marius, who did not want to learn Greek, since it was a language of those who had not been able to defend their liberty.

[703] I said: "Old books are for authors; new ones, for readers."

[704] You find in Corneille's *Dict[ionary]*,[1] at the word *sclavon: Sclavon*

[697]
1. "Put in the *Romans*" (M.), XV, 135; Caligula was emperor (from 37 to 41).

[698]
1. Cf. *pensée* 607.—HC

[699]
1. See *Universal monarchy,* X (*OC,* 3:369; *OC* Volt, 2:349).

[701]
1. Frederick William I of Prussia. (r. 1713–40); Charles IX of Sweden (r. 1697–1718).

[704]
1. Thomas Corneille (1625–1709), *Le Dictionnaire universel, géographique et historique,* in 3 volumes (1708; *Catalogue,* 2468).

means glory, a name that those peoples took because of their conquests; whence it arises that most of their family names end in *slaw: Stanislaw, Wenceslaw, Boleslaw.*

[705] If Hannibal had died immediately after the battle of Cannae, who wouldn't have said that without his death, Rome would have been ruined?[1] There is often an unknown force within States.

[706] In the book *Origo Gentis Romanae* {thought to be by Aurelius Victor},[1] the Latins, colonies of Alba Longa formed under the reign of Latinus Sylvius:[2] Praeneste, Tibur, Gabii, Tusculum, Cora, Pometia, Locri, Crustumium, Cameria, Bovillae, *caeteraque oppida circumquaque.*[3]

However, not all of these cities were of the Latin nation. Cora and Pometia were from the league of the Volsci. These cities often changed sides. Thus, Titus-Livy (1st decade, book II) distinguishes the ancient Latins from those who had entered into the alliance of these peoples. Crustumerium at first, in the league of the Sabines; then, in that of the Latins.

[707] The Catilinian conspiracy is only famous because of the number of villains who formed it and the great figures who sought to encourage it. For otherwise, it was an ill-conceived, ill-digested scheme, less the effect of ambition than of impotence and desperation.[1]

[708] [Men ought to be convinced of the happiness they are overlooking at the very time they are enjoying it.][1]

[709] The more the poem *The League* seems to be *The Aeneid,* the less it is.[1]

[710] There are men who go to the ends of the earth to convert, and at

[705]
1. Because Hannibal had defeated the Romans there.—HC

[706]
1. *Origin of the Roman Race*, XVII.6; Aurelius Victor, Latin historian of African origin, late fourth century (*Catalogue*, 2819a).
2. King of Latium and eponymous hero of the Latins.
3. "And other fortified places in the vicinity."

[707]
1. See *pensée* 1669.—HC

[708]
1. See *pensée* 31.

[709]
1. Voltaire's *Henriade* appeared in 1723 under the title *La ligue, ou henri le grand* [The league, or Henry the great].

first think only of converting princes. They want to submit the grandeur of kings to God because they are dazzled by it themselves. But he does not accept their offerings, and since he does not want worldly outlooks in the establishment of a religion made to offer different ones, he expels them from Japan and China. And content with the triumph of a few martyrs, he finds his glory more in the destruction of their work than he would have in its fulfillment.[1]

[711] A thought by Plutarch, in the *Life of Nicias:* that Plato, in acknowledging a superior mind that governs the world, silenced the slanderers, who regarded as atheists all those who subscribed to the stars' regular movement and explained celestial phenomena scientifically, who were called *meteorologues.*[1]

[712] M. Sainte-Aulaire said it well:[1] "We say: 'We cannot understand how matter thinks; thus, we have a soul different from matter.'[2] Thus, from our ignorance we derive a reason to make ourselves a substance more perfect than matter."

[713] If a corporate body that has a great reputation in the world were ever—entirely at its leisure—to write our modern history, I believe the princes who have entrusted their consciences and their affairs to them would loom very large, and the others very small.[1]

[714] That soldiers' custom[1] of electing emperors had its origins in Republican times. When a general had performed some splendid deed, his soldiers would proclaim him emperor. This was only an honorific title.[2] But when this name entailed power, the armies continued to confer it, and

[710]
1. This entry is a reference to the strategy and fate of the Jesuits.—HC

[711]
1. See also *pensée* 969, first paragraph.—HC

[712]
1. François-Joseph Beaupoil de Saint-Aulaire (1643–1742), member of the French Academy.
2. First version: "thus, our soul is thought, is a different substance."

[713]
1. "I had put this in the *Romans,* and I've removed it" (M.); cf. *pensée* 674. The reference is doubtless to the Jesuits.

[714]
1. "I've also removed this" (M.) from the *Considerations.*
2. "These two titles did not stop being still distinguished, for when an emperor had performed some splendid deed, his soldiers still saluted him as *Imperator* (marginal note)" (M.).

what happened is what we always see: that names make things and govern the world.

[715] One thing I cannot reconcile with the enlightenment of this age is the Jesuits' authority.

[716] In the acts of dissolution for the marriage of Louis XII and Queen Claude, Saint-Hyacinthe has found a petition in which it was revealed that the marriage was null because he had not slept *nudus cum nuda*,[1] but with a shirt on.[2] I say this is evidence that back then people slept that way. Our corruption has increased our modesty. The early times had a simplicity by which the whole family and the unmarried daughters slept with their father and mother in the same bed.[3]

[717] The books of the casuists of old were written because the tribunals in Spain and Italy—warm countries, where people like refined tastes—were full of those cases, and there was no knowledge of natural science. Thus, a release had to be found in scholasticism, and that science was bound to be the occupation of the bright people. (Fontenelle)

[718] I am not surprised by the sweet delights found at Court and the impossibility of changing one's way of life. You are all together at every moment. A hundred little things to amuse or engage you, and to enter into the petty ambition you have conceived; moreover, no more part in that lottery made of the Prince's graces bestowed upon the Nation; the pleasure of seeing that, whatever petty post you may hold, it is envied; in a word, this active life cannot be replaced by repose.

[719] I think we are jealous from a secret pain at others' pleasure when we are neither its cause nor its object;[1] or from a certain modesty, that is, the shame of our imperfections which has obliged us to hide certain things from sight—whence it happens that a husband has regarded his wife's se-

[716]
1. "Naked man with naked woman"—HC
2. Hyacinthe Cordonnier, called Thémiseul de Saint-Hyacinthe (1684–1746), was a journalist. Louis XII (1498–1515) had married Jeanne de Valois, disgraced daughter of Louis XI, in 1476; the annulment of his marriage was recognized by the pope, and he married Anne of Brittany. Claude de France (1499–1524) was the daughter of Louis XII and Anne of Brittany, and wife of Francis I.
3. "Look at my remark in my Ammianus Marcellinus extract" (M.). This extract is lost, but see *Considerations,* XVII and XVIII, for Montesquieu's use of Ammianus Marcellinus (*Catalogue,* 2812).

[719]
1. "I've put something approaching this in chapter XIV of the book on the *Laws,* on domestic servitude" (M.). See, in fact, *Laws,* 16.13, although nothing there corresponds directly to the content of this *pensée.*

crets as his own; or by an awareness that each of us has of the limited extent of the passions, too easily satisfied, and of that imbecility of nature by which the heart divided between two persons gives itself whole to one or disengages from both; or because of a property granted to the husband in the children born from a certain woman, a property whose uncertainty one seeks to reduce as much as possible; or from a certain fear of the ridicule that the jokers of all nations have heaped onto this matter, since everyone is always happy to bring up a passion which, once evoked in one man, has its effect on all others; (Speak about vengeance, and you will touch only the one who is steeped in an affront he has received. Everyone else will be like ice. But speak about love, and you will find all hearts open and all ears attentive;) or, finally, by a certain desire to be loved by persons that one loves, which is in the substance of the soul—that is, in its vanity—and is no different from the desire we have to be esteemed by everyone, especially by those who have the closest relation to us. A Frenchman likes to be esteemed more in Germany than in Japan, more in France than in Germany. And since nothing concerns us more intimately than the persons we love, it is therefore by them that we most wish to be loved.[2]

[720] Mathematical propositions are received as true because no one has an interest in their being false. And when someone has had such an interest, that is, when someone, by doubting them, has wanted to make himself head of a faction and, in overturning them, drag down all other truths, he has been doubted: witness Pyrrho.[1]

[721] When someone asks me if a word is French, I can answer. When someone asks me if the diction is good, I cannot answer, unless it violates good grammar. I cannot know the circumstance in which it will be good, nor the use that a smart man will be able to make of it. For in his works, a smart man is a creator of diction, of turns of phrase and concepts. He dresses his thought according to his fashion, forms it, and creates it by manners of speaking that are removed from the vulgar, but that do not appear to have been used for the purpose of being removed from the vulgar. A man who writes well writes not the way people have written, but the way he writes, and it is often in speaking poorly that he speaks well.

2. See *pensées* 506, 507, 733, and 757.

[720]
1. Pyrrho of Elis (ca. 360–ca. 270 B.C.), Greek philosopher and founder of the skeptical school known as Pyrrhonism.

[**722**] I know of a man {very ignorant} who, if he had employed in study the time and trouble necessary to pass for being learned, would be one of the most learned men in Europe.

[**723**] It was the Muslims (Moors of Spain) who brought the sciences to the West. Since that time, they have never wanted to take up again what they gave us.

Under the twenty-seventh Caliph, Al Mamoun, the Arabs began to study the Greek texts, and founded numerous academies in Africa. {I believe the destruction of the Caliphate has destroyed the sciences in the Muslim world.}

[**724**] THE VIRGILIAN FATES. Nothing better proves the Romans' great respect for Virgil. The first words of his that they would read were regarded as an oracle: *Sortes Virgilinae.*[1]

[**725**] A bad law always obliges the legislator to pass many others—often very bad as well—in order to avoid the bad effects, or at least fulfill the purpose, of the first one.

[**726**] The constancy of the Grand Alliance against France is a practically unheard of thing in history, and yet it did not really have the effect that might have been expected from such a success, which was to humiliate France.[1]

[**727**] {Often} those who have no religion do not want to be obliged to change the religion they would have if they had one, because they feel that this is an act of power that should not be exercised against them. The spirit of contradiction makes them find a pleasure in contradicting—that is to say, a good. Besides, they feel that life and property are no more their own than their religion or their manner of thinking, and that whoever can take away the one can even more easily take away the other.

[**728**] When I see Louis XIV—guided by the Jesuits—sending his enemies subjects, soldiers, merchants, workers, his commerce, and expelling the Huguenots,[1] I have more pity for him than for the Huguenots.[2]

[724]
1. "The Virgilian Fates."—HC

[726]
1. On the Grand Alliance, see *pensée* 562.—HC

[728]
1. First version: "the protestants"; cf. *pensée* 2023, dated October 20, 1729.
2. The reference is to the Revocation of the Edict of Nantes (1598) in 1685; see also *pensée* 954.

[729] Those ceremonies of the Egyptians and other peoples—of carrying in procession some human limbs or some testicles—were contrary to modesty, but they were not absolutely contrary to good sense. Peoples who did not believe in the creation thought that generation was the origin of everything, and they worshipped that generative faculty of nature that was to be their God. Thus, Priapus was set up in the gardens, as the God[1] of the fertility of plants and of all nature.

[730] The Jesuits defend a good cause, Molinism, through quite bad means.[1]

[731] The Ancients must have had a greater attachment to their Country than we do, for they were always buried with their Country. Was their city captured? They were made slaves or killed. As for us, all we do is change princes.

[732] [When Hannibal approached Rome, the Republic substantially inflated the currency.]

[733] We like to be loved and esteemed by persons who are present, because they make their love or esteem felt more often, and, so to speak, at every moment, an advantage we do not get from that of distant folks.

[734] Princes change the meanings of words: the King of Sweden, Charles XII, in the cruelest act of our age, the condemnation of Patkul,[1] took the title *very clement prince.*

[735] Sentences should not be too cruel, so that men are not accustomed to be affected only by the fear of cruel punishments. The king of Persia,[1] the most humane of all princes, who was dethroned by the Aguans, saw that his goodness was abused, because his nation was not accustomed to such mildness.

[729]
   1. First version: "as the symbol"; Priapus was the son of Dionysus, god of fecundity, guardian especially of orchards and vineyards.

[730]
   1. Molinism is a theological hypothesis by which the Jesuit Luis Molina (1535–1601), in his 1588 *De liberi arbitrii* [On freedom of the will], attempts to reconcile human free will with divine providence and the necessity of grace.

[734]
   1. See *pensée* 641.

[735]
   1. Hussein I, shah of Persia (1694–1722); after the seizure of Ispahan by the Afghan army of Mir Mahmud, he was dethroned and assassinated.

[**736**] The King of Sweden, defeated, still said of the Muscovites: "But the Muscovites were able to become men!"[1]

[**737**] A general corruption has spread everywhere. Those who approach princes make incessant demands. The gifts they come away with serve only to establish a luxury that those are obliged to accept who, lacking credit in the money markets or unconcerned about getting credit, seek to live within the means of their ancestral possessions.[1]

[**738**] It is no longer a prudent dispenser of public revenue who is called a {*great*} *minister,* but only someone who has ingenuity and what are called *expedients.*

[**739**] We have no minister, no functionary with a thousand-crown salary who is so petty that he does not have more public business than the grand viziers of the East who are at the head of the military, justice, and finances of the Empire.

[**740**] We can never have order in our finances, because we always know we are going to do something, but never what we are going to do.

[**741**] If I knew something that was useful to me and harmful to my family, I would banish it from my mind. If I knew something useful to my family but not to my Country, I would seek to forget it. If I knew something useful to my Country and harmful to Europe, or else useful to Europe and harmful to the human race, I would regard it as a crime.[1]

[**742**] Cardinal Richelieu's maxim to negotiate constantly, that maxim so fit for increasing mistrust among princes, has become more and more established. The treaties that result, and the clauses that are put in them {to foresee what never happens and to never foresee what does happen}, only multiply the occasions for rupture, just as the multiplicity of laws increases the number of trials among citizens.[1]

[736]
1. The reference is to Charles XII, defeated by Peter the Great in the Great Northern War (1700–1721).—HC

[737]
1. On luxury, see *Laws,* bk 7.

[741]
1. In *pensée* 350 there is a first draft of this *pensée* which, according to Shackleton, belongs to the *Treatise on duties,* X, "Duties of man." Montesquieu takes it up again in *Histoire véritable* [True history] (*OC,* 3:335).

[742]
1. See *pensée* 549.—HC

[743] Bad faith has become so reinforced in politics that it cannot be said that all the treaties continually being signed today have the slightest meaning.

[744] King Charles XII of Sweden could be compared to that cyclops from the myth, who had very great strength but was blind.

The same {king}, after having long misused his successes, was less than a man in adversity—that is, in that state of life when it is essential to be more than a man.

The same, always in the marvelous, never in the real; enormous, but not great.

[745] Louis XIV bought Dunkirk for four million.[1] He has scarcely ever paid a better price for a fortress that he has acquired.

[746] Look into France's proportion of troops to revenues, comparing it with the King of Prussia's ratio of troops and revenues.

[747] Great conquests, all in haste, are rather the work of rashness than of prudence, and are designed less for the monarchs of great States than for adventurers.

[748] What made Roman fortunes unalterable is that, sure of their superiority in the military arts, they made offensive wars with few troops and employed prodigious forces on the defensive.

[749] We are not in those warm climates where men and animals, virtually without needs, traverse boundless territories and leave one monarchy to go and attack another. Our conquests take a long time, and before they have been completed, there is always a certain reaction that puts the conqueror back in the situation from which he started.

[750] Asia was not as strong in the past as Europe is today;[1] she was hardly any stronger in the past when, in each state, the only concern was to secure the prince's place of residence. In the ancient histories, therefore, one finds expeditions but rarely wars, invasions rather than conquests.[2]

---

[745]
1. Louis XIV had Dunkirk ceded to France by the treaty of October 27, 1662.

[750]
1. First version: "Asia is not as strong as Europe by a long shot. Kandahar is the only barrier between the Mughal and Persia; Baghdad between Persia and the Turks; Azov between the Turks and Muscovites; and this part of the world"—HC
2. See *pensée* 300, first paragraph.—HC

[**751**] LIBERTY.[1] We must put these words *throne* and *senate* {or *estates*} out of our heads; that is not what characterizes liberty. There are points and moments of liberty in monarchies.

No one free in Turkey, not even the Prince.[2]

[No one free in Venice,[3] not even . . .]

In Venice, the senators free politically, but not civilly.

The Genoese aristocracy equal to that of the Algiers army.[4]

Holland is no longer free ever since it no longer has a stadholder.[5]

In Holland, the magistrates are free. In England, they are slaves as magistrates and free as citizens.

It is a bad thing when a magistrate is free as a magistrate, and this always happens if there is not some ordering and moderating power.

In England, the man who is being prosecuted, and who will be hanged the next day, is freer than any citizen in the rest of Europe.

In Spain, the Clergy free,[6] the people in a strange slavery.

Any overly small republic cannot be called free: *libertas non sua vi nixa.*[7]

In Rome, liberty of the ecclesiastics and of foreigners; mild though deficient government.

[**752**] CHARLEMAGNE. Under him, the Northern peoples were subdued, and the river flowed back toward its source.

[**753**] During the period of Charlemagne's first successors, there were no regular troops, no garrisons were put in the cities, and there were no citadels, so it was impossible to maintain fidelity in a distant nation, as the example of the Saxons and the Italians made clear.

[**754**] Ecclesiastics have an interest in keeping the people in ignorance; otherwise, since the Gospel is simple, people would say to them: "We know that {just} as well as you do."

[751]

1. Some commentators see this entry as the first trace of a larger essay on liberty from which the famous chapter on the English constitution, *Laws*, 11.6, is borrowed.

2. See *PL*, LXXX, 136.

3. On Venice, see Montesquieu's letter to Berwick of September 15, 1727 (*OC*, 3:912), and his *Voyages* (*OC*, 2:981).

4. See *Lettre sur Gênes* (*OC*, 2:1303–9).

5. See *pensée* 655 n. 2, on the stadholder.

6. First version: "the king and the clergy free"

7. "Liberty is not supported by its own strength"; this may be a reworking of Tacitus, *Annals,* XIII.19, also cited by Machiavelli, *The Prince*, ch. 13.—HC

[755]   A prince who makes himself head of a faction resembles a man who would cut off one arm so that all the nourishment goes to the other.

[756]   It is a bad maxim to make dictionaries from living languages; this limits them too much. All words that are not in there are considered improper, foreign or out of use. It is the Academy itself that has brought forth the *neological satires*,[1] or has caused them to be.

[757]   Jealousy seems to me necessary in warm countries, liberty in cold climes. Here is a natural reason for it.[1]

It is certain that women are nubile in warm climates at eight, ten, twelve years of age, and are immediately old; that is, that childhood and marriage are almost always together. Now since it is reason that provides control, and since reason is almost never present together with attractive charms, which exercise a still stronger control, women are necessarily subordinated. Now reason cannot enable them to regain in their old age the power they lost when they had their charms and beauty. In warm countries, in a word, women are rational only when they are old, and they are beautiful only when they are not rational. {Thus, they have never been able to assume a certain influence over men, and their rapid aging had inevitably to introduce polygamy.}

In cold countries, women marry at the age when their reason is strongest, and their attractions are better preserved, so that their husbands' aging follows their own. The use of strong drinks, which brings with it intemperance among the men, usually gives even women an advantage in reason over them. There are countries in which every night, the entire nation is drunk. Women, who have in this regard a natural reserve, because they always have to defend themselves, have therefore great advantages over men; since the latter also have their advantages, there results this equality.

That is why the Roman law that permits only one wife, which became a Christian law, conforms to the nature of the European climate but not to the nature of the Asian climate. And that is why Islam has found it so easy to become established in Asia and so difficult in Europe, why Christianity

[756]

1. Pierre-François Guyot Desfontaines, *Dictionnaire néologique* (1726); Montesquieu owned the 1731 edition (*Catalogue*, 1857); his friend Pierre Bel, councilor in the Bordeaux Parlement, was a collaborator.

[757]

1. "Put in the *Laws*" (M.), 16.2, a chapter which draws on this fragment of long standing and is textually similar but not identical. See Brèthe, 2:423 n. 1b, and, in this volume, *pensées* 719 and 2248.

has been maintained in Europe and destroyed in Asia, why the Muslims are making so much progress in China and the Christians so little.

Nature, which has not given men such attractions, has given them no limit but that of their strength and their reason. She has given women attractions; their limit is the end of their attractions. {For Eastern women, youth is at the beginning of their life cycle, whereas for our women youth is in the middle.} That is why it was inevitable for the plurality of wives to be established, as a thing in some sense necessary. On the other hand, if it had not been established, the law of a single wife would have given women a tremendous advantage, given the incontinence produced by the climate.

[**758**] The Germans are too indolent to be so expert at public business.[1] That is why they are less involved in it. They leave most things as they are. In Vienna, a government minister who has worked two hours in the morning goes and has dinner and plays the rest of the day. Public business remains in the ordinary tribunals, and no one dreams of either removing it from them or disturbing them. Unhappy vivacity of our nation, which sets the fashion even in financial schemes, council resolutions, and provincial administration! We dislike everything that is established, and a minister who does nothing is regarded as a bad minister.

[**759**] Great joy always has one of two effects: when it does not make others gay, it saddens them, as something out of place. The great secret is to parcel out only the convenient dose; otherwise, one is very often sadly gay. To be likeable, you must be able to lend your character to the occasion; when it does not put you on track, it derails you.

Likewise with constant joy: if I am sad, the joy of others afflicts me, because it pulls me away from the pleasure I get by indulging my sadness and thus does me violence, which is a type of pain.

[**760**] It is probable that what is called *heroic valor* is going to be lost in Europe. Our philosophy, the end of chivalry, indifference in belonging to one master or another for our fortunes. In the past, it was a matter of one's destruction, being sold into slavery, losing one's family, one's city, one's wife, one's children.

[**761**] That spirit of glory and valor is being lost little by little among

[758]
1. On the Germans, see the similar comment in *Voyages* (*OC*, 2:1233).

us. Philosophy has gained ground. The former ideas of heroism and the chivalric romances have been lost. Civil offices are filled by men who have wealth, and military offices are discredited by men who have nothing. In short, it is almost everywhere a matter of indifference for one's fortunes to belong to one master or another, whereas in the past a defeat or your city's capture was linked to destruction—it was a question of being sold into slavery, of losing one's city, one's gods, one's wife, and one's children. The establishment of commerce in public funds; the immense gifts of princes, which enable an enormous number of people to live in idleness and obtain esteem by their very idleness, that is, by their charm; indifference toward the afterlife, which entails flabbiness in this life, and makes us unfeeling and incapable of anything that takes effort; fewer occasions to distinguish ourselves; a certain methodical way of taking cities and engaging in battle—being merely a question of making a breach and surrendering once it is made; all of war consisting more in the technique than in the personal qualities of those who fight it—at each siege, the number of soldiers to be sacrificed is known in advance; the nobility no longer fight as a corps.[1]

[762] TO THE QUEEN OF ENGLAND.[1] "Your largeness of mind is so renowned in Europe that it seems no longer permissible to praise it.

"It is that happy talent, that seductive charm, that enables you to communicate with your subjects without losing anything of your rank and without confounding social conditions.

"You reign over a great people. Heaven, which has granted you the reign over so many realms, has granted none of your subjects the happiness you enjoy in your family."

[763] TO THE KING.[1] "Most amb[assadors] come with hidden designs and secret negotiations. As for me, I can reveal to Your Majesty all my instructions: I come only to cultivate friendship."

[764] I never judge men by what they have or have not done as a re-

---

[761]
  1. This *pensée*, the first written by secretary E, can thus be dated to early 1734.

[762]
  1. Written in English in Montesquieu's hand; Caroline, daughter of Johann-Frederick, Margrave of Brandenburg-Anspach, married George II in 1705. See *pensée* 662.

[763]
  1. Montesquieu puts these words in English; George II (1683–1760), George Augustus, Duke of Brunswick-Lüneburg (Hanover; r. 1727–60).

sult of the prejudices of their times.[1] Most great men have been subject to them. The problem is when they have added their own. For most of the time, I might add, they have not seen the prejudices of their times, because they have not wanted to see them. Who are the fools who claim to be smarter than the great men who have been subject to them? I do not judge Saint Louis by his crusades. It is indifferent to me that M. Arnaud was a Jansenist, if he reasoned well about Jansenism.[2] Nor do I respect a man because he has followed them; I set no store by Fabricius's poverty or Regulus's return (I speak only of his return), but I do set store by Plato's and Socrates' constancy and virtue.[3]

[765] I have no more esteem for a man who has devoted himself to one science than for someone who has devoted himself to another, if both have contributed intelligence and good sense to them equally. All the sciences are good and they assist one another. Molière's dancing master and master of arms are the only ones I know who argue about the dignity and preferability of their arts.[1]

I say all this against the geometers.

What shocks me about geometry and strips it of all sublimity in my eyes is that it's a family affair, and that geometers go from father to son. How many Bernoullis have we seen?[2]

[766] A prince wrote this letter: "I declare that you have become my friend. You have such great talent for fixing my wig and my stockings that I like you at the same time that I admire you. You never tell me anything but pleasant things, whereas those beastly ministers never have anything but impertinent things to tell me. I would do very well to entrust my affairs to your care. My ministers will report to you, you will report to me."

[767] ENGLISH. If I am asked which prejudices they have, I would in truth not know which to answer: neither war, nor birth, nor dignities, nor

[764]

1. See also *pensées* 911 and 1302 (section on Saint Louis).—HC

2. Antoine Arnauld (1612–94), Jansenist theologian and coauthor, with Pierre Nicole, of the well-regarded Port-Royal *Logic*.

3. Caius Fabricius, consul (282–278 B.C.), symbol of the simplicity and disinterestedness of the early Romans; on Regulus, see *pensée* 225.

[765]

1. In *Le Bourgeois Gentilhomme*, act 2, sc. 2.—HC

2. Bernoulli, family of mathematicians from Anvers who went into exile in Basel in the late sixteenth century to escape from the persecution of the duke of Alba.

men who get lucky,[1] nor the frenzy over ministerial favor. They want men to be men. They set store by the Duke of Marlborough, Lord Cobham, the Duke of Argyll, because they are men.[2] They respect only two things: wealth and personal merit.[3]

They have more pride than vanity; a neighboring nation has more vanity than pride.

When a foreigner is received there at the level of citizen, it is much better. No one mistrusts him, because his interests are not mingled with anyone else. They disdain you like mud, because they think you esteem only yourself.

They neither love nor hate their kings, but they do fear them or disdain them.

[**768**] We praise people in proportion to the esteem they have for us.

[**769**] It is surprising that the people so strongly cherish republican government, but that so few nations have it; that men so strongly hate violence, but that so many nations are governed by violence.

[**770**] They are the eternal monument of a friendship that touches me more than {all} the renown I might get from my writings.[1]

[**771**] In the last revolution in Constantinople, when the new emperor saw that the rebel Janissaries had committed enough outrages to make themselves odious, he exterminated and punished them.

[**772**] Frenchmen are agreeable, communicative, varied, abandon themselves in their discourse. They go out, walk, run, and are always on the go until they drop.

[**773**] On the fragments of Cicero's book *Of the Republic,* I said, "We owe many of these fragments to Nonius, who, in giving us the words, has preserved the things."[1]

---

[767]
   1. *Hommes à bonne fortune;* which may refer here to winning the favors of women.—HC
   2. Richard Temple, viscount Cobham (1669–1749), and John Campbell, duke of Argyll (1678–1743); on Marlborough, see *pensées* 300, 562, 593, 635, and 1648.
   3. See *Laws,* 19.27, 331, but also *Notes sur l'Angleterre* (*OC,* 3:286).

[770]
   1. See *pensées* 484, 1655, and 1820.—HC

[773]
   1. Nonius Marcellus, Latin grammarian of the early fourth century and author of *De proprietate sermonum* (*Catalogue,* 1932). On Cicero, see Montesquieu's *Discours sur Cicéron,* written ca. 1709 (*OC,* 3:15).

I am naturally curious about all fragments from the works of ancient authors, just as one likes to find the debris from shipwrecks that the sea has left on the beach.

Cicero, in my view, is one of the great minds that has ever existed: a soul always beautiful when it was not weak.

[774] For about a century, Sweden has done great things.[1] But her resources are easily exhausted; poverty prevents her from making up her losses. Her neighbors fear her, and her declared enemies are always encouraged by secret enemies.

She is fit only for serving in the designs of some great State. But if she has some success, she is soon halted by the very power that is making her act.

Charles XII, who employed only his own forces, determined his fall by forming designs that could only be executed through a long war, something of which his realm was not capable.

It was not an empire in decline that he undertook to overthrow, but an emerging empire. The Muscovites used the war he was waging against them as a school. With each defeat, they were approaching victory, and while losing abroad, they were learning to defend themselves at home.

Charles thought he was master of the world in Poland's deserts, where he was wandering around and where Sweden was stretched rather thin, while his main enemy was fortifying himself against him, tightening up his realm, establishing himself on the Baltic Sea, destroying or taking Livonia.

Sweden resembled a river whose waters are cut off at the source and diverted in its course.

It was not Poltava that ruined the King of Sweden; if he had not been destroyed in that place, he would have been in another. Accidents of fortune are easily repaired; accidents in the nature of things are not repaired.

But neither nature nor fortune was ever as strong against him as he was himself.

He did not follow the actual arrangement of things, but a certain model he had picked up; and he followed it very badly, too. He was not Alexander; but he would have been Alexander's best soldier.

[774]
1. "Put in book X of the *Laws*" (M.), 10.13, 147.

Alexander's plan only succeeded because he was sensible.

The Persians' failure in their invasions of Greece, the conquests made by Agesilaus, and the retreat of the Ten Thousand had made perfectly clear the Greeks' superiority in their manner of waging combat and in their types of arms, and it was well known that the Persians were incorrigible.[2]

They could no longer disturb Greece because of her divisions. At that time, she was united under a leader who could have had no better means of holding her together than to dazzle her with the destruction of her eternal enemies and the expectation of Asian conquest.

An empire cultivated by the most industrious nation in the world, which worked the lands because of religious principle and was fertile and abundant in all things, gave its enemy all sorts of means of subsistence.

One could reckon by the pride of those kings, always vainly mortified by their defeats, that they would precipitate their fall by still giving battle, and that flattery would never permit them to doubt their grandeur.

Not only was the plan wise, but it was wisely executed. Alexander, in the rapidity of his actions, in the fire of his passions {themselves}, had, if I dare use this term, a sally of reason that guided him, and that those who have wanted to write a novel out of his story, and whose minds were more vitiated than his own, have not been able to hide.

[775] Descartes taught those who came after him to discover his very errors.

I compare him to Timoleon, who used to say, "I am delighted that by means of me, you have obtained the freedom to oppose my desires."[1]

[776] What makes commercial people more independent is that their goods are further from the sovereign's reach.

[777] In his *History,* Pufendorf[1] says that, in States where the citizens are enclosed in a city, the people are more suited for aristocracy and de-

2. Agesilaus, King of Sparta (r. 400–360 B.C.); the retreat of the ten thousand Greek mercenaries after their defeat at Cunaxa (401 B.C.) and the death of Cyrus the Younger.

[775]
1. Timoleon, Greek statesman, general, and reformer of Syracuse during the wars with Carthage (ca. 410–ca. 336 B.C.).

[777]
1. Samuel Pufendorf (1632–94), German historian, jurist, and leading natural-law philosopher. Montesquieu owned the French edition of *De jure naturae et gentium* [Of the law of nature and nations], translated into French with influential commentary by Jean Barbeyrac in 1708 (*Catalogue,* 801), as well as Barbeyrac's 1708 translation of *De officio hominis et civis* [The whole duty of man], Claude Rouxel's 1710 French translation of Pufendorf's German work *Einleitung zu der historie der*

mocracy.[2] For if someone governs a city tyrannically, the people can unite against him in an instant, whereas in dispersed countries, they cannot unite. {I would add that since Sweden has not been subjugated like Muscovy, Hungary, Poland, Bohemia, Silesia, and other German territories close to the Baltic Sea, her peasants have not been made slaves. (Page 269)} I would offer another reason. When whoever has only one city is expelled by his subjects, the trial is over. When he has several cities and provinces and is expelled from one city, the enterprise has just begun. And it is a bad situation in the kingdom of Naples, where almost half the kingdom is in the City. (Page 245)

In Sweden, says Pufendorf, where there are few cities, the peasants attend the estates, because they are the body of the nation rather than the bourgeoisie. They attend solely to give their consent to taxes.

[**778**] The Mohammedan tradition that contains the reason why Mohammed prohibited the use of wine is no more true than is customary with other popular traditions.[1] Diodorus, on the public business of Demetrius, says the Arabs had always drunk water.[2] And in Niger's time, the Romans, after being defeated by the Arabs, said: "We have no wine; we cannot do battle; *Erubescite, inquit Imperator, qui vos vincunt aquam bibunt.*"[3] This should be examined in Diodorus.

[**779**] The establishment of monarchies produces politeness. But works of the mind appear only at the beginning of monarchies, since the general corruption affects even that part.[1]

[**780**] The English are busy; they don't have time to be polite.[1]

---

vornehmsten Reiche und Staaten in Europa [An introduction to the history of Europe's leading kingdoms and states], and the 1708 edition of Pufendorf's earlier work *Severini de Monzambano, de statu imperii germanici* [The present state of Germany] (*Catalogue,* 802, 2426, 2709, and 3107).

2. "Put in the *Laws*" (M.), 8.16.

[**778**]
1. See *Laws,* 14.10, 239.
2. Diodorus of Sicily, XIX, 97; Demetrius of Phalerus (ca. 350–ca. 283 B.C.), Athenian orator and statesman.
3. "'Blush,' says the commander, 'those who are conquering you drink water.'" Aelius Spartianus, *Life of Pescennius Niger,* VII, Roman historian in Diocletian's time; see *Catalogue,* 2819a, 2820, and 2842–44.

[**779**]
1. See *Laws,* 4.2, 32.

[**780**]
1. See *Laws,* 19.27, 331, and *Notes sur l'Angleterre* (*OC,* 3:292) on this theme.

[**781**] THE DIFFERENCE BETWEEN THE ENGLISH AND THE FRENCH. The English get along with their inferiors but cannot stand their superiors. We are accommodating to our superiors but insufferable to our inferiors.

[**782**] In the *Amsterdam Gazette* for February 12, 1734, which I have inserted into my *Spicilège,* there is a letter from the Grand Vizier to Prince Eugene on Polish affairs,[1] in which, speaking of the late king Augustus II, he states: "Now their king, surnamed *Nal-Kyran,* being deceased for a long time already"; on which, I say let someone go seek the {true} names of the Babylonian and Assyrian kings, since among the Turks, King Augustus {their neighbor} is called *Nal-Kyran!*[2]

One sees in this letter the imprint of great goodness and mildness.

[**783**] Government ministers always work against liberty; they hate the laws because these pose obstacles to all their passions.

[**784**] Free nations are policed nations. Those that live in servitude are polite nations.[1]

[**785**] When birth and dignities do not confer authority in a nation, everyone seeks a natural authority, which is that of personal merit.

[**786**] Frivolous things, which give nothing to those who enjoy them and degrade those who care about them.

[**787**] I am not surprised that Henry VIII had tyrannical power. That was the moment when the nobility's power had just been abolished and that of the people began to take wing.[1] During this interval, the king became a tyrant.

[**788**] Animal intelligence is proportional to the means they have of exercising it—the monkeys with their hands; the elephants with their trunk; the beavers with their tail; men with their arms and their tongue.

[782]
1. Ali Pasha, son-in-law of Sultan Ahmed III, was named grand vizier on April 27, 1713. He commanded the Ottoman troops in the campaign of Morea against the Venetians in 1715, and the following year, the alliance of Austria with Venice led him into a war where he met his death; see *Spicilège,* 619.
2. Demetrius Cantemir stated that *nal kiran* means "horseshoe-breaker" (*Histoire de l'Empire Othoman* [History of the Ottoman Empire], translated into French by M. de Joncquieres, 4 volumes [Paris: Ganeau, 1743], 3:50).—HC

[784]
1. The French pun contrasts *policées* (well-administered, well-governed, well-policed), and *polies* (polished, polite).—HC

[787]
1. The metaphor is *prendre le dessus,* which can mean either catching the wind in the sail or restoring health in someone who has long been ill.—HC

[789] In Europe, there is a sort of balance between the peoples of North and South.[1] The latter—with an abundance of all things, enabling them to dispense with everything, live close to home, and have but few needs—would have too many advantages over the former if climate and nature did not give them a laziness that equalizes them. The former, on the other hand, can enjoy the conveniences of life only through their work and resourcefulness, which nature seems to have given them only to equalize their condition and their fortune; without which, they could only survive as barbarians. Each part is defended by its climate as much as by its sources of strength.

[790] It took more than six thousand years to know how to do what the Grammar Master teaches[1] the Bourgeois gentleman: writing.

[791] As princes have discovered the arts of mastering our secrets, through the art of opening letters without anyone noticing, we have discovered the art of publicizing theirs through more secret methods of printing.

[792] In a nation in servitude, one works more to preserve than to acquire; in a free nation, one works more to acquire than to preserve.[1]

[793] The greatest misfortune for the commerce of certain States is that there are too many people who are in abject poverty and live on little. In a certain sense, they are nullities because there is practically no connection between them and the other citizens. {This is false; this is impossible. On the contrary, it is when, in a noncommercial State such as Spain, the land belongs to a few individuals and the people have none.}

[794] In my life, I have committed many follies but no iniquities.

[795] In his work on the beginnings of our monarchy, abbé Dubos reads only to seek the authority of kings and the dependence of the ancient French, and the right they had of fleecing the lords. That man never saw anything in that history but a pension.[1]

[789]
1. See *Laws,* 14.2.

[790]
1. The reference is to act 1 of Molière's *Le Bourgeois gentilhomme.*—HC

[792]
1. See the last sentence in *Laws,* 20.4, 340.—HC

[795]
1. Abbé Jean-Baptiste Dubos (1670–1742), whose four-volume history of the French monarchy (1742) Montesquieu owned (*Catalogue,* 2930). To follow Montesquieu's polemic against him, particularly on the origins of the nobility, see *Laws,* 28.3 and 30.10.

[796] I would like to render a judgment on the History of Hernando Cortez by Solis, with some reflections;[1] I already have it all done.[2]

[797] It would not, perhaps, be impossible to lose the compass someday.[1]

[798] When it is said that we are not sure there is a world because God could be a trickster and could affect us in such a way as to make us like dreamers, or like those who have had a leg cut off and who feel it without having it, this reasoning (I say) is conclusive only for those who believe that the soul perceives independent of the organs. For in the two cited cases, the soul perceives by means of the organs, and these two cases themselves prove that there is matter.

[799] The same error permeated the Greeks' whole philosophy; what made for bad science made for bad moral philosophy, bad metaphysics. It is that they did not see the difference that exists between positive and relative qualities. Just as Aristotle erred with his dry, his humid, his hot, his cold, Plato and Socrates erred with their beautiful, their good, their foolish, their wise. {Great discovery that there are no positive qualities.}[1]

[800] The Duke of Orleans only feared ridicule aimed at him.[1] It was the age of the one-liner; he conducted himself by the one-liner and others managed him by the one-liner.[2] The Parlement's cabal was destroyed when someone said to him that Mme de Maisons expected to have precedence over Princess ———. The Duke of Brancas destroyed the great talker M. de Canillac by telling him that a lackey—bored with M. de Canillac, who would make him spend whole nights listening to him—had come

[796]
    1. Hernando Cortez (1485–1547), Spanish conqueror of Mexico; Antonio de Solis y Ribadaneyra (1610–86), dramatist and historian whose *History of the Conquest of Mexico* Montesquieu owned in a French edition of 1714 (*Catalogue*, 3175).
    2. See *pensées* 1265 and 1268.

[797]
    1. Pierre Nicole, in his *Essais de morale* [Moral essays] that began to appear in 1733, argued of the compass and other modern inventions that it was "impossible they will ever perish once found." See Henry C. Clark, ed., *Commerce, Culture, and Liberty* (Indianapolis: Liberty Fund, 2003), 62.—HC

[799]
    1. See *pensées* 410 and 818.

[800]
    1. In the *Lettres de Xénocrate à Phèrés* (*OC*, 3:129–35), Montesquieu sketches a portrait of the Duke of Orléans. See also *pensée* 173.
    2. On this theme, see also *pensée* 1018.—HC

to offer his services to him. "And what did he talk to him about?" "His quarrels with M. de Luynes and the advice he gave M. d'Orleans."[3] Thus, the character of such a man cannot be defined. Why was he dominated by {abbé} Dubois? Those who have known him are obliged to cry out: "*O altitudo!*"[4]

[801] People who do not have their business affairs in order say: "I would be on easy street if I had ten thousand pounds more." If they had those ten thousand pounds more, they would immediately mess things up and say: "If I had those ten thousand pounds more!" *Et in infinitum.*

[802] Women obtain Court favors better than men, princesses more than princes. This is because they never hear the reasons offered for their refusal, so they always return to the charge and tire people out. [*M. de M.*]

[803] The peoples of Northern Europe, source of liberty. The peoples who came from Northern Asia brought servitude with them, as I have noted.[1]

[804] When I see a man of merit, I never dissect him; a mediocre man who has some good qualities, I always dissect[1] him.

[805] What an age is ours, when there are so many judges and {critics and} so few readers!

[806] The North must have changed a great deal in fifteen or sixteen centuries, and the land become more sterile.

The reports on Iceland that we have at present no longer square with what the ancient authors tell us. That is where the Herules[1] came from, and there were a large number of kingdoms on that island.[2]

What we have from Greenland and from the ancient Danish colonies in the country also does not comport with the reports we have today.

3. Marie-Charlotte Roque de Varengeville, marquise of Maisons (1681–1727); Louis de Brancas, marshal of France, marquis of Céreste (1672–1750), member of the Council of Dedans; Philippe de Montboissier-Beaufort, marquis of Canillac (1669–1725); Charles-Philippe d'Albert, duke of Luynes (1695–1758).
4. "O the heights" or "O the depths"; see Romans 11:33 for a classic use.—HC

[803]
1. See *Laws*, 17.2, for this theme.

[804]
1. The term is *décompose*, which can also mean to disconcert.—HC

[806]
1. The Herules, ancient Germanic people who appeared in the second century on the littoral of the Black Sea and in the region around the mouth of the Rhine.
2. "Check my extracts" (M.); these extracts are lost.

The ancient land of Asia[3] was highly subject to earthquakes in the past. It no longer is at present.

To which you may add the reflections I have made on the changes in the land that could make Pliny a liar today. The same will happen to the books by the Academy of Sciences.

Perhaps this is the true reason for the differences found in the North, which no longer sends colonies to the South as they used to, although Sweden has sent quite a few in the wars of the Gustavuses and the two Charleses.[4]

[807] Fools who follow the way of fortune always take the beaten path. Has a Royal tutor become prime minister?[1] Every petty ecclesiastic wants to be a Royal tutor, in order to be prime minister. Smart people follow their own route; they have new and hidden paths. They march where no one has been before. The world is new.

[808] I said: "One must regard one's property as a slave, but one must not lose one's slave."

[809] In despotic states, tranquillity is not peace; it resembles the silence found in cities that the enemy is ready to occupy.[1]

[810] Philosophy and, I dare say, even a certain commonsense have gained too much ground in this day and age for heroism to make much headway in the future.[1] Once vainglory has become a little ridiculous, conquerors—no longer consulting anything but their own interest—will never go very far.

Each age has its particular character: a spirit of disorderly independence was created in Europe with Gothic government; the monastic spirit infected the times of Charlemagne's successors; then reigned that of chivalry; that of conquest appeared with orderly troops; and it is the spirit of commerce that dominates today.

---

3. The comprehensive modern sense may be intended here (see *Encyclopédie*, 1:755), though Montesquieu may also mean Asia Minor.—HC

4. Gustavus II Adolphus, king of Sweden (r. 1611–32); Charles X Gustavus, king of Sweden (r. 1654–60); and Charles XII (r. 1697–1718).

[807]

1. Cardinal Dubois, the duke of Orléans's tutor.

[809]

1. See *Laws*, 5.14, 60, and *pensée* 826.

[810]

1. See *pensée* 761.

This spirit of commerce makes everything a matter of calculation. But glory, when it is all alone, enters only into the calculations of fools.

I speak here only of vainglory, not that which is founded on the principles of duty, virtue, zeal for the Prince, love of Country; in a word, I speak of the glory of Alexander, not of Epaminondas.[2] The latter, being real, is or ought to be for all nations and all times; the former, being chimerical, has the same vicissitudes as prejudices do.

[811] Please let no one accuse me of attributing to moral causes things that belong only to climate.[1] I know the role climate plays in the formation of character, but I am going to make some observations. Today's Romans have all the principles of character that the Romans had in the past, for they will never enjoy a play if there are no fights on stage.[2] The Athenians are just as subtle today, the Lacedemonians just as coarse. But what effect does this have?

I well know that, if moral causes did not interrupt natural ones, the latter would emerge and would act to their full extent.

I also know that, if natural causes had the capacity to act by themselves, as when peoples inhabit inaccessible mountains, they would not soon destroy the moral cause, because the natural cause often needs the moral cause in order to act.

[812] An ambassador cannot be tried by the host prince. The nature of his functions removes him in some sense from the civil state, because of natural law (by which the lips are sealed), because of fear, and even because of the law of nations. For since his functions could be disturbed at any moment by unjust accusations, a free prince would be speaking through the mouth of a man who did not have freedom.

[813] The grander the Prince, the pettier the Minister; and the grander the Minister, the pettier the Sovereign.

[814] In England, since you see an unbridled liberty in the newspapers, you at first think the people are going to revolt. But the people are unhappy with the ministry there as elsewhere; what is written there is what is thought elsewhere.[1]

---

2. Epaminondas (ca. 418–362 B.C.), Theban general and statesman.

[811]
1. On climatic influence on society, see *Laws*, bk. 14.
2. In contemporary French theater, violent actions were to occur offstage.—HC

[814]
1. See *Notes sur l'Angleterre* (*OC*, 3:287).

[815] In that State, punishment will be moderate because any punishment that does not derive from necessity is tyrannical.

The Law is not a pure act of power.[1] Any useless law is a tyrannical law, like the one that obliged the Muscovites to have their beards cut off.[2] Things that are indifferent in nature are not within the compass of the Law. Since men have a passionate desire to follow their will, the Law that obstructs it is tyrannical, because it obstructs the public happiness.

Moderate punishments have the same effect {as atrocious punishments have} on minds accustomed to atrocious punishments.[3]

The Romans can be believed on this—always so moderate in their punishments and with such a fine justice system. It was permissible for a person accused {before the people} to go away before his sentencing. Theft was punished only by double, and sometimes by quadruple.[4]

[816] England is agitated by winds that are made not for submerging but for leading to port.[1]

[817] What is beginning to ruin our comedy is that we want to find the ridiculous in the passions instead of finding the ridiculous in manners. But the passions are not ridiculous by themselves.

[818] When it is said that there are no absolute qualities, I believe this means not that there are none in reality but that our minds cannot determine them.[1]

[819] If men had remained in the little garden, we would have had a different idea of happiness and unhappiness from the one we have.[1]

[820] Van Helmont's experiment is that, when rain water is left to stand, a kind of sediment is found at the bottom of the vase.[1]

[815]
1. See *Laws*, 19.14, 316.
2. Decreed by Peter the Great in 1698.—HC
3. See *PL,* LXXX, 136, and *Laws,* 6.12, 84.
4. That is, by double or quadruple the value of the objects stolen; cf. Montesquieu's discussion of French feudal law at *pensée* 1826.—HC

[816]
1. See *pensée* 657.—HC

[818]
1. See *pensées* 799 and 1154.

[819]
1. See *pensée* 1153.—HC

[820]
1. Jean-Baptiste Van Helmont (1577–1640), Belgian doctor and chemist. Montesquieu describes this experiment in *Spicilège,* 40, and alludes to it in *Voyages* (*OC,* 2:991).

That being the case, I reason thusly {and say that} the rains fall constantly on the earth, {and since they} come from the sea, they leave a sediment which, being deposited in the earth, balances what the sea receives
from the earth. Otherwise, the earth would become dry, rocky, and bare.
All rivers, all streams large and small, flow ceaselessly into the sea. It is
quite useful for this balancing to occur, since the water deposits its sediment, which consists in light and angular particles that stop and become
attached to each other in the earth, and since the waters carry away the
sands, made of round parts easy to take away. This is why, although the fat
of the land is always being lost, the riverbeds have only sand, since the fat
of the land has gone with the water to the sea, and the sand has remained
in the rivers and the sea. If the sea did not give back, waterfronts would be
constantly having to recede and islands to shrink, which is not the case.
It is true enough that the great rivers are always increasing the territory
in front of them. But this is a special case, which arises from the fact that
they let out onto a single location—namely, their mouth—what they have
picked up from everywhere. An experiment ought to be done with a tube
on this sediment. Just as the sun lifts the rains, the interior heat lifts the
water from the seas, and this sediment rises up in natural water just as it
does in the rains.

Experiment. Take a vase of six square lines[2] at the base and several square
feet at the top. Through this experiment, see how many lines of sediment
fall on the earth.

The receding of the sea on the Italian coasts and on our Mediterranean
tells us nothing. This is because of a devastating catastrophe that occurred
in the past, which brought the sea onto the land. Now, equilibrium is restoring things little by little to the way they were.

It is easy to see the waters that descend from the mountains, and how
one can see that the rivers' sources do not come from the rain. A little
mountain in the Tyrol forms two rivers, as I have said.

This sediment rests in the earth, where the water flows as if into its
womb or its menses. The water discharged from there picks up sand particles in the earth. Since they are round, they are more fit for motion, so
that the water takes on particles of sediment, as analogues, and grains of
sand, as of a body that the water carries along. Now the particles of sediment stop and combine in the particles of earth, as analogues but not in

---

2. A line seems to represent half an inch in this context.—HC

the particles of sand, where they cannot stop. This is why the rain does virtually nothing for the vegetation in sandy terrain.

The rains carry sediment into the ground, and discharge it from the particles of sand that they drag into the sea. These particles of sand, which are deposited on the riverbeds, ensure that the sediment that remains in the water is not deposited there, but goes on to the sea. The sandy parts of the rivers that remain in the flood zones are deposited there because of their weight, but the particles of sediment cannot settle there because the sand is not analogous to it. This is why floods are harmful. {I am mistaken, I believe, on river flooding. It's been found by experience that floods destroy newly cultivated lands; the waters carry away all the fat of the land, and the sand settles in its place. The floods do no harm, I believe, to uncultivated land. I do not believe, however, that they do any good. Look into this.}

The land near rivers is fertile, because the river water communicates with it underground and infiltrates it as if through capillary tubes, disposing of its sediment there.

Thus, sediment comes from the sea and sand returns there.

{An experiment should be done as to whether this sediment mingles with the sand: mix them in a vase where sand and earth have been placed.}

Those who say that springs come from the rain have not traveled in mountain country. It is not necessary to prove that the water that falls on the earth is enough to make rivers. It is necessary to prove that the water that falls on the mountaintop is enough. The snows are beside the point, since the snows are only on the mountains because they do not melt there, especially in the summer. For as soon as they melt, there is nothing left of them.

The riverbeds should be lowered by machine. I have seen one in Venice, very good for this, made by Bonneval.[3]

The earth does not send all the water it receives back to the rivers; a lot of it remains in its womb, impregnating it. How much stagnant water remains in a pound of earth should be looked into. Now, since the numerous shoots do not fall to the ground at the same time, everything less than in the above-mentioned account is nil. This is because the water must reach a certain quantity for it to flow; otherwise, it forms into droplets and evaporates in the heat.

3. See *Voyages* (*OC,* 2:999).

It is readily seen how the effect of rainwater is prompt and discontinuous. In the Romagna, I have seen streams falling from the Apennines that swell in terrifying fashion when it rains.[4] If they are allowed to flow for an hour, they become streams again, unless the cause continues.

In a village in the Tyrol named *Mittenwald,* near the Bavarian border, I was shown snow that has been there for more than a hundred years; this is because it does not melt.[5] Now snow that does not melt is nil. Thus, we see that the effects of snowmelts are not moderate, as they would have to be in order to be continuous, but extreme.

I would say nothing to defend what I am writing here. I am not passionately in favor of opinions, except those that are in Euclid's books.[6] I am no more inclined to do battle for my work than for anyone else's. If what I say is true, it belongs to everyone, for truth is the property of all. If it is false, I do not intend to defend it. Besides, either the objection is valid, and in that case I do not intend to respond to it, or it is invalid, in which case the one who makes it, being an intelligent man, will himself find the response.

[821] [I was saying of abbé de S.: "A man lacking wit and discernment who, luckily for men of letters, has no letters, and who would dishonor the learned if he were learned; constantly condemned by that justice that has authority only over the vilest criminals; a man whose acquaintance is everywhere disavowed."][1]

[822] THE "LIFE OF MARIE ALACOQUE"[1] has this particular impertinence, that it is a man of composure, who presumably has some sense since he is a bishop, who recounts the biggest inanities in the world—apparitions, conversations, marriages, exchanges of hearts, and other frivolities; whereas Saint Theresa, Madeline Pazzi, and others talk about what they have seen, what they have felt; it is their own ecstasies, their enchantments.[2] Now,

4. Ibid., 1201.
5. Ibid., 1235.
6. See *pensée* 475.

[821]
1. See *pensée* 823.

[822]
1. Saint Marguerite-Marie Alacoque (1647–90), Visitandine nun who disseminated the devotion to the Sacred Heart; Jean-Joseph Languet de Gergy (1677–1753), archbishop of Sens in 1731, published his *Life of Marie Alacoque* in 1729.
2. Saint Theresa of Avila (1516–83), canonized in 1622; Saint Mary Magdalen de' Pazzi (1566–1604), Carmelite canonized in 1669.

someone who describes things that have affected himself is forgiven, but this is not forgiven in a bland storyteller.

[823] A man lacking wit and discernment, who finds the means of supporting his [wretched] life only by the slanders he sells his publishers; whose {wretched} works one reads only to learn by what stroke of malice he will attack some reputation; constantly condemned by that justice that punishes only the vilest criminals; a man that is not silenced,[1] out of fear of debasing the hand that would bring about this effect; a man, in a word, whose acquaintance is everywhere disavowed, and who makes one blush when one has spoken of him.[2]

[824] Because men are wicked, the laws are obliged to presume them to be better than they are.[1] Thus, the deposition of two witnesses suffices in the punishment of all crimes. Thus, every child born during a marriage is considered legitimate.

[825] What proves to me the necessity of a revelation is the inadequacy of natural religion, given men's fear and superstition. For if you place men today in the pure state of natural religion, tomorrow they would fall into some gross superstition.

[826] [The tranquillity of despotic governments is like the silence found in cities that the enemy is ready to occupy.][1]

[827] ENGLISH. The nation insolent, the individuals modest.[1]

[828] The men who enjoy the government I have spoken of are like fish who swim in the sea without constraint.[1] Those who live in a prudent and moderate monarchy or aristocracy seem to be in large nets, in which they are caught, though they think themselves free. But those who live in purely despotic States are in such tight nets that they feel themselves to be caught right at the outset.

[823]
1. First version: "that we cannot bring to reason."
2. See *pensée* 821.

[824]
1. "Put in the *Laws*" (M.), 29.16.

[826]
1. See *pensées* 809 and 829.

[827]
1. See the next to last sentence in *pensée* 1531.—HC

[828]
1. On the allegory of the fishes, see *pensées* 434n, 597, 874, and 943.

[**829**] When prosperity is merely external, the evidence of well-being is quite equivocal. For often a prince who has great qualities, but does not have them all, can do great things abroad for a State that he governs very badly.

[**830**] Authors are not good judges of their works. Here is the reason why: if they had thought that a sentence was bad, they would not have written it.

[**831**] The reason why most governments on earth are despotic is because this happens all by itself. But for moderate governments, it is necessary to combine and temper powers, to know what to give to one, what is left for another; in a word, a system is necessary—that is, an agreement of many, and a discussion of interests. Despotic government is uniform; it is plain to see everywhere.[1]

[**832**] BALANCE. Every State that sends out less than it receives puts itself in balance by impoverishing itself;[1] that is, it receives less and less until, in a state of extreme poverty, it is obliged not to receive anything more.

[**833**] How can princes be sure of winning battles? This depends on so many circumstances. You find a big obstacle like this bar? A squadron or batallion must be unleashed. There's an opening! Now, if you enter this little opening? Maybe a rank is too compressed; it's bent into an arc. You're too squeezed (big disadvantage). Ditto, too loose.

[**834**] The Germans have this going for them: they know how to rally. But they do not do as well by themselves as when joined with a nation that has more forward thrust, like the English or even the Spanish. They do not have that forward thrust and that strength of attack that other nations do.

{The large number of our officers contributes to giving us this forward thrust; our entire first rank is officers.}

[**835**] Quite a few professions[1] destroy themselves through imitation. The orators ruined themselves by imitating the poets, just as the sculptors ruined themselves by copying the painters.

---

[831]
1. See *Laws,* 5.14, 63, as well as *pensées* 892 and 935.

[832]
1. "Put in the *Laws*" (M.), 20.23, 352.

[835]
1. First version: "All professions."

[**836**] What M. Van Dale[1] says about priestly trickery concerning oracles seems to me in no way proven. There is every probability that they were themselves deceived. I base this on the {miracle of the} blood of Saint Januarius, which I can prove was not a scam.[2] The priests are of good faith; Naples is in good faith; and this cannot be otherwise. In a matter involving general and continuous credulity, it must be that the ministers are deceived. What M. Schot[3] says about the tripod {of Delphi}, which spoke through the mountain wind, entered the hollow of that machine, and seemed to be increased or decreased by some hidden spring, does not seem probable to me—unless the priestess herself was deceived (this is in the *Journal littéraire*[4] of November and December 1714). It may have happened naturally that the priestess, in her fury, was herself seduced by the persuasiveness of the gifts that had been brought to the temple, or by a tendency to welcome flattery, or even by a prejudice she conceived for one man over another. But that this could be fabricated by trickery, that cannot happen in any age. There may well have been an early con artist; but a continual and secret succession of con artists, under shadow of religion, this cannot be or is unlikely.

Nota: M. Hickman[5] explains the phial of Saint Januarius's blood by well-rectified oil of anise, mixed with, I believe, good spirits of well-rectified vitriol. This makes it so susceptible to changes in temperature that touching suffices. Now this was regarded as miraculous before the invention of thermometers, and it was believed to be blood because it was red.

Against me, there is the story from the *Book of Daniel*,[6] the trickery of the priests of *Darius Medus.* I do not know whether it is found in a canonical book. Absent that, it is going to have very much the air of a story contrived for amusement. And we see by these priests' lack of success how easy it was to convince them; in a word, it is an unusual event. But being

[836]
1. Antoine Van Dale (1638–1710), author of *De oraculis veterum ethnicorum* [On the oracles of ancient peoples] (1700); cf. *Spicilège*, 421.
2. See *Voyages* (*OC*, 2:1159–60, 1162) for Montesquieu's attendance at the liquefaction of Saint Januarius's blood in Naples on April 30, 1729.
3. Johann Carl Schott, librarian to the king of Prussia, author of the 1710 work *Explication nouvelle de l'apothéose d'Homère* [New explanation of Homer's apotheosis].
4. Cf. *Journal littéraire* (November and December 1714), VI, art. 347ff., for the review of Schott's book.
5. Henry Hickman, *Laudensium apostasia,* a work in English in 1660.
6. Daniel 14.

duped comes more easily to men than being imposters, especially when a large number of people are needed for that. The reason is that the number of accomplices is detrimental to trickery, but the large number of accomplices is useful for prejudice and credulity, and encourage it.

[**837**] I have the disease of writing books and being ashamed of them when I have written them.

[**838**] To be true everywhere, even about one's Country. Every citizen is obliged to die for his Country; no one is obliged to lie for it.[1]

[**839**] Fontenelle: "Nothing produces more cuckolds than the Parisian custom that gives the wife permission to be obliging[1] for her husband's sake."

[**840**] I say that rouge, far from being a sign that women are thinking more about their beauty, actually makes them think less about it. It is incredible how preoccupied women used to be with their complexions; how much they looked in the mirror; what precautions they took; how they lived behind a mask for fear of suntan. Since there were complexions at that time, and since beauty was individualized, the complexions offered great distinctiveness and great advantage. Today, all faces are the same.

Idem, since they no longer wear tailored bodices.

[**841–842**] Ideas that did not make it into my "Academy speech."[1]

[**841**] Like children who have lost a cherished father and who, while the public pays attention to their new wealth, see only the loss they have suffered.

[**842**] I hope that by my efforts I might convey to you the man of virtue, if I cannot convey the man of wit. Heaven has distributed different talents to men, and has thereby prescribed limits to each that he cannot transcend, but heaven has given us an equal right to virtue. All of us can acquire it because it is necessary, while talents are only useful.

How splendid it is to see this illustrious man who, able through his brilliant qualities to make a great name for himself in a day, neglected none of those virtues that confer reputation only slowly and with the help of an entire lifetime of action!

[838]
1. The pun in English is an alliteration in French: *mourir* vs. *mentir.*—HC

[839]
1. *S'obliger,* can have either a legal or a moral connotation.—HC

[841–842]
1. In 1728; cf. *pensées* 299 and 303.

[843] The political men[1] have studied their Tacitus in vain; all they will find there are subtle reflections on events that would require an earthly eternity to recur in the same circumstances.

[844] Here is why our works bring a sovereign pleasure to us, independent of self-love: it is because they cohere with all our other ideas, and are analogous to them. And the reason why they are no longer so pleasing to us after a certain time is that they no longer cohere so much with our other ideas and are not so analogous to them.

[845] When we read books, we find men better than they are, because each author, not lacking in vanity, seeks to make others think he is a more honorable man than he is, by always coming down on the side of virtue. In a word, authors are theatrical characters.

[846] I approve of the English nation's taste for short works. Since there is a lot of thinking going on there, one quickly finds that everything has been said. In nations where there is not much thinking going on, people find that after speaking, they sense their impoverishment, and that there is still something to say.

[847] From the submissiveness that we naturally have toward our confessor, we can judge how easy it was to move toward submission to the pope.

[848] Saint Louis[1] calls disavowal a *greate mortall sinne,* which leads *soul* and *feith* to perdition. In reality, since the lords' property in those days consisted solely in their vassals, to deny one's vassalage was to do them the greatest damage one could do.[2] That is why the old acts of recognition were so short, so general, so imprecise, since vassalage or the act of recognition was known by the fact, and possession was being exercised constantly.[3]

[849] Without syphilis, honorable women would be ruined; everyone would take the courtesans. {Thus, it is syphilis that produces gallantry.}

---

[843]

1. *Politiques,* which may connote active participants or detached analysts.—HC

[848]

1. Paul Viollet, ed., *Les établissements de Saint Louis,* 4 vols. (Paris: Renouard, 1881–86), II, 29 and 42; the underlined words are in old French. See F. R. P. Akehurst, ed. and trans., *The Etablissements de Saint Louis: thirteenth-century law texts from Tours, Orléans, and Paris* (Philadelphia: University of Pennsylvania Press, 1996).

2. On the origins of vassalage, see *Laws,* 30.3 and 30.4.

3. First version: "was being renewed constantly."

[850] I said: "To avoid being dishonored in this world, it is enough to be only half a fool and half a fraud."

[851] One should always leave[1] a place a moment before becoming the butt of a joke. It is the way of the world that causes this.

[852] Of all the pleasures, the only one the Jansenists allow us is that of scratching ourselves.

[853] Look at how, in Plutarch's *Life of Nicias,*[1] the scientists who explained lunar eclipses by natural causes were suspect to the people. They called them *weather fanatics,*[2] convinced that they reduced all of divinity to natural and scientific causes, until Socrates cut to the root of everything by subjecting the necessity of natural causes to a divine and intelligent origin. The doctrine of an intelligent being was thus discovered by Plato only as an antidote and a defensive weapon against the calumnies of the pagan zealots.

[854] Men are governed by five different things:[1] climate, manners, morals, religion, and laws. In each nation, to the extent that one of these causes acts with more force, the others give way proportionally.[2] Climate dominates over savages almost by itself; manners govern the Chinese; the laws tyrannize Japan; morals would set the tone in Rome and Lacedemon; and religion does everything today in Southern Europe.

The English nation scarcely has manners or even morals to call its own. She has at most an enlightened respect for religion.[3] She is tremendously attached to the laws that are particular to her, and these laws are bound to have unlimited force when they counter or favor the climate.[4]

[855] ENGLISH. Singular talents: they will not even imitate the Ancients, whom they admire, and their plays are less similar to the regular productions of nature than to those games in which nature has followed fortuitous chance.

[851]
1. First version: "I have always left"

[853]
1. *Life of Nicias,* XXIII.
2. *Météorolesches,* a French transcription not found in the dictionaries.—HC

[854]
1. See *Laws,* 19.27, and *pensée* 542.
2. "Put in the *Laws*" (M.), 19.4.
3. See *Notes sur l'Angleterre* (*OC,* 3:292) and *pensée* 1052.
4. See *pensée* 523.

[856] I have screened the essays to be sent to the Academy, so we would not be accused of being like those folks who live near the sea, and who survive only by scavenging through everything tossed up on their shores.[1]

[857] When the great cardinal to whom an illustrious academy owes its foundation[1] had seen royal authority solidified, France's enemies in consternation, and the King's subjects returned to obedience, who would not have thought that this great man would be content with himself? No! While he was at the height of his fortunes, there was in Paris, hidden away in an obscure study, a secret rival for his glory. He found in Corneille a new rebel, whom he could not subdue. It was enough that he had to suffer the superiority of another genius; nothing more was necessary to make him lose the taste for a great ministry destined to be the envy of generations to come.

[858] On a quarrel with a prince of the blood, I said: "As soon as a prince of the blood claims[1] to be offended, he is."

[859] Estates of Languedoc, tranquil: the bishops—who have no interest in the matter and who need to have the abbeys and some barons—entirely in the pockets of the Court.

Estates of Brittany, tumultuous but useful to the province.[1]

[860] Supplications used to be made from the income off the property of the condemned. That is why they were called *supplicia;*[1] that is also why sacred things were sometimes called venerable, sometimes execrable: *de bonis execrandorum.*[2] These confiscations[3] were made by means of the high priest, but by order of the consul or the magistrate {and, says the same

[856]
1. See *pensée* 1148.

[857]
1. Cardinal Richelieu (1585–1642).

[858]
1. First version: "means" or "intends"

[859]
1. The Estates of Languedoc, like those of Brittany, were so-called *pays d'état* which had the privilege of holding provincial estates which presented grievances to the king, voted subsidies and proceeded to the collection of the agreed-upon taxes. (The first manuscript volume of the *Pensées* ends here.)

[860]
1. "Offerings," one meaning of which is "punishments," especially capital ones.—HC
2. "Concerning the property of those about to be prosecuted."
3. See *Laws*, 6.5, 78.

Giraldus, the people had to be present, otherwise the confiscation would have been useless.}[4] And this again outlines for us an idea of the Roman distinction between the two powers, which I have spoken of in my work.

[861] See my Lilius Giraldus extract on these confiscations, p. 72.

[862] The Romans wanted the Latin name of the city of Rome to be unknown, as we see in Plutarch, who sought the reason for it.[1] Giraldus looks for the name of Rome's tutelary God, and he thinks it is *Ops consiva*.[2] But this is a great absurdity; it was no longer a name once no one knew it. As for the city's name, we have absolutely no knowledge of it, says Giraldus. {Among the Hebrews, the name of the Ineffable was not hidden, since it was written in all the books. It was merely prohibited, out of respect, to pronounce it. But among the Romans, the name was unknown; that is, it was not a name.}

[863] The Romans, says Lilius Giraldus, evoked the tutelary gods of the cities they besieged, either because they thought they were unable to take the City otherwise, or because they thought it was a sacrilege to make the gods captive.[1]

Now, from all this, I conclude that the Romans and the Pagans did not have the gross idolatry to believe that their statues were gods. For they saw clearly that, even though they had evoked the divinity, the statues still remained after the seizure of the city, and they doubtless did not figure that the statues were about to venture off.

[864] Lilius Giraldus (page 17) cites Festus, who said that the idol of Modesty was the same as that of Fortune.[1] Did the Romans believe that modesty was not a natural virtue, and that it could only be obtained as a result of chance?

[865] Priapus: Servius says he was from Lampsacus, from which he was

4. Lilius Giraldus, Latinized name of Lilio Gregorio Giraldi (1479–1552), author of a *History of the pagan gods* (cf. *Spicilège*, 164); Montesquieu owned his *Opera omnia* (Basel, 1580; *Catalogue*, 2245).

[862]
1. Plutarch, *Roman Questions*, 61.
2. "Bountiful sower."

[863]
1. "See what's said about all this in my extract of Lilius Giraldus, p. 73" (M.).

[864]
1. Sextus Pompeius Festus, a Latin grammarian of the second century; Montesquieu owned three editions of the *De verborum significatione* [On the meaning of words] (*Catalogue*, 1873–75).

expelled because of the size of his male organ. {He is, I believe, the first to whom such a thing happened.} He was unfortunate, that one.

[866] Lilius Giraldus says the temple of Diana of Persia at Castabalis was highly renowned, because the virgins who served in that temple walked barefoot over burning coals without doing themselves any harm. Many authors say the same thing happened on Mount Soracte, to a certain family of Hirpi, in the Temple of Feronia. (Pliny, Solinus, and Servius.) Pausanias assures us of having seen this miracle.[1] Trial by fire is {thus} quite ancient.

[867] *Barbata Venus:*[1] Because Roman women had an attack of a certain disease that made all their hair fall out. (Extract from Lilius Giraldus, page 54.) "At the time that I write this," says the author, "there is a disease going around that makes men and women lose their hair. They say this problem comes from intercourse with women."

This is doubtless[2] syphilis. Look into when Lilius Giraldus lived.

[868] In my extract from the same author, page 73, he says that among the Lindians, it was pious to vomit out curses against Hercules, and it was believed that the more you insulted him, the more honored he was. This makes it quite clear that the pagans thought they were honoring the gods in bringing their vices to the fore, whether they came from force or from cleverness.[1] It has been wrong, therefore, to criticize Homer over this, since he was merely following his theology. Cleverness and force are marks of power, and it is power that the pagans honored in their gods.

[869] The Arabs performed sacrifices on the altars of the unknown God, it is said in my Lilius Giraldus extract, page 73.[1] {The Athenians were thus not the only ones who had such a divinity.}

---

[866]

1. Solinus, Latin geographer of the third century, whose *Polyhistor* Montesquieu owned (*Catalogue,* 2718) in a 1554 Latin edition; Servius Honoratus, Latin grammarian of the late fourth century; Pausanias, Greek geographer of the second century whose *Description of Greece* Montesquieu owned in several Latin editions (*Catalogue,* 2639–40 and 2788–89).

[867]

1. "Bearded Venus."
2. First version: "perhaps."

[868]

1. See *Laws,* 24.2, 460.

[869]

1. Giraldus, *Opera,* I, col. 17.

[870] Among the Pedalians (an Indian nation),[1] there was no established priestly order, it is said in the same extract, page 76,[2] but whoever passed for the most prudent immolated the victims. {They were the Quakers of that era.}[3]

[871] The ancient myths are explained very well by the situation the earliest men found themselves in before they had discovered offensive and defensive arms.[1] They were weak and timid, prey to ferocious beasts, and their condition must have been uncertain or at least perilous until the invention of iron, or at least equivalent materials. That's why those who killed monsters were heroes. Occupied with ferocious beasts, men did not dream of attacking each other. They were too timid and too few.

[871a] In book two of his *Laws,* Cicero cites this passage from the Book of the High Priests: "*Sacrum commissum, quod neque expiari poterit, impie commissum esto; quod expiari poterit, publici sacerdotes expianto.*"[1] Thus, there were inexpiable crimes among the pagans, and apparently that is the basis of Zosimus's account, in favor of poisoning the motives behind Constantine's conversion.[2]

[872] Father Hardouin was a man whose head was on no straighter than that of the man who believed himself the Eternal Father in the Little-Houses.[1]

[870]

1. See *Laws,* 25.4, 483.

2. Giraldus, *Opera,* I, col. 527.

3. Quakers, a Protestant sect without formal clergy calling themselves the Society of Friends, founded by the cobbler George Fox in 1647.

[871]

1. See *pensée* 1336.

[871a]

1. Cicero, *On the laws,* II.ix.22: "Sacrilege which cannot be expiated shall be held to be impiously committed; that which can be expiated shall be atoned for by the public priests."

2. The inexpiable crimes are human sacrifices; see *Laws,* 24.13, 467; Zosimus was a Byzantine historian of the late fifth century and author of a history which Montesquieu owned in a Latin edition of 1531 (*Catalogue,* 2732); according to Zosimus, Constantine converted to Christianity out of gratitude for a religion that pardoned him of the crime of having condemned his natural son Crispus to death. On this theme, see Zosimus, *Historia Nova: The Decline of Rome,* trans. James J. Buchanan and Harold T. Davis (San Antonio: Trinity University Press, 1967), II.29. See also *pensées* 1777, 2192, 2195, and 2201, and Bréthe, 2:426 n. 33.

[872]

1. Fr. Jean Hardouin, S.J. (1646–1719), librarian of the collège Louis le Grand in Paris; the Little Houses (*Petites Maisons*) was an insane asylum founded in Paris in 1557; see *pensées* 1061, 1102, 1355, 1376, and 1610 for more references to it.

[873] Folly of the Portuguese, who just this year (March 1734) formed a company to support the price of diamonds, which will inevitably lower their price. It is said there: that only a certain number of workers will work in the mines, on pain of death; that the Company alone will sell the diamonds, and always at a price proportional to the old one. But who doesn't see that the high price of diamonds was based on the fact that they were thought to be rare in the world, and that they will lose their value as soon as it becomes clear that it belongs to a single company to raise it or lower it, to mine many diamonds or few?

[874] [A free government can be compared to a big net in which fish move around without thinking they are caught; the nonfree government, on the other hand . . .][1]

[875] At first, the works bring renown to the worker; afterward, the worker brings renown to the works.

[876] The new Christians, nurtured on idolatry, still had their minds filled either with gods who had left Heaven to come live among men, such as Apollo, Neptune, etc., or with men who had been raised to godly rank. This is what facilitated the establishment of the truth of the mystery of the Trinity. But people did not strongly adhere to these truths. As Christianity ridded itself of Jewish superstitions, it filled itself with pagan ones, in the same way liquors lose the odor they had contracted in the vase they are no longer in, to take on that of the vase they are now in. If the religion is ever established in China,[1] Oriental Christianity will be quite different from the Occidental.

[877] It is the idea of God's unity that has made for such an easy reception of the Christian and Mohammedan religions. When it is said that there are many gods, it is necessary to know what these many gods are all about. When it is said that there is only one, it suffices to know that there is only one; that says everything.

[878] My friend N. devoted himself to philosophy at the age of eighty. He was the hero of book III of Virgil:[1] stronger than the young folks.

[874]
1. See *pensée* 434.

[876]
1. See *Laws*, 19.18, and *Geographica* (*OC*, 2:949).

[878]
1. Anchises, father of Aeneas, is the hero of book 3 of the *Aeneid.*

[879] D***, who had certain goals, gave me to understand that someone would give me a pension. I said that, having done no servile acts, I had no need to be consoled by favors.

[880] On Mme L.'s affliction, I said: "Goodness of heart is the source of great maladies."

[881] "I am from a sect {I was having a Quaker speak to the King of England} that takes part in men's various calamities only by the tender compassion it has for them, and by its patience. In the unhappy times that agitated our island, it knew how to feel grief and never complain.

"Just as it knows how to suffer evils, it knows how to enjoy goods, and the feeling of happiness that it possesses under Your Majesty's reign cannot be separated from a feeling of gratitude toward the one who guides the hearts of Kings."

[882] At a dinner in Milan, at the home of Prince Trivulce,[1] an Italian said he had no esteem for French architecture. Count Archinto[2] said to me: "Sir, you are saying nothing about what Monsieur has just put forward." I responded: "Sir, this is because it is impossible to respond to such a proposition. Monsieur says he does not esteem French architecture, but this means he does not esteem architecture, for French architecture is the same as the Italian and that of all other nations. It consists everywhere of the five orders, whose proportions the French have neither increased nor decreased, and in this regard, they merit neither praise nor blame. And if I were to say to Monsieur that I do not esteem Italian geometry, he would do very well not to respond to me either."

This is by way of telling you, my dear President,[3] that the Ancients discovered that the pleasure we feel, in looking at a building, is caused by certain proportions that the different architectural elements that compose it have among themselves. They found that there are five different sorts of proportions that stimulate this pleasure, and they called these orders. When the column had a height seven times its diameter, they called this the Tuscan order; when it was eight, Doric order; when it was nine, Ionic

[882]

1. Antonio Tolomeo Gallio-Trivulzio (d. 1767); Montesquieu was hosted by him in Milan on September 27, 1728 (*Voyages, OC,* 2:1031–32).

2. Carlo Archinto (1670–1732), after traveling in Germany, France, Holland, and Italy, settled in Milan in 1700; he founded there the Società Palatina and financed the publication of Muratori's works; see *Voyages* (*OC,* 2:1029).

3. Doubtless Montesquieu's friend President Jean Barbot.

order; ten, Corinthian order; and it can be said that there are only four orders, because the composite has practically the same proportions as the Corinthian, differing only in that the column and other elements are made even more slender.

Whatever ornaments are added to these orders, whatever disguise is applied to them, this never changes them. Put oak leaves instead of acanthus leaves on the Corinthian capital—this will still be the Corinthian order, because its proportions will conform to the Corinthian order.

This makes it impossible to change the orders, to increase or decrease the number, because these are not some arbitrary beauties that can be replaced by others. This is taken from nature, and it would be easy for me to explain the scientific reason for this, and I will do it someday.

[883] Since one must be faithful to one's Country, one must also be faithful to one's prince or magistrates who govern it.

The authority of princes and magistrates is not only founded on civil law, it is also founded on natural law.[1] Since anarchy is contrary to natural law (because the human race is unable to survive it), the magistrates' authority, which is opposed to anarchy, must be in conformity with it.

What gives strength to the authority of princes is that often the harm they do can only be prevented by a still greater harm, namely, the danger of destruction.

[884] ON POLITICAL LIBERTY.[1]

This word *liberty* in politics is far from signifying what the orators and poets make it signify. Properly speaking, this word expresses only a relationship, and cannot serve to distinguish the different types of government. For the popular state is the liberty of poor and weak persons and the servitude of rich and powerful persons; monarchy is the liberty of the great and the servitude of the small.

Thus, in Rome, monarchical government was lamented by the children of the very consul who had established the government of the many. And when the Romans gave liberty to Macedonia, they were constrained to exile her nobles with as much care as with the King himself.[2]

[883]
1. On civil law, see *Laws*, 1.3; on natural law, see *pensée* 1266.

[884]
1. See *pensée* 751 and *Laws*, bk. 11.
2. See *Laws*, 11.13 and 11.14, on Rome.

And it must not be thought that the Swiss and Dutch nobility imagine themselves to be quite free, for the word *nobility* entails distinctions—real in monarchy, chimerical in the republican state.

Thus, the English nobility[3] buried itself with Charles I under the ruins of the throne. And before that, when Philip II thrust the word *liberty* into the ears of the French, the crown was still supported by that nobility that prides itself on obeying a king, but that regards sharing power with the people as a supreme disgrace.

Thus, when one says in a civil war that one is fighting for liberty, it is not that. The people are fighting for domination over the great, and the great are fighting for domination over the people.

A free people is not the one that has this or that form of government, it is the one that enjoys the form of government established by Law; there can be no doubt that the Turks would think themselves slaves if they were subjugated by the Republic of Venice, or that the peoples of the Indies regard it as a cruel servitude to be governed by the Dutch East Indies Company.

From this, it must be concluded that political liberty concerns moderate monarchies just as it does republics, and is no further from a throne than from a senate. Every man is free who has good grounds to believe that the wrath of one or many will not take away his life or possession of his property.

Just as, in a corrupt monarchy, the Prince's passions can become lethal to private individuals, so too, in a corrupt republic, the dominant faction can be as rabid as a wrathful prince. And on this, one can look at Thucydides' fine passage on the condition of various Greek republics.

[It is true that the evils of the corrupt republic are transitory—unless it changes, as often happens, into a corrupt monarchy—whereas the evils of the corrupt monarchy never end.]

[**885**] DESPOTIC GOVERNMENTS. It is only by dint of philosophy that a sensible man can support them, and by dint of prejudice that a people can bear them. These sorts of government are self-destructive.[1] Each day leads them into decline, and with them, there is virtually no middle ground between childhood and old age. It would be more difficult for the Emperor

---

3. "Put in the *Laws*" (M.), 8.9, 118–19, which reproduces this passage.

[**885**]

1. See *Laws*, 8.10.

to strip the Duke of Parma[2] of his states than it was for Mir Wais, with
ten or twelve thousand thieves, to destroy the formidable Persian Empire.[3]
The capital was besieged, only the bourgeois defended it, and with all his
power, the presumptive heir could bring only two or three thousand men
to his aid.

[886] Princes who do not like war have sought to distinguish themselves by another talent, namely, courtly mystery and deception. For there
are few men who have the good character to measure their personal merit
in virtue, candor and courage.

[887] ORDEAL OF CIVIL WARS. Don't tell me that in the middle of
two different factions I have only to keep my neutrality.[1] For what are the
means of staying sane when everyone else is mad, and keeping one's cool
in the general frenzy? Moreover, I am not isolated in society, and cannot avoid taking part in all kinds of things with which I am connected.
Besides, neutrality is not a prudent option, for I am quite sure of having
enemies, but I am not sure of having a friend. Thus, I must take sides.
But if I choose badly? In addition, the stronger party may not be stronger
everywhere, so that I may very well die a martyr to the dominant faction,
which is very disagreeable.

[888] [I don't believe there is a man in the world who brings to the
examination of things a more . . .]

[889] The perennial character of the English is a certain impatience
imparted to them by the climate, which permits them neither to act for
long in the same manner, nor to endure the same things for long[1]—a character that is not great in itself, but that can become very great when it is
mixed not with weakness, but with that courage furnished by climate,
liberty, and the laws.[2]

---

2. In 1545, Paul III, in detaching Parma and Plaisance from the Papal States, had made of them a
duchy for his son Pier Luigi Farnese, whose dynasty lasted until 1731.

3. Mir Wais Khan was intendant of the province of Kandahar when he shook off the Persian yoke
to found the realm of Afghanistan. Montesquieu, who draws on Fr. Du Cerceau's translation of Judasz
Tadeusz Krusinski's *Histoire de la dernière révolution en Perse* [History of the late revolution in Persia]
(1728), discusses him in *Spicilège*, 304, and in *Laws*, 3.9; see also *pensée* 1898.

[887]
1. See *pensée* 32 on this theme.

[889]
1. "Put in the *Laws*" (M.), 14.13, 242.
2. First version: "the liberty of the laws."

[**890**] On the Emperor's failures in the war of 1733 and 1734,[1] I said: "What causes the Emperor's true weakness is that that court is not accustomed to playing a leading role either in politics or in war. In the era of the Spanish monarchy, it was she who played this role in Italy and in the Low Countries; then, the Dutch; then, King William; then, Queen Anne.[2] They have been quite confounded when they have had to play a leading role. His monarchy was made all of a sudden out of bits and pieces. Ours is a monarchy made little by little; as a problem has appeared, it has been fixed. But the Viennese monarchy has not had the institutions necessary to preserve its power. Not having an engineering establishment, she has been unable to defend her fortifications. She has had adequate artillery ranks. She has regarded the Italian States as her revenue streams, but has consumed the income from those countries in pensions. All the revenues from that country should have been used to maintain it: to keep a permanent army of thirty thousand fully-equipped men in Lombardy; near the Papal borders, ten thousand men; in the kingdom of Naples, as well (near the Papal borders); and ten thousand more men {partly} astride the straits. That would in some sense have combined all his forces, and he would have projected them where he wanted to."

{In the past, Imperial salvation lay in the Empire and the Hungarian sector; the rest was scarcely part of their beat.}

[**891**] Ever since I saw in Amsterdam the tree that bears the sap called *dragon's blood*—big as a thigh when it was near the female tree, and no bigger than an arm when it was alone—I have concluded that marriage is a necessary thing.[1]

[**892**] It should not be surprising to see that virtually all the world's peoples are so far from the liberty they love. Despotic government is plain, so to speak, for all to see, and is established virtually all by itself. Since the

[890]
1. The War of the Polish Succession, after the death of Augustus II, king of Poland, and the election of two kings—Stanislas Leczinski in Danzig and Augustus III in Warsaw; it pitted France, Savoy, and Bavaria against Russia and Austria and ended with the treaty of Vienna in 1738.
2. Charles VI, German emperor (r. 1711–40); William III, stadholder of the United Provinces (r. 1672–1702) and king of England, Scotland, and Ireland (r. 1689–1702); Anne Stuart, queen of Great Britain and Ireland (r. 1702–14); Montesquieu treats the emperor's Italian policy in *Voyages* (*OC*, 2:1032–33).

[891]
1. See *Voyage to Holland* (*OC*, 2:1298).

passions alone are necessary to form it, everyone is fit for that. But to form a moderate government,[1] it is necessary to combine powers, temper them, make them act, and adjust them; to give ballast to one, so to speak, in order to put it in a position to resist another. It is a masterpiece of legislation that chance very rarely achieves, and that prudence is scarcely allowed to effect.[2]

[893] It seems to me that in the prettiest women, there are certain days when I see how they will be when they are ugly.

[894] In the last debates over the Ancients and the Moderns, M. Pope alone hit the target.[1] Mme Dacier did not know what she admired. She admired Homer because he had written in Greek. M. de La Motte lacked feeling, and his mind had been narrowed by regular contact with the circle of folks who engaged only in small talk, and neither he nor they had any knowledge or understanding of antiquity. As for abbé Terrasson, he was missing the five senses. Boivin was merely a scholar. As for the poet Gacon, a more contemptible one has never been known.[2]

[895] M. Pope alone perceived Homer's greatness, and that is what was at issue. It is true that M. de La Motte has been dragged into the details by Mme Dacier herself, who found them all completely divine in Homer.

[896] I said: "Voltaire is not noble;[1] he is only nice. It would be shameful for the Academy for Voltaire to belong; it will someday be shameful if he has not."[2]

[897] We can make goods out of all our goods, and we can also make goods out of our ills.

[898] In abbé de Bellegarde's *History of Spain,* when the grand inquisitor Torquemada {the first one} offered a general amnesty, more than seven-

[892]
1. See *Laws,* 5.14, 63.
2. See *pensées* 831 and 935 for the development of this idea.

[894]
1. Alexander Pope (1688–1744) translated the *Iliad* and the *Odyssey* between 1715 and 1726.
2. First version: "Gacon, he was the infamy of Parnassus"; abbé Terrasson (1670–1756), elected a member of the French Academy in 1732, leading representative of the Moderns for his *Critical essay on Homer* (1715); Jean Boivin de Villeneuve (1663–1726), professor of Greek at the Royal College and author of an *Apology for Homer* (1715); François Gacon (1667–1725) published *Homere vengé* [Homer avenged] against La Motte in 1715 under the name of the "unadorned poet."

[896]
1. *Beau* may here refer to character or deportment rather than appearance.—HC
2. Voltaire was admitted to the French Academy on May 9, 1746.

teen thousand persons came voluntarily to confess their crimes in the hope of absolution.[1] "But they were tricked": more than two thousand were burned, and the others ran off to various realms. {One cannot read these words, "But they were tricked," without feeling sadness in one's heart.}

[**899**] When you see the huge to-do made in Antiquity over a renowned philosopher or a scholar, and how folks came from all over to hear him, you might say we no longer have the same love for the sciences. This is because, since books and libraries were rare, the knowledge of those who were living books was more valued. "He knows history." "But I have history." It is the discovery of printing that has changed this: in the past, it was men who were valued; today, it is books.

[**900**] Admirable maxim: no longer talk about things after they are done.

[**901**] Dominion of the sea has always given the people who possessed it a natural pride,[1] because, feeling themselves capable of insulting everywhere, they think their power has no other limits than the Ocean.[2]

[**902**] The Monks: "*Genus hominum quod damnabitur semper et semper retinebitur.*"[1]

[**903**] It is not philosophers who disturb states, but those men who are not philosophical enough to know their happiness and enjoy it.[1]

[**904**] Timidity appears to be linked to avarice: thus, old men, eunuchs, women; all this comes from weakness of soul.

[**905**] It is odd that, in the climes of Southern Europe, where celibacy is more difficult, it has been retained, but in the climes of Northern Europe, where the passions are less lively, it has been rejected.[1]

[898]
1. Abbé Jean-Baptiste Morvan de Bellegarde (1648–1734), author of *History of Spain* (1726); Tomàs de Torquemada, Dominican (1420–98), Spanish inquisitor.

[901]
1. First version: "natural insolence"; the term Montesquieu uses for "pride," *fierté,* can be taken in a positive or a negative sense.—HC
2. "Put" (M.), *Laws,* 19.27, 329.

[902]
1. "A species of men who will always be condemned and will always be retained."

[903]
1. See *pensée* 945.—HC

[905]
1. See *Laws,* 25.4, 484.

[906] I would readily raise the question of whether men have gained anything by the custom of eating animal flesh, instead of feeding on their milk and on the fruits of the earth. I am convinced that men's health has been diminished by it. The meat had to be prepared; the stews, ragouts, and saltiness had to be enhanced; in addition, the pasture has to be employed in feeding the animals that must in turn feed man. Now if man were to feed directly from the fruits of the earth, the same territory would feed many more men. The experience in England is that the multiplication of pasture reduces the number of men, by reducing the number of those who cultivate the land. And I am convinced that the large number of people in China arises only from the fact that most people there live on rice,[1] which enables a field to feed a very large number of men.[2]

[907] As for my system on liberty, it will have to be compared with the other ancient republics,[1] and for this, read [Aristotle's *Politics*], Pausanias, Reinerius, Reicennius, *De Republica Atheniensium;* examine the aristocracy of Marseilles {which was wise, no doubt, since it flourished for a long time}, the republic of Syracuse, which was foolish, no doubt, since it was never preserved for more than a moment; Strabo, book IV, which seems to apply my system; [Plato, book III of the *Laws;*] Plutarch, *Life of Theseus,* on the republic of Athens; *Ibid.* Plutarch, *Life of Solon;* Xenophon, *Republic of Athens;* Julius Pollux, *Onomasticon, de Republica Atheniensi;* Kekermannus, *De Republica Atheniensium;* Sigonius, *De Republica Atheniensium; Thesaurus Republicarum* by Coringius.[2]

---

[906]
 1. "Put the end in my *Laws*" (M.), 23.14, 436; cf. also *Geographica* (*OC,* 2:944).
 2. "See the volume *Mythologia et Antiquitates*" (M.); it must mean extracts from Montesquieu's readings since lost.

[907]
 1. First version: "On my system of politics, one must study with care"
 2. The references are to Reinhart Reinecke Reicennius, *De Republica Athenensium;* Strabo (ca. 58 B.C.–A.D. 25), whose geographical works Montesquieu owned in a 1587 Latin edition (he had made an extract; cf. *pensée* 2189); Xenophon (ca. 430–ca. 355 B.C.), several of whose works Montesquieu owned (*Catalogue,* 2802–7); Julius Pollux, grammarian and sophist of the second century A.D., whose *Onomasticon* Montesquieu owned in a 1608 Latin edition (*Catalogue,* 2346); Bartholomaus Keckermann, whose works on logic and natural science Montesquieu owned in Latin editions of 1606 and 1610 (*Catalogue,* 1481–82); Carlo Sigonio (*Catalogue,* 1966–67, 2873–74, and 3074–75); and Hermann Conring (*Catalogue,* 1432, 2924, and 3108–10).

[**908**] Pericles[1] gave the people all judicial power, *consilia totiusque Reipublicae gubernationem,*[2] with remuneration. Good thing the civil judges were picked from among the people. It was, I believe, like that at Athens.[3]

[**909**] I no longer like oratorical speeches; they are works of ostentation.

[**910**] It is a mistake not to speak the truth when possible, for one does not always speak it when one intends to, and when one is seeking it.

[**911**] One will never think well of men if one does not give them a pass on the prejudices of their times.[1]

[**912**] Nothing better proves how easy it is to govern a large State than M. d'Orléans, despite the essential faults he had in the area of good administration.

{If M. the Duke[1] had not been so foolish as to think he had little ability, he would have governed just like anyone else.}

[**913**] At present, the Jews are saved. Superstition will not return, and they will no longer be exterminated out of a principle of conscience.[1]

[**914**] CARDINAL FLEURY. He succeeded in crushing Jansenism and achieving the reception of *the Constitution;*[1] [This has certainly changed.] and he did this, *per alluvionem,*[2] {by marching slowly and} not taking one step that did not move toward his goal. The self-contradictory paces of M. d'Orléans, the impetuosity of most others, would have put the evil beyond remedy. [I set aside everything there is to say about his candor, his modesty, and his gentleness—about war and peace since Pharamond

---

[908]

1. Pericles (ca. 495–429 B.C.), Athenian statesman during the Golden Age between the Persian and Peloponnesian wars.

2. "The counsels and government of the entire commonwealth."

3. See *Laws,* 11.6, 158.

[911]

1. See *pensées* 764 and 1302 (section on Saint Louis).—HC

[912]

1. Louis-Henri de Bourbon, called Monsieur le Duc (1692–1740). See also *pensées* 1964 and 2042.

[913]

1. On Montesquieu's ideas on the Jews, see Pierre Aubery, "Montesquieu et les Juifs," in *Studies on Voltaire and the Eighteenth Century* 87 (1972): 87–99.

[914]

1. The Papal bull *Unigenitus* (1713); on Fleury's role, see *Voyages* (*OC*, 2:1097).

2. *Per alluvionem,* by the action of water, by a river, for example.—HC

... What is extraordinary is that this was thought about him during his lifetime.]

[915] FRENCHMEN. Their character: Among the ancient Gauls, they set out on the highways to learn the news. Jesters: when Roman ambassadors came to inspire them to oppose Hannibal, their young people burst out laughing. Look at Anna Comnena's *History*.[1]

[916] Histories are false facts composed on the basis of true ones, or else on the occasion of true ones.

[917] Luther, having Princes in his favor, could not make them appreciate an authority lacking external signs of preeminence. And Calvin, having in his favor peoples kept in the dark under monarchy, or peoples living in republics, could scarcely establish dignities and signs of preeminence in religion.

This is because Lutheranism was established by the Northern kings, Calvinism in popular States and in those where certain people sought to make it so.[1]

Each of these two religions believed itself the more perfect—the Calvinist considering itself more in conformity with what Jesus Christ had said, the Lutheran, with what the Apostles had done.

The religious disputes made government no longer a constitution for living according to the laws, but instead a conspiracy of those who thought one way against those who thought another; a type of evil that we owe to our modern times, and on which the ancient men of politics have nothing to tell us.

[918] Every moderate government—that is, where one power is limited by another power—needs much wisdom to be established, and much wisdom to be preserved.

During certain disorders and disturbances, when every citizen is head of a faction, how can a government be set up—unless it is the one that is established, so to speak, by itself, namely, the tyrannical, or the one that is merely the deprivation of government, namely, the anarchical?

When the English people had overturned their constitution, passing

[915]
    1. Anna Comnena (1083–1148), Byzantine princess and author of the *Alexiade*, or life of Alexis Comnenus, her father.

[917]
    1. "Put in the *Laws*" (M.), 24.5.

from government to government and finding each one harsher than the last—free in appearance, slave in fact—they were obliged out of desperation to restore a monarch.[1] By the nature of the thing, it was necessary to arrive at a situation where the sects would be contained by the government, and not the government contained by the sects.

[**919**] I said: "Prigs are never wicked. This is because they admire themselves and are not irritated against anyone."[1]

[**920**] THE LEARNED. In their books, one would like them to have learned women's jargon. But they know all languages except that one. They are gauche when they want to be trifling, and foolish when they want to reason with machines that have never done anything but feel.[1]

[**921**] Animals are happier than we are. They flee difficulty, but they are not afraid of death, of which they have no idea.

[**922**] Most men are more capable of doing great deeds than good ones.[1]

[**923**] Those who make digressions think they are like those men who have long arms, and who reach further.

[**924**] The cases of conscience that the pagan philosophers set up for each other indicate such great sincerity of soul and such refinement that there are few Christians who dare judge themselves by their principles. Look at the case of the grain merchant in Cicero's *Offices*.[1] One sees with pleasure that Christian charity scarcely demands more of us than what the Pagans felt humanity and love of the common good demanded of them.

[**925**] If abbé Dubos's system is true, what would be the origin of servile conditions in France?[1]

[918]
1. Allusion to the Stuart restoration (1660) after Cromwell's death; cf. *Laws*, 3.3, 22.

[919]
1. "Put in the *Histoire véritable*" (M.), (*OC*, 3:334).

[920]
1. "Put, more or less, in the *Laws*" (M.).

[922]
1. See also *pensées* 959 and 967.

[924]
1. "See my *Traité des devoirs*" (M.). According to Shackleton, 434, this entry must have been part of chapter 3, "Duties toward men."

[925]
1. See *pensée* 795n.

[926] It is improbable that Maevius did not write against Virgil and against Horace.[1] Otherwise, those two great men would not have written against him. But time has not made the offensive writings of that mean poet pass into posterity.

[927] On the historians of France: "*Et, sicut prima aetas vidit quid ultimum in libertate esset, ita nos quod in servitute.*"[1]

[928] In the ode *Donec gratus eram tibi,*[1] which has been so much praised, Horace is inept in the dialogue. Horace says he has been dying for Chloë; Chloë responds that she would consent to die twice. That is not felicitously said.

[929]   *Jure perhorrui*
                   Late conspicuum tollere verticem[1]
[930]   *Virtutem incolumen odimus*
                   Sublatam ex oculis quaerimus invidi.[1]
[931]   *Iam nec spes animi credula mutui.*[1]

[932] The success of this book has amply fulfilled my ambition,[1] since all the criticisms that have been made are buried, after a month of life or of torpor, in the eternal darkness of the *Mercure,*[2] with the enigmas {and the accounts of the gazetteers.

[926]
1. Virgil, *Eclogues,* III.90; Horace, *Epodes,* X.2.

[927]
1. Tacitus, *Agricola,* 2.3: "and even as former generations witnessed the utmost excesses of liberty, so have we the extremes of slavery."

[928]
1. Horace, *Odes,* III.ix.1: "As long as I was dear to you."

[929]
1. Horace, *Odes,* III.xvi.18–19: "I have had a horror, quite rightly, of raising my head to an eminence that could be seen far and wide."

[930]
1. Horace, *Odes,* III.xxiv.31–32: "we reject virtue when it is alive; then, when it's removed from our sight, we long to have it back, jealous creatures that we are."

[931]
1. Horace, *Odes,* IV.i.30: "nor the fond hope of a kindred spirit."

[932]
1. The reference is to the *Considerations,* whose first edition was published in Amsterdam in 1734.
2. Four reviews of the work appeared in 1734, according to *Presse et histoire au XVIIIe siècle,* ed. Pierre Rétat and Jean Sgard (Paris, 1978), 105.

Hoc miserae plebi stabat commune sepulcrum}.[3]

[933] This great power that God has placed in the hands of the King, my master, does not make him any more fearsome to his neighbors. It is the guarantee of the peace of Europe. Prouder of the title *friend* than he would be of *conqueror,* Heaven, in causing him to be born, has made all his greatness; he himself adds only virtues. He believes that Kings are not only born to make their subjects' happiness, but that they are also destined to make the felicity of the human race. Such are the sentiments of the great soul of . . .

[934–935] SOME FRAGMENTS THAT DID NOT MAKE IT INTO THE "POLITICAL LIBERTY"

[934] I do not at all think that one government ought to make other governments repulsive. The best of all is normally the one in which we live {and a sensible man ought to love it}. For since it is impossible to change it without changing manners and mores, I do not see, given the extreme brevity of life, what use it would be for men to abandon in every respect what they have gotten used to.[1]

[935] What makes most governments on earth despotic is that such a government is plain for all to see, it is uniform everywhere.[1] Since violent passions alone are necessary to establish it, everyone is fit for that. But to establish a moderate government, it is necessary to combine powers, temper them, make them act, and adjust them; to give ballast to one in order to put it in a position to resist another. In short, it is necessary to make a system.[2]

[936] Whatever good thing I say, I relinquish it completely to the pride of those who would like to criticize it.

[937] People may think you put no fire into your thoughts because you put none in your manner of defending them.

[938] Nothing is closer to divine Providence than that general benevolence and that great capacity for love that embraces all men, and nothing more closely approaches animal instinct than those boundaries that the

3. Horace, *Satires,* I.viii.10: "Here was the common burial place fixed for pauper folk."

[934]
1. See *PL,* LXXX, 136.

[935]
1. "Put in the *Laws*" (M.), 5.14, 63.
2. To follow this thread, see *pensées* 831, 892, and 918.

heart gives itself when it is touched only by its own interest, or by what is right near it.[1]

[939] I have been working for twenty-five years on an eighteen-page book that will contain everything that we know about metaphysics and theology, and that our moderns have forgotten in the immense volumes they have offered on those sciences.[1]

[940] No one is free in Turkey, not even the Sultan.[1]

In absolute States where there is a nobility, slavery—increasing imperceptibly—extends downward from the Prince to the lowest subject.

In those states where there is no nobility, slavery—increasing imperceptibly and passing through all ranks—extends upward from the most wretched subject to the Sultan.

The aristocracy of Genoa is like that of the army of Algiers.[2]

Holland has become less free since it no longer has a stadholder.

In England, the magistrates are slaves as magistrates but free as citizens.

In a well-constituted government, the man who is being prosecuted, and who will be hanged the next day, is freer than a good citizen is in a bad government.[3]

The governments of Spain and Portugal are liberty for the clergy and a strange slavery for the people.

Any overly small republic cannot be called *free: fato potentiae, non sua vi nixae.*[4]

To remedy this, the ancient republics of Greece, Italy, Gaul, Spain, and Germany formed associations, as the Swiss and the peoples of {Germany and} the Low Countries do today.[5]

[941] A government is like a sum composed of many numbers. Add or subtract a single digit and you change the value of all the others. But since

---

[938]
1. "Put in the *Histoire véritable*" (M.).

[939]
1. "Put in the [*Histoire véritable*], the preface to the *Temple of Gnidus*" (M.).

[940]
1. See *pensée* 751.
2. Cf. *Voyages* (*OC,* 2:1089).
3. "Put in the *Laws*" (M.), 12.2.
4. "The fate of power not supported by its own strength." Cf. Tacitus, *Annals,* XIII.19; Machiavelli, *The Prince,* ch. 13, and *pensée* 751.
5. "Put in the *Laws*" (M.), 9.1, 131.

in arithmetic the value and relationship of each number are known, one is not deceived. It is not the same in politics; one can never know what will result from the changes one makes.

[942] Many people have examined what is best: monarchy, aristocracy, or the popular state. But since there are countless types of monarchy, aristocracy, or popular state, the question thus posed is so vague that awfully little reasoning ability is needed to deal with it.

[943] Pure liberty is more a philosophical than a civil condition;[1] which does not prevent there being very good and very bad governments, nor does it even prevent a constitution from being more imperfect to the extent that it is further removed from this philosophical idea of liberty that we have.[2]

An ancient compared the laws to those cobwebs that, being only strong enough to stop flies, are broken by birds.[3]

As for myself, I would compare good laws to those big nets in which fish are caught, while thinking themselves free,[4] and bad ones to those nets in which they are so squeezed that they immediately feel themselves to be caught.[5]

[944] There are few[1] in which those who govern do not in general have good intentions and want their administration to be good. For since they are on stage for all the world, however little feeling of honor they may have, etc.

In some, enlightenment may be lacking; in others, education or the aptitude for work. Many are guided by the prejudices of their country, their age, or their own state.[2] Others are dragged along by the problem that has already been caused, or demoralized by the difficulty of solving it. For it is difficult not to make a mistake when one wants to correct individual problems, and when one was not lucky enough to be born with the ability to fathom in a stroke of genius a State's whole constitution.

[943]
1. "Put in the *Laws*" (M.), II.4, 155.
2. See *Laws*, 12.2.
3. Solon the Athenian lawgiver, as quoted by Diogenes Laertius in "Life of Solon," X.—HC
4. For Montesquieu's use of this image, see *pensées* 434, 597, 828, and 874.
5. "Return page 17 (934): 'I don't think this at all'" (M.).

[944]
1. Governments. This is a continuation of *pensée* 934.—HC
2. *État* here might mean either social position or polity.—HC

[945] It is not philosophers who disturb states; it is those men who are not philosophical enough to know their happiness and enjoy it.[1]

[946] Though one should love one's Country supremely, it is as ridiculous to talk about it with prejudice as about one's wife, one's birth, or one's property, because vanity is foolish everywhere.[1]

[947] Montrésor says Saint-Mars's tattletale[1] was saying that one of his great crimes was to have sought to oust the Cardinal. "To deprive the Prince of his minister," he said, "is as if he were depriving him of his arm." As for me, I say that if servitude itself were to arrive on earth, it would not speak differently.[2]

[948] When the Abbasid caliphs wanted to restore the Temple with more magnificence, the learned men responded (it is said in Boulainvilliers's *Life of Mohammed*)[1] that the one who established the Temple in this place left it in its natural poverty for many centuries, that gold and rocks are equally the creatures of the same sovereign.

I say this is the first time that clergymen refused money. {This is the oddest event in the history.}

[949] All timid people readily make threats. This is because they know that threats would make a big impression on themselves.

[950] People were talking about Marivaux's play *La Mère confidente*,[1] in which the mores are admirable. I said: "The people[2] are honorable in their tastes, although not in their morals. We are delighted to find honorable folks, because we would like people to be that way toward us."

[951] Most people's vanity is as well founded as the vanity I would feel over an episode that took place today at Cardinal Polignac's, where I was

[945]
1. See *pensée* 903.—HC

[946]
1. See *pensée* 634 for a slightly different version.—HC

[947]
1. Claude de Bourdeille, Count of Montrésor (ca. 1606–63); Henri Coiffier de Ruzé, Marquis of Cinq-Mars (1620–42), condemned to death with de Thou on September 15, 1642, after a conspiracy with Spain against Richelieu.
2. "Put in the *Laws*" (M.), 12.8, 195.

[948]
1. Henri de Boulainvilliers, *La vie de Mahomet* (1730), 81–82 (*Catalogue*, 3124).

[950]
1. *The Confidante-Mother;* first performance, May 9, 1735.
2. *Le peuple*, the common people in general.

having dinner. He took the hand of the House of Lorraine's eldest son, the Duke of Elbeuf, and after dinner, when the prince was no longer there, he gave his hand to me.[1] He gives me his hand [because he has contempt for me]; that's an act of contempt. He took the prince's hand; that's an act of esteem. That is why princes are so intimate with their [most cherished] domestics. They think it's favor; it's contempt.

[**952**] I saw a fool who had returned from a diplomatic mission and who never spoke anymore except in monosyllables. If that man only knew how much he lost by acting like the Count of Avaux, and how much he would gain with us by being plain![1]

[**953**] A prince must never descend into the details. He must think, then let others and make others act. He is the soul, not the arm. It is a job that he can never do well, and if he did it well, it would make him do the other things poorly.

[**954**] When I see a great prince who has reigned in our time seduced by a blind counsel, despite his natural good sense, and suddenly send subjects, soldiers, merchants, workers, commerce to his enemies, I lament the Catholic religion more, and if I dare say so, I lament it even more than I do the Protestants.[1]

[**955**] When a State is prospering, it is essential not to make decisions without weighing with the utmost care all of their disadvantages. But when one finds oneself surrounded by difficult circumstances, when one does not know what to do, one must act, since at that point there is no mistake so pernicious as inaction.

[**956**] We do not have R[eligion] firsthand, but perhaps tenth-hand.

[**957**] Take away from a nation's general spirit the sentiments of honor, duty, love, and you do the same harm as when you take from a private individual all his principles.[1]

[951]
1. Emmanuel-Maurice de Lorraine, Prince of Elbeuf (1677–1763).

[952]
1. Jean-Antoine de Mesmes, Count of Avaux (1640–1709), had been ambassador to Venice, negotiator at Nimegen, and ambassador in Holland and in Sweden; see also *pensée* 1053.

[954]
1. See also *pensée* 728. The allusion is to Louis XIV and the Revocation of the Edict of Nantes, 1685, which ended France's limited toleration of the Protestants.

[957]
1. "Put in the *Laws*" (M.), 19.5 and 19.12.

And when you have done everything necessary to have good slaves, you will be left with nothing but bad subjects.

[958] France is no longer in the middle of Europe; it is Germany.

[959] Generous, liberal, magnificent, ready to do all sorts of splendid deeds, unless they were merely good ones.[1]

[960] Italy is no longer at the center since the discovery of the Cape and the West Indies; she is in a corner of the world. And since the Levantine trade is dependent upon that of the Indies, her trade is of only secondary importance.

[961] One finds in the earliest days of the Republic the explanation for what happened when it no longer existed. It was the same Romans in different circumstances. The historians, who for the sake of narrative brevity tell us the facts without going into the causes, depict the Romans after the Revolution as an entirely new people, and one who loved slavery, because they seemed to be seeking it.

[962] It is clear that a certain vanity among the Romans was not as ridiculous as it is with us. It is seen in that mania they had for demanding that their friends praise them, that they put them in their histories, their dedications.

The particular fact of Caesar's death seemed so splendid that people who were not even in on it boasted of it. Trebonius wrote to Cicero that, if the latter writes something on Caesar's murder, he hopes he will not occupy the least significant place.[1] {Cicero, who begs people to put him in Roman history, and even to lie for him![2] This immoderate love of celebrity comes from the education of that time.}[3]

[963] Look at *Ostendanae Obsidionis Diarium.*[1]

[959]
    1. See *pensées* 922 and 967 for variations on this thought.—HC

[962]
    1. See Cicero, *Familiar Letters,* XII.16; Caius Trebonius (d. ca. 43 B.C.) was a Roman general who participated in Caesar's assassination on March 15, 44 B.C.
    2. Cicero, *Familiar Letters,* V.12.
    3. "Put in the *Laws*" (M.), 19.9.

[963]
    1. Gaspar Ens, *Annalium mercurio gallo-belgico succenturiatorum tomus v in tres libb tributus (1603–1606)* [Of the annals of the sub-centurions in the Gallo-Belgian Mercury] (Cologne, 1606), contains the *Ostendanae obsidionis breviculum* [Brief account of the siege of Ostend]; Ostend was besieged by Spinola's Spanish forces, 1601–4.—HC

[964] [That constant train of vexations that the Emperors' subtly insatiable desires had conceived were seen to be reduced merely to a simple tax easily paid and as easily received, which was doubtless the reason for the facility they experienced in their conquests.][1]

[965] After the sovereign has made the most general and impartial laws that he can, he must conduct himself in such a way as to leave the details to others while being severe against important infractions, rise above the two parties {and not side with any party}, and not make himself suspect. Since he possesses more in trust, he has more need of confidence. Let him be especially afraid of falling in with private interests. This is revolting to Truth itself! Let him wait for the time, let him watch much, act little, and not think he is {doing} simply by virtue of doing; let him study the spirit of his nation. In things that are not frivolous, such a spirit is rarely that of the Court.

[966] One might believe that God, who loves men, [—and who is not bothered about whether his religion is held in glory or humiliation in terms of external power, because in either case, it is equally fit to produce its natural effect, which is to sanctify—one might believe, I say, that God, out of love for human nature],[1] endured at that time the frightful Muslim inundation of the Empire,[2] in order to deliver it from so many taxes, charges, and abusive exactions that were occurring there.

Men were astonished to see themselves under a government where they saw neither avarice nor larceny; where, instead of that constant train of vexations that the Emperors' subtly insatiable desires had conceived, they saw themselves subject merely to a simple tax, easily paid and as easily received, which was doubtless the reason for the facility they found in their conquests.

[967] A splendid deed is a deed that has goodness in it, and that[1] requires strength to do.

[968] In republics, a general spirit must always be dominating. As

[964]
1. See *pensée* 966.

[966]
1. For this deleted passage, see *Considerations,* XXII, 201.
2. See *Laws,* 13.16.

[967]
1. First version: "that is good and that"; see also *pensées* 922 and 959.

luxury becomes established in a republic,[1] the spirit of particularism becomes established as well. For people who need only the necessities, there remains nothing to desire but the Country's glory and their own. But a soul corrupted by luxury is an enemy of the laws, which always constrain the citizens. What led the Roman garrison in Reggium to bleed the inhabitants dry at the instigation of Decius, their tribune?[2] It is because in their sojourn in Reggium, they had begun to lapse into luxury.

[969] Paganism was at that time in decline. Founded on poetic delirium, it was incompatible with every kind of philosophical sect and human knowledge. Ignorance established it in the East and brought it to the Greeks. But since it is impossible for a country to flourish without there being countless people who, enjoying happiness, seek to cultivate their minds and acquire knowledge, it happened that in Greece people began to devote themselves to Philosophy. The Athenians, who saw that fear of the gods was going to be taken away from the people, condemned Protagoras and Diagoras, put Socrates to death, and banished Aristotle.[1] Plutarch tells us that all the scientists were regarded as atheists, because in teaching the people that the stars were merely bodies driven by regular movements, they destroyed the idea of the Divinities that Paganism had attached to them.[2]

Cicero, who was the first to put the dogmas of Greek philosophy in his language, dealt a mortal blow to Roman religion. It began to undergo a sort of civil war. Within the Empire, Pyrrho's sect is seen doubting religion and that of Epicurus is seen holding it up to ridicule. The sects of Plato, Socrates, and Aristotle enlightened the mind, and that of Zeno corrected the morals.[3]

It is in these circumstances[4] that Christianity spread through the Empire, and I cannot refrain from making a few observations about this establishment, which have not perhaps been made by the apologists of the Christian religion.

[968]
1. "Put this in the *Laws*" (M.), 7.2.
2. The city of Reggium, today Reggio, on the straits of Messina, was pillaged by the Romans in 282 B.C.; Decius Jubellius was a Roman military tribune.

[969]
1. Protagoras (ca. 485–ca. 410 B.C.), Greek sophist; Diagoras of Melos, called the Atheist, Greek poet and philosopher of the fifth century B.C.
2. See Plutarch, *Life of Nicias*, XXIII. See also *pensée* 711.
3. Pyrrho (ca. 365–275 B.C.), Greek philosopher and founder of the skeptical school; Zeno of Elea, Greek philosopher of the fifth century B.C.
4. See *Considerations*, XVI.

If the Christian religion is not divine, it is certainly absurd. How then was it received by those philosophers who were abandoning Paganism precisely because of its extravagance? What! Those philosophers, who were maintaining that Paganism was harmful to divine Majesty, accept the idea of a crucified God, after they had taught men about the immutability, the immensity, the spirituality, the wisdom of God? The torturing of a God, what a revolting idea! It was much more revolting than all the monstrous opinions in Paganism, which concerned beings that were merely superior to us, but still imperfect. Paganism became established because it had a reasonable origin at first, and because its extravagance emerged only little by little. But with the Christian religion, everything revolting to the human mind had to be said from the outset. Cerinth and Ebion are proof that it was said. Arius, who never denied the divinity of Jesus Christ but only his consubstantiality, makes clear that that divinity was the common opinion.[5] Thus, they began by proposing a crucified God. But this idea of the Cross, which has become the object of our respect, is far from being as damning for us as it was for the Romans. There is more: there did not exist a people so vile in the Roman mind as the Jews. All their works are full of the ignominy they heaped upon them. And yet it is a man from that nation that they are supposed to worship; it is the Jews who announce him, and Jews who offer themselves as witnesses. The Gospels are published, and are accepted by the Pyrrhonians, who say everything must be doubted; by the Naturalists, who believe everything is the effect of form and motion; by the Epicureans, who mock all the miracles of Paganism; in short, by the enlightened world, by all the philosophical sects. If the establishment of Christianity among the Romans were an event solely in the category of things of this world, it would be the strangest event of its kind that has ever occurred.

[970] State power is attached not to the conquering State that has been founded, but to the army that founded it.

[971] SENSIBLE PEOPLE. They have more reason to be disdainful, but they have less disdain.

[972] Two sorts of men: those who think and those who amuse.

[973] I have not wanted to make my fortune by means of the Court;

---

5. Cerinth, late first-century heresiarch; Ebion, supposed founder of the Ebionite sect of the first century; Arius (ca. 280–336), heresiarch who contested the divinity of Christ.

my design has been to make it by improving my lands, and to hold my fortune directly from the hands of the gods.[1]

[974] I said: "All women can please {someone}; each has a net after her fashion; some larger, others smaller; some with a mesh of one kind, others of another."

[975] Someone has said that God is only committed to the preservation of species, and not at all individuals.

[976] I see people who get discombobulated at the slightest digression; but as for me, I think those who know how to digress are like men with long arms who can reach further.[1]

[977] It has been fifty years since it was decided at the Council that the intendants are right. They say they are going into the provinces to win respect for the King's authority, but it is the King's authority that makes them respected.[1]

[978] If we only wanted to be happy, that would soon be done. But we want to be happier than others, and this is almost always difficult because we believe others to be happier than they are.[1]

[979] ASTRUC.[1] He has never said anything; he has always repeated himself.

[980] Religious polemicists defend the established religion for the sole reason that it is established; they combat those who attack it for the sole reason that they attack it.[1]

[981] PROPHECIES. If they are obscure, it is said they do not apply. If they are clear, it is said they [are too clear and] have been made after the fact.

[973]
1. See *pensées* 213 and 1003.

[976]
1. See *pensée* 923.—HC

[977]
1. The intendants were the monarch's chief officials in the provinces; Montesquieu does not discuss them in his published works, though there are about twenty references to them in his correspondence, mostly concerning individuals. For more on the intendant in this volume, see *pensées* 1353, 1572, 1835, 1840, 1846, 1898, 2066, and 2099.—HC

[978]
1. See *pensée* 30.

[979]
1. Jean Astruc (1684–1766), erudite naturalist, first royal physician of Poland, author of *De morbis venereis* [On venereal diseases] (1736). See *pensées* 1243 and 1647.

[980]
1. See *pensée* 1010.—HC

[982] Moderate States overturned in popular uprisings, when the people did not succeed and even when they did: witness England's devotion during the restoration of Charles II.[1]

[983] Those scholars whose whole knowledge is outside their souls, and who announce the wisdom of others without being wise themselves.

[984] {WOMEN AND} BIG TALKERS. The emptier a head is, the more it seeks to empty itself out.

[985] [I have always marveled at the facility with which princes do impious things but not devout ones.]

[986] In the present era, no more Greek, no more verse, no more sermons.

[987] The Academy will never fall: as long as there are fools, there will also be well-adorned minds.[1]

[988] *I never saw a nation* that thinks less than this nation. Unlike animals, she does not even know what does her good or what does her harm.[1]

[989] Nothing is so easy as destroying the sentiments of others; Bayle took the easiest path to glory.[1]

[990] Persons of wit, who have read a great deal, often lapse into a disdain for everything.

[991] The word *trinquer* doubtless comes from the noise that two glasses make in hitting each other. And if one no longer knew the correct pronunciation of the French *i,* one would [doubtless] find it by means of reading this word in books, just as the correct pronunciation of the *u* has been found by the word *cuculus.*[1]

[992] One may recognize how the Ancients' weights and measures have come down to us through the means by which the weights and measures

---

[982]
1. In 1660.

[987]
1. *Beaux esprits;* see translator's note for another possible interpretation here.—HC

[988]
1. The reference is to England; the italicized words are in English in the manuscript.—HC

[989]
1. On Pierre Bayle, see *Laws,* 24.2 and 24.6, as well as *pensées* 104n, 1230, and 1946.

[991]
1. *Trinquer,* to clink glasses together; *cuculus,* Latin for "cuckoo."

of the Indies have come to us since the East Indies trade has been engaged in directly by Europe.

[993] In France, nothing saves you from contempt: honors, dignities, birth. Princes are hardly exempt from the need for personal merit.

[994] People are much mistaken over the size and power of ancient States, because they often judge by the notions that fear conveyed to the peoples who had dealings with them: thus, the Jews' fear of the Assyrians, the Greeks' fear of the Trojans. The Greeks did not talk in the same way about the Assyrians and Babylonians.

[995] I said: "Supper kills half of Paris; dinner, the other half."

[996] An honorable man who produces *Characters* like La Bruyère should always do scenes, not portraits; should depict men, not one man. Even so, he will always be suspected of bad intentions, because the particular applications are always the first things fools notice, since they are made easily and as often as one wants; plus, their petty malice is more active.

[997] When I was in Florence and saw the simple manners of that country—a senator with his straw hat by day and his little lantern by night—I was enchanted; I acted like them and said: "I am like the great Cosimo."[1] In fact, you are governed there by a great lord who acts like a bourgeois; elsewhere, by bourgeois who act like great lords.

[998] I hate Versailles because everybody is small there. I love Paris because everybody is large there.[1]

[999] I said: "You can grumble as much as you want, as long as you don't have the air of doing so." It's the same with praise.

[1000] A man was consulting me on a marriage. I said to him: "Men in general have decided you would be foolish; most men as individuals have decided not."[1]

[1001] While I was in Chantilly, I said I was abstaining from the meat out of politeness; M. le Duc was being pious.[1]

[997]
1. Cosimo III de' Medici (1670–1723), grand-duke of Tuscany; on Montesquieu's trip to Florence, see *pensée* 677 n. 4.

[998]
1. See *pensée* 1078.

[1000]
1. See *pensée* 1034.

[1001]
1. Louis-Henri de Bourbon, Duke of Condé (1692–1740), led a luxurious life at Chantilly; after the publication of *Persian Letters,* Montesquieu frequented Chantilly.

[**1002**] In cosmetic matters, I said, one must always do less than one can.

[**1003**] [Continuation] I have always had a timidity that has often revealed some confusion in my responses. I have sensed, however, that I have never been as confused with smart people as with fools. I would get confused because I believed I was confused, and because I felt ashamed that they could get the better of me.[1]

On occasion, my mind, as if it had made an effort, would get by well enough. Once when I took a trip, I arrived in Vienna. Being {in Laxembourg}, in the hall where the Emperor was dining, the Count of Kinski said to me: "You, Sir, who come from France {and have seen Versailles}, you are quite surprised to see the Emperor so poorly lodged." "Sir," I said, "I am not upset to see a country where the subjects are better lodged than the master."[2] Indeed, the palaces of Vienna and Laxembourg are plain, but those of the leading lords are beautiful. Being in Piedmont, King Victor said to me: "Sir, are you related to the abbé of Montesquieu whom I saw here with abbé d'Estrades, during the time of Madame, my mother?"[3] "Sir," I said, "Your Majesty is like Caesar, who never forgot any name." The Queen of England said to me on a walk: "I give thanks to God that the kings of England can always do good, and never evil." "Madam," I said, "there is no man who ought not but give an arm for all kings to think as you do."[4] {Sometime later, I dined at the Duke of Richmond's. The gentleman ordinary Labaune, who was a smug fool, although French envoy in Holland, maintained that England was no larger than Guyenne.[5] The English were indignant. I abandoned my envoy on that one, and fought on the others' side. That evening, the Queen said to me: "I understand you defended us against M. Labaune." "Madam, I could never imagine that a country where you reigned could fail to be a big country."}

[1003]

1. See *pensées* 213 and 973.

2. Montesquieu arrived in Vienna on April 30, 1728, and was hosted by the emperor, Charles VI (1685–1740), on May 20 at Laxembourg, a hunting resort fifteen miles south of Vienna; see *Voyages* (*OC,* 2:967 and 969). For this same thought, see *pensée* 2134.

3. Montesquieu arrived in Turin in Piedmont on October 23, 1728. The other references are to King Victor-Amadeus II (1666–1732); Joseph de Secondat, abbé de Faise, Montesquieu's uncle; Jean-François d'Estrades (d. May 10, 1713), abbé of Moissac and ambassador to Venice (1675) and then to Piedmont (1679); Maria Giovanna di Savoia-Nemours, widow in 1675 of Charles Emmanuel II.

4. See *pensée* 662 for this thought.—HC

5. The references are to Queen Caroline, wife of George II; Charles Lennox, second duke of Richmond (1701–50), a frequent subject in Montesquieu's correspondence; and De Labaune, chargé d'affaires in Holland from 1728 to 1730.

[**1004**] To succeed perfectly well in the world, I have always seen that you have to appear mad while being wise.[1]

[**1005**] I have never liked to enjoy the ridicule of others.

I have not been hard on others' minds; I have been friend to almost all minds and enemy to almost all hearts.[1]

Timidity has been the curse of my whole life. It has seemed to bring confusion right down to my organs, to leave me tongue-tied, to cloud my thoughts, to muddle my expressions. I have been less subject to these weaknesses with smart people than with fools. This is because I have had the hope that they would understand me; this gave me confidence.[2]

[**1006**] It cannot be said that letters are an amusement for only a certain portion of the citizenry; they must be viewed from a different side. It has been noted that their flourishing is so intimately connected to the flourishing of empires that they are invariably either the sign or the cause of the latter. And if we want to take a look at what is presently happening in the world, we will see that, for the same reason that Europe is flourishing and is dominating the other three parts of the world while everyone else groans under slavery and misery, Europe is likewise more enlightened, relatively speaking, than the other parts of the world, which are buried in the depths of darkness. Now if we want to have a look at Europe, we will see that the states where letters are most cultivated also have, relatively speaking, more power. If we have a look only at our France, we will see letters being born or buried with her glory—giving a somber glow under Charlemagne, then dying out; reappearing under Francis I and following the brilliance of our monarchy. And if we limit ourselves to the great reign of Louis XIV, we will see that during the period when that reign was most flourishing, letters enjoyed their greatest success as well.

If you have a look at the Roman Empire, if you examine the works of art that survive, you will see sculpture, architecture, all the other arts decline and fall like the Empire—sculpture and architecture on the increase from Augustus to Hadrian and Trajan, but withering until Constantine.

If you have a look at the Caliphs' empire, you will see that those from

[**1004**]
1. See *pensées* 29 and 971.

[**1005**]
1. See *pensées* 1009 and 1290.
2. See *pensée* 1003.

the Abbas[1] family, whose general spirit was to make the sciences flourish—Almanzor, Rashid and his son Alamon, who surpassed all his ancestors in this love, who obtained all the Greek philosophy books from the Eastern emperor, had a large number of them translated . . .[2]

If you have a look at the Turkish empire, at its weakness in the same country where such a large number of powerful nations had been seen in the past, you will see that in that country, only ignorance equals the weakness that we have been discussing. And if we compare this state in its present condition with those states that had the power to conquer all and destroy all, you will see that this arises from that definite principle that there can be only two sorts of truly powerful peoples on earth: either entirely civilized nations, or entirely barbarous nations.

It is known[3] that those vast empires of Peru and Mexico perished only from their ignorance, and it is probable that they would have defended themselves against our arts if that same ignorance had not placed in their hearts a superstition that constantly made them hope for what they should not have hoped for and fear what they should not have feared. Proof positive of this is that the small barbarous peoples found on that vast continent could not be subjugated, and most still are not.

Thus, the sciences must not be regarded as a vain occupation in a large nation; they are a serious matter.

And we have no need to criticize ourselves for our nation not working diligently on this front. But just as, where empires are concerned, nothing is closer to decline than great prosperity, so too is there reason to fear that prosperity may lead to decline in our literary republic. We have only the drawbacks that we find in our prosperity itself, happy that we are no longer in those times when only the drawbacks produced by an opposite cause were found.

Knowledge, due to all the types of support we have had, has assumed among us an easy air, an appearance of facility that leads everyone to consider himself knowledgeable {or a fine mind} and to think he has acquired the right to disdain others. Hence that neglect toward learning what we

[1006]
1. Abbas, Mohammed's paternal uncle (d. 652–53). The Caliphs of the Abbasid family founded in 750 descend from him.
2. "Look into this" (M.).
3. "Look into what I've said about it in a separate fragment" (M.).

think we know. Hence that foolish confidence in our own powers, which makes us undertake what we are incapable of executing. Hence that frenzy for passing judgment, that shame at indecision,[4] that air of contempt toward anything we do not know about, that desire to debunk anything found to be too lofty, in an age when everyone thinks himself or sees himself as an [important] personage.

Hence—in those who think they are obliged to be know-it-alls[5] but who cannot help sensing their inferior merit—that mania for diatribe that has multiplied writings of that kind among us, which produces two sorts of bad effects: discouraging the talents of those who have them, and generating the {stupid} malice of those who do not.[6] Hence that constant tone that consists in turning good and even virtuous things to ridicule. Everyone has gotten involved in it, and taste has become all mixed up. By virtue of claiming to look for it, people have made it disappear; if we no longer have a Socrates, even less do we have any Aristophanes.

In their time, Virgil and Horace felt the weight of envy. We know it, and we know it only through the works of these great men. The diatribes written against them have perished, the works they attacked are eternal— like the insects that die drying out the leaves of the trees which, upon the return of Spring, always reappear green.

A certain delicacy has made people extremely difficult on anything that lacks that perfection of which human nature is not capable, and by demanding too much, we discourage talent.[7]

In a word, great discoveries made in recent times make people regard as frivolous anything that does not carry with it an air of present usefulness, without considering that everything is linked, everything holds together.[8]

[1007] GENERAL MAXIMS OF POLITICS.

I. Princes should never make apologias; they are always strong when they are deciding and weak when they are debating.[1]

II. They must always do reasonable things while reasoning very little.

---

4. First version: "shame at not passing judgment."
5. *Beaux esprits;* see translator's note.—HC
6. See *pensées* 1292 and 1541–42.
7. See *pensées* 1262, 1289, and 1292.
8. "Look at my work on *Criticism*" (M.); see also *pensées* 935 and 1260–61.

[1007]
1. For an application of this idea, see *pensée* 1132.—HC

III. The preambles of Louis XIV's edicts were more unbearable to the people than his edicts themselves.

IV. What can be done by mores must not be done by laws.

V. Fear is a resource that must be managed; one must never make a severe law when a milder one suffices.

VI. Useless laws weaken necessary ones.

VII. Those laws that can be eluded weaken legislation.

VIII. When correction suffices, removal must be avoided.

IX. The Prince should have his eye on public decorum, never on private.

X. Heaven {alone} can produce devout people; Princes produce hypocrites.

XI. A great proof that human laws ought not to obstruct religious ones is that religious maxims are highly pernicious when they are brought into human politics.

XII. There are countless cases in which the lesser evil is best.

XIII. [The best is the mortal enemy of the good.]

XIV. Correction presupposes time.

XV. Success in most things depends on knowing {well} how much time is needed to succeed.

XVI. Most princes and ministers have good will; they do not know how to take measures.

XVII. Hating *esprit* and making too big a deal of it: two things that a prince should avoid.

XVIII. The prejudices of the age must be well known, so as to avoid either offending them too much or following them too much.

XIX. Everything done must be reasonable; but great care should be taken not to do every reasonable thing.

XX. All my life, I have seen folks losing their fortune out of ambition and ruining themselves out of avarice.[2]

XXI. To see the manner in which Princes are raised, you would say they all have their fortunes to make.[3]

[1008] Practically all virtues are a particular relationship between one man and another. For example, friendship, love of Country, compassion

---

2. See *pensées* 1194 and 1214.—HC
3. See *pensées* 1072, 1077, 1081, 1083, 1088, and 1188.

are particular relationships. But justice is a general relationship. Now all the virtues that destroy this general relationship are not virtues.[1]

[1009] I said: "I am friend to almost all minds and enemy to almost all hearts."[1]

[1010] In unimportant points of controversy, quarrels where Religion makes war on itself.[1]

[1011] In the past, women were beautiful; today they are nice. They used to be constrained in their manner; little social exchange; thought only about their complexion; did not dare show their nose for fear of ruining their complexion, which held them in servitude; constant bathing. This perpetual attention narrowed their minds. The novels of those days always depict beauty, majesty, an aquiline nose, big eyes; they do not depict the graces. Today, our women cannot be criticized {for not having} great freedom of mind, manners, and morals.

[1012] When Madame la p—— de Lix had asked my opinion of her marriage with M. de M.[1] [I was of a contrary opinion and disapproved of it], I sent her these maxims:

I. Love never reveals the things that supreme friendship has made one say.

II. Even if it is true love, it has its rules; and in well-born souls, these are stronger than its laws.

III. The heart is entirely given over to love; the soul remains for virtue.

IV. Two ordinary beauties undo each other; two great beauties highlight each other.

V. It reflects extraordinary merit to be in one's element in the presence of such great merit.

VI. [I said: "I am in love with friendship."]

[1008]
1. According to Shackleton, this entry, along with *pensée* 220, belongs to chapters 7 and 8 of the *Treatise on Duties*.

[1009]
1. See *pensée* 1005.—HC

[1010]
1. See *pensée* 980.

[1012]
1. Anne-Marguerite-Gabrielle de Beauvau-Craon, born in 1707, married first to Jacques-Henri, chevalier de Lorraine-Marsan, who became prince of Lixin (1698–1734), then afterward to Gaston-Charles-Pierre-François de Levis, the marquis of Mirepoix, also alluded to here; Montesquieu was quite close to her, as his correspondence indicates (and see *pensée* 1242).

[**1013**] It seems to me the Romans had no word to express a dandy;[1] their gravity was too contrary to that kind of figure.

[**1014**] There must not be constant cross-purposes in conversations, or they become tiresome. Marching together is called for. Even if you do not march {side by side, or} on the same line, you keep to the same path.[1]

[**1015**] END THAT I WANTED FOR MY "ORATION TO THE KING."[1]

With these virtues appropriate for governing, how have you been able to combine all those necessary for pleasing? Permit me, Sire, to cease for a moment being dazzled by the majesty {grandeur} that surrounds you. You would be the most amiable private individual in the world if you were not the greatest of kings.[2]

[**1016**] A ridiculous thing is a thing that does not accord with life's ordinary manners and actions.

[**1017**] Old man Law, talking about all the fine geniuses ruined amidst the countless number of men,[1] said, as if speaking of merchants, "They died without displaying their wares."

[**1018**] When the Duke of Chartres took Quinault, people wanted to flatter the Regent:[1] "He is beginning to be like the others, he has vices" . . . "But how would he have vices?" said M. d'Orléans. "He doesn't even have virtues." Good line and very philosophical! That regent had a philosophy of one-liners.[2]

[**1019**] I don't know that I have yet spent four *louis* for the sake of giving airs, nor paid one visit out of self-interest. In what I have undertaken, I

[1013]
1. *Petit maître* (literally, "little master").—HC

[1014]
1. See *pensée* 1292.

[1015]
1. See *pensée* 1284.
2. See *pensée* 1281.

[1017]
1. The reference is to the speculative bubble of 1720; on John Law, see *pensées* 530 n. 2, 1610, and 2143.

[1018]
1. Louis I, duke of Chartres (1703–52), son of the regent Philippe of Orléans; Jeanne-Françoise Quinault (1699–1783) had debuted at the Comédie-Française in 1723.
2. For more on Orléans's one-liners, see *pensée* 800.—HC

have employed only common prudence, and have acted less to avoid missing out on affairs than to avoid failing in my own affairs.[1]

[1020] It is first of all necessary to cure oneself of the vices of one's
country and not resemble Ovid's Thrace.

Flagrat vitio gentisque suoque[1]

Otherwise, one is revealed as being among the common run of one's
compatriots, and thus, among the common run of men.

[1021] Saint Francis of Sales, very moderate in his morality. I said: "He
was too reasonable to be a saint. He thought that in conversations meant
to unbend the mind, there was no 'vain speech.'"[1]

[1022] I said: "Nature has offered the problem of squaring the circle to
bad geometers, in order to bring joy to their lives."

[1023] I had the good fortune of liking practically everyone, and this
trait was the luckiest thing in the world for me. For since my face was an
open book, since it was impossible for me to hide my love, my contempt,
my friendship, my boredom, my hatred, since I liked most people, they
found on my face a favorable account of themselves.

[1024–1049] LETTERS[1]

[1024] You send me word that you love me a little. If it has taken you a
year to love me a little, how long will it take you[1] to love me a lot?

[1019]
1. The last sentence rests on a pun, contrasting *manquer les affaires* and *manquer aux affaires*. Montesquieu wrote to Fleury and to Chauvelin in July 1728 to request entry into the diplomatic corps; cf.
also *pensées* 293, 973, and 1003.

[1020]
1. Ovid (43 B.C.– A.D. 17 or 18), *Metamorphoses*, VI.460: "he burns with his own vice and that of
his people."

[1021]
1. Saint Francis of Sales (1567–1622), author of *Introduction à la vie devote* [Introduction to the
devout life] (1608–9) and *Traité de l'amour de Dieu* [Treatise on the love of God] (1616); Montesquieu
owned the 1637 edition of his *Works* (*Catalogue*, 643). The phrase "vain speech" (*paroles oiseuses*) often
had this religious inflection.

[1024–1049]
1. It is unclear whether the following letters were ever sent.

[1024]
1. First version: "will it take you centuries"

[**1025**] [Why are you worried that I am not supping with you this evening? I love you and you love me. You are much more truly in my heart than in any other place in the world.]

[**1026**] [Mademoiselle de ***, who always distinguishes you from everyone, wants to bore you today, out of her preference for you: she asks you to have supper this evening.]

[**1027**] I have seen the afterlife up close. I cannot tell you about those who live in the heart of the country; but those on the frontier have a pale face, a grave air, and are big talkers, etc. {The Little One from Launay}

[**1028**] You cannot do better than to marry. Thus, get married quickly.

Necte, Amarylli, modo et "Veneris" dic "vincula necto."[1]

[**1029**] [It is my heart that is speaking, why does yours not respond?]

[**1030**] The rule is to request entry into the Academy. I know well that rules are not made for persons like you. But persons like you rarely want to abandon them.

[**1031**] [My uncle[1] just told me that he would send to have me go to sleep in two hours . . . I'll slip away and be able to spend at least two with the one I love.] I declare by the divinity that I adore you; you know my idolatry. [What! I'm sorry! . . . We have only a few days to see each other—that is, to live—and we have to spend them away from each other! . . .]

[**1032**] I'm sending you what you ask of me. However great the loss, I'll never criticize you for follies I can fix.

[**1033**] Transfer taxes![1] Good God! Transfer taxes! What diction! It's a barbarous word that ought never to pass the lips of a man such as you. I

[1028]
1. Virgil, *Bucolics*, VIII.78: "Weave them, Amaryllis, I beg, and say, 'Chains of love I weave!'"

[1031]
1. Doubtless Jean-Baptiste de Secondat, president at the Parlement of Bordeaux. See *pensée* 1035 n. 2.

[1033]
1. The *lods et ventes* were taxes owed the lord on the alienation of a fief and a manor; for Montesquieu's view of their origin, see *Laws*, 31.33, 718, where the Cambridge editors translate it as "permissions and sales."

especially don't want to know its signification, and I beg you not to talk to me anymore about transfer taxes.

[**1034**] [You consult me¹ over whether you ought to marry or not. I don't know what to tell you, because men in general have determined that it's folly to marry, but most men as individuals have decided the contrary.]

[**1035**] You inform me, dear father,¹ that you will not tell my uncles² about the grounds for complaint you have against me. I will comport myself in the future in such a way that you will no longer be in a position to grant me similar indulgences. [I wasn't ten years old] {I was very young when I wrote this letter.}

[**1036**] [We are two great examples of constancy: I love you always and you hate me likewise.]

[**1037**] You have done it in vain, I will never hate you. You can distress me but it is impossible for you to displease me.

[**1038**] [The old king¹ died generally lamented by all the abusive tax collectors and all the Jesuits.]

[**1039**] [Yesterday I was in a house where people were talking loudly about you. Everybody said you were very amiable. It was only me who said you were very wild.]

[**1040**] You have just lost your husband; you will no longer love me.

[**1041**] [Your devotion put me on bad terms a month ago with Mme ***. You have made every effort to spoil Mme ***'s view of me. If you continue, I'll go around saying you love me.]

[**1042**] *Asper eram, et bene dissidium me ferre loquebar.*¹
You well know the power you have over me. You are enjoying your usual influence. I intend to adjust.

[1034]
1. See *pensées* 1000 and 1028.

[1035]
1. This is the first known letter from Montesquieu and dates to ca. 1700.
2. Montesquieu had four uncles, his father's brothers: Jean-Baptiste de Secondat, president at the Bordeaux Parlement, from whom Montesquieu inherited the office; Joseph de Secondat (1646–1726), abbé de Faize; Armand de Secondat (1663–1714), a Jesuit; and Ignace, abbé de Fontguilhem in the diocese of Bazas.

[1038]
1. Louis XIV (d. 1715).

[1042]
1. Albius Tibullus (ca. 50–ca. 19 B.C.), elegiac poet, *Elegies* I.v.1: "I was angry. I vowed I could bear our severance well" (*Catalogue*, 2012).

[1043] [Your rival, but you have no rival, has the task of telling me something. I do not want a third party to negotiate with you. I want to learn everything, right down to rejection, from the most lovable mouth in the world.]

[1044] [Why do you complain about the title I give you? I call you my wife, because you are not. If you were, I would call you my mistress.]

[1045] [Your inconstancy pains me, but your choice consoles me. You no longer want to love me, but it seems to me you are doing everything you can to miss me.]

[1046] So, you're leaving me, and you're leaving me for a worthless man. Wretch that I am! What sadder thing could have happened to me than to see myself obliged to blush at having loved you? Usually, when one stops being in love, there still remains in the mind an agreeable memory of past pleasures. But here, the present brings shame, and the past, despair.

[1047] How just is the hatred you have for marriage! Reason has made you feel what experience alone has made others know.[1]

> When, by solemn ties,
> Two faithful lovers, whom equal ardor fires,
> Join together, before Immortal eyes,
> Love itself expires,
> Always the altar's sacrifice.

You know very well that in the past, sophisticated folks did not get married.

> You know old Coriolan,
> Amadis, Roger and Roland.
> Though in real love, true and well,
> They detested the sacrament,
> And content to please their belles,
> They wedded only their quarrels.

You see, Mademoiselle, that the chains of Hymen must not be confused with the chains of Love; one must not marry, but one must love, and everyone should belong to the same religion on that score.

[1047]
1. Cf. Montesquieu's letter to Mlle de Clermont in 1724 (*OC*, 3:770–72).

Iris, be not so hard on me.
Love and pine away, night and day.
The most adorable mystery
Is Love's mystery, far and away,
No salvation outside Kythery.²

On my word, Mademoiselle, love; I know what it's about.

Taste this sovereign delight:
It is alone a true felicity.
The gods themselves it makes feel right,
Lifts boredom from their immortality.

[1048] I'm desolate. Picture me still in that {horrible} state we were in
when we separated. Remember it, my dear child? Your anxiety allowed you
to perceive all of mine. I'll talk no more about that day we spent in tears,
but about that cruel moment when both the pleasure of weeping and the
consolation of lamenting each other were torn from us. Remember Juno
studying us constantly and seeking our sighs down to our very hearts? Remember that pirate who brought cruelty to the point of wanting to amuse
us? How I suffered! Still, if I'd been able in leaving you to clearly paint my
despair, I'd have found consolation in making you see that I'm not unworthy of all your love. I'm always afraid of not having made you aware of all
my own. I've told you a million times that I love you madly. I always think
I've not told you enough, and I'd like to die telling you.¹

[1049] I said: "A man who is quick-witted is a man who has his wealth
in ready cash. A man who is not is a man who has his wealth in land."

[1050] The more primitive and unperfected the art of music,¹ the more
surprising its effects have been. Here, I believe, is the reason: They had instruments that make more noise and would thereby strike the ears more forcefully, since the latter are not accustomed to music, or rather to better music,

2. Kythera (Cythera): Aphrodite's birthplace. The line is a play on the religious saying, "No salvation outside the Church."—HC

[1048]
1. Cf. the letter (1726?) by Montesquieu to an unknown female (*OC*, 3:830).

[1050]
1. On music's influence on mores, see *Laws,* 4.8, 41, and 14.2.

which is more pleasing even though it is less moving. But when this new music began to be more pleasing, the prior music began to be less moving.

[**1051**] I have in my head (and in truth, all the chronicles of France and Normandy compiled by André Duchesne[1] should be read closely) that Brittany was not given in its entirety to the Normans, but only the Nantes region and what surrounded the lower Loire.[2] It was the Normans' constant practice to seize an island at the mouth of a river where they were fortifying their positions. From there, they carried their brigandage everywhere. But the country close to the lower part of the river was singled out for ruin. From which I conclude that they were at first given the most ruined portion of Brittany. It even seems from Father Lobineau, book III, that at the same time, there were counts of Rennes, who remained.[3] It may even be, according to Father Lobineau's opinion, that only a part of Normandy was given to Rollo at first, such as the diocese of Rouen and neighboring lands, and that the Cotentin had already been given to the Bretons. For it seems to me that the eastern part of Normandy, being closer to the mouth of the Seine, must have been singled out for devastation.

[**1052**] Fiction is so essential to epic poetry that that of Milton, founded on the Christian Religion, only began to be admired in England[1] once Religion began to pass for fiction there.[2]

[**1053**] I was watching a fool return from a diplomatic mission {and puffed up}. I said: "Now he talks his nonsense only in monosyllables."[1]

[**1054**] I said: "M. de Cambrai's book destroyed in three words: love is a relationship."[1]

[1051]
1. André du Chesne (1584–1640), author of several works on the history of the Normans (alluded to here), on the Franks, and on the writing of history (*Catalogue*, 2542 and 2932).
2. "See my *Spicilège* (572), where Czar Peter I, with small vessels that contained forty horsemen, ravaged all the coasts of Sweden; they went faster than the coast guards" (M.).
3. Guy-Alexis Lobineau (1666–1727), *Histoire de Bretagne* (1707).

[1052]
1. See *Notes sur l'Angleterre* (*OC*, 3:292) and *pensée* 845; John Milton (1608–74), *Paradise Lost* (*Catalogue*, 2099–2100).
2. First version: "Religion has been most discredited there."

[1053]
1. See *pensée* 952.

[1054]
1. See Fénelon's *Explications des maximes des saints* [Explanations of the maxims of the saints] (1697 ed.; *Catalogue*, 539).

[**1055**] Prosperity turns one's head more than adversity; this is because adversity warns you, but prosperity makes one forget oneself.

[**1056**] There are many people for whom it is a great drawback to be known.

[**1057**] I said: "What good is it to write books for this little Earth, which is no larger than a point?"

[**1058**] One always hears it said: "Heaven and Earth." It is like someone saying: "Heaven and nothing."

[**1059**] In Paris, there was a casuist of such great reputation that everyone came to consult him; he was the arbiter of consciences and the great conductor on the road to salvation.[1]

He saw himself as a public man; he was of easy access, and everyone was satisfied with him.

He settled in a large office; he had a bureau in front of him, and on the two sides, parallel to each other, two large rows of books. Placed on one side, in neat order, were all the mild and benign casuists; on the other, the casuists who torment the heart and are in perpetual conflict with sinners.

The door was across from his bureau, and he saw from a distance those who were coming to consult him. He examined their air and countenance, and studied the situation of their heart, for having to serve them different dishes, he wanted to find something to their taste. When a man came with a composed air, a look that was fixed and a bit sad, his clothes in perfect order, he would turn to the right, to the side of the strict theologians, and serve him according to his pleasure. But if a worldly man, an abbé, a coquettish woman came to him, he would turn to the side of the lax theologians and serve them as well, according to their fancy; he made manna fall in the desert.

This craft was not without its drawbacks. One day, he fell into a frightful confusion. A man came to him who was so ambiguous that in greeting him with the usual civilities, it was impossible to decipher him. His confusion appeared; when the question was raised, he turned now to the right, now to the left, twenty times, taking an author and his antagonist. In fact, he was so flustered that he put an Escobar back in Sainte-Beuve's

[**1059**]
1. For a portrait of a casuist, see *PL*, LVII, 96.

slot, and a Grenoble *Morals* right next to Sanchez.[2] "Your question is difficult," said the casuist at that point, all distracted. "Difficult, how so?" said the client. "Can someone be exempt from paying me the damages?" "Ah! You're right," he said. "I wasn't sorry to see what you yourself were thinking." "But you have fine discernment, and if you're in doubt about it . . ." Just then, he brought down a heap of casuists, one after the other, and overwhelmed the client with quotations and authorities.

[**1060**] By the divinity, I declare I worship you; you know my idolatry.[1]

[**1061**] It is quite certain that love has a character different from friendship; the latter has never sent a man to the Little-Houses.[1]

[**1062**] I was asked why there is no longer a taste for the works of Corneille, Racine, etc. I answered: "It is because all things that require *esprit* have become ridiculous. The problem is more general. Nothing that has a specific object is bearable[1] anymore: men of war can no longer stand war; men of politics can no longer stand politics, and so forth. Only general objects are known, and in practice, that amounts to nothing. It is the company of women that has led us there, because it is in their character not to be attached to anything fixed. [Thus, we have become like them.] There is only one sex anymore; we are all women in spirit, and if we were to change faces one night, no one would notice that anything else had changed. Even if women were to move into all the employments that society offers,[2] and men were deprived of all those that society can take away, neither would be disoriented."

[**1063**] It is not surprising that Pompey and Caesar were jealous of each

---

2. Antonio de Escobar y Mendoza (1589–1669), Spanish Jesuit made famous by Pascal's *Provincial Letters;* Jacques de Sainte-Beuve (1613–77), French theologian; Thomas Sanchez (1550–1610), renowned moralist and canonist, especially on matrimonial matters. The *Morals* of Grenoble is probably *Theologie Morale, ou resolution des cas de conscience* [Moral Theology, or resolution of cases of conscience] (Paris: Pralard, 1689).

[1060]
1. See *pensée* 1031.

[1061]
1. The Little-Houses [*Petites-Maisons*] was an insane asylum in Paris; see other references at *pensées* 872, 1102, 1355, 1376, and 1610.

[1062]
1. First version: "It is because one can no longer bear the things for which *esprit* is needed: *esprit* has become ridiculous, and we have become so given to that way of thinking that we have no more taste for anything. It has happened that we cannot"
2. See *pensée* 1006.

other; neither of those world leaders could have any superior but the other. But as for us, why would we be jealous of someone? What does it matter whether he is above us or not, since so many others are already?

[1064] In a house, some women were talking about natural sentiments, a father's love for his children, that of the children for their father, a certain propriety in desertion, what is owed in marriage. I said: "Don't talk too loudly; you'll be taken for chatterboxes. These are things that one can think, but that are not in good taste to say . . ." It is certain that these days, integrity is no longer a matter of indifference, and that nothing alienates a man from more people than the knowledge that he is an honorable man. I remember that Commander Solar came to France after having taken the investiture of certain fiefs in Vienna for the King of Sardinia, his master,[1] who was at that time declaring his opposition to the Emperor. Since that man was regarded as an atrocious man—devious, subtle, treacherous, a man who had wickedly deceived the Viennese court—everyone welcomed him; people were throwing themselves at his feet. When they realized that he was merely an honorable man who had just been following orders, you cannot believe how people cooled toward him. He was only fashionable when he was thought to be a rogue.

[1065] Contades, low courtier even at death. Did he not write to the Cardinal that he was happy to die in order not to see the end of a minister such as him?[1] He was a courtier by force of nature, or thought he could pull through.

[1066] *I said:*[1] "I find nothing so difficult as to be smart[2] with fools."

[1067] On tyrannical and exploitative friends, I said: "Love has compensations that friendship does not have."

[1068] I can imagine that a man who has acted pusillanimously on

---

[1064]
1. The allusions are to Antonio Maurice Solar (1689–1762), ambassador to Vienna and to Paris, commander in the Order of Malta, whom Montesquieu had met in Vienna in 1728 (*OC,* 2:971 and 1085), and to Victor-Amadeus II (r. 1720–30).

[1065]
1. The references are to Georges-Gaspard de Contades (1666–1735) and Cardinal Fleury (1653–1743), Louis XV's prime minister (1726–43).

[1066]
1. The italicized words are in English in Montesquieu's text.—HC
2. Or "to be witty"; the French is *avoir de l'esprit.*—HC

some occasion might die with much courage. In the first case, he wanted to preserve a good that he thought was in danger; in the second, he abandons a good that he sees he cannot preserve.

[**1069**] [EASTERN WOMEN. Their youth is at the beginning of their life cycle, whereas with our women, youth is in the middle.][1]

[**1070**] On the new discoveries, I said: "We have been quite far for men."

[**1071**] You cannot believe just how far the sense of wonder has declined in recent times.

[**1072**] There is one thing that ought to make all the ministers in most European States tremble: it is the ease with which they could[1] be replaced.

[**1073**] Most of our Frenchmen who have written their own memoirs are so visibly vain that it is impossible for them to be true. They have done everything in war and in public affairs. But since men have virtually the same passions, the same anxieties, the same talents, it is not possible for them to relinquish to a single person the office of acting and thinking, without being held back by some overwhelming force.

[**1074**] I was saying that Philip V[1] owed his crown to the Andalusian horses ridden by his Spaniards, and to Spanish wine, which killed the English.

[**1075**] A noble pride sits well with men of great talent.[1]

[**1076**] In reading an extract from M. Freind's *History of Medicine*,[1] I noticed that the physicians he talks about lived long lives. Natural reasons: (1) Physicians are inclined toward temperance; (2) ward off their illnesses

[1069]
1. See *pensée* 757.

[1072]
1. First version: "can"

[1074]
1. King of Spain (r. 1700–1746).

[1075]
1. See *pensée* 384 and the beginning of *pensée* 1256.—HC

[1076]
1. John Freind (1675–1728), English physician and author of *History of Physic* (1725–26); cf. *Spicilège*, 561, where Montesquieu cites it as a book he has to read.

at the outset; (3) because of their position, they get a great deal of exercise; (4) in seeing many sick people, their temperament adapts to all types, and they become less susceptible of disturbance; (5) are more familiar with danger; (6) those whose reputations have come down to us were skillful; thus, they were guided by skillful men, namely, themselves.

[**1077**] It is quite amazing that Churchmen's wealth began with poverty as its first cause.¹

[**1078**] [I said: "At Versailles everyone is small; in Paris everyone is large."]¹

[**1079**] In Paris, one is numbed by the social world; only manners are known; there is no time to know vices and virtues.

[**1080**] A man said: "I do not love God, because I do not know him; nor the neighbor, because I do know him." I am not saying this impious thing, but I am indeed saying that those who argue over the love of God do not understand what they are saying if they distinguish this love from the sentiment of submission and from that of gratitude toward an all-powerful and beneficent being. But as for love, I can no more love a spiritual being than I can love this proposition: two and three makes five.

[**1081**] Smart people are managed by valets, and fools, by smart people.

[**1082**] A proof that irreligion has gained ground is that witticisms are no longer drawn from Scripture, nor from the language of religion; an impiety no longer has spice.

[**1083**] To do big things, it is essential not to be such a great genius; one must not be above men, one must be with them.

[**1084**] One must break up with women brusquely; nothing is so unbearable as a worn-out old affair.

[**1085**] Continual idleness should have been placed among the pains of Hell; it seems to me, on the other hand, that it has been placed among the joys of Heaven.

[**1086**] What orators lack in depth, they give you in length.¹

[1077]
1. See *pensées* 181, 214, and 273.

[1078]
1. See *pensée* 998.

[1086]
1. There is a bit of a pun: *profondeur* vs. *longueur.*—HC

[**1087**] The story of the soldier that Clovis killed[1] because he did not want to hand over a vase full of spoils that he had had a part in, which abbé Dubos uses to prove Clovis's authority,[2] does more to prove his impotence. Do not imagine that a Janissary might refuse something to the Sultan. The corps of Janissaries will indeed kill him, but one Janissary will never disobey him.

[**1088**] Simplicity {and minimal cultivation of the mind}, good for victories: witness the earliest Romans, the Tartars, the Arabs.

[**1089**] There is no fifty-year-old woman who has a good enough memory to recall all the persons with whom she has had a falling out, and with whom she has made up.

[**1090**] When a girl is seven, she seems to be smart, because she is afraid of nothing; at twelve, she falls into a kind of stupidity because she perceives everything. It is the same with those children who seem to be so smart, but become so foolish. They let out all manner of nonsense, because they neither know nor sense what they are saying; whereas those children who seem foolish have a kind of premature feeling for things, which makes them in some sense more reserved. Pay attention! What is pleasing in the child's discourse arises, at bottom, from the folly of the child, who has not been struck by what he says as he should have been, and has neither seen nor sensed what he should have. {Only those who are smart seem foolish.}

[**1091**] [How many people I see who are very smart but are not smart enough. How many I see who are not very smart but are smart enough.][1]

[**1092**] The four great poets: Plato, Father Malebranche, Lord Shaftesbury,[1] {Montaigne}.

[**1093**] I wrote to a person: "I believe the Graces have sent you to teach us what they are saying and what they are doing."[1]

[**1087**]
1. Clovis, king of the Franks (485–511); the allusion is to the vase of Soissons.
2. See *pensée* 795n.

[**1091**]
1. See *pensée* 1094 for a slightly different version.

[**1092**]
1. Anthony Ashley Cooper, third earl of Shaftesbury (1671–1713); Montesquieu owned the three-volume, 1714 edition of his *Characteristicks* (*Catalogue*, 696). On Malebranche, see *pensée* 156.

[**1093**]
1. See *pensée* 1333.—HC

[1094] How many people do I see who are not smart enough, but are very smart! How many do I see who are smart enough, but are not very smart![1]

[1095] On the front of the house of Chantilly, where M. le Prince retired for so long, I would like to put:

> *Haec limina victor*
> *Alcides subiit; haec illum regia cepit.*[1]

[1096] OBJECTIONS THAT ATHEISTS COULD MAKE, TO WHICH I WILL RESPOND.[1]

Since, when we see some watch or some other machine, we have always seen that it is some artisan who has made it, likewise, when we see the world, we judge that it is some superior being who has made it.

Since we see that everything made in the world has a cause, and since we see matter existing, we judge that there is some other being that is the cause of matter's existence.

Since this matter, with the exception of some portions that we see organically structured, appears to us in a state of inertia, we judge that another being must have given it motion.

Since we have seen that bodies that appear to be at rest changed the direction of their motion only when we put our hands there to move them, we have judged that motion in general is alien to matter and must have been imparted to it by another being.

Since, when we do not see a cause for something, we say that chance has produced it, we likewise say that if a being has not created matter, it is chance that has created it, and that if it has not imparted motion to it, it is chance that has done so.

Since, when we find laws in our societies, we always have the idea of a legislator, seeing laws constant in nature, we do not fail to say that it is a being other than nature that has established them.

In the end, our judgments on this immense universe are always based on the ideas we have derived from our human operations, and since we

----

[1094]
1. See *pensée* 1091 for a slightly different version.

[1095]
1. Virgil, *Aeneid*, VIII.362–63: "'These portals . . . victorious Alcides [i.e., Hercules] stooped to enter; this mansion welcomed him.'"

[1096]
1. See *Laws*, 24.2, against Bayle's defense of atheism.

see only particular effects everywhere, we judge that the universe is itself a particular effect.

Since we distinguish two things in every body, its essence and its existence, we make the same distinction concerning the universality of things—without considering that for an eternal, infinite, necessary extension without bounds, its essence is to exist, and conversely its existence necessarily presupposes its essence. It would not exist if it were not eternal; it would not be eternal if it were not necessary; it would not be necessary if it were not infinite; it would not be infinite if something could limit it; and if something could limit it, this something would not be infinite, either.

This universality of things, an atheist will say, must not have a cause, for if it were necessary to assume one, the same reasoning would assume a cause for this cause, and so on to infinity.

This existing matter will have properties, and these properties will be its laws, which we know by the result of the properties and of general necessary effects.

Since our perspective is very limited, and since we see only parts, we have no means of judging the properties of matter and, consequently, the laws of nature, except by the effects they produce. For in order to judge otherwise, we would have to know the whole, by which we would derive knowledge of effects from knowledge of cause, whereas we are obliged to derive knowledge of cause from some effects.

The properties of matter or laws of nature, the atheist will say, are: (1) extension; (2) force, which is motion; (3) the faculties that bodies have of attraction and repulsion; (4) gravitation; (5) the faculty matter has of vegetating; (6) its faculty of becoming organically structured; (7) its faculty of sensation; (8) its faculty of thought.

The faculty of these properties that constitutes the force that all bodies have to put themselves in action is found both in bodies that we call *in motion* and in those we call *at rest.* Motion and rest are different, but not contradictory. Bodies in both states have force. The difference consists entirely in the relations they have among themselves and with other bodies.

The faculty of vegetating is joined to the power of reproduction, which is found in all vegetation. Most plants produce by cuttings. They would all produce that way, if there were not many whose texture dries out immediately in the ground, which makes them spoil before being able to receive the juices that suit them. Such are the grasses and flowers. In this case, the seed is necessary. In a plant that produces by cuttings, there is no part that is not seed. Thus, it is a big mistake to say that the plant is contained in the seed, and a still bigger one to say that the first plant contained all those that were going to be born. As soon as any stalk can receive juices from the ground, you suddenly see a leaf push forth and reproduce, and the roots emerge as well.

Microscopes have enabled us to see in matter such a capacity to become organically structured that it is impossible to say which part of matter is not organically structured.

Such a tendency to attraction or repulsion has been found in matter {by observation} that it is impossible to say there is a single body that is not in some respect electric.

Now, an atheist will say that, with eyes such as ours and with such organs, it is seeing a great deal in matter to have discovered so many things. But how much new enlightenment would we need in order to conceive of how matter is capable of feeling and thinking?

But just as we judge that bodies are organically structured because we see their organs; that they have electricity because we see its effects; we should likewise say that matter is capable of feeling (an atheist will say) because we feel, and of thought because we think.

[1097] Those sermons by Maillard, Menat, Rollin, Barlette were written to be preached as seriously as ours are at present, even though we find a comedian everywhere in them, and scandalous applications of Scripture, and burlesque spread throughout the whole.[1] Those men preached what they knew, and taught what they had been taught. In those days, people did not read Scripture; they read only stories based on Scripture or legends about the Saints. Scripture was known only by plays performed on Scriptural stories or on the mysteries. Combined with these were books based on revelations, legends and other stories that were in the hands of the entire people. Most of these books perished during the renewal of the sciences, and few deserved to see daylight when printing was discovered. The appearance of the Protestants was the reason why all these books perished—except the most extravagant, which they preserved as a stain on the old religion—and the Catholics neglected them or hid them as soon as a greater enlightenment appeared. We must therefore transport ourselves

---

[1097]
   1. Olivier Maillard (ca. 1430–ca. 1502), Franciscan preacher (see *Catalogue*, 592); Michel Menat and Jean Rollin were also French preachers who died in the early sixteenth century; Gabriel de Barletta was a fifteenth-century Dominican preacher from Naples.

to those times when everything that might serve in the instruction of the people was of a different nature from all the works presently in their hands. This was bound to make for a new kind of preaching.

[1098] My belief has been that one should attempt to regulate one's conduct as if prospering in one's status and situation. For I have seen that most people lose their fortunes out of ambition and dissipate their estates out of avarice.

[1099] In Seneca's *Thyestes*, Thyestes asks to see his children. Atreus, showing him his children's remains, which he had served him in the meal, says to him:

> *"Venere. Gnatos ecquid agnoscis tuos?"*

To which, Thyestes responds:

> *"Agnosco fratrem."*[1]

Crébillon's translation is very good:

> "Do you recognize this blood?"
> "I recognize my brother."[2]

But through an imperfection in the language, the French does not make as much of an impression as the Latin. A feminine rhyme is too mild to express Thyestes' feeling. Besides which, the pronoun *my,* which our language unavoidably gives us there, spoils the thought: *my brother* is a term of endearment there, as of consanguinity. I would as much have liked to put:

> "I recognize Atreus."

[1100] *"Nec me divitiae movent in quibus Bonieri et Samueles Turennios et Warvicos superarunt."*[1]

[1099]
1. Seneca, *Thyestes,* V.1005–6: "Dost recognize thy sons?" "I recognize my brother."
2. Crébillon, *Atrée et Thyeste,* V.vii.11. The text is "Do you not recognize" and not "Do you recognize."

[1100]
1. "Nor do riches influence me, in which the Bonniers and the Samuels surpass the Turennes and the Warwicks." The entry may be a contrast between tainted wealth and military renown. Montesquieu

I would have put: *faex Gallica Bonieri et Samueles;*[2] but I would have said less, because when the thing says it all, one must not have new words.

[1101] I like it when a man of modest quality becomes vain and proud because he married the daughter of a knave who enjoys esteem. He prides himself on what ought to humiliate him. I have seen some of those types: *O foex hominum e sanguine Deorum.*[1] {Rosmadec,[2] who had married the niece of the Keeper of the Seals.}

[1102] [It is quite right to say that love is livelier than friendship; at least friendship has never sent anyone to the Little Houses.][1]

[1103] One must never respond; if the public does not respond for us, the response is worthless.

[1104] It seems to me that love is agreeable in that vanity is satisfied without being ashamed of itself. If a mistress talks to me about myself, if I talk about myself to my mistress, if she caresses me less than she does another, if she does not give me complete preference, the petty feelings of my vanity[1] are excited without my being able to criticize myself for it, which[2] would happen if I had the same feelings in other circumstances.

[1105] Flattery is a soporific music. I heard M. Coste say that M. Locke

---

seems to be adapting a passage from Cicero comparing wealthy slave merchants with the Roman generals Gaius Laelius and Scipio Africanus, heroes of the Carthaginian wars. Joseph Bonnier (1676–1726) was treasurer of the Estates of Languedoc and one of the richest men of his age; his son Joseph Bonnier de la Mosson (1702–44) inherited his father's estate and presided over a large cabinet of curiosities in the hôtel du Lude near the Boulevard Saint-Germain in Paris after his father purchased it in 1726. Since Montesquieu lived nearby at this time, he may have known of it firsthand. There were numerous wealthy Bernards named Samuel: Samuel-Jacques Bernard (1615–87), Samuel Bernard (1651–1739), and Samuel-Jacques Bernard (1686–1753), the latter being superintendent of finance for the Queen (1725). Turenne (Henri de la Tour d'Auvergne, Viscount of Turenne, 1611–75), French general under Louis XIII and Louis XIV. See also *pensée* 1222.—HC

2. "The Gaulish dregs of the Bonniers and Samuels."—HC

[1101]
1. "O dregs of men, coming from the blood of the gods."
2. Possibly Sébastien Rosmadec (1658–1700), Marquis of Molac, royal official in Brittany under Louis XIV.

[1102]
1. Little Houses (*Petites-Maisons*), Paris insane asylum; see also *pensées* 872, 1061, 1355, 1376, and 1610.

[1104]
1. First version: "the passions of my vanity"
2. First version: "being able to criticize myself for being a fool, which"

could no longer live except by flattery and by talking about himself;[1] that Lord Shaftesbury, after noticing that M. Locke had gotten so accustomed to this, fell into it himself without realizing it, from having lived for five or six years in the country with his inferiors; that when M. Locke had been at Lady Masham's[2] in the country with Sir Isaac Newton and himself, he was contained by M. de Newton; but that, as soon as the latter climbed into his carriage, M. Locke began to say: "As for me, I . . ." He was, I reckon,[3] a wound up spring suddenly let loose.

[**1106**] Why is it that the children of misers are spendthrifts? It is because the goal of the latter is to make a fortune; the former, to enjoy it. In addition, the former are accustomed to opulence; the latter have been raised in frugality. Which is so true that rich merchants' children are no more prodigal than their fathers.

[**1107**] A hard business, all these missions to the Infidels. If the King converts, he becomes an enemy of his people. If the people convert, they become enemies of the King.

[**1108**] The theologians write a chapter: *De Simplicitate Dei,* and in turning the page, you see the title: *De Deo uno et trino.*[1] {I heard M. Coste make this observation.}

[**1109**] I like peasants; they are not learned enough to engage in crooked reasoning.

[**1110**] Virgil inferior to Homer, as we know, in the greatness and variety of his characters; in invention, wonderful; equal in the beauty of his poetry. His first six books are fine. I admit that his last six give me much less pleasure. I think the reasons are, *primo,* that six books from the arrival in Italy are too much; this should have been dispatched in one, because once Aeneas has arrived, everything is over. Homer did not make that mistake. Once Odysseus has arrived in Ithaca, the poem ends almost immediately, even though the reader yearns to learn how he will be received.

[1105]
   1. Pierre Coste (1668–1747), from Uzès, Protestant refugee in London, translator of Montaigne (see *pensée* 1231); a friend of John Locke (1632–1704).
   2. Favorite of the queen of England; cf. *Spicilège,* 434.
   3. *Me semble,* which *DAF* (1762) describes as a "kind of parenthesis"; the best equivalent would be "methinks," no longer in use. Montesquieu uses this phrase also at *pensées* 1110, 1111, 1896, 1962, and 1966.—HC

[1108]
   1. "On the Simplicity of God" and "On God, one and triune."

Lavinia's marriage is of little interest to the reader, is no more interesting than Lavinia herself, whose character is cold and lifeless—quite different from that of Helen, so marvelous in her adventures, in the goddesses' quarrels, and in her beauty. I sense that Turnus should not have been defeated by Aeneas;[1] it is the poet who needed Aeneas to win, not Aeneas who really had to win. There are, I reckon, many reflections to make on Virgil, while leaving him all the merit that he has, and that has been so justly attributed to him.

[1111] HISTORY OF FRANCE. If I write it {I had thought of writing that of Louis XIV}, I will have to include the principal parts, will have to put the extracts from the documents in everywhere, more or less long according to whether they are more or less interesting. As for the rest, I thought I would succeed no less well than someone else, and particularly better than those who, having had a part in the events, have become interested parties. There are, I reckon, a thousand examples of this. It appears to me that Caesar, in the causes he assigns for the civil war, is in contradiction with Pompey; but I intend to examine that.[1]

[1112] I have not {yet} seen the letter by Scarron where he says: "I still remember that girl who came to my place, who had a dress on three inches too short and who was crying."[1] This has been published, M. de Fontenelle told me. I have to look at Scarron's letters. He was himself surprised at having married her. I have to know how she moved from Scarron's to the Court. She used to go to Ninon de Lenclos' place. It is said she's a descendant of d'Aubigné, who wrote the *History*.[2]

[1113] Most people who die from a kidney stone operation die from

[1110]
1. Lavinia, daughter of King Latinus, fiancée of Turnus when her father promised her to Aeneas; Turnus, legendary king of Ardia and the Rutulians, son of Daunus, and one of the heroes of the *Aeneid*.

[1111]
1. See *pensée* 1183.

[1112]
1. The allusions are to Paul Scarron (1610–60), a writer and Mme de Maintenon's husband, and to Mme de Maintenon herself (Françoise d'Aubigné Scarron, marquise de Maintenon, 1635–1719).

2. Anne, called Ninon de Lenclos (1620–1705), celebrated for her beauty, her wit, and her romantic adventures, kept a correspondence with Mme de Maintenon; Agrippa d'Aubigné (1552–1630) was Mme de Maintenon's grandfather; Montesquieu owned the 1626 edition of his *Universal history* (*Catalogue*, 2905).

fright; the abbé de Louvois, for example.[1] He was full of bluster, but his blood was so clotted that it never came through.

[1114] Rabelais jests naïvely, Voiture subtly. Thus, the former is always pleasing; the latter is tiresome over time.[1]

[1115] The geometers' methods are types of chains that bind them and prevent them from deviating.

[1116] You have to have studied much in order to know little.

[1117] One must know the value of money. Spendthrifts do not know it; misers, even less.

[1118] Polygamy is unreasonable in that the father and mother do not have the same affection for their children,[1] since it is impossible for a father to love fifty children in the way that a mother does two.

[1119] There is no country where there is more ambition than in France; there is no country where one ought to have less. The greatest dignities confer no esteem here: M. de Coigny, less esteemed since winning two battles; d'Asfeld, since he was made marshal; and likewise for everyone.[1]

[1120] M. de Fontenelle said it very well: "Good styles form bad ones."

[1121] Charlatans succeed. Here's how. There are excellent remedies that the physicians have abandoned because they are violent. They have a reputation to preserve. Thus, they have to use general remedies whose effect, if it goes badly, is not rapid. Now, a remedy that does not kill rapidly does not cure rapidly, either. Charlatans grab all these remedies, such as certain preparations of antimony, which produce sometimes miraculous cures. They do not have a reputation to preserve, but to establish. Now, this method does indeed establish a reputation, but does not preserve it. There you have why all the charlatans' remedies fail in the long run. The

---

[1113]
1. Camille Le Tellier, abbé de Louvois (1675–1718), third son of Louis XIV's war minister.

[1114]
1. Vincent Voiture (1597–1648), who frequented the salon of Mme de Rambouillet.

[1118]
1. "Put in the *Laws*" (M.), 16.6.

[1119]
1. François de Franquétoy, marquis, then duke of Coigny (1670–1759); Claude-François Bidal, Chevalier, then marquis of Asfeld, marshal of France (1665–1743).

people like charlatans, because they like the wondrous, and rapid cures fit with this sense of wonder. If an empiric and a physician have treated a patient, the people absolve the empiric—whom they like—of the patient's death and blame the physician. It sometimes happens that a remedy cures one ailment and produces another; medicine bans it, and charlatanry grabs it. Thus, it cures gout by shedding blood. Lastly, it is believed that when a physician treats a long illness, it is nature that cures; but for an empiric, it is believed to be art.

[**1122**] [Louis XIV,[1] neither pacific nor warlike. He had the forms of justice, politics and devotion, the subtleties of politics, the air of a great king. Mild with his servants, good with his courtiers, anxious with his enemies, greedy with his people, hard in his counsels, childlike in that of conscience, despotic in his family, king in his court, always governing and always governed, dupe of all who play games with princes—state ministers, women, the devout—born without taste, making the arts flourish without understanding them, seeking glory where he was told it was, miserable in his glory, infatuated with fools but suffering through the gifted, fearing smartness, serious in his love affairs, and pathetically weak in his last attachment; no mental toughness in his successes; some firmness in his reverses, and courage in his death. He loved glory and religion, but was prevented throughout his life from knowing either one. Of all his faults, he would have had hardly any if he had been better raised, or if he had been a little smarter.]

[**1123**] Kings, with all that equipage they have given themselves—those guards, those officers, that house—have been reduced to being subject to the hour and the ceremonial. It becomes a great commendation for a king to be punctual. His life has become his duties. There you have what Louis XIV gained over Henry IV: he lost his freedom, but his character as king was as attached to his person as his skin.

[**1124**] Authors are always using each other. They have three manners, like painters: that of their master, which is that of the secondary school; that of their talent, which makes them produce good works; and that of art, which among painters is called *manner*.

[**1122**]

1. See *pensées* 1145 and 1306, as well as *PL,* XXXVII, *Catalogue,* pp. 213–14, and *Spicilège,* 452 and 570, for other treatments of Louis XIV.

[1125] Regarding certain people who live with their lackeys, I said: "Vices do have their penance."

[1126] I said: "When a man has made a reputation for integrity and humanity, it happens that people seek to take advantage of it. They come to him with proposals that they would never dare make to someone else. They count on his generosity."

[1127] I am the dupe of neither Madame de Sevac's sorrow nor Madame de Berville's love for her son; all this is done to stir up gossip.

[1128] Inside the building of the Church of Saint-Sulpice, which presses against the Seminary, I like to see the ecclesiastics, after forcing the seculars to retreat, make themselves retreat, and engage in a civil war after a victory in the foreign war.

[1129] For a woman to pass as bad, she needs to have wit. A thousand arrows from a foolish woman are wasted; a single one from a witty woman connects.

[1130] I vastly prefer being tormented by my heart than by my mind.

[1131] Too much regularity—sometimes, indeed many times, disagreeable. Nothing is so beautiful as the sky, but it is strewn with stars in no order. The houses and gardens around Paris have only the defect of being too much alike; they are constant copies of Le Nôtre.[1] You always see the same ambience, *qualem decet esse sororum.*[2] If someone has a peculiar terrain, instead of using it the way it is, they have made it regular so as to build a house that would be like the others. Our houses are like our characters.[3]

[1132] On the writings that Lord Townshend and M. Walpole arranged to appear in the *Craftsman* and in Lord Bolingbroke's writings, I said: "Kings are strong when they are deciding, and always weak when they are debating."[1]

[1131]
1. André Le Nôtre (1613–1700), royal architect and landscaper, notably on Versailles.
2. Ovid, *Metamorphoses,* II.14: "as it should be with sisters."
3. See *Essay on Taste* (*OC,* 1:617).

[1132]
1. See also the first of Montesquieu's "General Maxims of Politics" in *pensée* 1007. The references are to Charles, viscount Townshend (1674–1738); Robert Walpole (1675–1745), prime minister, 1721–42; the *Craftsman,* Bolingbroke's paper that Montesquieu read in London (see *Spicilège,* 516–34 passim, and *Notes sur l'Angleterre* [*OC,* 3:285]); and Henry Saint-John, viscount Bolingbroke (1678–1751), a Tory leader exiled in France from 1714 to 1725, where he had ties to the Jacobites; Montesquieu knew him and owned his *Dissertation upon Parties* (1735; *Catalogue,* 2370); see Shackleton, "Montesquieu, Bolingbroke, and the Separation of Powers," in *French Studies* (1949): 25–38.

[**1133**] God has given me possession,[1] and I have given myself surplus.

[**1134**] What a business it is to be moderate in one's principles! I pass in France for having little religion and in England for having too much.

[**1135**] In England, they think half the Frenchmen are in the Bastille and the other half in the Poorhouse.[1]

[**1136**] The English are virtually never united except by the ties of hatred and the hope of vengeance.

[**1137**] Raymonde's *Essay* on poetry: there are two or three ideas that have made it out of a sterile mind.[1]

[**1138**] I said in Rome: "I am buying neither virginities nor Raphael paintings."

[**1139**] Men need a little logic and a little morality.

[**1140**] To perform a bad deed, devotion finds reasons that a simple honest man cannot find.

[**1141**] THE CASTRATI. For one who sings well, there are a hundred who do not succeed. "*Multi sunt vocati; pauci vero electi,*" Jacob used to say.[1]

[**1142**] *Mare liberum sive de Jure quod Batavis competit ad Anglicana Commercia.* {Book published in Leiden, 1689.} At first, they asked only for liberty; now they ask for dominion.[1]

[**1143**] I said of Madame de B[onneval] that no one better understood the etiquette of love and friendship than she did.[1]

[**1144**] Having an affair with a woman, I saw from afar that I was going

[1133]
1. *Bien;* "estate" or "goods" are other possibilities.—HC

[1135]
1. The Poorhouse, or "Hôpital" in the original, housed the poor and the transient as well as the sick; according to *DAF* (1762), it is said of "a man ruined by lawsuits, gambling or other foolish expenses, that *he is on his way to the Poorhouse.*" See also *pensée* 1610.—HC

[1137]
1. Rémond de Saint-Mard (1683–1757), *Réflexions sur la poésie* (1733).—HC

[1141]
1. On Hildebrand Jacob, see *pensée* 397 n. 2; the passage is Matthew 22:14, "many are called, but few are chosen." On the *castrati,* see also *Voyages* (*OC,* 2:1110).

[1142]
1. "The Free sea which the Dutch rightfully possess for the East Indian trade." See *Catalogue,* 2406, where Montesquieu appends the same sentence to the title.

[1143]
1. Judith-Charlotte de Gontaud-Biron, countess of Bonneval (d. 1741).

to have a successor, and soon I saw it up close. I sent back her letters and wrote: "Perhaps you will find as much pleasure in receiving these letters as you had in writing them."

[1145]   Louis XIV, neither pacific nor warlike. He had the forms of justice, politics, and devotion, and the air of a great king. Mild with his servants, liberal with his courtiers, greedy with his people, anxious with his enemies, despotic in his family, king in his court, hard in the counsels, childlike in that of conscience, dupe of all who play games with princes—state ministers, women, and the devout; always governing and always governed; unfortunate in his choices, loving fools, suffering through the gifted, fearing smartness, serious in his love affairs, and pathetically weak in his last attachment. No strength of mind in his successes, some firmness in his reverses, and courage in his death. He loved glory and religion, but was prevented throughout his life from knowing either one. Of all these faults, he would have had hardly any if he had been better raised, or if he had been a little smarter.[1]

[1146]   I have read in the *Relations*[1] that when some American savages see that their hunts are not going well, they tighten up their stomachs and thereby enable themselves to withstand hunger for a long time. You will see in Aulus Gellius, book XVI, chapter III, that to withstand hunger, the Scythians tighten their stomachs with little bandages, as the physician Erasistratus says, using this fact to prove that "*esuritionem faciunt inanes patentesque intestinorum fibrae, quae, ubi cibo complentur aut inanitate diutina contrahuntur, voluntas capiendi restinguitur.*"[2] The hunger is more pressing at first but diminishes afterward.

[1147]   In book XIV, chapter I, of Aulus Gellius, Favorinus, railing against astronomy, said he was surprised the planets were only seven in number: "*Posse enim fieri existimabat ut alii planetae pari potestate essent,*

[1145]

1. See *pensée* 1122.

[1146]

1. The reference would be to Fr. Louis Hennepin's *Recueil des voyages du Nord* [Northern voyages collection], published in many editions in the early eighteenth century.

2. Aulus Gellius, author of *Attic nights* (*Catalogue,* 1822–23); Erasistratus, Greek physician and anatomist (d. ca. 280); the passage, which Montesquieu condenses somewhat, is from Aulus Gellius, XVI.iii.3: "that the empty and open fibers of the intestines . . . cause hunger; but when these are either filled with food or are contracted and brought together by continued fasting, . . . the impulse to take food . . . is destroyed."

sine quibus perfecta observatio perfici nequiret."¹ He had surmised the existence of the moons of Jupiter and Saturn.

[1148] [I thought I should screen a pile of essays that are going to arrive, so we would not be accused of being like those people who live near the sea, who survive only by scavenging . . .]¹

[1149] Examine closely the *vis comica* in action, and examine it in speech.¹

[1150] *Ego odi homines ignava opera et philosopha sententia.*¹

Verses, cited by Aulus Gellius.

It seems to me these are our monks.

[1151] Dampier says the great lords of Tonkin all wear a long gown made of English wool, without which they would not present themselves at Court.¹ It is curious that our European cloths, so appropriate for our colder climes, are hardly in use anymore among us, giving way to the silks and cottons of Tonkin, but that they are brought to Tonkin, where nature has provided so many silks and cottons, which we wear even though it runs counter to our climate.

[1152] It is unfortunate that there is too little interval between the time when we are too young and the time when we are too old.

[1153] *Est miser nemo nisi comparatus.*¹

[1147]

1. "He thought it might possibly be the case that there were some other planets of equal power, without which a correct and final observation could not be completed." *Attic nights*, XIV.i.12. Montesquieu's version is approximate.

[1148]

1. See *pensée* 856.—HC

[1149]

1. *Vis comica*, "power of comedy," a phrase used, for example, in discussions of Terence and the Greek comic authors (see Suetonius, *Life of Terence*).—HC

[1150]

1. Pacuvius, cited by Aulus Gellius, XIII.8.4: "I hate base men who preach philosophy." See *pensée* 1656 and *Catalogue*, p. 46, above entry 602.

[1151]

1. William Dampier (1652–1715), English navigator, whose *New Voyage Round the World* (1697) Montesquieu owned in a five-volume translation (1711; *Catalogue*, 2740); in *Geographica* (*OC*, 2:295–96), Montesquieu gives extracts of the first three volumes but declares he has not read the last two and a half volumes.

[1153]

1. "No one is unfortunate, save as compared with others." Seneca, *Troades*, 1023.

If we had remained in the earthly Paradise, we would have an idea of happiness and unhappiness different from what we have.[2]

[**1154**] When it is said that there are no absolute qualities, this does not mean that there are none, but that there are none for us, that our minds cannot determine them.[1]

[**1155**] I said to Madame de ———, "I want to have the best share in your friendship; I need the lion's share."

[**1156**] In Pithou, I have read *Sextus Rufus,* which is a summary of Roman history written in favor of Valentinian.[1] It all amounts to a detailed account of the manner in which each piece that made up the Roman Empire came to be attached to it, and in that regard it is curious.

[**1157**] Physicians say that for one sick man, there are two women. It seems the ratio is equal in the countryside.[1] Whence one can conclude quite naturally that half of women's maladies are imaginary.

I am not talking about childbirths, which are voluntary maladies.

[**1158**] This did not make it into my *Memoir on Rome's Inhabitants:*[1]

"Wine, by the joy it inspires, encourages intemperance and, bringing us imperceptibly back toward itself, regenerates our debauches or at least our taste.

Mohammed, who had been a merchant, rendered a great service to his Country by prohibiting wine; he made all of Asia drink the wine of his country—very good reason for enacting his law, if he had thought of it."[2]

[**1159**] In America, the peoples subject to despotic kings, such as those

---

2. See *pensée* 819.—HC

[1154]
1. See *pensées* 799 and 818.—HC

[1156]
1. Pierre Pithou published Sextus Rufus's *Breviarium* (*Epitome*) in his 1609 *Opera sacra, juridica, historica, miscellanea* [Sacred, juridical, historical and miscellaneous works] (*Catalogue,* 2343); Flavius Valentinianus, Roman emperor (364–75).

[1157]
1. Montesquieu seems to assume here that physicians practice mainly in the city.—HC

[1158]
1. See *Réflexions sur la sobriété des habitants de Rome* [Reflections on the sobriety of Rome's inhabitants] (*OC,* 3:357–60).
2. See *Laws,* 14.10, 239.

of Mexico and Peru, have been found down south, and the free nations have been found up north.[1]

[1160] There is no agreement on *esprit* because, although *esprit* insofar as it sees is something very real, *esprit* insofar as it pleases is entirely relative.[1]

[1161] Talk in England about Government, and you will please as if you were talking about War at the Invalides.[1]

[1162] In the arts, and especially in poetry, there are certain felicities that cannot be recaptured.

[1163] I said Bohemian leagues are long because it is men who were not thinking who marked them out.[1]

[1164] I said {in Italy}: "The French are misers and spendthrifts; they are Florentines and Milanese all at the same time."[1]

[1165] I said that if a Persian or an Indian came to Paris, it would take six months to make him understand what a commendatory abbot who pounds the pavement in Paris is all about. {This is by me; it has been attributed to abbé de Mongaut.}[1]

[1166] Anticipation is a chain that links all our pleasures.

[1167] Marshal Villeroy always talked to his ward about his subjects, never his people.[1]

[1168] [1]

[1159]
1. See *Laws*, 14.3, 234.

[1160]
1. See *pensée* 1682 and the translator's note glossary.—HC

[1161]
1. The military hospital founded in Paris under Louis XIV.—HC

[1163]
1. See *pensée* 381.

[1164]
1. See *pensée* 474.—HC

[1165]
1. An abbot *in commendam*, or provisionally, who draws Church revenues without exercising spiritual authority. On abbé Mongault, see *pensée* 291 n. 2.

[1167]
1. Nicolas de Neufville, marquis of Villeroy, marshal of France (1598–1685), governor of Louis XIV. See *pensée* 1185.

[1168]
1. Deleted and illegible.

[1169] I said: "Truth has no clients;[1] it has only martyrs."

[1170] The big problem with the Constitution is that all the bishops had conceived the hope of making a fortune, like all the lords in Mississippi.[1]

[1171] I find in Tacitus, *De Moribus Germanorum*, the quite natural reason for the great authority that the bishops assumed among the Frankish converts to Christianity.[1] This was in their ancient mores. "*Reges ex nobilitate, duces ex virtute sumunt; nec Regibus infinita aut libera potestas . . . Ceterum neque animadvertere, neque vincire, neque verberare quidem, nisi sacerdotibus est permissum; non quasi in poenam, nec ducis jussu, sed velut Deo imperante, quem adesse bellatoribus credunt.*"[2]

The same Tacitus shows us the origin of our custom of always being armed: "*Nihil . . . neque publicae neque privatae rei, nisi armati agentes.*"[3]

Likewise, the custom of hiring oneself out in war: "*Si civitas in qua orti sunt longa pace et otio torpeat, plerique nobilium adolescentium petunt ultro eas nationes quae tum bellum aliquod gerunt.*"[4]

[1172] As to what Tacitus says about the Germans—"*Omnibus iis idem habitus*"—this proves that they had not been defeated, and that they had only sent colonies elsewhere, without receiving any.[1]

[1173] Since the vessels of the human body, the veins and arteries, are of {conical or} pyramidal shape, the blood goes through the arteries from

[1169]
1. *Client* may mean someone who hires a lawyer, or someone who seeks the protection of powerful persons as in its ancient Roman usage.—HC

[1170]
1. The Constitution is the bull *Unigenitus* (1713), against Jansenist doctrine; the Mississippi refers to John Law's *Mississippi Company*, a trading company that went bankrupt in 1721.

[1171]
1. "Put in the *Laws*" (M.), 18.31.
2. Tacitus, *Germania*, 7.1–2: "They take their kings on the ground of birth, their generals on the basis of courage: the authority of their kings is not unlimited or arbitrary; . . . But anything beyond this—capital punishment, imprisonment, even flogging—is permitted only to the priests, and then not as a penalty or under the general's orders, but as an inspiration from the god whom they suppose to accompany them on campaign."
3. Tacitus, *Germania*, 13.1: "They do no business, public or private, without arms in their hands."
4. Tacitus, *Germania*, 14.2: "Should it happen that the community where they are born be drugged with long years of peace and quiet, many of the high-born youth voluntarily seek those tribes which are at the time engaged in some war."

[1172]
1. Tacitus, *Germania*, 4. "The same characteristics in each one." See *Laws*, 28.17, 552.

bottom to top and returns through the veins from top to bottom. Look into what effect this must have on the movement of the blood.

[1174] All the origins in the epoch of Creation, all those little animals seen in the microscope, whose number is no less astonishing than their tininess, made on the same day as the lamias and the whales: "*Creavit Deus cete grandia et omnem animam viventem atque motabilem.*"[1]

[1175] It is easier to write a micrography like messrs. Hooke, Atrocquer, and Joublot than to learn to play those games that idle people[1] have invented to while away the time that weighs so heavily on them.[2]

[1176] THE TWO WORLDS. This one is ruining the other one, and the other one is ruining this one. Two is too many; there should only have been one.

[1177] I said of a man: "He does good, but he does not do it in a good way."[1]

[1178] I said: "It's an extraordinary thing that all of philosophy consists in these three words: 'Couldn't care less.'"

[1179] On the Roman law permitting fathers to give strangers their estates, I said:[1] "That's an unloaded cannon; *brutum fulmen.*"[2]

[1180] "God makes the thunder groan," says Seneca, "*paucorum periculo et multorum metu.*"[1] The Legislator, in the establishment of punishments, should do the same thing.

[1181] Extremely happy and extremely unhappy people are equally inclined to harshness: witness monks and conquerors. It is only a middling condition, or a mixture of good and bad fortune, that yields pity.[1]

[1174]
1. Genesis 1:21: "God created the great sea monsters and every living creature that moves, with which the waters swarm."

[1175]
1. First version: "worldly people" (i.e., *gens du monde*).—HC
2. Robert Hooke (1635–1703), *Micrographia* (1667); Louis Joblot (1645–1723), *Descriptions et usage de plusieurs nouveaux microscopes* [Descriptions and use of many new microscopes] (1718).

[1177]
1. "Put in the *Laws*" (M.), 28.41, 595. The remark is a pun on *le bien* (the good) and *bien* (well).

[1179]
1. See *Laws*, 27, 523.
2. "Unfeeling thunderbolt," an empty threat.—HC

[1180]
1. Seneca, *De Clementia* [On clemency], I.viii.5: "dangerous for the few, though feared by all."

[1181]
1. See *Laws*, 6.9, 83.

[1182] I would not be able to console myself for not making a fortune if I had been born in England. I am not at all put out at not having made one in France.

[1183] I am in the most suitable circumstances imaginable for writing history.[1] I have no eye toward a fortune. My estate and my birth are such that I have neither to blush at the one nor to envy or wonder at the other. I have not been employed in public affairs, and I do not need to speak for either my vanity or my self-justification. I have lived in the social world, and have had connections, even friendly ones, with people who have lived at the court of the prince whose life I am describing. I have known a great many anecdotes in the social world where I have lived part of my life. I am neither too far from the period that monarch lived in to be ignorant of quite a few circumstances, nor too near to be dazzled by them. I am living in a time when admiration for heroism is very much in retreat. I have traveled to foreign countries, where I have collected some good memoirs. Time has in any event brought out of the secret corridors of power all the various memoirs that men of our nation—where people love to talk about themselves—have piled up. And from these different memoirs, one draws out the truth when no memoir is followed and when all of them together are followed; when they are compared with more authentic monuments such as the letters of ministers and generals, the instructions for ambassadors, and the monuments that are like foundation stones for the edifice, within which all the rest is set. Lastly, I came from a profession where I acquired knowledge of the law of my country, and especially public law—if that is what we must call those feeble and wretched remnants of our laws, which arbitrary power has been able to hide up to now, but which it will never be able to annihilate except with its own demise.

In an age when everything is offered for amusement and nothing for instruction, there have been writers who have sought only to make their histories enjoyable. For this, they have chosen to treat a single point in history, such as some revolution, and they have written history as one writes a tragedy, with a unity of action that pleases the reader because it offers effortless movement, and because it seems to instruct without the need for memory or judgment. And this has put people off from that whole train of facts with which history is filled, and which weary the memory and are not all interesting.

[1183]
1. This design for a preface was perhaps destined for a *History of Louis XIV* that Montesquieu planned to write; see *pensées* 111 and 1302.

[1184] REMARKS ON COUNT BOULAINVILLIERS' "HISTORY."[1]

It seems the English custom that everyone must be judged by his peers, called *juries*,[2] and the entire judicial order, used to be the same in France. It is found in the charters granted by Louis the Headstrong concerning the widespread nonsupport he found in the realm on the death of his father, Philip the Fair.[3] In his *History of Government,* the Count of Boulainvilliers gives an account of these charters. In the second one, granted to the Lord of Cayeu and La Varenne, the King declares that his bailiffs and other officers will not have a voice in judicial decisions but will leave these to fief-holders, after assembling them and entreating them to it, and that they will be obliged to give their letters of judgment in conformity with their opinion.

These charters granted to various lords and territories are still in the Treasury of Charters, and among others, the one called *Norman Charter,*[4] the most troublesome for kings. There remain eight. They were granted after royal deputies were sent into the provinces to redress the grievance that had given rise to associations formed against Philip the Fair, and it seems the King's principal aim was to obtain the original of these associations; the ones in the Treasury of Charters are the ones obtained at that time. Count Boulainvilliers says these documents are the principal monument of our liberty, and would have preserved that liberty had it not been for our nation's constant inattention.[5] It seems indeed that it did more than that, says the Count. He says Nicholas Gilles informs us[6] that, beyond this, the Headstrong made a declaration in which he recognized, both for himself and his successors, that he could levy no taxes without the consent of the three estates, which would themselves undertake their collection and use. There are authors, says the Count, who cast doubt on this declaration because it is not found in the Treasury of Charters. But it is clear that it was

[1184]

1. Boulainvilliers, *Histoire de l'ancien gouvernement de France* (1727); cf. *pensée* 948n and *Catalogue,* 2912; see also *Laws,* 30.10.

2. On English juries, see *Laws,* 6.3, and David Hume's April 10, 1749, letter to Montesquieu in *The Letters of David Hume,* 2 vols., ed. J. Y. T. Greig (Oxford, 1932), 1:135.

3. Louis X le Hutin (r. 1314–16); see *pensée* 1302.

4. The two charters of Louis X known by the name of the *Norman Charter* are dated March 19, 1314, and July 1315.

5. "Look into what he says chapter II, page 97" (M.).

6. Nicholas Gilles, secretary to Louis XI (d. 1503). He published an account of the Gauls, of which Montesquieu owned two sixteenth-century editions (*Catalogue,* 2950–51).

the foundation of the authority the three estates have acquired since that time; besides which, it is so connected to the above-mentioned charters that without it, they could not endure. The King declares in that place that he renounces any imposition of a taille or levies without obvious necessity or obvious utility. Now wouldn't this be pointless if he had been the sole judge of both?[7]

Associations were prepared against Philip of Valois,[8] as they had been against Philip the Fair. The Normans, slower to choose sides, were also the slowest to come to terms. They obtained confirmation of the charter granted by the Headstrong, with the declaration that no taxation would be permitted without the consent of the estates. This firmness was common throughout the realm. Nicholas Gilles and *The Rosebush of France*[9] say that in that year, 1338 and 1339, before Easter, it was decreed before the three estates, with the King present, that the taille could be neither imposed nor levied if urgent necessity or obvious utility did not require it on the part of the estates.[10]

I would add and observe something peculiar here. While everyone rises up on the occasion of the taxes that the kings want to establish, which indicates that the rights of liberty were known, we see, on the other hand, acts of cruelty and barbarism by the kings that produce not the slightest peep throughout the nation. In one day, Philip of Valois has fourteen lords of Brittany and Normandy arrested and their heads cut off, without any formal trial, because he suspects them of taking the side of John of Monfort—and this, despite their being under the safeguard of a tournament, where they had been guests. His son King John begins his reign by having the Count of Eu, Constable of France, the flower of chivalry at that time, kidnapped and decapitated in his presence without due process.[11] I say these things could not have made as much impression in that period, when the lords themselves were accustomed to engaging in similar bold strokes of authority against their vassals or others as they wished. This appears in countless examples—among others, in the example of the quarrel between Saint Louis and Enguerrand de Couci, whom that king arranged

7. "See this *Histoire du gouvernement* by the count, pages 127, 128, 129" (M.).
8. Philip VI of Valois, King of France (r. 1328–50).
9. Pierre Choisnet wrote two works on this theme in the 1520s.
10. "Look at the same author, pages 185, 186, 187" (M.).
11. *Formalité de justice,* which of course would not have been as specific and extensive as the English phrase *due process* might connote.—HC

to be taken and tried for having hanged without due process three Flemish hunters in Couci's forest.[12]

I will say next that the charters cited by Boulainvilliers are curious in that they give us an idea of the origins of our French law, and of the forms of royal and seigneurial justice, and of the changes that have taken place in them, and by what route we have arrived at those changes. Thus, they should be looked at; I'll make an extract of them.[13]

It must be remarked that the kings mainly rose only by the immense profits they made on the currency,[14] which went so far that they often tripled or quadrupled, to their benefit, all the money possessed by private individuals. This put them in a position to buy up everywhere cities, lands, castles, seigneuries, counties, duchies. This often made them richer than all the lords put together. The very remedies that the estates brought to bear on this only made things worse: they set up subsidies so the King would be able to produce a strong currency, which enabled him to claim weakness at the outset and thus make new gains. {The lords, who wanted a strong currency, consented to taxes on the People, so that a strong currency would be given them. I have cited Budé in the *Spicilège*,[15] where he criticizes our nation for its constant inattention.}

[1185] What usually gives princes a very mistaken idea of their greatness is that those who raise them are themselves dazzled by them; they are the first dupes, and the princes are duped only afterward.

{Marshal Villeroy always talked to the King about his subjects, never about his people.}[1]

[1186] I said: "Those who have little vanity are closer to pride than are the others."

[1187] The fibrous tips of our brains receive a small disturbance, which produces a feeling or a slight stimulus in us. This is enough to explain everything. For example, we see a square for the first time. Perceiving that we see it is enough to give us an idea of it, because otherwise, we would

---

12. The allusions are to John of Monfort (1295–1345), Duke of Brittany; John II the Good, King of France (r. 1350–64); Raoul of Brienne II, Constable of France, beheaded in Paris in 1350; Enguerrand IV of Coucy (d. 1311).

13. This extract, if it was made, is lost.

14. See *Laws*, 22.2.

15. See *Spicilège*, 672.

[1185]

1. See the end of *pensée* 1167.

not see the square. To see the square, we need to perceive that four equal angles are being presented. We thus have an idea of the square's properties, and as soon as the stimulus of the square comes to us, an idea of its properties immediately comes to us as well. We do not see a square by itself, we see a square of other things. Our soul, which sees them together, cannot avoid comparing them, for if it did not see that the square has angles and the circle does not, it would not see either the circle or the square. For our soul to see real relationships, it inevitably sees that there are others that are not. For it to see that a square has four sides and a circle does not, it must see that a square does not have eight sides, and that a circle does not have fifty.[1] Thus, it sees the relationships that exist, and it sees that there are relationships that are not there. Sometimes, there are certain relationships of which it cannot tell very well whether they are there or not. Sometimes, it lets itself be touched by what makes it see that they are there, and then, by what makes it see that they are not there. It sees a square, and afterward another one. It says: "If this one were that one, then when I turned my eyes away from this one, I would no longer see that one; thus, there are two of them; another, there are three of them, and so forth."

When it does not know how many there are, it uses an idea that corresponds to the idea of confusion, and sees many squares. In the end, it can let itself be stimulated by {all} the squares it sees, but also by the squares that could be in the adjacent space. Thus, it sees squares that do not exist but that are possible. It can envision all possible squares, and it will see squares in general, that is, the square insofar as it is not placed where I have seen one. Then, it will effect an abstraction and will see the quadrature—just as, when it sees a circle in general, it will see roundness. Now, one man will see a great many of these relationships at once; another will see few.

A man will be made to feel the stimulus of a false relationship, by virtue of renewing it and accustoming his soul to it, since all this is nothing but habit.

But if what I just said is quite true, why do animals not reason as men do?[2]

[**1187**]

1. See also *pensée* 1341.—HC

2. Compare this with *L'Essai sur les causes qui peuvent affecter les esprits et les caractères* [Essay on the causes that can affect minds and characters] (*OC*, 3:397–430), used by Montesquieu in *Laws*, bk. 14.

[**1188**] I said: "There are so few bad deeds that a man of thirty thousand pounds in income has an interest in committing that I cannot imagine how he does it."

[**1189**] THE LANDES. On the map of Charlemagne's empire, nothing is found from Bordeaux to Adour except *Ager Syrticus,* Basato in the west, and Aire, a river that goes from west to north into the Ocean, running parallel to the Garonne, emptying into the Médoc, and on the map of the Island, passes by Belin and flows into the Arcachon basin.

On the map of the councils, one city is found in these parts: Nugariolum.

[**1190**] A minister {of the Gospel} presently in Berlin had never been a poet. He falls into a hot fever; now he speaks only in verse. Good health had hidden his talents.[1]

Give him whatever topic you want, he will dictate on it as fast as you can read. There is a volume of his impromptu works published.

He must have been born a poet without being aware of it, and that fever, in giving him boldness, uncovered the talent which the man then turned to advantage. For we love to do an extraordinary thing, and the minister attributed to the fever what was only the effect of nature. For the thing in itself is not extraordinary; witness the Italian improvisers.

[**1191** and **1192**] THIS DID NOT MAKE IT INTO THE ESSAY ON THE "DIFFERENCES BETWEEN TALENTS."

[**1191**][1] A Spanish author, who perhaps will no longer be known by the time I cite him {it's Huarte},[2] tells a tale of Francis I, who, being dangerously ill and disgusted by the Christian physicians and the impotence of their remedies, sent a request to Charles V for a Jewish physician. The good Spaniard seeks the reason why the Jews have a mind better suited for medicine than the Christians, and he strongly believes that this comes from the great quantity of manna that the Israelites ate in the desert. He then presents himself with a very strong objection, which is that the descendants of those who ate manna must, little by little over time, have lost

[1190]
1. First version: "This cured fever was hiding his talents."

[1191]
1. See *OC,* 3:413.
2. Juan Huarte de San Juan (ca. 1529–ca. 1588), whose popular 1575 *Examen de ingenios* [The tryal of wits] Montesquieu owned in the 1668 French edition (*Catalogue,* 1474).

the dispositions that this diet had introduced among them. He answers that it seems from Scripture that manna had so disgusted the Israelites that in order to destroy the alteration that it had made in one day, they needed to follow a contrary diet for an entire month. On which, he makes this calculation: to destroy the qualities that manna had impressed upon the bodies of the Israelites over forty years, four thousand years and more were necessary, which means that the men of that nation still have, for some time yet, a special disposition for medicine.

[**1192**] How can anyone claim that a Carthusian's mind is made like that of other men? It is made precisely to lead the athletic life; it is given no other function but to feed itself. All the body's pleasures, all the mind's activities that it is deprived of, are so many eliminated distractions that might prevent it from eating. The soul turns completely in the direction of the one pleasure remaining to it. It is at the age of sixteen that it is chosen[1] for this type of life.

While on the one hand, its fibers are engrossed and thickened, on the other hand, they are left in a perpetual torpor, and my man is made to dream about Being in general throughout his whole life.

This is not all. Those same fibers are loosened because his brain is struck with continual fear. For now it is intimidated by a bizarre and pitiless superior, now by the vain scruples that monkishness always brings with it. The loosening of the fibers in the state of fear is perceptible, for when it is immoderate, the arms fall, the knees fail, the voice is poorly articulated, the muscles called *sphincters* slacken; in short, all parts of the body lose their functions.

While all moderate movements are eliminated from it, they are replaced by intermittent violent ones, of a sort that continence and regimens produce. During these attacks, spirits are brought to the brain; they tug at the fibers there and excite there a rather confused feeling; they do not awaken ideas there.

[**1193**] A great deal of wit is needed for conversations with princes. Since these are always men whose reputation is made, it is necessary in praising them to say only things that the listeners might think as well as the speaker.

[**1194**] [How many men lose their health by taking cures, who lose

[**1192**]
1. First version: "they are taken."

their fortune through ambition, their property through avarice, who fall into contempt by seeking distinction.]¹

[**1195**] Father Malebranche's system is finished.¹ When extraordinary things like that are not new, it is impossible for them to last.

[**1196**] I believe I have remarked that many persons who have had the true pox have never had the small one:¹ Prince Eugene is one. The . . .

[**1197**] You must never do something that might torment your mind in the moment of its weakness.

[**1198**] [As for our poets, I compare Corneille to Michelangelo, Racine to Raphael, Father Le Moyne to Joseph Pin, La Fontaine to Titian, Despréaux to the Carraci, Marot to Corregio, Crébillon to Guercino, Fontenelle to Bernini, Capistron to Guidi, La Fare and Chaulieu to Parmigianino, Voltaire to Pietro da Cortona, La Motte to Rembrandt, Régnier to Giorgione; Rotrou is better than Albrecht Dürer, but Chapelain is not better than X, that painter who painted in the Vatican library. {If we had a Milton we would compare him to Giulio Romano; if we had Tasso we would compare him to Dominicini; if we had Ariosto, we would compare him to no one, because no one can compare with him.}]¹

[1194]
    1. First version: "ambition, which impoverishes itself through avarice"; cf. *pensées* 1007, XX, and 1214.

[1195]
    1. Fr. Nicholas Malebranche, Oratorian (1638–1715).

[1196]
    1. This is a pun; the true pox, *vraie vérole,* is syphilis; the smallpox is the *petite vérole.*—HC

[1198]
    1. The references are to Michelangelo Buonarotti (1475–1564) and Raphael (1483–1520), Florentine artists; Fr. Pierre Le Moyne (1602–71), preacher and Jesuit writer; Jean de La Fontaine (1621–95); Tiziano Vecellio, known as Titian (ca. 1490–1576), Venetian painter; Nicolas Boileau, called Boileau-Despréaux (1636–1711); the Caracci, Italian painters and decorators; Clément Marot (1496–1544); Antonio Allegri, called Corregio (1489–1534); Giovanni Francesco Barbieri, known as Guercino (1591–1666); Gian Lorenzo Bernini (1598–1680); John Capistrano (1386–1456), Franciscan preacher; Guido Reni (1575–1642), Baroque painter; Claude-Emmanuel Lhuillier, known as Chapelle (1626–86), poet and libertine; Charles-Augustus, Marquis de La Fare (1644–1712); Nicolas du Bourget de Chaulieu (1642–1721), Latin poet; Francesco Mazzola, Il Parmigianino (1503–40), and Pietro Berrettini da Cortona (1596–1669), painters; Antoine Houdar de La Motte (1672–1731), poet and translator; Rembrandt Harmenszoon van Rijn (1606–69), Dutch painter; Mathurin Régnier (1573–1613), French satirist; Giorgio de Castelfranco, Giorgione (ca. 1477–1510); Albrecht Dürer (1471–1528), German artist; Jean Chapelain (1595–1674), French poet; Giulio Romano (1492–1546), disciple of Raphael; Ludovico Ariosto (1474–1533), Italian writer. For Montesquieu's judgments, see *Voyages* (*OC,* 2:1023, 1096, 1118, 1124, 1128, 1135, 1139, 1203, 1208, 1324, and 1332); *Essai sur le Goût* [Essay on taste]; and *pensée* 1215.

[**1199**] It is the constitution of the climate that makes customs. The Muscovites, who have very thick blood, are not bothered by the use of eau de vie; on the contrary, they need it. This would burn and inflame the blood of an Italian or a Spaniard. They need severe punishments; they need to be flayed before they feel anything.[1] Another effect of the grossness of blood that has no spirits.

[**1200**] AVARICE. It is so foolish that it does not even know how to count.

[**1201**] When everything is good, we easily get tired of this good. This is because we are never doing so well that there is not something going amiss, and this is distasteful. Now, when things are good, we easily sense this distaste and do not sense the good very much. But when things are bad, we sense only the bad. The new bad that arrives does not make itself felt, either. Whence it arises that there are no domestics, or subjects, who enjoy changing masters more than those who are happy.

[**1202**] Ovid and Bussy, two exiles who have not known how to bear misfortune.[1]

[**1203**] King William, in a debate[1] at which someone said, "But Sire, it might well happen that we make ourselves a republic," answered with his usual aplomb, "Oh, that is what I am not afraid of; you are not honorable enough men for that." Good line! And I am surprised that a king said it. This was also a newly created king. He saw clearly that virtue and love for the public good are needed to make a republic. Also, after Cromwell, one could not be made in a day. There was a change of government every week; everyone thought only of his own interests; in the end, the King had to be recalled.

[**1204**] I said: "Rameau is Corneille, Lully is Racine."[1]

[1199]
1. See *Laws*, 14.2, 233.

[1202]
1. Roger de Rabutin, count of Bussy (1618–93), who, after publication of *Amorous history of the Gauls* (1665), spent seventeen years in exile.

[1203]
1. First version: "in a quarrel with the leading figures of the nation, at which"; the allusion is to King William III of England (r. 1689–1702).

[1204]
1. Jean-Philippe Rameau (1683–1764) and Jean-Baptiste Lully (1632–87), composers; see *pensée* 1209. On Racine, see *pensées* 1198 and 1215.

1205. *Mr. Locke said:* "It is necessary to waste half one's time to be able to employ the other half."[1]

[1206] I said: "One proof of the Greeks' novelty is those sayings that have brought such renown to the ones who said them, and that seem so common to us that they would not be noticed today if an artisan said them."

[1207] The precepts of Lycurgus and Socrates on boys' pure love make us see the decided Greek penchant for that vice, since legislators thought to make use of this penchant by regulating it, in somewhat the way Mme de Lambert and today's moral systems have thought to make use of the love for women and women's love for men, by purifying this love and regulating it.[1] When a legislator employs a motive, he must judge it to be very strong.

[1208] I am not among those who regard Plato's Republic as an ideal and purely imaginary thing, whose execution would be impossible. My reason is that Lycurgus's Republic seems to be {just} as difficult of execution as Plato's, and yet it was so well executed that it lasted as long as any republic we know of in its vigor and splendor.

[1209] Lully makes music like an Angel; Rameau makes music like a Devil.[1]

[1210] In conversations, I never respond to proofs[1] based on comparisons; they are only good in oratory and poetry, and serve only to say the same thing, and worse.

[1211] I said: "Fortune is our mother; docility, our governor."[1]

[1212] I said: "It is only common works that are boring; the bad ones we don't count."

[1213] I said: "How women calculate in changing lovers! The successor,

[1205]
1. The italicized words are in English in Montesquieu's text.—HC

[1207]
1. Anne-Thérèse de Marguenat de Courcelles, marquise of Lambert (1647–1733), hostess of a Parisian salon frequented by Montesquieu from 1724 onward. See also *pensées* 203 n. 1, 677 n. 4, and 1655.

[1209]
1. See *pensée* 1204.

[1210]
1. First version: "speeches"

[1211]
1. *Gouverneur*, tutor to a grandee.—HC

with more merit, is always worth less to them than the predecessor; the awkwardness of making a change; a man they make unhappy; always less esteem for themselves; the danger of soon having to change again; etc."

[1214] I constantly see people who destroy their health by taking cures, who become objects of contempt by seeking distinction, who lose their property by virtue of avarice, who destroy their good fortune by virtue of ambition.[1]

[1215] If one has to size up the quality of our poets, I compare Corneille to Michelangelo, Racine to Raphael, Marot[1] to Corregio, La Fontaine to Titian, Despréaux to the Dominicini, Crébillon to Guercino, Voltaire to Guidi, Fontenelle to Bernini, Chapelle, La Fare, and Chaulieu to Parmigianino, Father Le Moyne to Joseph Pin, Régnier to Giorgione, La Motte to Rembrandt, Chapelain[2] is below Albrecht Dürer. If we had a Milton, I would compare him to Giulio Romano. If we had Tasso, we would compare him to the Carraci. If we had Ariosto, we would compare him to no one, because no one can compare with him.[3]

[1216] I said: "It is the Marais that cost M. de Saint Mars his neck (gentlemen of the Marais).[1] He could not live without the Marais; today, you cannot live in there."

[1217] It is very amusing that in England, when it was uncertain whether inoculation for smallpox would succeed, everyone wanted to have himself inoculated, but now that success is assured, no one thinks about it. We love to have done something out of the ordinary, and moreover, we become stubborn about something we see contradicted improperly or through bad reasonings—such as in this case, where people saw the doctors for, and the theologians against.

[1218] LOUIS XIV.[1] He had to perfection all the middling virtues and the

[1214]
1. Cf. *pensées* 1007, XX, and 1194.

[1215]
1. First version: "La Fontaine to Corregio, Marot to Titian, Despréaux to the Caracci"
2. First version: "Rotrou is better than Albrecht Dürer, Pinturichio is our Chapelain."
3. See *pensée* 1198 for an earlier version of this entry.

[1216]
1. Cinq-Mars was beheaded with de Thou in 1642.

[1218]
1. See *pensée* 1122.

beginnings of all the great ones . . . ; not smart enough for a great man . . . ; big with his courtiers and foreigners, small with his ministers.

[1219] I said: "I esteem men not because they have no faults, but because they have corrected the faults they had."

[1220] The pr—— of Au——was telling me to speak. I responded: "Madam, if I were to speak, you would not speak."

[1221] *I said to a lady:*[1] "You have none of the qualities that prevent you from being lovable; you may have some of those that prevent you from being loved."

[1222] On the sale of Turenne, I said: "In his affairs, Bernard should calculate how much richer he will be, but M. de Bouillon should calculate how much greater a lord he will be."[1]

[1223] On Father Tournemine,[1] I said: "He had no good quality, and he was even a bad Jesuit."

[1224] M. de Fontenelle was telling me of his belief that prophecies derived from the entrails of sacrificial victims came from the fact that peoples going off to colonies and wanting to stop in a place would examine animals' entrails beforehand to see if the air and the terrain were healthy. From this, they could move easily into regarding one or another condition of the entrails as a good or bad omen. *Idem,* for bird flight: when they came from one place to another, it was conjectured that this was to search for food, and consequently, that this place was better than the ones they were coming from. From this, the good augur followed naturally. I said: "There is still another cause of the slitting of victims' throats: warrior nations, and that is most of them, must have imagined a god who resembled them, who took pleasure in blood, who was cruel like themselves, who demanded victims' blood, who demanded enemies' blood, citizens' blood, etc."

1. Doubtless Catherine de Belrieu, married to Henry d'Augeard, president of the Parlement of Bordeaux (d. 1739).

[1221]
1. Emphasis in original, which appears in English in Montesquieu's text.—HC

[1222]
1. In 1738, Charles-Godefroy de La Tour, duke of Bouillon, sold the viscounty of Turenne to the king of France; Samuel Bernard, count of Goubert (1651–1739), was a renowned French financier. See also *pensée* 1100.

[1223]
1. See *pensée* 472.

[**1225**] On the news making the rounds in January 1738 that the King was going to eliminate appeals to the Parlement against abuse of ecclesiastical authority,[1] I said: "The King cannot do everything he is able to."[2]

[**1226**] There is scarcely anyone I have heard reasoning on the present affairs, I will not say sensibly, but with a full knowledge of what they are talking about. For more than ten years now, it has no longer been a question of the Constitution;[1] it is a question of knowing whether there is going to be a schism or not. Although the Court and the Parlement are opposed in the paths they are taking, they both have none other than the same objective, which is to prevent schism, but they go at it in different ways. Their objectives are so much the same that the same things the Parlement condemns, the Council is obliged to condemn. The Court and the Parlement know that once there is a schism, penal laws will have to be established, all of us on both sides will have to be hanged, and when you start down that path, no one knows where it will lead. The Jansenists, for their part, are still pushing ahead and seem to be seeking nothing else but to go and get themselves hanged; the Molinists[2] are {already} preparing the ropes with which they will hang or be hanged. The Court of Rome, committed (it knows not how) in this affair, is following its principles of always driving things to extremes. All good Frenchmen, all true citizens, shudder at seeing the danger—both to Religion and to the Nation. One cannot erect enough statues to Cardinal de Fleury, who saw the problem, the causes, the effects, and who sought throughout his entire ministry to minimize the problem—and did so.[3] And it can be said that he prevented the schism which the frontline troops[4] of the two sides wanted to hasten with all their might. He gave employment to moderate folks, or at least he

[1225]

1. The *appels comme d'abus,* appeals to French secular courts against encroachments by ecclesiastical judges. The French parlements were particularly vigilant about claiming these "liberties" of the Gallican Church against Rome. In 1738, the King wanted to assign such appeals to the Great Council.

2. *Peut* means "may" or "can" and is used in both senses here, so the remark is a witticism.—HC

[1226]

1. The bull *Unigenitus;* cf. *Mémoire sur la Constitution Unigenitus* (*OC,* 3:469–76), as well as *pensées* 273, 426, 914, 1170, 2158, 2164, and 2247.

2. On Molinism, see *pensée* 730n.

3. For Montesquieu's research on Fleury's role in this affair, see *Voyages* (*OC,* 2:1097–1127).

4. *Enfants perdus,* literally, "lost children"; the 1694 *DAF* defines the phrase as "detached soldiers who begin the attack on the day of combat," often used metaphorically.—HC

sought to do so. He put a stop to the outbursts of the Molinists and gradually eliminated the forces of the Jansenists, by depriving them of their best
excuses. It is true that the Ministry greatly embittered the Parlement. Two
things need to be thought about: first, calming people down; next, filling
vacant posts with prudent people to the extent possible.

I always hear it said that the King has only to suppress, change, eliminate, quash the Parlement. It is ignorant people who talk like that, or
people who have an interest in talking like that because of their fortunes in
Rome. One of the good things done in our time is that which has most revolted the public, namely, the red hat given to the Cardinal of Auvergne;[5]
this has made the clergy understand that the excesses of individuals in today's affairs would not lead on to dignities those who devour them.

It must not be thought that the Parlement of Paris is acting solely out of
caprice and spite. Since, when we are irritated {by being contradicted}, we
throw ourselves more strongly behind the opinion we hold than we were
before, I admit that there can be and there were in the Parlement some
petty minds who let themselves get worked up over the Jansenist idiocies
and trivialities. But I cast my eyes not on the Parlement of Paris but on
the magistracy of the Realm, and I find that magistracy in the principles
of the Parlement.

Why so? Because for four centuries, {all} the books have been full of
Parlementary principles; because that is what people have studied, that is
how they have formed their minds, and men do not renounce their principles altogether and all of a sudden; because the disputes between Philip
the Fair and Boniface VIII established the principles of France; because the
Pragmatic confirmed them;[6] because the misfortunes of the religious wars,
the excommunications of Henry III and Henry IV rendered the magistrates more attached to these principles; because the peace in the reign of
Louis XIII and the beginning of Louis XIV had kept minds within the
dependence and respect necessarily due—both for the interest of Religion,
and for our interest, including our civil interest, at the Court of Rome—
when Louis XIV effected the famous assembly of the Clergy, which did

---

5. Henri-Oswald de la Tour d'Auvergne (1671–1747), abbé of Cluny and archbishop of Vienna,
promoted to cardinal on December 20, 1737.
6. Boniface VIII was pope from 1294 to 1303; the Pragmatic refers to the Pragmatic Sanction of
Bourges, promulgated by King Charles VII in 1438 to limit the powers of the pope in French church
affairs.

more harm in Rome than the Parlements had done; because then Father Le Tellier arrived and wanted to make Frenchmen forget all their maxims in one day.[7]

But the magistrates have not forgotten them. They are not ill-humored, but they have knowledge. Thus, it is through reason and mildness that they need to be worked on, and brought imperceptibly back to the right path, in matters where disputes have carried them too far.

One must especially be on guard against losing the scent, where we move from the main question over to questions in which people have a vested interest, and where the Clergy might seek, in the shadow of the Constitution, to move on to other claims, on the pretext of implementing the aforementioned Constitution. A good citizen ought to seek, on the one hand, to calm people down, and to maintain each of the orders of the Realm within its limits. And when I say this, I am not speaking against the bishops. I have always thought their jurisdiction over the correction of morals was only too limited. I even believe that the Pope's authority is, politically speaking, even infinitely useful to us. For what would become of us in this turbulent nation, where no bishop thinks like his neighbor? But this does not mean that you are going to be violently hauled off, and despotically, to an authority that we are told is always without limits (because it is sometimes), and on all occasions (because it is on some occasions).

(I have scribbled this out based on the ideas that came to me on the occasion of a dispute over the suppression of the offices of president of the Great-Council, January 1, 1738,[8] against an Avignon man who was asserting that the King was going to eliminate the appeals to the Parlement against abuse of ecclesiastical authority; to whom I said that this would not happen, because the Council was too prudent not to see that this would make Jansenists out of all prudent men, who had no desire to be. And when he said to me, "Can't the King abolish the Parlement?" I responded, "Sir, take it from me that the King cannot do everything he is able to.")[9]

[**1227**] It is against the nature of things, in a federative constitution

---

7. The assembly occurred in 1681; Michel Le Tellier (1643–1719), Jesuit, prolific anti-Jansenist, royal confessor as of 1709; cf. *Laws*, 5.10, 2.4, 18. See also *pensées* 1958 and 2144.

8. These venal offices were perennial subjects of jurisdictional dispute between Parlement and Crown.—HC

9. See *pensée* 1225 for the last sentence.

like Switzerland, for the cantons to conquer each other,[1] as they have done recently, the Protestants vis-à-vis the Catholics.[2] It is against the nature of a good aristocracy for the citizens from whom the magistrates, the Senate, the Councils are elected to be so few that they make up a very small part of the people, as in Berne, for in that case, it is a many-headed monarchy. Again, it is against the laws of nature for a republic that has conquered a people to continue treating it as a subject and not an ally when, after a considerable period of time, all sectors of one people have become allied with the other through marriage, customs, laws, general meeting of minds. For the laws of the conqueror are only good and tolerable because those things do not exist, and because there is such an estrangement between the nations that the one cannot trust the other.[3]

[1228] I said: "Dinners are innocent, suppers are almost always criminal."

[1229] I envy the temerity of fools; they are always talking.

[1230] It is foolish of Bayle to say that a republic of good Christians could not last; it is rather that there could not be a republic of good Christians.[1] Likewise, when it is said that a republic of philosophers could not last, it is rather that there could not be a republic of philosophers. Everything is mixed up.

[1231] "M. Coste," I said, laughing, "thinks he has written Montaigne's work, and he blushes when someone praises Montaigne in his presence."[1]

[1232] I said: "It is nature that makes us pleasing and displeasing: Mlle de Clermont cannot be displeasing; the Duke of Villars cannot be pleasing."[1]

[1227]
1. "Put in the *Laws*" (M.), 10.6, 143.
2. The inhabitants of Toggenburg rebelled in 1705 against the abbey of Saint-Gall, of which they were a dependency, and were supported by most Protestant cantons.
3. "Put in the *Laws*" (M.). See *Laws*, 10.3.

[1230]
1. See *pensée* 989n and *Laws*, 24.6, on Bayle.

[1231]
1. Coste had published an edition of Montaigne's *Essays* in London in 1724; see also *pensée* 1441.

[1232]
1. Marie-Anne de Bourbon-Condé, maiden of Clermont (1697–1741), daughter of Louis III of Bourbon-Condé and Louise-Françoise de Bourbon; Claude-Louis-Hector, marquis, then duke of Villars (1653–1734).

[1233] A great change must have been made in the Athenian mind by Socrates' philosophy, since Plato thanked the gods for having been born in his time.

[1234] Mme *of Mort. take the deffense of an honest man injustly injuried. I said to her:* "Madam, I was well aware that you had lovely qualities, but I did not know that you had virtues." People wanted to criticize this. *I said:* "Virtue is not ranked among the virtues."[1]

[1235] Nephews are children when we want them to be; children are children in spite of ourselves.

[1236] I am going to begin with a foolish thing, my genealogy.[1]

[1237] [Mr. of Nieu, very big man, said to a priest, "I have the arms," *les bras longs.*][1]

[1238] Bloodletting from the jugular vein is revulsant, not relative to the side of the vein where the bloodletting takes place, but to the opposite side. For a clearer idea, let us suppose that the bloodletting takes place from the carotid on the right, for example. Relative to this vein, it will only be evacuative in its effects, for if it is diversionary from the head region, it is also diversionary from the heart region. These two opposite diversions will cancel each other out. But this bloodletting becomes revulsant relative to the left carotid. This is because the same quantity of blood always passes through the two carotids taken together, so that if more passes on the right because of the bloodletting, that much less will pass on the left. Thus, the bloodletting of the right carotid is revulsant to the left carotid.

Bloodletting is called *diversionary,* insofar as it calls forth the blood from the region where it is occurring, and *revulsant,* insofar as it reduces the course of the blood going toward the opposite side. Thus, the bloodletting of the right arm is diversionary from the right side and revulsant to the left side.

[1234]
1. The italicized words are in English in Montesquieu's text; "virtue" (singular) may refer to chastity here.—HC

[1236]
1. See *pensée* 213.

[1237]
1. This passage, carefully deleted by Montesquieu, is written in English except for the final three words, which mean "the long arms."—HC

People respond to the explanation I have given by saying that the jugular vein on the right side communicates with the jugular on the left side. But what does that prove? My principle still holds, as it does against the objection that the common trunk of the two carotids is so big that very little blood rises from it, less through the left carotid. But less rises from there; that is enough for my argument.

I must look at the treatise on bloodletting by M. Silva and the treatises of those who have written against him.[1]

[1239] Why do the thymus and the adrenal glands become smaller with adulthood? Why does the venous canal dry out? Why does {the} umbilical cord become a ligament? It is because everything is full in the animal, everything is in motion, everything presses against each other. As the neighboring parts grow, those whose functions are useless shrink and harden, and even dry out. {In the human body, everything depends on everything else.}

[1240] The blood in the coronary artery does not pass by the lungs. This makes a third circulation, different from the other two. I have found the reason: the blood is taken from the left auricula or ventricle and has not been venous; it is from the arterial blood. It has no need to pass by the lungs.

[1241] There is no communication of the mother's blood to the fetus, but the placenta's veins anastomose in the mother's arteries, and the mother's veins in the placenta's arteries. In that way, the subtlest and best prepared of the mother's fluids pass through, and not the red corpuscles. Today, this is the common opinion.

But a mother who has died of a hemorrhage, where no blood was found in the fetus, has been raised as an objection.

To this, I respond that, given the system of communication that we have worked out, the full supplied the empty, not the empty the full. The entire aqueous and lymphatic part of the child's blood has therefore passed into the mother's veins. The red corpuscles, which are in very small quantity in comparison with the other fluids of the blood, have remained in the fetal canals, where no one sees them.

[1242] I said of Mme de Lixin that she has a nice manner of being witty.[1]

[1238]
   1. Jean-Baptiste Silva (1682–1748), physician, associate member of the Bordeaux Academy (1742), author of a 1729 treatise on methods of bloodletting.

[1242]
   1. See *pensée* 1012.—HC

[1243] I talked about Astruc and his obsession with always wanting to teach things he does not know about to those who do know about them.[1]

[1244] The tone of the social world consists largely in talking about trifles as serious things, and about serious things as trifles.

[1245] Bourgeois women are looking for titles in their lovers; Court women are looking for other qualities besides those of heraldry.

[1246] When someone was saying that men do not love the truth, I said that instead of "You must believe it, because it is true," one ought to say "You must believe it, even though it is true."

[1247] Look at the destruction the Roman Empire caused! Titus-Livy says that in his time, one could scarcely find in the land of the Samnites —— men of war. Plutarch says that in his time, one could scarcely find in all of Greece —— men of war. This is because before the Romans, the world was divided into countless small States. The Macedonians and Carthaginians destabilized many; the Romans destroyed them all. Now, in all these small republics, etc.

[1248] Lycurgus did all he could to make his citizens more warlike; Plato and Thomas Morus, more honorable; Solon, more equal; the Jewish legislators, more religious; the Carthaginians, more wealthy; the Romans, more magnanimous.[1]

[1249] Saavedra, *Corona Gothica*. Look at this book.[1]

[1250] The Franks immediately blended in with the defeated nations; not so, the Saxons or Britons. And the Goths,[1] during the three hundred years they ruled in Spain, did not contract marriages or mix together with the Spaniards. From this, I derive the origin of their decline and of the superiority of the Franks.

[1251] OATHS.[1] Oaths take the place of the pledge that one is naturally

[1243]
1. Jean Astruc (1684–1766), French physician and theologian. See *pensées* 979 and 1647.

[1248]
1. See *pensée* 1911 for the same idea.—HC

[1249]
1. Diego Saavedra Fajardo (1584–1648), Spanish statesman and author of *Corona gothica* [Gothic crown], a history of Gothic Spain (see *Catalogue,* 3176, for the 1646 edition).

[1250]
1. See *Laws,* 28.7.

[1251]
1. "These are fragments from my projected *Treatise on duties*" (M.). According to Shackleton, 435 n. 1, it is a discarded fragment from the *Treatise.*

inclined to give for a promise, for men have always needed to procure the trust of others. Thus, they have often made the following agreements: "If I do not do what I promise you, I will lose the pledge that I am placing in your hands." "If I do not do what I promise, I want my friend to take offense and be compelled to repair the damage I have done to you." "If I do not do what I promise, I submit to the greatest of misfortunes, namely, God's vengeance. And in this case, if I am not a believer, I am giving you a false pledge, and am deceiving you in two ways: for you have neither the thing that I have promised you, nor the pledge that you think you have."

Those who say that oaths add nothing to the promise are greatly mistaken, for your promise binds you only because it commits me to believe you. The bond therefore strengthens with the motive of trust: I counted on what you were saying to me not only because you were saying it, but also because I believed that you had religion, and because you gave me no grounds for thinking you were an atheist.

If it is false that the oath is a new bond, it is also false that the word is a bond; for the word binds only through the degree {of credibility} that it offers the recipient.

[**1252**] ON THE GOVERNMENT OF ENGLAND.[1] On the question of whether it is permissible to resist tyranny, the English may ask: "Is it more useful to the human race for there to be an established opinion in favor of blind obedience than of limiting power when it becomes destructive?"

Was it better for flourishing cities to be drenched in blood than it would have been for Pisistratus to be exiled?[2] Dionysius expelled? Phalaris stripped of power?

Let us suppose for a moment that a cruel and destructive government finds itself established throughout the whole world, and that it endures not by tyrannical force, but by a certain popular credulity and superstition. If someone came to disabuse men of that superstition and teach them about the fundamental and immutable laws, would he not be precisely the benefactor of the human race? And what hero would have a more just claim to the oak-leaf cluster?[3]

[**1252**]

1. See *Laws*, II.6.

2. Pisistratus (ca. 605–ca. 527 B.C.), Athenian tyrant.

3. *Autel* ("altar"); but Furetière and the 1762 *DAF* both envision the more secular option used here.—HC

There is no good sense in wanting the Prince's authority to be sacred and that of the Law not to be.

Civil war is caused when the subjects resist the Prince; civil war is caused when the Prince does violence to his subjects; each is an external violence.

But, it will be said, no one disputes the right of peoples; but the miseries of civil war are so great that it is more useful never to exercise it. How can one say that? Princes are mortal; the Republic is eternal. Their dominion is transitory; the Republic's obedience does not end. There is therefore no evil that is greater, or that has more disastrous consequences, than the tolerance of a tyranny that perpetuates itself into the future.

[1253] ON FRIENDSHIP.[1] The Stoics used to say that the Sage loves no one. They carried the reasoning too far. I nonetheless believe it is true that if men were perfectly virtuous, they would not have friends.

We cannot attach ourselves to all our fellow citizens. We select a small number, to whom we limit ourselves. We arrange a sort of contract for our common utility, which is merely a retrenchment of the one we have arranged with the entire society—and even seems, in a certain sense, to be detrimental to it.[2]

In fact, a truly virtuous man ought to be inclined to assist the most un-known man as his own friend. He has in his heart a commitment that does not need to be confirmed by promises, oaths, external testimony, and to limit him to a certain number of friends is to divert his heart from all other men; it is to separate him from the trunk and attach him to the branches.

If that is so, what can be said about those shameful souls who betray even this commitment, which has been established only to bring aid to our imperfect nature?

Friendship was the Romans' distinctive virtue; one finds its traces in the history of their most corrupt ages; never more the hero than when they were friends. {Look at how far Lucilius carried his friendship for Brutus and Antony, Saint-Réal, 290.}[3]

[1253]

1. "What follows, up to page 134 [i.e., *pensée* 1280—ed.] are fragments left over from what I wrote on the *Duties*. I made a beginning of it, which I presented to the Bordeaux Academy as an essay. Since, by all appearances, I am not going to continue with it, I think I ought to break it off and connect it here" (M.).

2. See *pensée* 1267 on the social contract.

3. Marcus Junius Brutus (83–42 B.C.), nephew of Cato of Utica and adoptive son of Caesar; César Vichard, abbé of Saint-Réal (1639–92), diplomat, and author of, among other things, *Césarion, ou entretiens divers* [Caesarion, or various dialogues] (1684).

The constitution of the State was such that everyone was driven to make friends for themselves. The eternal need for friendship established its rights. A man was powerful in the Senate or among the People only because of his friends; he went on to public office only through his friends; and when the time of his administration was over, and he was exposed to every accusation, he needed his friends still more. Citizens were linked to citizens by all sorts of chains: they were bound together with their friends, their enfranchised, their slaves, their children. Today, everything is abolished, right down to paternal power; every man is isolated. It seems that the natural effect of arbitrary power is to particularize all interests.

In the meantime, those ties that detached man from himself to attach him to another brought forth great deeds. Without that, everything is vulgar, and there remains only a base interest that is properly speaking merely the animal instinct of all men.

Among us, those who can do good to others are precisely those who neither have nor can have friends. I am talking about Princes and about a third kind of men who occupy the middle between the Sovereign and his subjects; I mean the Ministers—men who experience only the misfortunes of the Princely condition and who have the advantages of neither private life nor sovereignty.[4]

[1254] The custom of Court women serving as power brokers has produced much harm: (1) It fills all sorts of positions with worthless men. (2) It has banished generosity, candor, good cheer, nobility of soul. (3) It has ruined those who were not engaging in this shameful traffic, by obliging them to rise at others' expense. (4) Women being better suited to this commerce than men, they made a private fortune, which is what contributes most of all to the ruin of morals, to their luxury and their love affairs.

[1255] The love of money so debases a prince that it leaves no sign of any virtues in him. This is what made the great Condé's father the laughingstock of Europe.[1] There was as much song and story about the father's avarice as about the son's heroic deeds.

[1256] We like a noble pride that comes from that inner satisfaction

---

4. "What I am saying about ministers I've put in my treatise on the *Prince*" (M.); cf. *Reflections on the character of some princes* (*OC*, 3:537–51 passim).

[1255]
1. Henry II of Bourbon, prince of Condé (1588–1646).

left by virtue; it befits the great nobles, it gives luster to dignities.[1] A great soul cannot avoid showing itself whole; it feels the dignity of its being. And how could it not know its superiority over so many others degraded in nature?

These proud men are the least arrogant, for it is not they whom one sees annihilated before the great, low as grass under their equals, raised like cedars over their inferiors.

A base soul that is arrogant has descended to the sole point of baseness to which it could descend. A great soul that abases itself is at the highest point of greatness.

One cause of the feebleness of our affections is our education, in which we have not sufficiently distinguished greatness of soul from arrogance, and from that vanity—unsuited for any good—which is founded on no motive. This has led us to weaken the principle of action, and the more motives we have eliminated from men, the more we have demanded of them.

[1257] The ways of dressing and lodging oneself are two things in which both too much affectation and too much casualness must be avoided.

The table contributes not a little to giving us that gaiety which, combined with a certain modest familiarity, is called *politeness.*

We avoid the two extremes that the nations of the South and North are prone to: we often eat together, and we do not drink to excess.

[1258] In France, we have not ceased to have those rare men who would have been acknowledged as Romans. Faith, justice, and greatness of soul ascended the throne with Saint Louis. Tanguy du Châtel abandoned his posts as soon as the public voice rose against him; he left his Country without complaining, to spare it his murmurs. Chancellor Olivier introduced Justice even into the Kings' Council, and Politics gave way before it. France has never had a better citizen than Louis XII. Cardinal Amboise found the People's interests in the King's, and the King's interests in the People's. Even in his youth, Charles VIII understood all the vanities of his youth. Chancellor de l'Hôpital was as wise as the laws in a court that was only calmed by the most profound dissimulations, or agitated by the most violent passions. In La Noue, we see a great citizen in the middle of civil

[1256]
1. See *pensées* 384 and 1075.—HC

discords. The Admiral was assassinated with only the State's glory in his heart, and his fate was such that after so many revolts, he could only be punished by a great crime.[1] The Guises were extreme in the good and evil they did to the State: how fortunate France would have been if they had not felt the blood of Charlemagne flowing through their veins! It seemed like the soul of Miron, head of the merchants' guild, was that of all the People. Henry IV, I will say nothing about him; I am speaking to Frenchmen. Molé showed heroism in a profession that usually rests only on other virtues. Caesar would have been compared to M. le Prince if he had come after him. M. de Turenne had no vices, and if he had had any, perhaps he would have carried certain virtues further; his life is a hymn to the praise of humanity. The character of M. de Montausier has something of the ancient philosophers in it, with their excess of reason. Marshal {de Catinat} bore victory with modesty and disgrace with majesty, still great after the loss even of his reputation. M. de Vendôme never had anything of his own but his glory.[2]

[1259] ON REWARDS. I do not intend to speak of the posterity of those six bourgeois from Calais who offered up their lives to save their Country, and whom M. de Sacy has rescued from oblivion.[1] I do not know what has become of the posterity of that woman who saved Amiens in Charles VIII's time. Those bourgeois are still bourgeois. But if there has been some noteworthy knave in our France, you can be sure that his posterity is held in honor.

But virtue should nonetheless be the eternal object of our pursuits. It has almost always been left unrewarded; it has been shunned, feared, persecuted. It scarcely arrives before it is disdained.

[1258]

1. These allusions are to Tanguy III du Châtel, viscount of La Bellière (d. 1477); François Olivier, chancellor of France (1487–1560); George I of Amboise, archbishop of Rouen (1460–1510); François de La Noue (1531–71); Admiral Gaspard II de Coligny (1519–72), one of the first victims of the Saint Bartholomew's Day massacre of August 24, 1572.

2. Robert Miron (1569–1628); Mathiew Molé (1584–1656); Henry of La Tour d'Auvergne, viscount Turenne, marshal of France (1611–75); Charles de Sainte-Maure, marquis of Salles, then duke of Montausier (1610–90); Nicolas Catinat, marshal of France (1637–1712); Louis-Joseph, duke of Vendôme (1654–1712).

[1259]

1. Louis-Silvestre de Sacy (1654–1727), author of *Traité de l'amitié* [Essay on friendship] (1703), in numerous English and French editions. For Montesquieu's relationship with him, see *pensée* 299.—HC

[**1260**] ON HISTORY. It is fitting that everyone read history, especially that of his country. We owe this to the memory of those who have served their Country and have thereby contributed to giving virtuous people that reward which is their due, and which has often encouraged them.

The sentiment of admiration that their fine deeds excite in us is a kind of justice that we render them, and the horror we feel toward the wicked is another. It is unjust to grant the wicked oblivion for their name and their crimes. It is unjust to leave great men in that same oblivion that the wicked have seemed to desire.

Historians are severe examiners[1] of the deeds of those who have appeared on earth, and they are an image of those Egyptian magistrates who would call to judgment the souls of all the dead.

[**1261**] It is not only serious readings that are useful, but also agreeable ones, given that there are times when one needs an honest relaxation. Even the learned must be paid, in the form of pleasure, for their fatigue. Even the sciences benefit from being treated in a delicate and tasteful manner. It is therefore good that people write on all subjects and in all styles. Philosophy must not be isolated; it has connections with everything.

[**1262**] What still holds back our progress is the mockery associated with knowledge and the fashionableness of ignorance.[1]

The talent for mockery, a talent so common in our nation that it is easier to find people who have it in some degree than people who are totally deprived of it.

This taste for parody clearly proves it: {a type of work} in which even a mediocre mind cannot fail.

In a nation, one must be on guard against the penchant one may have for mocking good things. One must reserve that penchant as an arm against those things that are not good. Thus, fanaticism in England was destroyed by this. Therefore, it can at most be for men's good that one may make use of human malignity.

This method of proving or combating decides nothing, because a joke is not a reason.[2]

[1260]
1. The term Montesquieu uses, *examinateur,* has a legal inflection.—HC

[1262]
1. "Continuation of p. 34" (M.), that is, of *pensée* 1007.
2. "Go to page 136 of this volume" (M.), that is, to *pensée* 1292.

[1263] Cicero divides the honorable into four headings: attachment to the sciences[1] and the pursuit of truth, the maintenance of civil society, greatness of soul, and a certain propriety in acts, *secundum ordinem et modum.*[2]

He thinks that a good citizen should exert himself for his Country, rather than devote himself to the acquisition of knowledge. But he does not attend to the fact that the learned are very useful to their Country, and all the more worthy of esteem for the fact that they almost always serve it without self-interest—being compensated for their efforts neither by monetary rewards nor by dignities.

The sole difference between civilized and barbarous peoples is that the former have applied themselves to the sciences; the latter have absolutely neglected them. It is perhaps to the knowledge we have, and which savage peoples do not have, that most nations owe their existence.

If we had the mores of the peoples of America, two or three European nations would soon have exterminated or eaten all the others.

[1264] There is a body in a neighboring State[1] that examines the state of the Nation every year. Let us examine here the present state of the Republic of Letters.

[1265] SPECIFIC EXAMPLES OF SPANISH CONQUESTS IN THE INDIES.[1] If one wants to know what philosophy is good for, one has only to read the history of the conquests of two great empires: Mexico and Peru.

If a Descartes had come to Mexico a hundred years before Cortez, rest assured that he would have taught the Mexicans that men, constituted as they are, cannot be immortal; that he would have had them understand that all of nature's effects are a consequence of laws and communications of motion; that he would have made them recognize in nature's effects the impact of bodies rather than the invisible power of spirits. Cortez, with a

[1263]
1. By "sciences" in this entry, Montesquieu means any field of systematized knowledge.—HC
2. "According to order and method." Montesquieu wrote *Discours sur Cicéron* [Discourse on Cicero] in 1709 (*OC*, 3:15–21).

[1264]
1. The reference is to England.

[1265]
1. According to Shackleton, 434, this entry belongs to chapter XI of the *Treatise on duties*, on violations of man's duties.

handful of men, would never have destroyed the vast empire of Mexico, and Pizarro that of Peru.[2]

When the Romans saw elephants in combat against them for the first time, they were astonished, but they did not lose their heads as the Mexicans did at the sight of horses.

In the Romans' eyes, the elephants appeared merely as larger animals than those they had seen. The impression those animals made on their minds was only what it should naturally have made. They perceived that they needed greater courage because their enemy had greater strength. Attacked in a new way, they sought new means of defending themselves.

The invention of gunpowder in Europe gave such a modest advantage to the nation that used it for the first time that it is still not determined which nation had this initial advantage.

The discovery of the spyglass served the Dutch only once.

In all effects, we find merely a pure mechanism, and for that reason, there are no devices that we are not in a position to elude by another device.

Those effects that an ignorance of philosophy attributes to invisible powers are pernicious not in creating fear but in making people despair of winning, and they do not permit those struck by them to make use of their strengths, since they make them deem these strengths to be useless.

Thus, there is nothing so dangerous as to hit the minds of the people too hard with miracles and prodigies. Nothing is more capable of generating destructive prejudices than superstition, and if it has sometimes happened that wise legislators have used them to advantage, the human race in general has lost a thousand times more than it gained by them.

It is true that the first kings of Peru found great advantage in passing themselves off as children of the Sun, and that they thereby made themselves absolute over their subjects and respectable to foreigners, who vied with each other in arraying themselves in obedience under them. But the same advantages that the Peruvian monarchs had derived from superstition, superstition also made them lose. The mere appearance of the Spanish demoralized Atahualpa's subjects and himself, because it seemed to be a sign of the Sun's wrath and of his abandonment of the Nation.[3]

2. Hernan Cortez (1485–1547), Spanish conqueror of Mexico, and Francisco Pizarro (ca. 1475–1541?), Spanish conqueror of Peru; see *Laws*, 10.4, 142.
3. Atahualpa, last Inca emperor, whom Pizarro put to death in 1533; see *Laws*, 26.22.

Against the emperors of Mexico and Peru, the Spanish made effective use of the veneration or rather the inward devotion that their peoples paid them, since as soon as they had taken them as prisoners—by the most infamous tricks—the entire Nation was demoralized and gave hardly any more thought to defending itself, believing it useless to oppose the angry gods.

Montezuma, who would have been able, by using force, to exterminate the Spanish on their arrival if he had had the courage, or could even have had them starved to death without risking anything, instead attacked them only with sacrifices and with the prayers that he arranged to be said in all the temples.[4] He sent them all sorts of provisions, and let them tranquilly make leagues and subjugate all his vassals.

It is true that the Mexicans had no firearms, but they had bows and arrows, which were the strongest arms of the Greeks and Romans. They had no iron, but they had gunflint, which cut and pierced like iron, and which they put on the end of their weapons. They even had something good as far as military technique is concerned: they made their ranks very tight, and as soon as someone was killed, he was immediately replaced by another, in order to hide their loss from the enemy.

As evidence for my thesis, the Spanish who went on the conquest of Peru thought they were going to be exterminated by small barbarous peoples they had raided, and they saved themselves only by a hasty retreat, after having been really manhandled. On the other hand, they met with no resistance in Peru and very little in Mexico, where superstition stripped these empires of all the strength they would have been able to draw on from their size and their civilized order. To make themselves revered as gods, the Princes had made their peoples as stupid as animals, and they perished by that same superstition that they had authorized for their advantage.

Virtually everywhere the Peruvians defended themselves, they had the advantage over the Spanish. All they lacked, then, was the expectation of success, and deliverance from the evils attending weakness of mind.

[1266] CONTINUATION OF SOME THOUGHTS THAT DID NOT MAKE IT INTO THE "TREATISE ON DUTIES."[1]

4. Montezuma, or Moctezuma the Younger (1446–1520), Aztec emperor upon Cortez's arrival in Mexico in 1519.

[1266]

1. According to Shackleton, 434, *pensées* 1266–67 belong to chapter V of the *Treatise,* on principles of philosophy, and in part to chapter II, on God.

Let us make an effort to uproot the idea of God from our hearts; let us once and for all shake off this yoke that error and prejudice have imposed on human nature; let us very well fortify our belief that we are no longer in that state of dependence. Look at what we have achieved! From that moment, we lose all resources in adversity—in our illnesses, our old age, and, still more, our death. We are going to die, and there is no God. Perhaps we will enter into nothingness. But what a horrifying idea! Or perhaps our soul survives—isolated, without support, without assistance in Nature; what a sad state it will be in! By the loss of its body, it has just been deprived of all the pleasures of the senses, which rendered this life so delicious, and there can only remain what is still more specific to it: that irritating desire to be happy, and that impotence to become so; that dolorous view of itself which reveals only its pettiness; that void, that disgust, that anxiety that it finds in itself; that impossibility of achieving satisfaction in itself, by the sole force of its being. Excruciating immortality! If it is not absolutely certain that there is no God, if our philosophy has managed to leave us some doubt on this, one must hope that there is one.

We are a great proof that this God that we hope for is a beneficent being. For he has given us life—that is, a thing that not one of us wants to lose; he has given us existence and, what is much more, the feeling of our existence.

If God is a beneficent being, we must love him, and since he has not rendered himself visible, then to love him is to serve him with that inner satisfaction that one feels when giving someone signs of one's gratitude.

This being would be quite imperfect if he had not created or, if you will, had merely moved or arranged the universe from some point of view, and if, acting without design or disgusted with his work, he abandoned us once we left his hands.

This providence that watches over us is extremely powerful. For since an infinite power was necessary to put the universe in the condition it is in, it is inconceivable how God, once having exercised such a power, would have lost it since then, or how, still having this power over the universe, he would not have it over us.

Above all, God has been able to make us happy. For since there have been moments when we have experienced that we were happy in this life, it is scarcely conceivable that God has been able to make us happy once, but has not been able to do so all the time.

If he could, he would, because our happiness costs his own happiness nothing. If he would not, he would be more imperfect in that regard than men themselves.

Nonetheless, a great genius has promised me that I will die like an insect.[2] He seeks to flatter me with the idea that I am merely a modification of matter. He uses a geometrical framework and reasonings that are said to be very bold, but that I have found very obscure, to elevate my soul to the dignity of my body. And instead of this immense space that my mind embraces, he gives me to my own matter and to a space of four or five feet in the universe.

According to him, I am not a being distinguished from another being; he deprives me of everything I had believed most personal. I no longer know where to find again this "me" in which I used to be so interested. I am more lost in the expanse than a particle of water is lost in the sea. Why glory? Why shame? Why this modification which is not one? Does it mean, so to speak, to make a body apart in the universe? It is neither this nor that; it is nothing distinct from being, and in the universality of sub- stance, there have been—there have passed by without distinction—the lion and the insect, Charlemagne and Chilperic.[3]

This same philosopher very much wants, in my favor, to destroy freedom within me. All the actions of my life are merely like the action of aqua regia, which dissolves gold; or magnetite, which sometimes attracts and sometimes repels iron; or heat, which softens or hardens mud. He takes from me the motive of all my actions and relieves me of all morality. He honors me to the point of claiming that I am a very great villain, without crime and without anyone having the right to find it bad. I have many good offices to bestow on this philosopher.

Another one, much less extreme and therefore much more dangerous than the first (that's Hobbes),[4] warns me to mistrust all men in general, and not only all men, but also all beings that are superior to me. For he tells me that justice is nothing in itself, that it is nothing more than what the laws of empires ordain or prohibit. I am upset about this, because,

2. The reference is to Spinoza (1632–77), *Tractatus theologico-politicus* (1670) and *Ethics* (1677); for more on him, see *PL*, LXXVI; and *Considerations*, XII.

3. Chilperic, king of Neustria (561–84).

4. See Thomas Hobbes, *De Cive* [The citizen] (1642) and *Leviathan* (1651); Montesquieu owned a 1651 French edition of the former, a 1660 French compilation of his political writings, and a 1668 Latin edition of his philosophical works (*Catalogue*, 1473, 2393–94).

since I am obliged to live with men, I would have been delighted had there been in their hearts an inner principle to reassure me about them, and, not being sure that there are not other beings in nature more powerful than me, I would have been glad for them to have a rule of justice that prevented them from harming me.

Hobbes[5] says that, since natural right is merely the freedom we have to do everything that serves our preservation, man's natural state is the war of all against all. But aside from the fact that it is false that defense necessarily entails the necessity of attacking, one must not imagine men, as he does, as if fallen from the sky or arising fully armed from the earth, a little like Cadmus's soldiers, to destroy each other; this is not the condition of men.

The first and the lone man fears no one. This lone man, who would also find a lone woman, would not make war against her. All the others would be born in a family, and soon in a society. There is no warfare there; on the contrary, love, education, respect, gratitude—everything exudes peace.

It is not even true that two men who stumble on each other in a desert seek, out of fear, to attack each other in order to subjugate each other.[6] A hundred circumstances, combined with the particular nature of each man, could make them act differently. The air, the demeanor, the bearing, the particular manner of thinking would all make a difference. First of all, fear would lead them not to attack but to flee. The signs of mutual fear would soon make them approach. The boredom of being alone and the pleasure that any animal feels at the approach of an animal of the same species, would lead them to unite, and the more wretched they are, the more they would be resolved to do this. To this point we see no impetus against settlement. It would be like other animals, which make war against members of their species only in special cases, even though they find each other in the forests every day, somewhat like Hobbes's men. The first feelings would be for the true needs one would have, not for the commodities of domination {Natural prayers}. It is only when Society is formed that individuals, in peace and plenty, having occasion at every moment to feel the superiority of their minds or their talents, seek to turn the principal advantages of that society in their favor. Hobbes would have men do what lions themselves

---

5. See Brèthe, 1:236 n. 6, for an extract from this entry.
6. "Put, in large part, in *The Spirit of the Laws*" (M.), 1.2.

do not do. It is only through the establishment of societies that they mistreat each other and become the strongest; before this, they are all equal.

If they establish societies, it is by a principle of justice. Thus, they
had it.

[**1267**] In considering men before the establishment of societies, we
find that they were subject to a power that nature had established.[1] For
childhood being a condition of the greatest conceivable weakness, children
had to be dependent upon their fathers, who had given them life, and who
were still giving them the means of preserving it.[2]

What is said about the unlimited power of fathers is not just; it is not so,
and there is nothing like that. Fathers have preservation as their purpose,
like other powers and even more than other powers.

[Since the natural law that yokes that age to all imaginable needs has
established this dependence, children could never escape from it. For such
an authority, having preceded all convention, originally had no limits,
and if age imperceptibly reduced paternal power, this could only be done
through progressive disobedience. Now the father who commanded and
the son who obeyed could never agree on the time when blind obedience
should cease, or on the method by which it should diminish.

Thus, children have never been able to limit this power. Paternal authority is limited all by itself, because as children emerge from youth, fathers
enter old age, and the children's strength increases as the father weakens.
It is only the fathers' reasoning that has done this when, in the establishment of societies, they have modified paternal authority by civil laws,
and the modifications have sometimes gone so far that the laws are almost entirely abolished, as if the intention was to encourage ingratitude in
children.]

Nature itself has limited paternal power by increasing, on the one hand,
children's reason and on the other, fathers' weakness; on the one hand, by
decreasing children's needs and on the other, by increasing fathers' needs.

Families became divided; the fathers, once dead, left collaterals independent. It was necessary to unite by convention and to do by means of civil
laws what natural right had done at the outset.

Chance and the imagination of those who entered into conventions

[**1267**]
1. "This is good for the *Laws*" (M.), 1.2. See also *pensée* 1318.
2. On paternal power, see *PL*, CXXIX, 217, and *Laws*, 1.3, 8.

established as many different forms of government as there were peoples—
all of them good, since they were the will of the contracting parties.

What used to be arbitrary has become necessity; now, only tyranny and
violence are permitted to change a form of government, even for a better
one. This is because, since all the associates could not change their way of
thinking at the same time, there would have been a period between the
establishment of the new laws and the abolition of the old ones, fatal to
the common cause.

All changes to the established laws had to be an effect of these established laws. Whoever abolished the old laws could do so only by the force
of the laws, and the people themselves could retake their authority only
when this was permitted by the civil or natural law.

What used to be merely convention became as strong as natural law.
It became necessary to love one's Country as one loved one's family; it
became necessary to cherish the laws as one cherished the will of one's
forefathers.

But since the love of one's family did not entail hatred of others, so
too the love of one's Country should not have inspired hatred of other
societies.

[1268][1] The Spanish forgot man's duties at each step they took in
their conquests of the Indies, and the Pope, who put the weapons in
their hands, who gave them the blood of so many nations, forgot them
even more.[2]

I would gladly erase the memory of that conquest; I cannot abide reading those histories tinged with blood.[3] The account of the most wondrous
things always leaves something sad and melancholy in the mind.

At Thermopylae, at Plataea, at Marathon, I love to see a few Greeks destroy the Persians' vast armies; those were heroes who sacrificed themselves
for their Country, who defended it against usurpers.[4] Here, these are brig-
ands guided by a burning avarice, who exterminated a prodigious number

[1268]

1. Shackleton, 434, sees this entry as part of chapter XI of the *Treatise on Duties,* "Violations of
man's duties."

2. See *Laws,* 10.4, 142.

3. See *PL,* CV, 176.

4. Thermopylae, where the Greeks under Leonidas resisted the Persians in 480 B.C.; in 479 B.C.
the Greeks under Pausanias and Aristides defeated the Persian army at Plataea; Marathon was the first
great Greek victory over the Persians, in 490 B.C.

of peaceful nations in order to satisfy it. The Spanish victories do not elevate man; their defeats of the Indians cause his pathetic debasement.

The Spanish conquered the two empires of Mexico and Peru by the same treachery; they had themselves brought before the kings as ambassadors, and made them prisoners.

One is indignant to see Cortez talk endlessly about his equity and about moderation, to peoples whom he afflicted with countless barbarities.

In a previously unheard-of extravagance, he takes as the purpose of his embassy the abolition of the dominant religion. In saying constantly that he seeks peace, what is he laying claim to but a conquest without resistance?

The fate of Montezuma is deplorable; the Spanish preserve him merely to aid in making them masters of his empire.

They burn his successor Guatimozin to oblige him to reveal his treasures.[5]

But what shall we say about the Inca Atahualpa? He comes with a numerous retinue before the Spaniards. A Dominican gives him a declamation that he finds impertinent because the interpreter cannot well explain it, and that he would have found even more impertinent if the latter had explained it well. That angry monk goes around and fires up the Spanish, who take Atahualpa, with a horrible massacre of his family, who never defend themselves. Nonetheless, that monk cried out with all his might to stab those Infidels, instead of contenting themselves with some sabre-rattling.

The unfortunate prince agrees on his ransom, which was as much gold as he could hold in a large room, at a height that he marked off. Despite this accord, he was condemned to death.

This verdict, rendered with reflection in order to give correct form to injustice, seems to me a heinous assassination.

But the charges are odd: he is told that he's an idolater, that he has waged unjust wars, that he maintains many concubines, that he has embezzled his imperial taxes since his imprisonment. He is threatened with burning if he does not get himself baptized, and as the reward for his baptism, he is strangled.

---

5. Guatimozin, last Indian emperor of Mexico, succeeded his uncle Montezuma in 1520 and was hung by the Spanish in 1522.

But what is revolting in these histories is the constant contrast between devotions and cruelties, crimes and miracles. They claim heaven guides those scoundrels—who preach the Gospel only after dishonoring it—by a special grace.

But if it is true that love of Country has in all times been the source of the greatest crimes, because men have sacrificed more general virtues to this particular virtue, it is no less true that, once rectified, it is capable of honoring a whole nation.

It is this virtue which, when it is less outlandish, gives Greek and Roman history that nobility which ours does not have. It is the constant spring behind all actions, and we feel pleasure in finding it everywhere—that virtue dear to all those who have a heart.

When I think of the pettiness of our motives, the baseness of our means, the avarice with which we seek out vile rewards, that ambition so different from love of glory, one is astonished at the difference in the spectacles. And it seems that ever since those two great peoples are no more, men have become a cubit shorter.

[1269] Civic spirit[1] does not consist in seeing one's Country devour all Countries. This desire to see his city swallow up all the wealth of nations, to feast his eyes constantly on the triumphs of captains and the hatred of kings, all this does not make for civic spirit. Civic spirit is the desire to see order in the State, to feel joy in public tranquillity, in the exact administration of justice, in the security of the magistrates, in the prosperity of those who govern, in the respect paid to the laws, in the stability of the Monarchy or the Republic.

Civic spirit is loving the laws, even in cases where they are harmful to us, and considering the general good they always bring us rather than the particular harm they sometimes bring us.

Civic spirit is exercising with zeal, with pleasure, with satisfaction, that type of magistracy entrusted to everyone in the body politic; for there is no one who does not participate in government—whether in his employment, or in his family, or in the management of his property.

A good citizen never thinks of making his private fortune except in the same ways that the public fortune is made. He regards whoever acts otherwise as a despicable rogue who, having a skeleton key to the common treasury, filches part of it and refuses to share legitimately what he prefers to steal completely.

[**1270**] I next treated duties founded on propriety and serving to render social life more pleasant:

"We can gauge what our fellow citizens should demand of us by that which we ourselves demand of those with whom we want to live in any kind of close liaison—and which we derive, for this purpose, from the bosom of society as a whole. We do not only want them to be just, enemies of fraud and deception, at least toward us—for as luck would have it, we are much less concerned that they be this way toward others. We also want them to be assiduous, obliging, tender, affectionate, sensitive, and we would regard a friend as a dishonorable man if he were to rest content with observing the rules of an exact justice toward us. Thus, there are certain duties that are different from those that come directly from justice. These duties are founded on propriety, and derive from justice only in the sense that it is just in general for men to have consideration for each other—not only in the things that can make society more useful to them, but also in the things that can make it more agreeable.

For this, we must seek to predispose all men by our consideration, all men with whom we live. For normally, since we have no more right to demand complaisance of others than they have of us, neither of the two parties would have consideration for the other if they were to wait for each other, which would render society harsh and make a people barbarous.

Whence arises that mildness and ease of mores in a society that makes the society happy, and that makes everyone in it live content both with himself and with others.

And the great rule is to seek to please as much as one can without one's integrity being at stake. For it is a matter of public utility that men have credit and influence over each other's minds, which will never be achieved by a rude and austere temperament. And such is the arrangement of things and of minds in a polite nation that however virtuous a man may be, if he has only harshness in his mind, then he will be virtually incapable of all good, and will only on very few occasions be able to put his virtue into practice."

[**1271**] OF POLITENESS. This internal disposition has produced in all peoples an external etiquette called *politeness, civility,*[1] which is a sort of code of unwritten laws that men have promised to observe among themselves. And they have agreed that they would take as a mark of esteem the use made of these rules on their behalf, and that they would take offense if they were not observed.

Barbarous peoples have few of these laws, but there have been certain nations in which they are so numerous that they become tyrannical and come to do away with all liberty, as among the Chinese.

In France, we have greatly reduced our etiquette, and today, all of politeness consists, on the one hand, in requiring little of people, and, on the other, in not giving beyond what is required.

The change has come on the part of women, who regarded themselves as dupes of an etiquette that made them respected.

[**1272**] OF THE CHANGE IN MORES IN THE FRENCH NATION.[1] As royal power grew stronger, the Nobility vacated its lands. This was the main cause of the change in mores that occurred in the Nation. The simple mores of earlier times were abandoned for the vanities of the cities; women renounced wool and disdained all pastimes that were not pleasures.[2]

The disorder arose only imperceptibly. It began under Francis I; it continued under Henry II. The luxury and flabbiness of the Italians increased it under the regencies of Queen Catherine. Under Henry III, a vice that unfortunately is unknown only in barbarous nations showed itself at Court. But the corruption and spirit of independence continued in a sex that sometimes draws advantage even from scorn. Never was marriage more insulted than under Henry IV. Louis XIII's devotion froze the problem where it was; Anne of Austria's grave gallantry also left it there; Louis XIV's youth added to it; the rigidity of his old age suspended it; its dikes were broken at his death.[3]

Daughters no longer heeded their mothers' traditions. Women, who in the past came only by degrees to a certain liberty, now obtained it whole

[**1271**]
1. For a distinction between these two terms, see *Laws,* 19.16; see also 4.2, 32.

[**1272**]
1. See *Laws,* 19.5, for an elaboration of this entry, and *pensée* 1340.
2. See *Laws,* 19.8.
3. Anne of Austria, queen of France, married to Louis XIII in 1615.

from the first days of marriage. Women and idle youth stayed up all night every night, and often the husband would begin the day when his wife was ending it. Vices were no longer recognized; only mockeries were felt, and numbered among these mockeries was an inhibiting modesty or a timid virtue.

Each part of the evening repast concealed some new convention, but the secret lasted only as long as it took to agree upon it. With women of rank, dangers were no longer avoided. Amidst this constant change, taste was worn out, and in the end it was ruined by the search for pleasures.

The education of children no longer ranked among mothers' concerns. The wife lived in complete indifference toward the affairs of the husband. All ties of kinship were neglected; all consideration was eliminated; no more visits for propriety's sake; all conversations became impudent. Everything one dared to do was openly avowed, and the sole impoliteness was to lack daring, will, or capacity.

A woman's virtue was totally useless for her; sometimes, it was even like a kind of persecuted religion.

All this was not the end of the disorder. They were unfaithful in recreation as in their love affairs, and they combined that which dishonors their sex with everything capable of debasing our own.

[1273] OF DIGNITIES. Another change that has occurred in our time is the degradation of dignities. There is a certain cast of mind that is the support of all dignities and all powers. When an office has had authority but loses it, we still revere it between its loss and the time when some petty circumstance reveals our error. Then, we are angry at ourselves and want to bring down in a single day what we think we have respected for too long.

As soon as Louis XIV died, jealousy against ranks appeared. The People added to what royal authority had already done. They were willing to abase themselves before the Prince's minister, but they did not want to concede anything to the Crown officer, and they regarded with indignation any subordination that was not a form of domestic service.

The grandees—astonished—found consideration nowhere; every dignity became burdensome, and in place of the honor that had been attached to it, there was only ridicule to claim.

The untitled high nobility, which contributed the most to this degradation, thought to gain much by it. But in making the titled fall back toward themselves, they also raised to the same level a crowd of folks who would never have thought about it. Everybody was a Montmorency; everybody was a Châtillon.[1]

[1274] OF RAILLERY. Every man who jests is claiming to have wit; he is even claiming to have more than whoever he is joking with. The proof is that if the latter responds, he is disconcerted.

On this score, there is nothing so slight as what separates a chronic jester from a fool or an impertinent.

Nonetheless, there are certain rules one can observe in jesting which, far from making the character of a jester odious, can make him very likeable.

One must touch only upon certain faults that a person is not sorry to have, or that are compensated by greater virtues.

One should spread the jesting equally over everyone, to make clear that it is the effect only of the gaiety we are feeling, and not of a fully formed design to attack someone in particular.

The jesting must not be too long or recur every day, for then one is thought to despise a man, from the sole fact of having given him the continual preference over all others in receiving one's sallies.

The goal must be to make the one you are jesting with laugh, not a third party.

One must not refuse to be joked with, for it often livens up conversation, but one must also not have the baseness to offer oneself excessively and to be, as it were, the butt of everyone's joke.

[1275] GALLANTRY. The lack of propriety in women[1] has always been the most certain sign of the corruption of mores.

A great deal of wit is needed for gallantry, and for preparing women for the conversations they might sustain.

The nations that have most abused that sex are those that have most spared it the trouble of defending itself.

They are exposed to insults from which they cannot protect themselves.

[1276] With regard to the grandees: in the past, they had only to pre-

---

[1273]
1. The houses of Montmorency and Châtillon were among the most ancient families of the French nobility.

[1275]
1. Compare *Laws,* 7.8.

serve their liberty. Today, it is difficult to combine the familiarity in which everyone lives, with the marks of consideration that they must draw forth from that familiarity.

[1277] OF CONVERSATIONS. The pitfalls we are accustomed to fall into in conversations are felt by virtually everyone. I will say only that we should be mindful of three things:

First, that we are speaking before people who have vanity just as we do, and that theirs suffers to the extent that ours is satisfied;

Second, that there are few truths important enough to be worth the trouble of mortifying someone by criticizing him for not knowing them;

And lastly, that any man who monopolizes every conversation is a fool or a man who would happily be one.

[1278] GENEROUS DEED DONE IN OUR TIME. When a Northern king[1] had struck an officer of his troops with a baton, that man retreated in despair without saying anything. A half-hour later, he returned with a pistol, presented it toward the prince, and suddenly turned it toward himself. What a lesson!

[1279] OF FORTUNE. This goal must not be discouraged; only most of the means must be discouraged.

Suppose there is a country somewhere on earth so fortunate that offices, employments and favors are given only to virtue, and that cabals and secret methods are unknown, and that a guileful man is born there who, for his own fortune, comes to put in use those ploys that seem so innocent to us. Wouldn't this man be regarded by all reasonable people as a disturber of the public welfare, and as the most dangerous man this earth could produce?

Indeed, what satisfaction for good people to have to think only of being deserving, and to be relieved of the trouble of obtaining.

The reason meritorious people make a fortune more rarely than those of little merit is that they care less about it. People of merit go for consideration independent of fortune; they are loved and esteemed. Thus, fortune does not seem to them to be as consequential a matter as it does to those who can only obtain esteem in a certain post and by virtue of honors and properties.

[1278]
1. Frederick William I of Prussia (r. 1713–40), called the Sergeant-King, father of Frederick II (the Great).

[**1280**] OF BUSINESS AFFAIRS.[1] The true method of succeeding in one's affairs is to seek also to ensure the success of one's contracting party, in order to act in concert to good advantage.

There needs to be much simplicity in agreements and much facility brought to bear in them. That way, we engage honorable people to contract with us, which is the greatest advantage of civil life.

We owe it to the memory of our ancestors to preserve, as much as we can, the houses they possessed and cherished. For by the care they have taken, by the expenses they have made in building and embellishing them, we can be all but certain that their intention was to make them pass to their descendants.

Now there should be nothing more sacred for children than this ancestral spirit, and one may believe—if not literally, at least for our own satisfaction—that they take part from on high in the affairs here below.

End of the fragments on *Duties*.

[**1281**] Sire,[1] when your Majesty judged it appropriate to declare war, all the powers of Europe concurred in your designs—some, by the assistance You received from them; others, by their respect and by their silence.

Your soldiers . . .

Your nobility hastened from all parts . . .

Your other subjects envied each other the sweet satisfaction of showing you their love, and, certain that after the peace you would enable them to enjoy superfluity, they have supported without difficulty the retrenchment from the necessities.

No more zeal is brought to the salvation of the Country in peril, than was shown in defending the honor of your Majesty.

Wondrous thing! While you were bringing terror everywhere by your victories, no one in Europe ceased for a moment to count on your moderation.

There would be nothing so sad for a great monarch as to hear it said

---

[1280]
1. See *Laws*, 20.2.

[1281]
1. "Almost all of this didn't make it into my speech" (M.). *Pensées* 1281–84 are materials for a speech Montesquieu addressed to Louis XV on June 3, 1739, during a solemn homage rendered to the king on the occasion of the signing of the treaty of Vienna, ending the War of the Polish Succession; see also *pensée* 1505.

incessantly that he can do anything, and to see that he does not do good. In flattery itself, he would find constant criticism, and in this sense it is only good kings who can be indulged great power.

[1282] Madam,[1] even if the French nation had not taken part for its own sake in this war, it would have taken part in the various occasions of sadness and joy that your Majesty has experienced in its various episodes.

This peace is as glorious for the King, your father, as it is sad for faithful subjects who, losing the sight of their monarch, have thought they were seeing the dissolution of their monarchy.

It is distinguished equally by the regrets of the people who had called for it and by the joy of those who have received it.

[1283] We hope, my Lord,[1] that of all the events in the reign of the King, your father, the one on this day will be the one you recall the best. And since Providence, which has done everything for you, has already placed you above other men, you can place yourself there by yourself only through greater virtues. And emulation, which in you can no longer attach itself to honors, places, and ranks, should have no other object than personal merit.

[1284] Sire, you are king of a people who love you, who look upon you with admiration, and who obey you with pleasure; who regard your virtues as the greatest good that heaven could do for them; who would want no happiness that they would not share with you; who believe they love the Country in loving you, and whose prosperity announces your glory.

If your Majesty had lost merely a great minister,[1] You would find more than enough in yourself with which to repair that loss. But You have lost a friend, and this is something princes find even less than other men.[2]

[1285] Conversations are a constructed work, and everyone must contribute to this work. If someone disturbs it, he makes himself disagreeable. There are some minds that are constantly demolishing as others are build-

---

[1282]
1. Marie Leczinska (1703–68), daughter of Stanislas Leczinski (king of Poland); she was the queen of France.

[1283]
1. Louis, dauphin of France (1729–64), son of Louis XV.

[1284]
1. Perhaps Cardinal Fleury; the prime minister received extreme unction in September 1738, though he recovered and remained in power for five more years.
2. See also *pensée* 1015.

ing. They do not respond to the point; they obsess on minutiae; they are always going off on tangents; their objections are not derived from the matter at hand; in short, they help in nothing and obstruct everything. For it must be observed that good objections contribute, just as approbations do.

In a word, do freely in conversations what is done methodically in dialogues.[1]

[**1286**] An English gentleman is a man dressed in the morning like his valet; a French gentleman is a man who has a valet dressed like him.[1]

[**1287**] I have seen ten thousand men in Paris who were smart enough to criticize the works of M. de La Motte, and out of all of them, there were none who were smart enough to write the least of his works.[1]

[**1288**] Pardon me, Sir, if I tear myself away from my topic; I must deprive myself of the pleasure of speaking of you any further.

[**1289**] In criticism, we must help each other, not destroy each other; seek the true, the good, the beautiful; illuminate or reflect {reflect and return} the light by its nature; outshine only by chance; turn things.[1]

[**1290**] I dare say it: if I could make a character for myself, I would be a friend to virtually all minds and an enemy to virtually all hearts.[1]

[**1291**] I would not advise devoting oneself entirely to criticism. Caesar had written three books of it against Cato; they have been lost and have been unable to escape the contempt that posterity always attaches to these sorts of work—neither by the great name of Caesar, nor by the name of Cato:

Hoc miserae plebi stabat commune sepulcrum.[1]

[1285]
1. See *pensée* 1014.

[1286]
1. See *Notes sur l'Angleterre* (*OC,* 3:292).

[1287]
1. The first version included both La Motte and Fontenelle; see *pensée* 119.

[1289]
1. See *pensée* 1006.

[1290]
1. See *pensées* 1005 and 1009.—HC

[1291]
1. Horace, *Satires,* I.viii.10: "Here was the common burial-place fixed for pauper folk." This passage is also cited at *pensée* 932.

[1292] The flourishing of letters makes them decline; it is like the flourishing of empires. This is because extremes and excesses are not made to be the ordinary course of things.[1]

[1293] We have seen men of letters attack each other with defamatory writings so horrible that there is not talent enough in nature to save a man from the humiliation of having written them.

[1294] M. de Fontenelle, as far above other men by his heart as he is above other men of letters by his mind.

Comperit invidiam supreme fine domari.[1]

[1295] The illustrious abbé de Saint-Pierre has proposed various schemes, all designed to bring good. It is surprising that he has not thought of a journalists' society, and given rules for it.[1]

[1296] That bellicose spirit that climate used to give the Roman people is today limited by moral causes to the taste they have for the conflicts they see on stage. And the climate that used to make the Athenian people so turbulent now serves only to show us some perhaps slightly less stupid slaves. Nature acts at all times; but it is greatly outweighed by mores.

[1297] What is more, I have not meant in all of this to praise or blame our nation. When I act, I am a citizen; but when I write, I am a man, and I regard all the peoples of Europe with the same impartiality as the different peoples of the island of Madagascar.

[1298] An honorable man (M. Rollin) has enchanted the public with his works of history.[1] This is because in them, heart is speaking to heart; it is the friend of mankind who is speaking to mankind. One feels a secret satisfaction at hearing virtue speak. There would be pleasure in being

[1292]
1. See *pensées* 1006, 1014, and 1285.

[1294]
1. Horace, *Epistles*, II.i.12: "found that Envy is quelled only by death that comes at last."

[1295]
1. Abbé Charles-Irénée Castel de Saint-Pierre (1658–1743), author of many reform proposals, including *Plan to perpetuate peace and commerce in Europe* (1713); Montesquieu owned a 1737 edition of his tax reform plan (*Catalogue*, 2432).

[1298]
1. Charles Rollin (1661–1741), *Histoire ancienne* (1730–38) and *Histoire romaine*, a sixteen-volume work completed by Jean-Baptiste Louis Crevier (1693–1765) in the 1750s.

criticized by a man who looks to see all men improve. He is the honeybee of France . . .

[**1299**] *Le Cid.* The splendid critique by the Académie française, which has offered the finest model we have in the genre: a critique harsh but charming.[1] It was a case of morality demanding that before thinking of what it owes the public, the Academy should think of what it owes Corneille, and perhaps what it owes the great Corneille. It is there that one finds praise of beautiful passages so close to criticism of defects, such natural simplicity on both sides, etc.

[**1300**] I said to Mme du Châtelet:[1] "You keep from sleeping in order to learn philosophy; you ought instead to study philosophy to learn to go to sleep."

[**1301**] OBSERVATIONS ON THE MAPS OF FATHER DU HALDE AND THE JESUITS, AND THAT OF CAPTAIN BEHRING SENT BY THE CZAR, AND THAT OF M. DE L'ISLE CONCERNING TARTARY.[1]

Father Du Halde's map of Chinese Tartary runs to the 55th degree north.

Captain Behring's map runs from the 50th degree south up to Cape Schelinskoy,[2] which is at the 73rd degree less a few minutes.

The mouth of the Sakhalin or Amur or Mur is not placed on Father Du Halde's map at 52 degrees north, 50 minutes. And since this map is more precise, because the Jesuit Fathers have not measured there, the Sakhalin must flow into the sea further south.

Captain Behring gives us the course of the Lena only to the 60th degree.

[1299]

1. Chapelain edited and published the *Sentiments de l'Académie française sur la tragédie du Cid* [Sentiments of the French Academy on the tragedy of Le Cid] in 1638; the first performance had been in December 1636.

[1300]

1. Emilie Le Tonnelier de Breteuil, marquise du Châtelet (1706–49), scientist and Voltaire's mistress.

[1301]

1. On Fr. Du Halde, whose 1735 study of China was extracted by Montesquieu in *Geographica* (*OC*, 2:943–51), see *pensée* 374 n. 2; Vitus Behring (1681–1741), Danish explorer, explored the Pacific Ocean in the service of Russia; Guillaume de l'Isle (1675–1726), geographer for the king of France who was involved in the *Atlas Russicus,* brought out in Latin, German, and Russian, with some French introductory material, in 1741.

2. Perhaps Cape Szagalinskoi, which occupied the 73rd parallel on some contemporary maps of Russia, such as the 1741 *Atlas Russicus* cited in the previous note.—HC

Thus, it does not appear that the Muscovites had a mouth of the Lena at Cape Schelinskoy.

Since the northernmost extremity of Japan is at 40 degrees north, the Muscovites have quite a route to take by sea from north to south, to go from Cape Schelinskoy to the Korean Sea.

It appears that from Tobolsk on the Irtysh to the Cambakka Sea,[3] there is a route of only about a thousand leagues, which one can take almost everywhere by water because of how the rivers are situated.

This new map extends land more than two hundred leagues further east than it was on M. de L'Isle's map.

From the Baikal Lake or Sea, all along the Angara till it flows into the Yenisei, everything is horribly misarranged on M. de L'Isle's map.[4]

The Lena, which runs east-northeast for about three hundred leagues from its source, is found going directly from south to north on M. de L'Isle's map, which lapses into bigger errors as it moves further from Muscovy.

According to M. de L'Isle's map, the Amur river flows into the sea at the 46th degree latitude north, whereas on the Jesuit Fathers' map of Tartary, it flows there only at the 52nd degree, 50 minutes. And as we have said that this mouth is not found on Captain Behring's map, which begins at the 50th degree and goes north, it could be that M. de L'Isle's positioning is even better than that of the Jesuit Fathers.

[1302] EXCERPTS OF WHAT I INTENDED TO WRITE ON THE HISTORY OF FRANCE.[1] It was not a people but an army which, under Clovis, conquered the Gauls. It was composed of volunteers, who had chosen chieftains among themselves more to lead them than to command them. Their first act of independence was to expel Chilperic, and when Clovis's family parceled out the realm, lords were seen everywhere making themselves arbiters of war and peace.

Brunhilde, a skillful woman, carried royal authority further, and she astonished the lords by her boldness and her crimes. Her government was,

---

3. The Kamchatka Sea on eighteenth-century maps.—HC

4. Amur, river of the Far East, 4,354 kilometers long and serving as a boundary between Russia and China; Lena, river of central Siberia that runs from the Baikal mountains into the Arctic Ocean; Tobolsk, river running from the Atlai in China over the Irtysh to western Siberia; Baikal, lake in eastern Siberia; Angara, river of eastern Siberia, outlet of Lake Baikal that runs into the Yenisei, a Siberian river, originating in Mongolia in the Saïan mountains and into the Arctic Ocean.

[1302]

1. "Our courage is not so abased that we dare not speak the truth even under a good prince" (M.); see also *pensées* 1111 and 1642 for Montesquieu's intention to write a history of France.

furthermore, good. Everywhere, she created projects worthy of a Roman proconsul. Fredegund rivaled her in iniquity; but she inflicted it more on the royal family than on the subjects.[2]

Hereditary government came to be envisioned by the lords as a sequel to slavery. Thus, they were delighted to transfer all authority to the mayors of the Palace, leaving the name of *King* to those of Clovis's family. In doing so, they merely returned things to the original order, for as Tacitus said (*De Moribus Germanorum*): *Reges ex nobilitate, duces ex virtute sumunt.*[3] The Kings were civil magistrates; the chieftains, military magistrates. Now Clovis had joined these two functions, but the French deemed it appropriate to separate them.

Thus, it must not be thought that all those kings called *do-nothings* were without intelligence because they were without authority, unless we want to say that the kings of Poland, Sweden, and Denmark have been without intelligence every time they have been either exposed to their subjects' attacks or weighed down by the dominion of the laws.

Pepin's victories made him resolve to collect again in his person the title of *King*—a title that gave him no more authority than he had, an elective title like his own—whether because in some sense he already was or because, as an accessory to an elective title, he had become so.[4] I do not believe, however, that the title of *King* was elective in nature before Pepin, and for three reasons: first, because it was so hereditary that each child had a right to a share; second, since the title had so little authority (because no king had the power by himself to have it conferred upon himself), it would have been odd for people to submit to the rules of birth if the title had been elective; third, because this is expressly indicated in Tacitus: *Reges ex nobilitate, duces ex virtute sumunt.*[5]

OF THE SECOND RACE

The continual victories of Charlemagne, the mildness and justice of his government, seemed to found a new monarchy.[6] He avoided dissension,

---

2. Brunhilde (543–613), queen of Austrasia; Fredegund (ca. 545–97), queen of Neustria.

3. Tacitus, *Germania,* VII, 1–2: "They take their kings on the ground of birth, their generals on the basis of courage": cf. *pensées* 1171 and 1548.

4. Pepin the Short, king of the Franks, first of the Carolingians (751–68).

5. See note 3 above.—HC

6. See *Laws,* 31.18, 697.

often assembled the Nation. The arts and sciences seemed to reappear. One might have said that the French people were going to destroy Barbarism.

Under this second race, the lords exercised the same authority as over the first. But several causes humbled and destroyed this double power, of king and chieftain, that Pepin had combined in his person and that of his successors.

1. The great officers, those who had employments in the provinces, in the cities, became hereditary.

2. The bishops, who had had much authority under the first race, much increased it under the second. The origins of this authority must be sought even before the era of the establishment of the Christian religion. We see in Tacitus (*De Moribus Germanorum*)[7] that those peoples did nothing without having consulted their priests. Thus, the French lords, having become Christians, found themselves disposed to consult the bishops, as they had consulted their priests. This authority spread in two ways: (1) it was propagated with the Religion and acquired new defenders with each convert; (2) ecclesiastical assemblies became better ordered; their corporate body separated itself more and more, and their interests became more cohesive, which put them in a position to cause revolutions in the Nation by themselves, and to depose Kings even by unheard-of pretexts, such as penitence and discipline.

OF THE THIRD RACE

The history of the first race is the history of a barbarous people. The history of the second is that of a superstitious people. The beginning of the third is the history of a people that lives in a kind of anarchy, that has a bad government and that does not even follow its rules.

The lords once again left nothing to Kings but the name. But instead of forming a monarchical body under a mayor, as at the end of the first race, they left it in tatters, dividing that authority which they had enjoyed in common under a mayor.

Thus appeared a body composed of pieces brought together without harmony and without connection: no authority in the head; no union in

7. See Tacitus, *Germania,* X.

the members; each lord ruling his particular state with the same defects as the Monarchy; majesty without power; wars waged with courage, it is true, but without purpose and without design.

But what seemed destined to annihilate royal authority forever was the cause of its recovery, something which has never failed to happen throughout this entire third race, as the sequel to this will make clear.

When the lords formed various states, they nonetheless still intended to bequeath a body and form a nation. But at that time, there were no state-to-state alliances. They were not even known. Every union consisted of many placing themselves under the protection of one alone, with each one, likewise, having other lesser figures in descending order under his protection. At that time, this was the distinctive character of Europe. All French lords placed themselves under the protection of their king; that is to say, they consented that their tenure came from him. The Crown became the dominant fief in the entire State, and according to the law of fiefs, each fief that came immediately from it was revertible to it, which was not a burden to the French princes or lords because they exercised the same right over their vassals; and in any case, this condition did not concern either them or their posterity.

But it thus happened that, since chance made these unions occur very rapidly, because many houses came to an end while the posterity of Hugh Capet remained perpetual, it happened, I say, that the King succeeded to the authority of the leading French lords and united both powers in himself, which is perhaps the most innocent means of acquisition.[8]

{Through this very system, moreover, it was inevitable that the Crown engulf everything in the end, for it had a right to everything, and it was bound to happen that everything would end up being swallowed up by it like the rivers in the Ocean.}

And it must not be thought, as some historians have said, that Hugh Capet gave the lords privileges in order to obtain the crown from them, for he would only have been giving them what they already had, and what he himself did not have. He had only his particular rights in his county of Paris and his duchy of France, which were an emanation of that general authority that each lord had had, with slight changes, since the beginning of the Monarchy.

8. Hugh Capet, king of France (987–96), founder of the Capetian dynasty; see *Laws*, 31.16, 695, and 31.32, 717.

Having the crown, Hugh Capet found that he had a great title but without power; it was even uncertain—it was not assured to his race, but only to his person. In this, his condition was worse than that of the other lords. Thus, the history of the beginning of this race is less the history of the king of France than of the count of Paris. The kings were humiliated to the point where they had the shame, over several reigns, of defeating the lord of Dammartin,[9] and they lost respect right down to the villages.

[There has never been a constitution as defective as that of the realm of France under this race.] The constitution under this race, as we have said, was a work worthy of chance, which had formed it. It was a monstrous body which, within a large fief where no one obeyed, contained an enormous number of petty states, in which obedience was sometimes unlimited and sometimes scarcely known. The public good consisted only in the exercise of certain private rights that some men claimed to have over others, and was founded on no general view.

The Nation's assemblies were merely conspiracies and constant pretexts for vexation—now to fleece a lord, now to ruin him. Everyone sought to oppress each other; no one to aid each other.

The grandees, who had no notion of politics, approved of the practices by which their peers' lands were confiscated, because they themselves engaged in the same practices on their lands.

If, at that time, the laws had been as prudent as those of the Germanic Corps are today,[10] and an assembly of lords and an assembly of city deputies had been joined to the assembly of Peers—which corresponds to that of the Electors—the gothic government would have endured.

For even since the power of kings has become so great, there has appeared, on the one hand, the simple association of towns that brought ——[11] to despair, and that of the Public Good that brought Louis XI to the point where he was ready to quit the realm.[12]

One thing happened in the early days of that race that enhanced somewhat the power of our kings: the folly of the crusades. Every lord conceived

---

9. Hugh I of Dammartin, eleventh-century Norman lord.

10. Germanic Corps, another name for Holy Roman Empire.—HC

11. The words "Philip the Fair" (r. 1285–1314) had been crossed out here.—HC

12. The League of the Public Good, formed by the nobility against Louis XI (1461–83), was ended after the battle of Montlhéry (1465) by the treaties of Conflans and Saint-Maur (1465).

a distaste for his Country: on the one hand, the hope of distant conquests and lands more extensive than those of their fiefs; on the other, the hope of salvation acquired in the path of glory, a means much more seductive than that of purchasing it through self-renunciation.

It happened that Philip, who was reigning at that time, was untouched by these ideas. He was in love with Bertrade, Countess of Anjou, and he was happy in his love affairs. Historians speak of that princess's charms as of those of a Circe. Thus, unreasonable passion led Philip to do what consummate policy might have suggested to him.[13]

At the French court, there appeared for the first time the reign of that mildness of mores that love inspires even in barbarous nations. While so many heroes carried war to the ends of the earth, the king languished in lethargy and pleasure.

[Bertrade ruled her husband's heart, just as she ruled her lover's heart.] Never has a woman carried further the sovereign dominion that beauty bestows. She ruled her husband's heart, just as she ruled her lover's heart. Love pardoned crime, silenced despair, extinguished vengeance; laments were prayers; criticisms were tears. Fulk became more tender as he was more cruelly insulted.

Soon the quarrels with the English arose. The hatred conceived toward them was the reason why, for a long time, there was no jealousy toward the kings' aggrandizement, and why men even hastened to put the kings in a position to resist the English.

Once they were expelled, it was seen that the foundations of royal grandeur were raised high, and the lords marveled at how they had thus managed to pass from such an extreme license to such an extreme servitude with nothing in between. Someone who looked at the reign of Charles VII and that of Louis XI would say that it is a different people being governed. Arbitrary power arose and was formed in an instant. At the end of the latter reign, there was not a lord who could be assured of not being assassinated.[14]

---

13. Bertrade de Monfort, wife of Fulk IV, count of Anjou and Touraine (1060–1109), was kidnapped from her husband in 1092 by Philip I, king of France (1060–1108).

14. On Louis XI, see *Reflections on the character of some princes* (*OC*, 3:538–39), where Montesquieu draws a parallel between Louis XI and Tiberius in the style of Plutarch. Montesquieu's Italian friend abbate Ottaviano di Guasco reports what happened to Montesquieu's projected history of Louis XI: "As he was composing, he would toss into the fire the memoirs he had been using. But his secretary

One of the things one should notice in France is the extraordinary facility with which she has always recovered from her losses, her maladies, her depopulations—and with what resourcefulness she has always endured or even surmounted the internal vices of her various governments.

Perhaps she owes this to such diversity itself, which has brought it about that no problem has ever been able to take strong enough root to eliminate entirely the fruit of her natural advantages.

Few princes have known the duties of royalty better than Saint Louis. If he gave vent to bigotry, this was the weakness of his time and not his own; if he undertook crusades, this too was the error of his age. He must be judged on the virtues that he would have had in all times.[15]

CHARLES VII

{Under this reign fought} Count Dunois, a man whom we may regard as having as much claim to be the founder of our monarchy as Pharamond and Clovis.[16]

LOUIS XI

The death of Charles VII was the last day of French liberty.[17] In an instant, there appeared a different king, a different people, a different policy, a different patience, and the passage from servitude to liberty was so great, so prompt, so rapid, the means so strange, so odious to a free nation that one can only regard it as a spirit of dizziness suddenly descending upon this realm.[18] Especially when one reflects that, in subduing so many princes

---

made a crueler sacrifice to the flames: having misunderstood that Montesquieu told him to throw the rough draft of his history of Louis XI into the fire, of which he had just finished reading the edited copy, he tossed the latter into the fire; and the author, in finding the rough draft on the table upon getting up, thought the secretary had forgotten to burn it, and tossed it as well into the fire . . ." For the source of this story, see H. Barckhausen, "L'Histoire de Louis XI," in *Revue philomathique de Bordeaux et du Sud-Ouest* (1897–98): 569–78. Guasco dates this event to 1739 or 1740.

15. See *pensées* 764 and 911.—HC

16. Jean, Count of Longueville and Dunois (ca. 1403–68); Pharamond, legendary Frankish chieftain from the early fifth century.

17. See *pensée* 195, where Montesquieu compares this change to Rome in Caesar's time.—HC

18. First version: "people."

and so many cities, he employed no army that was not wretched, he used merely a few lousy ruses, and he always buttered up someone with the same hand with which he had struck him.

He seemed to be given to his father only to cast bitterness upon his victories and correct the arrogance of his successes. He obtained permission to enter Dauphiné, about which, extraordinarily enough, the rights he possessed were not known.[19]

When he acceded to the throne, France was in a condition she had not seen herself in since the earliest Carolingian kings. The English, our eternal enemies, had been chased from our provinces; all they possessed now was Calais;[20] their divisions were reassuring us even more than they were avenging us. {Such was the fate of the two monarchies that the unhappiness of the one seemed to be attached to the happiness of the other. England was agitated with troubles as soon as France began to breathe.} Relieved of our fears, we had almost lost hatred itself. Germany could only involve itself in our affairs either as our ally or as an enemy of the House of Burgundy. The latter's different estates, governed by entirely different laws, of which they were supremely jealous, hardly left their princes the internal authority that makes for an enterprising policy abroad. Thus, the dukes of Burgundy were respected, but all the other feudatories were feared. The kings of Aragon, of Castile, of Granada, of Navarre, of Portugal, restricted their ambitions to the mainland of Spain. The Italian States were even weaker, more divided, more timid; the cities made war inside their walls— now the theater of tyranny, now of liberty. The Duke of Brittany was asking only to grow old in peace; he was approaching that imbecility that would end his life. The Duke of Savoy was the King's brother-in-law, and if he had attacked us, we could dispose of the Milanese territory against him.[21] The height of good fortune was that, while we were enjoying a peace that it seemed nothing would disturb, we had scarcely any neighbors who were not in a state of fear, frenzy or war-weariness. Our finances were in

19. The last dauphin, Humbert II (1333–49), lacking issue, sold his state to the King of France; Dauphiné was not incorporated into the royal domain but became the traditional appendage of the king's eldest son.

20. The city had been seized by the English in 1347; it was taken back from them only in 1558 by François de Lorraine, Duke of Guise.

21. François II, duke of Brittany (1458–88); Amadeus IX, duke of Savoy (1465–72), had married Yolanda of France, Louis XI's sister.

good shape. Our troops were numerous, battle-tested, disciplined, and accustomed to victory, and we were profiting from the knowledge acquired in a long war. The states of the leading lords were virtually all surrounded by royal power. Most of the great fiefs were reunited; others were going to be reunited. The limits of dominion and obedience were well-enough known; the reciprocal rights, well-enough settled. Thus, it was easy for Charles VII's successor to combine justice with grandeur, to make himself dreaded in his very moderation—in short, to be the European prince most beloved by his subjects and most respected by foreigners.

But he saw in the beginning of his reign only the beginning of his vengeance; he renounced even his dissimulation and revealed all his joy. He left the Burgundian estates, followed by the duke and his son, and went to Rheims for his consecration. In an instant, he changed everything his father had done: he mortified all his servants, protected all those who had distinguished themselves against him by their crimes, showed favor to doctor Fumée—accused of having poisoned him—doubled taxes, abolished the towns' privileges, made the Nobility anxious, eliminated offices or reduced their prerogatives. And what vengeance or avarice, which can have their limits, did not change, he changed through anxiety.[22]

He abolished the Pragmatic Sanction—that is, the product of Religion and Liberty.[23] He refused a royal territorial inheritance convenient for Monsieur; he made anxious the Duke of Burgundy; he restored the Duke of Alençon.[24]

Suddenly he appeared with an army in Brittany, and he made such unreasonable demands of the Duke as to make it quite clear that he had no more intention to do harm to him than to the other lords. The Duke, surprised and terrified, humbled himself and promised so many things that he thought of deceiving the King by virtue of making promises. But during this time, he sent his emissaries everywhere. He expressed to the lords that they must not think Brittany alone would be insulted; that he had no particular quarrel with the King,[25] that he was his enemy solely because he was his vassal; that he was coming across his border to demand

---

22. Philip the Good, duke of Burgundy (r. 1419–67) and his son, Charles the Bold (r. 1467–77); Adam Fumée (1430–94) was physician to Charles VII and Louis XI.

23. On the Pragmatic Sanction, see *pensée* 1226 n. 6.

24. John V, duke of Alençon (1409–76).

25. "Too long" (M.).

previously unheard-of rights; that he was prosecuting his claims with arms; that such an active, hidden, and unquiet mind could be halted only by fear; that as for his justice, one had only to judge by the justice he rendered his brother,[26] and his moderation by the attacks against the late King; that he had marked his childhood by disobedience and merited punishments beyond his age; that at the age of eleven, he had made himself a factional leader; that in the English wars, there had been a dispute in the choice of a lord, but that at present there was nothing more to choose, except between the preservation of his rights and subjection.

No one was as easy to persuade as the Count of Charolais.[27] Those two princes had seen each other, had known each other. Born to be unequal in dignity but virtually equal in power, they nursed the seeds of a great hatred during the entire time the Dauphin enjoyed—in the Burgundian lands— the only refuge he had on earth. He had been insulted by the King's ambassadors even in the palace of the Duke, his father, and that prince, who had every passion except the petty ones, could not swallow this affront.

The Count, who had sent word to the King that he would make him regret this before year's end, seized this occasion eagerly. He entered the League.[28] Public animosity would soon have created this. On all sides, the King saw only enemies: the Duke of Burgundy, the Duke of Brittany, the Duke of Bourbon, countless other lords; and, what managed to confound him, Monsieur escaped from Court and carried off to the enemy side a great name,[29] compassion for its misfortunes, and a certain confidence that an oppressed son of France gives to any faction.

While the King was attacking the Duke of Bourbon, the Count of Charolais entered France. His army encountered the King's at Montlhéry.[30] The King, who had everything to lose, did not want a battle; the Count, who was waiting for the Duke of Brittany, was not seeking it either; but it was engaged in spite of them. The two armies had all the signs, all the disadvantages associated with defeat. The runaway soldiers on the two sides brought consternation everywhere: some were saying the King had been

26. Charles of France, duke of Berry (1446–72), fourth son of Charles VII.
27. Charles the Bold.
28. The League of the Public Good, whose leaders were Charles of Berry, the duke of Brittany, and the duke of Bourbon, and whose soul was Charles the Bold, was formed against Louis XI in 1465.
29. "Nota: stop here" (M.).
30. This indecisive battle at Montlhéry (Essonne) occurred in July 1465.

killed, others the Count. The latter considered retreat, the former retreated in fact, so little confidence did the two sides have in their forces.

The King advanced toward Paris—resolved, if the gates were closed to him, to retreat into Italy. It is likely that he would never have returned to the realm, and that the Duke of Burgundy would have established whatever form of government he pleased.

That retreat gave the lords the idea that they had prevailed, and this idea gave their faction the kind of renown that confers power itself—always based on the way of thinking of those who hope, or who fear.

[The army of Brittany arrived with Monsieur and.] Monsieur was a name formed by the voices of the oppressed lords, and at the head of the Public Good, it seemed to be the public good itself; but that name became, I know not how, a fatal symbol of weakness.

He arrived with the army of Brittany; but his presence did his faction more harm than good. The King was received in Paris. It is there that he employed all his ingenuity to win over hearts.

The Duke of Burgundy had long had an alliance with the English, and in the course of these wars, the French, and especially the Parisians, had become accustomed to regarding the Burgundians as enemies. Thus, if they did not love the King, they loved the Burgundians even less; they remembered former problems. The King was pouring his charm on the Parisians, and his vices seemed to disappear along with his fortune. He told them that he had come to them as his leading subjects, that he intended to treat them as a father would, that the princes in league sought only the sacking of the great cities and the dissolution of the Monarchy, that as for himself, he regretted the lack of a peace that would have enabled him to do the greatest good for them, that he was not refusing a royal territorial inheritance for his brother, but that he could not consent to give him Normandy and see the Royal forces diverted from the Crown. Thus, should he multiply taxes on the provinces that were to remain in his domain, or see France again in the state of weakness from which she had just emerged? He could see near their walls those Burgundians whom they had so long seen among the English.

The French lords did not cease to be confounded. Their recourse was the assembly of the estates. But the People and the Clergy were always against them on this, because they feared civil war and the lords' ambition; they feared a war whose costs they would have borne. Thus, the estates held during this reign at the request of the lords decided that the King's brother would content himself with a monetary allocation.

When princes are not at the summit of power, nothing brings them there with more certainty than fear of an invasion by a foreign nation. The people are jealous of their privileges only in the idleness of peace, which is as burdensome to those princes who are not absolute as it is favorable to those who are.

Peace was made,[31] and you might have said it was the work of discord itself. The King gave everything and reserved for himself only the hope of vengeance, the tears of his people, and the slavery of his subjects. {It is certain that if those princes had been able, for even six months, to cast off their jealousies and their mistrust and to work on the matter at hand, they would have put the King in a position where he could not disturb them. If, instead of demanding new lands, they had merely sought to assure themselves of the possession of their own, to put limits on the vague crime of "treachery" and on arbitrary confiscations, they would have secured the present constitution and forced the King to swallow his ambition.}

It is astonishing that the King dared to place himself in the Duke's hands during the time that he was preparing unpardonable offenses against him. He soon felt all the danger of this trick. He learned that he had been too well served on the Liège front.[32] He redoubled his charm offensive toward the Duke's men, and it is certain that he never had more need for his talent at creating protégés.[33]

The Duke led the King against the Liégeois. They had only the usual strength of the People—that is, the occasional fifteen minutes of fury. The city being taken, Religion spared the houses of worship, but Humanity did nothing for the citizens.

The Count of Saint-Pol was a clever man who chose his dupes very badly.[34] For he undertook to trick three men, of whom the first prided himself on deceiving all the others; the second was the man who least enjoyed being tricked in the whole world; and all three were infinitely more

31. Treaty of Conflans and Saint-Maur (October 5 and 29, 1465).
32. Having revolted against the Duke of Burgundy, the Liégeois cooperated with Louis XI, who abandoned them. Charles the Bold sacked Dinant (1466), defeated the Liégeois at Brustheim (1467), and burned their city in 1468.
33. *Créatures,* clients wholly dependent for their position on, in this case, the king.—HC
34. Louis of Luxemburg, count of Saint-Pol (1433–75).

powerful than he. He therefore deprived three great princes of the interest they would have had in protecting him.

It is surprising that the Duke of Burgundy wanted to remove this thorn in the King's side, which would have hampered him all his life; for he certainly experienced that the rest of the French nobility were faithful.[35]

The Duke of Burgundy entered the Realm, and the man who had been at the head of the Public Good of the Realm reduced everything there to fire and sword.

The King let his rival exhaust himself with his wars, his defeats, his victories; he would rather give him assistance to help him ruin himself. In fact, that prince—incapable of learning the lessons of either good or bad fortune, a prince easier to destroy than to correct—was creating dangers for himself everywhere, and was taking on his neighbors' quarrels as well as his own.

Louis savored the pleasure that ungenerous souls have when they see the moment arrive for a vengeance that fear had stifled. He prepared himself against Burgundy, and as if he had intended to call to judgment Duke Charles's ancestral spirits—he who, as long as he drew breath, had never had the daring to find him guilty—accused him of treachery and confiscated the lands that were appendages of his feudal possessions.

He made a show of piety, not against the crime but against repentance for it. As he was filling the prisons, inventing tortures, increasing taxes, he was also redoubling his pilgrimages, vows, and foundations, covering himself with relics, making new cults of the saints. It seems he wanted to compromise with Heaven for his compensation, and that which can only serve to prevent others from despairing formed the basis of his boldness.

Well, his fears, his mistrust, his ill health, led him to the castle of Plessis-les-Tours, where it seems he was the most wretched of all men. Miserable prince, who trembled even at the sight of his son[36] and of his friends, who saw peril where others find their security, who entrusted his life only to sword-bearing henchmen—as if, in order for him to live, it was necessary that he inflict violence on all good people.

He was madly afraid of death. It seems, however, that the terrible reckoning that he had to make was the least of his concerns, for he did

---

35. In 1469, he encroached on Haute-Alsace; in 1473, he seized the main fortified cities of Lorraine.
36. The future Charles VIII (r. 1483–98).

not want people to pray to God for his soul. He could not face the end; he covered himself with relics against death. In his last breaths, he was still establishing his power; without hope for life, he still feared for his authority.

He was fortunate enough to have had an historian[37] who has honored his vices and adorned them with the names of *prudence* and *wisdom*. His wit consisted particularly in finding all souls venal and paying them. He bought fortified towns and would have given nothing for the glory of conquering them. He also knew just how to debase his dignity. He excelled at making and unmaking friendships and enmities. He was restrained only by adversity. He was not among those princes who leave insinuations to inferiors while maintaining themselves in their majesty. He made his devoutness the first instrument of his tyranny, more implacable when he thought himself more pious.

{Cromwell had a great mind; Louis's was a tissue of petty deceptions, without issue and without sure purpose. The two best pieces of advice that Louis took—the one, to confuse the Duke of Burgundy; the other, to let him act—were suggested to him by Sforza and Commines, respectively.[38]

Sforza did not have the audacity of the great criminals, but he had a darkness that they never had. His crimes were the effect not of his passions, but of his reflections, his deliberations, his habitual thoughts. That is the man Louis undertook to go and console himself with, and Fate has scarcely better joined together two souls that she had so well matched. Louis recognized him as his master.}

.

LOUIS XII

Here we find ourselves in a reign that good people will always remember with pleasure—where virtue finds its history, where one is delighted to write in order to reveal to one's fellow citizens that monarchies also have their happy ages, and that subjection has its advantages just as liberty has its disadvantages.

37. The reference is to Philip of Commines (1447–1511), whose *Memoirs* on the reigns of Louis XI and Charles VIII Montesquieu owned in three editions (*Catalogue,* 2920–22).
38. Galeazzo Maria Sforza, Duke of Milan (1444–76).

It is then that he uttered that saying that will never be forgotten: "A king of France does not avenge the injuries of the Duke of Orléans."

The Venetian republic was daily increasing its wealth and its insolence. At that time, she had the power that the nations engaging in the commerce of the Orient take turns having.

But the day that the battle of —— took place was destined to be its last day, as the battle of Cannae ought to have been the last day of Rome.

LOUIS XII. [Louis XII was the adornment of his age and indeed of all ages.] That prince would have made men love subjection if it were odious; he would have been able to make arbitrary power more bearable than other princes liberty. He had a minister after his own heart. He governed his subjects like his family—without passion, like the laws; and without noise, like Heaven. He never thought anything except what a man of integrity would have wanted to think; he said only what a great king ought to have said; he did only what a hero would have gloried in having done. In brief, if you want to find something that exhibits to you the golden age of the Roman emperors—that of the Trajans or the Antonines—you must read about the reign of Louis XII.

{Never did the gates of Hell prevail more against the Church than when the wickedest of all men (Alexander VI) ascended to the premier seat in the world. And we would still be indignant at that scandalous election if we did not regard it less as the result of a cabal than as a secret judgment of God upon the faithful.}

FRANCIS I

The courts of the Duchesses of Etampes and Valentinois were rivals:[39] the ostentatious rule of the one, the ambition to rule in the other, the luxury and avarice in both. Those two women envied each other's pleasures and even each other's vices. Sovereigns over the heart of their prince, they were both jealous of a conquest they did not contest.

39. Anne de Pisselieu, duchess of Etampes (1501–80), favorite of Francis I, and Diane de Poitiers (1499–1566), favorite of Henry II.

HENRY II

The Duchess of Valentinois combined great beauty, which brought her lovers, with all the wiles that keep them. The influence she had over the King was a public calamity; she used the King's heart against itself. She did not have that timid youthfulness nor that decent modesty that is more engaging but less irritating.

Charles V retired to monastic solitude. He had convinced himself that public affairs were overwhelming him because they were occupying him. But that soul, which had been so strongly agitated, soon grew bored with the silence of the cloister and the emptiness of his new occupations.

CHARLES IX

HENRY III[40]

The Dutch shake off the yoke of Spain.[41] This was the result of their naval forces. The land has been given to monarchies; the sea, to free peoples. Philip II grew indignant to see two petty provinces against which his power was being smashed.

Don Juan of Austria died,[42] whether of poison or of sorrow, for he had formidable virtues for his brother the King; odious, for having wanted to rule even over imaginary realms: Tunis and England, by marriage with Mary Stuart.

The Duke of Alençon's life was one of constant despair:[43] he loved pleasure; he always had grand designs; but in charge of these designs, he had only the ministers of his pleasure. Called to the Low Countries, and unhappy that the *Protector of liberty* there was not being given all the power of tyr-

---

40. "Look into what I said in a little work on this entitled *Parallels*" (M.); that is, *Reflections on the character of some princes* (*OC,* 3:545–51).

41. Zeeland and Holland, Calvinist refuges, seceded with William of Orange from Habsburg rule in 1572.

42. Natural son of Charles V.

43. François, duke of Alençon (d. 1584), last son of Henry II.

anny, he moved against the main cities and was chagrined to have revealed his treachery uselessly. Thus, those people, who saw servitude existing as much with him as without him, returned to that ancient hatred of the French which they had under the House of Burgundy.

Don Carlos was the greatest victim of the Inquisition, even if it is true that it pardoned Charles V's ancestral spirits.[44] Thus, in Philip's heart, superstition completed what jealousy had begun. It is said that after vainly putting his father's pity to the test, he gave back in his blood a life that had been a burden to him ever since he had asked for it.

That prince was violent, but impetuosity of mind is less incurable than its weakness, and this weakness in the kings who came afterward made Don Carlos's death fatal to the Monarchy.

It was the fate of England to be twice ruined by the Popes' impetuosity.[45] The great power that Rome had exercised over that realm rendered her less tractable in her quarrels with her kings. Adapting the degree of dominion to that of disobedience, she was incapable of all the manipulativeness that works so well for a power that reigns only over souls.

HENRY IV

The Sixteen, bold men who did not know whom to make accountable for the misfortunes of their party, went and seized Brisson, Tardif, and Larcher, and had them hanged.[46] The People regarded this execution impassively, and the Sixteen were never able to make them share their rage.

The Duke of Mayenne,[47] finding himself in a party where the title of *King* was odious to the leaders, did not dare take it; but he did not reflect that he

44. Don Carlos, son of Philip II (1545–68).
45. Allusion to the schism of Henry VIII in the 1530s.
46. The Sixteen were a committee elected in Paris (1587) on the proportional basis of one for each of the sixteen neighborhoods; it supported Henry of Guise. After his assassination, the Sixteen engaged in excesses and formed an insurrectionary committee of ten members who made terror reign and who had to be subdued by Mayenne.
47. Charles of Lorraine, marquis of Mayenne (1554–1611), Henry of Guise's brother.

was leaving it to the legitimate prince. In fact, the latter's person was becoming sacred for all Frenchmen whom frenzy could abandon, for those whom disgust could overtake, for those who could honor their ambition with the name of *loyalty*, for those who might remember the glory of the Monarchy—in short, for that nobility who take it as a matter of honor to obey a king, but who find it ignominious to share power with the People.[48]

It is certain that in having Cardinal Bourbon declared *King*,[49] he accustomed the People to revere that house again and recalled them to their ancient loyalty.

When the Duke of Mayenne hanged the Sixteen, he followed justice and not politics; he eliminated that spirit of faction that had elevated him, and all the ardor animating his party. The loss of battles can be repaired, but the spirit of a faction in decline can scarcely be restored. Soon that boundless opposition in the minds of the two parties was no longer the same, especially when the King of Spain had revealed his designs and demanded the crown for his daughter; every extremist Leaguer was regarded as a traitor.

It is certain that, if Philip[50] had supported only the Duke of Mayenne's interests, if he had made him king as he could have, he would have made the Houses of Lorraine and Bourbon eternal rivals and forced the king to remain in his religion. But the fate of France decreed that he not take that side, that the faction itself be divided, and that the House of Lorraine be no less divided.

While the House of Lorraine was preparing its power and forming a new monarchy in the realm, the Huguenots, relieved of the weight of royal power, were able to divide themselves with impunity and give their enemies advantages which, at any other time, would have ruined them without recourse.

Henry converted and saw nothing more sacred than his crown.[51]

---

48. "Put in the *Spirit of the Laws*. It is seen in the Continuation of the *Journal* of Henry III that only two noblemen of the Paris provostship were Leaguers" (M.), *Laws*, 8.9.

49. Charles, Cardinal of Bourbon (1523–90), Antoine de Bourbon's brother and Henry IV's uncle, proclaimed king of France by the League under the name of Charles X (1588).

50. Philip II, king of Spain.

51. Henry IV abjured Protestantism on July 25, 1593, in Saint-Denis.

Once Henry IV was assassinated,[52] the Spanish were relieved of an immense weight. They saw themselves liberated from a prince who had big
plans, who was allying with oppressed princes and had the confidence of
Europe. It is certain that they were mixed up in Ravaillac's enterprise, that
the Leaguers, banned in Naples and in the Low Countries, did not stop
their conspiracies—especially since the Spanish, informed of the King's
plan against them, thought they no longer had anything to manage. As
for the Society,[53] it is likely, despite the public gossip, that it was not an
accomplice, and that it counted even the King's death among its misfortunes. For that death, reviving the memory of countless misdeeds that time
had not yet been able to erase, regenerated public suspicions and placed
the entire corps in danger, especially its main leaders. Moreover, the King's

52. "Killed May 14, 1610, at 4 PM. — Ravaillac [François, 1578–1610.—HC] searched: three-quarters
of a shield, with a wax heart wounded in three places. He asks if the king is dead; he's told no. 'Did I
give him a bad hit?' He banters and says: 'Watch out that I don't say it was yourself.' (De L'Estoile, page
305). — At 5 PM, the Queen declared regent by the gathering Parlement. (Ibid., page 306). — Forebod-
ing of the king. (Ibid., pages 307, 308). — Fr. Coton asks if the scoundrel isn't a heretic. (Ibid., page
309). — Dr. Duret made Queen's physician: the man the king liked least in the World. Conchine, said
to be constantly angling for the King's death; believed to have contributed to it. (Ibid., pages 309, 310).
— The coldness of the late King toward a poor woman. (Ibid., page 311). — De Vicq obtains the King's
bloody shirt. (Ibid., 310). — A note left on an altar three years before to warn the King about Ravaillac.
(Ibid., page 312). — The young King: 'I would like,' he used to say, 'not to be king, and that it be my
brother: for I'm afraid they're going to kill me.' (Ibid., page 314). — The King goes to the Parlement
to confirm the Regency on May 15. The First President and Servin make very fine speeches: the First
President, on the protests of the Duke of Guise, thanks him, and says he'll have the registers attended
to, to make a record of it. — A man put in prison for having said Ravaillac's act was good: he was from
the house of the Duke of Epernon [Jean-Louis, Duke of Epernon (1554–1642).—HC] and the Constable; put outside by the importunity of the leading nobles. The People's talk about these two lords.
(Ibid., page 316). — Another imp seized, who had shown a woman several of the King of Spain's spies
dressed as poor people; among others, Ravaillac, who had a false arm hidden. Trial. (Ibid., page 319).
— Fr. D'Aubigny, confessor, interrogated, says he has the gift of forgetting confessions. (Page 320). —
Jesuits accused in sermons by some Paris priests. — Much information sent to the Chancellor, incred-
ibly half-witted. — Heart carried to La Flèche. (Page 325). — M. . . (De l'Estoile, pages 307 and 309).
— d'Epernon, on good terms with the Jesuits and on their behalf. Cause to suspect M. d'Entragues
and Marquise de Verneuil. (Ibid., pages 327, 328). — Affairs of war. (Ibid., page 329). — Divisions
between the Prince of Conti and the Count of Soissons, supported by d'Epernon, who possessed the
mind of the Queen. Epernon preserved in his administration of Metz. (page 331). — Affliction of the
Pope at this news. (Page 332). — Epernon rejuvenated since the death of his master. (Ibid., page 334).
— The Count of Soissons threatens to stab in the chest those who say the Jesuits had the late King
killed. (Ibid., page 337). — The Jesuit Gontier preaches intolerance against the Huguenots. Epernon
emboldens him. Huguenots fear a Saint-Bartholomew's. (Ibid., page 338). — The money collected by
the late King given to the grandees. (Ibid., page 341). — Baldwin, a Jesuit, who knew more news about
the assassination of the late King than any man in the World, is arrested for the powder conspiracy.
(Page 343). — Coton mistreated by the King. (Page 355)" (M.).
    53. The Society of Jesus, the Jesuits.—HC

conduct was for them Religion itself, for he gave them money, and, what was even more catholic, they directed his conscience[54] and often his affairs. The Society had powerful friends at Court, and the King, who liked it when people gave him tokens of their affection, was, from that standpoint, entirely content with them. The King himself was on very good terms with Rome, which had achieved with his conversion the most fortunate situation it could wish, namely, the preservation of the Catholic Religion within the realm, and the independence of Spain.

The lords of the Realm were also not involved (except that one or two were gravely suspected). For beside the fact that those deeds came neither from their hearts nor their minds, no penchant for disorder was seen in them; on the contrary, they offered all their enmity to the common calamity.

Ravaillac maintained to the last moment that he had no accomplices, and he received absolution on condition that if he were not telling the truth, he would be damned.

But what gave birth to suspicion was the great negligence in the pursuit of certain people accused of being accomplices. But it was thought prudent to cease prosecutions where no one was gaining anything, where quite a few people could be slandered, where they ran the risk of finding a great enemy whose enmity would have to be hidden in order to avoid making him irreconcilable with them. Those in charge of the government were thinking only of their present interests. They therefore ceased to expose people to an accusation that would be terrifying to innocence itself.

LOUIS XIII

King James[55] had succeeded to the states of Elizabeth, but not to her authority. Dignity without strength; a great name without power, which makes for the saddest condition in the world. Elizabeth was the last English monarch.

Having renounced military power, Italy counted on her policy in facing disturbances to the balance of power: seeking two masters, from fear of

---

54. "Look into this" (M.).
55. James I, king of England (1603–25), son of Mary Stuart.

one; working to divide the forces of Europe, as Europe had parceled out her own. Spain divided her through the Milanese territory and held her by one end through the kingdom of Naples. The Papal States were of no consideration as far as a league was concerned, since no one wanted to be allied with princes whose imbecility was successive, and who offered only the prospect of a few days in a time of life when everything—including prudence itself—is in decline, when experience leaves many difficulties but no expedients, doubts but no resolutions.

The Spanish, masters of the Valtelline,[56] confined Italy by the Alps, by the sea. They were able to receive support through the State of Genoa, a dependency of theirs, because of the dependence in which they held their private individuals; they were going to make the Lombards in Italy . . .

War of the Valtelline.

The Pope,[57] who has power only by the ostentatious display of his power, pretended to take arms, well aware that he was not at risk of making war at the moment of peace. The two kings negotiated without the Savoyards and the Venetians. The monarchs made sport of the petty princes, as Fortune makes sport of monarchs.[58] Peace was made without the parties who had so happily made war, and contempt for the allies was called *dignity.*

Protection of great princes, for whom defense is subjugation, something which is true even among individuals.

Charles-Emmanuel, Duke of Savoy,[59] in a petty State where fortune was rather shackled, had the soul of Caesar. He inveighed against Fate, which had made him sovereign only to render him dependent—all the less free for having been born to be free; in a situation all the more bleak because he could neither command nor obey. That prince, gauging his power by his dignity or his ambition, dared—despite the whole of Europe—to make war on the Duke of Mantua and display pride before the Spanish. At that time, France was forging common interests with Spain—as if it was not already bad enough not to be aiding the Italian princes, without also assisting in their oppression. But at that moment, politics was employed only in

56. It was occupied by the French from 1635 to 1637.
57. Urban VIII, pope from 1623 to 1644.
58. "V. Nani, p. 312" (M.). Giovanni Battista Felice Gasparo Nani (1616–78), whose 1663 history of the republic of Venice Montesquieu owned (*Catalogue,* 3090).
59. Charles-Emmanuel, the Great, duke of Savoy (1580–1630).

assuring the fortunes of an unworthy favorite. Concino was thinking only of a retreat that he was already anticipating would be necessary.[60] He was assassinated, as if he had been a Duke of Guise.

Shortly thereafter was revealed that conspiracy against Venice which has not dishonored its author, because men are horrified only by the crimes of the mediocre. He had conspired against that republic as one conspires against the life of an individual. While she was defending herself only against conquest, which is always long, he was contemplating destruction, which takes only a night. While the accomplices were being executed, the ambassador's character made him fearsome. The People were threatening to tear him to pieces. Bedmar, heaped with curses, was still upholding the pride of his rank; he was still threatening, because he had been unable to destroy.[61]

The Duke of Osuna, viceroy of Naples, a man whose whims entered into the framework of his designs.[62] He had the policy of letting people doubt whether he was rational, and he thought to make himself king at a time when he was being judged scarcely capable of being governor.

By the treaty of Ulm, France established that great power of the House of Austria in Germany.[63] The Catholic League was making surprising progress in Germany. The Protestant princes, in consternation, were not making use of their forces; they were not even aware of them. They were merely adventurers who, having neither property nor reputation nor states to lose, were annoying the victors but not stopping their progress. Only Mansfeld distinguished himself by his facility in recovering from his defeats.[64] King James, as unfortunate in negotiation as his son-in-law was in war, did him more harm than good. And in making him negotiate constantly, giving him only meager support, he denied him even the expedients of promptitude and despair. The House of Austria was disposing of the estates of those she labeled *rebels,* and was going to dispose of those who were not yet to that point. She thought she already held the tail of the universal mon-

---

60. Concino Concini, marshal of Ancre (1575–1617); Louis XIII had him arrested and executed in 1617.
61. Don Alonso della Cueva, marquis of Bedmar, Spanish ambassador to Venice (1572–1655).
62. Don Pedro, duke of Ossuna, or Osuna (1579–1624).
63. Treaty of Ulm, March 14, 1647.
64. Ernst von Mansfeld (1580–1626).

archy through Germany, when France suddenly resolved to cut down that monarchy, which only stood up to Louis XIII, but which, under the reign of Louis XIV, was mixed in with the ranks of his enemies.[65]

One may say that Cardinal Richelieu resuscitated the Protestant Religion, which was heading toward its destruction, and that in striking Madrid and Vienna he struck Rome with the same blows. The popes of that time did not stop being torn between Religion and Empire. That same house[66] which had carried the Catholic Religion everywhere was going to become mistress of Italy. The interests of the Church were found to be different from the interests of Religion; the Prince was not in agreement with the Pontiff. Each pope accepted or rejected his predecessors' views, depending on whether he had more ambition or more zeal. Thus, Urban was not as obsessed with the Valtelline affair as Gregory.[67]

King James thought that with a long peace, he would eliminate his people's anxieties. But if that people is sometimes unruly toward kings it fears, it is even more so toward those it disdains. It never respects the throne so much as when it sees it covered in glory.

The King of Bohemia[68] had against him: the House of Austria; the French Crown, to which his house was odious because of the support she had always accorded the Protestants; the negotiations of his father-in-law; his indecisions, often companions of adversity and often more fatal than adversity itself.

Stuart, a house that Fate strikes constantly in order to astonish all kings; whose grandeur has been made only for disgrace; which has suffered outrages unknown to sovereigns; which has had misfortunes of mythic dimensions.

The marriage of the French princess with Charles I, a marriage which had alarmed the Spanish at the outset, was happy neither for France

65. Cf. *Universal monarchy.*
66. The house of Austria.
67. Pope Gregory XV (1621–23).
68. Ferdinand II, king of Bohemia (r. 1619–37) and Holy Roman Emperor (r. 1619–37).

nor for England, nor even for the two spouses. In the trip that Bucking-ham, the King of England's favorite,[69] had made to seek his queen, he had seen the young Queen of France; he had had the audacity to love her—and Richelieu, to be jealous over it. The hatred of the two favorites passed into the hearts of the two kings. The Queen of France was always insulted by Richelieu; the Queen of England, by Buckingham. They de-nied the first her most cherished servants; they quibbled with the second over her religion. In a word, the two courts lost no occasion to inflict that petty vengeance which is as exquisite as the passions that give birth to it, and which sometimes brings as much relief to hatred as does open warfare.

Epernon was a man equally arrogant in good fortune and bad, in favor and in disgrace, with his superiors, his equals, and his inferiors.[70] He knew how to rise, but he was absolutely ignorant of how one might fall.

The Queen Mother had nothing to put her below the common run of women, nor anything to put her above them.[71] Never was there a less Ital-ian princess. She saw nothing through her prejudices. Her complaints and her eternal bitterness alienated rather than moved her husband and son.

Louis,[72] lacking mind and even more lacking in strength of mind. He amused himself with inanities but was jealous of government; he took on all the suspicions and sorrows that his ministers wanted to lay on him; he swallowed all his own; he owed his name *the Just* to his discharge of the Cardinal's vengeances. Devout instead of pious, he had that devotion which comes not from strength of mind, but from weakness.

The King's character was not very different from that of Monsieur.[73] But Monsieur's craft was more difficult to practice than that of King, which was in a class by itself, since nothing does more to cut problems down to size than power.

69. George Villiers, duke of Buckingham (1592–1628).
70. Jean-Louis de Nogaret, duke of Epernon (1554–1642).
71. Marie de' Medici (1575–1642), queen of France (1600–1610) and queen Mother thereafter.
72. Louis XIII; cf. *Reflections on the character of some princes* (*OC,* 3:546).
73. Gaston d'Orléans, Louis XIII's brother.

Monsieur always entered affairs with anxiety about exiting them. He was plotting against the Cardinal and conducting himself in such a way that all he displayed to him was useless animosity. He knew how to be neither innocent nor guilty; he thought he was losing nothing in losing only his servants [and looked upon their loss with an indifference that has scarcely ever been equaled]; to the factions that he joined, he brought only his fears and a spirit that was susceptible sometimes to all impressions, sometimes to none.[74]

Richelieu, a private individual who had more ambition than all the world's monarchs. He regarded peoples and kings as mere instruments of his fortune; he waged war less against enemies than against the intrigues of peace. France, Spain, Germany, Italy, all of Europe, the entire world were nothing to him but a theater fit for distinguishing his ambition, his hatred, or his vengeance.

He governed as a master, not a minister; this was royal conduct not in its flattery, not in its attachment, but in its ambition. He made slaves to enjoy them; through mistreatment, he drove the princes of the blood to resentment and drew advantage from it. He was even jealous of his master, and usurped from him that authority which he made him take back from the grandees. A favorite, but without the King's heart, jealous even of mediocre talents, thinking less of exercising than of distinguishing his ministry—a man, in short, who always had influence over minds but never dominion over hearts. He maintained his position without favor, solely by his own talent and by the greatness of affairs. He made his monarch play the second role in the monarchy {but the first in Europe}. He abased the King but honored the reign, and stripping the laurels from all the King's victories.

It must be admitted that the means he employed to take hold of the King's mind were not those commonplace means that succeed so well with base souls at court. He treated the post of favorite as beneath him; he went after the Prince from the angle of security, of glory, and thereby made himself master of a man who was equally suspicious, jealous and ambitious— but ambitious in the way that a private individual is avaricious—and who had nothing of the great man in him except some desire to become one.

74. "See *Memoirs* of Montrésor, volume I, page 162; letters of Monsieur, the King and the Cardinal" (M.); a 1723 edition of Claude de Bourdeille, count of Montrésor's memoirs was in Montesquieu's library (*Catalogue*, 3018).

He managed to put the Prince in that situation where his interests were no longer separate from those of his minister—who, having irritated all the grandees, was making his victories against external enemies a necessity for the King. In the end, the latter was nothing more than the instrument of the Cardinal's grandeur, and, as I said, his secret was always to give the King more affairs than he could handle.

Marillac took to the scaffold the good repute of his innocence. Marshal Montmorency was lamented even by those who condemned him, while the implacable Cardinal was inveighing against the universal compassion, and making the King as inflexible in his justice as he himself was in his hatred. Thus, in the presence of a prince, it takes only a day to efface the deeds of a thousand years.[75]

M. Cinq-Mars had a great soul, a noble air, friends, and ambition, even before being favorite.[76] The Cardinal had placed the King's favor in his hands as a deposit that he would have to return to him; he wanted him to rest content with the honor of amusing the King. But such moderation was not made for M. Le Grand, who was seeking to distinguish himself by everything that can make great men; for he demanded to command in the armies and wanted to enter political affairs. In the end, these two men took their enmity so far that·they no longer left the King free to put up with both of them.

The Huguenots, quite torn under Louis XIII. The grandees in their party had abandoned the spirits of their forefathers: Condé for money, La Force for the baton of Marshal of France; Lesdiguières to be constable. Rohan alone was reliving the Admiral at a time when foreign support was no more;[77] when James was only a hollow shell of that hero known under the name of *Elizabeth;* when zeal had slackened; when peace had enervated the spirits; when captains and soldiers had become citizens; when the new

---

75. Louis de Marillac, marshal of France (1572–1632), executed at the Place de Grève in May; Henry II, duke of Montmorency, marshal of France (1595–1632), executed in Toulouse in October.

76. Henri Coiffier de Rezé, marquis of Cinq-Mars (1620–42).

77. Henri de Nompar de Caumont, duke of La Force (1582–1678), opposed Louis XIII in 1621–22; François de Bonne, duke of Lesdiguières (1543–1626); Henry I, duke of Rohan; the admiral in question is Coligny.

religion was beginning to take on the lukewarm quality of the old; when the air of the Court had put ambition where superstition used to be; when ministers were known less for their sermons than for their avarice and their weakness; when subordination was ruined; when every bourgeois wanted to be a captain, and every captain, a courtier; when the Catholic party, which had been unable to destroy royal authority, had, so to speak, managed to encircle it. But everything was rekindled by the ardor, the activity, the presence of the Duke of Rohan—a great reader,[78] a great captain. Montauban defended itself with that fury and patience found only when there is a religion to defend.[79] The Catholic army was almost destroyed without yet being weary.

Buckingham, who attacked the Île de Ré in vain, denied provisions to La Rochelle and facilitated its capture. La Rochelle was defended by its situation, its reputation, its religion, the courage of a people of soldiers and citizens, the assistance it received, even the fury of the sea, finally by the natural ardor to defend one's independence. On that patch of land was to depend the fate of Europe. Richelieu contemplated its subjection. The difficulty of the enterprise aided in its success, because no one at home or abroad considered thwarting it. And if one thinks carefully about it, the least sensible plans are often those that are most successful. We create a thousand obstacles against enterprises that we can fear, or that we can foresee.

The capture of that city changed the entire face of Europe. From that moment, the genius of France rose against that of Spain. The latter, it is true, washed her hands of the frequently made accusation that she had no other religion than that which advanced her grandeur or her policy. The fall of the Huguenot party, the expulsion of the Moors justified her. But what did it not cost to justify her?

The ministry of the Count-duke Olivares was a perpetual decline.[80]

The war was made not for the glory of princes, the utility of peoples, or the good of Religion, but for the vanity of two ministers who made sport of their respective Countries and abused the human race.

---

78. *Homme de cabinet,* a man who enjoys the tranquil life of study.—HC
79. Montauban was besieged by Louis XIII (1621–22).
80. Don Gasparo de Guzman, count of Olivares (1587–1645), Spanish statesman.

The two most wicked citizens that France has had: Richelieu and Louvois.[81] {I would name a third. But let us spare him in his disgrace.}

LOUIS XIV

Cardinal Imperiali, who had offended the King, found everywhere the wrath of a great prince.[82]

At the peace of ——,[83] France was given Upper and Lower Alsace and the ——. The French ambassadors protested at how little this was. "Come on," said M. Foscarini, Venetian plenipotentiary.[84] "It is more than twelve hundred years since any French ambassador sent his master three provinces in one letter."

An army of one hundred thousand Turks suddenly appeared before Vienna. There was more astonishment than consternation. The Emperor, in retreat at Linz, asked for and found support everywhere. He even dared to refuse ours. Sobieski arrived with ——, support that was all the more agreeable in that it was not suspect, it had scarcely been asked for, scarcely expected, and could have been refused for reasons of self-defense.[85]

Thus, we took no other part in the Viennese affair than that which it pleased the Imperials to arrange for us. They spread the rumor that we had ourselves attracted this scourge to the name of Christianity; they claimed to have found proof in the privy purse of the Grand Vizier. Let us say this was true; how well suited something like that was to excite hatred.

Louis worked only to arouse Europe's jealousy against him. He seemed to have devised the project of alarming her rather than conquering her. The genius of a great political strategist is to seek to establish power before making it felt; the genius of Louis was to make it felt before having established it.

81. On Louvois, see Montesquieu's short portrait in this entry on page 386, below.—HC
82. Giuseppe Imperiali (1651–1737), whom Montesquieu met in Rome; cf. *Voyages* (*OC,* 2:1184).
83. Westphalia, in 1648.
84. Michele Foscarini (1632–92).
85. Jan III Sobieski, king of Poland and Lithuania (1674–96), in 1683; at the battle of Kahlenberg he stopped three hundred thousand Turks who were besieging Vienna.

He seemed to have power only for ostentation.[86] Everything was swagger, even his policy. And if one wants to read Count Estrada's letters to Cardinal Mazarin, and then to the King,[87] one will see that the swaggering spirit had gained as much ground with the King as it had gained little with the Cardinal.

He had such a misguided ambition that he ruined himself taking fortified towns that he knew he would be obliged to give back; his ambition was for a certain kind of heroism of which the histories have not yet given us examples.

Louvois, perhaps the worst Frenchman who has yet been born,[88] made him wage war only to make himself necessary—a crime that includes all those that the justice of war alone makes legitimate. The princes who would have upheld the King's grandeur in respect, he drove to despair with his insolence.

The Prince of Orange[89] did not have a warrior's talents; but he had so many elements of a great man that his mistakes were ranked among his misfortunes. And whereas it is customary to blame the other generals for the failures of Destiny, the continual defeats of this one were laid to the account of Fortune—whether for his glory or against our own.

Bâville, man from a family that has produced great men;[90] a great instrument of arbitrary power, who had established himself in a large province as a sort of dictator over the troop commanders and the sovereign companies—like an inquisitor over the faith, like a rigid quaestor for public funds; the fittest man to extinguish an aging religion and to provoke the zeal of an emerging one; a man who spilled blood over his tribunal the way warriors shed it on the battlefield; who constantly confused civil and military power; talent more dangerous than a mediocre one, because he pushed principles to extremes; a man, for all that, who loved order and did not neglect the good when it was compatible with his prejudices; diligent,

---

86. See *PL*, XCV, 157, and the commentary in Vernière, 196 n. 1.
87. Godefroy, count d'Estrades (1607–86), marshal of France and diplomat.
88. François-Michel Le Tellier, marquis of Louvois (1639–91). See page 385, above.
89. William Henry of Nassau, king of England under the name of William III.
90. Guillaume de Lamoignon, lord of Bâville (1617–77).

hard-working, fit for breaking enemy enterprises and promoting those of the Ministry.[91]

[**1303**] I said: "Temperament is the passion of the mind."

[**1304**] In writing a letter of recommendation to M. de Fontenelle, I used to end this way: "I ask you to take up the interests of a man of merit and of honesty; I know of nothing to say that would be more seductive to you."

[**1305**] [See p. 34 of this volume.[1] As we have demanded more of authors, we have demanded less of critics.]

[**1306**] Until now, Fortune seems to have taken pleasure in corrupting the King's heart; she has gotten tired of it. Before the battle of Hochstädt,[1] France had risen to that phase of grandeur that is regarded as immutable, even though it is near the moment of decline. It is certain that the League was formed out of desperation. We lost at Hochstädt, then, that confidence we had acquired from thirty years of victories: ―― battalions surrendered as prisoners of war; we regretted their lives, as we would have regretted their deaths.

It seems that God, who wanted to put limits on empires, gave the French facility of acquisition along with facility of loss—that ardor that nothing can resist, along with that discouragement that yields before everything.

MME DE MAINTENON. Time took away her beauty, but a certain grace she possessed, never; her ingratiating mind achieved that great conquest by itself, and despite her appearance. She served her family with moderation and had no attachment to wealth. She demanded nothing except the heart, and in her middling condition, she enjoyed the greatest of all fortunes. Exposed constantly to the King's woes when he became difficult, she seemed rather to soften them than to suffer them. It is true that the King had a soul greater than her own; this meant that she was constantly humbling that of the King.

91. "See above, the character portrait of Louis XIV" (M.); cf. *pensées* 1122 and 1145.

[**1305**]

1. *Pensée* 1006.

[**1306**]

1. This is the second battle of Hochstädt, won by the Anglo-Austrian troops under Marlborough and Prince Eugene against France under Tallart and Marsin on August 13, 1704.

The King had lost the hearts of his subjects because of the intolerable taxes with which he had burdened them—necessary support for a useless war. For such is the nature of things that those who begin by fighting for glory usually end up fighting for the State's survival.

That war is often initiated without cause made people believe that all those wars he subsequently undertook had just as little legitimacy, and when they were fighting for the survival of the realm, they still thought they were fighting for the King's passions.

He had an inordinate desire to increase his power over his subjects; on which score, I am not sure I should blame him so much for a sentiment common to virtually all men.

He had more the mediocre qualities of a king than the great ones:[2] a noble form, a grave air, accessible, polished, constant in his friendships, not liking to change ministers or methods of governing, sticking to the laws and rules as long as they did not clash with his interests, liking to preserve the rights of his subjects vis-à-vis his subjects, liberal toward his servants—well-suited, in short, to uphold the externals of royalty, but born with a mediocre mind. He often mistook false grandeur for true. He knew neither how to begin his wars nor how to end them. In an age and in a part of the world where heroism has become impossible, he had a weakness for seeking it. Determined in his military ventures by his ministers' interests, he knew neither how to wait for pretexts nor how to use them. Heaven gave him ministers and generals; his own choice never did. His confessors, who always adjusted his devotion to his present situation, [made him think, when he made treaties in which he was abandoning everything, that devotion consisted in moderation; when he suffered reverses, that it consisted] when he made war, they spoke to him only about David; when he made peace, they spoke to him only about Solomon. That devotion managed to take away from him the little talent that Nature had given him. His Council of Conscience, with its hard-line governance, made him odious and ridiculous; he swindled it for forty years in plain view of all Europe; he was caught in the act without losing his dupe. People marveled at the boldness of the Council of Conscience and the feebleness of the other councils. In the former, everything was ardor; everywhere else, it was lukewarmness and consternation. The idiotic ministry of Chamillard

2. See *pensées* 1122 and 1145.

managed to degrade him.[3] Very easy to fool, because he expressed himself little. M. de Cambrai, by his devotion, thought to become his prime minister.[4] Toward the end of his days, difficult to amuse; incapable of either seeking or finding resources within himself; devoid of reading, devoid of passions; made melancholy by his devotion, and, with an old wife, abandoned to the sorrows of an old king. He had a quality which, among the devout, transcends devotion itself—namely, letting himself be deceived by them. In the different choices he made, he always consulted his heart before his mind.

REGENCY

The Duke of Orléans had all the qualities of a good gentleman.[5]

Cardinal Dubois was a real pedant.[6] The Regent was so tired of him that he would have ousted him if he had lived two months longer. But why did the Regent make his career? It is a question that should be asked, because the answer is not visible. He was the most timid man in the world. The English ministers used to amuse themselves spouting false news that would keep him from sleeping, and telling him the next morning that the news was false. The Duke of Orléans would sometimes say to him: "Abbé, you are telling me nothing about this country." He used to go dictate a letter to his secretary, then carry it to the Duke of Orléans. At his death were found three weeks' worth of unopened letters from the Grand Vizier, which had been there for a year. He was careful to ensure that dispatches came directly to him alone. He used obscure men unable to get to the bottom of them. When the Duke of Orléans proposed something, he had those men write down difficulties, and then he made them stop, in such a way that the Duke of Orléans was enchanted by his mind.

One day, he told the Duke of Orléans that foreign ministers had no con-

---

3. Michel Chamillart (1652–1721), controller-general of finances in 1699, secretary of state for war in 1701, minister of state in 1709.

4. Cambrai, that is, Fénelon.

5. For Montesquieu's view of Orléans, see *Letters from Xenocrates to Pheres* (*OC,* 3:129–35), his letter to Bulkeley, January 1, 1726 (*OC,* 3:758), and *pensées* 29 and 800.

6. See *pensées* 173, 1390, and 1407.

fidence in him because he had never worked alone with the King. "What a b—— and a scoundrel you are!" said M. d'Orléans. "I'll give you twenty kicks in the butt if you talk to me that way again."

It is said that M. d'Orléans's plan was at first to form a Royal Council made up of Marshal Villeroy, M. d'Uxelles, Tallard, and some others, by means of which Dubois would not have been prime minister; but Marshal Villeroy did not want to go along.[7]

Cardinal Dubois was a bad copy of Cardinal Mazarin. What infamy to have revealed the accomplices of the Bishop of Rochester's conspiracy! Did he not use the Pretender to have himself made cardinal?[8] And did he not write in England that, once he became cardinal, he would make sport of the imbecile?

After what I have seen, I will never again put any stock in the praises bestowed on the minister in office. I saw the most sensible people admire Cardinal Dubois as if he were a Richelieu, but three days after his death, everyone agreed he was a pedant, lacking the capacity for any part of the ministry.

People took their respect as far as they had at first taken their contempt, and without examining the reasons for such rapid progress, they took that rapidity itself as a demonstration of his great genius.

Here is the reason for this sort of reputation: one wants to pass for a wise man; sometimes, one wants to pass for a man of the Court; a very small number of persons can set the tone for the public; as soon as this small number of interested persons has stopped talking, the public retracts its judgment.

Cardinal Dubois died, leaving no one after him to recall his memory. The Duke of Orléans took his place, knowing that it suits only the King to have prime ministers, and that the third level was too close to the second.[9]

[**1307**] I said of Shakespeare: "When you see such a man soar like an eagle, it is he. When you see him creeping along, it is his era."

[**1308**] When one wants to look something up from Antiquity, one

---

7. François de Neufville, marshal, duke of Villeroy (1644–1730); Nicolas du Blé, marquis of Uxelles (1652–1730), marshal of France; Camille d'Hostin de La Baume, duke and marshal of Tallard (1652–1728); see *pensées* 1390 and 1407.

8. Pretender, Prince James Stuart (1688–1766), Jacobite claimant of the English throne; Francis Atterbury, high Tory bishop of Rochester, who plotted a Jacobite rising in London during the election of 1722.—HC

9. "Look in the *Spicilège* for some anecdotes I have not put here" (M.); cf. 745–69.

must take care that the things cited as proof by the authors not always be taken as literally true, because their need for these things may have made the author give them a broader meaning than they really have.

[**1309**] Greenlanders find great delight in drinking whale oil. This is because in such extremely cold countries, the fibers of their stomachs are strong enough to withstand the oil diet, which would ruin the stomach in southern countries.

[**1310**] Just as the miser says that his heirs would not have more pleasure in dissipating his fortune than he had had in amassing it, an author may say that no one will find more pleasure in reading his book than he has had in writing it.

[**1311**] *I said of* Mme de L——,[1] "Those who hear about you admire you; those who see you love you."

[**1312**] The great martyrdom that is shame, when one suffers in one's character.

[**1313**] John of Antioch said that Diocletian, offended by the Egyptians, had all their ancient books burned "*de chemia auri et argenti conscriptos,*" so they would no longer have grounds for revolt,[1] and too much wealth would not come their way.[2]

This malady, then, is quite ancient, and it is not true, as some have said, that it is modern.

[**1314**] DROPSY. Dropsy, common disease in the South Sea. Captain Dampier (volume 1, page 193) says: "Many of ours had died from that disease."[1] He was in that area. "I was laid and covered all but my head in the hot sand: I endured it near half an hour, and was then taken out, and laid to sweat in a tent. I did sweat exceedingly while I was in the sand, and I do believe it did me much good, for I grew well soon after."

[1311]
1. Doubtless the Princess of Lixin, who later became Mme de Mirepoix; cf. *pensée* 1012n. The italicized words here are in English in Montesquieu's manuscript.

[1313]
1. John of Antioch, seventh-century Byzantine chronicler, contemporary of Heraclius and author of a *Universal history* of which only fragments remain; Diocletian was a Roman emperor (r. 284–305). An earlier account can be found in *Polybii, Diodori Siculi: excerpta ex collectaneis Constantini Porphyrogenetae* [Polybius, Diodorus Siculus: Excerpts from the collections of Emperor Constantine Porphyrogenitus]. The passage reads: "written on the chemistry of gold and silver." H. Valesius (Paris, 1634), 834.
2. "Extracts *Universal history,* p. 311 v°" (M.).

[1314]
1. On William Dampier, see *pensée* 1151n, *Geographica* (*OC,* 2:925–26), and *Catalogue,* 2740. (The passage Montesquieu cites in this paragraph has been reproduced in Dampier's original.—HC)

He then says the extreme diet he was obliged to follow on the ship from the South Sea to the Larron Islands managed to cure him. It's in the same volume.

Like all violent remedies, this remedy has doubtless been neglected because on the one hand, patients refuse it, and on the other, doctors, who do not want to risk their reputation, are afraid to give it. {This should be put after a passage from Aulus Gellius (book XIX, chapter viii) which talks about the cure of a man's dropsy by hot sand. He does not explain how.}

[1315] It will be found that in giving my judgment on various authors, I praise more than I criticize. I have rarely given my judgment except on authors I esteemed, having as much as possible read only those I have thought the best.

Besides, without indulging here in a display of fine-sounding sentiments, I have been so plagued my whole life by those petty know-it-alls who have talked my ears off with their criticisms of what they have badly read, and what they have not read, that I believe I am partly in their debt for the singular pleasure I find in seeing an excellent work, in seeing a good work that will perhaps approach the excellent, even in seeing a mediocre work that one might render good.

Moreover, I confess, I have no predilection for old or new works, and all disputes in this regard prove to me nothing except that there are some very good works, both among the ancients and among the moderns.

[1316] Lawyers' citations disturb the spirit of judicial decision-making instead of aiding it.[1] Common sense tells us that the facts and not matters of reasoning are subject to authority. For example, it can be proven that a disturbance was made, or a crime was committed, by the authority of witnesses; that a contract was entered into, by the signature of the notary public; that a man is of age, by the authority of the baptismal registry. But as soon as you engage in reasoning, authority must be abandoned. For in order for you to be able to use it, it would have to follow, as a necessary consequence of the fact that an author has thought that a thing is just, that it really is just—something all the more difficult to believe in that there are not perhaps two opinions universally agreed upon by the jurisconsults.

[1316]

1. For Montesquieu's ideas on the exercise of justice, see his *Discours sur l'équité qui doit régler les jugements et l'exécution des lois* [Discourse on the equity that ought to guide the judgments and execution of the laws], delivered before the Parlement of Bordeaux on November 11, 1725 (*OC,* 3:209–19).

It takes a judge much less trouble to decide the question in itself, than to unravel all the authorities cited before him; to contrast the strong and the weak; to seek the reasons that determined one author to give a decision contrary to another's; the authority that a certain author ought to have in this country or in another; finally, the exactness of the application he has made of it.

If a pagan theologian, in reading Homer, had wanted to resolve that famous quarrel that reduced Asia to ashes, and decide who was right between the Greeks and Trojans, and if he had said:

"I do not have a profound enough mind to resolve this great question; but there are intellects more perfect than mine who saw that quarrel, several of whom even got involved in reconciling them. Let us see what they thought. First, if I knew the opinion of Jupiter, the father and greatest of the gods, I would be well along; but as luck would have it, he was neutral.

"But Juno, Jupiter's wife and sister, and Neptune, brother of the same god, were for the Greeks. But one cannot say that Juno and Neptune lined up on that side out of a spirit of equity. Is it not true that Juno wanted to take revenge on the affront that had been committed against her charms? And that Neptune, who did not intend to do the job of mason for nothing, was again demanding his wages? And besides, Mars and Venus were for the Trojans." "But in your view," one would reply, "did a motive other than that of love and gratitude engage Venus on the Trojan side? In addition, are you surprised that Mars follows Venus's lure and fights for her?"

"But look at Vulcan, who is for the Greeks." "Exactly so," one would reply. "Don't you see in this conduct the distress of a jealous husband? And it is not without reason that he is jealous."

"But we have Pallas for us," the Trojans would say. "I believe it," one would reply; "you had a good token of her protection: you had the palladium."

It is clear that this way, there would never be an end of it, whereas if one were to take the question in itself, nothing would be simpler. A Greek king had a very beautiful wife; the Trojan king's son arrives there and cuckolds him on his arrival; he abducts the wife; the husband is good enough to ask her back; the Trojans refuse. It's the Trojans who are in the wrong.

[**1317**] [I said: "There are likeable people, there are detestable people, and there is an even more extensive class of unbearable people."]

[1318] In considering men before the establishment of societies, one finds they were subject to a power that nature had established.[1] For childhood being the weakest conceivable condition, children were bound to be dependent upon their fathers who had given them life, and who were still giving them the means of preserving it.

Although this dependence, preceding all convention, seemed in its origins to be bounded only by the fathers' love, it was limited in two ways: (1) by the fathers' reason, when, in establishing societies, they bounded it by civil laws; (2) by nature, because as children leave youth, fathers enter old age, and the children's strength increases as the father weakens. The same love and gratitude remain, but the right of protection changes.

The deceased fathers left the collaterals independent. It was necessary to combine by convention and to do by civil laws what natural right had done at the outset.

It was necessary to love one's Country, as one loved one's family; it was necessary to cherish the laws, as they cherished the will of their fathers.

[1319] The people who produce those works of eloquence to enlarge or diminish things! Who would want to have an outfit so large or so small? Would it not be better for it to be just right?

[1320] Mairan, so superior to everyone in the sciences, who employs all the little expedients on all sides to make his reputation.[1] I compare him to that Breton, Marquis de Comaduc, who had a hundred thousand pounds in income but would ask for alms. Those who are so afraid for their reputation and are wounded by the pettiest things, they are like M. Newton's bodies, which are acted on *in distans*.[2]

[1321] One likes to read the Ancients' books to see other prejudices.

[1322] I call the flatterer a slave who is no good for any master.

[1323] I said of B—— that you ought not have him for either a friend or an enemy; that he is heeded by no one, and yet he is heeded by everyone.

[1324] THE KINGS OF SPARTA. There have perhaps never been kings

[1318]
1. See *pensée* 1267.—HC

[1320]
1. Jean-Jacques Dortous de Mairan (1678–1771), physicist, member of the Academy of Sciences in 1718; three of his memoirs were published by the Bordeaux Academy: on the barometer, on ice, and on light (1715–17).

2. At a distance, a reference to Newton's theory of gravity, in contrast to the mechanistic theory of action promoted by Descartes and others.—HC

whose lives were more exposed to danger, or perhaps longer—Agesilaus lived to the age of ——.[1] The age of the kings of Sparta must be looked into, and compared with that of the kings of Persia and Egypt.

[**1325**] ADVANTAGES OF TEMPERATE COUNTRIES. In extremely hot countries, little water, because it is lost or evaporates before it comes together or after having come together. In extremely cold countries, water cannot seep through the earth.

[**1326**] I said: "The English are not sufficiently superior to us not to be inferior."

[**1327**] Those who raise men dishonored by their morals to the highest positions offer quite a bad opinion of themselves.

[**1328**] Everyone works on the mind, few on the heart; this is because we are better at perceiving the new knowledge than the new perfections that we acquire.

[**1329**] The Court, where everyone thinks he is an important personage.

[**1330**] It is easy to paint at Court. If one is sometimes too hidden there, one is almost always too exposed there.

[**1331**] Le ——, equally beneath favor and disgrace. He was unable to hold firm against either of those great trials.

[**1332**] I won my lawsuit![1] Behold a pleasant letter in which I will speak to you only about myself. But to truly speak about me, I must speak about yourself.

[**1333**] It seems to me that the Graces have sent you to teach us what they are saying and what they are.[1] Do not take this letter as a declaration of love, but as the only way that exists of writing to you. It seems to me that this is ordinary speech, and that I have done nothing but talk about you.

[**1334**] The irony should not be constant in a work; then it no longer surprises.

[1324]
1. Agesilaus II, king of Sparta (398–358 B.C.), who died in a storm.

[1332]
1. Montesquieu pursued a number of cases in defense of his prerogatives as a landowning lord; it is not clear which one was meant here.

[1333]
1. See *pensée* 1093.—HC

[1335] In the _Saints' Maxims,_ the true is so close to the false that you don't know where you are.[1] The role of M. de Meaux was easy: he had a big target to hit.[2]

[1336] I am not surprised by ancient stories where you see men made reputable for having killed monsters devastating the countryside. That must have been in lightly populated territories typical of those times, when crocodiles could enter by the rivers and survive in the territory—they were called _dragons,_ and they engaged in that sort of devastation. See Thomas Gage's _Relations_ (volume II, part IV, chapter 4):[1] how, in passing by a lake, they were pursued by a caiman or crocodile going as fast as their horses. Men and beasts sought to destroy each other, and contested the land. These lands here are too populous for caimans to be allowed to become established in them; our rivers are not wide enough; they would have been immediately destroyed. And let there be no doubt that, if the French or English were to inhabit Egypt, they would soon find the means of purging it of crocodiles. Sharks are another species of animal {seems to me}.

[1337] Ariosto collected the chivalric tales of his time and made a whole out of them, just as Ovid collected the myths and made a whole out of them.

[1338] What makes {seems to me} Holy Scripture venerable is the true-ness to life in the depiction. The lives and mores of the Patriarchs are true, because even today, the Arabs and the peoples of the lands of the Patriarchs have lived that way. This is a great presumption in favor of the truth of the entire book.

[1339] The crime[1] of sodomy must not have been as ridiculous in the past as it is now. The ordinance of a grand-duke of Florence: _poi che, nei_

[1335]
1. Fénelon published _Explication des maximes des saints_ [Explication of the saints' maxims], a subtle defense of Quietism, in February 1697. Jacques-Bénigne Bossuet (1627–1704), bishop of Meaux, and others referred the work to Rome for censure; Louis XIV demanded Innocent XII's condemnation of the work in July 1697; it was granted in 1699.
2. Bossuet maintained a polemic with Fénelon after publication of the _Maxims,_ marked by his _Relations sur le Quiétisme_ [Account of Quietism].

[1336]
1. Thomas Gage, English Dominican, missionary to Mexico (d. 1655). After some disagreements with his superiors, he returned to England, where he became a Protestant pastor. His _New Survey of West Indies_ (1648) is highly critical of the Catholic missions and Spanish administration of America.

[1339]
1. First version: "the vice"

tempi di dietro, nostri fidelissimi sudditi non si sono punto guardati de la sodomia,[2] he established penalties that were (I think): a fine of twenty-five gold crowns for the agent; less for the passive one. Such a law would no longer be enacted.

[1340] CHANGE OF MORES IN A CERTAIN NATION.[1] As political power grew stronger, the Nobility vacated its lands. This was the main cause of the change that occurred in the Nation. The simple mores of earlier times were abandoned for the vanities of the cities; women renounced wool and disdained all pastimes that were not pleasures.

The disorder arose only imperceptibly. It began under Francis I; it continued under Henry II. The luxury and flabbiness of the Italians increased it under the regencies of Queen Catherine. Under Henry III, a vice that unfortunately is unknown only in barbarous nations showed itself at Court. But the corruption and spirit of independence continued in a sex that knows how to draw advantage even from scorn. Never was marriage more insulted than under Henry IV. Louis XIII's devotion left the problem where it was. Never was a prince less suited for setting the tone for his age. Anne of Austria's grave gallantry could change nothing. Louis XIV's youth added to the problem; the rigidity of his old age suspended it; the dikes were broken at his death.

Daughters no longer heeded mothers' traditions. Women who used to come only by degrees to a certain liberty now obtained it from the first days of marriage. In the fear of blushing at jealousies, one blushed at attentions. Vices were no longer known; only mockeries were felt, and numbered among these mockeries was an inhibiting modesty or a timid virtue. Ignorance of mores was a kind of persecuted religion.

Conventions were followed by conventions; the secret lasted barely as long as it took to agree upon it. Amidst constant change, taste was worn out; it was ruined by the search for pleasures. Half the nation began the day when the other half was ending it. Idleness was called *freedom,* and *pastime* was the name given to the immoderate enjoyment of pleasure. There was a desire to carry over into life that joy made manifest at banquets.

---

2. "That, in times past, our very faithful subjects did not take care to refrain from sodomy."—HC

[1340]
1. See also *pensée* 1272.

[1341][1] After M. Cheseldam had reduced the cataract of a man blind from birth, the latter could not judge distances and thought that objects were about to touch his eyes, like what touched his skin; he did not know the shape of anything and could only recognize it by sight after examining the shape by touch.[2]

It is known that, although the soul at first sees the left side of every object on the right, the right side on the left, the top on the bottom, the bottom on top, it rectifies everything by experience.

To M. Cheseldam's man, a painting did not represent a figure in relief.

It would certainly seem that the soul relates sounds to acoustic bodies only by reiterated observations in childhood, in which it links the sense of sound to the bell that produces it.

The sensation of touch did not give M. Cheseldam's man an accurate idea of the shape of things. The sensation of sight did not give it to him, either. Thus, it was from these two senses that his soul derived its idea of them.

The soul is thus a philosopher that begins to instruct itself, that learns to judge by its senses themselves and by the nature of the warnings they should be giving it.

At first it receives a sensation, and then it makes a judgment about it; it adds, it corrects itself, it adjusts one of its senses by another, and based on what they tell it, it learns what they meant to tell it.

Having formed these natural judgments, the soul likewise forms all the ones it can create with the same facility, and they are such, for the most part, that it cannot avoid forming them.

It sees a square; it does not see it all alone, but with other things. Seeing them all together, it can compare them. For if it did not see that the square has angles and the circle does not, it would not see the shape of either the square or the circle. As soon as it sees real relationships, it will see others that are not real; so that, from the fact that it sees that a square has four sides and a circle does not, it also sees that a square does not have eight sides and that a circle does not have fifty.[3] It will have an idea of number,

[1341]

1. This is the last entry in the hand of secretary E, who served Montesquieu from 1734 to 1738.

2. William Cheseldam (1688–1752), English surgeon who in 1729 performed a cataract operation on a man born blind. See *Spicilège,* 342, for Montesquieu's own eye problems.

3. See also *pensée* 1187 for much of this paragraph.—HC

because, seeing a square near another one, it will say: "If this were that, then when I moved my eyes away from this, I would no longer see that; these are thus two things. Another; these are thus three." When it does not know how many there are, it will have an idea that corresponds to the idea of confusion. After seeing some squares in a certain space, it might think there are that many in another space; it will therefore see possible squares when it does not see squares, as if placed in a certain location rather than another; it will see squares in general. It will be likewise with all general conceptions.

These things are again types of natural judgment. The soul will have only a sensation of them; it will not develop them; in some sense, it will not know that it knows, because it will not have learned them by reflection.

[1342] In monarchies, things in common are regarded as another's things, but in republics they are regarded as everyone's things.

[1343] I said to a man who was speaking ill of my friend: "Attack me, and leave my friends alone."   .

[1344] My daughter said quite rightly: "Bad manners are only hard the first time."[1]

[1345] Europe will be ruined by her men of war.[1]

Here is an incident that was stifled at the time, and that has hardly been spoken of since.

Soldiers in 1714 or 1715, on learning of the intention to give them bread instead of money, wrote to each other from regiment to regiment, and one fine day, they left their officers there, created some officers from their own ranks, went on guard all the same—all the officers remaining where they were. The King's fortified towns remained in their power for four days. Marshal Montesquiou finessed that.[2] He spoke to them. A soldier drew a line and said: "If you cross that line, you are dead. Speak!" A soldier from Navarre or some other regiment came to make some proposals. A soldier from Champagne slapped him in the face: "Is it up to you to speak while the soldiers of Champagne, the premier regiment of France,

[1344]
1. Montesquieu had two daughters: Marie (1720–84), married in 1738 to Vincent d'Armajan; Denise (1727–1800), married in 1745 to her cousin Godefroy de Secondat.

[1345]
1. First version: "by her militaries."
2. Pierre de Montesquiou, count of Artagnan (1645–1725), marshal of France.

are here," and pursued the negotiation. This was finessed, silenced and suppressed.

The Dutch garrison in Lille has done something similar in our time,[3] in 1737 I believe; a Swiss regiment got up and left.

So many troops will someday feel their strength.

[1346] I said: "I have an enormous amount of business that I do not have."

[1347] I said: "One can hide one's pride, but one can't hide one's modesty."

[1348] I said: "When one has been a woman in Paris, one can't be a woman elsewhere."

[1349] It has been demonstrated that there can no longer be a great man of war in France. This is because no one does what he is supposed to do. The general communicates nothing of what he is doing to the general officers; the secret is between him and the army's sergeant and the deputy chief of staff. But if good general officers are not being formed, where will a general be found? There's more: the general himself is not being formed, because the Court wants to do his job. *Idem,* the ministers.

[1350] [I think I have discovered why stags cry when they are cornered; it is out of pity at the folly of those who spend their lives pursuing them.]

[1351] Flanders and Artois, *Sylva carboniana,*[1] great-governor of early medieval Flanders. When good country has become desert through some accident, it is at first covered with woods, and is quite difficult to clear.

[1352] I am convinced that the Angels do not despise men as much as men despise each other.

[1353] I said of the intendant Boucher: "I agree that the intendants are being made all-powerful; but if they are going to be made gods, they must at least be chosen from among men, not beasts."[1]

---

3. The Dutch occupied Lille from 1708 to 1713 as part of the European alliance against Louis XIV in the War of the Spanish Succession.—HC

[1351]
1. "Burnt forest."—HC

[1353]
1. Claude Boucher, intendant of the generality of Bordeaux (1720–43), was in conflict with Montesquieu in 1726–27, attempting to prevent him from planting vines in the commune of Plessac, near Bordeaux. For more on the royal intendants, see *pensées* 977, 1572, 1835, 1840, 1846, 1898, 2066, and 2099.

[1354] In my extract from the *Journal des Savants,* August 1736, is a song about the Greeks:[1]

"The first of all goods is health; the second, beauty; the third, wealth acquired without fraud; the fourth, youth spent with friends."

There is no talk here of wit, which is a principal attribute of our modern times.

[1355] Little houses for gallantry, well-devised for the Nation's taste; you have an air of mystery there without having its disadvantage, which is the mortification of vanity.[1]

[1356] Big difference between Asia and Europe. In the latter, the warm and the cold are just about proportional to the latitude, so that one passes through the warm, the temperate, the cold. But in Asia, there is no temperate land between the warm and cold lands; in leaving the heat of China, one passes to the fortieth, forty-first, and forty-second parallels, where it is colder than in Norway; so much so[1] that wheat often cannot grow there, because of the altitude and the niter in the soil. Now this has influenced the differences in character, in mores; it has been easier to invade from north to south. There have only been two sorts of people: uncouth and ferocious peoples, or peoples softened up by the heat.

[1357] What accounts for the fact that nowadays, there are no more devotions, confraternities, [pilgrimages,] church assemblies, sermons, is that gallantry no longer needs it; women are seen everywhere.

[1358] I said: "When you run after wit, you catch up with folly."

[1359] It is the great knowledge of navigation that accounts for the fact that geography, after having advanced so far, is coming to a halt. The routes are so well known, {and the rules for following them are so certain,} that it is rare for a vessel to stray off course. Thus, nothing is discovered by

[1354]

1. This extract is lost. See the August 1736 *Journal des savants,* 486–89, for La Nauze's *Premier et second mémoire sur les chansons de l'ancienne Grèce* [First and second memoir on the songs of ancient Greece].

[1355]

1. The *petites maisons galantes* were houses of prostitution, sometimes high-toned, in eighteenth-century Paris. Their self-ascribed term was a play on the Little Houses (Petites-Maisons), a Parisian insane asylum, as they emphasized the "follies" of love; for the latter, cf. *pensées* 872, 1061, 1102, 1376, and 1610.—HC

[1356]

1. "Put in the *Laws*" (M.), 17.3, 280.

chance anymore, and ships have to be sent out expressly to make discoveries in order for them to occur.

[1360] I said: "One must have opinions, passion; then, one is in harmony with everyone. Every man who has moderate sentiments is {usually} in harmony with no one."

[1361] I said: "Princes get bored with everything that amuses us, and amused with everything that bores us."

[1362] On the misfortunes of hail or frost, I said that it is in the nature of things that this is bound to happen from time to time, and that one has to know this in general; that it is therefore indifferent whether it happens this year or some other year; that those who agonize over these things are bound to agonize over them the first day they become involved in their business.

[1363] I said of the Volteromania: "That is too strong to have its effect."[1]

[1364] I was saying of Rousseau:[1] "All his epithets say much, but they always say too much; he always expresses himself and more."

[1365] I defined M. de La Trémouille: a great lord, who has many petty talents.[1]

[1366] Churchmen are always the flatterers of princes, when they cannot be their tyrants.

[1367] The inhabitants of islands are always {more} disposed to liberty than the inhabitants of the mainland. This is because on islands, there are never large empires; besides which, they think they are the only people in the world.[1]

[1368] Cardinal de Retz was better suited to be at the head of a faction, and Cardinal Mazarin was better suited to be in an inner circle.[1]

[1363]
1. The *Voltéromanie* was a lampoon against Voltaire from the 1730s, attributed to his nemesis the abbé Desfontaines, over which Voltaire went to court.—HC

[1364]
1. Jean-Baptiste Rousseau, the poet.

[1365]
1. The French contrast is between *grand* and *petit* ("big" and "small").—HC. Charles-Armand-René de La Trémouille, Duke of Thouars (1708–42); cf. *pensée* 1381.

[1367]
1. See *Laws*, 18.5.

[1368]
1. Jean-François-Paul de Gondi, cardinal of Retz (1613–79), played a leading part during the French civil war known as the *Fronde* (1648–52), on which his *Memoirs* are an important source of information.

[1369] I said to a man: "Come now! You have sentiments as low as a man of quality."[1]

[1370] I was saying of the D[uchess] of Aig[uillon]: "She has *esprit,* but it is of the poorest kind; she has the arrogance of a pedant and all the faults of a lackey."[1]

[1371] I was saying of the ch—— of Play——: "So mild! It seems I see a worm spinning silk."

[1372] We see from Diodorus how ancient the arts are. Among the earliest Assyrian kings, we see riches so great that it is clear they could not have acquired them except by their plundering of the nations they subjugated. During the foundation of their empire, for example, the three solid gold statues that Semiramis placed on the temple of Belus that she built:[1] Jupiter had a height of forty feet and weighed a thousand Babylonian talents, one-seventh heavier;[2] that of Rhea, on a golden chariot, was the same weight. Golden table (five hundred talents) and other prodigies of wealth. The kings of Persia pillaged all that. In all these buildings by Semiramis, look also at how perfected the arts were: sculpture, . . . gardens in the air: three beds, the last made of lead, to prevent the earth's humidity from tilting the walls. Wall in the middle, cavities from top to bottom, in the depths of which there had been placed pumps which went down to the river and raised water into the garden. {They therefore already had the use of pumps. It is true that this garden was later than Semiramis.} Stone of 130 feet long and 25 feet wide and thick, which she got from the Armenian mountains and made an obelisk out of it in Babylon. All this taken from Diodorus (book II). Notice also that Semiramis drew maritime workers from Phoenicia, Syria, island of Cyprus.

The nature of the country is for all time.

[1373] I said: "The Czar was not tall, he was enormous."[1]

[1369]
1. *Homme de qualité* is a synonym here for nobility by birth.—HC

[1370]
1. Anne-Charlotte de Crussol Florensac, duchess of Aiguillon (1700–1772); in 1718 she married Armand-Louis de Vignerot, count of Agenais, duke and peer of Aiguillon in 1736. Friend of Maupertuis, Voltaire, and Montesquieu, she was at Montesquieu's deathbed.

[1372]
1. Diodorus of Sicily, *Library of History,* II.9; on Semiramis, see *Laws,* 21.6, 357.
2. Montesquieu seems to mean one-seventh heavier than the more familiar Greek talent.—HC

[1373]
1. Peter the Great of Russia (r. 1697–1725).

[1374] I was saying of the Marquis of M——: "He has an indecent familiarity, which displeases those above him and those below."

[1375] [I said: "One reads only books that ought not to be read."]

[1376] On the spirit of witticisms: if one were to go around collecting witticisms from the Little-Houses, one would find a lot of them.[1]

[1377] I said of M. de For[calquier]: "If he did not have a great deal of wit, he would have none at all."[1]

[1378] One must reflect upon Aristotle's *Politics* and the two *Republics* of Plato, if one wants to have an accurate idea of Greek laws and mores. To look for them in their historians is as if we wanted to find ours by reading about the wars of Louis XIV.

[1379] EDUCATION. Through education, men are taught their duties, to the extent they are in a position to know them; they are taught in a few years what the human race has only been able to possess after a very large number of centuries, and what savage peoples are still ignorant of today.

[1380] It seems to me that Voltaire believes in attraction because it is an extraordinary thing, like one believes in miracles. In his book, he is obsessed solely with making us see prodigies. It is clear he wants to sell his snake oil.[1]

[1381] I said of M. de La Trémoille: "No one in the world does what ought not to be done better than he does."[1]

[1382] Voltaire's works, like those ill-proportioned faces that sparkle with youth.

[1383] The advantage of love over debauchery is the multiplication of pleasures. All thoughts, all tastes, all feelings become reciprocal. In love, you have two bodies and two souls; in debauchery, you have one soul which is disgusted even with its own body.

[1384] Besides the pleasure that wine brings us by itself, we also owe to the joy of grape harvests the pleasure of comedies and tragedies.

[1376]
1. For the Petites-Maisons, a Paris insane asylum, see *pensées* 872, 1061, 1102, 1355, and 1610.—HC

[1377]
1. Louis-Basile de Brancas, the count of Forcalquier (1672–1750).

[1380]
1. Montesquieu may be referring here to Voltaire's *Elements of the Philosophy of Newton* (1736), where the theory of attraction, or gravity, is spelled out; see also *pensée* 1320.—HC

[1381]
1. See *pensée* 1365.

[1385] Sire, . . . you help me speak the truth every day.

[1386] Inscriptions for a pyramid that I intend to have erected on the borders of my land:[1]

> Tutatis Dynastiae Finibus,
> Repressis Praedam Quaerentibus,
> Hoc
> Gallici Senatus Aequitatis Monumentum
> Carolus
> In Rei Memoriam Erexit.[2]

On the other side:

> Stet Lapis Hic, Donec Fluctus Girunda Recuset
> Oceano Regi Generosaque Vina Britannis.[3]

On the third side:

> Deo Terminali,
> Judici, Indici, Testi,
> Perpetuo
> Fines Regenti,
> Dormientibus Vigilanti,
> Hoc Sacrum
> Juris Cultor Et Pacis Amans
> Posuit.[4]

[1387] Moderation is a virtue for every status:[1] for since it is properly

---

[1386]

1. On the occasion of Montesquieu's trial, acting as lord of Martillac, against the city of Bordeaux's attempt to delimit the lordship of Martillac and the county of Ornon. A Parlementary decree of August 28, 1743, ruled in Montesquieu's favor.

2. "Having preserved the boundaries of his dynasty, / And repressed those who sought plunder / This / Monument to the Justice of the French Senate / Charles / Has erected in remembrance."

3. "Let this stone rest here until the Gironde refuses its waves / To King Ocean, and its generous wines to the Britons."

4. "To the God of Borders, / To the judge, the guide, the witness, / The Everlasting one / Who rules the frontiers, / Who keeps vigil for those who sleep, / An adept of the law and friend of peace / Has consecrated this."

[1387]

1. See *Laws*, 5.5, 47; Montesquieu's word for *moderation* is *médiocrité*.

speaking merely a prudent and orderly management of the present condition, it is able not only to bring sweet pleasures into the lives of the humblest individuals, but also to make the felicity of Kings.

It is usually a misfortune to have more riches than is fitting to one's status, because one can hardly dispense them without insolence or keep them without avarice.

A man who is of low condition, and who would like to have great wealth, does not stop to think that he would have precious little use for it, and that practically all the things his money would procure him would be for him as the purple was in the past, whose use was permitted only to kings.

For as we want a man of high birth to preserve a noble pride in disgrace, we likewise want a man of no birth to preserve some modesty in his fortune.

Otherwise, one is sure to lose the most precious of all goods, namely, the good will of the People, and to lapse into a great misfortune, namely, the scourge of ridicule that they heap on those who have offered themselves to their scorn.

If a nouveau riche immediately goes and builds a sumptuous house, he will offend the eyes of all who see it; it is as if he were making this declaration to the people:

"I am alerting you that I, who in the past was the most commonplace of all men, I am today making myself a man of consequence. I am going to put between you and me a vast courtyard and five rooms on the same level; in vain will you expect to find me sooner, because I will make my residence in the sixth. I will have people better dressed than you whom you will find on your path, like new obstacles to reaching me. Instead of my lousy gray outfits, I am going to dress in the richest fabrics. The only thing you will find left of me from now on is a rather ugly face; I couldn't change that. But as for my name, that name that used to be so dear to me, I will abandon it. May I lose my memory of it, and may you lose it as well!"

After the great houses that have no origin and that seem, so to speak, to have been born in Heaven, the best families are those that have emerged imperceptibly out of the low condition they were in, and whose first founders did not have the insolence to make themselves noticed. For nothing dishonors a family like a perennial anecdote or popular rumor, and, if I dare use this term, a denouement in the beginning.[2]

2. *Catastrophe,* literally, the last and principal event of a tragic play; figuratively, a disaster or catastrophe.—HC

Once they become rich, those who used to blush at their poverty now have to blush at their birth—all the more mortified in that they no longer believe they are made to be mortified.

The children who inherit such a large fortune bear the weight of the memory of the one to whom they owe so much. And this is so true that nothing appears so heroic on our stage as the deed of a prince who, in his glory, rediscovers with pleasure a shepherd whom he believes to be his father, and who does not make him blush.

I admit I have too much vanity to want my children to make a large fortune someday; only by dint of reason could they maintain a mental image of me. They would need all their virtue to acknowledge me; they would regard my tomb as the monument of their shame. I can believe they would not destroy it with their own hands; but they would doubtless not restore it if it were to collapse. I would be the perpetual stumbling block of flattery, and I would reduce its courtiers to confusion. Twenty times a day my memory would be uncomfortable, and my unhappy shadow would torment the living without end.

Thus, those who have so much ambition, and such foolish ambition, think as madly as Agrippina, who used to say to the soothsayers: "Let me die, provided my son be emperor!"[3]

[**1388**] The only man that Saint-Sernin acknowledged as admirable was Marshal Villars. It is not that he had no merit; perhaps more than Saint-Sernin recognized.[1]

[**1389**] People have thought they have noticed that in certain countries, diseases arrive with the doctors. It is rather the doctors that have arrived with the diseases. Diseases have arrived in proportion to people's divergence from simplicity and innocence of mores. In a frugal life, there are few diseases, as well as few changes, varieties, and metamorphoses in the diseases. A few commonplace observations, two or three remedies suffice to guide one to old age in those countries. There are few mass diseases because the inhabitants' good constitution makes them resistant to a bad year's inclement weather, whereas when mores are corrupted, countless

---

3. Agrippina (16–59), Germanicus's daughter and Nero's mother.

[**1388**]
1. Jean-Benoît-César-Auguste des Porcelets de Malhane, marquis of Saint-Sernin (1675–1750), lieutenant-general in 1734.

bodies are ready to be disturbed by a bad season's disturbance or the least natural accident that occurs.[1]

[1390] The sultans of Egypt destroyed the Crusaders. They were very powerful because they had the East Indies trade.[1]

[1391] THE KNIGHTS. Since the lances, in order to be used, needed quite a few men, those who carried them were like the Greeks and Trojans who went and mounted the chariots—troops who cut the finest figure in the armies.

{Whence arose—both in chivalry and among the Homeric heroes—the colloquies between the main characters.}

[1392] {The abbé of Trianon said:} "M. de La Rochefoucauld tells us: 'Man is made like that.' The abbé of Gamaches tells us: 'He is fatefully made like that.' Raimon: 'He is truly like that.'" I add: "M. Pope tells us: 'He cannot be better than to be like that.'"[1]

[1393] Maupertuis says Voltaire is the man of his acquaintance who shows the most wit in a given time.[1] I also said the Duchess [of Aiguillon] was the woman in France who lies the most in a given time.

[1394] DU——[1] OF AIGUILLON. I said: "She is a much better friend of her enemies than of her friends."

[1395] There are many people who regard as necessary only what is superfluous.

[1396] THE DUKE OF ORLEANS. He had no sequel; he was indefinable; one can define him only by not defining him.

[1397] DIFFICULTY OF TRANSLATING. At first, one must know Latin well; then, one must forget it.

[1389]
1. See also *pensée* 1813.—HC

[1390]
1. See *Laws*, 21.19.

[1392]
1. Louis-Adolphe Rouault, abbé of Gamache (1672–1756); Alexander Pope (1688–1744), the English writer.

[1393]
1. Pierre-Louis Moreau de Maupertuis (1698–1759). On his recommendation, Montesquieu was elected a member of the Berlin Academy; cf. Montesquieu's letter to him on November 25, 1746 (*OC*, 3:1071). See also *pensée* 2010.

[1394]
1. Duchess

[1398] [The only man that Saint-Sernin recognized was Marshal Villars. It is not . . .][1]

[1399] Rome, slave after Tiberius, Caligula, Claudius, Nero, Domitian. All the blows struck against tyrants; none against tyranny.[1]

[1400][1] The bulk of players win as much as they lose, except for the expense of the cards. But what makes it a bad business is that those who lose make very bad deals in order to pay or make amends, and those who win also make very bad deals in order to spend.

[1401] The late Duke of Antin never put money in any raffle, gave to any collection plate, gave any New Year's gift, any present, never gave a tip or a little gratuity to anyone in his life.[1]

[1402]

> *Francorum Regis socero diadema negasti,*
>   *Carole! Quid genero, si tibi sceptra neget?*[1]

[1403] I said that what makes the English have better doctors is that, since women do not make reputations there, chattering does not lead to esteem. I set great store on a man who, without being a fine talker, still acquires esteem.

[1404] I said that businessmen are very fortunate to have the kind of pride that leads them to form marriage alliances with the nobility. Otherwise, they would be like a special caste. This is useful to them in that it makes them disgorge themselves.

[1398]
1. See *pensée* 1388.—HC

[1399]
1. "Put in the *Laws*" (M.), 3.3.

[1400]
1. This is the first entry in the hand of secretary H, who was in Montesquieu's service from 1740 to 1743.

[1401]
1. Louis-Antoine de Montespan, Duke of Antin (1665–1738).

[1402]
1. "You have refused the diadem to the father-in-law of the King of the Franks, Charles! What will you do to your son-in-law if he refuses you the scepter?" Probably a reference to Charles VI, Habsburg emperor until 1740. For the complex diplomatic context, see the German political periodical *Die Neue Europäische Fama* [The new European [goddess of] rumor], 61 (1740): 1005 and passim.—HC

[1405] I call devotion: a disease of the body that gives the soul a madness whose character is to be the most incurable of all.

[1406] I said[1] *of* Mme {d'Aiguillon} that she is now a dream, now a delirium.

[1407] I said of M. d'Orléans {Regent} that he did some good, but he did not do good.[1]

[1408] I said that the pulpit is getting more worn out than the theater, because vices are not changing the way jokes are.

[1409] I said to an angry[1] man: "Show me your true face."

[1410] I said of La Popelinière: "There are people who are fools because they want to have too much wit. This man would not have any wit if he did not think he had a great deal."[1]

[1411] "Good taste," I said, "is what is analogous in speech and manners to what is called *not having an accent* in language."

[1412] He is the one with good form, of whom one cannot say what it is.[1]

[1413] In the past, when science was not so filled with geometry, women, who understood something of it, despised it. Now that they can understand none of it, they esteem it highly and want to know about it.

[1414] I said: "I am among neither the twenty people who know those sciences in Paris, nor the fifty thousand who think they know them."

[1415] By way of boasting, Mme d'Aiguillon was telling us something that she had neither done nor said, even though she claimed it. I said: "How is it that one is modest enough with oneself to be vain with others?"

[1416] For one to be able to grasp ridicule at the theater, it is not enough that the character say ridiculous things, he must himself be ridiculous: Don Quixote, Sancho, Ragotin.[1]

[1406]
1. First version: "*I said*" (in English). Here, the word "*of*" is in English.

[1407]
1. A pun on the difference between *faire du bien* and *faire le bien.*—HC

[1409]
1. *Fâché*, alternative reading: *caché*, "hidden."—HC

[1410]
1. Alexandre-Joseph Le Riche de La Popelinière (1692–1762), farmer-general of taxes.

[1412]
1. The "it" (*il*) may refer either to the "good form" or to the subject "he".—HC

[1416]
1. Ragotin, a character in Scarron's *Roman comique* [*Comic novel*] (1651–57).

[**1417**] I said: "I like houses where I can withdraw from business with my everyday spirit."

[**1418**] TO LORD WALDEGRAVE. "I have run into you in Paris as minister of a great king. You are so well liked that those who have not seen you as a minister at Court would take you as a citizen in Town."[1]

[**1419**] I said: "The grandees have pleasures; the people have joy."

[**1420**] When one wants to govern men, one must not chase them from behind; one must make them follow.[1]

[**1421**] Our body is like any other instrument, which lasts in proportion to its use.

[**1422**] A corrupt monarchy: that is not a State, it's a court.[1]

[**1423**] There is the same difference between a man of *esprit* and a *bel-esprit*[1] as we express between a beautiful woman and a beauty.

One is never a *bel-esprit* when one does not claim to be one.

[**1424**] What makes us so prejudiced for our moderns is that the new discoveries seem more surprising to us than the ancient ones, which no longer move us and which are always our starting point. We have become familiar with them, and it seems to us that everyone could have made those discoveries. But add up the total for the ancients and moderns, and you will see.

[**1425**] I said of the Princess of Rohan: "I always begin with an admiration for her that I do not complete."[1]

[**1426**] I have often noticed that, for the children to have a great deal of

[1418]
1. James, count of Waldegrave, maternal grandson of James II and Arabella Church, and nephew of the duke of Berwick. After being ambassador to Paris, where Montesquieu met him, he was sent to Vienna for the exchange of preliminaries signed in Paris on May 31, 1727. On April 15, 1728, Montesquieu left Paris with him for Vienna, where he remained as English minister until 1740. Montesquieu caught up with him again in Hanover on September 24, 1729; cf. *Voyages* (*OC,* 2:1272) and Montesquieu's letter to Berwick at the end of September (*OC,* 3:933).

[1420]
1. See *pensées* 597, 828, and 943.—HC

[1422]
1. Cf. *Laws,* 8.6, 117.

[1423]
1. See the translator's note for the ambiguities in this entry. One non-ironic possibility: the second item in each pair is intensive.—HC

[1425]
1. Anne-Geneviève de Levis-Ventadour, princess of Turenne, then of Rohan; wife of Louis-Charles de La Tour, prince of Turenne, then of Hercules Mériadeck de Rohan-Soubise, prince of Rohan (1673–1727).

esprit, the mother has to be a bit crazy and have some *esprit,* and the father be dull-witted—or else the reverse: the Corneilles' mother and their father, who was just a simpleton,[1] who wrote down his son's published plays by hand; the father of Fontenelle, whose mother was a Corneille; Marshal de Brancas, somewhat sluggish, and his wife, quite mad; ———, M. de Forcalquier's father.[2]

[**1427**] Mme de Boufflers said of Lemaure that, in hearing her sing, she pronounces so well that one learns the correct spelling.[1]

[**1428**] Here is how I define talent: a gift that God gives us in secret, and that we reveal without knowing it.

[**1429**] I said that M. Walpole always had a thunderbolt in his hand and a woolly arm: *Dii lanatos pedes habent.*[1] The lords who used to protest against him would say there has never been a minister more enterprising in domestic affairs and more timid in foreign affairs.

[**1430**] A man who keeps his word becomes as similar to the gods as is possible.

[**1431**] We have seen the House of Austria work continually to suppress Hungarian liberty. She did not know how valuable that liberty would someday be to her. When all her Estates were divided and invaded, all the pieces of her monarchy—immobile and inactive—fell, so to speak, one on top of the other. There was life only in that nobility that forgot everything as soon as it thought the crown was insulted, and as soon as it was a matter of its glory to serve and forgive.[1]

[**1426**]
  1. Literally, *bon homme,* which could refer derisively to a peasant or old man (*DAF,* 1694), or to a man naïve and easy to dupe (*DAF,* 1835), as I have rendered it here.—HC
  2. The Corneilles' mother was a bailiff's daughter, and their father was a private master in the waters-and-forests department; François Le Bovier de Fontenelle, esquire, lawyer in the Parlement of Rouen; Martha Corneille, the Corneilles' sister; and Louis de Brancas, marquis of Céreste (1671–1750), marshal of France.

[**1427**]
  1. Madeleine-Angélique de Neufville-Villeroy, duchess of Boufflers, married to Joseph-Marie, duke of Boufflers; Catherine-Nicole Lemaure (1704–83), celebrated opera singer.

[**1429**]
  1. Literally, "the gods have woolly feet." Montesquieu cites and translates a Latin proverb that Erasmus had explained (*Adages,* I.x.82).

[**1431**]
  1. These remarks refer to the Hungarian nobility's show of loyalty to the Austrian Empress Maria Theresa at the meeting of the Diet in Pressburg on September 11, 1741, after the invasion of Habsburg Silesia by Frederick II (the Great) of Prussia; for a similar assessment, see *Laws,* 8.9, 119.

[1432] It is not by speechifying that despotism must be attacked, but by making clear that it tyrannizes the despot himself.

[1433] FRAGMENT OF A PREFACE. When I was able to envision my subject in all its extent, everything I was looking for came to me, and I saw my work grow, move forward, and come to an end.[1]

[1434] [The abuse is very often preferable to the convention . . .][1]

[1435] I said of —— : "He is the strangest man in the world, but he is the least ridiculous man in the world."

[1436] Such is the nature of things that the abuse is very often preferable to the correction, or at least that the good that's established is always preferable to the better that is not.[1]

[1437] I am a good citizen, but I would have been one whatever the country of my birth.

I am a good citizen because I have always been content with the condition I am in, because I have always approved of my lot, and because I have never blushed at it or envied that of others.

I am a good citizen because I love the government I have been born under without fearing it, and because I expect no favors from it except this boundless good that I share with all my compatriots; and I thank Heaven that, having put mediocrity in me in all things, it was willing to put a bit less of it in my soul.

[1438] Some people have regarded the reading of the *Temple of Gnidus* as dangerous.[1] But they fail to realize that they are imputing to a single novel the defect of all. If there are licentious things in a work of verse, that is the poet's vice. But if passions are aroused in it, that is a function of the poetry.

Reading novels is dangerous, no doubt. What isn't? Would that one had only to reform the bad effects of reading novels! But to command an

[1433]
1. See the preface to *Laws,* xlv.

[1434]
1. See *pensée* 1436.—HC

[1436]
1. See the preface to *Laws,* xliv.

[1438]
1. The official permission for Montesquieu's short work *Temple de Gnide* is dated February 8, 1725. The work was published almost simultaneously in the *Bibliothèque française,* volume 4, second part (Amsterdam, 1724); a review was published in the *Journal des savants* (May 1725): 293–94.

always-sensitive being not to have sensations; to want to ban the passions without even allowing them to be rectified; to propose perfection to an age that is worse every day; to revolt against mere weakness in the midst of so much wickedness[2]—I am really afraid that such a lofty morality may become merely speculative, and that in showing us from such a distance what we ought to be, it will leave us as we are.

[1439] There are among us few fools who are at the same time stupid; on this score, folly is that close to wit.

This is what produces among us a prodigious number of readers. In other countries, those who have wit know it, and those who do not have it know that as well. In those countries, many people would be well-equipped to amuse others; they hardly consider themselves capable of being amused themselves. Whatever agreeable work one presents to them, they would not even deign to read it.

I am stating here the true reason why I have all my life had a particular esteem for our young court dandies. I am speaking here only as a man of State. For although they promote the main branches of our trade, based on constant change in fashions and outfits, they perform a service to their Country without demanding the least gratitude.[1]

Of all known nations, none is less pedantic than ours, but all we can do is rattle on about the fashionable folks.

It is they, in the final analysis, who polish that most charming of European peoples. It is they who forge our sociability, who bring about a happy harmony between persons whom the old mores would have made incompatible.

It is to them that we owe that vivacity which accounts for the fact that our witty folks seem more likeable to us, and that our fools are not completely stupid.

Some present us with a certain action that changes even our amusements into occupations; others are a kind of highly delightful spectacle.

It is they who, instead of that arrogance that appears in private individuals among some peoples, change our pride into a pleasing impertinence produced in a thousand ways.

---

2. *Méchanceté* puts the emphasis on social vices, connoting nastiness, malice, etc.—HC

[1439]
1. See also *pensée* 1553.—HC

They inspire young people, offended by the seriousness of their forefathers' judicial robes, to shed their blood in service to Country and to gain
access to the Prince.

Lastly, it is from their heads, albeit a bit harebrained, that arises the main
branch of our trade, founded on that good taste that makes us change fashions and outfits with an authority too absolute for us not to believe we are
changing for the better.

It is principally to them that I consecrate this little work. Most people
dedicate their books to those who read them; as for me, I dedicate this
one to those who will not read it—hoping that, if by chance they learn
that it concerns them, they will kindly refrain from criticizing it, and will
candidly admit that they have not read it.

I will not, however, despair if the gravest men do me the honor of reading me. If my hero does not have a philosopher's outfit, he sometimes has
some tolerably philosophical ideas.[2]

[**1440**] Melon spoke amusingly about how man is a monkey *manqué*.
This has a meaning in the report where men have imperfections that animals do not have.[1]

[**1441**] Among my friends, there is a good man who has made some
fine notes on Montaigne.[1] I am sure he thinks he wrote the *Essays*. When I
praise Montaigne in front of him, he assumes a modest air and gives me a
little bow {and blushes a little}.

[**1442**] Victory Plaza is a monument to frivolous vanity.[1] These sorts
of monument need to have an object: Trajan's Bridge, the Appian Way,
Marcellus's Theater.

[**1443**] I said: "Vivacity makes for fine repartee, composure makes for
fine deeds."

---

2. This fragment is perhaps a projected preface for the *Histoire veritable* [True history], Montesquieu's whimsical work probably from the 1730s on the transmigrations of a soul.

[**1440**]
1. Jean-François Melon (1675?–1738), inspector of the farms in Bordeaux, one of the founders of the
Bordeaux Academy, whose 1734 *Essai politique sur le commerce* [Political essay on commerce] was one
of the most influential French works on economics before the Physiocrats.

[**1441**]
1. Pierre Coste; cf. *pensée* 1231n.

[**1442**]
1. La Place des Victoires, created in 1685 on the initiative of Marshal de La Feuillade by the architect
Prédot, under the direction of J. Hardouin-Mansart; a statue of Louis XIV stands in the center.

[**1444**] To offer quite concrete images yields strength; to offer ideas drawn from the soul's conceptions yields finesse.

[**1445**] I said: "Descartes is like the man who would cut the bonds of those who are attached. He would run with them; he would stop along the way; perhaps he would not arrive. But who would have given to the first the faculty of arriving?"

[**1446**] Voltaire will never write a good history. He is like the monks, who write not for the subject they are treating but for the glory of their order; Voltaire writes for his monastery.

[**1447**] I said of M. de Belle-Isle's plan: "It's a plan made of lead; it is constantly being raised, but it always falls down again."

I said it was like the monkeys, which are always climbing up the tree until, having reached the top, they show their bottoms.[1]

[**1448**] How many occasions where one does the most with the least? It is said that when Ruyter[1] learned that the English had declared against Holland, he ordered a supplement of forty vessels; when he learned that France had joined England, he demanded no more than thirty.[2] King Richard, when he learned that his rival was descending upon England with an army, said, "Fine! We'll beat them!"[3] Someone came to tell him his rival was coming with fifteen hundred men, and he threw himself on his great chair and said: "I am ruined!" He figured he had secret contacts in his army. Add to this Boccalini's scale, where Spain always weighs less.[4]

[**1449**] What makes beauty is regularity of features; what makes a woman nice[1] is the expression on her face.

[**1450**] One must always choose a good subject. The brainpower you invest in a bad subject is like the gold you might put on a beggar's outfit, whereas a good subject seems to lift you onto its wings.

[1447]
1. Charles-Louis-Auguste Fouquet, duke of Belle-Isle (1684–1761), marshal of France, wanted to dismember the house of Austria. Montesquieu applies to him a saying attributed to Chancellor Olivier and to Chancellor de l'Hôpital, and that Montaigne cites in the *Essays*, II.17; see also *pensées* 1452 and 1466.

[1448]
1. Michiel Adriaanszoon Ruyter (1607–76), Dutch admiral.
2. First version: "fifty."
3. Richard III, last Plantagenet king of England (1483–85).
4. See *Spicilège*, 248.

[1449]
1. *Jolie* may also mean "pretty."—HC

[**1451**] When one sees an active man who has made his fortune, this is due to the fact that, out of countless mostly failed paths that he has used, one has succeeded. From this, one infers that he will be fit for public affairs. That is not accurate. When one errs in some schemes concerning one's fortune, that is merely a waste of time. But in enterprises of State, there are no wastes of time.[1]

[**1452**] I hear it said every day: "We must make war to humble the House of Austria." It is for that purpose that Belle-Isle has persuaded the government to send one hundred million pounds and eighty thousand men into Germany. This is stupid. You have only to ennoble yourselves by good government, and you will humble the House of Austria. This is the sole equitable means of humbling one's neighbors. Isn't everything relative?[1]

[**1453**] The despotic monarch must be religious, rigid, just. If he is courageous as well, he will be a hero: Shah Abbas, Mohammed II, Shambi, Aureng-Zeb.[1]

[**1454**] God is like the monarch who has many nations in his Empire; they all come to bring him tribute, and each speaks to him differently in its own language and religion.[1]

[**1455**] I heard a good remark by the Turkish ambassador on February 18, 1742. I was telling him (at Locmaria's, where we were having dinner)[1] that I found it contrary to the maxims of a good government for the Great-Lord to have his pashas strangled at will. "He has them strangled," he said, "without stating the reason, in order not to reveal or make

[1451]
  1. The idiom translated as "wastes of time" here is *coup d'épée dans l'eau*, "hit the water with one's sword."—HC

[1452]
  1. The reference is to the War of the Austrian Succession (1740–48). See Montesquieu's letter to Barbot on February 2, 1742 (*OC,* 3:1016), which permits us to date this entry to early 1742; cf. also *pensées* 1447 and 1466.

[1453]
  1. Shah Abbas (1588–1629, legendary Safavid ruler); Mehmet II (1444–46, 1451–86), who conquered Constantinople on May 29, 1453; Aureng-Zeb (1618–1707), grand mogul who reigned from 1659 until his death.

[1454]
  1. See *pensée* 1699.—HC

[1455]
  1. Jean-Marie-François Du Parc, marquis of Locmaria (1708–45).

known his servant's faults." What do you say about men who gild even the statue of Tyranny?

[**1456**] I wrote about a loss of memory: "I am distracted; I have memory only in my heart."

[**1457**][1] I find in Tertullian the dogma concerning passive obedience. "Jesus Christ tells us," he says: "'Judge not, that ye be not judged.'[2] Now who is this one who does not judge another, if not he who is patient enough not to defend himself?"

[**1458**] I like what abbé de Mongault said: "In youth, we judge men by offices, and in old age, offices by men."[1]

[**1459**] It is impossible for someone who grasps jokes so well not to have frivolity in his mind; this is because he is affected only by incidentals {says abbé de Mongault}.

[**1460**] I said: "Voltaire is always strolling in gardens; Crébillon advances over mountains."[1]

[**1461**] Critics are like that painter who, having painted a rooster, forbade his apprentices to let roosters approach his painting.

[**1462**] Since the discovery of printing, there are no more true histories {says Father Cerati}.[1] The princes used to pay no attention, and the police used to remain uninvolved. Today, all books are subject to the inquisition of that regulatory system which has established rules of discretion. To violate them is an offense. Princes have thereby been taught to be offended by what people are saying about them. In the past, they did not worry about it; thus, people spoke the truth.

[**1463**] It is odd how, in our country, we constantly do everything we can to keep the people in ignorance and deny them all kinds of knowledge on the affairs of the State and of Europe; and how at the same time we fol-

[1457]
1. This entry is the last in the hand of secretary H (1740–43).
2. Matthew 7:1.—HC

[1458]
1. Nicolas-Hubert de Mongault (1674–1746), on whom, see *pensée* 291 n. 2.

[1460]
1. "Advances" (*marche sur*) may evoke a military metaphor here.—HC

[1462]
1. Montesquieu had known Fr. Gaspare Cerati (1690–1769) well in Rome; cf. *Voyages* (*OC*, 2:1191). Superintendent of the University of Pisa, he later traveled in France, England, and Germany, maintaining a correspondence with Montesquieu. See also *pensée* 1525.

low so closely the prejudices, the impressions, and the frivolousness of the talk of that same people—especially the people at Court. This is the same talk that made us undertake the two wars of 1733 and 1741.[1]

[1464] [The aptitude to grasp the joke proves the futility of wit. One is not so strongly attached to the petty incidentals when one is struck as one ought to be by the main issue. {This thought is from abbé de Mongault.}][1]

[1465] The Nobility is moved by battles and victories won {like the peasants are moved by having nice bells. Mongault}.

[1466] I will always regret not having solicited some position in foreign affairs after returning from my travels. It is certain that, thinking the way I did, I would have been at cross-purposes with the plans of that madman Belle-Isle,[1] and would thereby have rendered the greatest service a citizen can render his Country. There are ponderous fools, and there are vivacious fools, but it is the vivacious fools who give birth to the stupidest plans.

[1467] Princes are always in prison. Clement XI used to say: "When I was a private individual, I knew everybody in Rome, and the merit of each one. Now that I am Pope, I no longer know anyone."[1]

[1468] *Morbus castrorum,*[1] which Vegetius talks about, is no longer experienced today. This is because the Romans did not have fortresses back then; their camps were fortresses divided into neighborhoods, streets; they were crowded. When they stayed there for a long time, that caused disease. Today, our camps take up a large field; they are usually on favorable locations, and sometimes cover many leagues. No disease.[2]

[1469] ATTACKED LINES, FORCED LINES. A proverb that has become

[1463]
1. The reference is to Villars's campaign in Italy and the War of the Austrian Succession, respectively.

[1464]
1. See *pensée* 1459.—HC

[1466]
1. On Belle-Isle, see *pensées* 1447 and 1452.

[1467]
1. Giovanni Francesco Albani (1649–1721; r. 1700–1721).—HC

[1468]
1. "Camp sickness"; Flavius Vegetius Renatus (late fourth, early fifth century), *Epitome rei militaris* [Summary of military matters], which Montesquieu owned in a 1553 edition (*Catalogue,* 1742). See also *pensées* 1496, 1527–28, and 1532.—HC

2. At some point, perhaps at the time of this entry, Montesquieu began the process of revising his *Considerations.*

false. In the past, there were not such big armies as at present. When a fortified place was besieged, there was the same terrain to guard with a small army as there is today with a big one, and they descended with their strongest forces on the weakest parts they picked out. That is how Arras was aided.[1] Today, the big armies mean there are no more weak spots. You build big entrenchments in front of you, tossing all the earth to one side; you build pits to halt and confuse the cavalry, launch a terrifying barrage on the attackers. There is no way to get through.

[1470] I said: "The French are presumptuous and the Spanish as well—the Spanish because they think they are great men; the French because they think they are lovable.[1] The French know that they don't know what they don't know; the Spanish know that they know what they don't know. What the French don't know, they scorn; what the Spanish don't know, they think they know."

[1471] I think what made Porphyry write against Jesus Christ is that he was a Pythagorean, and he viewed the Savior's miracles as being in rivalry with those of Pythagoras.

[1472] Regarding the currency exchange,[1] notice that its rise or fall depends {on the change} in the perfection of the coins or in their face value. I call this *constant variation*. It depends on something still more variable, namely, whether the money is rare or common in a country. This rarity is a relative rarity: when there is more need to send funds into a country than receive them from it.

[1473] Armed merchant vessel, uselessly pernicious thing! This destroys the trade even of those who capture booty. The trade is led into a port where the merchandise is not in demand. This makes it too cheap in one place and too expensive in another. In addition, it does infinitely more harm than good—everything gets spoiled, pillaged, perishes, sells poorly. These are dupes' injustices.

[1474] Nice verse of Ovid (*Fastes*) [where Lucretius recounts his adventure].

[1469]
1. The city of Arras (Pas-de-Calais), besieged by Condé in 1654, was liberated by Turenne.

[1470]
1. "*Aimable*" may also mean likable, kind, amiable, or nice in this context.—HC

[1472]
1. "Put in the *Laws*" (M.), 22.10, 405.

Restabant caetera; flevit,
Et matronales erubuere genae.[1]

It is said that the pentameter is not in its place, and that She should have blushed before crying. It seems to me that the poet does well to place the blush on the *restabant caetera;* this is an enhancement of the blush. *Matronales* is wonderful.

I have heard a good observation. Hexametric and pentametric verses inevitably attract the epigram. Thus, Ovid puts more wit into his heroines' letters than in the *Metamorphoses.*

[1475] Titus-Livy is a bit bombastic, and what is remarkable is that he is not that way in his fine orations. This is because there, one does not seem so bombastic.

[1476] In Venice, as in Rome, the monarchy existed before the republic. Titus-Livy says that, without the kings, the empire would not have been founded. I do not know if the observation is accurate. Those elective kings did not oppress the people. They always kept them at war, because their principal function was to command. They hardened them; they aggrandized them. Their government had much force mixed with much mildness.[1]

[1477] I said: "I would very much like to be the confessor of the truth, not the martyr."

[1478–1480] FRAGMENTS THAT DID NOT MAKE IT INTO MY "ROMANS."[1]

[1478] On Tarquin, I said:[1] "At that time, there was an alienation from the government of one. For having given themselves a king, the Veiians were abandoned in all the cities of Tuscany. Alba had already liberated itself. Porsena's realm did not endure."[2]

[1474]
1. Ovid, *Fastes,* II.827–28: "The end she left unsaid, but wept and a blush o'erspread her matron cheeks." See also *pensée* 1680.

[1476]
1. See *Laws,* II.12, 170.

[1478–1480]
1. These fragments date from the period when Montesquieu was preparing the new edition of the *Considerations,* which appeared in Amsterdam (Wetstein) in 1746.

[1478]
1. On Tarquin (d. 579 B.C.), see *Considerations,* I, 26.
2. Porsena, King of Clusium in Etruria (sixth century B.C.).

On his character, I said: "Everything is extremely mixed up in the world. The private iniquities in a properly established State always bring a certain contraction in public virtues, and the virtues seen in a corrupt republic likewise take on something of its corruption."

[**1479**] Servius had transferred the right of electing kings, and that of naming judges in civil affairs, from the Senate to the People;[1] he had paid the debts of private individuals, given lands to those who had none; he had eliminated the arbitrariness in taxes and had exempted poor citizens from them; he had admitted the enfranchised slaves into the assemblies of the People, and the Plebeians into the Senate.[2]

[**1480**] Cato was the executor of the infamous law that confiscated the king of Cyprus's treasures; he put all his virtue into not robbing kidnappers.

[**1481**] "It is highly probable that what used to be the sea is now earth. Beds of shells are seen on virtually every mountain. In the cabinets of the curious, there are fish shells found in the earth, of unknown species. One even finds animals here that are only in China. Those things are not explained by the Flood, however one presents it, but by some still greater accident. If, for example, the Earth's center of gravity came to be altered—as, for example, if the waters in one place on the Earth were to break through and enter a cavity filled with air—at that moment the sea would be transported elsewhere, and since there are precipices in the sea, mountains would be found, and everything would emerge as land, with mountains and valleys; what is now rock and sandbank would emerge as mountain."

It is by M. de Réaumur that I heard this said.[1] [I would like to ask him how there can be high and low solely from inequalities in the earth.]

Indeed, the change in the center of gravity might well carry off the

[1479]

1. Servius Tullius was the sixth king of Rome (578–535 B.C.); cf. *Laws*, 11.12, 171.

2. "See Dionysius of Halicarnassus, book IV, and Zonaras" (M.). Dionysius of Halicarnassus (first century B.C.), Greek historian and critic whose *Works* and *Roman Antiquities* Montesquieu owned (*Catalogue*, 2831–32) in Latin and French editions of 1586 and 1722, respectively; he also owned the twelfth-century Byzantine Zonaras's *Annals* in a 1560 French translation by Jean Millet de Saint-Amour (*Catalogue*, 2731).

[1481]

1. René-Antoine Ferchaut de Réaumur (1683–1757). See Montesquieu's early plan for an *Histoire physique de la terre ancienne et moderne* [Natural history of the ancient and modern earth] in *OC*, 3:87–88, of which only the prospectus appeared in the *Mercure* of January 1, 1719, and in the *Journal des savants* (1719): 159ff. Montesquieu seems to have burned the manuscript of this projected history.

waters from one place to another. But in that case, if what was sea became earth, the inequalities in the terrestrial globe would not produce high and low. It is certain, however, that the sea is always lower than the earth, since the water from all the rivers flows to the sea, etc.

[1482] I said of princesses: "They love little marvels."

[1483] Establishment of Roman power—that is, of the longest conspiracy against the World ever made.

[1484] In a fragment of Sallust's *History*, I found a passage that fits marvelously with the character of the late Cardinal de Fleury: "*Modestus ad omnia alia, nisi ad dominationem.*"[1]

[1485] I could compare the proportion that exists today between copper and silver with that which existed in the past. The Roman denarius is one sixty-fourth of our half-pound mark. Now the Roman denarius weighed 10 asses, or 120 ounces of copper, until the First Punic War. Thus, this proportion must be seen as the basis for how different today's proportion is between copper and silver. If no new mines were discovered, the proportion ought to endure, because copper is almost always found to be mixed with silver. The proportion today between the value of a pound of copper and a pound of silver should be looked at.

The sesterce was a quarter of the denarius. It was worth two and a half asses when the denarius was worth 10; it ought to have been worth 4 when the latter was worth 16. One would need to know if, when the denarius was 16 asses, the sesterce changed, or if it remained at two and a half—that is, if it ceased to be real money in order to be money of account.

The *nummus* and the sesterce are the same thing. The *aureus* is 100 sesterces (or *centum nummi*) and 25 denarii. Budé notes that Otho gave *aureum* to every soldier of the guard; Tacitus and Plutarch say *centenos nummos.*[1] Suetonius says that Domitian *addidit et quartum stipendium, au-*

[1484]

1. Caius Sallustius Crispus (ca. 86–35 B.C.), *History,* fragment CLXXV; the passage reads: "Modest in everything else, except in domination." Fleury had died on January 29, 1743; see *pensées* 472, 914, 1019, 1065, 1226, 1284, 1509, 1595, and 1976 for more on him.

[1485]

1. Guillaume Budé (1467–1540), author of *De Asse* (1514), of which Montesquieu owned the 1542 edition (*Catalogue,* 3217); Marcus Salvius Otho (32–69), Roman emperor in 69; Tacitus, *Histories,* I.24; Plutarch, *Life of Galba,* XX; the passage from Suetonius that follows (*Domitian,* VII.3) reads: "He increased the pay [of the soldiers] one fourth, by the addition of three gold pieces each year." See also *Laws,* 22.3.

reos ternos; that means 75 denarii, which corresponds to Zonaras's passage on this.

[1486] Although one sees shells of which the animal's identity is no longer known, M. de Réaumur believes that the species is not, on that account, gone; it is just that, since the animal lives at the bottom of the sea, that species can only be found in catastrophes.

[1487] What causes the most sensible people to be moved as soon as someone pays preferential respects to their dignity is that they feel their dignity demands these honors, and that they easily imagine that when these respects are not paid, it is the person's fault, which greatly humiliates them.

[1488] It seems to me that there is always something lacking in the works we have been given on the history of France. One may perhaps say of most of the authors who have written on it that some had too much erudition to have enough genius, and others had too much genius to have enough erudition.

[1489] There must have been very little gold in Italy in the past, since the Romans, who had pillaged and devastated so many nearby cities, had so little. Pliny, book XXXIII, article 5, remarks that at the capture of their city by the Gauls, they could muster only one thousand pounds of gold, which is nothing in comparison with the immense sums that came to them in the triumphs, especially the triumphs from Asia.[1]

[1490] Who would have said it—that it would be a people that boasts of being free that would establish the cruelest maxims of despotism against their wretched subjects?

In their treaties, the Corsicans[1] have been obliged to stipulate Natural Right, but the Republic of Genoa has signed the treaty that will forever cover them with embarrassment—by which she engages no longer to put the Corsicans to death without trial or on the informed conscience of the Governor.

That republic, impotent at subduing mistreated peoples, sends around

---

[1489]
1. "See Pliny, *ibidem*" (M.).

[1490]
1. See *Laws*, 10.8, and *Spicilège*, 611.

from court to court to importune all the kings and buy the lives of these people from them, after having so often sold them.

[1491] It seems to me that in France, only ridicule is feared.

[1492] One must not make one's equals unhappy, and one must make those who depend upon us happy.

[1493] ABBE DU VAUBRUN.[1] With a somber mien and a serious air, he was the most frivolous man of his age. He had none of those oddities that give pleasure, but all of those absurdities that bring pity. With the body of a deformed man, he had all the sweet talk of a woman. Idiot in praise and blame; impertinent in admiration. His vanity gave him claims to fortune, and that same vanity spoiled them all. He headed off, but although he took the easiest way, he never arrived.

Wit might be debased to the point of saying that he had some; but it is impossible to degrade good sense to the point of thinking he had any. And yet, admirable in company because he had few vices and no virtues. He had the favor of a petty court, but was the only one not suspected of enjoying its confidence.

[1494] I have no doubt at all that in a small republic, one could provide an education[1] such that the republic would be entirely composed of honorable people.

The laws make good and bad citizens. The same spirit of timidity that makes a man exacting in his duties in one republic will make a man cunning in another. The same spirit of boldness that makes a man love his Country and sacrifice himself for it in one State will make a highway robber in another.[2]

Let us imagine a savage man, who has never lived anywhere but in the forest, encountering for the first time in his life another man of the same species as himself, and neither of them can flee. Chance, based on the smallest gesture, on an expression, will make these two men seek either to destroy each other or to lend each other assistance. Thus, the slightest circumstance will at the outset make for a cannibalistic people or a people with morals.

[1493]
1. First version: "Here lies he who, with." Nicolas-Guillaume Bautru, abbé of Vaubrun (d. 1746).

[1494]
1. See *Laws,* 4.5.
2. See *Laws,* 19.16.

What usually makes a man wicked is that he finds himself in circumstances in which he is more influenced by the utility of committing crimes than by the shame or danger in committing them. Good laws can make these circumstances rare; bad laws multiply them; indifferent laws leave all those circumstances that chance may bring forth.

[1495] There are things that could be done in the past that are no longer done at present. For example, Titus Martius, in Spain, surprised two camps of enemies on the same night, one after the other.[1] The noise of the musketry and cannon would no longer permit it.

[1496] Vegetius has made the very good observation that licentious armies are rebellious. His reason . . . There is another: it is that they are less accustomed to authority.[1]

[1497] Just as the Swiss have given us the art of war by shaping our infantry, it is not surprising that the Romans had done likewise in the past.

[1498] The peace conditions imposed by the Romans were derived from the ideas of those times, when men sought less to aggrandize themselves than to weaken their enemies. Thus, the peace that the Lacedemonians offered the Athenians was such that they would have the same friends and enemies, the same galleys, etc.

[1499] Perseus, King of Macedonia, had qualities that at first dazzled his age; but his mind seemed to be designed for his own ruin. As soon as he had the least success, he deceived his allies; at the slightest reverse, he fell into a consternation that deprived him of common sense. He had a stupid avarice that made him consider the preservation of his treasures to be independent of that of his realm. He thought his mind was sharp enough to love public affairs; but his heart was base enough to prevent him from succeeding at them.

Private individuals often need only qualities of mind; princes, more exposed to the whims of Fortune, also need qualities of soul. They can find qualities of mind in their ministers; sentiments—they find these only in themselves.

[1500] The situation of Italy favored the Romans. It is very narrow

---

[1495]
1. Probably Lucius Marcius Septimus, left in temporary charge against the Carthaginians upon the death of the Scipio brothers in 212 B.C. See Livy, *History of Rome,* 25.12–15.—HC

[1496]
1. Vegetius, *Summary of military matters;* see *pensées* 1468, 1527–28, and 1532.

from north to south, and is cut from east to west by the Apennines. The Romans positioned themselves on the mountains, where they had an eye on the entire plain and on Hannibal. Polybius says that at the siege of Capua, they did great things because, being entrenched, they were not afraid of the Numidian cavalry.[1]

[**1501**] [The intimate liaison, the greatest possible, that existed between the Carthaginians and the Tuscans—which Aristotle tells us about, and which dated to his time.] Intimate liaisons of the Carthaginians with the Tuscans from Aristotle's time. Common matters among them. Their treaties. (second volume of *Politics,* page 106 vº).

It could be that the Tuscans' destruction put the Carthaginians in a state of anxiety.

[**1502**] The Roman Republic had a big advantage over the Carthaginian: during the Second Punic War, the former was a democracy governing itself according to the order and rules of an aristocracy; the latter was an aristocracy turning into an oligarchy.[1]

[**1503**] "Baal reigned for ten years over the inhabitants of Tyre. After which, various magistrates on fixed terms governed the city of Tyre under the name of *judges.* They were called *suffetes,* a name familiar to the Carthaginians. This name is derived from the Hebrew word *shophetim,* which means *judge.*" Page 168, *History of the Jews* by Prideaux.[1] Pages 11 and 12 [*Hist.*], vol. [*universal*].

This may explain how the men of Carthage, after Dido, changed their government into a republic. Tyre, their capital city, had done likewise.[2] In the mores of these people, royalty must have been regarded as merely one species of magistracy, which could easily be changed into another.

[**1504**] HANNIBAL. He conceived and initiated with boldness; a mind precise but extensive; ordered but fertile; prudent but bold; his influence over mind and heart was equal.

[1500]
1. Polybius, Greek historian (ca. 201–120 B.C.); only five or six of the original forty books of his *History* survive (see *Catalogue*, 2635, for a 1558 French edition); the siege of Capua occurred in 215 B.C.

[1502]
1. "See my Aristotle extract" (M.); this extract is lost.

[1503]
1. Humphrey Prideaux (1648–1724), *History of the Jews,* 6 vols. (1728; *Catalogue,* 3189).
2. Dido, princess of Tyre in the ninth century B.C.

Imagine a Dutch general who, five or six hundred leagues from home, leads some Swiss and Germans for twenty years, without their even thinking about complaining. Hannibal formed the only good army that Carthage had during the entire war. The jealousy of an opposing faction strips him of all reinforcements; in his genius, he finds them. These long-awaited reinforcements finally arrive; they are destroyed; Hannibal remains firm with his old army. After the peace, Hannibal flees Carthage; he finds Romans everywhere, and the Romans find Hannibal everywhere. He goes from court to court to give courage to spineless princes, and it seems his presence alone, whatever advice he gives them, increases their power and makes them formidable.

[**1505**] ORATIONS.[1]

Sire, when your Majesty declared war, the various powers of Europe entered into Your designs—some through their assistance, others through their respect and their silence. Your nobility hastened from all parts, disconsolate if they found no place from which to shed their blood in your service. A new ardor appeared in your troops. Everything that was occupying the Nation touched them no more; every other idea but that of your glory disappeared before it. Your clergy lavished its goods. All your subjects rivaled each other over the sweet satisfaction of being useful to you. Certain of your Majesty's desire to enable them to enjoy superfluity, they would have supported retrenchment from the necessities without difficulty.

You are, Sire, the King of a people who love you. Monarchs are easily worshipped, but they are never so great as when they are loved.

This peace that you have granted us—we cherish it in its own right, and because it is one of your benefactions. It is the character of our good fortune to be inseparable from your own. We regard all of your virtues as the greatest favor that Heaven could have bestowed upon us, and we are ecstatic to see in your person the father of the Country and King of the French.

[1505]
1. "Only the first was pronounced" (M.). This speech was addressed to Louis XV by Montesquieu as director of the French Academy on June 3, 1739, marking the signature of the treaty of Vienna between France and Austria (November 18, 1738), ending the War of the Polish Succession. See also *pensées* 1281–84.

Madam, this peace is as glorious for the King, your father, as it is sad for the faithful subjects who, losing the sight of their monarch, have thought they were seeing the dissolution of their monarchy.[2]

Daughter of a king so long famous for his reverses, wife of a monarch who has seen only successes, Heaven has chosen you to make the happiness of the one and to fulfill the happiness of the other.

Your Royal Highness, we hope that, of all the events in the glorious reign of the King, your father, it is this day's event that you will remember the best.

Ladies, we appreciate how difficult it is to enjoy complete satisfaction when we come to speak to you of our joy—that joy that is disturbed by our regrets. Ladies, all of Europe awaits with impatience that age, perhaps far from us, when you will be the felicity of princes and of peoples; we would like, if we were able, to prolong the moments. But whatever your destiny may be in this regard, the French people will always contend for your heart with all the nations of the world.

[**1506**] I am very glad that the {new} King of Prussia has treated the subject of anti-Machiavellism, and it is nice that these maxims, which have until now brought horror to subjects, are also bringing horror to princes.[1] A king who writes such a work is making a kind of oath to reign well; {it is} much stronger than those established by custom, since this oath is made to himself.

[**1507**] The People do not follow orators' logic.[1] They can be struck by images and by a moving eloquence, but nothing is good at leading them to action except spectacles, and if one follows the history of the passions of the Dominating People,[2] one will see that all these great movements arose only from the sight of some unexpected act. Lucretia's death brings the expulsion of Tarquin. The act of Brutus, who puts his children to death, establishes liberty. The sight of Virginia, killed by her father, brings the

---

2. The references are to Maria Leczinska and Stanislas Leczinsky.

[**1506**]

1. The reference is to Frederick II, king of Prussia (1740–86), whose *Anti-Machiavel* was published in the Hague in 1740.

[**1507**]

1. Most of this entry was used in *Laws*, 11.15.

2. *Peuple dominateur,* an expression Montesquieu uses for the Romans in *Laws*, 13.12, 221.—HC

expulsion of the decemvirs.³ The spectacle of that debtor who leaves prison with his clothes all torn apart by violence makes the people withdraw from the City. The spectacle of that young man whose modesty was assaulted by a creditor causes new laws to be passed. When Manlius is accused, the people, who see him extend his hands toward the Capitol that he had saved, cannot bring themselves to find him guilty, and in order to have him condemned, it becomes necessary to hold the assembly in a place from which this great scene cannot be viewed.⁴ Caesar's bloody gown⁵ enraged the people and ruined everything.

[**1508**] CARDINAL POLIGNAC. We owe him that immortal work in which Descartes triumphs a second time over Epicurus.¹

[**1509**] CARDINAL FLEURY. History will always have a soft spot for the man who was the delight of the Roman people.¹

[**1510**] An idea that enters into the empty head of a writer fills it completely, because it is neither destroyed nor interfered with by any collateral idea. This is how the least bubble in an otherwise empty container¹ spreads everywhere and inflates all bodies.

[**1511**] MARSHAL BELLE-ISLE AND CHAUVELIN.¹ Because they were ambitious, they rose. Because they were foolish, they fell.

3. Brutus was a semi-legendary hero of Rome, sixth century B.C.; Lucretia, Roman lady, wife of Tarquinius Collatinus; dishonored by Sextus, the son of Tarquin the Proud, she is said to have taken her own life in 509 B.C. See also *Considerations*, I, 25. Virginia, young Roman woman whom the decemvir Appius Claudius had wanted to violate; to prevent her dishonor, her father killed her, then took refuge among the plebs and the soldiers on the Aventine until the fall of the decemvirate (ca. 449 or 441 B.C.); see also *Laws*, 6.7.

4. Marcus Capitolinus Manlius, died in Rome in 384 B.C.; accused of aspiring to tyranny, he was pushed from the top of the Tarpeian rock.

5. See also *Considerations*, XII, 114.

[1508]
1. The *Anti-Lucretius, sive de Deo et natura* [Anti-Lucretius, or, on God and nature] (Paris, 1747) was published after Cardinal Polignac's death by Charles d'Orléans, abbé of Rothelin. See Montesquieu's letters to President Barbot on November 20, 1741 (*OC*, 3:1008), and to Maupertuis in 1747 (*OC*, 3:1101).

[1509]
1. On Louis XV's prime minister, see *pensées* 472, 914, 1019, 1065, 1226, 1284, 1484, 1595, and 1976.—HC

[1510]
1. *Machine du vide,* which may refer to a period instrument, such as Torricelli's barometer, that greatly reduced air pressure.—HC

[1511]
1. Germain-Louis Chauvelin (1685–1762), keeper of the seals and secretary of state for foreign affairs in 1727. On Belle-Isle, see *pensées* 1447, 1452, and 1466.

[**1512**] ON JUSTINIAN. If Caesar had executed his plan to compile the books of the ancient jurisconsults, he would have done it much better than Justinian, who was not firm enough.[1]

[**1513**] There is no nation that does not love its laws, because its laws are its customs.

[**1514**] In our time, those men who judged Charles I virtually all had a tragic end.[1] It is impossible to engage in such acts without having mortal enemies on all sides—that is, without running endless risks.

[**1515**] This idea of deifying men was not new, and Caligula was not as wrong as is imagined in finding it {strange} that the Jews did not want to place his statue in their temple. That prince, who laughed so hard at their not eating pig, must have regarded as pure obstinacy the fact that they did not want to do for him what the peoples of Asia and Greece had done for their Roman magistrates.

Sejanus went all the way with this system: he made sacrifices to himself.

[**1516**] The inconvenient footwear of the Romans was the reason for the square-stoned highways.

[**1517**] One may gauge the enchanting Roman sojourn by Cicero's *Letters* in exile,[1] and by Ovid's *Sorrows* and *Epistles from Pontus*.[2]

[**1518**] Since Galba, Otho, and Vitellius were made emperors one after the other by soldiers, and these latter two at virtually the same time, a new problem was experienced during their reigns which had not appeared before, namely, the power of election arrogated by various provinces and armies.[1] And although these emperors were not more wicked than the others, the name of *tyrant* was lavished upon them, and the ordeal of the thing itself was imputed to their persons.

[1512]
1. Alternative reading: "was not formed (or trained) enough."—HC

[1514]
1. Charles I, king of England, condemned to death and executed in January 1649.

[1517]
1. After the formation of the first triumvirate by Pompey, Crassus, and Caesar in 60 B.C., Clodius was elected tribune of the people in 58. His first act was to slake his vengeance against Cicero by bringing a law that punished with death any Roman citizen convicted of having put another person to death without the people's consent. Cicero, frightened by this threat, went into exile (March 20, 58 B.C.), and was only recalled in August 57.

2. Works written after he was exiled by Augustus in Tomis in the year 8.

[1518]
1. Galba, Roman emperor (68–69); Vitellius, Roman emperor in 69.

[1519]

THE PERSIAN LETTERS
Per servir sempre, o vincitrice, o vinta.[1]

THE TEMPLE OF GNIDUS
Neque enim Dea nescia nostri
Quae dulcem curis miscet amaritiem.[2]

THE DECLINE OF THE ROMANS
Ut lapsu graviore ruant.[3]

THE LAWS
Lex est ratio summi Jovis.[4]

[1520] 1741 SCHEME.[1] I could likewise reveal that the things that have ruined our realm have come from people who were too smart to be smart enough, who saw far but did not see from afar,[2] and who did not perceive that big things differ from small ones only in their object, resembling each other in their manner of execution.

[1521] In abandoning Italy, Pompey was wrong to boast of following Themistocles' example.[1] For he fled before 6,000 men; Themistocles,

---

[1519]

1. Vincenzo da Filicaia (1642–1707; Italian poet born in Florence), Sonnet *"All'Italia,"* V.14: "To serve always, o victor, o vanquished."

2. Catullus (ca. 87–ca. 54 B.C.), "To Manlius: written in affliction," LXVIII.17–18: "[N]ot unknown am I to the goddess who mingles with her cares a sweet bitterness"; Montesquieu owned a 1559 edition with commentary by Antoine Muret (*Catalogue,* 2009).

3. Claudian, *In Rufinum* [Against Rufinus], I.23: "that he may be hurled down in more headlong ruin." Claudius Claudianus (ca. 370–ca. 404); Montesquieu owned two editions of his *Opera* (*Catalogue,* 2015–16).

4. Cicero, *De legibus* [On the laws], II.10: "Law is the right reason of Jupiter" (see *pensée* 1874). In fact, Montesquieu used a different epigraph for the *Laws,* from Ovid's *Metamorphoses,* II.553: "Prolem sine matre creatam" ("a child [born] without a mother").

[1520]

1. The alliance with Frederick II, in the War of the Austrian Succession.

2. They were visionaries without prudential foresight.—HC

[1521]

1. Pompey fled to Greece after Caesar's crossing of the Rubicon in 50 B.C.; Themistocles (525–460 B.C.), unpopular because of his extravagance, had to go into exile.

Ceci a esté imprimé sur une mauvaise copie. Je le fais reimprimer sur une autre selon les corrections qui [sont] faites icy.

REFLEXIONS

SUR LA

MONARCHIE

UNIVERSELLE

EN

EUROPE.

[signature: Le President de Montesquieu]

Title page for the sole remaining copy of *Reflections on universal monarchy in Europe,* a short 1734 work that continued Montesquieu's investigation of the relevance of the Roman Empire for modern Europe, an investigation begun in the *Considerations.* The note in Montesquieu's handwriting reads: "This was printed from a defective copy. I am having it reprinted from another one based on the corrections made here." Elsewhere, he explained that he had halted printing altogether "out of fear that some passages would be misinterpreted." The work was printed in Amsterdam but was not authorized for sale in France. On the censorship question, see *pensée* 1525.

before 900,000. Doesn't Plutarch say something about that? {Look into Plutarch.}[2]

[**1522**] After the first capture of Constantinople, Europe, fearing for her, recognized that she had herself weakened her barrier, and this was a defect that she sought in vain to repair.[1]

[**1523**] This custom (of making oneself worshipped) could not have been more ancient among the Greeks than Alexander's reign, since his madness in this regard so strongly aroused the nation. It is probable that this mania passed from him to the Greek kings, his successors, and thence to the Roman magistrates.[1]

[**1524**] LAWS; EDUCATION. Sallust, *Catiline's Conspiracy,* speaking of the earliest Romans: "*Ingenium nemo sine corpore exercebat.*"[1]

This is how it should be in States that are not corrupted by luxury.[2]

[**1525**] It is a real question whether or not printing has contributed to the truth of history.[1] In the past, partisan authors disguised the truth more boldly. Their works were not widely disseminated and were hardly read except by a few people from their own sects; thus, they were less fearful of saying absurd things, more likely to exaggerate character traits, and they spoke out more loudly because they were less heard.

On the other hand, princes have made of this art the principal object of their administration; the censors they have set up direct all pens. In the past, one could speak the truth but did not speak it; today, one would like to speak it but cannot.

[**1526**] In the Punic wars {I speak only of the first two, for the third was not a war, but a conspiracy}, Carthage undoubtedly had just as big victories as the Romans.[1] The whole difference was that the former made peace while they were doing well; the latter, while doing poorly.

---

2. Plutarch, *Life of Pompey,* LXIII; *Comparison of Agesilaus and Pompey,* IV.

[**1522**]
1. Constantinople was seized in 1204, during the fourth crusade.

[**1523**]
1. "See if abbé Mongault made this observation" (M.).

[**1524**]
1. Sallust, *Catilina,* VIII.5: "their minds were never employed apart from their bodies."
2. See *Laws,* 7.1.

[**1525**]
1. See *pensée* 1462.

[**1526**]
1. The three Punic wars (264–241, 218–201, and 149–146 B.C.) pitted Rome against Carthage.

[**1527**]   Vegetius has observed that armies that work are not unruly.[1] This concerns military government, and the reasons for it are natural: work presupposes discipline, which in turn presupposes the force of command. The goal of the one who works is the pleasure of relaxation; but when one is idle, one has many other ways of seeking happiness.

[**1528**]   All armies that have lived voluptuously are unruly, for work is unbearable to them. But those accustomed to exercises obey, for combat is not onerous to them. On the contrary, they desire it, so as to have some rest, whereas the others flee it in order to recapture the scene of their voluptuous delights.[1]

[**1529**]   Fright made us do in Turin the most prudent thing in the world: abandon Italy and defend the Alps.[1] By the nature of things, we had grounds to expect to wage war exceptionally well in Spain. We were unassailable in Alsace. We had only to defend Flanders and let that ardor reawaken which so much misfortune had extinguished.

[**1530**]   THE HUMOR of the English is something independent of wit and distinguished from it, as will be seen by examples.

This humor is distinguished from pleasantry and is not pleasantry; it is rather the pleasant in pleasantry. It is not the comic force, the *vis comica;* it is rather the manner of the comic force. In pleasantry, I will define it as the manner of rendering pleasant things pleasantly—it is humor's sublime— and in ingenious things, the manner of rendering ingenious things pleasantly. What images are in poetry, humor is in pleasantry. When you engage in pleasantry without humor, you sense that something is missing, as when you make poetry without images. And the difficulty in humor consists in enabling you to find a new sentiment in the thing, which arises, however, from the thing itself.

Here are some examples. Rousseau's epigram which begins:

A mandarin of the Society[1]

[1527]
1. See *pensées* 1496 and 1528; on Vegetius, see also *pensées* 1468 and 1532.

[1528]
1. See *pensées* 1496, 1527, and 1532.

[1529]
1. After the battle of Turin (September 7, 1706), during the War of the Spanish Succession, the French troops evacuated Italy.

[1530]
1. Jean-Baptiste Rousseau, *Epigrammes,* IV.21.

is ingenious, it is even pleasant if you will; but there is no humor. The one

> *Between Racine and the eldest Corneille*[2]

is similar: it is ingenious and pleasant, but there is no humor. In the one about the monk, where a penitent comes and accuses himself of having made some admirable things by virtue of a recipe,[3] to whom the monk says:

> *"Now give me the jolly recipe!*[4]
> *And I promise you my absolution"*

the idea is pleasant, and the author has added some humor by the word *my*. If he had said *the absolution,* the epigram would have been merely pleasant. The monk says *my absolution* to make the swap. Rousseau's other epigram, about the drunk and the hapless young surgeon,[5] is pleasant in substance. Rousseau adds humor in the way he recounts it:

> *"Now, Hippocrates counts it as a unique method."*

You see the village surgeon's effort to appear skillful.

> *When the man with the fever said to him: "Master Clement,*
> *This first point isn't the most necessary."*

This term, *Master Clement,* indicates the gravity of a deliberation.

> *"And as for my thirst, that will be my affair."*[6]

This last verse marks the importance of the resolution. It is a pleasing moment that is incidental to the pleasantry, the humor; but it must be found within the thing itself.

2. Rousseau, *Epigrammes,* I.23.
3. *Recette,* which here means a drug cocktail for curing some ailment.—HC
4. Rousseau, *Epigrammes,* IV.7.
5. The term is *frater,* a Latin word connoting contempt.—HC
6. Rousseau, *Epigrammes,* I.13.

Likewise, in this epigram:

> *Was she not all sleepy,*
> *That unfortunate Academy,*
> *When she took Jean Chamillard.*

It is the word *Jean* that makes the humor, and there would have been none if it had read:

> *When she chose Chamillard.*[7]

In brief, humor is the pleasant sentiment added to the pleasant sentiment, just as epithets are the particular image added to the general image.

[**1531**] ENGLISH.[1] They speak little, and yet they want to be heard. Simplicity, modesty, restraint are never ridiculous among them. They attach more importance to personal merit than any nation in the world. They have their whims, but they get over them. If you send them petty men, they think you want to deceive them. They are authentic, and open, and even indiscreet, but they cannot stand being deceived. Everything called an *air* is disagreeable to them. They like to see simplicity and decency; they like to reason more than to converse. Naturally honest, if the Court and necessity have not corrupted them; brave, without valuing bravura; equally capable of scorning money and of loving it; incapable of amusing themselves, they like to be amused by others. When foreigners do not have the faults they thought they had, they are the sort of people who will love them madly. They like talent and are not jealous of it. All this is covered with eccentricity, which is like a costume that envelops all their virtues.

So much for the individuals!

Now for the Nation and the Ministry:

Deceive them; since they do not expect to be able to pay you back in kind, you drive them to despair.

The nation, insolent; the individuals, modest.[2]

---

7. Jean-François Chamillard (d. 1714), bishop of Dol, then of Senlis, elected to the French Academy in 1702.

[**1531**]
1. See *Notes sur l'Angleterre* (*OC,* 3:283ff.).
2. See *pensée* 827 for the same thought.—HC

438 *Pensée 1532*

Let us never fear a king of England who does not have personal merit.

[1532] Items cut from the book "*Considerations on the greatness of the Romans*" in the new edition that I will bring out, or that did not make it into the additions.[1] What is published is marked by a cross.[2]

But the greatness of Rome soon appeared in the public buildings: *the projects[3] which have presented, and still today present, the loftiest idea of its power were built under the kings. The eternal city was already beginning to be built.

Note p. 7 *The Romans regarded foreigners as enemies; *hostis,* according to Varro, *De lingua latina,* bk. IV, in the beginning meant a foreigner who lives under his own laws.[4] P. 9 *What happened to Italy is what America has experienced in our time. Since the indigenous peoples, weak and dispersed, had given up their lands to new inhabitants, she was peopled by three different nations—the Tuscans,* the Gauls and the Greeks. The Gauls had no relationship with the Greeks or with the Tuscans. The latter assembled an association that had a particular language, manners, and mores; and the Greek colonies, which derived their origins from different, often mutually hostile, peoples had quite separate interests.

Note *It is not known for sure whether they were indigenous or came from elsewhere. Dionysius of Halicarnassus thinks they are natives of Italy. Bk. I.

*The world at that time was not like our world today: the voyages; the conquests; the commerce; the establishment of large states; the inventions of the postal service, the compass, and printing; a certain general law and order have facilitated communications and established among us an art called *Politics.*[5] Everyone sees at a glance everything that is causing disturbance in the world, and however little ambition one people may manifest, it immediately frightens all other peoples.

There used to be a disease called camp sickness;[6] it arose from the fact

[1532]

1. A revised and corrected edition appeared in Paris in 1748.

2. *Une croix* in Montesquieu's manuscript. We use asterisks in the present volume.—HC

3. "Its sewers, its walls. See Dionysius of Halicarnassus's astonishment, Bk. III" (M.).

4. Marcus Terentius Varro (116–27 B.C.); Montesquieu owned the 1581 and 1593 editions of his *Works* (*Catalogue,* 1978–79).

5. See also *pensées* 8, 145, and 2207.—HC

6. "See Vegetius (*Military Art,* III.3). We are no longer familiar with it. Our camps today have a different expanse from those of the Romans" (M.). See *pensées* 1468, 1496, and 1527–28.

that, since the Romans did not have fortresses, their camp had to take their place. They were enclosed and packed together. To prevent this disease, they often changed camps, and this itself made them more robust, by multiplying their labors.

P. 68 *Macedonia was surrounded by inaccessible mountains. The Senate divided it into four parts, declared them free, prohibited all sorts of contact among them, even for marriage, had the nobles transferred to Italy, and thereby reduced that power to nothing.

P. 70 *Note. When Claudius Glycias had granted peace to the Corsican peoples, the Senate gave orders to renew the war against them, and delivered Glycias to the island's inhabitants, who would not receive him. We know what happened at the Caudine Forks.[7]

P. 72 *Divitiarum tanta fama erat,* said Florus, *ut Victor gentium populus, et donare regna consuetus, socii vivique regis confiscationem mandaverit,* I.3, c. 9.[8]

P. 87 *The census, or enumeration of citizens, was in itself a very wise thing; it was a reconnaissance by the state of its own affairs, an examination of its power. It was established by Servius Tullius; before him, says Eutropius, I, the census was unknown in the world.[9]

[1532a] The Citizens could be distinguished in three ways: by origin, as the Patricians were from the Plebeians; by order, as the senators were from the knights and the knights from the rest of the people; and finally, by the right of visual representation,[1] possessed by those whose fathers had obtained curule magistracies, which has some connection to our nobility today.

P. 99 *In the world at present, there is one Republic that virtually no one knows about but that, in secrecy and in silence, is increasing its strength every day.[2] It is certain that, if it ever arrives at the position of greatness

---

7. The Samnites, having defeated the Romans at the Caudine Forks in 321 B.C., fell in a quandary as to what to do with them; see Livy 9.2–6.—HC
8. Florus, *Histories,* I.44: "Such was the fame of its riches . . . that a people which had conquered nations and was accustomed to make gifts of kingdoms ordered . . . that the property of a king, allied to themselves and still living, should be confiscated."
9. Flavius Eutropius (fl. in the late fourth century), *Breviarium historiae romanae* [Abridgment of Roman history], I.7.—HC

[1532a]
1. *Droit d'image,* or right of having an image of themselves made, which some elites, such as the Capitouls, or aldermen, of Toulouse, continued to exercise in the eighteenth century.—HC
2. "The canton of Berne" (M.).

destined for it by its wisdom, it will inevitably change its laws, and this will be the work not of a legislator, but of corruption itself.

P. 100. Note. There are people who have regarded the Government of Rome as defective, because it was a mixture of monarchy, aristocracy, and the popular state. But the perfection of a government consists not in relating it to one of the types of administration found in the books of the political analysts, but in corresponding to the purposes that every legislator should have—namely, the greatness of a people and its felicity. Was the Government of Lacedemon not also composed of these three?

1532b. Nota. Note removed by the censor from the Paris edition.[1]

*If Charles I, if James II had lived within a religion that permitted them to kill themselves, they would not have had to bear such a death, in the one case, or such a life in the other.

P. 148. Note *The Grandees of Rome were already poor at the time of Augustus—they no longer wanted to be aediles, or tribunes of the people; many did not even bother about being senators.

P. 158. Although gladiators had the most shameful origins and the most shameful profession there has ever been—for they were slaves or criminals who were obliged to expose themselves to the danger of death in combat at the grandees' funerals—the passion for these exercises, which were so closely comparable to those of war, became such that it can only be regarded as a kind of mania. Emperors, senators, the great, even women appeared in the arena, *nec virorum modo pugnas sed et foeminarum,* Suet. *In. Domit.*[2] The Romans had no less taste for athletes.

P. 162 *There is no authority more absolute than that of the Prince who succeeds the Republic, for he finds that he has all the power of the people, who had not been able to limit themselves. Today, therefore, we see the kings of Denmark exercising the most arbitrary power that exists in Europe.

[1533] Voiture has raillery but not gaiety. Montaigne has gaiety but not raillery. Rabelais and the *Roman comique* are admirable for their gaiety. Fontenelle has no more gaiety than Voiture. Molière is admirable for both

[1532b]

1. The reference is to the discussion of suicide in the next sentence.—HC
2. Suetonius, *Life of Domitian,* IV.1: "Not only combats between men but between women as well."

of these qualities, and the *Provincial Letters* as well.[1] I dare say the *Persian Letters* bring both laughter and gaiety, and have been pleasing on that account.

[**1534**] The patriarchs' lives were very long. But this lifespan seems to be contrary to the order of nature, because the longer men live, the fewer births must be produced, so that there not be too many inhabitants on the earth. But the longer men survive, the more the human race multiplies.

[**1535**] The situation of the realm of France is difficult[1] in that it has 170 leagues of border to guard, 170 posts on these borders, 93,000 men to guard these posts; the money this costs is consumed on the extremities of the Realm and does not return; it takes a general staff to maintain these posts; beyond that, it takes troops for the interior to form the armies, it takes a recruitment of not less than 25,000 to 30,000 men every year; the Ocean coasts are close to two great maritime powers, and are thereby exposed; it is therefore necessary to have a navy and guard the ports; these coasts are accessible. That adds up to immense and necessary expenses! She cannot wage war without waging it on all of Europe. Luxury of the Court, unavoidable upkeep of the Nobility. Ease of borrowing, which causes her to borrow.

Spain has no need of forts, no need of a large army. She defends herself all alone; most of her Ocean coasts are inaccessible, like the Galician, etc.; the Mediterranean coast is distant from the great sea powers. Surprising wealth that comes to her from the Indies. She owes nothing; she has woollens, which everyone needs, oils, wines, iron, salts, potash, gold and silver mines; if she wanted, as much silk as she would like, as much wheat as she would like, etc. She could spare as much of her revenue as she wants, to create whatever establishments she wants. She needs nothing from abroad; everyone needs to come to her.

[**1536**] I said: "It is only out of ambition that most people lie. They want to make themselves estimable by the success of some tale."

[**1537**] I give thanks to Messrs Grotius and Pufendorf for having so well

[1533]
1. Paul Scarron's *Comic Novel* was published from 1651 to 1657 (see *pensée* 1416); Pascal's *Lettres provinciales* appeared anonymously in 1656–57 (see *pensée* 1059).

[1535]
1. But see *Laws,* 9.6, 135.

executed what a part of this work demanded of me, with that loftiness of genius which I would not have been able to attain.[1]

[1538] That irritated impotence which inspired the Persian kings to give prizes to those who invented new sensual delights led some Roman emperors to establish an office of *tribune of sensual delights*, spoken of by Cassiodorus.[1]

[1539] In Rome, the unjust {accuser} was condemned to punishment in kind[1] and to infamy, with the letter *K* on his forehead, by the Law Remmia. Whence it arises that the *K* was pronounced like a *C*.[2]

[1540] I have read the *Mores of the French* by M. Legendre.[1] Here are the reflections that have come to me.[2]

Trial by man-to-man combat had some rationality grounded in experience: (1) The refusal to engage in combat could prove something, as long as weak individuals were subject to another trial or took a champion, and whoever had not found a champion was bound, by that fact alone, to generate a bad opinion of himself. (2) If he accepted combat, one had to presume in favor of the victor. In a warrior nation, cowardice presupposes other vices, since it presupposes that one has resisted the education one has received, and has not been sensitive to honor, nor guided by the principles that have governed the other citizens; so that one does not fear their contempt, and counts their esteem for little. And as for skill, a man who has counted honor for something will always have practiced something without which it cannot be obtained. {In addition, you will notice that, in a warrior nation, where strength, courage and feats of valor are honored, there are hardly any crimes established except those that arise from treachery, trickery, and cunning, that is, from cowardice.}

JUDGMENT OF GOD. As for trial by hot iron or boiling water, after lift-

---

[1537]
1. See *pensée* 1863; the reference is to the *Laws*.

[1538]
1. Cassiodorus, *Variarum*, VII.10.

[1539]
1. *Talion*, or the law of an eye for an eye.—HC
2. *C* for "calumny."—HC

[1540]
1. Louis Legendre (1655–1733), canon of Notre-Dame of Paris; the work Montesquieu refers to, *Mœurs et coutumes des Français dans les différents temps de la monarchie française* [Manners and customs of the French in the different periods of the French monarchy], appeared in 1712 (*Catalogue*, 2949).
2. "Put in the *Laws* up to the line" (M.). See *Laws*, 28.17, 552–53, for this entry.

ing a hot iron once or several times, or putting one's hand in boiling water, one wrapped one's hand in a sack and sealed it. If, three days later, there appeared no burn mark, one was innocent. Who does not see that, among a people practiced at handling heavy arms, the rough and calloused skin, for such it was, was bound not to receive enough of an impression from the hot iron or the boiling water for it to appear three days later, and that if it did appear, that was a sign that this was an effeminate man? The peasants, with their calloused hands, handle the hot iron at will. It will be said that women, more delicate, handled the hot iron. But laboring women were in a position to be able to pick up the iron without difficulty, and women of quality[3] usually had a champion.

As for trial by cold water, it is known that old women, who are usually thin, should float. Experience thus revealed that those whom the voice of the people had accustomed everyone to call *witches* always floated. Well, people are convinced that magic and witchcraft are attached to old women. If they are by chance pleasing, it is witchcraft; if they are displeasing, people are inclined to attribute an odious character to them. It has to be an old woman, because it is not a young one. It has to be a woman, because women, who prepare the meals in simple times, are more familiar with herbs than men are.

It has surprised people that a hot iron could be handled without a problem; they have imagined a miracle. *Idem,* about Saint Januarius's head. A miracle worked in favor of an accused man proves his innocence.[4]

There are differences in lungs which cause some to float, others not.

[**1541**] In dedicating oneself to the art of criticism and presuming to direct the public's taste or judgment, one must examine whether, once the public (after deliberating) has decided, one has often been of their opinion; for their judgments, sealed by time, are almost always good. Thus, if you have only extraordinary opinions, if you are usually alone in your opinion, if you reason when feeling is called for, if you feel when reasoning is called for, if the public pronounces and you do not pronounce, if they do not pronounce and you do pronounce—then you are not fit for criticism.[1]

3. *Femmes de qualité,* connoting nobility.—HC
4. See *pensée* 871; the blood of Saint Januarius (d. ca. 305) was and is said to be liquefied by the archbishop of Naples in ceremonies commemorating his martyrdom each year in the cathedral there.

[**1541**]
1. See *pensée* 1542.

[1542] As more has been demanded of authors, less has been demanded of critics.[1]

One must not criticize poets because of the defects of poetry, nor metaphysicians because of the difficulties of metaphysics, nor scientists because of the uncertainties of science, nor geometers because of the dryness of geometry.

Everyone takes part today in the treasures that used to belong to a few persons. But with that small part, they think they have everything. A scruple of gold[2] has seemed like the philosopher's stone; with the shared riches—marvelous thing!—everyone has thought himself too rich; the Republic of Letters has been like that of Athens, where the poor were more esteemed than the rich.

One disdains, in order to display wit. Why is the wit that you have a proof that others have none? What! your taste will always be infallible, and others' wit will always fail them? How so, such a different allotment: you always judge well, without exception, and without exception they always think badly? You are free. Then be free to do justice to others.[3]

[1543] The Fatherland believes it has lost its father; each citizen, his friend; each hapless wretch, his protector . . . If you have not made good every ill, you have at least obliged those who come after you to seek to finish what you have begun, or forgo glory . . . Your grants and your refusals were always in favor of the Fatherland. You refused like the father of a family refuses his children. You refused like a father, and you granted like a friend.[1]

[1544] Problems arising in China from the introduction of the sects of Fo and of Lao-Chium:[1] the wars and bloody executions that were generated. An emperor of China was obliged to put to death a hundred thou-

[1542]

1. See *pensée* 1006.

2. A scruple was twenty-four grains.—HC

3. See *pensée* 1541.

[1543]

1. This is the text of a letter Montesquieu sent to Jean-Frédéric Phelypeaux, count of Maurepas (1701–81), at the moment of his dismissal as minister of the royal household and navy minister in 1749. For Maurepas's May 20, 1749, response, see *OC,* 3:1231.

[1544]

1. Fo, name given in China to Buddha, according to Fr. Du Halde; Laochium, or Lao-Tsu, legendary founder of Taoism in China; see *Laws,* 24.11n.

sand bonzes at the same time. The Chinese people were living under the most perfect and practical morality of any people in that part of the world. Men came and dizzied them—them and their emperors—with illusions about a quietism and a metempsychosis that prohibited putting even criminals to death, and that made all the duties of morality consist in feeding the bonzes.

[**1545**] After winning my case against the Jurats,[1] I wanted to put on a pyramid:

Deo Terminali,
Recto, Justo,
Semper Vigilanti,
Semper Clamanti,
Testi, Indici, Judici,
Perpetuo
Sacrum.[2]

On the reverse side:

Finibus Dynastiae Defensis,
Calumniis Litium Repressis,
Hoc Gallici Senatus Aequitatis Monumentum
Carolus
In Rei Memoriam Erexit.[3]

On the other reverse side:

Stet Lapis Hic, Donec Fluctus Girunda Recuset
Oceano Regi Generosaque Vina Britannis.[4]

[**1546**] I have quickly glanced at part of a manuscript attributed to Fra

[**1545**]
1. On this trial, see *pensée* 1386 n. 1.
2. "For ever consecrated / To the God of Borders, / To the right, the just, / The always vigilant, the always assertive, / To the witness, the guide, the judge /"
3. "Having preserved the boundaries of his domain / And repressed the calumnies of the trials, / Charles / Has raised this monument to the Justice of the French Senate / In remembrance."
4. "Let this stone rest here until the Gironde refuses its waves / To King Ocean, and its generous wines to the Britons."

Paolo, which contains opinions on the government of Venice—demanded of him by some principal officer of that republic, on the means of perpetuating its glory.[1]

He has divided it into three parts: that which concerns the Sovereign; that which concerns the State, that is, the subjects; and the manner of conducting itself with foreigners. He finds that the Grand Council, being composed of a very large corps of nobility, without room for choice, has too much authority. He would like the authority of the Senate and the Council of Ten, chosen on their merits, increased. And he believes that the *avogadore*—a magistrate who can summon the Senate and the Council of Ten before the Grand Council—is a magistracy that needs to be restrained, and that people need to be picked for this magistracy who do not have too much credit, or who even have some flaw, so they will be restrained by fear of the Senate or the Council of Ten.

It is certain that the Council of Ten and the Senate pertain to aristocracy, and the Grand Council, to oligarchy; one does not arrive there by virtue, but by birth.

Fra Paolo would like the senators to be chosen for more than one year, and in this he is right. That is how it was in Rome and in Lacedemon.

The State Inquisitors judge without due process, and can put to death the Doge himself if all three of them are of the same opinion, but the Council of Ten follows due process.[2]

[1547] "The Cretans had kings. They have gotten rid of them, and it is the ten cosmi who command in war," says Aristotle (chapter x, *De Republica Cretensium,* book II).[1] {Same lack of resourcefulness as in Holland, since she has been without a stadholder.}[2]

[1548] THE GERMANS. "*Reges ex nobilitate, duces {ex} virtute sumunt,*" says Tacitus, *De Moribus Germanorum.*[1] That is what made the difference between the mayors' power and the kings', and their different titles. This is

[1546]
1. Fra Paolo Sarpi (1552–1623) wrote much on his native Venice.—HC
2. See *Voyages* (*OC,* 2:977ff.).

[1547]
1. From *cosmus,* a term used in some Greek cities for a supreme magistrate.—HC
2. The reference is to the second so-called era of liberty, a period free of the stadholder, which began in 1702 and ended in 1747 (the first such period was 1651–72).—HC

[1548]
1. "They take their kings on the ground of birth, their generals on the basis of courage." Tacitus, *Germania,* VII, 1–2; see *pensées* 1171 and 1302, and *Laws,* 31.4.

what caused the kings of the second race to be elective, because the crown was combined with the mayoralty of the Palace.

[**1549**] The disputes over the agrarian laws did not attack the foundations of the constitution.[1] On the contrary, the laws made or proposed on this subject were a renewal of the ancient discipline, the mores of the ancestors, and a correction of the problem caused by evasion of the laws. Individuals could not even complain about it, because, although societies have mainly been established only so that each individual may preserve his property, nonetheless no one could call what he had acquired in committing fraud against the Law *his property.*

[**1550**] The leader of a republic is a civil magistrate. Chance and necessity gave Holland a military leader {*stadholder*}, and she did great things. The Republic of Venice, with its civil leader from the hereditary nobility, cannot but fall into languor; the Grand Council is an assembly of civil tyrants; they cannot be great men, and they prevent others from becoming so.[1]

[**1551**] But in the end, this democracy (Rome) was corrupted, and in its ruination it followed the same path as virtually all democracies do.[1] The people, who already had all legislation, wanted to have all execution; they eliminated power from all the magistracies, evaded all the laws, and to eliminate morals, they enervated the censorship itself. All public affairs were brought before the people, were debated before them; nothing, before the Senate. The tyrannies of liberty became so unbearable that the leaders defended it without courage, and the people lost it without regret.

[**1552**] There are some surprising examples of Roman vanity. There is nothing as ridiculous as Trebonius, who wrote to Cicero that, if he describes something about Caesar's murder, he hoped he would not have the least place.[1] There is nothing as ridiculous as Cicero himself, who begged to be put in the Roman history, and even to have lies told in his favor.

[1549]
1. On agrarian laws, see *Laws,* 7.2, and 27, 521.

[1550]
1. For Holland, see *pensées* 751 and 940; for Venice, see *pensée* 1546 and *Voyages, OC,* 2:980.

[1551]
1. On the corruption of democracies, see *Laws,* 8.2, 112.

[1552]
1. Caius Trebonius (d. ca. 43 B.C.), Roman general who participated in the assassination of Caesar.

This vanity is entirely different from the vanity that some peoples have today. The latter bears only on the present moment; the former was always joined to the idea of posterity. A fashionable outfit for a certain day suffices for the one; a name engraved in stone was needed to flatter the other. These things are the result of the education of that age and of ours, and are related to the foundings[2] of the two peoples.

[**1553**] I will gladly conform to the ideas of the man who wrote the fable of the Bees,[1] and I will ask to be shown grave citizens, in any country, who do as much good there as their dandies do for certain commercial nations.[2]

[**1554**] FATHERS' PREJUDICES. It is not the prejudice of man; it is that of nature.

[**1555**] Savages: men but not citizens. They breathed the air but did not live. Taken from my *History of Jealousy*.[1]

[**1556**] I used to look at the list of merchandise that European merchants transport every year to Smyrna. I would see with pleasure that those good folks took four hundred bales of paper to package sugar, but only thirty bales of paper for writing.[1]

[**1557**] Plato tells us that the belief in Hell is well-suited to softening up courage.[1] It may eliminate it; it may encourage it.[2]

[**1558**] Contradiction in Plato, who regards poets as pernicious, but who on the other hand says that the main cause of the horror toward incest arises from the tragedies we have seen performed on stage.[1]

[**1559**] Proselytizers love large empires, where those who have true zeal

2. *Institution,* defined by the *DAF* as "action by which one institutes, or establishes."—HC

[1553]

1. Bernard Mandeville (1670?–1733) published *The Fable of the Bees* in 1714; it appeared in French in 1740. See *Laws,* 7.1, 97, where Montesquieu cites the 1732 English edition, the basis of the F. B. Kaye edition of 1924 reprinted by Liberty Fund (1988). See also the third paragraph of *pensée* 1439.
2. See *PL,* CVI, 179.

[1555]

1. All that is left of this history are fragments inserted into *pensées* 484–509, 719, 1622, and 1726. This comment is a reprise of *pensée* 498.

[1556]

1. See *pensée* 1888.—HC

[1557]

1. Plato, *Republic,* III.1.
2. Cf. *Laws,* 25.2, 480.

[1558]

1. Cf. *pensée* 1766.

find great opportunities, and those who have hardly any zeal find the delights of a great court.

[**1560**] The law of nations is established among nations that know each other, and this law should be extended to those nations that chance or circumstance bring to our acquaintance—a rule that civilized peoples have very often violated.[1]

[**1561**] All religions introduced into China are received not as new religions, but as supplements to the ancient one. Confucius, in letting stand the cult of the Spirits, left a door open to these supplements.[1]

[**1562**] So many people who have taken literally the Church Fathers' rantings have imagined that the Emperors' entire attention was occupied in impeding the progress of the Christian religion. It was the least of their affairs; they hardly thought about it. In vain have people talked about the credit of the pagan priests; that credit was very small in itself, and Lucian's works are evidence that the philosophers had discredited them in such a way that they were never able to recover. Most of the persecutions were occasioned by particular accidents, and a lot of them must have occurred in an empire where so many tyrants reigned. Our writers have amassed all the incidents and have produced a body of history from all the sufferings of their own. But it is still true to say that, in a State where a part was constantly proscribed by a part, where the thirst for gold, vengeance, and blood made people look only for guilty parties most of the time, religion was often merely the pretext rather than the cause of so many murders.

I know very well that the early Christians did not defend their own cause; that they bore witness not to their innocence but to their faith. But I say that the Emperors had no zeal for their religion; that most were monsters who had no plan; that Nero wanted only to shift the blame onto them for his crimes and folly, and that even Diocletian at first persecuted them only as State criminals; that Decius persecuted them only for being devoted to Philip, and Licinius, for being too devoted to Constantine,[1]

[**1560**]
1. See *Laws,* 1.3, 7.

[**1561**]
1. Confucius (ca. 555–ca. 479 B.C.), Chinese sage.

[**1562**]
1. Decius (r. 249–51); Marcus Julius Philippus (r. 244–49), defeated and killed at Verona by Decius; Licinius (r. 307–23).

and perhaps likewise Valerius and Maximian[2] only out of jealousy toward Constantine. And this was an occasion for governments to commit countless injustices and hear countless secret denunciations.

[1563] In despotic government, commerce is founded on the momentary necessity of what nature demands for food and clothing.

[1564] *Deuteronomy,* ch. xxviii. *"Reducet te Dominus classibus in Egyptum; . . . ibi venderis inimicis tuis in servos suos et ancillas, et non erit qui emat."*[1] In fact, the Romans were not very interested in the Jews as slaves, says Hegesippus. Thus, after the capture of Jerusalem, many for sale, few buyers. Josephus says twelve thousand died of hunger while those working on public projects were being separated from those who were to be sold.[2]

It is impossible to present more striking threats and promises than those of the legislator, unless it is to employ those of the afterlife. See chap. xxviii of *Deuteronomy,* toward the end.

[1565] I had put in my work (*The Prince*):[1]

"Speaking of politic princes, M. Zamega said they have always had an odious image in history—witness Tiberius, Louis XI, Philip II. The reason is that nothing is so opposed to greatness of soul as trickery, and it is greatness of soul that we like.

"'That is why,' he said, 'in our theaters, a conquering prince is often a favorable character, whereas a politic prince is never depicted except to attach hatred to him.

"'Most politic deeds do not excite our surprise, cannot serve as spectacle, . . . When a sultan gropes for words, we feel this is an act we could perform as easily as he.

"'Trickery is a defensive weapon; it is the recourse of weak people, and we find it intolerable for a prince to employ this resource at the same time that he uses his power. These are too many advantages in one hand.

"'Strength can be useful to the very men who submit to it; it can be

2. First version: "even Gallienus, and Maximian"; that is, Publius Licinius Egnatius Gallienus and Galerius Valerius Maximinus (r. 260–68 and 305–11, respectively).

[1564]
1. Deuteronomy 28:68: "And the Lord will bring you back in ships to Egypt, . . . and there you shall offer yourselves for sale to your enemies as male and female slaves, but no man will buy you."
2. Hegesippus, Greek orator (d. 325 B.C.); Flavius Josephus, *The War of the Jews,* VI.44 (see *Catalogue,* 3188, for the 1611 edition of the *Opera*).

[1565]
1. The *Reflections on the character of some princes* (*OC,* 3:538–41).

useful to the vanquished as to the victor. He has picked up courage by resistance itself and has thereby made himself similar to the conqueror, or worthy of him. But cunning is not useful to men. It is not useful for them to be deceived, nor to deceive. Cunning debases human nature; it makes the victor the subject of contempt, and the vanquished the object of pity. {Look (please) at how sad it is to see a Moghul who gives you a *burleik* or little sachet, which is a sign of his favor, which one is obliged by duty and gratitude to carry on one's nose, and which is often poisoned. How easy it is to commit crimes, and big crimes!}'"

[**1566**] It could be that the constancy of the Japanese during torture might be due to the fact that physical suffering is perhaps not so great there, that the bodily machine is not so susceptible to pain there.[1]

[**1567**] What happened to Hannibal is what always happens when wars last too long: the two sides become battle hardened; the war always terminates in favor of the one that has the truest forces, and more constancy.

[**1568**] Since great booty was taken in the capture of cities, it often happened that the people from a city that sensed it was being captured would burn themselves with all their wealth, their women, their children, so the victor would have nothing to mark his victory, and would have nothing but his losses, with no profit.

In Numantia, says Orosius, "*unum Numantinum victoris catena non tenuit; unde triumphum dederit Roma non vidit.*"[1]

[**1569**] In France, the craft of a pleader is a profession, for once you have begun to plead, you plead throughout your whole life. It is even a status that passes from father to son, like nobility. That profession goes around and takes its subject matter from all professions.

[**1570**] The English kill themselves at the least setback, because they are accustomed to good fortune. Unfortunate people preserve their lives, because they are accustomed to misfortune.

[1566]
1. See *Laws*, 6.13, 86.

[1568]
1. Numantia, city of ancient Spain, near present-day Soria; after a long siege (134–133 B.C.), Scipio Aemilianus razed it. Orosius was a Christian historian and apologist (b. ca. 390) in Tarragonia; the passage is from his *Histories*, V.7: "The chains of the victor did not hold a single Numantine. Rome did not see any reason for granting a triumph." Paulus Orosius, *The Seven Books of History against the Pagans,* trans. Roy J. Deferrari (Catholic University Press, 1964), 188.

[**1571**] It is the nature of our State's constitution that makes us need a man to guide us at every step. The head of household's good sense does him no good. It is taken away from us for the conduct of our conscience; it is taken away from us for the conduct of our health; it is taken away from us, in a word, for the conduct of our business.[1]

[**1572**] Collection of taxes by state functionaries has many advantages, if what Duverney told me is true.[1] No tax collector has made a fortune. They have not been odious to the people. The money has been brought and brought again into the Royal treasury. They have been able to press rigorously or not, according to need. As for expenses, never in the Realm have more than five hundred thousand francs been paid in expenses for enforcement, because it was seen every week which parishes were paying and which not, and because the order came from here and not from the intendant[2] or the taille collector; whereas ever since, we have been at seven or eight million.

[**1573**] I said: "In France, any talking you cannot do in front of women is low and obscene. General rule."

[**1574**] Liberty, that good which makes for the enjoyment of other goods.

[**1575**] The grandees in France—they must always be either our valets or our masters.

[**1576**] When it comes to obtaining honors, we row with personal merit, but we sail in the open waters with birth.[1]

[**1577**] [I don't know who said: "Tastes are misers but passions are spendthrifts."][1]

[**1571**]
1. Cf. *pensée* 1857.—HC

[**1572**]
1. There were several efforts at a system of direct taxes (the *régie*) in old-regime France, but the practice of farming out the collection to private contractors prevailed. See Montesquieu's apparent defense of the *régie* in *Laws*, 13.19, a position criticized by the farmer-general Claude Dupin in his *Réflexions sur quelques parties d'un livre intitulé de* l'Esprit des lois [Reflections on some parts of a book entitled *The Spirit of the Laws*] (1749, rev. 1750). Joseph Pâris Duverney (1684–1777) was a financier who tried in vain to oppose the system of John Law by creating a general assembly of shareholders.
2. For other commentary on the intendant, see *pensées* 977, 1353, 1835, 1840, 1846, 1898, 2066, and 2099.

[**1576**]
1. See *pensées* 1778 and 1802.—HC

[**1577**]
1. See *pensée* 1590.

Montesquieu's library catalogue was also a manuscript he maintained assiduously through his life. Here, he heads a page of political titles with a device from the Neapolitan jurist Gian Vincenzo Gravina, *Originum juris civilis* [On the origins of the civil law] (Naples: Liguori, 2004 [1713]), II.18 (vol. 1, pp. 267–68), which reads: *Res est sacrosancta libertas et divini juris: . . . ut eam tentare scelus sit, impium circumvenire, occupare nefarium* [Liberty is sacrosanct and derives from divine law, . . . to the point where violating it is infamy, stifling it is sacrilege, and seizing it is an abominable crime]. See *pensée* 1574. For more on Montesquieu's interest in Gravina's work, see *pensées* 1761, 1763, 1912, and 1913.

[**1578**] M. de Vaudémont told King William that Monaco is a rock that has a perpendicular league in the sea.[1]

[**1579**] I said: "There are some people who have their souls on their faces; others, in the back of their heads."

[**1580**] I said: "Wealth, birth, etc., are medals; public esteem and personal merit are legal tender."

[**1581**] It is Paris that makes the French. Without Paris, Normandy, Franche-Comté, Picardy would be more German than the Germans.[1]

[**1582**] In this war of 1741, we have seen that the French, bad warriors the first three years, become wonderful the fourth.[1] They learn this craft and forget it. It is Paris and the small cities that make it forgotten, but when they have seen the camps, they learn it.

The Italians, bad warriors because they all live in cities.

[**1583**] Our valets: they have the charm of vanity without the disadvantages of honor.

[**1584**] It is the capital that {especially} makes the mores of peoples; it is Paris that makes the French.[1]

[**1585**] Mme du Deffand said it very well: "One may be a liar, but one must never be false."[1]

[**1586**] I said: "I like Paris. One engages in no reflection there; one gets rid of one's soul."

[**1587**] In Paris, I don't like the organized dinners. They are like the monks' vows; the sacrifice only counts for something the first time.

[**1588**] In Paris, one goes through life with tastes. In foreign countries, passions are needed {said M. Lomillini}.[1]

[1578]
1. Charles-Henri de Lorraine, prince of Vaudémont (1649–1723); William III of England (r. 1689–1702).

[1581]
1. See *pensées* 1584 and 1903 for a more elaborated version.

[1582]
1. The War of the Austrian Succession (1740–48). The French won an important victory at Fontenoy in 1745.

[1584]
1. See *pensées* 1581 and 1903 for an elaboration.

[1585]
1. Montesquieu was one of the most welcomed guests at the salon of Mme Du Deffand (1697–1780); see her letter to him of November 8, 1751 (*OC,* 3:1404).

[1588]
1. Agostino Lomelini, extraordinary envoy of the republic of Genoa in Paris from 1739 to 1742.

[**1589**] I said of V[oltaire], "This is a real question: namely, who has rendered him more justice, those who have given him a hundred thousand praises, or those who have given him a hundred blows of the cane."

[**1590**] I don't know who said: "Tastes are misers and passions spend-thrifts."[1]

[**1591**] The late King of Prussia's father was magnificent. He died at eleven o'clock; dinner was not served; it "served" for the next eight days.[1]

[**1592**] I have heard it said, I don't know where, {or have read} that Mme de Montespan felt some attack of devotion and came to Paris. People did not want her to return to Court. M. de Meaux[1] was of the opinion that she should return, but on condition that she always be amongst three or four prudes. The King came, spoke to her in a doorway; from there, passed into the private office. Whence was born this face—half love, half piety[2]— that is Madame d'Orléans.[3]

[**1593**] I said of V . . . ,[1] whose character was wretched: "He resembles {those} cochineals that offer the loveliest color in nature, though they are only worms."

[**1594**] I said of those who, through some injustice, had left service: "These are dead men in the service of ministers."

[**1595**] I said that, in the Cardinal's time, one had every inconvenience of order, but none of its advantages.[1]

[**1596**] Scaramouche is crying.[1] He is asked the reason. He says: "*Il*

[**1590**]
1. See *pensée* 1577.

[**1591**]
1. The late king of Prussia is Frederick-William I (r. 1713–40), whose father was Frederick I (r. 1701–13).

[**1592**]
1. Bishop Bossuet.
2. The word I translate as "piety" is *jubilé,* which describes someone who has completed fifty years of profession or service, usually of a religious nature.—HC
3. Françoise-Marie de Bourbon, often called Mlle d'Orléans (1677–1749), daughter of Louis XIV and Mme de Montespan and wife of the regent.

[**1593**]
1. Voltaire.

[**1595**]
1. Perhaps a reference to Cardinal Fleury, first minister (1726–43); see *pensées* 472, 914, 1019, 1226, 1284, 1484, and 1509.

[**1596**]
1. Scaramouche is a character in the *commedia dell'arte,* the popular theater of the period, imported from Italy.

Mondo s'imputanisce, ed io son vecchio."[2] It is the ingenuousness that is pleasing, beyond the expression.

[1597] One of the great delights for men's minds is to make general propositions.

[1598] [On several petty authors who were criticizing me, I said: "I am a large oak tree at whose trunk the toads come to cast their venom."][1]

[1599] Upon someone saying to me that I was going to England to receive plaudits for *The Spirit of the Laws,* I said: "One must seek approbation, never plaudits."

[1600] We wanted to dissuade M. de Fontenelle from having his comedies published during his lifetime.[1] I said to him: "Your reputation must be very great, since you don't even have to publish admirable works."

[1601–1608] REFLECTIONS ON THE EARLIEST HISTORIES.[1]

[1601] Those were quite extraordinary times, the earliest ages. Only princes had brains; all other men lacked common sense. Kings had to teach all the arts to their peoples, who were so thickheaded that they could not even conceive of the simplest things.

You are always reminded of the idea of a shepherd who lived alone in a desert with his flocks, and of whom one might say that he invented a sheepfold to take them to, to dry out the grass and put it away to feed them in the winter, to shear the wool that was bothering them. In this way the peoples are presented to us as beasts, while the princes alone enjoyed the light of reason.

Isis taught the Egyptians how to sew, spin, sow, bake bread.[1] Equally subtle inventors are found in other countries: a king of Macedonia— what an absurdity!—invented weights and measures;[2] and it is said

---

2. "The world is going to hell and I'm an old man."

[1598]
1. This would seem to be the first entry clearly written after the publication of *Laws* in 1748.

[1600]
1. See Montesquieu's letter to Guasco, December 8, 1754 (*OC,* 3:1527), and Guasco's note.

[1601–1608]
1. These entries are all that remain of the "Reflections."

[1601]
1. Isis, Egyptian divinity represented as a woman alone or nursing Horus.
2. "Syncellus reports this fact" (M.); probably Georgius Syncellus, or Synkellos, Byzantine ecclesiastic and chronicler of the late eighth and early ninth centuries; see *pensées* 142 and 2193.

that Mnemosune[3] taught them how to speak, as if they had whistled beforehand.[4]

Once the Kings had provided these common inventions, they devoted themselves to more refined researches: they became excellent doctors, good astronomers, perfect engineers. Everything that was discovered was owing to them. In those days, they levied taxes only on the learned.

When I reflect that we do not know precisely who it is that discovered the compass, gunpowder, printing—those things so useful or so harmful, those things, too, that are practically in our time and before our eyes— what can I think of those people who exhaust themselves in seeking out, in the most obscure and distant times, the names of those who discovered the most common things?

Is it not clear that the most common arts have experienced only imperceptible progress, and that each inventor must always have been lost among the great number of those who have added to his invention?

[1602] The earliest heroes were beneficent: they protected travelers, purged the earth of monsters, undertook useful projects; Hercules and Theseus were like that.

Afterward, they were merely courageous: like Achilles, Ajax, Diomedes.[1]

After that, they were great conquerors, like Philip and Alexander.

Finally, they became amorous, like the ones in novels.

At present, I don't know what they are. They are no longer subject to the whims of Fortune. An empire is exploited the way a farmer exploits the land; one gets the most one can from it. If one makes war, it is made by commission[2] and solely to have lands that provide subsidies. What used to be called *glory, laurels, trophies, triumphs, crowns,* is today ready cash.

[1603] The earliest histories are histories of the gods.[1] Those gods

---

3. Mnemosune, personification of memory, mother of the nine muses.

4. "This conforms to what Diodorus of Sicily says, book V, chapter 15" (M.); that is, the *Universal History.*

[1602]

1. Achilles, Homeric hero, king of the Myrmidons; Ajax, name of two Homeric heroes, namely, the king of Salamis and the king of the Locrians; Diomedes, fabled king of Thrace.

2. *Par commission,* by delegation from the prince or sovereign, a phrase used more commonly during the old regime than it would be after the Revolution.—HC

[1603]

1. This is a fragment from a *Persian letter,* of which Louis Desgraves found the autographed manuscript in the archives of the La Brède castle in May 1950; the text of the letter differs significantly from that of the present entry.

change into heroes as the times become less unrefined. Those heroes have only men for children, because the world is beginning to become more enlightened, and because children are seen at a closer distance than fathers.

The mythologists, confused about how to sort out the history and generation of the gods, formed two different sects. Some distinguished and multiplied divinities; such were the poets and scholiasts. Others, more subtle, wanted to simplify everything, reduce everything, blend everything together; among these were the philosophers.

But it must be admitted that there was precious little philosophy involved in taking on the tiresome job of systematizing superstition and organizing what was constantly being scrambled by the poets' digressions, the painters' fantasies, the priests' avarice, and the prodigious fecundity of the superstitious.

This was not the only branch of that endless trial: some, the cruder ones, wanted to understand everything literally; others, more metaphorical, found only allegories, and related everything to morality and science.

The rebel philosophers wanted to restrict that prodigious number of divinities, which had come to include even the abstract names of substances. But what great difference was there between themselves, who animated all of nature, and the theologians, who divided it completely?

[1604] What is most striking about the ancient authors is that their episodes practically all resemble each other. It is either a prince who has invented some art; another who has consulted an oracle; another who goes to look for his daughter, his wife, or his sister who has been abducted from him; a last one, finally, who has overcome some monster—always the same adventures, recurring under different names.

Since Greek territory, which was the scene of a goodly portion of the ancient histories that have survived, was divided into a countless number of small islands, those who first populated it did not inhabit it as a people. They were adventurers who traveled the seas and established themselves in those deserted islands. Each came with his oracle, undoubtedly an Asiatic method, and chose the location that suited him. And since such adventurers brought hardly any women, they very well had to abduct some in that earliest state of virtue, in those ages closer to innocence. Those heroes took those wild women as cities are taken at present.

Abductions were so common in Greece that before Paris had abducted Helen, Greece had already committed itself by oath to make war on whoever dared abduct her.[1]

[**1605**] One used to be a philosopher on the cheap. There were so few known truths; one reasoned on such vague and general things.

Everything turned on three or four questions:

What is the sovereign good?

What is the origin of things: either fire, or water, or numbers?

Whether the soul is immortal.

Whether the gods govern the world.

Whoever had come to a resolution on one of these questions was immediately a philosopher, however baby-faced he may have been.

[**1606**] The world no longer has that cheerful air that it had in Greek and Roman times. Religion was mild and always in accord with nature. Great gaiety in the ritual was joined to complete independence in the doctrine.

Games, dances, festivals, theater, anything that can arouse, anything that can create feeling was part of religious ritual.

If pagan philosophy wanted to afflict man with the sight of his miseries, theology was much more consoling. Everyone flocked into that school of the passions. The philosophers appealed in vain to their disciples, who were fleeing; they were left to weep alone, in the midst of the public joy.

Today, Mohammedanism and Christianity, made solely for the afterlife, are annihilating all that. And while religion is afflicting us, despotism—spread out everywhere—is overwhelming us.

This is not all. Frightful diseases, unknown to our forefathers, have swooped down on human nature and infected the sources of life and pleasure.

The great families of Spain,[1] which had survived so many generations, have been seen to perish to a great extent in our time—a devastation that war has not caused, that must be attributed only to an evil that is too common to be shameful, but that is nothing less than lethal.

[1604]

1. Paris, younger son of Priam and Hecuba, perpetrator of the abduction of Helen, wife of Menelaus, which caused the Trojan War.

[1606]

1. "Put (I think) in the *Laws*" (M.); see *Laws,* 14.11.

[**1607**] What charms me about the earliest times is a certain simplicity of mores, a natural naïvete which I find only there, and which at present no longer exists in the world (at least that I know of) among any civilized people.

I like to see in man himself virtues that have not been inspired by a certain education or religion, vices that luxury and indolence have not caused.

I like to see innocence endure in customs when greatness of courage, pride, and wrath have expelled it from hearts themselves.

I like to see kings stronger, more courageous than other men, distinguished from their subjects in combat, in counsel; aside from that, mixed in with them.

But most people know only their own era. A European is shocked at the simple mores of heroic times, just as an Asiatic is shocked at European mores.

[**1608**] In the ancient histories, one can notice a certain taste in early men for the marvelous, and a mark of singularity in princes' minds that always made them seek a sort of eternity in their enterprises.

If Ninus builds a city, it is to create a project that would have had no equal up to that time, and that also cannot have one in the future.[1]

When the kings of Egypt raise their immense pyramids, they make difficulties for themselves—they select a sandy terrain so they will be forced to have stones brought from Arabia, and so it might be said that the pyramid was only put there by the gods.

If Semiramis travels the length and breadth of Asia, it is to make constant changes in the nature of the terrain—to flatten out mountains and create others in flat country, to square off rocks that are seventeen stadium-lengths high, and create an elevation with the equipment from her army to climb up there.

Note how princes always sought the marvelous; the useful came in second. If they made public highways, it was so they would extend across valleys and precipices. If they made rivers navigable, it was for the glory that was bound to redound to the Prince. It seems that by Alexander's time, men had become somewhat cured of this taste for marvels of that sort,

[**1608**]
1. Ninus, King of Assyria, mounted the throne of Nineveh ca. 2000 B.C.

for in the earliest ages, a conqueror would never have refused the proposal made to Alexander to chisel Mount Athos and carve his statue out of it.[2]

At a time when the arts were unknown, tasteless men labeled as *beautiful* everything that was big, everything that was difficult, everything that had been made by a large number of hands.

[**1609–1619**] FRAGMENTS OF OLD MATERIALS FROM THE "PERSIAN LETTERS." I HAVE DISCARDED THE OTHERS OR PUT THEM ELSEWHERE.[1]

[**1609**] THE KING OF TIBET TO THE CONGREGATION OF PROPAGANDA, IN ROME. You sent me here a man who has told me his religion demands he be dressed in black. You sent me another who brags about being dressed in gray. They hate each other so much that, even though they are thousands of leagues from home, they see each other only to insult each other; and although my empire is of prodigious extent, both of them can't live in it. I told them they could divide it between them and one go off to the Orient, the other to the Occident. But they don't want one to be in a place where the other will never go. I admit they have some knowledge of mathematics. But couldn't they be that learned without being so foolish? Since they told me it was their costume that inspired such great fury in them, I have made them take it off, and have decreed that they dress like two mandarins. Moreover, I considered that, since they have no commerce with women, this was giving them an unrefined mind. Thus, I resolved to marry them and to give each of them two women, etc.

[**1610**] At last,[1] they have just published the ordinance that puts the Foreigner in the Little-Houses and all Frenchmen in the Poorhouse.[2] Shares

2. The reference is to Dinocrates of Rhodes, Alexander's architect who actually was instrumental in the building of Alexandria, starting in 332 B.C.—HC

[1609–1619]

1. The manuscript of the *Persian Letters* is lost; there survive only notebooks of corrections preserved at the Bibliothèque Nationale in Paris (Nouv. acq. fr. 14365). In the manuscript of *Laws,* V, fol. 255, one finds the text of this letter, which has not been inserted into any edition of *Laws,* although it should have figured at the end of 25.15. For more on this, including textual variations, see Brèthe, 3:440–41 n. 43, and Derathé, 2:481–82.

[1610]

1. See Antoine Adam's edition of the *Persian Letters* (Geneva, 1954), 408, for the suggestion that *pensées* 1610–11 are in fact one entry, with a postscript.

2. The ordinance (*arrêt*) is the order in council of May 21, 1720, terminating the Law System (on John Law, see also *pensées* 530, 1017, and 2143); the Foreigner (*l'Étranger*) is the Scotsman John Law, whose bold financial operations are the subject of this entry; the Little-Houses (*Petites-Maisons*) refers to a Parisian insane asylum (see *pensées* 872, 1061, 1102, 1355, and 1376). For the Poorhouse (*Hôpital*), see also *pensée* 1135.

and bank notes are losing half their value. Subjects are being stripped of thirty times a hundred million with the stroke of a pen, that is, a sum that barely exists[3] in the world, and with which one could buy all the real estate[4] in the realm {of Persia}. The whole Nation is in tears. Darkness and mourning cover this wretched realm. It resembles a city seized by assault or ravaged by flames. In the midst of so many calamities, the Foreigner alone seems content with himself, and still speaks of supporting his disastrous system. Here, I inhabit the land of despair. My eyes see only miseries that overwhelm the Infidels. A wind picks up and carries away their wealth. Their false abundance disappears like a phantom.

[1611] I learned at this moment that the ordinance I was telling you about has just been revoked. This change should not seem extraordinary to you. Here, schemes chase after schemes like clouds chase after clouds. The ordinance is revoked,[1] but not the harm it has done. The Ministry has just shared a secret with the people from which it will never recover. —Farewell.

From Paris, the 21st of the moon of Rabia Ist, 1720.

[1612] You tell me our great monarch is occupied only in rendering inviolable justice to his subjects, in rescuing the small from the oppression of the great, and in making the great respected by the small. Eternal glory to that generous prince! May Heaven grant that his power be no more limited than his justice.

[1613] You ask me what the Regency is all about.[1] It is a succession of failed projects and disconnected ideas; of witticisms given an air of system; an incoherent mélange of weakness and authority; all the ponderousness of a ministry without its gravity; command that is always too tight or too loose; emboldened disobedience alternating with righteous trust demoralized; an unfortunate inconstancy in abandoning evil itself; a council that shrinks and then multiplies, that appears and disappears from public view in a manner that is silent or resounding, as different in the persons who compose it as in the end they propose for themselves.

3. First version: "that does not exist"
4. First version: "buy three times the real estate"

[1611]
1. By the order in council of May 27, 1720, the paper currency was restored to its full denomination.

[1613]
1. On the regent, the Duke of Orléans, see *pensées* 29, 800, and passim.—HC

[**1614**] There is a type of turban that accounts for half the follies committed in France. The candidate who wants to have the hat at any cost imagines that it will cover all the bad moves he makes to obtain it.[1]

There is scarcely a prince who does not feel honored by it. There is scarcely a good-for-nothing who cannot aspire to it. Its purple confounds all conditions and arrogantly allies itself with them.

[**1615**] I remember that when we arrived in France, Hagi Ibbi looked upon the King with scorn when told that he had neither women, nor eunuchs, nor seraglio; that no one fled when he passed by somewhere; that, when he was in the capital, most people barely distinguished his coach from that of a private individual.

[**1616**] Page 64 of the *Persian Letters,* Ist volume, I had thought of continuing the story of the Troglodytes,[1] and this was my idea. It was a great spectacle to see all the Troglodytes in joy, while the Prince was dissolving in tears. The next day, he appeared before the Troglodytes with a face indicating neither sadness nor joy. He no longer seemed occupied with anything but the task of government. But the secret grief that was devouring him soon sent him to the grave. Thus died the greatest king who has ever governed men.

He was mourned for forty days. Each person thought he had lost his own father. Everyone was saying: "What hope is left for the Troglodytes? We are losing you, dear Prince! You thought you were not worthy of commanding us. Heaven has revealed that we were not worthy of obeying you. But we swear, by our sacred ancestral spirits, that, since you did not want to govern us by your laws, we will conduct ourselves by your examples."

Another prince had to be elected, and there was something remarkable— namely, that of all the relatives of the deceased monarch, none claimed the throne. The wisest and most just in that whole family was chosen.

Toward the end of his reign, some people thought it necessary to establish[2] commerce and the arts among the Troglodytes. The Nation was assembled, and that decision was made.

[1614]
1. The allusion is to Dubois, who obtained the cardinal's hat in 1721.

[1616]
1. *PL,* XI–XIV.
2. First version: "Toward the end of his reign, it was noticed that the people were so numerous that the land"

The King spoke thusly: "You wanted me to take the crown and believed me virtuous enough to govern you. Heaven is my witness that, since that time, the Troglodytes' happiness has been the sole object of my worries. I glory in the fact that my reign has not been sullied by the baseness of one Troglodyte. Would you today like to prefer riches to your virtue?"

"My Lord," said one of them, "we are happy; we are working on an excellent foundation. Dare I say it? It is you alone who will decide whether riches are pernicious to our people or not. If they see that you prefer wealth to virtue, they will soon accustom themselves to doing likewise, and in that, your taste will govern theirs. If you raise a man to office or bring him into your confidence solely because he is rich, be assured that you will be striking a mortal blow to his virtue, and that you will be imperceptibly creating as many dishonest people as there are men who will have noticed that cruel distinction. You know, my Lord, the basis on which your people's virtue is founded: it is education. Change that education, and whoever was not bold enough to be criminal will soon blush at being virtuous.

"We have two things to do: namely, to stigmatize both avarice and prodigality. Each individual must be responsible to the State for the administration of his property, and the louse who sinks to the level of avoiding an honest subsistence must not be judged less severely than the one who dissipates his children's patrimony. Each citizen must be an equitable dispenser of his own property, as he would be of another's."

"Troglodytes," said the King, "wealth is going to enter your midst. But I declare that if you are not virtuous, you will be one of the unhappiest peoples in the world. In the state you are in, I need only to be more just than you; this is the mark of my royal authority, and I can find none more august. If you seek to distinguish yourselves solely by wealth, which is nothing in itself, I will certainly have to distinguish myself by the same means, and not remain in a state of poverty that you disdain. Thus, I will have to overwhelm you with taxes, and you will have to employ a large part of your subsistence in maintaining the pomp and glitter that will serve to make me respectable. At present, I find all my wealth within myself; but at that point, you will have to exhaust yourselves to make me rich, and that wealth—which you were making so much of—you will not enjoy it; it will all come into my treasury. O Troglodytes! we can be united by a beautiful bond: if you are virtuous, I will be; if I am virtuous, you will be."

[**1617**] (This letter could not be put into the *Persian Letters,* first, because it resembles others too much; and second, because it only restates what is better said elsewhere. I put it here because of certain fragments that I will perhaps be able to pull from it, and some vivid passages in it.)

The great Eunuch to Janum, at ***.

I pray Heaven that he take you to those places and shield you from all dangers.

Destined to fill a position in the seraglio under my control, you will perhaps move someday to the post that I occupy; it is there that you should bring your views.

Thus, think very soon about shaping up and attracting your master's attention. Affect a strict face; drop some somber looks; speak little. Let joy shun your lips. Sadness well suits our condition. Tranquil in appearance, let an anxious mind appear from time to time. Do not await the wrinkles of age before showing its sorrows.

It is in vain that you would adapt to a base complaisance. We are all hated by the women, and hated maniacally. Do you believe this implacable rage is the result of the strictness with which we treat them? Ha! they would pardon our whims if they could pardon us our misfortunes.

Do not pride yourself on a fastidious integrity. There is a certain delicacy that suits scarcely anyone but free men. Our condition does not leave us with the capacity to be virtuous. Friendship, faith, oaths, respect for virtue are victims that we have to sacrifice at every moment. Obliged to work constantly to preserve our lives and deflect the punishments that are looming over us, all means are legitimate: trickery, fraud, cunning are the virtues of wretches like us.

If you ever arrive at the premier position, your main goal will be to make yourself master of the seraglio. The more absolute you are, the more means you will have of breaking up the cabals and the mania for vengeance. You must begin by quelling courage and burying all passions in astonishment and fear. You will never do better on this score than by arousing your master's jealousy. You will share little secrets with him from time to time. You will focus his mind on the slightest suspicions. Then, you will fix it there by some new circumstances. Sometimes, you will abandon him to himself and leave his mind floating in uncertainty for some time. Then you will appear, and he will be delighted to find in you a mediator between his love and his jealousy. He will ask your advice; mild or harsh, you will give yourself a protector or humiliate an enemy.

It is not that you can always cast suspicion at will about some criminal intrigue; women beaten down by such scrutiny can scarcely be plausibly accused of certain crimes. But these must be sought in the measures that desperate love procures itself, when the furious imagination latches onto every object it finds. Don't be afraid of saying too much about it; you can be bold at dissembling. In the many years I've been governing, I have learned about—I have even seen—some incredible things. My eyes have been witness to everything that madness can invent, and to everything that the Daemon of Love can produce.

If you see that your master, capable of the yoke of love, fixes his heart on one of his wives, relax your ordinary harshness a little toward her; but bear down on her rivals, and try to make both your mildness and your harshness agreeable to her.

But if you see that, inconstant in his loves, he uses like a sovereign all the beauties he possesses; that he loves, leaves, and retakes; that he destroys in the morning the hopes of the evening; that caprice follows choice and contempt caprice—then, you will be in the most fortunate situation possible. Master of all his wives, treat them as if they lived in perpetual disgrace, and have no fear of a favor that is lost as it is being dispensed.

It is thus up to you to contribute to his inconstancy. It sometimes happens that a beauty triumphs and arrests the flightiest heart. It escapes in vain, she always calls it back. Such constant returns threaten to become an undying attachment. These new chains must be broken at all costs. Open the seraglio; bring in waves of new rivals; cause distractions on all sides; confound a proud mistress by sheer numbers, and reduce her to fighting again for what the others could no longer forbid.

This policy will almost always work for you. By this means, you will use his heart so well that he will sense nothing. The graces will be ruined; so many charms, secret for the whole world, will be even more so in his own eyes. In vain will his wives, out of emulation, attempt the most fearsome maneuvers against him. Useless at love, they will cling to his heart only out of jealousy.

You see that I hide nothing from you. Though I have scarcely ever known that commitment called friendship, and have wrapped myself entirely within myself, you have nonetheless made me aware that I still have a heart, and while I had a heart of stone toward all those slaves living under my laws, I was watching with pleasure as you passed through childhood.

I took care of your education. Harshness, always inseparable from instruction, long made you unaware that you were dear to me. But you were, nonetheless, and I would say that I loved you as a father loves his son if these words "father" and "son" were not better suited to conjure up a frightful memory in the two of us than to point to a gentle and secret sympathy.[1]

[**1618**] RICA TO USBEK. Here is a letter that has fallen into my hands.

"My dear cousin,[1]

"Two men have suddenly left me. I have attacked the one you knew about, but he has been like a rock. My heart is indignant at the affronts it receives every day.

"What haven't I done to attract him? I have outdone my customary courtesies by a hundredfold. 'Good God!' I said to myself, 'can it be that I, to whom so many niceties were uttered in the past, am today making so many restitutions for nothing!'

"My dear cousin, you are two years younger than I, and your charms are well above my own. But I implore you not to abandon me in the resolution I have taken to quit the world. You are the confidante of so many secrets; I am the depository of so many others. It has been more than thirty years since our friendship triumphed over all the petty tiffs that the variety of intrigues and the multiplicity of interests inevitably produce in a society.

"I have often told you: these dandies I have so much loved, I can't stand them anymore. They are so satisfied with themselves, and so little with us. They put such a high price on their folly and their appearance . . . My dear cousin, spare me their contempt.

"I'm beginning to develop such a taste for the company of the devout that it is now my entire consolation. I've not yet sufficiently broken with the world for them to trust in me. But as I distance myself from it, they've been approaching a bit. What sweetness in this new way of life, instead of the tumult and noise of that phony world!

"My dear cousin, I'm going to surrender myself to them completely. I'll reveal to them the condition of a heart that takes on all the impressions

---

[**1617**]
1. This entry is a first draft of *PL*, XV. See Adam, 415n.

[**1618**]
1. The French makes clear that the recipient is female.—HC

that are given to it. I don't have it in me to extinguish all my passions; it's just a matter of regulating them.

"There's one thing that's the fundamental principle of the devout life: the total suppression of alien attractions. For although, just between you and me, these attractions are always more innocent during the period one is leaving them than when one is beginning to make use of them, they nonetheless always indicate a certain desire to please the world, which devotion detests. It wants us to appear before the world in all its stormy weather, to show it just how much we disdain it. As for us, dear cousin, it seems to me that we can still display ourselves as we are. I've told you a hundred times that you're charming when you seem most unadorned, and that there is much art in your not manifesting it.

"May this letter touch your heart and inspire in you resolutions that I've made only after having long combated them. Farewell."

Devotion, which in certain souls is a sign of strength, is in others a sign of weakness. It is never indifferent, for if, on the one hand, it adorns the virtuous, it completes the degradation of those who are not.

In Paris, the 25th of the moon of Rabia, 1717.[2]

[1619] USBEK TO ZELIS.

You demand your separation before the judge.[1]

What kind of example are you giving your daughter! What a topic of conversation for the whole seraglio! You insult me much less by displaying how little love you have for me, than how little respect you have for yourself.

Do you think virtue costs less to your girlfriends than to you? that their lives are less burdensome? Doubtless not. But the struggles endured are unknown; the pains of a hard-fought victory are secret; and virtue, even when it is being tyrannical, appears in them under a modest mien and a tranquil face.

I can well believe you are suffering all the rigors of continence [but how can you be so imprudent as to divulge this secret that women who have a little modesty so carefully hide?]. I count on the vigilance of my eunuchs.

---

2. See Adam, 417, for the suggestion that this *pensée* belongs between letters CI and CII, or between CIV and CV.

[1619]

1. For the rarity of such demands, see Adam, 408, who traces Montesquieu's source to Jean Chardin, *Voyages en Perse* (Amsterdam, 1711), 2:272.

They respected your age; they believed you mistress of your passions. But now that they know the dominion of those passions, have no doubt that they will redouble their efforts to prop you up. They will treat you as if you were still in the perils of youth, and will again begin to adapt you to an education from which you have strayed so far.

Thus, get rid of your ideas, and know that there is nothing left for you but repentance and my love; for I am not a man to put up with a woman I love passing into the arms of another, when I ought to be regarded as the cruelest of all men . . . I say nothing more about it; you know my heart, and you understand me.

From ***, the 1st of the moon of Zu'lhijjah, 1718.[2]

[**1620**] CONTINUATION OF MY REFLECTIONS. What makes me unable to say that I have spent an unhappy life is that my mind has a certain activity that makes it take a sort of leap to pass from a state of sorrow to a different state, and to take another leap from one happy state to another happy state.

[**1621**] In the past, epistolary style was in the hands of the pedants, who wrote in Latin. Balzac picked up the epistolary style and the manner of writing letters from those people.[1] Voiture was put off by it, and since he had a subtle mind, he put some subtlety and a certain affectation into it, which always happens in the transition from pedantry to worldly sophistication. M. de Fontenelle, a near contemporary of those people, mixed Voiture's subtlety and a little of his affectation with more knowledge and enlightenment, and more philosophy. Mme de Sévigné was not yet known.[2] My *Persian Letters* taught how to write a novel in letters.

[**1622**] NEW FRAGMENTS OF A "HISTORY OF JEALOUSY".[1] I sometimes read an entire history without paying the slightest attention to the shots and shocks of battle, or the thickness in the walls of the captured cities; careful only in scrutinizing men, my pleasure is in looking at their lengthy sequence of passions and fantasies.

---

2. Adam, 481, sees this entry as belonging between letters CVIII and CIX.

[1621]
1. Jean-Louis Guez, lord of Balzac (1595–1654), a leading writer of the period.
2. Marie de Rabutin-Chantal, marquise of Sévigné (1626–96); her *Letters* appeared for the first time in 1726 (*Catalogue*, 2306).

[1622]
1. "Look at what's in volume I, page 483" (M.), that is, *pensée* 719; see *pensée* 1555n.

It will be seen in the *History of Jealousy* that it is not always nature and reason that govern men, but pure chance, and that certain circumstances that do not at first seem weighty have such an influence on them and act so forcefully and persistently that they can impart a certain cast of mind to human nature itself.

When Darius made a law prohibiting adultery, the Massagetes represented to him that they could not obey it, because their custom was to treat their guests to their wives. Whatever the force of this custom may have been, it is quite certain that a Massagete who loved his wife, whom he was prostituting to a stranger, would have been quite angry had she loved that stranger more than himself. He was happy to fulfill an external duty; but he doubtless wanted his wife to stick purely to the formalities, and to preserve for him a heart that was dear to him. They were so honorable in that country that they wanted to make a stranger see that they were giving him what they loved best—and this itself must make us think that a man would have been quite upset to lose forever the love of a woman who was abandoning him for a moment.

Large societies had to be formed in order for certain prejudices to become general and to set the tone for all the rest.

There were two peoples who argued with each other about their antiquity: the Egyptians and the Scythians.

Isis and Osiris reigned amidst the Egyptians; they were ranked among the gods. Isis had preeminence over her husband, and through her, her entire sex was respected. Egyptian men submitted to their wives in her honor, and were so compliant with this servitude that they took care of the house and left them all the external business; the wives succeeded to the realm with their brothers.

As for the Scythians, history informs us that some women killed their husbands, calling marriage not an *alliance,* but a *servitude.* They founded the Amazons' empire, built Ephesus, and conquered almost all of Asia.

Nations have the same prejudices as empires. It takes next to nothing to give one people another's prejudices, and the progression can be so great that it changes, so to speak, the entire character of human nature. This is what makes man so difficult to define.

Is it not true that, if Mohammedanism had subjugated the entire world, women would have been everywhere confined? That manner of governing them would have been regarded as natural, and people would be at pains to imagine that there might be another way. If the Scythian women had continued their conquests, if the Egyptians had continued theirs, the human race would be living under the servitude of women, and one would have to be a philosopher to say that a different government would be more in conformity with nature.[2]

[1623] I said of T——: "He is false of heart, hypocrite in his body, gauche of mind, childishly low, stupidly high, deceptive without insight, subtle but clumsy."

[1624] A woman is obliged to please as if she had created herself.

[1625] A game of biribi is being played.[1] If the money bothers you, throw it out the window. If I asked someone if he wants to play seventy louis against sixty-three, he would laugh. But that's biribi. You don't calculate.

The English are calculators; this is because they have two ends that surround the middle: merchants and philosophers. Women are nothing there; here they are everything.

[1626] Princes are so tightly enclosed within the circle of their courtiers, who steal everything from them and blind them to everything, that the one who came to see clearly would be like Descartes, who emerged from the darkness of the old philosophy.

[1627] I said: "I don't like bawdy witticisms."

[1628] There are people who see everything as exaggerated, and whose minds, moreover, exaggerate things. This is how Mme Du Ch[atel][1] depicted Lironcourt.[2]

[1629] A witty man can say some foolish things in front of women; but he must elaborate so imperceptibly that one cannot be more upset with the second than with the first. Likewise, when one attacks them; likewise, when one complains to them. By preparing minds, one can say and do anything.

2. See *pensée* 1630.

[1625]
1. Biribiri is a game of chance played between a banker and any number of players. A board divided into seventy numbered squares receives the players' stakes. Out of an equal number of numbers, the banker draws one, which is the sole winner. The player who has placed on that number receives sixty-four times his stake.

[1628]
1. Perhaps Emilie Du Châtelet; see *pensée* 1300.—HC
2. Lironcourt was a nobleman attached to Cardinal de Polignac; he was named an associate member of the Bordeaux Academy on December 15, 1737.

[**1630**] JEALOUSY.[1] Once women are guarded, it naturally happens that one will seek to guard them still better every day; the effect will itself become the cause, and vigilance the greatest motive for vigilance.

The more you take measures, if it happens that they do not work, the pain will increase in proportion to the measures thwarted. People who have always kept themselves on guard, who have always congratulated themselves on some imaginary means of protecting themselves, who have eliminated all pretexts, who have chosen their guardians, who have watched over their tasks—if, given all of this, they find themselves taken in, they become furious. In the futility of what has been done, one thinks about what remains to do; one begins again on a new plan; one invents, embellishes, corrects, and always surpasses oneself.

The pain felt by a jealous man arises especially from the satisfaction a woman has found in driving him to despair. The more jealous a man is, the greater is the affront that he feels; and by a just consequence, the more jealous he is, the more he has reason to be, and the more he should become so.

Soon a certain prejudice based on honor and religion will persuade a man that it would be a smaller misfortune to lose his life and property than to bear another man, a father even, seeing the face of a woman that he himself does not even bother to see. This prejudice cannot be better compared than with the one we have in Europe, that a man who has been called a liar merits being avenged by death—a prejudice that is founded on nothing, but that is nonetheless established, and much better established than more reasonable things. For often, nothing does more to disturb the progress of an opinion than this consideration that it is reasonable and, consequently, unexceptional.

Just as the servitude of women has given birth to a greater servitude among the Asiatics, their liberty has given birth to a greater liberty among us. What makes us take fewer precautions with our women is that, to the extent that they threaten us with the affronts they can commit against us, they make us subject to ridicule if we fear them. The more liberty they have, the more they are in a position to introduce this ridicule and give us the cast of mind that suits them.

[1630]
1. See *pensée* 1622.

[1631] THE PRINCE.[1] He should consider that whole villages are not enough to pay a pension that they give to great lords who are about to become wretches or wretches about to become great lords, and who often have no other merit for obtaining it than the effrontery of asking for it.

It has been put into the head of a great monarch that, provided the money does not leave his realm, the realm—whatever subsidies he may levy, whatever prodigality he may engage in, whatever pensions he may pay—the realm can never become poor. But to take away money that is necessary for the cultivation of the land, in order to give it to those who will only use it in the encouragement, through their luxury, of the luxury arts—does this not impoverish the State? It is as if one were to say that twenty horses, each carrying a hundred pounds, will not be more bothered when ten carry the whole load, and five carry the other five in a wagon.

Give enormous benefits to some individuals, and you weigh down the others through deprivation; those individuals, again, weigh down the latter by their luxury, which they communicate to them and compel them to accept.

[1631a] CONTINUATION OF MY REFLECTIONS. 3rd VOLUME.[1] I have put down what did not make it into my dialogue *Lysimachus,*[2] what did not make it into my *Romans,*[3] on Happiness,[4] what did not make it into *The Spirit of the Laws;*[5] after which, there is a continuation[6] and it will go further. See also p. 341.[7]

Doubts.[8]

Reflections on *The Prince,* which did not make it into my works.[9]

[1631]

1. "I copied it for the novel *Arsace*" (M.). To compose *Arsace et Isménie,* Montesquieu drew on fragments he had assembled before his voyages, under the title *The Prince.* He hesitated to publish this "Oriental story." See his letter to his friend Guasco on December 8, 1754 (*OC,* 3:1527); in the end, it was published only in 1783, by his son Jean-Baptiste de Secondat (*OC,* 3:477–535).

[1631a]

1. With this entry begins the third and last manuscript volume of the *Pensées.*
2. *Pensée* 2161.
3. *Pensées* 1669–74 and 2183–202.
4. *Pensées* 1661–62, 1675, and 2010.
5. *Pensées* 1690–1877.
6. *Pensée* 1943.
7. That is, *pensée* 2052.
8. *Pensées* 1945–48.
9. *Pensées* 1983–2003.

Some fragments of a work that is no more.[10]

Things that did not make it into my *Défense.*[11] Things that did not make it into my novel *Arsace.*[12]

Apologia and preface to the *Persian Letters.*[13]

Fragments of an essay: *Differences between Minds.*[14]

Various materials.[15]

Literature and belles-lettres.[16]

Materials from essays for the Bordeaux Academy, which should not appear.[17]

Various materials.[18]

[1632]　To love to read is to make an exchange of the inevitable hours of boredom in one's life, for some delightful hours.

[1633]　I like those men who know how to do great, contradictory things. Sixtus V could put as an inscription on many of his fine works: *"Primo Pontificatus Anno,"*[1] but that same Sixtus V put six million in gold in the Castel Sant'Angelo, to be used in time of danger to the Holy See. Thus, that man knew how to act quickly and for his glory; he knew how to act slowly and for others' glory.[2]

[1634]　There are three types of prince: the first care only about themselves and view their state only for themselves, without considering their people; the next think first about the people's good, and derive their own from it; the next, to achieve their own good and in considering their own good, consider that of their people to enhance their good. Here, the people are in second place; in the previous case, they are the primary object; and with the first, they are in no way the object. Genuine prosperity is found among princes where the people are the primary object. The prince and

---

10. *Pensée* 2004.

11. *Pensées* 2005–8.

12. *Pensées* 2025–31.

13. *Pensée* 2033.

14. *Pensée* 2035.

15. *Pensée* 2165.

16. *Pensée* 2178.

17. *Pensée* 2245.

18. *Pensée* 2246.

[1633]

1. "The first year of the pontificate."—HC

2. Sixtus V (Felice Peretti, 1521–90; r. 1585–90), known for his aggressive fiscal and administrative reorganizations and for his prodigious public works.—HC

the people derive little utility when the people are the second object; they are sheep fed to be killed.

[1635] I wrote to Mme de Talmont on[1] the loss of her son:[2] "Our misfortunes shrink in proportion to our reason, which means that, just as past good fortune does not create the good fortune to come, likewise with past misfortune."

[1636] IN 1748 AND '49. It is a very odd phenomenon, what we see in the Swedish nation[1]—a nation which, by the most extraordinary good fortune, has obtained a free government, and which enjoys it for two reigns, which has been weighed down by arbitrary government for a reign, where it has seen practically all its subjects perish through the obstinacy and pigheadedness of an arbitrary king, and where a powerful faction arises to deprive this nation of its free government and reestablish arbitrary government.

Ambitio tantum potuit suadere malorum.[2]

[1637] Gravity is the shield of fools. But once it is pierced here and there, it is the most contemptible weapon in the world. One becomes angry at a man because he has hidden, and one overwhelms him because he is revealed.

[1638] I don't know how it happened that a Turk one day found himself with a Cannibal. "You're quite cruel," the Mohammedan told him; "you eat the prisoners you have taken in war." "What do you do with yours?" answered the Cannibal. "Ha! we kill them. But when they're dead, we don't eat them."

It seems that there is no people that does not have its particular cruelty; that each nation is moved only by the cruelty of other nations, as if barbarism were an affair of custom, like fashions and clothes.

[1635]
1. First version: "a lady, on"
2. Marie-Louise, Princess Jablonowska (d. 1773), had married Anne-Charles-Frédéric, prince of Talmont; Louis-Stanislas, count of Taillebourg, died on September 17, 1749.

[1636]
1. After the death of Charles XII (1718), his sister Queen Ulrika Eleanora (r. 1718–20), and then her husband Frederick I of Hesse (r. 1720–51), had to accept the constitution of 1719, which left power to the Riksdag, led by the nobility, and to the Council, whose members were designated by this assembly.
2. Lucretius, *On the Nature of things,* I.102: "So much can ambition counsel crimes," although Montesquieu substitutes "ambition" for Lucretius's "religion" in the passage.

[**1639**] Everything in Europe is full of change. Since woollen fabric is not as widely used anymore in England, and is consumed mainly in the Levant and in the Orient, the farming of land has been increased in England, and people have cultivated bad lands not hitherto cultivated, so that at present it is reckoned that England exports 200,000 pounds sterling of wheat more than it exported in the past. Less is cultivated in Sicily, in Sardinia, in Barbary, in Poland, so that Holland, France, even Italy (through Leghorn), even Spain need English wheat.

For twelve years in England, it has been found that about 100,000 pounds sterling worth of silver, separated by mercury, has been drawn from the lead mines,[1] and that they could preserve the lead after the operation. There is only some scrap metal (a tenth), and the lead itself is more malleable after the operation. When a ton of lead, which is, I believe, 200 thousand weight,[2] yields 5 ounces of silver (each ounce is 5 shillings), there is some profit. But sometimes as much as 14 ounces are drawn. Lord Bath told me this.[3]

He also told me that in Cromwell's time, the postal revenues in England amounted to only 30,000 pounds sterling per year; that after the restoration, Charles II gave them to the Duke of York, his brother,[4] for his right of succession;[5] that since then, they have been farmed out; that the farmers eliminated the abuses and made the revenues more profitable. Then, they were placed under direct administration, and at present, the State gets 150,000 pounds sterling from them per year. From which it must be concluded that the best way is to begin by farming, because the farmers, as self-interested men, begin by eliminating abuses and bringing the tax up to its value; after which, one must move to direct administration.

[**1639**]
1. Throughout this article, Montesquieu substituted the word *lead* for *tin*.
2. First version: "When a hundred pieces, which are, I believe, twenty thousand weight"
3. William Pulteney, count of Bath (1682–1764); Montesquieu had gotten to know him in England (see *Notes sur l'Angleterre* in *OC*, 3:285). Montesquieu's friend President Barbot wrote to Montesquieu on April 7, 1749: "The famous Pulteney . . . has cited, my dear President, as an authority in the full Parliament of England, a passage from the treatise of *The Spirit of the Laws*. When will we see this book cited in the King of France's Council?" (*OC*, 3:1216). In a letter to Montesquieu three days later, David Hume specifies that the subject was state debt (*OC*, 3:1221). See Bulkeley's letter to Montesquieu on May 5 for Pulteney's broader approval of Montesquieu's interpretation of the English constitution (*OC*, 3:1229), an approval shared by William Domville, who writes in a June 4 letter to Montesquieu, "You are perhaps the only foreigner who has untangled such a complicated system and such variable features." (*OC*, 3:1235). For the payment of public debt, see *Laws*, 22.18.
4. The brother of Charles II, the future James II.
5. The French term is *apanage*, which usually connotes a territorial rather than a monetary transaction.—HC

(This must be put in *The Spirit of the Laws,* in the chapter on direct administration.)[6]

[1640] Lord Bath says that England and Scotland have yielded {in some years} as much as II million sterling; that nonetheless, they make up scarcely a third of the realm of France in area. Now France, he says, is far from paying as much proportionally; and figuring eight million inhabitants in England and Scotland and twenty million in France,[1] it is found that France is far from paying as much either in proportion to its inhabitants or in proportion to its land. He attributes this: (1) to commerce; (2) to the government, which makes these self-taxing people tax themselves above their capacity out of a love of liberty; (3) to the wealth from their mines.

I added: that France has a large part of its country in forest; that England replaces this with its coal mines, which make up the extra lands that would form large provinces; our government, which cannot tax the Nobility too much (because they are needed for war and for the Court, for the exercise of civil charges), nor the merchants, whom an abusive tax[2] is crushing already. The tax thus falls on the lower classes, who are crushed, and everyone is more crushed because we begin by weighing people down, and because no one has the time to get rich.

[1641] For twelve years, people in England have applied themselves to getting silver from lead. When a ton of lead, which is about 200 thousand weight, yields 5 ounces of silver, which (at 5 shillings per ounce) makes 25 shillings, there is neither loss nor gain in the operation; but all the surplus is profit. Now there are sometimes 14, 20, 24 ounces of silver. Thus, the surplus is profit, and every year 100,000 pounds sterling in silver is brought to the Mint.[1] In expenses, which run to 5 ounces, scrap metal of one-tenth of the lead is reckoned; but that is somewhat compensated by

---

6. See *Laws,* 13.19; for the contrast between farming and directly administering tax revenues (i.e., the *régie*), see also *pensée* 1572.

[1640]

1. See *pensée* 1747, where Montesquieu himself estimates fourteen million Frenchmen.—HC

2. The term is *maltôte,* a term of abuse which connoted an extraordinary and unwarranted tax. See *Laws,* 13.7, 217, and 13.14, for methods of taxation, and 25.5, 485, and 30.12, 630, for other uses of this term.

[1641]

1. The term translated here as "Mint" is *Hôtel de la Monnaie,* of which there were twenty-nine in France at the time of Montesquieu's writing; here, however, he probably means the English Royal Mint.—HC

the value of the lead which has passed through the operation—it has a higher price because it is more malleable.[2]

[**1642**] SHORT PREFACE FOR THE "HISTORY OF FRANCE."[1] A doctor at the University of Salamanca has found, through an exact calculation, that from the death of Henry IV to the Treaty of the Pyrenees, the leagues, associations of the nobility, deliberations of the parlements, different expeditions, treaties of peace and war cost only 118 minutes of reflection to all the French leaders; that in going further back, to the reigns of Henry III, Charles IX, Francis II, they were in a state of general distraction and they killed each other, always without thinking about it.[2] When one of their kings—who, as it happens, did a great deal of thinking—found himself head of a nation that did not engage in thinking, he undertook to subjugate it, succeeded, and put himself, as he used to say, beyond reach.[3]

[**1643**] I was complaining about the countless bad criticisms of my *Spirit of the Laws,* which came from the fact that they did not understand me.[1] I was mistaken; they came from the fact that they did not want to understand me. Countless petty minds had some moral commonplaces they wanted to peddle. Now for that, it was essential not to understand me. For example, if he took the word *virtue* in the sense that I presented it to him, it would not have been possible to hold forth on the necessity of the Christian virtues and the moral virtues in all types of government.[2] Moreover, in not understanding me, they had a clear field for their rants. Now of all types of work, this is the easiest.

[**1644**] To write a treatise on happiness,[1] it is essential to lay down the

2. See *pensée* 1639.

[1642]

1. On Montesquieu's plan to write a History of France, see *pensées* 1111 and 1302 n. 1.

2. Henry IV died in 1610; the Treaty of the Pyrenees was signed in 1659; the others named were kings of France from 1559 to 1589.

3. The reference is likely to Louis XI (r. 1461–83), of whom the phrase *le roi hors de page* (the king beyond reach) was first and most memorably used. For Montesquieu's view of Louis XI, see *pensées* 195, 390, and especially 373; see also the section on him in *pensée* 1302. See 364–71.—HC

[1643]

1. The book was criticized by financiers such as the farmer-general Dupin (see *pensée* 1572 n. 1), by the Jansenists in their *Nouvelles ecclésiastiques* [Ecclesiastical News], and by the Jesuits in their *Journal de Trévoux.* The book was condemned to the Papal Index on November 29, 1751; in Paris, the Sorbonne theology faculty took up the case without reaching a formal condemnation.

2. On Montesquieu's use of the term *virtue,* see *Laws,* 3.5, 25, and Derathé, 2:456–57.

[1644]

1. *Réflexions sur le bonheur,* of which only some fragments are preserved in the *Pensées.* See *pensées* 30, 69, 658, 819, 978, and 1181.

limit to which happiness can go by man's nature, and not begin by requiring that he have the happiness of Angels or other Powers happier than we imagine.

Happiness consists more in a general disposition of mind and heart, which opens up to the happiness that man's nature can offer, than in the multiplicity of certain happy moments in life. It consists more in a certain capacity to receive these happy moments. It does not consist in pleasure, but in an easy capacity to receive pleasure, in a well-founded expectation to find it when one wants to, in the experience that one is not generally put off by the things that make for the felicity of others.

Two things compose moral misfortune: general ennui, which arises from a distaste or a disdain for everything; general discouragement, which comes from the feeling of one's own baseness.

[1645] ENGLAND. One of Chancellor Yorke's sons, who is a very renowned lawyer in England, has enlightened me on many things with great precision.[1]

There are four courts of justice in England: the Court of King's Bench, which is for criminal cases; the Court of Common Pleas, which is for civil cases; the Chancellery Court, which is for cases where it is a question of moderating the rigor of the law for wills and movable property cases; and, finally, the Court of the Exchequer, which concerns fiscal cases, whether the King be a defendant or a plaintiff.

Cases are brought to these courts—at least to the first three—when juries remand them because the question, not being properly one of fact, needs to be judged by the law. I do not know whether the Court of the Exchequer judges by a jury remand, or whether in that case there are juries.

The Court of King's Bench has a chief justice, and the Court of Common Pleas has another chief justice, and in each of these tribunals, there are four judges, including, I believe, the chief justice. Notice that the House of Lords has jurisdiction to moderate the law, like the Chancellery Court.

[1645]
1. Philip Yorke, first earl of Hardwicke (1690–1764), lord chancellor from 1737 to 1756, and his son Charles (1722–70), who died several days after having been elevated to the rank of lord chancellor. In a letter of April 22, 1750 (*OC,* 3:1300), Charles Yorke wrote to Montesquieu to announce the shipment of various works, including his *Some Considerations on the Law of Forfeiture for High Treason* (1745), and on May 9, 1751, he wrote to Montesquieu to thank him for having read it so closely and for having placed a copy in the royal library (*OC,* 3:1380). Brèthe, 2:333 n. 22, expresses doubts about the thoroughness of Montesquieu's understanding of this dimension of English civil law.

But it has jurisdiction only through the appeals brought to it from the Chancellery Court, whose judgments are carried out if there is no appeal. Commerce having become extensive in England, many claims arose over movable property cases. These cases were remanded to the Chancellery.

Notice also that, around the time of Henry VIII, the Court of Common Pleas did not want to recognize fideicommissum. This word is taken in the same sense as among the Romans. This was a great folly committed by that court: cases of fideicommissum were transferred to the Chancellery.

Notice that in these courts, judgment is made, *primo,* by the feudal law; by the Roman law; and by the customs or practices of England based on previous judgments. Needless to say, acts of Parliament are also used as models, but that source is not of great moment.

Lawyers earn a great deal in England, especially those who represent the Crown, and M. Yorke told me that the chancellor, his father, being {I believe} solicitor general, earned up to seven thousand guineas a year, and that a renowned lawyer could earn up to five thousand guineas. The reason is the large number of cases that a lawyer can try. They do not have big trial folders[2] sent to their office, as in France, for studying the case. There is another category of professionals employed in that task, who bring the lawyer a memorandum all prepared. He adds his citations, his observations, and he tries the case; and that puts him in a position to try a very large number of cases.

Under the reign, I believe, of Charles II, all military laws were eliminated, and this was not, it seems to me, a big loss. When M. Yorke told me that a foreigner could not understand a single word of Lord Cook and of Littleton,[3] I told him I had observed that, compared with the old and feudal laws of England, it would not be difficult for me to understand them—no more than those of all other nations, because, since all the laws of Europe are gothic, they all had the same origin and were of the same nature; that on the other hand, modern laws and jurisprudence are difficult to understand, because times and circumstances have changed and modified the gothic law within the country, and that law has everywhere taken on a Country and changed like the political laws. He agreed.

---

2. *Sac de procès,* literally, trial sacks, where legal papers were kept.—HC

3. Sir Edward Coke (1552–1634), leading legal authority in early Stuart England, and Sir Thomas Littleton (d. 1481), on whom Coke wrote a 1628 commentary. For more, see Steve Sheppard, ed., *The Selected Writings of Sir Edward Coke,* 3 vols. (Indianapolis: Liberty Fund, 2004).—HC

By acts of Parliament, it has been decided that all real estate in England is *socage,* which has done very great damage to the feudal law. All patrimonial justice has been eliminated, all *nobility* of estates also, or dependencies as well. On the one hand, everything is royal justice; on the other, everything is commonalty.[4] They have just eliminated, in 1748 and 1749, all seigneurial justice in Scotland, which is more consistent with a government that is taking after the republican form and moving away from monarchy.

M. Yorke told me that the best work written on feudal laws was *Cragii Jus feudale,*[5] written in the time of James I, and that there was a fine new edition; that this work was clear and luminous.

[**1646**] Mme de R—— was complaining about some pimples. I said to her: "Ha! what are some pimples on a face that has behind it such a beautiful soul."

[**1647**] I said of Astruc and d'Aube:[1] "d'Aube thinks only about what he is saying, and not at all about what you are saying. Astruc thinks only about what you are saying, and never about what he is saying.

"I like d'Aube better. He does not offend you, but he bores you; Astruc bores you and offends you." {I add: d'Aube seeks the true, Astruc the false.}

[**1648**] Lord Bath told me that, in the war that the Duke of Marlborough and Prince Eugene waged in Flanders,[1] a gambler, who became mad and devout, thought he could gamble only against Jesus Christ. He lost ten thousand florins against Jesus Christ, and wanting to pay, he went to find the Jesuits, who told him that being from the Company of Jesus, they would receive the money. He counted it out, took his receipt, and went away. Two weeks later, he came back and said he had played again and had won twenty thousand florins from Jesus Christ. The Jesuits did not want

4. The French term is *roture,* which means non-noble.—HC

5. The first edition of *Jus feudale* [Feudal Law] by Thomas Craig (1538–1608) was published in 1603.

[**1647**]

1. Jean Astruc (1684–1760), physician and theologian (see *pensées* 979 and 1243); René-François Richer d'Aube (1668–1752), jurisconsult and magistrate, nephew of Fontenelle, and author of the 1743 *Essai sur les Principes du droit et de la morale* [Essay on the principles of law and morals], which he accused Montesquieu of having plagiarized; he was one of the first to criticize *Laws.* Letters to Montesquieu by Mme de Tencin (December 2, 1748, in *OC,* 3:1149 and 1176) and the chevalier d'Aydie (January 6, 1749, in *OC,* 3:1159) report d'Aube's hostility toward the book.

[**1648**]

1. During the War of the Spanish Succession (1701–13).

to pay. Trial—and by the credit of the order's generals, the Jesuits were obliged to give back what they had received.

[1649] Lord Bath told me that the Nation's debt,[1] in 1749, was 81 million sterling—which, at 4 percent, amounted to about 4 million to pay out in returns; that the amortization fund and the civil list made up about 2 million more; that for this purpose there were earmarked funds, because as the debts have been incurred, a fund for interest payments has been established, and with the interest payments being reduced, the amortization fund has been formed from them—which, consequently, also has funds earmarked for it. The civil list also has its earmarked funds, and for that, there is no need for any act of Parliament or any levy upon the people. Now for extraordinary expenses, such as upkeep for the troops, which are extraordinary expenses, there are funds applied as the Parliament wants, and according to circumstances—such as the land tax, greater or lesser, which reaches 500,000 pounds sterling for each shilling per pound, and a tax, I believe, on beer.

[1650] I am going to offer some reflections on the amortization funds.[1]

It has just been said that interest in England is at 4 percent. Lord Bath told me that they were thinking in England of reducing it to 3½ at first, then to 3, which would raise the amortization fund to 2 million and would mean they would be able to pay the Nation's debt in a short enough time, because of the interest on the interest.

Now I will examine the question, namely, what would be more appropriate: to combine this million in reduction with the amortization fund, or to reduce by a similar amount the taxes levied on the people. This has led me to offer some reflections on the nature of amortization funds.

An amortization fund is good only when it is perpetual. It is perpetual only when it is permanently applied; otherwise, it is an amortization fund that does not amortize. The more continuous a government is, the lighter the amortization fund should be, because fifty years of a continuous government can be equal to two years of a government that is not. I call a *continuous government* one that can make its operations continuous, that

[1649]
1. England's.

[1650]
1. See Montesquieu's *Mémoire sur les dettes de l'Etat adressé au Régent* [Memoir on state debt] (*OC*, 3:23–31) and *Laws*, 22.18, 419.

is, independent of a prince's death or a minister's fall. A State can owe
only up to a certain point. If the State approaches that point, it is in great
danger. Since the smallest danger can raise the interest rate on money, it
borrows only with difficulty, because it is left with only meager funds to
apply as collateral for its loans, and because the old debts fall in value.
There is more. When, through certain efforts, that State could increase a
moderate amortization fund, it should not do so; this is because, making
a sudden large payment, it runs the risk of obliging its subjects to send
their funds abroad, or at least of reducing the capital in the public funds,
which every State should maintain because it is the public wealth. And
when a State is organized in such a way that the citizens have a certain
number of funds invested, you must not suddenly leave a large number
of individuals empty-handed. If that State, by its prudence and its good
government, finds the means to reduce the interest on its public funds, it
must not increase its amortization fund, for reasons that have just been
stated. It is better for it to employ the returns from the interest on public funds in reducing taxes by the same amount, in order to lighten the
burden on lands, commerce, and industry, and reduce the high cost of
manufactures; and thereby to proceed in such a way that the public funds
do not take too much priority over private funds. On the other hand,
one can bring order to the public funds and increase confidence in them;
by increasing the confidence the State vests in its amortization fund, it
will increase the assets in the fund, and one can even say that this is the
same thing as increasing its capital. For that, such a State should enact a
quite simple law: it is a crime of high treason to apply the amortization
fund [to any other use] {or to propose to apply it to any other use} than
to payments on the public debt, for whatever cause, even if the enemy is
at the gates. By this means, one can forget the debt and the amortization
fund by making arrangements for the future with the remaining assets,
because a State that has only certain known assets manages with its assets, and realizing that it cannot touch its debts or its amortization fund,
it conducts itself as if it had that much less power. The postponement
in total payment of the public funds likewise increases, in this case, the
solidity and value of the public funds. The less certain the debt is by its
nature, the more the expectation of prompt payment increases its value.
The more certain it is by its nature, the more the expectation of payment
increases its value.

That way, the State will become free of its debts in a manner that is imperceptible to both itself and its creditors; there will be no sudden shock. Every year, a moderate sum will come in through trade, which will likewise suffice to procure the State an imperceptible increase, which is perhaps better than rapid increases (which are very often difficult to sustain, and which bring about the downfall of some branches even as these branches are forming others); which do not cause nations' jealousy and do not attract their attention; which do not give a State too much boldness and too much confidence in its own strength; which do not make it undertake overly big enterprises—in a word, which give it health, but not too much girth; in a word, which they nourish but do not inflate.

A State that is increasing its strength little by little enjoys prosperity in comparison with States that are preserving theirs, just as the latter does in comparison with those that are losing theirs.

A State that increases its strength all of a sudden is subject to all the disadvantages of a change in fortune, which demands countless other changes; these various other changes demand other principles. Now since wisdom is a sequence of principles that experience has well applied, it is more difficult for a State that enhances its fortunes rapidly to conduct itself with wisdom than a State that enhances its fortunes imperceptibly. {Combine this with other reflections that are in my folder on the new edition of *The Spirit of the Laws.*}[2]

[1651] When one examines the men of our nation, one is surprised to see people who never consider themselves as ruined, and who never consider themselves as wealthy.

As for me, I consider myself fortunate to have —— thousand pounds in income that has nothing to do with anyone.

[1652] Miserable condition of men! Hardly has the mind reached the point of its maturity when the body begins to weaken.

[1653] "My merit has made a breakthrough," said a man who had become wealthy; "I have made more friends since yesterday than I had made in my whole life. How could it be that I was as scorned as I was a week ago! It was probably not my fault; it was the fault of those obscure people, lacking taste and education, whom I was seeing at that time. But surely I will give up bad company; {or else: but surely, I will no longer see them.}"

---

2. These "other reflections" were not found in the notes collected by Henri Barckhausen in *Montesquieu, "l'esprit des lois" et archives de la Brède* (Bordeaux: Michel and Forgeot, 1904).

[**1654**] *Mémoires de Trévoux* (January 1736, article 10) is an inscription (found in Malta, by abbé Guyot from Marne) which is Phoenician, and since all the characters of our Arab numerals are found there (1, 2, 3, 4, 5, 6, 7, 8, 9, 0), abbé Guyot concludes that, after the fashion of the Oriental languages, the numbers were taken from the alphabet; so that 1, in the Phoenician alphabet, was *alep* in the Hebrew alphabet; 2 was the *beth,* etc. He thinks the Arabs, before bringing the numbers we have into Spain, had picked them up from the African peoples, Phoenician in origin, whom they had conquered, considering them more convenient than their ancient Arab numerals.

[**1655**] This was for my work on *Consideration:*[1]

"It is about twenty-five years ago that I offered these reflections to the Bordeaux Academy. The late Marquise de Lambert, whose great and rare qualities will never leave my memory, did this work the honor of taking an interest in it. She gave it a new order, and by the new turns that she imparted to its thoughts and expressions, she elevated my mind up to her own. Since Mme de Lambert's copy was found among her papers after her death, the booksellers, who were not well-informed, have inserted it into her works[2]—and I am delighted that they have done so, so that if chance should make both of these writings pass into posterity, they will be the {eternal} monument of a friendship that touches me much more than would glory."[3]

[**1656**] The King of Sweden:[1]

Illi robur et aes triplex
Circa pectus erat . . .[2]

[1655]

1. The *Mémoire sur la Considération et de la réputation* [Memoir on Consideration and reputation] was read by Montesquieu at the Bordeaux Academy on April 25, 1725; it was reviewed in the *Bibliothèque française* in May–June 1726, p. 47. It was edited for the first time in *Deux opuscules de Montesquieu* [Two small works of Montesquieu] in 1891 (47–56); the manuscript, sold in 1939, seems to be lost. See *OC,* 3:201–8.

2. The *Works* of Mme de Lambert published in 1748 contained *Discours sur la différence qu'il y a de la Réputation à la Considération* [Discourse on the difference between Reputation and Consideration], which was considered tantamount to plagiarism of Montesquieu's text. But in order not to tarnish his friend's memory, Montesquieu treats the affair as appears here.

3. See also *pensées* 484, 770, and 1820.—HC

[1656]

1. Charles XII (r. 1697–1718).

2. Horace, *Odes,* I.iii.9–10: "Oak and three layers of brass were wrapped round the heart of that man."

M. le Prince:[3]

Qualem ministrum fulminus alitem.[4]

Luther:

Caelo tonantem credidimus Jovem.[5]

Charles V:

Huic, post tres consultatus et totidem triumphos, fortunae fuit exitus, tantum in illo viro a se discordante Fortuna, ut eadem tellus, quae modo victoriis defuerat, pene deesset ad sepulturam.[6]

Sermones Marianae, by Benedict XIII:[7]

Caelum ipsum petimus stultitia.[8]

Civil Wars of France, by d'Aubigné:[9]

Neque
Per nostrum patimur scelus
Iracunda Jovem ponere fulmina.[10]

Life of Philip, Duke of Orléans:

Atque metus omnes et inexorabile fatum
Subjecit pedibus, strepitumque Acherontis avari.[11]

---

3. Louis II de Bourbon, prince de Condé (1621–86), called the Grand Condé.
4. Horace, *Odes,* IV.iv.1: "Like the winged deliverer of the thunderbolt."
5. Horace, *Odes,* III.v.1: "Because Jove thunders in heaven we have always believed."
6. Velleius Paterculus (ca. 20 B.C.–A.D. 31), *Roman history,* II.53: "So died this man after three consuls and as many triumphs . . . Such was the inconsistency of fortune in his case, that he who but a short time before had found no more lands to conquer now found none for his burial."
7. Pietro Francesco Orsini, Pope Benedict XIII from 1724 to 1730.
8. Horace, *Odes,* I.iii.38: "In our folly we aspire to the sky itself."
9. The *Universal history* in 3 vols. (1616–20; Montesquieu owned the second edition of 1726; see *Catalogue,* 2905).
10. Horace, *Odes,* I.iii.38–40: "And by our crimes we do not allow Jove to lay aside his bolts of wrath."
11. Virgil, *Georgics,* II.491–92: "and he has cast beneath his feet all fear and unyielding Fate, and the howls of hungry Acheron!"

Life of Queen Mary of England:[12]

> *Tantum Religio potuit suadere malorum.*[13]

Turkish religion:[14]

> *Te nascente, novum Parcae cecinere puellis*
> *Servitium.*[15]

Poland:

> *Magis sine domino, quam in libertate.*
> (Tacitus, book II)[16]

Muscovites:[17]

> *Saxa—quis hoc credat?—*
> *Ponere duritiem copere . . .*[18]

Chinese:[19]

> *Major et longinquo reverentia.*[20]

12. Mary Stuart, that is, Mary I of Scotland (Mary Queen of Scots; 1542–87).

13. Lucretius, *On the Nature of things:* "So potent was Superstition in persuading to evil deeds." See also *pensée* 1636.

14. In *Catalogue,* p. 226, Montesquieu applies this quotation to *Turcicae historiae scriptores et mahometanae* [Writers of Turkish and Mohammedan history].

15. Fragment of Sulpicia, according to Montesquieu's *Catalogue;* the passage is by Tibullus in *Catullus, Tibullus, Pervigilium Veneris,* III.xi.3–4: "When thou wast born, the voices of the Fates proclaimed that now there was new slavery for woman . . ."

16. Tacitus, *Annals,* II.iv: "rather without a ruler than at liberty."

17. In the *Catalogue,* p. 229, Montesquieu applies this citation to the *Moscovitarum rerum scriptores* [Writers on Muscovite matters].

18. Ovid, *Metamorphoses,* I.400–401: "And the stones (who would believe it . . .) began to lose their hardness . . ."

19. In the *Catalogue,* p. 229, Montesquieu applies this quotation to the *Sinarum rerum scriptores* [Writers on Chinese matters].

20. Tacitus, *Annals,* I.xlvii: "always most venerable from a distance."

Spain:[21]

Effice quidquid
Corpore contigero fulvum vertatur in aurum.
(Ovid, *Metamorphoses*)[22]

The Pope:[23]

Rex Anius, rex idem hominum Phoebique sacerdos.
(Virgil, book I)[24]

The Jews:[25]

Eorum prospera res, regnante Saturno.
(Tacitus)[26]

The Monks:[27]

Ego odi homines ignava opera et philosophica sententia.
(Pacuvius, in Aulus-Gellius)[28]

Juriconsulti:[29]

Monstrum horrendum, ingens.[30]
Rescindere nunquam

---

21. In the *Catalogue*, p. 231, Montesquieu applies this citation to the *Hispanicarum rerum scriptores* [Writers on Spanish matters].

22. Ovid, *Metamorphoses*, XI.103–4: "'Grant that whatsoever I may touch with my body may be turned to yellow gold.'"

23. In the *Catalogue*, p. 14, Montesquieu applies this quotation to the *Scriptores historiae ecclesiasticae* [Writers on ecclesiastical history].

24. Virgil, *Aeneid*, III.80: "King Anius—at once king of the people and priest of Phoebus."

25. In the *Catalogue*, p. 6, Montesquieu applies this citation to the *Interpretes critici et commentatores Judaei* [Critical interpreters and Jewish commentators].

26. "Their prosperity under the reign of Saturn."

27. In the *Catalogue*, p. 97, Montesquieu applies this quotation to the *Ascetici* [Ascetics].

28. Aulus-Gellius, *Attic Nights*, XIII.8: "I hate base men who preach philosophy"; cf. *pensée* 1150.

29. In the *Catalogue*, pp. 52, 60, and 183, Montesquieu applies these three brief citations to the *Jurisconsulti*, the *Constitutiones regiae*, and the *Daemonologi, Physionomici, etc.*, respectively.

30. Virgil, *Aeneid*, III.658: "a monster awful . . . huge."

Diis licet acta Deum.
(Ovid)[31]
. . . *Acheronta movebo.*[32]

[1657] What is not useful to the swarm is not useful to the bee.[1]
[1658] Savoy:

> *Quum faber, incertus scamnum faceretne Priapum*
> *Maluit esse Deum . . .*[1]
> (Bolingbroke, at the Treaty of Utrecht)[2]

[1659] . . . And our fortune, though modest, is such that I, you, and yours will always have to love, honor, and serve our prince, and ask of him nothing.[1]
[. . . was in the Parlement of Bordeaux . . .]
the grandest and finest profession that men can practice among men.
. . . that you do not have to blush over your fortune and your birth, and still less to puff yourself up over it.
. . . that we have neither to caress Fortune nor tempt it.
. . . because one is always great with the majesty of virtue and in-nocence.
Since this is the first time my mouth has spoken of these things.
I never wished on you more brilliant employments. I do not wish greater employments on you, my son; one is always great with the majesty of vir-tue and innocence.
[1660] It is much less rare to have a sublime mind than a great soul.

---

31. Ovid, *Metamorphoses*, XIV.784–85: "it is never permitted to gods to undo the acts of gods."
32. Virgil, *Aeneid*, VII.312: "then Hell I will arouse!"

[1657]
1. See *pensée* 1694.

[1658]
1. Horace, *Satires*, I.viii.2–3: "When the carpenter, doubtful whether to make a stool or a Priapus, chose that I be a god."
2. "Nota that there are others at page . . ." (M.); cf. *pensée* 1786. The Treaties of Utrecht ended the War of the Spanish Succession (1701–13); the Tory Bolingbroke negotiated an accommodating agree-ment that Whigs attacked as pro-French.

[1659]
1. This entry is addressed to Montesquieu's son, Jean-Baptiste de Secondat; see *pensée* 5.

[**1661**] ON HAPPINESS.[1] In his seraglio, the king of Morocco has white women, black women, and yellow women.[2] The poor man! He only just needs one color.

[**1662**] ON HAPPINESS. A man went to ask the Duke of Orléans for permission to wear a special court outfit. "I approve," he answered, "provided your tailor agrees." That's the way it is with all the things we desire or possess in life. There is always some tailor who does not agree.

[**1663**] Here is a good line by Henry IV, and I believe it was cited by Lord Bolingbroke. The King asked the ambassador from Spain if his master had any mistresses. "Sire," the ambassador said gravely, "the King, my master, fears God and respects the Queen." "What?" said Henry IV, "doesn't he have enough virtues to get one vice pardoned?"

[**1664**] To explain what a *Committee* is, it must be understood that there are private committees, that is, deputies named for private business. But there is something else. Business is treated in the House of Commons as a chamber, and at that time, the Speaker of the House is in charge, and a member can speak only once on the same matter; or else the House forms itself into a committee, and in that case, the Speaker descends from his chair, and the affair is discussed in such a manner that everyone can speak as many times as he thinks appropriate, and the House names a President instead of the Speaker; and after the matter has been adequately discussed, the Speaker resumes his place, and they deliberate in the House. All affairs that concern contributions to the sovereign are treated in the committee of the whole. Every time one brings a bill, it is deliberated on three times; three times people can speak for and against the bill.

[**1665**] M. Yorke, lawyer, son of the chancellor, has well explained to me what the bill of attainder was.[1]

It must be understood that the House of Commons sometimes makes itself a party against a private individual and comes to accuse him before the House of Lords, proceeds against him before them, and performs the function of lawyer through some member of its body. In that case, it is prosecutor and not judge.

[1661]

1. See *pensée* 1675.

2. This sentence is taken up in *Laws*, 16.6; according to Dodds, its source is Francis Brooks, whose *Barbarian cruelty* (1693) came out in a French edition in 1737.

[1665]

1. Montesquieu's discussion is in *Laws*, 12.19; see also *pensée* 1645 and n. 1.

Sometimes, it proceeds by a bill of attainder. In that case, it is acting as legislator and not judge. It must be understood that in all the tribunals of the Realm, it is not enough that there be evidence against the accused such that the judges be convinced. This evidence must also be of proper form, that is to say, according to the law. Thus, there have to be two witnesses to convict an accused; any other proof whatsoever would not suffice, even written evidence. Now, if a man presumed guilty of a high crime has found a method of sidelining the witnesses in such a way that it is impossible to have him condemned according to the law, one may bring against him a private bill of attainder—that is, pass a private law on his person. And here is how one proceeds:

A member of the House of Commons declares that a man has committed a crime, guarantees that he can prove it, and proposes to pass a bill of attainder against him. At that point, they proceed to this bill as with any other bill. The accused has his lawyers speak against the bill, and anyone in the chamber may speak for the bill. If the bill passes in the House of Commons, it is brought to the House of Lords. And there, they proceed as in the House of Commons. If it is rejected in the House of Lords, the case is over, and there is no bill. If the King rejects it, there is again no bill. If the King gives his consent, the law is passed, and the accused is condemned, even though the evidence was not according to due process, but was merely among the evidence that convinced the two Houses and the King. The bill may also begin in the House of Lords, but this is rare.

[**1666**] [Did not make it into my discourse entitled *Lysimachus:* The laws were silent; necessity spoke; and we obeyed.][1]

[**1667**] It is very expensive to live in Lisbon, even though people live for practically nothing in the provinces. This is because the realm is only a strip of land, and the rivers enter it widthwise. The provinces that should supply it are separated from the capital. Thus, a great deal must be drawn from abroad. The King's palace overlooks the Tagus. The least squadron—two English vessels—could overthrow it. M. de Chavigny was saying there would be nothing so easy as taking the King.[1] There is a special gate for leaving the Palace. The reigning King, who did not want people to know what he was doing, never wanted to let a sentinel be placed there.

[**1666**]

1. See *pensées* 563 and 2161; for *Lysimachus,* see Allen, 76–81.

[**1667**]

1. Anne-Théodore Chevignard de Chavigny (1687–1771), ambassador to Lisbon from 1740 to 1749. The king being discussed is John V (r. 1707–50).

Portuguese workers carry out what they do well enough, but they do not know how to invent. They chisel stone very well and make very fine moldings.

The system of that court is one of perpetual neutrality.

[**1668**] People are so accustomed to hearing certain things spouted out with an air of authority that they find themselves defeated before they begin the contest. Respect has taken the place of examination. These propositions have begun to be accepted as true, and the host of objections that have been presented have been regarded merely as objections. These objections themselves have become contemptible; since they are presented to everyone, smart people have been ashamed to present them. They no longer make an impression because they are too natural, that is, because they are too strong.

[**1669–1674**] THIS DID NOT MAKE IT INTO THE "ROMANS."

[**1669**] Catiline's conspiracy was a design that was ill-conceived, ill-digested, difficult to begin, impossible to end, and less the effect of ambition than of impotence and despair.

But it is remarkable in being such a general conspiracy to destroy Rome, the Republic. All those to whom Sulla had given land and all those from whom he had taken it away, all the great who had ambition, all those who had no property, and all those who hated Pompey, all those of the Senatorial party, all those who were for the People desired a revolution.

We find in Cicero's letters a quite authentic monument of Roman corruption . . .[1]

Catiline's conspiracy is famous only for the number of wicked men who formed it, the great characters who sought to encourage it; for otherwise, it was a design that was ill-conceived, ill-digested, and less the effect of ambition than of impotence and despair.[2]

[**1670**] Being consul, Sulla drew lots for the provinces with his colleague and was commissioned to go off and make war on Mithridates.[1] To deprive him of it, Marius sought to introduce more disorder into the Republic than there was already. He won over the tribune Sulpicius,[2] and after summoning the common people to Rome from the Italian cities with

[**1669**]
1. Cicero, *Letters to Atticus*, XVIII.4; cf. *Considerations*, IX and X.
2. See *pensée* 707.—HC

[**1670**]
1. Mithridates VI Eupator the Great (ca. 132–63 B.C.), defeated by Pompey definitively in 66 B.C.
2. Publius Sulpicius Rufus (124–88 B.C.).

new laws and with these acts of violence, he arranged to receive Sulla's commission. [He spread out the eight tribes of the peoples of Italy . . .]

That man rushed to the army; that man rushed to Capua, where the legions intended for him were, and he so well represented the offense that Marius wanted to commit against them—of giving the honors and advantages of that war to other soldiers—that they followed him to Rome, whence he expelled Marius and his partisans.[3]

[**1671**] Justinian and another prince that I will not name are two princes that historians can praise and blame as much as they want.

[**1672**] One might perhaps want me to go into detail here on the political government[1] of the Roman Republic. But I will refer to Polybius, who has admirably explained what part the consuls, the Senate, the People took in that government—all the better in that he speaks of a time when the Republic had just escaped such great perils and was presently doing such great things.

[**1673**] The places accorded by posterity are subject, like others, to the whims of fortune. Woe betide the reputation of any prince who is oppressed by a party that becomes the dominant one, or who has attempted to destroy a prejudice that survives him.[1]

If ever a body, which has much reputation in the world, should— entirely at its leisure—write our modern history, I believe that the princes who have depended upon it for their consciences and their affairs will loom quite large, and the others quite small.[2]

[**1674**] The people of Rome,[1] with an always-active hatred toward the nobles, changed means without changing ends. They thought of debasing them at first by reducing their privileges; then, by increasing the authority of one alone.

---

3. "Appian, *On the Civil War,* book I (55–60)" (M.). See *Considerations,* XI, 101, for Montesquieu's use of the late first-century Greek historian Appian on the conflict between Marius and Sulla. See also *Laws,* 11.18, 183.

[**1672**]
1. First version: "civil government"

[**1673**]
1. The first paragraph is from *Considerations,* I, 26; the second is similar to *pensée* 713.—HC
2. The reference seems to be to the Jesuits, whom Montesquieu treats frequently elsewhere in this collection; see *pensées* 11, 55, 104, 180, 293, 394, 395, 453, 482, 544, 581, 713, 715, 728, 730, 1038, 1223, 1301, 1302 n. 52, 1959, and especially *pensées* 180, 395, and 728 for overtly critical treatments.—HC

[**1674**]
1. See *Considerations,* VIII, 83.

The people of Athens had a natural jealousy toward all those who served them with some glory. They would get rid of them once, so as not to fear them all the time. In Rome, on the other hand, the people worshipped those who by their exploits had placed themselves above others; always showering them with new honors, they themselves seemed to want to lead these men on to tyranny. This is because the people of Athens, composed of select citizens, felt themselves free, but that immense populace of Rome considered themselves slaves. The former feared nothing but the ambition of their leading citizens; the latter hoped only for the favor of those who had done great things, and every time they heard talk about the victories of some general, they summoned him into their hearts against a haughty nobility. Since the people of Athens were not numerous, sensible people made themselves heard and found the means to remind the people of their interests; but that populace became so immense that they could not be informed, advised or corrected.

The Senate was in the sort of situation where it was not even defended by those who composed it. Many, who wanted to make their fortune, agitated the people as the tribunes did, and most had so many other interests that their interests in the Senate were constantly subordinate. A few people who had distinguished themselves in civil functions, who were of limited fortune, were alone the true senators. But love of the Republic had become awkward. Everyone followed Sulla, Marius, Caesar, Pompey, Crassus, while only Favonius and Cato remained to speak of the former customs and the laws.[2]

[1675] ON HAPPINESS.[1]

To be happy, one must have a goal, because this is the means of giving life to our actions. They even become more important according to the nature of the goal, and that way, they occupy our souls more fully.

Look at that good line in Plutarch: "Yes! if happiness were for sale."[2]

One is happy in the pursuit of a goal, even though experience reveals that one is not happy with the goal itself; but that illusion is good enough for us. The reason for this is that our soul is a sequence of ideas. It suffers when it is

---

2. "Nota that other fragments have been put on page 456 that did not make it into the *Romans*" (M.); see *pensée* 2183.

[1675]

1. See *pensées* 1661–62.

2. Plutarch, "On Love of Wealth," in *Moralia,* VII, 1 (523D).

not occupied, as if that sequence were interrupted and someone were threatening its existence. What causes us not to be happy is that we would like to be like the gods; but it is quite good enough for us to be happy like men.

Those who, because of their status, do not have necessary occupations must seek to give themselves some. The most suitable one for those who have had an education—reading—takes from us some hours that would be unbearable in the emptiness of each day, and can often make the hours spent at it delightful.

The big cities have this advantage, that you can always change course. Have you chosen your company badly? You find others.

In republics, one has friends and enemies; one has neither in monarchies. In the former, there is mutual hatred; in the latter, mutual contempt. In the former, friendship is founded on interests; in the latter, it is founded on pleasures.

One is happier with amusements than with pleasures. This is because amusements give us a respite from both pains and pleasures.

The soul has its existence to manage, like the body.

Animals are types of stringed instruments; their nerves serve the function of strings in musical instruments. Those who play the latter need to give them the proper tension in order to play them. If this is not found in man, the commerce between the soul and the object is in some sense interrupted, or at least that commerce becomes so burdensome to him that his condition is unbearable to him.

Great lords usually have a great dearth of pleasures of the soul. This is why they are much attached to the pleasures of the body, because it is these almost alone that are favored by their status, and that can result from their grandeur. But that same grandeur puts the amusements of the mind at such a distance from them that they do not reach them. Their grandeur commands them to be bored. Conquests would be necessary for their amusement; but their neighbors prohibit them from amusing themselves. Charles V and King Victor[3] sought retreat, to save them from the trouble they were in. They soon found that retreat was more unbearable to them than their anxieties, and that it was better to govern the world than to be bored by it, that a state of agitation is more fitting for the soul than

---

3. Charles V, Habsburg emperor (r. 1517–55) and Victor-Amadeus II, king of Sardinia (r. 1720–30).

a state of annihilation. If some Carthusians are happy, this is certainly not because they are tranquil; it is because their souls are thrown into action by great truths.[4] Impressed by the condition of our life, they can experience its joy—just as a wretched prince, ousted from the throne, becomes happy when he sees that throne become accessible to him.

Let us seek to accommodate ourselves to this life; it is not up to this life to accommodate itself to us. Let us be neither too empty nor too full.

If we are destined to bore ourselves, let us know how to bore ourselves. And for this, let us correctly assess the pleasures we are losing, and let us not subtract their value from the pleasures we can procure for ourselves. When I became blind, I understood immediately that I would know how to be blind.

One can expect that in most misfortunes, it is only a matter of knowing how to change course.

In that case, most misfortunes will fit into the framework of a happy life. With a bit of reflection, it is very easy to get rid of sad emotions.

Rousseau[5] has said it very well: "I have seen that it is easier to suffer than to take revenge."

Most people hurt you without having the least intention of hurting you. They send shafts of enmity, but they are not your enemies. They spoke against you, but they meant only to speak. It was one of their needs, and they satisfied it. They spoke against you because they were powerless to be silent. Those people who have shown you little good will would gladly serve you if you urged them to, and would rebuke with all their hearts those they have praised against you. Do justice! Are you made to be praised by everyone? What someone has said—is it not offensive because you have too much sensitivity? Do you not begin to deserve it as soon as you have the weakness to complain about it? If someone has not shown you enough consideration, they are impolite; it is not you who is impolite. Even if it were true that someone lacked esteem for you, no one has obliged you to measure yourself by the degree of esteem that a certain person has for you. You are perfectly capable of not holding yourself to that price scale. Most scorn is worth only scorn. The things that bring dishonor have that effect only because it is a given that one cannot scorn them, and that not to

4. *Mise en activité,* "thrown into action," was (according to Féraud) an informal, journalistic expression.—HC

5. Jean-Baptiste Rousseau (1671–1741), the poet.—HC

indicate one's resentment is to accept them. Thus, do not array against you the whole business of dishonor; cling with precision to what it prescribes.

Do you have a nascent passion? Compare carefully the sequence of happiness and the sequence of unhappiness that can naturally result from it. I am not talking with religion in mind; there would be nothing to deliberate about there. I am talking with this life in mind. But at least, if you have to entrust your happiness, to whom do you entrust it? And is this not the situation in which love of yourself commands you to choose well? It is very rarely true that the heart is made only for one, that you are fatally destined for one alone, and that a little reason cannot destine you for another.

In treating happiness, I thought I should take common ideas, content myself with making others feel what I was feeling, and bring into others' souls the peace of my soul. You do not need a lot of philosophy to be happy; it is just a matter of taking up some tolerably sound ideas. A minute's attention per day is enough, and for that, you do not need to go into a private study to collect yourself; these things are learned in the tumult of the world better than in a study.

I have seen people die of distress at not being given positions that they would have been obliged to turn down if offered to them (Lord Bolingbroke).

Fine words of Seneca: "*Sic praesentibus voluptatibus utaris, ut futuris non noceas.*"[6]

Has a mother lost her beauty? You see she prides herself on that of her daughter.

One is happy in the social circle in which one lives—witness the galley slaves. Each individual makes his own circle, in which he places himself to be happy.

Just as pleasure is often mixed with pain, pain is mixed with pleasure. It is incredible how delightful false afflictions become when the soul senses that it is attracting attention and compassion; this is a pleasant feeling. This expedient of the soul comes through quite ingenuously in play. While one person prides himself on winning and thinks himself a more important figure because he is the winner, you see the losers seek endless petty consolations by their petty whining, their petty heckling of all around them. They are talking about themselves; that is enough for the soul.

---

6. "Use present pleasures in such a way as not to do harm to future ones."

There is more. True afflictions have their delights; true afflictions are never boring, because they keep the soul very busy. It is a pleasure when they like to talk; it is a pleasure when they like to keep silent, and it is such a great pleasure that you cannot distract anyone from the pain without causing him greater pain.

The pleasures of reading, when the soul identifies itself in objects, with the objects in which it is interested. There is a kind of love in which the depiction has given more pleasure to those who have read about it than to those who have experienced it. There are few gardens so agreeable that they have given more pleasure to those who walk around in them than is found in the gardens of Alcidas.

The soul is an eternal worker, which labors without end for itself.

As for women's beauty, there are few men who, when their passions are tranquil, are not sent into more raptures by a beautiful portrait than by the sight of the original.

[**1676**] I said it is very natural to believe there are intelligences superior to us. For in assuming the chain of creatures we know, and the different degrees of intelligence from the oyster up to ourselves, it would be the most extraordinary thing if we formed the last link, and if, among creatures, it was we ourselves who held first place, and were the end of the chain, and there were no intermediate being between us and the oyster that could reason as we do. It would always be 2, 3, 400,000, or 400,000,000 to one against this being true.[1]

It is true that we are first among the beings we know. But when we conclude from this that we are the first among beings, we are parading our ignorance, and the fact that we do not know about communication of our globe with another, nor even everything that exists on our globe.

M. Fontenelle has a very nice idea about this. He says it may be that the intelligences that have occasioned all the stories about communication with unknown beings cannot live for long on our globe, and that it's like divers who can go into the sea but cannot live in the sea. Thus, communication with aerial Spirits, for example, will have been short; it will have been rare; but it will have occurred sometimes.

[**1677**] In a conversation among M. Fontenelle, M. Yorke, and me,

[**1676**]

1. Montesquieu makes the same comparison in an October 12, 1753, letter to Mme Du Deffand (*OC,* 3:1475).

M. Fontenelle asked me to explain the origin of the idea of the purity and impurity of bodies {that bring a sullying to the soul}.

Here is the explanation I gave.[1]

The origin of the purity and impurity of things arises because it is natural to have had an aversion to things disagreeable to our senses. Mud, a dead body, a dog, women's monthlies—all this must have seemed to us to sully the bodies of those who touched it. In times when people scarcely had an idea of the nature of the soul and its real distinction with the body—a distinction which has hardly been well established except since Descartes—one could naturally believe that what sullied the body also sullied the soul and placed the affected being in sort of a state of sin, and rendered it disagreeable to God, just as the sullying made us disagreeable to each other. But when the soul was well distinguished from the body, it was clearly seen that only the body is sullied.

M. Fontenelle's idea is different, and it is very ingenious if not solid. He says it arises because murderers were usually stained with blood; that in the early days, when men were dressed in animal skins, a great deal of washing was needed to get rid of the blood; that those who were impure, that is, stained with blood, were the murderers, and that men got used to linking these two ideas—crime and staining—and thus moved from one idea to the other.

We then spoke of sacrifices, and I said that the idea of sacrifices arose because since God is master of everything, one cannot give him anything except by denying it to oneself. {M. Yorke said this idea arose from human sacrifice; that people had believed a man could take upon him all the sins of others, and that they had then believed that the animals being sacrificed were being burdened in like manner.}

I also think people may have believed that divinities enjoyed the odor from the victims' blood and their burnt flesh and smoke.}

[1678] SPAIN. Patino made a blunder, namely, to put all naval forces at Cadiz.[1] That cost more. The sailors of Biscay and Catalonia have 200 leagues before arriving home, from the time they have disembarked.

The king of France does not have all his vessels in a single port.

[1677]

1. See Usbek's treatment of this issue in *PL*, XVII.

[1678]

1. Joseph Patino (1667–1736), Spanish minister of the navy and the Indies from 1726 until his death.

[**1679**]   The air is very bad in Madrid. It is losing population constantly. Likewise, it is only repopulated by the foreigners who go there. Child-births are hardly happy there; women have miscarriages and die. There are barely two children per family; in Italy, three; in the more northern countries, four.

[**1680**]   In the *Calendar,* Ovid has Lucretia recount Tarquin's attack to her relatives. When she comes to his crime, the poet says:

> *Caetera restabant; voluit cum dicere flevit,*
> *Et matronales erubuere genae.*[1]

I have heard these two lines criticized in two ways: some claim that this last line is useless and only weakens the effect; others say that the order of things is confused, and that the blushing should have been put before the tears. As for myself, I say these two lines are wonderful, perhaps the loveli-est Ovid wrote; and that however he might have turned them, they would have been less lovely if the poet had preemptively responded to one or the other of these criticisms.

As for the first, I will say that there are several sources of beauty in rela-tion to works of the mind, that one must make distinctions, and that one must not make a thought belong to one kind of beauty when it belongs to another. It is true that there are occasions when the beauty of the thought consists in brevity. The "Let him die!" of old Horace, the "Me!" of Medea,[2] have a beauty that depends on brevity, by reason of the fact that it concerns a forceful action and a moment when the soul is in a kind of transport, and when it expresses everything in a moment because it seems to have only a moment to itself, because it is outside itself. The speech should be im-petuous because the soul is impetuous. But here, it is a matter of Lucretia's grief—a slow and silent passion, a passion one describes, a state of the soul one depicts. And here, it was not enough to make Lucretia weep; she had to be made to blush. We are too struck with that type of beauty that makes us desire that everything end in an epigram. Everything does not have to end in an epigram. Here, the epigram is not in the last words; if one wants an epigram, it is in the whole.

[**1680**]
1. "And a blush o'erspread her matron cheeks." Ovid, *Fastes,* II.827–28; cf. *pensée* 1474.
2. Corneille, *Horace,* III.v.48, and *Médée,* I.iv.316–17.

As for those who say the order is confused, it is not at all confused, because it could not be otherwise. The poet has to depict Lucretia's condition. It is wonderful in that, as soon as she arrives at what seems to her the most frightful detail, she can no longer speak, she weeps. The poet thus had two things to do: to depict Lucretia's condition, and all the impressions grief was making upon her. Lucretia stops when she has come to the most frightful idea, and she begins to weep. This is what the poet had to express at the outset—whether the blushing led up to the tears, whether the tears ensued upon the blushing, whether (which is much more natural) the blushing and tears were provoked at the same time. Now here, the poet was not obliged to follow the order that would involve beginning with the weakest expression in order to move to the strongest expression; one must follow not the order of the thing, but the order of the thought. Since he had to make Lucretia silent, Ovid had to begin by making her weep, because it was tears and not blushing that prevented her from speaking. The order of things must be taken from this: Lucretia was inevitably going to blush, and the poet was bound to say so; but he neither would nor could say so until afterward. These two simultaneous emotions have, here in this particular case, a particular order. Change the order and put: "The rest had to be said, but when she wanted to speak, she blushed and wept," and the entire thought is ruined. "When she wanted to speak, she blushed." The effect of the blushing is not to prevent speaking; it is the tears that have that effect. Thus, it is essential to begin by halting the speeches with her sobbing. But the depiction demands that the poet describe Lucretia's blushing, and he does it with the most beautiful line in the world:

Et matronales erubuere genae.

[1681] I have read a translation of Homer's *Odyssey* by M. de La Valterie; I have not compared it with that of Mme Dacier. It seems to me that this translation is done with more ardor, and I admit that in reading it I felt enormously enchanted, such that I do not remember Mme Dacier's translation making me feel the same way.[1] But I will compare them. I have been told that M. de La Valterie's translation is not accurate. That says noth-

---

[1681]
1. Fr. La Valterie's translation of the *Odyssey* appeared in 1681; that of Mme Dacier, in 1731.

ing against Homer. For if, in removing the literalism obstacle and giving Homer some genius and some French expressiveness, one has made him more pleasing, then one has made him more similar to himself. For no one has ever said that Homer did not employ in his poem all the charms of the Greek language, which cannot be conveyed in another language. Thus, the substance of the poem remains wonderful. In vain would one put similar charms into a bad poem, the poem will still be bad.

[1682] The spirit of conversation is what is called *esprit* among the French. It consists of a dialogue, usually gay, in which each person, without listening to each other much, speaks and responds, and where everything is treated in a manner that is choppy, rapid, and lively. The style and tone of conversation are learned—that is, the dialogue style. There are nations in which the spirit of conversation is entirely unknown. Such are those nations in which people do not live together, and those in which gravity is the foundation of mores.

What is called *esprit* among the French is therefore not *esprit,* but a particular kind of *esprit.* In itself, *esprit* is good sense combined with enlightenment. Good sense is the just comparison of things, and the distinction between the same things in their absolute and relative conditions.

[1683] I will always rank among my commandments never to speak of self in vain.

[1684] A man who was listening to an old shyster recount his exploits said to him: "I understand from all this, Sir, that if you demand half my estate, I will leave it to you; if you demand all of it, I will kill you."

That man was a great philosopher and was reasoning perfectly well.

[1685] [Fragments that did not make it into *The Spirit of the Laws.*]

[1686] I would not at all be of greater fortune. But as for the fortunes of those business men:

Non equidem invideo; miror magis . . . [1]

[1687] I cannot understand how princes so easily imagine they are everything, and how peoples are so given to believing they are nothing.

[1688] Chirac used to be asked if commerce with women is unhealthy.[1]

[1686]
1. Virgil, *Eclogues,* I.11: "Well, I grudge you not—rather I marvel."
[1688]
1. Pierre Chirac (1652–1732), physician to Louis XV.

He would say: "No, provided you don't take drugs; but let me alert you that change is a drug."

He was right, and this is well proven by the seraglios of the Orient.

[**1689**] I was saying that, up to seven years {or six}, nothing should be taught to children, and that even this could be dangerous; that you must think only of amusing them, which is the sole felicity at that age. Children receive the ideas furnished by the senses from everywhere. They are very attentive, because many things surprise them, and for that reason they are extremely curious. Thus, you must think only of distracting them and relieving them of their attention through pleasure. They engage in all the reflection that is within their capacity; their extraordinary progress in language proves evidence of it. Thus, when you want to make them share your own reflections, you impede theirs, which nature makes them engage in. Your art disturbs the process of nature. You pull them away from the objects of attention they give themselves, so they will pay attention to you. The former please them; the latter displease them. You plunge them into abstract ideas, for which they lack understanding. They have particular ideas, and you generalize them before their time. For example, the ideas of happiness, justice, integrity—all of that is beyond their ken. Don't make them see anything bad! You have nothing else to do. At a certain age, the brain or the mind develops all of a sudden. Work on it at that point, and you will do more in a quarter of an hour than you would have done in six months up to that time. Let the body and mind be formed by nature.

[**1690**] Materials that did not make it into *The Spirit of the Laws.*

PUBLIC BANKS AND TRADING COMPANIES.[1] In the manner of Giannone, who wrote the *Civil History of the Realm of Naples,* could I here offer that of the realm of Algiers?[2] That history is so short that it could scarcely bore the reader. It is true that it has very little variety. A few thousand caning sessions more in one reign than in another make up all the difference in events. There is only one incident that might be transmitted to posterity.

The dey Mehmet-Géry was a young man. He had a Christian slave who often supported him from the wealth and commerce of several European states. That struck him; he was indignant to see that he was the absolute

[**1690**]

1. On chartered companies and the banks that service them, see *Laws,* 20.10.

2. Pietro Giannone (1676–1748), whose history was published in 1723; see *Voyages* (*OC,* 2:1162).

master of a large country, but that he had no money. At first, he had his prime minister strangled; the latter had said to him, while shrugging his shoulders, that he was no poorer than his predecessors, nor could he be any richer. He chose a new vizier, who spoke to him this way in council:

"You've put me in the ministry in place of a man who didn't know how to conduct either his affairs or yours. It's been two nights already that I've spent devising a plan that will distinguish your reign forever. It's a matter of setting up a bank in Algiers, so that all the money in the country will be in a public depository. The whole problem consists in engaging the merchants to bring it there. For they're scoundrels, who are always afraid of being insulted somehow; bad subjects, who overlook nothing to deprive you of what they have, and who'd see you hanging around the streets before offering you ten ducats. There are expedients for all of them. I'll have them all abducted one night, they'll be weighed down with chains, and they'll be beaten with a stick a hundred times a day until they've declared their money. In its place, we'll give them a paper that will be signed by the six most senior military officers. I don't doubt that we'd effect a violent setback to Europe's banks, which can barely support themselves because the merchants who form them are constantly defying the Government and, without being courageous, are as insolent as janissaries; whereas our people will be very flexible. If this plan succeeds, I have another that will bring still more honor to the Algerian nation. It's to establish a Company of the Indies. Your wives will be covered with precious stones, and you'll see rivers of gold flow into your home. May Mohammed, servant of the powerful God, assist you!"

He sat down. An old counselor rose, and after placing his hands on his chest, bending over, and bowing his head, he said in a lower voice:

"Lord, I don't approve of your minister's plan; if the military knew you had money, they would strangle you the next day."

He sat down, and the dey dismissed the assembly.

[**1691**] It is quite remarkable that, just as the Goths were defeated in Italy by the Romans because of their military disadvantage, they were exterminated through the same cause in Gaul by the French.[1] The latter had a weapon that was specific to them, namely, the ax, which they threw with

[**1691**]

1. "Agathias, book I" (M.); that is, *Histories II.* Agathias was a sixth-century Byzantine author, whose *History of Justinian* Montesquieu owned (*Catalogue*, 2808) in a 1594 edition.

exceptional skill and which smashed all defensive weapons. They also had various kinds of short javelin, called *ancones,* which they used with much success.

[1692] {This is a fragment of a work I had begun, entitled: *Journals of little-known books.*}[1] Often a prince who punishes someone believes he is engaging in an act of justice, when he is committing an act of cruelty.

M. Zamega does not mean by this that a prince should not sometimes be strict.[2] His habitual goodness depends so much on his being firm on certain occasions that without this, it would be merely a weakness of soul capable of weakening the State or precipitating its fall. It can be restored only by the Prince's firmness. If license has entirely gotten the upper hand, and authority is scorned, at that point the Prince has no virtues left but courage and obstinacy itself. Some great and unexpected deed is necessary to restore the dying laws. By some desperate stroke, one must restore the throne or be buried under it. It is not necessary to live, but to do, to perish, to reign. Daring and boldness can alone succeed against timid insolence.

[1693] LAWS THAT EXTERMINATE THE FAMILY. It is the practice in many parts of the Orient to exterminate the guilty party's family. In those countries, women and children are regarded merely as tools, and as accessories of the family. They are confiscated in the way property is confiscated among us; they are the husband's or father's property.

[1694] THAT IN ESSENCE, EVERYTHING IS EXCHANGE (COMMERCE BOOK). To appreciate this, it is necessary to consider that a nation trades with a nation. The latter sends some wine and receives some wheat. What has the currency done? In the constant series of different transactions that have taken place, it has been the common measure of both wheat and wine. If that state has sent less wine than it has received in wheat, money has fixed the boundary where that nation has received enough wheat for its wine, that is, has fixed the moment when the exchanges on one side or the other were just[1]—that is, where that same nation has received enough wheat for

1. This collection seems to be the same as the *Bibliothèque espagnole* [Spanish library], preserved in *pensées* 524–26; it is also similar to *Reflections on the character of several princes* (*OC,* 3:537–51).

2. On Zamega, see *pensées* 540, 1565, and 2002.

[1694]
1. *Juste* may also mean exact, precise, accurate.—HC

its wine. But if it is still receiving wheat, the currency no longer has that same function to fulfill. Now, money must be given as barter, and no longer as a sign. In a word, in the monetary balance that is being made all the time, money must no longer be considered as a sign, but as merchandise.

It follows from this that a state that ruins others is ruining itself, and that if it neglects the common prosperity, it neglects its own. The reason is clear. A ruined state cannot make exchanges with others; nor can others make exchanges with it. What causes us not to appreciate this very well is that we only strongly feel the harm that comes to us from the loss of the immediate trade. All nations hold together in a chain and communicate their goods and their ills to each other.[2]

I am not speechifying, I am stating a truth: the world's prosperity will always constitute our own, and as Marcus Antonius said, "What is not useful to the swarm is not useful to the bee."[3]

[**1695**] HUGH CAPET. His name is lost in a time period that has itself been lost and is now in night, silence, darkness, and oblivion.[1]

[**1696**] HUGH CAPET. It is to know oneself very poorly in the matter of flattery to mix myth with the most firmly established genealogy that we know. Hugh Capet was not from the Carolingian house; he was from his own. As soon as this type of grandeur could be distinguished, he, his father, and his grandfather appeared in grandeur. As soon as perpetuity of fiefs served to distinguish the greatness of houses, the Capetian house appears with great fiefs, and it has the advantage that, always great in its course, its origin lay in the abyss of those times when night, darkness and oblivion reign.

[**1697**] CHARLEMAGNE. I cannot here forebear formulating some regrets over a silver table—of greater weight than the others of his palace (said Charlemagne in his will), of more exquisite art, and where the world shaped in three globes was seen.

If only he had committed to stone things which avarice has since turned into secrets. We would see the exact position of peoples after the movement of so many nations, the situation of cities; and what we can now only conjecture, we would know.

2. See *Laws,* 20.23, especially 352.
3. See *pensée* 1657 for this image.—HC

[**1695**]
1. On Hugh Capet, see *pensée* 1302 n. 8.—HC

[1698] Plutarch, *Life of Aratus* (at the beginning): "Thus, the city of Sicyon, once it emerged from the pure government of the nobility, which is proper for Doric cities . . ."[1]

[1699] We may consider God as a monarch who has many nations in his empire. They all come to bring him their tribute, and each speaks its language to him.[1]

[1700] We have heard about Phrynê's game.[1] She was at a great feast. This game was being played where each guest in turn orders what he wants from the others. She had noticed that some women at the feast were wearing makeup. She had some water brought, took a cloth, and washed their faces. Those women appeared hideous and full of wrinkles; Phrynê remained with the sparkle of her natural beauty. There you have Religion and Superstition.

[1701] Drawn from a chapter on Egypt, where I had written: "The Egyptian kings' lives were subjected to a certain ceremonial regime, and night and day, they had hours marked for certain duties prescribed by the laws. If the laws had drawn from them only this advantage—namely, that they appreciate that their will, which should regulate so many things, should itself also be regulated—they would have gained much by it, and their people as well."[1]

[1702] That nobility that has marked with its blood all the steps it has taken to maintain it . . .[1]

Sacred rights! since the one which God has taken for his image has recognized them as such . . .

Which has preferred the happiness of serving always to that of pleasing once . . .

[1698]
1. See Plutarch, "Life of Aratus," in *The Parallel Lives,* XI, 2.1.

[1699]
1. See *pensée* 1454. See also Brèthe, 3:437 n. 32, for manuscript evidence that *Laws,* 25.9, began here.

[1700]
1. Phrynê, fourth-century B.C. Greek courtesan, a flute-player in Athens, Praxiteles' mistress, who served as a model for his statues of Aphrodite; see *pensée* 1725.

[1701]
1. "See if that's by me or by Diodorus" (M.); cf. Diodorus of Sicily, *Historical Library,* I.xx.

[1702]
1. "The monarchy" (M.).

Who have thought of ruining this monarchy by virtue of misunderstanding it . . .

I would have dragged these men from obscurity . . .

[1703] ROMANS. On the change made in the time of the Empire, of dividing military and civil functions in offices, this reflection should be added: that in a republic, it would be dangerous to divide civil and military functions; that military functions must be merely an accessory to the civil magistracy; that a man must feel more like a citizen than a soldier, a magistrate than an official, a consul or senator than a general. But in a monarchy, these qualities must be separated. The military corps must form a separate body. And this is equally necessary for the subjects and the Prince: for the subjects, to have civil magistrates; and for the Prince, to put his defense in the hands of military officers.

[1704] You tell me that at the end of my career, I need to sing the praises of Clovis's conquest and Charlemagne's government. But who is this other one who was a victor at Fontenoy, and demands peace?[1]

[1705] PREFACE. I never stopped casting to the winds ———, wasting my efforts reshaping what was never going to see daylight.[1]

[1706] What good would it do me to have made reflections for twenty years, if I missed the first reflection of all: that life is short? I do not even have time to abridge what I have written.

[1707] By parading whatever readings I might have done, I would do more damage to my readers' minds than I could make up for by any enlightenment from my research.[1]

[1708] ROMANS. Examine the Romans in the period when they were given grass wreaths, and in the period when they received gold wreaths. It is again history's whole experience that the rewards that have led to the greatest things are those that in reality had the cheapest price. {This did not make it into the book on *Conquest*.}[1]

[1704]
1. In 1745, during the War of the Austrian Succession, Marshal Saxe, French commander, defeated the English and the Dutch at Fontenoy in present-day Belgium.

[1705]
1. This entry and the next seem to be drafts of *Laws*, Preface, xlv, where Montesquieu writes, "a thousand times I cast to the winds the pages I had written."

[1707]
1. See *Laws*, Preface, xliv.

[1708]
1. The reference is probably to *Considerations*, VI.

[**1709**] What I said about the despots who have their own army for containing the Timariots can be said of Rome,[1] which had an army in its midst, namely, its people, to contain the troops of the allied cities.

[**1710**] ROMANS. In granting peace to the Carthaginians during the Second Punic War, Scipio required of them that they not be able to hire mercenary troops from Gaul, nor from Liguria.[1]

[**1711**] This did not make it into *Religion:*[1]

"Julian took quite useless pains. Rays of light had appeared in the world. Philosophy had been established, and if he had overthrown Christianity, he could well have established a third religion, but not reestablish the pagan one."

[**1712**] DICTATOR. In his presence, the laws were silent and the Sovereign bowed his head. He would have been a tyrant, if he had not been chosen for a short time, and if his power had not been limited to the purpose for which he had been chosen.

DICTATOR. Extreme remedy for extreme problems. He was a Divinity who descended from Heaven for the unraveling[1] of tangled affairs.[2]

[**1713**] Czar Peter I joined the Black Sea to the Caspian Sea by a canal that goes from the Tanais to the Volga. But what needs to be joined are nations to nations, not deserts to deserts.

[**1714**] It was Alexander's conquests that made the Orient known to the Occident; it was the Carthaginian and Roman wars that made the Occident known to itself. Hannibal's passage through the Pyrenees, Gaul, the Alps, brought with it an astonishment that marks the novelty of the enterprise.[1] It is quite true that the Gauls had crossed the Alps before Hannibal;[2] but this nonetheless shows the lack of communication, because

[1709]
1. The Timariots were possessors of military benefices.

[1710]
1. "Appian, *In Libycis,* page 30" (M.); see Appian, *Punic Wars,* LIV.

[1711]
1. The reference seems to be to *Laws,* bks. 24 and 25.

[1712]
1. The French *dénouement* here has a theatrical association.—HC
2. See *Laws,* 2.3, 16.

[1714]
1. In 218 B.C., during the Second Punic War, Hannibal crossed the Alps and fought the Romans at the Ticinus and Trebia rivers.
2. The Gauls had settled in the Po valley in northern Italy in the third century B.C.

once those mountains were crossed, there was no more communicating with each other.

All that Homer recounts on the dangers of Ulysses' voyage—the Circes, the Lestrigons, the Cyclops, the Sirens, Charybdis and Scylla—were myths spread throughout the world and established by navigators who, engaging in the commerce of economy,[3] wanted to repulse other peoples from engaging in it after them.

[**1715**] Just as we have said that the principle of Government becomes corrupted, the principle of Religion can be corrupted as well. As long as it is piety, Heaven has made nothing better; when it becomes superstition, the Earth has given birth to nothing worse.

[**1716**] NATURE OF THE TERRAIN. There are three kinds of country: wheat country, poor; wine-growing country, populous and poor; pasture country, unpopulated and rich.

Nota that the factor in favor of temperate country is that pastureland is more abundant, and thus more large livestock, which are a big source of wealth and offer bigger possibilities than small livestock.

[**1717**] MORES AND MANNERS. Constantine Porphyrogenitus decrees that beautiful women be hidden from the Barbarians.[1] Nothing more is needed to change the mores and manners of a nation.

[**1718**] Abbé de Saint-Pierre says: "One must choose good people"; just as one says when one enlists: "One must take a man of 5 feet, 6 inches."

[**1719**] By the melting of medallions, one finds that the debasement of silver currency began with Julian; that of copper currency, with Caracalla.[1]

There is nonetheless a fragment from Dio, in the *Extract of Virtues and Vices,* book LXXVII, page 309,[2] which says that instead of silver, Caracalla provided lead covered with silver tinsel, and instead of gold, gilded copper. The medallions, which prove that the first item is true, prove that the second is false.

3. On the "commerce of economy," as opposed to the "commerce of luxury," see *Laws,* 20.4–5, 20.8, 20.10, and 20.11.—HC

[1717]
1. Constantine VII Porphyrogenitus, *Extracts of the ambassadors,* preliminary chapter.

[1719]
1. "See Savote" (M.). Louis Savot (1579–1640), whose 1627 work on ancient medallions Montesquieu owned (*Catalogue,* 3230). Caracalla was a Roman emperor (r. 211–17).
2. Dio Cassius, *Roman History,* LXXVIII.14.4; see *Laws,* 22.13.

[**1720**] Monarch from the Orient, who wants to be happy all alone! Whoever all alone wants to have power, but pleasure all alone, often has no power, and never pleasure—the pleasures of a moment and the distastes of a day. Wretched is he who spends his life with himself because he wants the whole World to spend its life with him; who lives in the silence of everything that surrounds him; who commands but cannot speak; who seeks blind obedience and finds frightful solitude.

[**1721**] Defeat of the Huns by Charlemagne in 788 and 789. Destruction of the Lombards by Charlemagne in 777. He confirmed the donation that his father had made to the Roman church.[1] The Lombards' realm had lasted 200 years.

[**1722**] On page 207, make the observation that, in Lower Germany, Bohemia . . . , the peasants are serfs and have a different language.

[**1723**] If I may be permitted to predict the fortunes of my work: it will be more approved than read. Such readings can be a pleasure; they are never an amusement.[1]

[**1724**] The Chinese legislators provided music for morals, like the Greeks.[1] They did not, however, copy each other.

[**1725**] Princes play Phrynê's game in politics.[1] She was at the table with some women wearing makeup. That game was being played where each guest in turn orders what all the guests must do. She ordered that water be brought and that they wash their faces. Phrynê remained in her natural beauty, but all the rest became hideous.

[**1726**] DRAWN FROM THE "HISTORY OF JEALOUSY":[1] GOOD FOR "DOMESTIC SERVITUDE." It must be noted that, except in cases which

[1721]
1. The Donation of Pepin (756) rewarded the papacy for its support in the Frankish king's conflict with the Lombards by confirming territories in the Romagna to the papacy, making them temporal rulers over extensive territory for the first time.—HC

[1723]
1. See also *pensée* 1861. For a distinction between pleasure and amusement, see *pensée* 1675.—HC. The work referred to here is the *Laws*.

[1724]
1. For his discussion of music in Greek moral education, see *Laws*, 4.8, 39–41.—HC

[1725]
1. See *pensée* 1700.

[1726]
1. On the *History of Jealousy*, see *pensées* 483n, 484–509, 719, 1555, and 1622.

certain circumstances have brought forth, women have hardly ever claimed equality. For they already have so many other natural advantages that equality of power is always dominion for them.

[**1727**] Tacitus, who has left us that excellent treatise *De Moribus Germanorum*, where we still see our mores depicted and our laws described ... One wishes that someone had left us a treatise *De Moribus Gothorum*, because those are primitive nations and we find them described only when they have intermingled among themselves or with subject peoples.

[**1728**] FRENCH NOBILITY. O you who, among future races, must take care of them—ministers of those kings, etc.—beware of casting jealous eyes on their honors or fiscal hands on their property.[1]

Ministers of those to whom alone, to whom this nobility would yield in courage and in generosity, ministers of those, etc.

[**1729**] ARMIES.[1] When an army has weakened the defeated people, the terrors that have ceased to be caused by the conquered people now come from the army's side. Here are the means that have been used to keep them within faithful bounds.

The army is separated and arranged into many, so that, according to Tacitus's expression, they will communicate to each other neither their forces nor their vices. (*Nec vitiis, nec viribus miscebantur. Histories,* book I.)[2]

Again, experience has revealed that idleness makes soldiers seditious. "By frequent expeditions," says Tacitus, "the legions of Brittany learned to hate their enemies, and not their captains." {*Doctae crebris expeditionibus hostem potius odisse. Histories,* book I.}

When the army has become rich by conquest, it will lapse into dissolution or disobedience. The harshness of the soldier's craft is incompatible with luxury and riches. Alexander, setting off for the Indies, had all his soldiers' equipment burned; Thamas Kouli-Kan, conquering the same Indies, obliged his soldiers to give back all their gold.[3] These are very bold initiatives.

[**1728**]
1. See *pensée* 1702.

[**1729**]
1. Cf. *Laws,* 11.6, 165.
2. Montesquieu translates before citing these passages from Tacitus, I.9.
3. Thamas Kouli Khan, also known as Nadir Shah, king of Persia (1688–1747). He conquered India, seized the imperial treasure, confiscated the properties of the lords and the rich, but restored the Moghul emperor to the throne; cf. *Laws,* 10.17, 153.

The Roman emperors retained a part of the soldiers' pay,[4] with the army's flags, as a pledge of their loyalty; it was given to them only upon their discharge. I do not see that this produced great results. The soldiers knew that in rebelling, they would be even more the masters of this treasure.

It is very dangerous not to pay the army: at first it revolts, and then by a new misfortune it apologizes, and one does not dare punish it.

When the whole array of laws, manners, and morals does not prevent malcontents moving from one army to another, seditions are less frequent. When there cannot be any desertion, malcontents remain, hide their hatred, or make it burst forth. (This has been deleted from the book on *Offensive Force.*)[5]

[1730] CLIMATE. CONQUEST OF THE CHINESE AND THE MOGOLS. {I have put in my essays folder all the authorities necessary for proving this.}[1] The whole difference is that the Tartars founded the Mogol empire only after adopting Mohammedanism, but that Japan was conquered before that epoch.

This needs to be explained.

These two empires were founded by a Tartar invasion.

{It cannot be doubted that Japan was a Tartar conquest. Same government and same constitution as that of the Mogol, founded by the Tartars. The Japanese are originally from Tartary, like the Mogols. The Deiro correlates entirely with the Tartars' Great-Lama. Minstrels, or hunters of Devils or diseases, are common in Japan, as among the Tartars. Genghis Khan had his enemies thrown into a scalding boiler, a common punishment among the Japanese.[2] The two peoples have virtually the same dogmas; they are also little attached to ritual, and with regard to dogmas, they have an equal indifference. The Tartars never argue over Religion; neither do the Japanese. Before Christianity, freedom of religion was complete

---

4. "*History of the world* by Pufendorf" (M.); that is, *Einleitung zu der Historie der vornehmsten Reiche und Staaten in Europas* [Introduction to the history of the principal kingdoms and states of Europe] (1710 French edition; *Catalogue,* 2709).

5. *Laws,* bk. 10.

[1730]

1. Doubtless an allusion to a notebook entitled "Everything in this envelope makes for very appropriate materials for essays, being composed of chapters that did not make it into my book on the *Laws,*" now lost, but included in the "Catalogue of manuscripts sent [by Joseph-Cyrille de Montesquieu] to my cousin [Charles-Louis de Montesquieu]," March 10, 1818 (*OC,* 3:1577).

2. Genghis Khan (1175–1227) established his domination in Asia from the Black Sea to Korea, taking over China in 1212 and Persia in 1221.

there. Likewise, the Tartars, from a principle of conscience, protect them all. Whatever the histories of the Chinese may say, what one sees today proves clearly that they would never have been capable of conquering Japan. Moreover, there is no relationship between those peoples.}

The conquerors made themselves proprietors of landed estates, and the Prince or General gave them out as types of fiefs. It seemed natural that they not be hereditary. Since they were distributed to the army, and it was up to the Prince to choose his officers and soldiers, it seemed that the reward for positions should not be more hereditary than the positions themselves. It is the idea of every conquering army; it was the way of thinking of our Franks, of all the Goths who conquered the Roman Empire. But in the Occident, it was soon appreciated that lands held so precariously would become uncultivated. The spirit of liberty inspired the spirit of property; our fiefs became hereditary. This could not be done in Asia, because the spirit of liberty did not reign there. Fiefs remained for life, or rather, continued to be given out or taken away by the Prince's capricious will. Soon the spirit of sufferance[3] destroyed villages, peasants, lands in Indolestan,[4] and turned it into the greatest desert in the world.

The same thing would have happened in Japan if the climate and religion had not introduced some differences there.

[1731] The valor that Alexander displayed in his conquest of the Indies has been praised.[1] I would rather see people praise his conduct—how he linked together the Indies with Persia, with Greece; how he pursued Darius's murderers right into Bactria and the Indies themselves; how he had the skill to begin by subduing the territory north of the Indies and returning, so to speak, by the Indies; how he descended along the rivers so as not to be stopped at their crossings; how he thought to make his conquests relate to his conquests.

This project of the Indies trade that Alexander had engaged in through Babylon and the Persian Gulf, the Ptolemies engaged in by the Red Sea, as everyone knows.[2]

---

3. *Esprit précaire,* simple holding of a property by temporary concession.

4. *Indolestan* seems to be Montesquieu's coinage, a play on *indolent* perhaps—lethargic, apathetic, etc.—HC

[1731]

1. See *Laws,* 10.14 and 21.9.

2. See *Laws,* 21.16, especially 384ff.

[**1732**] The hours in which our soul employs the most energy are the ones set aside for reading, because instead of abandoning itself to its ideas—often without even realizing it—it is obliged to follow others'. Ha! we spend our lives reading books that have been conceived for children. How could we not be frivolous, since we are so in the very things whose natural effect would be to prevent us from being so?

[**1733**] The main reasons for the superiority of the French over the other peoples were that, after the destruction of the Romans, there was not a single state in Europe that had a firm footing; that everything assisted it, even Religion—since the Gauls could not live under the Arian tyrants, and Italy could not bear the oppressors of the Roman Pontiffs. Finally, their type of weapons and their agility gave them an advantage against the Gothic cavalry, which we have discussed at length in the previous work.

[**1734**] When the conquest is mediocre, the State can remain or become monarchical. The conqueror must seek to maintain his conquest by fortresses.[1]

Fortresses, as we have said, belong more to monarchical government, because they are opposed to military government.[2] Moreover, they presuppose much confidence in the grandees, since the latter are being entrusted with so much. They presuppose an even greater confidence in the People, since the Prince has less to fear.

When I talk this way about a fortress, I am not talking about a petty tyrant, master of a city, who builds a fortress there that makes him even more cruel. He is himself its governor. The military and despotic governor is found equally in the petty prince of a city and in the master of a vast empire.

Vitiza, King of the Goths, demolished all the fortresses in Spain; Gelimer, King of the Vandals, destroyed them all in Africa.[3] Consequently, those two states were conquered, so to speak, in a day. Instead of weakening the defeated peoples, they had weakened the empire.

I believe that what caused the Goths and the Vandals to make this bad decision is that, coming from a country where fortresses were unknown,

[**1734**]
1. See *Laws,* 10.10.
2. See *Laws,* 9.5.
3. Wittiza (d. 709); Gilimer (r. 530–34).

they regarded the ones they found in their conquests as means of avoiding their violence, not as suitable means for stopping foreigners.

[**1735**] Let us closely examine the fate of large monarchies that, after their surprising strength, have been surprising in their weakness. This is because, when there still remains a spark of liberty in the rapidity of arbitrary power or despotism, a state can do great things, because what remains of its motive force is brought into action. But when liberty is entirely lost, one sees, after such a degree of strength, an equal degree of weakness. This is because the love of good things and of great things is no more. It is because in each profession, it is established—what am I saying? it is sometimes decreed—that they not be done at all; because people are demoralized in general, and they are demoralized in detail; because the nobility is without feeling; the men of war, without interests; the magistrates, without zeal; the bourgeois, without trust; the people, without hope. Odd thing! everything trundles along but everything is idle. Each citizen has a status, but no one has a profession. From each subject, it is the body, not the mind and heart, that is wanted. It is then that a monarchy shows all its weakness, and is itself surprised by it.

[**1736**] One proof of what I am saying is that the nations where ignorance is established by a special tribunal are also the ones that have made the biggest mistakes in political matters, and this cannot be otherwise. When the governed are in a state of ignorance, the governors have to have a special inspiration at every moment in order not to be ignorant themselves, since they belong to the body of the Nation and are not, as Caligula would have it, shepherds endowed with intelligence guiding flocks who are not.

When one considers most of our nation's men, one always marvels to see so much wit and so little enlightenment,[1] such narrow boundaries and such energy for going beyond them.

[**1737**] I was reading in the *Cyropaedia* that Cyrus rejected the use of those chariots from Troy that were used in combat, because —— men and —— horses were needed for a single combatant.[1] In reading that,

[1736]
1. See also *pensée* 1867 for this formulation.—HC

[1737]
1. Xenophon, *Cyropaedia,* VI.i.

I made this observation: Without those chariots from Troy, however, we would not have had Homer's poem, which consists entirely in the actions and speeches of those heroes on those chariots, by means of which they are always distinguished from the plebeians in the army. For a good epic poem, it is immaterial whether the general armor is good, provided that of the main characters is.

Likewise the system of chivalry.

[**1738**] Sheep for currency, as the Romans did it at first {where do these words *peculium* and *peculatus* come from?}. But ever since the Mohammedans founded empires, that law has destroyed commerce in those empires; we find commerce ruined by Religion and by the constitution of the State.

The law of Mohammed, which confused lending with usury, was good for the Arabian countries,[1] and it was good like the law of the Jews, which was introduced in that country. The Arabs are scarcely familiar with money; they make their payments in livestock, as the Tartars also do.

[**1739**] ON PUBLIC CREDIT IN POPULAR GOVERNMENT.[1] Governors are ordinarily more skillful managers of public money because they are more skillful managers of their own—they have fewer passions, fewer fancies, and thus fewer needs.

In the government of one, the ruin of public credit can come from an imprudent act, a momentary advantage, or a bad piece of advice. In popular government, it comes from the despair of those who are watching the fall of the Republic. One saves oneself in the skiff because the ship is going to perish.

[**1740**] ON THE ROMANS' PROUD WORK. If it were possible to doubt the misfortunes that a great conquest brings in its train, one has only to read the history of the Romans.

The Romans dragged the world from the most flourishing condition it can be in; they destroyed the finest establishments in order to set up a single one, which could not support itself; they extinguished the liberty of the planet and then abused their own, weakened the entire world—as usurpers and as the despoiled, as tyrants and as slaves.

[1738]
1. See Brèthe, 3:397 n. 71, for Chardin's travel account as a possible source here.

[1739]
1. See *Laws,* 22.18.

[**1741**] Judges were drawn from the order of Senators up to the time of the Gracchi.[1] I find no law that gives this privilege to the Senators. It is probable that, as soon as judges had been established, the art of jurisprudence began to be formed. {This establishment was very old. Dionysius of Halicarnassus says the people would complain about the decemvirs, about the fact that they mingled among the judges.}[2] Senators were selected as judges because they were found to have knowledge that others did not have. By the act of Flavius, who revealed to the People the formulas behind legal action, it is known how far the art of jurisprudence was shrouded in mystery before the People. Since the parties were given judges that they agreed upon, they selected the most enlightened and the best-versed in affairs—that is, the Senators—and this continual practice of choosing them gradually became a law.

[**1742**] This did not make it into the book *The Nature of the Terrain:*[1] "In Europe and Asia, the only savage peoples are those which are obliged to be by nature. Such are the peoples of Lapland and Siberia. They inhabit a climate so cold that even trees cannot grow there. These are savages that do not inhabit the forests. Dispersed throughout the most barren terrain in the world, in country that is open and defenseless, they form little nations, and they would be free if they had not been subjugated by neighboring princes—not by their armies, but by the tax collectors."

[**1743**] Ammianus Marcellinus, who situates cannibals near Muscovy, says that peoples retreated from their vicinity out of fear and horror at their diet; which is why that country is desert up to the Seres.[1] This could well be the cause of that depopulation that exists through all of Great Tartary, and that still endures today. And I will say that it may be easier for peoples who live by their hunting to be cannibals. {Did not make it into the book on *Nature of the Terrain.*}

[**1744**] JUST IDEA OF SOME GOVERNMENTS. What then is the consti-

---

[**1741**]
1. See *Laws*, 8.12, 121.
2. Dionysius Halicarnassus, *Roman antiquities,* X.60.

[**1742**]
1. *Laws*, bk. 18; for this entry, see especially 18.11.

[**1743**]
1. Ammianus Marcellinus, *Roman history,* XXXI.2; Latin historian of Greek origin (ca. 330–ca. 400) (see *Catalogue,* 2812).

tution of England?[1] It is a mixed monarchy—just as Lacedemon, especially before the creation of the ephors, was a mixed aristocracy;[2] {The ephors were established to strip the king and senate of the lion's share of the judgments, as appears through Euripides' apothegm in Plutarch.[3] These ephors were drawn from the lower classes. The judgments, and the greatest magistracy of the Republic, were thereby transferred. By Lycurgus's institution, the Senate kept a bridle on the kings and the people; by Theopompus's institution, the ephors kept a bridle on the Senate and the kings. Cleomenes abolished the Senate and the ephors, and tyranny was immediately born.}[4] just as Rome, sometime after the expulsion of the kings, was a mixed democracy. {The various time periods of Rome must be considered. At first, after the expulsion of the kings, she was a mixed aristocracy. She was then a mixed democracy; offices and honors were passed on to the Plebeians. In the beginning, the People's decisions had to be confirmed by the Senate. On the other hand, it was established afterward that the Senate's decrees would only have force if they were confirmed by the People.}

England, as we have seen, inclines more toward monarchy. Rome, where the People decided and discussed affairs, inclined more toward democracy. Lacedemon, where the People had only the decision, inclined more toward aristocracy.

In Rome, dictators were created;[5] censors were named; wars were waged to bring the democracy back toward aristocracy. In Lacedemon, ephors were created to bring the aristocracy back toward democracy.

[**1745**] There is an odd thing. The tour of Africa had been made in the past.[1] However, that trip was forgotten to the point where, in the time of Ptolemy the Geographer,[2] who lived in Egypt, only a small part of the

[**1744**]

1. See *Laws*, 11.6, and Derathé, 1:472–78 n. 6, for context.

2. The ephors were the five magistrates elected annually in Sparta; see *Laws*, 5.8, 55.

3. It is Eurycratidas and not Euripides whom Plutarch cites in his *Apophthegms of the Lacedemonians*.

4. Theopompus, King of Sparta (r. ca. 720–670 B.C.); Cleomenes, King of Sparta (r. ca. 235–222 B.C.), wanted to restore Lycurgus's law and suppressed the ephors.

5. Cf. *Laws*, 2.3, 15–16.

[**1745**]

1. "The tour of Africa" is the title of *Laws*, 21.10.

2. "Book IV, chapter vii, and book VIII, tab. IV of Africa" (M.); Montesquieu owned a 1541 edition of the Greek astronomer, mathematician, and geographer Ptolemy's *Opera* (*Catalogue*, 1777) and his *Geographicae* (*Catalogue*, 2642).

Ocean near the Red Sea up to the Prassum Promontory was known,[3] and even less was known in the time of Arrian,[4] who placed the border of that sea at the Raptum Promontory. Herodotus knew[5] that Africa was connected to land only by the isthmus that is today called the *isthmus of Suez.*[6]

He knew that in leaving Egypt by the Red Sea, one returned to Egypt by the Ocean and the Mediterranean. He knew it, I say, but Ptolemy the Geographer, who lived in Alexandria, did not know it. It is clear that under the Greek Kings, it passed for a certainty that the African sea, after some distance, was not navigable. Of all the writers of that time, Juba[7] is the only one who suspected it was possible to go from the eastern to the western coast of Africa.[8] Anyway, it is clear that the Egyptian Greeks were content to sail the Indies, and to engage in the African trade by land.

When we say the Ancients knew about a thing, we must know which ancient people we mean. What the Persians knew, the Greeks did not know; what the Greeks knew in one period, they were ignorant of in another. Writing has carried men's discoveries from one people to another; but the art of printing has sealed, so to speak, the knowledge of them. The Ancients made giant steps, but they went backward the same way; they wrote on sand, we write in stone.[9]

M. Huet, in his *History of Commerce,* assumes some things that I find in no way proven.[10] He says the Edomites[11] prohibited all nations from sailing

---

3. The promontories of Prassum and Raptum are situated on the coast of Mozambique on map 1 of *Laws;* the former at the 7th degree and the latter near the 6th degree of latitude south; cf. *Laws,* 21.10, 373.

4. "*Periplus of the Erithrean Sea.* He lived under Hadrian" (M.); Arrian, second-century Greek writer whom Montesquieu cites in a Latin edition (*Catalogue,* 2767–70). [Though the work, derived from a tenth-century Byzantine manuscript, was long attributed to Arrian, modern scholarship treats it as anonymous. See Lionel Casson, ed., *The Periplus Maris Erythraei: Text with Introduction, Translation, and Commentary* (Princeton University Press, 1986).—HC]

5. "Book IV" (M.). See Herodotus, *The Histories,* IV.42.

6. "Look into when Ptolemy lived. Look also at Arrian, *Periplus of the Erythraean Sea*" (M.). On this text, see notes 4 and 13 elsewhere in this *pensée.*

7. Juba II (952–ca. 923 B.C.), king of the two Mauritanias and of a part of Getulia, author of works on history and archeology.

8. "At Cerné" (M.). Cerné was located at the far end of the bay of Rio de Oro.

9. Literally, in bronze (*airain*), though Montesquieu's metaphorical intent is clear.—HC

10. Pierre-Daniel Huet (1630–1721), bishop of Avranches, author of *L'Histoire du commerce et de la navigation* (1716). For Montesquieu's criticism of his ideas, see *Laws,* 21.14, 382, and Brèthe, 3:368 n. 29.

11. *Idumée,* Montesquieu's term, is the ancient name of the land of Edom in southern Judea.

on the Red Sea with more than one vessel. (Look into this episode.) He says a fleet that departed from Alexandria arrived in the Red Sea. This item seems to be false; it indeed departed from Alexandria, but it arrived only in Coptus.[12] Finally, he cites Arrian (*Periplus of the Erithrean Sea*) as describing with precision both the Red Sea and the trade that took place in the Indies, and that a certain pilot was the first to risk abandoning the coasts.[13]

[**1746**] FOR "THE OFFENSIVE FORCE":
"We have seen above that the size of the State determined it to despotism. Conquests, which shape this aggrandizement, thus lead by a natural path to that form of government.

"We must remind ourselves here of all the horrors of despotism, which constantly dumps its calamities on Prince and subjects; which devours itself like the Dragon; which tyrannizes the Prince before the State, the State before the slaves; which bases the ruin of one on the ruin of all and the ruin of all on the ruin of one. We must look at the pallor and the terror on the despot's throne, always ready to mete out death or undergo it, made stupid by fear before becoming stupid by pleasure. Now if this state is frightful, what do we say about the blindness of those who work constantly to procure it for themselves, and who take so much trouble to exit a situation in which they are the most fortunate of all princes, in order to become the most miserable."

[**1747**] NUMBER OF INHABITANTS.[1] Fifty million inhabitants could live without difficulty in the realm of France; {there are only fourteen million}.[2]

The land always yields in proportion to what is demanded of it. The fertility of the places in the vicinity of the cities should enable us to conjecture what one could expect from other places. The flocks grow with the populace that takes care of them.

Wheat from Africa is not for the Africans, Northern wheat is not for the peoples of the Septentrion. It is for all those who want to exchange the product of their arts for it.

---

12. Coptus, city of Upper Egypt, on the right bank of the Nile.
13. On this text, see *pensée* 1745 n. 4.—HC

[**1747**]
1. See *PL,* CXII–CXXII, and *Laws,* bk. 23, for this general theme.
2. Cf. *pensée* 1640, where Montesquieu reports Lord Bath's estimate of twenty million Frenchmen.—HC

The more workers you have in France, the more farmers you will create in Barbary. But a farmer will feed ten workers.

The sea is inexhaustible in fish; all that is missing are fishermen, fleets, merchants.

If the forests run out, open up the earth, and you will have combustible materials.

How many philosophers and voyagers have made discoveries that have become useless because ordinary resourcefulness was sufficient to meet the needs of the present situation?

Philosophers have not discovered these things for us; these things will only be good when there is a great People on earth.

Why do you send to the New World to kill oxen, solely to have the skin? Why do you let so much water that could have irrigated your lands run to the sea? Why do you leave so much water on your lands that could have run to the sea?

Animals, which all have separate interests, are always harming each other. Men alone, made to live in society, lose nothing of what they share.

There are a thousand advantages for me to live not in a large state but in a large society.

Famine is not less felt in sparsely populated countries than in others. Often, indeed, it causes more devastation, because on the one hand, commerce does not procure foreign assistance for them promptly, and on the other, poverty prevents them from making use of it.

[1748] NUMBER OF INHABITANTS. Romulus and Lycurgus gave a certain number of acres to each head of household; I assume it was 5 acres. (I will look into this.)

On this reckoning—assuming a league of 3,000 geometric paces—a square league would have 9 million square geometric paces. Put the geometric paces at 500 feet; in 7-foot laths, that makes 6,428,572 square laths, which, divided by 512, would make 12,556 acres in a square league, and at 5 acres per family, that would make 2,511 families in a square league who would make their living from the soil.

Now since Catalonia has around 24 leagues of 3,000 geometric paces, in reducing her shape into square, and length, and height, she has 576 square leagues. That is, on the Romans' and Greeks' plan, at 5 acres per family, she could contain 576 times 2,511 families: 1,446,336 families—that is, more than one finds these days in all of Spain. To which you can add all the people who live by their resourcefulness, who in a nation thusly adminis-tered would amount to at least a third—whether slave or free.

It is true that the uncultivated lands are possessed by the Clergy, who have made them uncultivated by the property they have acquired in them, and who prevent them from being cultivated by the possession they have in them, having scarcely any right in them except the impediment they place against others cultivating them.

But in that case, Plato's rule would have to be implemented, namely, that no one can inherit from other families, and that as soon as a peasant has an inheritance from another distribution, it should be given to the nearest relative.[1] Besides which, 5 acres are sufficient to maintain the mas-ter, and they are sufficient to occupy him and to receive from him all the cultivation possible.

The laws of the Romans were not as prudent as Plato's; they permitted (or tolerated) that citizens, under assumed names, could acquire the citi-zens' inheritances, which was to evade the law. But if this law had not been evaded, Rome would not have fallen into corruption.[2]

[**1749**] I say this, knowing full well that men are always confounded when it comes to governing men.

I speak to magistrates as one good man speaks to another. If one is obliged to depart from the law, it is at least necessary to return to it as soon as possible. If one is obliged to do things which by their nature are not good, it is necessary to make them do the least harm possible.

[**1750**] The French law that does not permit interest to exceed princi-pal[1] is an Egyptian law on contracts,[2] enacted by Bocchoris, legislator of the Egyptians,[3] and it is very humane.

[**1751**] It cannot be doubted that the wealth given to the Clergy[1] contrib-

---

[1748]
1. Plato, *Laws,* V.10.
2. "Nota that what I call acre is our *journal*" (M.); the "journal" was a little over 3 square kilometers.

[1750]
1. "Look at the circumstances under which it does not permit it" (M.).
2. "Diodorus, book I, part II, chapter 3" (M.); Diodorus of Sicily, *Library of History,* I.79.
3. Bocchoris, founder and sole pharaoh of the twenty-fourth Saite dynasty (720–715 B.C.), whom Montesquieu cites in *Laws,* 20.15.

[1751]
1. See *Laws,* 25.5 and 31.10, on this theme, and *pensées* 214 and 273.

uted to the extinction of that feeble light that appeared from time to time. The excessive wealth of a corporate body is always followed by excessive ignorance, because that body always seeks to hide the weakness of its titles.

[**1752**] The Goths, admitted by Valens into the Empire, devastated Thrace, Macedonia, and Thessaly[1]—country that is so great and of such quality, and *in ea tam multa aratra terram versant ut nulla oratione earum fertilitas exprimi posit.*[2] That country, with the exception of some fortresses, is so devastated, *ut incoli, adiri amplius non posit.*[3]

Under the Turks, it is still the way the author described it.

[**1753**] Why the Chinese books burned? Because the learned defended the ancient constitution.[1]

[**1754**] I am not saying that change is always sequential, and that when the political government is destroyed, the civil government is immediately destroyed. I am saying that it would be natural for this to be so, and that this is so among peoples that have had good legislators.

[**1755**] I have put in my extract from Cragius: "It seems that Cragius explored Lacedemon's civil government more deeply than the political. This is either because the monuments were lacking, or because the Republic was based more on its original founding than on the civil government, and more on the civil government than the political."[1]

[**1756**] "There has never been such need to build fortifications as at present, with the discovery of so many kinds *telorum, tormentorum et machinarum ad urbium expugnationes.*"[1] They thus did not have them in the time of Lycurgus. {I don't know where this passage is from.}

[**1752**]

1. Flavius Valens, Roman emperor (364–78) after his brother Valentinian conferred the eastern part of the Empire upon him; cf. *Considerations,* XVII, 163.

2. "In which there is so much arable land that words cannot express its fertility." "*Excerpta de legationibus, ex historia Dexippi, Atheniensis,* Pièces diverses, p. 406" (M.). That is, *Excerpts of laws from the history of Dexippos, Athenian;* Dexippos (ca. 210–73) was a Greek historian of Rome.

3. "That one can no longer inhabit it or go to it."

[**1753**]

1. "*Lettres édifiantes,* 2nd volume *Geographica,* p. 332 v°" (M.); the reference is to the Jesuit mission's collection of "Edifying Letters" (1703–41), which Montesquieu extracted in *Geographica* II, f. 303–38 (*OC,* 2:955–63).

[**1755**]

1. Montesquieu's extract of Nicholas Craig, or Cragius (1549–1602), *History of the Republic of the Lacedaemonians* (1593), is lost.

[**1756**]

1. "Of weapons, engines, and machines for taking cities by storm."

[1757] The emperors of China shorten their days.¹

[1758] Every aristocratic assembly is always dividing itself into the people and the leaders.

[1759] How Zeeland covered the sea with her vessels; how necessity, caused by the vexations of the Spanish in Europe, obliged the Dutch to go seek their subsistence far away; how it happened that they destroyed the commerce of those same Spanish.¹

[1760] Reasons why republics become more flourishing than countries governed by a single person:¹

1. More security for what one has acquired;

2. More love of the public good and of Country, which belongs to us, not to another;

3. More equality of conditions, and consequently, more equality of fortunes;

4. More means of succeeding by personal merit, and consequently, fewer means by servility.

To fashion a monarchical state, a rich nobility with authority and privileges over a poor people is necessary—luxury and expense in the Nobility; misery in the People. In a republic, where conditions are equal, each person shares or can share the common riches. Each person, having an honest subsistence, enjoys the substance of the Nation's goods and seeks to enlarge it.

[1761] ADULTERY.¹ Adultery was severely punished by the Romans' ancient mores. "*Ex injuriis enim privatorum publica res maxime vexatur: per labem alieni thori ita exasperantur animae ut Civitatem distrahant in seditionem.*"² They thus believed that modesty contributed a great deal to

[1757]
1. "See my 2nd volume *Geographica*, p. 174" (M.); cf. *OC*, 2:947.

[1759]
1. Cf. *Laws*, 20.5.

[1760]
1. Cf. *Laws*, 5.3, 44.

[1761]
1. See *Laws*, 7.10, 106, on this theme.
2. Gravina, *Origins of Law*, III.86: "The public good, in fact, is much disturbed by private injustices. Minds are so irritated by the taint of an illicit bed that they draw the state into sedition." Montesquieu's quotation is approximate. Giovanni Vincenzo Gravina (1664–1718), Italian jurist, renowned in the eighteenth century, whom Montesquieu cites twice in *Laws*, 1.3. He wrote *Originum juris civilis* (1713), and Montesquieu owned his *Della Ragion poetica* (1716; *Catalogue*, 2047). In a two-volume 2004 edition edited by Fabrizio Lomonaco (Naples: Liguori), see 2:680–81. See also Derathé, 1:421 n. 25,

public tranquillity. They permitted the husband who found his wife in adultery to kill her, as is seen in Cato's oration, in Aulus-Gellius, book I, chapter XXVIII.[3] But by the law *Cornelia, de Sicariis,* the husband who killed his wife was punished.[4]

The punishment of the husband was established during the monarchy, when they couldn't be bothered to watch over women's chastity.

[**1762**] NUMBER OF SENATORS. Romulus instituted a hundred senators; Priscus, a hundred more; Brutus, a hundred more.

A numerous senate is more like a democracy.

[**1763**] GLORY, HONOR, EMULATION. It was the custom to place the crown on the corpse not only of the victor, but of his father. That is how, in Greece, whoever had been a victor acquired glory not only for himself but for his father and for Country.[1]

That is how it is in China.

[**1764**] Because God had reserved an immediate government for himself, Moses made but one and the same code for his laws and his religion.

Mohammed as well.

[**1765**] JUSTINIAN. When the Easter feast of the Jews fell before that of the Christians, he did not let them observe it at the time prescribed by the Law.[1]

This idea of certain preferences and honors that are given to one's own religion over another is derived from human ideas, and it is useless to be revolted by it.

[**1766**] Why is it that brothers, fathers, and children or girls are so horrified at incest,[1] if not because they are exposed to the myths of Thyes-

---

for more on Gravina's importance. Robert Shackleton (*Montesquieu: A Critical Biography* [London: Oxford University Press, 1961], 111) suggests it was while in Naples in 1729 that Montesquieu became acquainted with his fame; on the extract Montesquieu made of his work, see *pensée* 1912.

3. Aulus-Gellius, *Attic Nights,* X.23.

4. "Gravina, article 86, book III, p. 46" (M.). See the Lomonaco edition, 2:681. The law referred to was passed under Sulla in 82 B.C.

[**1763**]

1. "Gravina, art. 8, book II" (M.). The discussion does not seem to be there.—HC

[**1765**]

1. "Procopius, *Secret histories,* various documents, p. 148" (M.). Procopius of Caesarea, Byzantine historian and author of *Arcana historia* (*Catalogue,* 2862).

[**1766**]

1. On incest, see *Laws,* 26.14.

tes, Oedipus, and Macareus (who had polluted his sisters), which horrify everyone?[2]

Plato thus contradicted himself[3] in banishing the poets from the Republic.[4]

[**1767**] A government is like a sum of numbers. Subtract one or add one, and you change the value of all. But since the value of each number is known precisely, one is not fooled. Whereas in politics, one can never know what will result from the changes one makes.[1]

[**1768**] Volume II *Politica:* Different sorts of government in relation to the different sorts of military.[1]

[**1769**] A small change in the civil laws often produces a change in the constitution. It appears small, but has immense consequences. For example, the transfer of power from one part of the State to another, by changing the census.

A wagon that has four wheels can go with three, even with two, but they have to be arranged differently. Likewise with the change in Chinese civil laws, in permitting the entry of foreigners.

[**1770**] I am going to treat the relationship that political laws have with civil laws, which is something that I'm not aware anyone has done before me.[1]

[**1771**] MILITARY GOVERNMENT. The Prince must be his own general, like the Mogul.

[**1772**] Despotic military government—the Mogul, the Tartars. Aristocratic military government—Alger. Democratic military government— Are there any?

[**1773**] It is easy to see how Lycurgus managed to get his laws accepted

---

2. Thyestes, younger brother of Atreus, whose wife he seduced; Oedipus, son of Laius, the king of Thebes, and of Jocasta, with whom he slept after killing his father, in fulfillment of an oracle's prophecy; Macareus, son of Aeolus, committed incest with his sister Canace.

3. "Plato, *The Laws,* p. 40, and 841 of the author and the extract 177" (M.); this extract is lost.

4. See *pensée* 1558.

[**1767**]

1. "Page 19, II volume *Politica*" (M.); the *Politica* are lost and are known only by the passages in the *Pensées* where Montesquieu refers to them. See *pensée* 941 for the same thought.

[**1768**]

1. "Page 137 r⁰ and v⁰" (M.).

[**1770**]

1. See *Laws,* 1.3, 1.9, 26.15–17, and 29.13 on this theme.

by the Lacedemonians, however harsh they may have been: the Nobles were being oppressed by the multitude, and he won over the Nobles. (Look closely at his life in Plutarch.)

[1774] *Meng-Tse* or Mencius,[1] fourth Book of Order II (in Father Du Halde, volume II), reports on how feudal princes were punished in the past. For the first offense, they were abased by one degree; for the second, their income or territory was cut; for the third, an army was sent to depose them; often, in fact, neighboring kings were charged with this deposition. This last system is still observed in Germany.[2]

[1775] CHINESE AND JAPANESE. Very little connection in the customs. Same turn of mind; manners, everything different. The Chinese is peaceable, modest, judicious, deceitful, and avaricious; the Japanese is soldierly, restless, distracted, suspicious, ambitious, and full of big plans. The religion of the Buddhists, which is common to the Japanese and the Chinese, only came to Japan very late, and channeled through Korea. (Kaempfer)[1]

They may very well have come via Tartary.

[1776] Volume II *Politica,* page 81. Jewish representatives: Senate of seventy, for life; twenty-four thousand representatives who propose to the Senate, which decides. This is just the opposite of what was done in Greece and Italy. The Senate proposed; the People decided. Another oddity: the proposal is from the State, in the representatives chosen for a term, and the decision is in the representatives chosen for life. Look into the Republic of the Hebrews. See about its conformity with the laws of Egypt.

[1777] In speaking this way about Constantine, I admit I fear being ranked among those whom Orosius wrote against who would accuse the Christian Religion of ruining the Empire, and being charged with consulting only Zosimus, our declared enemy.[1] But it seems to me that Constantine's actions are hardly in dispute, and that Zosimus and Constantine's panegyrists agree well enough about the facts, even though they look at

[1774]

1. Mencius (ca. 380–ca. 295 B.C.), author of the fourth of the Chinese books in the Confucian tradition.

2. "II volume *Geographica,* p. 212" (M.). Montesquieu refers here to his extracts from Fr. Du Halde's *Description of China* (*OC,* 2:943–51).

[1775]

1. "Volume I, p. 91" (M.); on Engelbert Kaempfer, see *pensée* 374n.

[1777]

1. On Zosimus's *Roman history,* see *pensées* 871a and n. 2, 2192, 2195, and 2201.

them differently. When the Fathers say that Constantine had a great love for the Christian Religion, this is exactly what Zosimus says when he accuses him of abandoning Paganism. When they say that Constantine had much respect for the bishops, this amounts to what Zosimus says, that he was always surrounded by them. The truth is covered by praise and by ridicule, so you have to unveil it.

Constantine created a new design, just as Augustus had created one.

[**1778**] I am obliged to hug the coasts, when I would like to sail the open sea.[1]

[**1779**] Since the laws of any religion are of such a nature that they cannot be changed, a prudent legislator must not overturn, but instead must evade those that are detrimental.[1]

[**1780**] When one eliminates some natural liberty, the visible advantage derived from this must be adequate consolation for the loss of that faculty.

When a good thing has a disadvantage, it is usually more prudent to eliminate the disadvantage than the thing.

[**1781**] Since magic has been discredited, it has degenerated into witchcraft, which in our time and place is the people's version of the marvelous.[1] It is the accusation that makes the crime, and all others of that sort. The people owe these crimes solely to the guidance of their magistracies. "It must be the case," they say, "that magic exists, since the legislator, whose wisdom I trust, has made a law to punish it. It must be the case that this act of magic took place, since the judges, who bring to their judgments the greatest attention that human nature is capable of, have so decided."

[**1782**] Enfranchised slaves. Multitude of new poor who were not poor before. It was a revolution, what Christianity did.[1]

[**1778**]
1. See *pensées* 1576 and 1802.—HC

[**1779**]
1. See *Laws,* 25.11; Derathé, 2:480, reports the existence of an additional paragraph on moderate government in the manuscript of *Laws.*

[**1781**]
1. See *Laws,* 12.5, 192.

[**1782**]
1. See *Laws,* 15.7, 252.

[1783] SCHISM OF THE GREEKS.[1] The Popes had already cast their lot with the Western princes, and both had thereby done their business. That caused the Greeks to create a schism and regard the Popes' power as dangerous, in that it was foreign. This brought great hatred between the nations of the two rites.

Charlemagne had placed the Pope as a barrier against the Greeks.

[1784] Phocas,[1] who got along badly with his clergy, established the Pope's primacy.

The Pope's authority was a relief, next to the Patriarchs' tyranny. There were constant schisms over encroachments, real or imagined.

[1785] Without changing anything in the form of the former Chinese government, the Tartars have obliged them to conform to the form of their clothing.[1]

This is so that the difference in number would not be noticed.

[1786] On the book on *Religion*.[1]

> *Regum timendorum in proprios greges,*
> *Reges in ipsos imperium est Jovis.*[2]

On the book about the *Means of preserving Liberty:*[3]

> *Quasi aliena libertas sua servitus esset.*[4]

On the book on *political Liberty:*

[1783]
1. Reference to 1054, when the Roman Pope and the Patriarch of Constantinople excommunicated each other, ratifying divisions that had existed since the fourth century.

[1784]
1. "See the Byzantine History" (M.); perhaps a reference to the *Historiae Byzantinae* (1615; *Catalogue*, 3121). Phocas was a Byzantine emperor (r. 602–610).

[1785]
1. "Du Halde, volume II, p. 89" (M.).

[1786]
1. See *pensée* 1656; the reference is to *Laws*, bks. 24–25.
2. Horace, *Odes*, III.i.5–6: "Dreaded monarchs have power over their own flocks; monarchs themselves are under the power of Jove."
3. *Laws*, bks. 11–12; in the *Catalogue*, p. 222, Montesquieu applies this sentence to the *Thuscarum rerum scriptores* [Writers on Tuscan matters].
4. "As if foreign liberty were their own slavery." Attributed to Florus by Montesquieu's *Catalogue*, p. 222, but see also Justin, *Pompeius Trogus*, V.x.

Res olim dissociabiles, principatus et libertas.[5]

On the book about the *Laws on Climate,* and on *civil Servitude:*[6]

Non in avem Progne vertatur, Cadmus in anguem.[7]

On *domestic Servitude:*[8]

Fiet aper, . . . ignis.[9]
. . . Hanc tu compesce catenis.[10]

[1787] In the Mogul—every man, father's profession; daughters who do not get married, because they find no match in another profession, believed to be less noble.

Besides, the squalor prevents one from placing oneself with a master. One has only paternal instruction.[1]

[1788] CLIMATE. In the fragments of Nicolaus of Damascus, collected by Constantine Porphyrogenitus,[1] look into how ancient is the custom in the Orient of sending someone to strangle provincial governors on the least suspicion. The government demands this harshness, and the climate destroys the government.[2]

[1789] The first Roman who repudiated his wife, it was because she bore no children;[1] the second, because she had veiled her head, or had not

5. Tacitus, *Agricola,* 3: "things long incompatible, the principate and liberty."

6. See *Laws,* bks. 14 and 15, respectively.

7. Horace, *Ars poetica,* 187: "nor Procne be turned into a bird, Cadmus into a snake."

8. See *Laws,* bk. 16.

9. Horace, *Satires,* II.iii.73: "he will turn into a boar . . ."

10. Horace, *Letters,* I.ii.63: "check it, I pray you, with chains."

[1787]

1. "P. 296, II^d vol., *Geographica,* Bernier" (M.); that is, François Bernier (*OC,* 2:954). See also *Laws,* 20.22, 350.

[1788]

1. This text is edited in the *Fragmenta historicum graecorum* [Fragments of Greek history] (Paris, 1849), vol. 3, frag. 10. Nicholas of Damascus was a Greek writer of the first century B.C., friend of Herod the king of Judea.

2. See *Laws,* 14.4n for this entry.

[1789]

1. On this theme, see *Laws,* 16.16, 276.

veiled her head (I'm not exactly sure which of the two); the third, because she attended funeral games.

In these three causes, you see how pure the mores were at that time.[2]

[1790] Strabo says that most of the Cretans' institutions no longer survive, *cum, ut in reliquis fit provinciis, pleraque romanis constitutionibus gubernentur.*[1]

I am quite unhappy with the Romans for having destroyed the institutions of virtually all the earth's peoples, in order to establish their own.[2]

[1791] Plutarch, *Life of Dion.* Old Dionysius married two women at the same time: one a Locrian, the other a Syracusian.[1] By the Locrian, he had three children; by the Syracusian, four: two boys and two girls. The Syracusian's son married his sister.

Thus, it was not the Athenians alone who married two women, and whose brothers married their sisters.[2]

[1792] In China, where the fundamental principle is the love of ancestors, the laws enjoin people to populate. Thus, Father Du Halde (volume II, page 119, *History of China*) says: "A father is without honor if he does not marry off his children; a son fails in a son's duty if he has no descendants." But the system permits fathers to sell or expose their children, and this is something that necessity has exacted in order to make up for the overly extensive effects of that morality and those laws.

[1793] The people of Germany are a good people. Machiavelli tells us that in his time, when the city magistrates wanted to impose some tax, everyone put in a sack the portion of his revenue covered by the tax. The Magistrate trusted the People, and one proof that this trust was not always abused is the continuation of that practice. I have heard that this is still observed today in Danzig. {Look closely at this, and at what places this is still observed.}

---

2. "Plutarch, p. (of extract) 251" (M.). The citation refers not to Plutarch but to Valerius Maximus, *Factorum et dictorum memorabilium* [Memorable doings and sayings], II.1 and VI.3.

[1790]
1. "Since, as it happens in the other provinces, the majority are administered under Roman ordinances"; Strabo, *Geography,* X.4.22.
2. Cf. *Considerations,* VI, and *Laws,* 21.12, 380.

[1791]
1. The term "old" in this sentence is intensive and not descriptive; Dionysius was thirty-five at the time of the two marriages.—HC
2. See *Laws,* 5.5, 45.

[**1794**] There are main laws and subordinate laws, and in each country there takes shape a kind of generation of laws.[1] Peoples, like each individual, have a sequence of ideas, and their total manner of thinking, like that of each individual, has a beginning, a middle, and an end.

This topic would have no limits if I did not impose some. I have taken an example, which concerns the origin and generation of the Roman laws on inheritance, and that example will serve here as the method.

I have taken up my pen to teach not the laws, but the manner of teaching them. Thus, I have treated not the laws, but the spirit of the laws.[2]

If I have done well in presenting the theory of the Roman laws on inheritance, it will be possible by the same method to look at the birth of most people's laws.

It is natural to believe that the jurisconsults, in rendering their decisions on property ownership, began with the condition of things within the constitution at that time, and that in this way the Romans, in passing laws on inheritance, passed them according to the political law, which had created an equal distribution of the lands.

[**1795**] USEFULNESS OF THE KNOWLEDGE OF THINGS PAST. One must know about ancient matters not in order to change the new ones, but to make good use of the new ones.

It is a sure principle that the general opinions of each age are always extreme. The reason is that they have become general only because they have been very striking to people's minds. Now to put them back within the framework of reason, it is necessary to examine the status that the dominant opinions from that framework had in other ages. This can make them very useful—on the one hand, in employing the ardor they inspire, and the action they lead to, for good; and on the other, in preventing them from spreading prejudices for ill.

The preceding books[1] have led to this one, where I will offer a small essay on the history of the laws of France, as I have just offered the history of some Roman laws. I would like to see better works written on each

[**1794**]
1. This entry and the next can be considered an introduction to *Laws,* bks. 27–28.
2. See Derathé, 1:424, for more on this passage.

[**1795**]
1. For more on the structural questions surrounding *Laws,* see Brèthe, 1:cxix ff. and 4:1 ff., and Derathé, 2:538 n. 1.

country's laws. To understand modern times well, one must understand former times well; one must follow each law within the spirit of every time period. Giving men laws has not been a matter of sowing dragons' teeth to get them to emerge from underground.[2]

[**1796**] CHARACTER OF THE LAWS IN CERTAIN CLIMES. Two Ethiopian kings, who reigned in Egypt at different times, abolished the death penalty there. (This must likewise have been established in their countries.) Those princes reigned with all kinds of humanity, of justice. The relations we have with Ethiopia today show us more mildness in that government, and a better system of administration, than in any other country in Africa.

[**1797**] Diodorus, book {I}, section II, page 129:[1] "After Amasis reigned...,
Ethiopian, good prince.[2] In order not to impose the death penalty for thieves, he had their noses cut off and sent them to live in a city named *Rhinocorura.*"[3]

Page 139, *ibidem:*[4] "Several generations after Bocchoris, we find Sabacon in Ethiopia.[5] He abolished the greatest of judicial punishments, which is the death penalty, wanting criminals to be condemned to urban work projects. He wanted to change a fruitless severity into something from which Egypt would draw great advantage. He retired to Ethiopia."

[**1798**] MILDNESS OF PUNISHMENTS IN ETHIOPIA. Mildness of punishments. Hanging or beheading. Sometimes loss of property, with prohibition against offering them anything to drink or eat, which makes them wander like beasts. The Emperor often extends grace. He is just; he believes that the exact justice meted out in this realm, and its administration, bring forth innocence in mores.[1]

Korea. Mildness of punishment.[2]

---

2. The reference is to Jason's pursuit of the Golden Fleece in Greek myth.—HC

[**1797**]
1. Diodorus of Sicily, *Historical library,* I.60.
2. Amasis, next to last pharaoh of the twenty-sixth Saite dynasty (ca. 568–526 B.C.).
3. *Rhinococura,* "city of broken noses."—HC
4. Diodorus of Sicily, *Historical library,* I.65.
5. Bocchoris, founder of the twenty-fourth Saite dynasty (720–715 B.C.); Sabacon or Chabaka, Egyptian sovereign of the twenty-fifth dynasty, called Ethiopian (perhaps late eighth century B.C.).

[**1798**]
1. See *Geographica* (*OC,* 2:956), in the extract from the *Edifying and curious letters,* a paragraph "Mœurs des Ethiopiens" drawn from *Voyage d'Ethiopie* by M. Poncet, a French physician in 1698–1700.
2. Vol. II, *Geographica.*

Notice, then, that in Ethiopia, the mildness of mores has been from all time.

[1799] COMMERCE. Conquests are more suited to establishing the same mores everywhere than to providing good ones. It was one of the regrettable features of the Romans' world conquest that those countless peoples they subjugated took on Roman mores, and that each people lost the original character it possessed from its general spirit. The Spanish conquests in America have metamorphosed all the peoples of that part of the world into Spaniards.

There is plenty of difference between the mores that commerce inspires and those that a vast conquest forces people to take on.[1]

[1800] COMMERCE. THAT IT IS OFTEN USEFUL TO PEOPLES CULTIVATING THE ARTS THAT OTHERS BE CULTIVATING THEM AS WELL.[1] The establishment of manufactures in nations that had not had them should not so greatly alarm those that do. The former buy little; but if they establish manufactures, they will soon be in a position to procure those which they cannot imitate, and which will immediately figure among their needs.

The Hungarians were poor. They had no manufactures. They bought only three or four outfits throughout their lives; these outfits were of very low value and seemed to have been made only for frugality's sake. Let Hungary discover—or let them be provided with—some means of enriching themselves, and you will soon find all the merchandise in the world there.

[1801] COMMERCE. What Aristotle says—that whenever you have farmers, you have mariners[1]—is no longer true today. A great deal of commerce—that is, a great deal of industry—is needed in order to have a navy. It is no longer possible for a people to pass suddenly, like the Lacedemonians, from land war to sea war.

In any case, the opinion of the Ancients—that the souls of those who drowned themselves in the sea perished, because the water extinguished their fire—was well suited to repulse people from sailing. There were people who, when faced with the threat of shipwreck, killed themselves by sword. {I believe this is found in Petronius.}

[1799]
1. See *Laws*, 20.1.

[1800]
1. See *Laws*, 20.23, especially 353, and the discussion in Brèthe, 3:354 n. 64.

[1801]
1. "*Politics*, book I, chapter vi" (M.).

[1802] [I am obliged to hug the coasts, when I would like to sail on the vast seas.][1]

[1803] COMMERCE. The situation of the ports of the Dutch and most of the peoples of the Baltic Sea, where the ports have little depth and where the vessels are obliged to enter by the rivers and shoals, makes the vessels flat . . . and wide-bottomed; whereas the construction of French and English vessels, which have good ports, makes them narrow; so that they penetrate deeply into the water and will penetrate, for example, at a 70 to 30 ratio with the Dutch or Muscovite ones.

[1804] COMMERCE. One of the big advantages of our commerce over that of the Ancients is the rapidity of our sea voyages. We have perfected the art at present, just as they had perfected it themselves. Countless observations have made us familiar with all the sea lanes that we know about. They could not trade merchandise that perishes and is not easily preserved.

[1805] I had conceived the design of giving greater breadth and greater depth to certain sections of this work; I have become incapable of it. My reading has weakened my eyes, and it seems to me that what light still remains to me is merely the dawn of that day when they will close forever.

I am very close to the moment when I must begin and end, the moment which reveals and hides everything, the moment mixed with bitterness and joy, the moment when I will lose even my very weaknesses.

Why would I still occupy myself with some frivolous writings? I seek immortality, but it is within myself. My soul, elevate yourself! Throw yourself into the immensity! Return to the great Being! . . .

In the deplorable state I find myself in, it has not been possible for me to put the finishing touches on this work, and I would have burned it many times over if I had not thought it was noble to make oneself useful to men right up to one's last breath . . .

God immortal! the human race is your worthiest work. To love it is to love you, and in ending my life, I dedicate this love to you.[1]

[1806] The appeal is favorable to liberty. It is good for the criminal judge who performs the first procedures and the civil judge who gives the first instructions to be afraid of being corrected.

[1802]
1. See *pensées* 1576 and 1778.

[1805]
1. This is a fragment from the preface of *Laws* which Montesquieu did not retain.

[**1807**] Whoever killed a tyrant could demand what he wanted, besides the prize at the Olympic Games.[1] It was noble[2] for a prize given by the entire Greek nation to be given out in this way, and for them to take on the responsibility of rewarding a city's avenger.

[**1808**] Women could not be common property among great peoples. Kavadh, King of Persia, enacted a law to make all women common property. This aroused the entire Nation, and he was deposed[1] (based on some idea, I believe, of Manicheism; look into that).

[**1809**] The booty from Veii was put in the quaestors' hands,[1] to the discontent of the soldiers, who had a mixture of admiration and hatred for Camillus's virtue.[2] This is because they began, at the siege of Veii, to provide salaries to the soldiers. Seven acres of Veiian land was distributed to each free man, to give them more desire to have children.[3] {It seems to me that the Romans distributed sometimes seven, sometimes five acres.}

[**1810**] RELIGION. Monks and priests {in the Spanish Indies} were allowed a kind of concubinage.[1]

The force of climate.

Naturam expellor furca . . .[2]

[**1811**] *Vos vero, novo genere ambitus, adorationem miseria captatis.*[1] Monks.

[1807]

1. "Cicero, *Rhetoric*, book II" (M.).

2. First version: "peculiar"—HC

[1808]

1. "Procopius's *History*, various pieces, p. 243" (M.). See *Laws*, 16.4. The reference is to Kavadh I (r. 488–531), whose support for the communistically inclined Mazdakite sect led to his imprisonment in 496.—HC

[1809]

1. Veii, one of the most important cities of Etruria; enemy of Rome, it was seized by the Roman general Marcus Furius Camillus after a siege of ten years (405–395 B.C.); cf. *Considerations*, I, 30.

2. "P. 48, extract from Titus-Livy, book V, volume II, p. 43" (M.), which is lost.

3. "P. 66, extract from Titus-Livy, book V, volume II, p. 45" (M.).

[1810]

1. "Frézier, Volume *Geographica*, p. 376" (M.). Montesquieu refers to the first volume, which is lost; Amédée-François Frézier (1682–1773), author of a 1716 account of sea travel around Peru and Chile (*Catalogue*, 2742).

2. Horace, *Letters*, I.x.24: "You may drive out nature with a pitchfork . . ."

[1811]

1. Quintilian (ca. 35–ca. 95), *Declamations*, CCLXXXIII: "But you and your like have a new style of self-promotion: you seek veneration out of misery" (*Catalogue*, 1953–55).

[**1812**] NUMBER OF INHABITANTS. The more the earth is devastated, the more it happens that empires aggrandize themselves; just as we have said elsewhere that the more empires aggrandize themselves, the more the land is devastated.

[**1813**] The great communication among peoples has spread, and is spreading every day, some destructive diseases.[1]

[**1814**] ON THE NATURE OF THE THINGS THAT DEPEND ON THE LAW OF NATIONS.[1] The things that depend on the law of nations are of such a nature that they can be regulated only by force or by a suspension of force, that is, by treaties.

They could also be regulated by a superior iniquity. But since it is as necessary to the world that nations preserve themselves as it is necessary to each nation that its citizens not be destroyed, these means had to be rejected by civilized nations. Thus, it is contrary to the law of nations to poison wells and fountains, to assassinate a monarch in his court, in a word, to do all the things that depend neither on force nor on convention.

War presupposes natural defense. Thus, the law of nations establishes that one declare war before waging it. From this arises security for the heralds, who are the ministers of the law of nations in time of war.

War requires a convention to terminate it. To effect this convention, ministers are needed. These ministers are the ambassadors.

The object of war is peace. Thus, one must be able to make peace. The ministers of the law of nations in time of peace are the ambassadors.

The only ambassadors known in the past were those sent to certain peoples for a specific occasion. The invention of the post, the currency exchange, the extraordinary communication among peoples, the great knowledge they have of each other's affairs, have made them want to know each other better. Whence the establishment of ministers permanently established in the various courts.

These ministers are spies, but they are spies among friends; and what is demanded by the laws of friendship among friends who are present (complain about each other, enlighten each other, reassure each other, form

[1813]
1. See *PL*, CV, 175. Also on the history of disease, see *pensées* 77, 216, 366–68, 1389, and 1606.

[1814]
1. This entry was destined for a chapter in *Laws* by the same title, which Montesquieu deleted; see Brèthe, 3:451 n. 59.

one's suspicions, drop them) is done by means of ambassadors among friends who are at a distance.

It is hardly the custom today for a prince who is making peace to demand hostages. It was a constant practice among the Romans, which arose because they regarded victory as entailing a right of subjection—which is not today's idea.

The law of nations ends war by treaties. When the great princes violate them without cause, they reveal that they are not great enough, and that they have many things to hope and fear. When they observe them, they reveal that they are so great that they depend only on themselves.

[1815] ON THE RELATIONSHIP THAT THE LAWS HAVE WITH THAT PART OF THE SYSTEM INCLUDED IN POLITICAL ADMINISTRATION. Our medium-sized states enable men to preserve themselves despite vexation, and to pass from one country to another, whereas in large states, men and peoples perish without recourse—they are enveloped in tyranny.

Moreover, Princes think they are losing nothing. Among many examples, I will cite the act of Augustus, who gave his soldiers all the property in eighteen or twenty cities in Italy, which he could not even bring himself to lament. The Romans, considering themselves to be the entire world, believed they were losing nothing by destroying cities; they thought they were doing nothing but robbing Peter to pay Paul, without depriving themselves of either. Today, we see very well that when we ruin one of our cities, it is as if we were going off to build it among our enemies.

[1816] ON THE SIZE OF THE CAPITAL.[1] A city that is too large is extremely pernicious in a republic; mores are always being corrupted there. When you cause a million men to come to the same place, you can no longer exercise any administration but that which provides bread to a citizen, and which prevents him from having his throat slit. Put men where the work is, not where the pleasure is.

In despotic States, the capital grows inexorably larger. Despotism, which presses and weighs more upon the provinces, channels everything toward the capital. In some sense, this is the only asylum that exists against the governors' tyranny. The Prince is a strange star—he warms from up close and burns from afar. The unfortunate thing is that so many people assem-

[1816]
1. See *Laws*, 17.8.

ble there only to perish all at once by war, disease, famine. In that State, all causes are destructive, and all consequences.

The most deplorable situation[2] is when the capital, which attracts everyone from the provinces, is for its part destroyed. Constantinople is in this situation. {Madrid is in the same situation. Childbirths are not successful there. I have spoken about it in my *Reflections.*}[3] Epidemic diseases, which are neglected there, cause the people to perish; it is useless to lead colonies there, the city is not growing.

In a monarchy, the capital can grow in two ways: either because the provinces' wealth attracts residents there (this is the case with a certain maritime realm) or because the provinces' poverty sends them there.[4] In this latter case, if one does not have an eye on the provinces, everything will be equally ruined. (See vol. I of my *Thoughts,* p. 223,[5] the reasons why Asia's cities may be more populous.)

A monarchy that has rules and laws is not ruined by the capital. It may even draw its splendor from it. The Prince has a thousand means of restoring equilibrium and bringing the people back into the provinces, and to speak only of those that come immediately to mind: let him reduce the taxes on commodities in the provinces and increase them in the capital; let him allow cases to be concluded in the provincial tribunals, without constantly appealing them to his councils or his special tribunals; let him return to their posts all those who have employment and titles of whatever kind in the provinces. And let him make this observation: that the more people there are who leave a place, the more people there are who still desire to leave, because what remains has fewer attractions.

In the city of Naples,[6] there are fifty thousand men who are absolutely nothing. Those wretches ruin the provinces because they are not there; they ruin the capital city because they are.

Often States that appear to be booming have found themselves to be very weak. Men were poorly distributed in them, so while the cities overflowed with useless residents, the countryside lacked necessary ones. Unhappy effect, which prosperity itself produces!

2. See *PL,* CXIV, 192.
3. See *pensée* 1679.
4. The maritime capital would be London, and the depopulation of the French provinces by the capital was a frequent lament of contemporary commentators.—HC
5. See *pensée* 213.
6. See *Voyages* (*OC,* 2:1161).

[**1817**] PROPAGATION OF THE SPECIES. Aelian cites a Theban law, *qua capitis poena sancitur civi infantem exponenti aut in solitudinem abjicienti,*[1] and if a man was so poor that he could not raise his child, he was obliged—as soon as the child was born—to bring him to the magistrates, who gave him for raising to a man who became his master.[2]

This law has been established in Scotland.

[**1818**] ROMANS. One can exterminate by the laws just as one exterminates by the sword. In 150 years' time, the Roman Emperors destroyed all the ancient Roman families. One of their greatest tyrannies was that of their laws.[1]

[**1819**] LÈSE-MAJESTÉ.[1] Jurisconsult *"Paulus poena legis Corneliae plectendum esse ait quisquis monetam quae effigiem Principis impressam haberet, nec adulterina esset, accipere detractaret."* This is because, as Ammianus Marcellinus observes, as soon as a prince was selected, the custom was to have currency minted in his name.[2]

The law of Constantine that condemned to the flames those who refused his currency considered perhaps that this crime would have some connection with that of lèse-majesté.

[**1820**] PREFACE. From the moment I had the honor of seeing you for the first time, at the court of Vienna,[1] I felt that impression that a rare merit makes on others, and although you did not have the same reasons, my good fortune was such that I saw that as I was advancing toward you, you were quite willing to approach me.

And such was my situation that I was virtually obliged, out of gratitude, to cherish what I was admiring. Behold what made me resolve to

[1817]
1. "That [a Theban] could not expose his child or leave it on waste land, condemning it to death."
2. Aelian, *Various Histories,* II.7. Aelian was an Italian writer in the Greek language whose *De animalium natura* [On the nature of animals] Montesquieu owned in a 1616 edition (*Catalogue,* 1788).

[1818]
1. Cf. *Considerations,* XIV, 130, for this Tacitean saying.

[1819]
1. On this theme, see *Laws,* 12.7–10.
2. "Paul says that whoever refuses an unadulterated piece of currency bearing the effigy of the Prince should be sentenced to the punishment provided for by the Cornelian law." Montesquieu's comment seems to refer to Ammianus Marcellinus, XXVI.7.11.

[1820]
1. Probably Prince Eugene of Savoy, whom Montesquieu met in Vienna in 1728 (*OC,* 2:968 and passim).

dedicate this little work to you; for if chance makes it pass into posterity, it will be the eternal monument of a friendship that touches me more than glory.[2]

[1821] Good stipulation of the ordinance of 1735, article 76,[1] which abrogates the use of waiver clauses. In fact, these clauses represented the quite precious liberty of being able to change one's intention right up to death, especially in the case of a will[2]—quite different from donations, where one contracts, so to speak, with the recipient.

Good stipulation of the ordinance, of article 37 of the new ordinance, which abrogates the use of mutual wills. In the past they would continue on, despite a second will, when the one had not publicly declared the revocation to the other, which was very fair.

[1822] Good stipulation of the Customary of Normandy, which quashes the will when the testator does not survive for three months.[1] This term ought, however, to be reduced, especially if the testator is not on his deathbed, which is itself subject to ambiguity.

[1823] It is foolish to oblige the parties to defend themselves through counsel, because if lawyers are free not to plead, the parties must themselves be even freer to plead.

[1824] LETTERS OF REPRIEVE.[1] They should take place only in cases of absence for the Republic, and in cases where they are given to a man who is present, they should take place only where it is a matter of debtors' imprisonment, not pursuit of property.

[1825] It must be noted that it is not the same with civil laws as it is with the laws of religion. It is difficult to move from one religion to another, because reasons of convenience are not powerful enough to make the resolution and overcome strong motives. But in matters of civil law, one may easily prefer to live under a different law, because reasons of con-

---

2. See *pensée* 1655 for similar language.—HC

[1821]
1. See Isambert et al., *Recueil général des anciennes lois françaises* [General compendium of former French laws], 29 vols. (Paris, 1822–33), 21:386, no. 478.
2. On wills, see *Laws*, bk. 27.

[1822]
1. Montesquieu owned a French edition of this work from 1660 (*Catalogue*, 897).

[1824]
1. Letters of reprieve permitted debtors to obtain a delay in order to discharge their debts.

venience count for everything in that area. Thus, in Italy, the Lombards and then the Germans and the French became Romans.

[1826] I will set down here the different characteristics of the laws of these various peoples.[1]

"The Salic laws[2] fulfilled their purpose very well. They distinguished the various cases with great precision. If someone stole a pig from the first or second litter, he paid 3 sols; if it was from the third, he paid 15.[3]

"In cases of theft, the settlement terms in the Salic law did not always follow the price of the stolen object. Thus, for three sheep or more, 1,400 denier were paid, and for fifty or more, 2,500. Since the law always made the person give back the stolen object, and since it established terms only for the offense incurred, it considered that, to fix this offense, it was not necessary to follow the proportion of the scale of the theft—that is, the proportion of the wealth of the person who had been robbed.

"They weighed the circumstances to the last degree. If a sparrow hawk on a tree was stolen, 3 sols; if it had been locked away, 45 sols.[4] The law considered, on the one hand, the security of the house, and, on the other, a sparrow hawk on a tree seemed to have recovered its natural liberty.

"The Ripuary Law is distinctive in that it accords a bit more with the Roman Law than does the Salic Law; its terms are usually milder than those of the Salic Law. {Among other examples, Salic sols are 40 deniers; Ripuary sols are 12 deniers, *secundum antiquam consuetudinem* [according to ancient custom], says title XXXVI—that is, according to Roman custom, which had 12 ounces in the *as*.}

"The Ripuary Law seems to conform to Roman laws in that, *si homo regis infidelis extiterit* [if a king's man has been unfaithful], confiscation (book LXIX, p. 80), and title LXXVIII, on a thief hanged for having perjured himself, no confiscation; which conforms to Roman laws, which

[1826]

1. See *Laws,* 28.1, for what follows. In this entry, English translations of short Latin passages will be placed in brackets.—HC

2. Montesquieu cites the barbarian laws according to the Linenbrog collection of 1613 (*Catalogue,* 820); they have since been reedited in the *Monumenta Germaniae historica.* The first version of the Salic law seems to date to the reign of Clovis. But the prologue is of later date and has a legendary character; it evolved from its first version to the last version, the *Lex emendata,* which was done under Charlemagne; see Brèthe, 2:446 n. 38.

3. "*Salic Law,* title II, §§ 1 and 2" (M.).

4. "*Salic Law,* title VII, §§ 1 and 3" (M.).

allowed confiscation only for crimes of lèse-majesté (pp. 80 and 81 of the above-cited extract).

"Against abbé Dubos's system, this again proves: the Salians were therefore not as friendly with the Romans as the Ripuarians were.[5]

"When a man set fire to a house, he paid 600 sols, besides expenses and damages; and if he denied committing the crime, he swore with seventy-two witnesses. If the criminal was a slave, he paid only 36 sols, besides the damages and trial expenses; and if he denied it, the master swore with six witnesses.

"This law is peculiar in that the slave paid less than the freeman. But this is because they followed not the proportion of the resources but the nature of the thing, and they did not want the master to be ruined by his slave's crime, by paying beyond his value.

"But what is quite jarring is the difference in the number of witnesses necessary for the freeman to swear (when he would deny it) and the number necessary for the slave. It was ridiculous to follow the proportion of the terms on this point, since in both cases the necessity of proof was the same. But the slave was thought to have hardly any relatives or friends.

"Title XLIX of the Ripuary Law conforms entirely to Marculf's formulas, which makes me think that this law was at least as generally accepted as the Salic Law—even more so: witness the procedure on combat.[6]

"The justice and impartiality of the Burgundian laws is admirable. I will cite what it decrees on hospitality.

"{It is known that hospitality} was a common thing among the Germans, '*et qui modo hospes fuerat monstrator hospitii,*' says Tacitus.[7] When the Burgundians had founded a monarchy, it was necessary to regulate the abuses that could arise from the exercise of that right. The law requires that, when someone hosts an individual who is traveling for the public business, each resident of the village reimburse him for his part of the expense; it requires that this right of hospitality not be refused even to those who are traveling for their private business; that whoever refuses him

---

5. Montesquieu criticizes Dubos's *Etablissement de la monarchie française* [Establishment of the French monarchy] in *Laws*, bk. 30.

6. Marculf, Merovingian monk, who established, ca. 650, a collection of models of juridical acts; Montesquieu owned three copies of the 1613 edition of his work (*Catalogue,* 967–68) and consulted the 1665 edition from the Bordeaux Academy library.

7. Tacitus, *Germania*, 21.2: "he who had been your host points out your place of entertainment."

pay a fine of 3 sous, and that if a Burgundian, instead of hosting a guest, shows him a Roman's house, he pay the Roman another settlement of 3 sous, besides the 3 sous fine. If whoever is hosted wreaks havoc inside the house, the law requires him to pay nine times the thing's value. The entire Burgundian Code is full of good sense.

"Those Burgundian laws were extremely wise. They thought only of restoring to the body of the State that unity which conquest had taken away.

"*Romana puelle, si sine parentum [suorum] voluntate aut conscientia, se Burgundionis conjugio sociaverit, nihil se de parentum facultate noverit habituram.*[8]

"Marriages between Burgundians and Romans were therefore permitted, but they wanted to prevent the Burgundians from marrying Roman women without their fathers' consent (title XII of the above-cited laws, § 5).

"Here, I will observe the conformity of the law I am citing with what Tacitus tells us about the Germans: '*Qui modo hospes fuerat monstrator hospitii*' ['he who had been your host points out your place of entertainment'], which shows us that that author had a perfect understanding of those mores.

"Title XLIII of the Burgundian Law is entirely drawn from the Roman law on the form of wills and public donations. The Germans had neither wills for property, nor donations; when these were established, they took the stipulations of Roman Law, and the Burgundians were all the more willing to choose this law because such conduct could reconcile the minds of the conquered people to them.

"*Additamentum Legis Burgundionum* [An addition to the Burgundian laws], on the theft of a dog and a sparrow hawk (titles X and XI), very strange law,[9] and one that indicated the simplicity of those peoples (pages 122 and 123 of the extract).[10]

"The Law of the Visigoths[11] had said it well in decreeing that courtesans

8. "If a Roman girl, without the will or consent of her parents, is united by marriage to a Burgundian, she will possess nothing of the property of her parents."

9. "Book III, tit. 4, § 17" (M.).

10. This extract is lost. The law of the Burgunds, which Montesquieu calls Burgundian, is called the Gombette Law, because it was prepared on the orders of King Gondebaud (474–516).

11. Visigoth law was drawn up at first on the orders of King Euric (466–84); for more, see Brèthe, 4:310 n. 7.

be given in servitude to a poor man. The infamy of the profession could not be better punished than by the infamy of the condition.[12]

"Widows who took the religious habit upon the death of their husbands, and placed folded bands under this habit as evidence that they had not abandoned the worldly habit, were obliged by the Law to guard the monastic habit and monastic continence—because, said the Prince, one must judge by the external habit.[13] The reason for the law is no more sensible than the law itself. It is by the intention that they ought to have judged.

"In the German laws, we find crimes and misdemeanors punished by the same terms as in the Salic laws, as well as the fines or *freda* paid to the public. Corporal punishment was not in use. Everything follows the spirit of the early Germans on this score.

"This German law is very humane.[14] It decrees that if a free German woman marries a slave of the Church and feels repugnance toward the servile life, she can leave. But if she remains for three years without making a claim, she and her children will be slaves. The law of these peoples considered liberty to be as natural as marriage. The tie of nature was stronger than the tie of will, which became a tie of nature only through will. This claim is similar to those we make against monastic vows within five years. But our claim assumes violence and demands proof of it, whereas the German Law, founded on fragility, dispensed with this. A free woman who has tolerated servitude for three years, who has consented to seeing her soul beaten down for so long, who has not found a single moment when she could form a generous sentiment, has rendered herself unworthy of liberty.

"The German Law is everywhere very mild. These laws are quite a bit milder than the laws of the Visigoths. It might be that these Northern peoples, transported into Southern country, would have needed harsher laws.

"In any case, all these laws exude mildness. Such are the pecuniary penalties against whoever neglects the command of the Duke or the Centurion: 12 sous; 6 sous; 3 sous.[15]

"The German Law allowed negative proofs, like that of the Ripuarians.[16]

"Same mildness in the German Law if the Duke's son rebels against his

12. "Book III, title IV, § 17" (M.).
13. "Laws of the Visigoths, book III, title V, § 4" (M.).
14. "§ 18" (M.).
15. "Law of the Germans, § 29" (M.); it should read title 28.
16. "Law of the Germans, §§ 24 and 30" (M.); it should read title instead of §.

father at a time when he is of a condition to mount a horse. For those nations, mounting a horse was the greatest qualification for government.

"The German Law established combat.[17] When a free man accuses another of great crimes before the duke or before the king, and when the accuser does not prove his case but rests content with saying that the crime has been committed, the accused could vindicate himself by combat. It seems to me that the law of combat is much moderated by this law. In any case, it permitted combat like the Ripuary Law, but it did not admit of abuses. Thus, it did not have room for crimes of less consequence.

"In title LII of the German Law, it seems to be a very bad deed to marry the fiancée of another. This law accords very well with that of the Visigoths.

"The German Law provided great scope for repudiations. The husband gave terms of 40 sous.

"These German laws pay heed to the harm done to the Public by the diminution of families. If a free man is killed, and leaves children, 160 sous are paid for his *Weregilde,* and if he does not leave children, ——. One senses the reason for the Law: it is one less family. Thus, that same law prohibits with great care the transfer of slaves into foreign countries. The large number of peoples that had departed from Germany made them want to make whole those that remained.

"See the asterisk in my extract, page 197, on the character of the Bavarian Law, at title VII, § 15.

"Two quite odd laws in the Bavarian Law. Evidence of the correction that has been made to the Bavarian Law is that at title XIV, § 8, the Old Testament is cited.

"The Saxon Law also allows negative proof.[18]

"General law of these barbarian peoples against those who betrothed or raped girls betrothed to another.[19]

"The Saxon Law also allowed trial by combat.[20]

"Here, a free woman sold, the terms are not steeper than for a man:[21] they are 600 sous, whether for a noble man or a noble woman.

---

17. "I've put the citations in *The Spirit of the Laws*" (M.).

18. "*Caput Ium,* § 1" (M.).

19. "Law of the Saxons, § 9" (M.).

20. "§ 15 (of the extract) page 218" (M.).

21. "Law of the Angles, title I, § 1, and title X, § 3. It is true that this takes place only *pro faemina nundum pariente, vel quae parere desiit; nam, si sit pariens* [for a woman not yet bearing offspring, or else who has ceased to bear (them); especially if she might be bearing offspring] three times 600 sous. (*Ibidem*)" (M.).

"The Angles' Law had doubtless been corrected, since we see in it the establishment of donations and wills. *Libero homini liceat haereditatem suam cui voluerit tradere* [it is permitted to a free man to transmit his own inheritance to whomever he wants],[22] which was contrary to the right of the Germans, as we see in Tacitus: . . . *nullum testamentum* [no will], etc.

"One notes in the Frisian Law that the terms of settlement are beginning to be reckoned in pounds.[23] The Frisians were situated on large rivers, abutted large nations, and were able to engage in an extensive commerce, like the peoples that inhabit that territory today. (Look into the relationship, however, between these settlements in pounds and other peoples' settlements in sols.)

"It seems to me that this payment in pounds does not entail more money than fixing it in sols does in other peoples' laws. Thus, my observation will be useless.

"This law shows us the Frisians governed by a duke, under the king; like the Saxon Law [and the Bavarian] shows us the Saxons.

"Whoever sells a free man outside the country *componat ac si interfecisset* [let him make restoration . . . as if he had killed him]."[24]

[1827] Laws may still have a similarity of origin that needs to be known. How can one apply a law if one does not know the country for which it was made, and the circumstances in which it was made? Most of those who study jurisprudence follow the course of the Nile, overflow with it, but are ignorant of its source.

[1828] In the Lombard Code, one finds laws against those bearing enchanted arms.[1] They bear a pretty close relationship with the time when armor became heavier among the Franks. There may have been arms of such good stamp that they seemed to derive their force from some enchantment. This provided the origin for countless novels, which were the subject of those which Ariosto and others have transmitted down to us—

22. "Title XIII" (M.).
23. "Title XV" (M.).
24. "*Frisian Law,* title XXI" (M.).

[1828]
1. The Law of the Lombards, established in the North of Italy at the end of the sixth century, is constituted by the code of Rotharis (643), completed by the laws of his successors up to 755; it is a mixture of Germanic customs and Roman law.

all the more ridiculous today, now that firearms have made all the paladins disappear.

[**1829**] When one thinks about these three princes: Pepin, Charles Martel, and Charlemagne![1] Under them, the always-victorious Nation saw no more enemies. But after them, there happened what had been seen in the Roman Empire—when, after Marius, Sulla, Pompey, and Caesar, Rome had nothing to subjugate. There happened what had been seen among the Greeks after Alexander—the Franks destroyed themselves by civil wars.

[**1830**] In a letter to Louis the Debonair, Agobard complains that the canons of the French councils, written by such saintly bishops, were regarded by many people as superfluous and useless because, since they had been written without the participation of the Pope, the Roman canonists made no mention of them.[1]

But if the problem was already so large, what was it going to be in the centuries that followed?

[**1831**] I still have many things to say, but I am afraid this would become a matter of pure erudition. I would like to speak not to my readers' memory but to their good sense, and one has finished sooner when one speaks to good sense than to memory. I would prefer to teach how to consider laws in their origin, than to write a book on the origin of the laws.

[**1832**] The Normans having desolated the entire Realm, a sort of anarchy that arose from the public misery brought that public misery to its peak. Hugh Capet was elected.

[**1833**] The Sultan is accustomed to attend the Great Chamber[1] behind a tapestry. He thereby strips his subjects of freedom of thought in the one matter in the whole world on which it is most important to him that they be free, namely, the deliberations of his council.

[**1834**] In M. Barbeyrac's collection of ancient treaties, article 35,

[1829]
1. Charles Martel, mayor of the palace (ca. 688–741).

[1830]
1. Agobard (ca. 779–840), archbishop of Lyon, lived under the Burgundian Law; Louis I the Pious, or Debonair, Western Emperor (814–40).

[1833]
1. *Divan,* the chamber of the state council in Ottoman Turkey; see also *pensée* 1992.—HC

year 848 or thereabouts before Jesus Christ{, p. 192 v° of my extract},[1] it is said:

"*Treaty between the Locrians, who came from Greece, and the Siculians from Italy.* The Locrians landed in this corner of Italy, near the cape of Zephyrium, possessed by the Siculians. There, they made an alliance and swore that, as long as they walked on this earth, {and} had heads on their shoulders, they would possess the territory in common. The Locrians had put some soil from their country into their shoes and some garlic bulbs on their shoulders, under their clothes."

In those times, one sees all manner of oaths eluded in the same fashion: ignorance produces superstition, and superstition, which leads people to honor the gods in an outlandish manner, also leads them to dupe the gods.

Superstition is the mother of the literal sense, enemy of the allegorical sense.

In a period of comparable ignorance, the children of Clovis (I believe)—intending to violate the oath they were making on the saints' reliquaries—secretly had the relics pulled out of them.[2]

[1835] INTENDANCIES. How have they repaired the highways? They have employed a fast authority, even though they could not have employed one that was too slow. They confused quickness in execution . . .

If it is true that public works must be quickly executed, the undertaking cannot be too carefully deliberated.[1]

[1836] I would like people to follow the path that a trial takes among us, from tribunal to tribunal. It goes along, marches, climbs, goes in reverse, climbs again to a higher level, without counting the longer trips to the Prince's Council. It goes on for thirty years, without being able to wrap up its final decree.[1]

[1834]

1. Jean Barbeyrac (1674–1744), French Calvinist jurist, exiled in Berlin after the Revocation of the Edict of Nantes in 1685, whose translations and commentaries of the major works in the natural-law tradition by Grotius and Pufendorf helped shape their reception. Here, Montesquieu refers to the *Supplément au corps universel du droit des gens* [Supplement to the universal body of the law of nations] (Amsterdam, 1739; *Catalogue*, 2366); the extract cited is lost.

2. "Drawn from my volume *Polit.-Hist.*, p. 192 v° and 193" (M.), a volume that is lost; see *pensée* 1930.

[1835]

1. For other comments on the intendant, see *pensées* 977, 1353, 1572, 1840, 1846, 1898, and 2099.—HC

[1836]

1. Montesquieu pursued numerous court cases in his life.

[**1837**] Aristotle[1] censures the inequalities in female wealth in Lacedemon, and he blames Lycurgus, who, while prohibiting a citizen from selling his estate or buying that of another, had permitted bequeathing it by will. {I would rather believe what Plutarch says (*Life of Agis and Cleomenes*), where it was one Epitadius who had this law passed. Aristotle, who was writing to attack Lycurgus's system of laws, could not be regarded as impartial. He needed to find that those laws were bad.}

If that were the case, then Lycurgus, who had so striven to establish equality, would have grossly contradicted the laws, and it would be quite extraordinary that with such a principle of corruption, his republic had endured so long without being corrupted, and that with such a principle of inequality, fortunes had been equal for so long.

It is better to say, with Plutarch, that the principle of inequality was introduced by one of the ephors.

[**1838**] THE SENATUS CONSULTUM SILANIANUM,[1] IN ROME, AGAINST THE SLAVES. In Rome, those deeds of fidelity, of virtue, of courage by most Roman slaves were owing to such harsh laws. You see them kill themselves after having killed their master by his order. But the Law would have put them to death in any case. (Look into those Laws here.)[2]

[**1839**] Landed property, mother of all. The reason why China has a better government and is not in decline, like all other Asian states, is that landed property is established there, whereas it is not in Turkey, or in Persia, or in Mogul, or in Japan, at least not completely. The reason why it is in China is that the contrary would lead to revolt, whereas in the other states, it leads only to imperceptible ruin.

[**1840**] Tacitus, *De Moribus Germanorum: "Sororum filiis idem apud avunculum qui apud patrem honor."*[1]

This indicates a people that is not corrupted. Among the earliest Romans, first cousins regarded themselves as brothers, which came about be-

[**1837**]

1. Aristotle, *Politics,* II.vi.8–11.

[**1838**]

1. A group of enactments passed as a Senatorial decree during the consulship of Silanus in A.D. 10 that resolved, in part, that if a slave owner was murdered in his home, his slaves would be tortured and executed.—HC

2. See *Laws,* 15.16, on these laws.

[**1840**]

1. "Sisters' children mean as much to their uncle as to their father." *Germania,* 20.4.

cause the children remained in the house and got married there. Corruption makes interests become more private and lessens love of family.

Tacitus continues: "Some even regard this tie as being more sacred. *Haeredes tamen successoresque sui cuique liberi, et nullum testamentum.*"[2]

Wherever there is less luxury and more poverty, families love each other more, and distant relatives are more connected than in monarchies, where each individual wants to live for himself and pursue only the conveniences of life.

[**1841**] The perpetual soldier has depopulated the North, and Germany, and Spain.

The Indies have depopulated Spain and populated Holland, England, and France, by a particular trade they have provided them.

[**1842**] When a French officer, a prisoner of war, had said the time would arrive when he would wash his hands in Venetian blood, they hanged him, and he was slashed with a knife on the bottom of his feet so the place would be bathed in his blood—a circumstance more cruel than torture.[1]

This rash or indiscreet remark, which might be the occasion for a crime of lèse-majesté when pronounced against a monarch, cannot be pronounced against the People, because a single man may not exterminate a people. Anyway, this remark meant nothing more than that, having waged war against the Venetians, he would do so again, which is a legitimate thing to the French.

[**1843**] The Serf has altars to which there are temples attached, from which one would not dare abduct even thieves. Enemies who flee—if they are able to embrace a statue of the gods or rush into a temple—are assured of their lives. But the superstitious one, etc.

It was indeed the fitting situation of the asylums to save the lives of the defeated.[1]

[**1844**] RELIGION. In the farmers' caste, when they pierce their ears or

---

2. "However, so far as heirship and succession are concerned, each man's sons are his heirs, and there is no will." *Germania,* 20.5.

[**1842**]
1. "*Histoire du Gouvernement de Venise,* by Sieur de La Houssaye, page 358, and from the extract, page 70" (M.); see *Catalogue,* 3084, for this 1676 volume, the extract of which is lost. Nicolas Amelot de La Houssaye (1634–1706) had been secretary in the embassy at Venice in 1669.

[**1843**]
1. "Page 120, and (from the extract) page 228" (M.).

get married, they have to have two fingers on their hand cut off and presented to the idol, if they would prefer not to present two fingers of gold to the Divinity.[1]

It is strange that those who most need their fingers are the ones who have them cut off. This is taken from the idea that one can give to God only by depriving oneself.

[**1845**] Mores are never really pure in monarchies. That nobility, with its luxury and the virtues it fashions for itself, is the source of all corruption.

[**1846**] Volume II *Geographica:* Impoverishment of provinces attributed to the change of governors into intendants. They are like our own, who think only of treasure and not of the people. The governors were managing the province, which they regarded as their patrimony. Depopulation that followed from this. Nothing is feared from the intendants. They obtain their positions by virtue of presents and by doing better at collection. One must keep one's word and support the patrons. Chardin, p. 150.[1]

Those intendants very much resemble our own.[2]

[**1847**] The enslavement of the peasants in Germany clearly shows that it was a conquest of people who were not cultivating the land.

[**1848**] Volume I *Geographica:* The Spanish government's abuses in the Indies are attributed to the change of governors, which occurs every three, five, or seven years.[1] But it would be dangerous to leave them in there longer. Thus, one needs wise laws that prevent the drawbacks involved in changing them.

[**1849**] The type of dependence that the Carlian house[1] established was established in the past in China, and we do not see that that sort of govern-

---

[**1844**]

1. "Sixteenth Collection, *Edifying letters,* page 132" (M.).

[**1846**]

1. Montesquieu owned 1687 and 1711 editions of Jean Chardin's accounts of his travels to Persia and the East (*Catalogue,* 2738–39).

2. Also on the intendants, see *pensées* 977, 1353, 1572, 1835, 1840, 1898, 2066, and 2099.—HC

[**1848**]

1. "P. 371, Frézier" (M.); on Frézier, see *pensée* 1810 n. 1. Vol. 1 of *Geographica* is lost.

[**1849**]

1. The Carolingian dynasty of the Franks.—HC

ment has had bad effects. That made for a monarchical body, instead of a despotic state. This is also Germany.[2]

[1850] The Prince, who makes the civil laws, can indeed grant letters of pardon, because he can set the example, and because condemnation itself is an example, and because letters of pardon are likewise an example.[1]

[1851] OPPOSITION. Intervention or opposition did not go unpunished in the Roman Senate, if it was reckless: "*Cum enim in rem non esset publicam, aut remittere cogebantur eam, aut poenam aliquando subire.*"[1] Caesar (*De Bello civili*) says: "*De tribunis Plebis gravissime fuisse decretum.*"[2]

The abuse in Poland's laws is that they have not punished the reckless opposition.

[1852] SENATUS CONSULTA.[1] Since the Senate had become a court of judicature, it scarcely had authority except to make the civil laws. Thus, the number of senatus-consulta was very large.

[1853] The Czar has made the system in his states work in favor of the human race but not his empire. If that empire were civilized, inhabited, cultivated, it would be impossible for it to survive.

[1854] In monarchies, things in common are regarded as the things of someone else; in republics, they are regarded as the things of each individual.[1]

[1855] Plutarch has remarked that ancient philosophy was nothing else but the science of government.[1] The Seven Sages, he says, if one makes a single exception, devoted themselves only to Politics and Morality. Although the Greeks devoted themselves later on to the speculative sciences, it is

2. Probably a reference to the Holy Roman Empire.—HC

[1850]
1. On letters of pardon, see *Laws,* 6.16, 92.

[1851]
1. "In fact when (the opposition) was against the state, they were compelled either to pay a fine or to undergo punishment at some point."
2. "Decrees of the severest . . . character are passed affecting . . . the tribunes of the people." See Caesar, *De bello civili* [On civil war], I.5, for an approximation.

[1852]
1. "Decrees of the Senate."—HC

[1854]
1. See *pensées* 1760 and 1891.

[1855]
1. See Plutarch, *Life of Solon,* III; *Life of Themistocles,* II.

clear that their highest degree of esteem was for the active philosophy, and their true cult was for city governors and their legislators.[2]

[1856] Even in cases where the laws have force, they always have less of it than honor. Duty is a cold and studied thing. But honor is a lively passion, which animates itself, and which, moreover, is attached to all other passions. Tell subjects they must obey their prince because religion and the laws ordain it, and you will find cold people. Tell them they must be faithful to him because they have promised to, and you will see them become animated.[1]

[1857] Art is establishing itself and taking the place of the good sense and prudence that ought to guide citizens. The jurisconsults are quite happy to see us obliged to have recourse to them at each step we take in our affairs, and the judges are not upset to exercise their authority over those the jurisconsults send them.[1]

[1858] INFAMY. In Sparta, there was a question after Leuctra whether the mark of infamy prescribed by the Law would be imposed on those who had fled, for the Law declared them incompetent for any office.[1] It is infamy to give them any woman or to take any of theirs. Whoever encounters them on the way can strike them if he wants, and they must bear it, bowing their heads. Gown patched up; half shorn. Agesilaus put the Law to sleep one day.[2]

That sort of mark was quite repressive, and quite capable of bringing credit to valor and courage.

[1859] OF THE PURPOSE OF THE LAWS. It is a wonderful thought by Plato, *Republic,* book IX, that the laws are made to announce the orders of reason to those who cannot receive it immediately from itself.

[1860] EPISTLE. {I had thought to dedicate it to the Prince of Wales:}[1] When one sees the King, your father, govern with the same moderation

---

2. See also *pensées* 1871 and 1940.—HC

[1856]
1. See *Laws,* 3.7, for this theme.

[1857]
1. Cf. *pensée* 1571.—HC

[1858]
1. Leuctra, Boeotian city where the Spartans were defeated by Epaminondas (July 371 B.C.).
2. "Plutarch, *Life of Agesilaus*" (M.); XXX.

[1860]
1. Frederick, prince of Wales (1737–51), son of George II and father of George III.

both the realms in which his power has limits and the states subject to his will, one perceives that in the latter, he wills only what the laws will, and it seems that in the others, the laws have established in advance all that he might will.

[**1861**] PREFACE. We reflect little. Our interest in having accurate ideas about things gives way to another interest, which is a certain repose and a pleasant self-abnegation.

If I may predict the fortunes of this book, it will be more approved than read. Such readings can sometimes be a pleasure; they are never an amusement.[1]

[**1862**] It was necessary to read much, and to make very little use of what one read.[1]

[**1863**] I give thanks to Messrs Grotius and Pufendorf for having executed what a large part of this work demanded of me, and with that loftiness of genius which I would not have been able to attain.[1]

If everyone does not perceive what I am saying, I am wrong.

Not everything that is new is bold.

I believe most things are good, and the best is very rare.

[**1864**] This work would not be useless in the education of young princes, and would perhaps be worth more to them than vague exhortations to govern well, to be great princes, to make their subjects happy— which is the same thing as exhorting a man who does not know the first propositions of Euclid to resolve some nasty geometry problems.

[**1865**] This book having been written for no state, no state can complain about it. It is written for all men. Being offended by a treatise on morality is unheard of. It is well known that there were several emperors in China who wanted to have the books of Philosophy and the Rites burned—solemnly proscribed. They were more solemnly restored. The State needed them more than any individual whatsoever.

[**1866**] The style of my mind is not to give up on what everyone knows. But the boldest things are not offensive when they have been said often,

[**1861**]
1. See *pensée* 1723.—HC

[**1862**]
1. See *Laws,* preface, xliv, for a similar thought.

[**1863**]
1. See *pensée* 1537 and *Laws,* preface, xlv.

and the most innocent can shock petty minds because they have not yet been said.

[**1867**] There are nations in which it seemed that nature had done everything for men, and which seem to deprive themselves of her. She seemed to have placed them above others, but they place themselves below. Never has so much wit and so little enlightenment been seen.[1] But just as the heart leads the mind, the mind in its turn leads the heart. The mind, then, must be perfected.

[**1868**] This work is the fruit of my entire life's reflections, and perhaps out of an immense labor, a labor engaged in with the best intentions, a labor engaged in for public utility, I will derive only sorrows, and will be paid only out of the hands of ignorance and envy.[1]

Of all the governments I have seen, I have no bias toward any, not even the one that I love the most because I have the good fortune to live there.

I had read barely a handful of works on jurisprudence before I regarded it as a country where Reason wants to reside without Philosophy. [I conceived a design . . .]

[**1869**] Know in which situation an abuse can become the law and the correction[1] can become an abuse.

[**1870**] I esteem ministers; it is not the men who are small, it is the affairs that are big.

[**1871**] In our age, such a degree of esteem has been bestowed upon the natural sciences that mere indifference has been preserved for the moral. Since the Greeks and Romans, moral good and evil have become an opinion[1] rather than an object of knowledge.

The Ancients cherished the sciences; they protected the arts. But the esteem they had for those who invented something on the subject of government—they brought that up to a kind of cult.[2]

[**1867**]
1. This formulation is used to describe the French at *pensée* 1736.—HC

[**1868**]
1. See the first lines of *Laws,* preface, xliii.

[**1869**]
1. *Correction* may also mean "punishment" here.—HC

[**1871**]
1. *Sentiment,* which can also be translated as "feeling."—HC
2. See *pensées* 1855 and 1940.—HC

[**1872**] I have labored for twenty straight years on this work, and I still do not know whether I have been courageous or reckless, whether I have been overwhelmed by the size or sustained by the majesty of my subject.[1]

[**1873**] When you see causes of prosperity in a state that is not prospering, shortage prevailing where nature had put abundance, base vanity where the climate had promised courage, evils instead of the goods expected from the country's religion, it is easy to perceive that they have diverged from the Legislator's goal. The difficulty is to know when, how, and by what path one needs to recover.

It is in an age of enlightenment that Statesmen acquire the great talent of doing good things appropriately. Everyone can seek to project a few rays of this light, without having the arrogance of becoming a reformer.

All I have had before my eyes is my principles; they guide me, and I do not lead them.

I am second to none in my belief that those who govern have good intentions. I know there is such and such a country that is badly governed, but also that it would be very difficult for it to be better governed. In the end, I see more than I pass judgment on; I reason on everything and criticize nothing.[1]

[**1874**] Law is the right reason of the great Jupiter.[1]

[**1875**] France should support the Catholic religion, which is inconvenient to all other Catholic countries but does her no harm. Thereby, she preserves her superiority over the other Catholic countries. If she became Protestant, all would become Protestant.[1]

[**1876**] Continuation of the material that did not make it into *The Spirit of the Laws. For the Composition of the Laws.* Abbé Saint-Pierre, who was the best good man who ever was, has nothing to say about any problem except that you must assemble ten good people.[1] You might say this is

[1872]
1. See *Laws*, preface, xliii, and *pensée* 1920.

[1873]
1. See *Laws*, preface, xliii–xliv.

[1874]
1. "Cicero, *De legibus*" (M.). Montesquieu had thought of using this sentence from *On the Laws*, II.4, "Lex est ratio summi Jovis," as the epigraph of *Laws*. See *pensée* 1519.

[1875]
1. On religion and regime, see *Laws*, 24.5.

[1876]
1. On abbé Saint-Pierre (1658–1743), see *pensées* 1275, 1718, and 1940.

like a major who chooses the soldiers, and who says: "They must be 5 feet, 8 inches." The laws must begin by working at making good people, before thinking about choosing them. One must not begin by talking about those people. There are so few of them that it is not worth the trouble.

[**1877**] For book XIII, chapter xxi: *Dangerous practice*. When the Prince begins by welcoming the tax collectors and gives them the wherewithal to go after his subjects, he brings to the door of each one of them an enemy who is strengthened by tears, and whom poverty seems to encourage.[1] When the prefect of the praetorium, says Ammianus Marcellinus (book XVII), promised to make up for the entire shortfall in the head tax in Gaul, Julian said he would rather lose his life than stand for that. For he knew the incurable wounds that these sorts of provision cause in provinces (they caused Illyria's ruin, says the same author), and when the augmentation rolls were presented to him, he threw them on the ground. Ammianus Marcellinus, who writes this, says (book XVI) that when that prince entered Gaul, people were paying twenty-five gold crowns per head; when he returned from there, it was no more than seven, for every type of charge. Now those who are familiar with the Romans' financial condition in that period well know that they were in no position to sustain losses. The reduction was not on the tax, then, but on the collection expenses, and of these two arrangements, the one was the happy effect of the other.

[**1878**] For book XIII, chapter xviii.[1] *Of the Assistance the State can get from tax collectors*. In monarchies, the Prince is like the private individuals, who have credit as a combined result of their wealth, their conduct, and the prejudices toward their condition.

A monarch who has not made himself unworthy of public credit has some, provided that he can recognize he has some, and that he not think the tax collectors can provide him with some.

The property of a large State is so immense, compared with that of one or several individuals, that when these two "credits" join forces, that of the individual is no more. If the Prince has credit, he imparts some to the individual; if he does not, he ruins that which the individual used to have.

[1877]
1. On tax collectors, see *Laws*, 13.20, a view criticized by Claude Dupin (see *pensées* 1572 and 1643) and by the tax-farmer and man of letters Charles-Etienne Pesselier (1712–63) in the *Encyclopédie* article "financier," 6:815 (1756); see Derathé, 1:494 n. 24.

[1878]
1. In fact, it is chapter 20.

Tax collectors can procure credit for the prince only on the bad transactions they make him engage in. It is the money they draw from the Prince's coffers that has this credit, and if it had been kept, that money would have had it anyway.

I have seen great lords often need credit from a valet who had stashed away fifty crowns. Such will be the Prince who has recourse to his tax collectors.

[1879] CHINA. By the nature of the country, China can hardly be divided into many states, unless it is divided like a fief, to make the parts of a single body. As we have said, there is no country in the world where men's subsistence is so little assured and so precarious. Thus, there is no province that can imagine being able to dispense for two years with the support of another. Need is a chain that links them all and keeps them under an empire.

One sees laws by which the Emperors prohibit kings from arresting the course of rivers that flow into another realm, which would make them perish.

Isolated on three sides by the sea, by deserts, and by mountains, the Empire can have enemies only from the north. This has caused the seat of empire to be established in the North. The Northern provinces are vastly more bellicose than those of the South, and their people more courageous. Thus, the South can only with difficulty separate itself from the North.

[1880] CHAPTER VI. BY WHAT CAUSE CHINA, DESPITE ITS VAST EXTENT, HAS SOMETIMES BEEN OBLIGED TO TEMPER ITS DESPOTISM.[1] The Empire did not at first have too great an extent, which meant that luxury and wealth had a less harmful effect on princes. They possessed only the Northern provinces—the least delightful provinces, where there is less flabbiness, where people are more inclined to work, and where consequently mores are simpler.

The entire South was in a barbarous condition. It was the Chinese people's prosperity and good fortune that engaged the Barbarians to seek to live under their domination. (One finds hardly any conquests in the history of China.)

As we will show, China is situated in a climate where one is naturally inclined toward servile obedience. Thus, although the circumstances we

[1880]
1. For Montesquieu on China, see *Geographica* (*OC,* 2:927–43) and *Laws,* 8.21.

are going to talk about ought to have led her to the principle of republican government, she was not a republic.

China is a mixed government, which much resembles despotism in the Prince's immense power; which resembles the republic a little, in the censorship and in a certain virtue founded on paternal love and respect; and which resembles monarchy in the fixed laws and regular tribunals, and in a certain honor attached to constancy and to the danger of speaking the truth. These three things, well tempered, and the circumstances derived from the nature of the climate, have made it endure. And if the size of the Empire has made of it a despotic government, it is perhaps the best of all.

The eighth emperor of the second dynasty repressed the peoples of the southern part, who were pillaging the provinces. Thus, the South had not been subjugated.[2]

The eleventh emperor of the third dynasty—separated from China by the Yangtze river, some southern nations which had laid waste the Empire were repressed. Thus, the southern provinces were not part of the Empire.[3]

The emperors of the third dynasty reigned wisely enough. It is just that the times were difficult; their authority was limited; the tributary princes were demanding to be accommodated; the Empire was less extensive.[4] Its size must indeed have weakened it, for it is only since it became that extensive that it has been subjugated twice by the Tartars, who founded the twentieth and twenty-second dynasties. Before then, the Tartars, in the frightful discord of civil war, had made some incursions or invasions, but never establishments.

[1881] ARMORICANS. I believe Father Hardouin was quite happy when, in one of Horace's odes, he discovered the Jacobins.[1] It must not have been a lesser pleasure for abbé Dubos when he saw for the first time the role that the Armorican republic was going to play in the world.[2]

---

2. "Volume II, *Politica,* Du Halde, 126" (M.).
3. "Volume II, *Politica,* p. 131" (M.).
4. "Volume II, *Politica,* p. 133" (M.).

[1881]

1. Fr. Jean Hardouin (1646–1729) attributed Horace's *Odes* to a medieval Benedictine monk; "Jacobin" here refers to the Dominicans (not the Benedictines), who resided on the rue St. Jacques in Paris.

2. In his *Critical History* (especially 1.8, 2.3, and 2.5), abbé Dubos singled out the role of an Armorican tribal confederation in Brittany and Normandy in the founding of the fifth-century French monarchy.—HC

[1882] ON THE BOOKS ON CLIMATE.¹ Look into what the republics of the Indies were like at the time of Alexander's arrival. In Diodorus (book III, page 296),² look at the Indians' laws, which are greatly similar to what we are told about them today—whether concerning the caste differences, the conditions, the mildness of slavery, the landed property belonging to the Sovereign, etc.³ Look also at what it says about them in book II, page 246. What it says—that famine has never been seen there—has certainly changed. That is why there is no talk of rice.

This shows clearly that what the *Nouvelles ecclésiastiques* has said about what I said against the mildness of Indies government⁴ makes for a not very enlightened censure.

[1883] "BOOK XX ON COMMERCE." ON THE PROHIBITION OF CERTAIN MERCHANDISE.¹ When a specific reason engages a state to prevent the import of some item of merchandise, it is usually more appropriate to impose a substantial tax on it than to prohibit it. This removes a certain image of enmity and gives less cause for alarm, for reprisals. The State mostly fulfills its purpose. It increases or decreases the tax according to circumstance, and can easily return to the point from which it started. In brief, the State finds advantage in the tax.

It is not the same when one decides that it is appropriate to forbid the export of an item of merchandise. Such a thing is so offensive to the common views on, and the natural purpose of, commerce, it is in general so contrary to the State's prosperity, that it can take place only in a situation where the reason that determines it is of sovereign importance. Then, a complete prohibition will be better than a tax on the merchandise. It is not a question of offering accommodations or sweeteners; this is a matter of rigor.

Such are the laws of England that prohibit the export of wool, unneu-

[1882]

1. The reference is to *Laws*, bks. 14–17.

2. It should read book II of Diodorus's *Library.*

3. On caste differences, see *Laws*, 24.22.

4. See *Laws*, 14.15; the Jansenist journalist abbé Fontaine de La Roche had accused Montesquieu of natural religion in the October 9 and October 16, 1749, issues of the *Nouvelles ecclésiastiques* [Ecclesiastical news].

[1883]

1. See Brèthe, 3:350 n. 39, for the suggestion that this entry could have been placed in *Laws*, 20.12, as a sequel to the discussion of England.

tered horses, uncastrated rams,[2] etc. (Look into whether the prohibition against these two items is true or precise. Someone told me not for the rams and horses.)

[**1884**] COMMERCE. It is natural for France to tolerate trade in Holland rather than elsewhere. She has a general tie with France, which is that of commerce, while the ties she has with England are particular ties, such as the Stadhouder's alliance, the money she has in public funds, etc. Moreover, it is in France's interest to be able on certain occasions to equip a navy. She finds all she needs for that in no time, because Holland is the general store. Money is so common there that everything brought there is immediately bought up. Thus, France finds everything there instantly and avoids the tedious delays involved in going far away to look for things, to Norway and elsewhere; and besides, France can always wage war two years before Holland declares it.

[**1885**] There is no one so stupid in commercial matters as the Parisians. These are businessmen who, having suddenly and effortlessly gotten rich, find it entirely easy to continue to get rich. They even believe that they owe their riches to their intelligence. They are even prompted to undertake trade by the merchants from the maritime cities. The latter propose big projects to them, in which they enter for very little but earn a hefty commission on everything. And if they were to lose everything they have invested, they would earn six or seven times more in commission—besides which, they dispose of huge funds.

The Insurance Company in Paris {in 1750} has no common sense; it is obvious to me that it cannot succeed.

1. In the seaports, a company of merchants joins together to take out some insurance. They understand their task and they enlighten each other. They know whether the vessel being insured is good or bad, whether the equipment is good or bad, whether the captain is experienced or prudent, whether he is ignorant or a scatterbrain, whether the shippers are suspect, of good reputation, or may be suspected of fraud, whether it is supposed to be a long voyage, whether the season is favorable or not; they know everything, because each one makes himself informed. In Paris, they know nothing, and for the Company to have all that knowledge, it would lose as much in the cost of the letters and correspondence as it would gain by the premium.

---

2. Before they have been turned into mutton. See Féraud under "belier."—HC

2. Moreover, it is folly to create a fund of three million. There should be no fund, but in fact there should naturally be money in the coffers, since the premium goes in up front, and it is only afterward that the losses and damages are paid out.

3. It will happen that the good insurance risks will be handled in the seaports, and claims will be filed in Paris only on the bad ones. The merchants who have news through their private correspondence that the business might be dangerous will file claims with the Company, which will not know. In the seaports, even though no fund is set up, the insurance Company insures on its credit, and knowing that all the insurers are not going to fail at the same time, there is peace of mind, as if there were money in the coffers. The money in the coffers does not have a pacifying effect. For who can know the particular condition of those coffers?

[1886] I have heard that in our American islands, they were beginning to employ more horses and mules than in the past, at least in Santo-Domingo, and there are lands that have enough depth to withstand the plowing. Mules eat less than horses and work more.

The Negroes are so naturally lazy[1] that those who are free do nothing, and most are supported or raised by those who are serfs, or ask for alms, or are destitute. Horses, moreover, are employed to bring the sugar to port.

Better trade is always hoped for after peace. But the year after peace, commodities usually fall because, with trade becoming free, no one is in a hurry to buy.

[1887] HISTORY OF COMMERCE. The sea traffic in the Mediterranean and in the Black Sea were the only ones known; that of the Ocean was impractical; the compass had not yet brought the world together.

The trips that a merchant from Constantinople or Smyrna now make in two months provoked the wonder of the world in that period, and were celebrated by all the poets. Thus, one must not be surprised to see so many imperfections in the ancient histories, and so many empires and kingdoms in oblivion.

It was not like it is now, when all peoples are so bound together that the history of one always illuminates that of the others. Every large nation regarded itself as virtually the only one: the Chinese believed their empire

[1886]
1. See *Laws*, 14.3, 234, and 15.7–8.

was the world; the Romans believed themselves the monarchs of the universe; the impenetrable continent of Africa, that of America, constituted the entire planet for their conquerors.

Philosophy did nothing but demoralize those who would have wanted to attempt some discoveries. It taught that, out of five parts of the earth, there were only two that were habitable, and that people who were in one could not reach as far as the other. In the meantime, all obstacles have given way before the voyagers.

Often they protected themselves from the blazing sun by placing themselves in the middle of the torrid zone, and often they saved themselves from the great cold by approaching closer to the pole. Often, on the same mountain, they found the torrid zone on one side and the glacial zone on the other.

The sea has come to light in passages where only land was thought to be, and large continents have appeared in places where only vast seas were suspected.

The eclipses of the stars have been a source of knowledge, and what men thought had occurred in the heavens only to intimidate them now appeared there only to guide them.

[1888] I used to see the list of merchandise that Europe's merchants transport every year to Smyrna. I would see with pleasure that those good folks took four hundred bales of paper to package sugar, but only thirty bales of paper for writing.[1]

[1889] DESPOTISM. European kings ought not expose themselves to the despotism of Asia; that petty gratification of having irrevocable wishes is bought so dearly that a sensible man cannot envy it.

European kings govern like men, but they enjoy a condition as unalterable as the gods'. Asian kings govern like gods, but they are constantly exposed to the fragile condition of men.

[1890] DUEL. SUICIDE.[1] Plato's law (book IX of the *Laws*) required

[1888]

1. See *pensée* 1556.—HC

[1890]

1. On the duel, there was a campaign in France from Cardinal Richelieu (1624–42) onward against it. See *PL*, XC, 150–51; *Laws*, 28.20, for Montesquieu's views. On suicide, see *PL*, LXXVI, but also LXXVII, added in the 1754 edition, apparently to address criticisms of Montesquieu's seeming approval of the practice. The original edition of the *Considerations* (Bordeaux municipal library, P.F. 8031 Rés, p. 131) also contains a note favorable to suicide, which was deleted in subsequent editions. In the *Laws*, see 14.12, a position criticized by both Jansenist and Jesuit journals and censured by the Sorbonne.

burial without any honor for those who killed themselves.[2] Our canon law refuses them burial, as well as those killed in a duel.[3] These laws do very well to punish with infamy crimes that are committed most of the time out of pride.

[**1891**] To prove that morals comport better with the good republic than with the good monarchy: it is because in good republics, one says *We,* but in good monarchies, one says *Me.*[1]

[**1892**] In melancholy, one experiences difficulty in carrying one's body, as would be the case if one were obliged to carry another's body.

[**1893**] Monarchy usually degenerates into the despotism of one;[1] aristocracy into the despotism of several; democracy into the despotism of the People.

[**1894**] COMMERCE. I have heard that the English get Persian silk through Muscovy at a much better price than when they got it through the Persian Gulf and Gombroon.[1] It comes by way of Archangel, the ice and the sleds, at much less cost than by making the circuit around the Cape of Good Hope—all the more so because the provinces where there is more silk are distant from the Persian Gulf, and therefore it is more expensive there, whereas the provinces of Guilan and Mazandaran are close to the Caspian Sea. Thus, the distance from Persia is in some sense equivalent to the distance from Muscovy.

The prohibition on the export of silk from Spain, in England's last war with Spain,[2] made them think about procuring silk more easily from Persia. And the English claim that, if they eliminated all tariffs on silk, the silk would not cost them more than the domestic silk crop costs our manufacturers—which can be the case only because we do not have enough domestically, which causes the price to be fixed by the price of foreign silk.[3]

2. See, however, Derathé, 2:546 n. 9.
3. "Look at the canon law in chapter II" (M.).

[**1891**]
1. See *Laws,* 5.2, as well as *pensées* 1760 and 1854.

[**1893**]
1. See *PL,* CII, 169.

[**1894**]
1. Now Bandar Abbas, on the straits of Hormuz.—HC
2. The War of Jenkins' Ear (1739), which continued into the War of the Austrian Succession (1740–48).
3. "Written in Paris, this November 8, 1750" (M.).

[**1895**] DECEMVIRS. Zonaras says: "*Decemviros pauca quaedam in hasce tabulas sua auctoritate adscripsisse, non ad concordiam, sed majores dissensiones pertinentia.*"[1]

Thus, marriage between Plebeians and Patricians is prohibited in this table. The author treats Zonaras as ignorant in this regard, and cites the passage from Tacitus: "*Finis XII Tabularum juris aequi.*"[2]

Nota also that it could be that Zonaras had evidence for this which no longer exists; besides, the passage from Tacitus is not at all contradictory with what Zonaras says.

[**1896**] ROYAL LAW IN DENMARK.[1] M. La Beaumelle, French refugee in Denmark, told me that after the law that ceded sovereignty to the royal family of Denmark, a law was then enacted that was called *the royal Law*.[2] That law permitted him to change, interpret, annul the laws of the country, to do it at his whim. That law is such that people are ashamed of it nowadays in Denmark, and it is being repealed as much as possible.

That law, I reckon, was concerned with the Nobility, who were feared at that time, and who had the major share of legislative power. Now that everything is settled, people find the law ridiculous.

[**1897**] CRUELTY OF PUNISHMENTS. When punishments have been set up in such a way that they are too cruel, the best manner of restoring mildness to them is to do so imperceptibly, and by particular ways rather than general ways. That is, the public ordinance should be preceded by commutation of sentences; *secundo,* by reduction of sentences in the most favorable cases—leaving that to the arbitration of judges—and preparing minds in this way up to the entire revocation of the law. All this depends on circumstance, on the spirit of the Nation, on the frequency of the violation, on indulgence, on changes, on the relationship with the principles of the government. That is where the Legislator's wisdom should shine

[1895]

1. Zonaras, *Annals,* VII.18: "On their own authority, the decemvirs wrote on these tables certain things tending not toward concord, but toward greater dissension."

2. Tacitus, *Annals,* III.27: "the Twelve Tables . . . , the final instance of equitable legislation."

[1896]

1. The royal law in Denmark had been signed by Frederick III on November 14, 1665.

2. Laurent Angliviel de La Beaumelle (1726–73), Protestant man of letters from the Cévennes and author of a defense of Montesquieu's *Laws* with sequel. He and his brother Jean visited Montesquieu on November 10, 1750, just before his departure for Copenhagen.

forth. (I have put the gist of this in an addition I've made to chapter 13 of book VI.)[1]

[**1898**] DESPOTISM. It is said that the rebel Mir Wais is making surprising progress in Persia, and that the People are following him from all over.[1]

Up to now, our princes have exercised their power with so little restraint, they have made such a mockery of human nature, that it does not surprise me that God lets the People tire of it and shake off an overly heavy yoke. Wretched condition of the subjects! They have virtually no legitimate means of defending themselves against vexation; when they are right in substance, it turns out they are wrong in form.

Take at random the history of some disturbance in the State. There is a thousand to one chance that the Prince or his minister is the cause. The People, naturally fearful and with reason to be, far from thinking of a frontal attack on those who have fearsome power in their hands, have difficulty even in resolving to complain.

In Persia, we are so persuaded by the following maxim that we make use of it constantly: in the turmoil that occurs in the provinces, the Court will always decide for the People against those who have the Prince's authority.

In fact, despotic authority should never be imparted. Arbitrary orders should not be executed arbitrarily, and it is in the interest of the unjust prince that whoever executes his wishes, even the most tyrannical ones, observe the rules of the most exact justice in his manner of executing them.

In despotic states, one is for the People against the governor or the intendant.[2] It is just the opposite in monarchical states.

[**1899**] OF MILITARY GOVERNMENT. Military government is established in two ways:[1] either by a conquest by an army that still wants to

---

[**1897**]

1. See *Laws*, 6.13, 87 and n. 36, for this addition to the posthumous 1757 edition.

[**1898**]

1. Mir Wais Khan rebelled against Shah Hussein-Mirza and defeated a Safavid army at Kandahar in 1713. After his death, his son Mahmud in 1722 sacked Isfahan and had himself declared shah of Persia. There is some thought that this *pensée* is a fragment of a Persian letter. See Adam, 423–24, as well as *pensée* 885 and n. 3.

2. For the intendant in France, see *pensées* 977, 1353, 1572, 1835, 1840, 1846, 2066, and 2099.—HC

[**1899**]

1. On this theme, see *Laws*, 6.15, 90.

remain in arms—such as the government of Algiers today—or else it is despotic government's abusive excess and, so to speak, the corruption of that government.

The government is always still military in the interval that exists between the overthrow of the civil government and the establishment of another civil government—as was Rome's government from Sulla's usurpation until his abdication, and from the Triumvirate until Augustus's establishment. And after the subversion of that establishment, Rome became an empire that destroyed its own cities, giving them over to sacking and destruction for their soldiers' wages. How to pay for it afterward? This is how they acted . . . This is how they act in the civil war between Vespasian and Vitellius, when the sacking of Verona was given over to the soldiers. In the Triumvirate, wasn't the sacking of three cities promised?[2] Look into this.

[1900] This has been eliminated, with reason, from chapter xxiv of book XXVI: *On the Laws considered in the Order,* etc.[1]

"Now if it happened that a State were to abandon itself and were not to make a political law to preserve its independence or prevent partition, and if such negligence could put other nations in peril, let there be no doubt that in this case, it would be necessary to regulate that succession—not by the political law, but by the law of nations, which requires that the various nations do all they can to preserve themselves, and which does not permit their ruin to depend upon the negligence of a particular nation."

[1901] VENAL PENS. For a ministry that does not need them, there are venal pens that have claimed to prove that in France, despite the acquisition of so many provinces, the State is not levying more today than under Francis I (look into this). If that were true, it would prove great servitude. But it was not said to approve of it, but to establish it.

> *Wretched writers, the most pernicious thing*
> *That celestial wrath could offer to a king.*[1]

---

2. Titus Flavius Vespasianus, Roman emperor (69–79); the Second Triumvirate had been established in 43 B.C. by Octavian, Antony, and Lepidus.

[1900]
1. According to Brèthe, 3:452 n. 62, this entry was to be placed at the end of 26.23 of *Laws.*

[1901]
1. Montesquieu here adapts two lines from Racine, *Phaedra,* IV.vi.1325–26, changing the first two words from *Détestable flatteurs* (detestable flatterers) to *Malheureux écrivains* (Wretched writers).

[1902] CONQUESTS. Conquests get rid of the faculty of conquering by a natural process. I consider a conqueror to be like an ardent young man in a seraglio who makes new acquisitions every day at the expense of the first ones, until they all become useless to him.[1]

[1903] GENERAL SPIRIT.[1] It is especially a large capital that forms a nation's general spirit. It is Paris that makes the French. Without Paris, Normandy and Picardy and Artois would be German like Germany; without Paris, Burgundy and Franche-Comté would be Swiss like the Swiss; without Paris, Guyenne and Béarn and Languedoc would be Spanish like the Spanish.

[1904] PROPRIETIES. I do not know why I have not spoken about proprieties. They are manners established to exclude the notion of contempt from one's status, or from one's duties, or from virtue. They are rigorous both among peoples who have bad mores, and among those who have good ones. Among the latter, they are established to inhibit vices; among the former, to prevent them from being suspected. In the second case, the proprieties convey innocence; in the first, they are mere justifications.[1]

They are the only hypocrisy allowed; they are a light homage that vice pays to virtue.[2] We do not want to appear better than we are, but less bad than we are. They deceive no one and attest rather to the general conscience than to each individual's conscience.

A man who was not nearly as sublime as M. de La Rochefoucauld offered this reflection: "I don't know why M. —— pays me so many compliments when he wants to put his hat on my wife's bed, and so few when he wants to sleep with her." Indeed, one is quite surprised. But however disordered a nation may be, it always sets down its proprieties, sometimes stronger in proportion to the disorders.

[1905] PUNISHMENTS.—NATURE OF PUNISHMENTS.—ARRANGE-MENT OF THE LAWS. I notice that the distribution of the various praetors—

[1902]
1. See *Laws,* 10.3, 139, for this topic.

[1903]
1. See *pensées* 542 and 854 and *Laws,* 19.4, for some of Montesquieu's different approaches to the general spirit.

[1904]
1. See *Laws,* 19.16, 317.
2. This is a variation on La Rochefoucauld's *Maxims* (1678), 218: "Hypocrisy is a homage that vice pays to virtue."—HC

especially the one made under Sulla, who added four *quaestiones*[1]—led people to include under the same name crimes that had little connection with the main crime.[2] Whence it happened that crimes that ought to have received a lesser penalty were punished with the same one. What ought to bring about equal punishment is not that one crime may, because of some similarity, be ranked in another's place, but that there has to be the same degree of ill intent to commit these crimes. Thus, in establishing punishment, they followed rather the distinctions involving the jurisdictions and the praetors than the factors that might lead to an increase or decrease in the punishment. Look at the Cornelian law and the other laws that establish a *quaestio.* One will become convinced of this in looking at Sigonius, book II, *De judiciis,* and the *Digest.*[3]

[**1906**] POLITICAL LIBERTY. In his *History of the French Monarchy,* volume I, chapter VI (page 59, 1st edition), abbé Dubos says that before Constantine, he is unaware of there being not only any emperor, but he doubts there was even any foreign king who had separated civil functions from military functions in their officers.[1]

He has therefore not read what Socrates says in Xenophon about the Persian monarchy, where two different officers usually governed the provinces, and the problems that were noticed when that was not the case.[2]

He has therefore not read what Diodorus says about the Egyptian monarchy, where the priests have the civil, whereas the military forms a separate body.[3]

He next says, following Cassiodorus (*Variarum,* title VIII, no. 3), that this distinction did exist in the Italian monarchy of Theodoric, King of the Ostrogoths.[4] He adds that it is clear from some passages in Procopius that this practice was maintained there. But he says it was abrogated in Gaul by Clovis and his successors.

[1905]
1. Standing tribunals.—HC
2. See *Laws,* 6.15, 89, on Sulla.
3. Carlo Sigonio, *De Judiciis Romanorum* [On Roman courts] (1574).

[1906]
1. For Montesquieu's criticisms of Dubos, see *pensée* 1826 and *Laws,* 30.23; Voltaire defended abbé Dubos in his 1764 *Philosophical Dictionary* ("*Esprit des lois*"); see Derathé, 2:554 n. 20.
2. Xenophon, *Economica,* IV.
3. Diodorus of Sicily, *Library of History,* I.73.
4. Flavius Magnus Aurelius Cassiodorus, Latin writer (ca. 480–ca. 575); Theodoric (ca. 455–526).

572   Pensée 1907

He says it will be seen by many facts in the continuation of his history
that under these princes, the dukes and other military officers meddled
in purely civil affairs, mainly in financial affairs; that it was natural in this
respect for our Merovingian kings to follow the practice of their nation,
which was not familiar with the method of separating sovereign authority
between two representatives in the same region.

He therefore does not know what Tacitus so well says (*De Moribus Germanorum*) about the difference among the Germans between the functions
of the King, who had the civil authority, and the functions of the Duke,
who had the military—which is the key to the beginnings of the French
monarchy.[5] It is quite true that it was the Nobility and the Clergy who had
the judicature and the finances under the first and second races, because
the Third Estate was nothing; that the dukes, the counts, etc., adminis-
tered justice. But note that Europe was an aristocracy.

Abbé Dubos begins the division into two powers only with Louis XII.
But is it not necessary instead to begin it from the time when the Nobility's
ignorance gave the Third Estate most civil functions? He says the distinction came from Louis XII and his successors, who enacted many royal
ordinances to stop those who had the military power in a certain district
from meddling in matters of justice. There is no foundation for anything
he says about this—except that there were not two estates in the Empire
after Constantine's change: the one robe, the other sword, mutually exclusive, so whoever had taken on one could no longer take on the other; that
Emperor Avitus, who at first was a praetorian prefect, was afterward master
of the military, and passed, as Sidonius says, from the tribunals of justice
into the camps.[6] It is true that in the past, the distinction was in the functions, but that today it is in the estates.

[1907] MORALS. I have heard that the Spanish law (know the fact) that
confiscates the money passed fraudulently in Cadiz used to be explained
this way: "We give a third to the infamous informer." There is no stronger
proof of public honesty than the words in that law. It seems that the law
itself is suffering, and that it is indignant that the punishment of a guilty
party is owing to the loss of morals.

---

5. Tacitus, *Germania*, VII; see *pensées* 1171 and 1302 n. 3.
6. Sidonius Apollinaris (ca. 430–after 489), bishop of Clermont (472–?) and author of *Carmen* (i.e.,
"Panegyric on Avitus"), VII.295ff. (see *Catalogue*, 378–79). He had earlier married Avitus's daughter
Papianilla (452?).

The laws on proscription, which overturned the Valerian, the Sempronian, and the Porcian laws—and which all of a sudden eliminated that security which the Roman people had constantly defended even against their magistrates—were not less fatal to morals.[1] They set free every atrocity of the soul. They announced rewards for all those who would carry the head of an outlaw, or who would reveal the places he had been hiding.

[**1908**] COMMITMENT BETWEEN PRINCE AND SUBJECTS. Grotius has said (*works of the learned*, by Basnage, no. 1688, art. 7) that the subjects' rebellion is not a valid reason to exclude them, by the formalities of reparations, from the advantages of a prior agreement, because the return to obedience effaces the injury.[1] I add that this could take place only in contracts that are not reciprocal, and in situations in which a prince would give everything without receiving anything. Absent that, one of the two parties would be sole judge of a mutual commitment, which would destroy its nature. Besides, since this mutual commitment is made to last forever, the punishment of a crime against this commitment should not be its destruction.

[**1909**] WOMEN AND EUNUCHS.[1] In China, it has been noticed that it is less pernicious for the Prince to surrender to his wives than to his eunuchs. {In Father Du Halde, look at a work by the scholar Tang-King-Tchuel, written under the Ming dynasty.} Once he has abandoned himself to the latter, they make themselves masters of his person. The abuses and excesses of their governance cause an uprising. The Prince, even if he would like to remedy things, no longer can; his orders can no longer get out. This creates civil wars, and if the party opposed to the eunuchs is victorious, the Prince is embroiled in the eunuchs' ruin.

But when the Prince is under his wives' control, the problem is less great. The wives' interests are not the same; they cannot band together; they destroy each other; the eunuchs discredit them. Their designs are less

---

[1907]
1. The Porcian and Valerian laws, beginning in the sixth century B.C., and the Sempronian laws, from the late third century B.C., guaranteed various civil and political rights to Roman citizens.

[1908]
1. Henri Basnage, Sieur de Beauval (1656–1710), *Histoire des ouvrages des savans* [History of the works of the learned] (1687–1709; *Catalogue*, 2588). [See also Hugo Grotius, *The Rights of War and Peace*, ed. Richard Tuck (Indianapolis: Liberty Fund, 2005), 3:1539.—HC]

[1909]
1. See *Laws*, 15.19, 263.

coherent, less profound, less thought out, more reckless. In brief, it is rare in a monarch for weakness of heart to do as much damage as weakness of mind. (This chapter should not be made so general, but apply it only to China.)

In a work by the scholar Tang-King-Tchuel, written under the Ming dynasty, which Father Du Halde has provided us, one finds these fine reflections:

"When a prince abandons himself to the eunuchs, he regards as strangers the virtuous, skillful, and zealous people he has at his court. They retreat. Does the Prince open his eyes and seek the assistance of officials from outside? They don't know how to go about it, for the Prince is like a hostage. If the outside officials' enterprise does not prevail, an ambitious man finds the means of wrapping the Sovereign up in the eunuchs' cause, and he seduces the people's hearts while exterminating those scum."

To abandon himself to his wives is less of a problem, for if the Prince comes to his senses,[2] the evil can be cured. But if, through excessive confidence, he has abandoned himself to his eunuchs, he cannot pull back without ruining himself. From the Emperor Qin Shi Huang to Xian Di, the Empire was governed, or rather was toppled, at the eunuchs' whim.[3]

[1910] TAXES. The higher taxes are, the more inclined good people are to shun collecting them.[1] The higher taxes are, the less inclined good people are to scruple about cheating on them.

You say your burdened subjects will work better. I understand you. You would like to make a long-distance voyage with oars, not with sails.

To put at the head of the book: Caesar, _On civil war_ (look up the citation): _Cujus modo rei nomen re periri poterat, hoc satis esse ad cogendas pecunias._[2]

To think you can increase power by increasing taxes is to think, fol-

2. _Se reconnoit,_ literally, "recognizes himself" or "discovers himself."—HC
3. Qin Shi Huang (d. 210 B.C.) established a centralized bureaucratic government and had the Great Wall built; Xian Di, last Chinese emperor of the dynasty of the eastern Han (189–220), deposed by Cao Pi after the revolt of the "yellow turbans."

[1910]
1. Taxes are the topic of _Laws,_ bk. 13.
2. "Any mode of exaction, provided a name could be found for it, was deemed a sufficient excuse for compelling contributions." Caesar, _On Civil War,_ III.32; Montesquieu omits the last word of the sentence, _videbatur._

lowing the expression of a Chinese author cited by Father Du Halde (*On informers,* volume II, page 503), that you can lengthen a skin when you stretch it until it breaks.

[**1911**] LEGISLATORS. Lycurgus did all he could to make his citizens more warlike; Plato and Thomas Morus, more honorable; Solon, more equal; the Jewish legislators, more religious; the Carthaginians, more wealthy; the Romans, more magnanimous.[1]

[**1912**] Those Laws of the XII Tables had many death penalties. This was no doubt a leftover from the royal laws, whose rigor the Republic moderated. Whoever set fire to a pile of wheat, punished by fire. There were even some superstitious ones: it was thought possible to bewitch a field, "*Si quis malum carmen incantasset venenumque faxit, parricida esto.*"[1] See article 38, p. 24 of my Gravina extract.[2]

[**1913**] See article 58, page 24, from Gravina: "The Greeks punished perjury with only a fine or infamy. The Decemvirs tossed the guilty from the Tarpeian Rock. Afterward, this was relaxed to exile and banishment."

It seems to me that all these punishments from the Law of the XII Tables had been moderated by the *Porcian* Law, which prohibited putting a Roman citizen to death.[1]

[**1914**] Bodin rejects the practice of small cantons like Zug and Appenzell, where in matters of consequence, each senator has the task of leading with him to the Council two or three whom he will advise, and who also have a deliberative voice—which sometimes makes four hundred or five hundred, so the affairs cannot be secret.[1]

The experience is the opposite in the senates of Venice and Rome, where the number was large.

[**1911**]
1. See *pensée* 1248 for the same thought.—HC

[**1912**]
1. "If anyone has chanted an evil spell and made a potion, he shall be deemed a parricide." The Law of the Twelve Tables (449 B.C.), one of the earliest laws of Rome; see *Laws,* 6.15, 89.
2. This extract of Gravina, probably his *Origins of Law,* is lost; see *pensée* 1761.

[**1913**]
1. See *Laws,* 6.15, 89, and *pensée* 1907 on the Porcian Law.

[**1914**]
1. Jean Bodin (1520–96), *Six livres de la république* [Six books of the Commonwealth] (1579; *Catalogue,* 2371).

Nothing better proves this practice than the good morals of the People. Fol. Verso 315.

[**1915**] Article 60, page 41: Tribonianus's bad faith, in having placed under the title *On the Laws*¹ the law that freed the Emperor from the *caducaria lex*.² One piece of evidence that he was not freed from all the laws is what Dio tells us: "*Quod a Senatu veniam legis Voconiae peteret.*"³ Thus, to prove that the Prince was not subject to the laws, he offers a law that proves that he was, since he asks dispensation from it.

The *Julian* Law, under Augustus, freed the Prince from the constraints of the laws on enfranchisement.

[**1916**] In a chapter on Egypt, I had put: "The slaves had the Law to guarantee their lives. It punished with death even a master who would take it away from them. They were not citizens, but they were men." (See if this reflection comes from me or from Diodorus.)¹

[**1917**] Virtually all the nations of the world go around in this circle: at first, they are barbarous; they conquer, and they become civilized nations; this civilization makes them bigger, and they become polite nations;¹ politeness weakens them; they are conquered and become barbarous again. Witness the Greeks and Romans.

[**1918**] Extract of Coringius, page 53: Quarrel between Martin and Bulgarus—whether the Emperor had property or dominion.¹

[1915]
1. Tribonian (d. 546), Byzantine jurisconsult and councilor of Justinian I; the reference is to the *Digest*, I.iii.31, in S. P. Scott, *The Civil Law* (Cincinnati Central Trust, 1932), 2:225.
2. The *caducaria lex* was part of the Julian laws on inheritance passed under Augustus, ca. 18–17 B.C., by which goods belonging to no one, or to individuals who had lost the right to possess them, would be distributed to the people.—HC
3. Dio Cassius, *Roman History*, LVI.32; literally, "he was seeking an exception to the Voconian law from the Senate." The Loeb passage reads: "he [i.e., Augustus] had asked the senate for permission to leave her [i.e., Livia, his widow] so much [i.e., one-third of the estate], which was more than the amount allowed by law." See *Laws*, 27, 525–30, on the Voconian law.

[1916]
1. The reference is doubtless to *Laws*, 21.9–10.

[1917]
1. In French there is a possible pun: "civilization" (*police*) becomes "polite" (*polie*).—HC

[1918]
1. Martinus Gosia and Bulgarus are two of the famous Four Doctors of the University of Bologna law school in the twelfth century (Hugo and Jacobus were the others).—HC

Frederick thought he had succeeded the ancient Roman emperors, just as abbé Dubos has thought that Clovis succeeded the ancient Roman emperors.[2]

[**1919**] *"Tarentini,"* says Aristotle, *"jumenta et possessiones cum egentibus communicant."*[1]

This is because it was a Lacedemonian colony.

[**1920**] I have employed twenty years of my life on this work. I am far from having put in enough time on it.[1]

[**1921**] CORRUPT MORALS. It is then that a good man spends his life in a kind of unhinged state; that he is, so to speak, alone in the world; that all the ties of humanity terrify him, because he finds no man by whom he would like to be protected, none for whom he would like to be the protector, no sociable man he would like to have as a friend, no woman whose husband he would like to be, no child whose father he would like to be.

[**1922**] OF NEW LAWS. New laws demonstrate the attention of those who govern. But the execution of the old laws would demonstrate it even better. I would not want, however, to blame the Romans for the great changes that occurred in their jurisprudence; they changed the government, and their civil laws had to follow their political laws.

[**1923**] THE PRINCE. He loves when he thinks he is loved; thus, one must persuade him that he is loved.

[**1924**] It could be that, in foreign and distant affairs, the executive power's ministers would reveal only what they want to and with the coloration they want. It was not that way in Athens, where, since the People reserved the executive power to themselves in some fashion, the orators were always abreast of things. But they were hardly the better for that. Here the speechifiers would be dupes; there, they were scoundrels.

Such a people would not calm themselves by the cure of actual ills; they would need all sorts of remedies and precautions against those they might

---

2. Frederick I Barbarossa, German Roman emperor (1152–90), leader of the House of Hohenstauffen; the extract is lost.

[**1919**]
1. Montesquieu's Latin text means: "[The Tarentines] share their beasts of burden and their property with the needy," a slight variant of Aristotle, *Politics,* VI.v.1320b.9–11.

[**1920**]
1. See *Laws,* preface, xliii, and *pensée* 1872.

fear. (Nota: I have not put this in *The Spirit of the Laws,* in the chapters on England.[1])

[**1925**] In despotic countries, all men are equal, because they live equally in political slavery. There is a difference among men in civil slavery only, and even that difference is less in those countries.[1]

[**1926**] GREEK MEN OF POLITICS. In fact, the science of the arts that have some utility to men who live in society is subordinate to the great art that shapes and gives order to societies.

[**1927**] Without any restriction, limitation, interpretation, the crown has passed to males in three consecutive races, and in the third, always to the eldest of the males.[1]

[**1928**] M. Du Tillet is quite right to say that the Court of Peers was established by Louis the Younger to judge the affairs of his domain, those that concerned the dignity of the peerages, and other big cases.[1]

The object of that court was not to reverse the sentences that emanated from the lords' jurisdiction, but to correct their breaches of trust and their denials of justice.

That is why the lords themselves were summoned in person to answer for the sentence, and why they ran the risk of a fine to the King. But when Saint Louis abolished trial by combat in civil matters, sentences began to be appealed even in civil matters. Then it appeared extraordinary for the lords to be summoned to account.

[**1929**] It seems to me that in criminal cases, the oath was employed for unfamiliar cases, the duel for uncertain ones, and war for certain ones; that in civil cases, the oath was employed for cases of no consequence; that for others, testimony was employed—and combat, when the testimony was denied—and also combat, in case of appeal.[1]

[1924]
1. In *Laws,* 11.6 or 19.27.

[1925]
1. Cf. *Laws,* 15.1, and *PL,* XXXIV, 59.

[1927]
1. The Merovingian, Carolingian, and Capetian are the three races.

[1928]
1. Jean du Tillet, court clerk (d. 1570), author of *Recueil des rangs des grands de France* [Compendium of the ranks of the grandees of France] (1580); Montesquieu cites p. 542; Louis VII was king of France (r. 1137–80).

[1929]
1. See *Laws,* bk. 28, on these themes.

[**1930**] OATH ON EMPTY RELIQUARIES. Extract from the *Continuation of Fredegarius,* page 92.[1]

This is the period when men no longer feared perjury, but still feared its ill effects.

[**1931**] The bishops had already put in place there all the laws that we see established in Spain in the Inquisition Tribunal. But the bishops did not profit as much from them as they thought. The monks arrive and wrest the devotion of the people. The superstitious people run to them and find them more Catholic than the bishops. They become the inquisitors, and subject even the bishops to their authority.

It is the fate of those who abuse power that it soon be abused against themselves, and since injustice passes into different hands, it will forever be the wisdom of men to exercise moderation and take refuge in equity.

[**1932**] JUDGMENT OF GOD OR DIVINATION BY A PASSAGE FROM THE PSALMS, THE PROPHETS, THE GOSPELS. But since there are more misfortunes and threats in the Prophets and the Psalms than in any other books, the unfortunate found little consolation there. Chram and Merovech, son of Childeric, consulted in that fashion. Extract from Gregory of Tours, pp. 33, 34.[1]

[**1933**] Here I am at book XXIX, and I have not begun it without making new sacrificial offerings and without having built a temple to Boredom and to Patience.[1]

[**1934**] When a law seems bizarre, and there is no sign that the Legislator has had an interest in making it so (which can be presumed when

[1930]

1. This anonymous chronicle, a work of at least three authors and presumably written in the eighth century, was placed in the sixteenth century under the name of Fredegarius. It relates the events of the years 584–642 and was continued, by three contributors, until 678. Montesquieu read it in the collection by André Duchesne, *Historiae francorum scriptores* [Writers on French history], 6 vols. (1636–49); see *Catalogue,* 2932.

[1932]

1. Chram (d. 600), Frankish prince, son of Clotaire I; Gregory of Tours (538–ca. 594), whose *Historia francorum* [History of the Franks] Montesquieu owned in a 1610 edition (*Catalogue,* 2955); the extract is lost.

[1933]

1. Book 29 was designed to serve as the conclusion to *Laws,* instead of being placed between two long historical studies. See the 1817 *Observations de Condorcet sur le vingt-neuvième livre de* l'Esprit des lois [Condorcet's Observations on the twenty-ninth book of *The Spirit of the Laws*], a sequel to Destutt de Tracy's highly critical *Commentaire de l'Esprit des lois,* which was published first in English in 1811, then in 1817. For manuscript passages left out of the published version, see *OC,* 3:625–31.

that law is neither fiscal nor tyrannical), one ought to believe that it is more reasonable than it appears, and that it is based on a sufficient reason.[1] Genghis Khan's law prohibited the Mongols from approaching water during a thunderstorm. In a country where thunder was very frequent, he wanted to prevent the Mongols from immediately heading into the water and drowning. See Pétis de La Croix, *Life of Genghis Khan.*[2]

[1935] It is only extremely vice-ridden and extremely virtuous people who have a certain energy, and just as this energy always goes too far in the first, it may fail to stop itself adequately in the second.

[1936] How the former advantages have been compensated by different ones; how the military spirit has remained in the army and has disappeared from civil government; how the military spirit has not stifled the spirit of commerce; how skillful ministers have preserved the spirit of the monarchy and avoided offending it or even letting it weaken; how they have regarded this spirit as the most sacred State treasure—as its energy, as its soul—with which everything can live, without which everything can become deadened; how, in matters of government, more is almost always less, and less almost always more; how skillful men in our monarchy have seen what had to be done before seeing what could be done; the reasons why this monarchy has always seen its well-being increase; the reasons why this well-being might be made perpetual . . . But I am . . .

[1937] In reading the Barbarian law codes, I was looking for jurisprudence in its cradle.

[1938] When Michelangelo saw the Pantheon for the first time, he said he would put it in motion. In some way and after my fashion, I will imitate that great man. These antique laws, lying on the ground—I will expose them to the view of all.

[1939] In warlike nations that did not have the art of writing, people were obliged to make formulas out of all the various acts bound to occur in the civil state, and it is especially in these formulas that one finds the difference between the primitive laws and the laws added on. There you have the source of the Merovingian laws! One finds a few insights in the capitularies

[1934]
1. See *Laws,* 29.16, 614, and 616.
2. Alexandre-Louis-Marie Pétis de La Croix (1698–1751), French orientalist, author of *Vie de Gangis-Khan,* which Montesquieu cites also in *Réflexions sur la monarchie universelle en Europe* [Reflections on universal monarchy in Europe]; see *OC* Volt, 2:351 n. g.

of the Carolingian kings. But this is a sterile source, which gives only a few regulations for the priesthood and for the empire, fastidiously repeated and better suited for giving us an idea of the household management of the government of that time than of the civil laws—all the more so, in that the kings left virtually all of them alone without touching them. You arrive there, and it seems that the entire body of jurisprudence is collapsing, and everything is crumbling beneath your feet. A majestic river is going underground and vanishing.[1] Wait a moment; you will see it reappear and give back its waters to those who were no longer looking for it.

Reddit quaesitas jam non quaerentibus undas.[2]

[1940] Among the Greeks and Romans, admiration for the political and moral sciences was raised to a kind of cult. Today, we have esteem only for the natural sciences; we are occupied solely with them, and political good and bad are for us an opinion rather than an object of knowledge.[1]

Thus, not being born in the age I should have been, I have resolved to make myself a partisan of the sect of that excellent man the abbé de Saint-Pierre, who has written so much these days about Politics—and to persuade myself that seven or eight hundred years from now, there will arrive a certain people for whom my ideas will be very useful; and in the tiny portion of that time that I have to live, to engage, for my own use, in an ongoing employment of my modesty.[2]

[1941] It is said that Charlemagne's various wives were successive; a means should also be sought to prove that the three queens and the concubines of Dagobert,[1] who was as pious as he (see the *Chronicle of Fredegarius* for the year 628), came from hand to hand and were successive. I am not attacking Charlemagne's sanctity, because I do not know the boundaries

---

[1939]

1. See *Laws,* 28.11 for a similar discussion; for the river image, see *pensée* 1827.

2. "From the emperor Nero" (M.). The passage may be translated: "He restores the sought-after waters to those not seeking them." It was preserved in a scholium of Lucan's *Pharsalia,* III.261–63.

[1940]

1. For a similar theme, see *pensées* 1855 and 1871; again, Montesquieu's *sentiment* may be translated "feeling" as well as "opinion."—HC

2. On abbé de Saint-Pierre, see *pensées* 1295, 1718, and 1876.—HC

[1941]

1. Dagobert I was a Frankish king (r. 628–38).

on the mercy toward those who have violated the laws of the Gospel in following the laws of their country.

I will make a conjecture here. Fredegarius (for the year 626) says that with the mayor Warnachar being dead and his son Godinus having married his mother-in-law, the King flew into a rage, saying that he had violated the canons. But I do not believe that King loved the canons enough to send in an army against him on that occasion. The King decreed that an oath of fidelity be sworn to him. Godinus's act was therefore a political violation, and his incestuous marriage offended a certain royal prerogative. I have spoken of it in my *Spirit of the Laws*—in the book, I believe, on *The Nature of the Terrain* or in the book on *Fiefs,* on the subject of the Frankish kings' plurality of wives.[2]

[1942] Would it be an overly bold thought to say that that special benediction by which God multiplied the race of the Patriarchs was connected to the ideas provided them by the pastoral life? The land was open to all, and when the number of children increased, they were given a certain share of livestock, which enlarged the family without overburdening it; and with each family forming a petty empire, the enlargement of the family made for the security of the family.[1] Couldn't one say that God, wanting to bless the Israelite people, placed their rewards in a thing that the Israelites believed to be and felt to be their happiness? No doubt God has revealed to us grander designs and a grander household economy. But couldn't one admire his wisdom even in those cases where we seem to be considering things in a human manner? Among the Israelites, a large number of children was the sign of a special benediction from God. Today, it is merely the sign of a general benediction. God assigned a special benediction to a thing that was linked among the Israelites to the notion of their security. Today, he does not assign a special benediction to a thing that is so often linked to notions of our pride.

I will add that this special benediction was also suitable to a people chosen to be separate from all others—a people which, when established, was to maintain itself by its grandeur, and when dispersed, had to bear great witness forever.

---

2. *Laws,* bk. 31.

[1942]

1. On religion and population, see *Laws,* 23.21, especially 448–49.

[**1943**] By land, Greece was of invincible strength. You had to cross two mountain ranges, which go from one sea to the other. She was invincible to the Persians, for once those mountains were crossed, they found themselves in strongly fortified country, between those mountains and the isthmus of Peloponnesus, which they could not cross. With small armies, they were unable to conquer; with large armies, they were even less able to do so.

[**1944**] Greece was invincible to the Persians. With small armies, they were unable to conquer; with large armies, they were still less able to do so. They had to cross the Thermopylae, which separated Phocis and Locris from Thessaly. They had to cross the mountain range that separated Thessaly from Macedonia. After which, they had to live in the [barren] country between those mountains and the isthmus of Corinth, which is very narrow.

[**1945**] DOUBTS.[1] If it sometimes happens that God predestines—which can happen only rarely, for it happens only rarely that God takes away our liberty—he can never predestine us except to salvation.[2] Those who are predestined are saved. But it does not follow that all those who are not predestined are damned. Saint Paul, who has carried predestination furthest, is for what I am saying: "*Scimus autem quoniam diligentibus Deum omnia cooperantur in bonum, iis qui, secundum propositum, vocati sunt sancti.*"[3] Note well the words that follow: "*Nam quos praescivit, et praedestinavit . . . Quos autem praedestinavit, hos et vocavit; et quos vocavit, hos justificavit; quos autem justificavit, illos et glorificavit.*"[4] This is only to say: "*Quos praedestinavit, hos glorificavit.*"[5] Predestination is a sign of salvation. What I could say on this subject is not worth as much as what one of the best interpreters of Saint Paul has said. It is Sedulius,[6] who wrote a commentary on the *Epistles* of Saint Paul, almost all of it drawn from Origen, Saint Jerome,

[**1945**]

1. "Up to page 256" (M.), that is, to *pensée* 1948.

2. On predestination, see *Laws,* 25.2, 480.

3. Romans 8:28: "We know that in everything God works for good with those who love him, who are called according to his purpose."

4. Romans 8:29–30: "For those whom he foreknew he also predestined . . . And those whom he predestined he also called; and those whom he called he also justified; and those whom he justified he also glorified."

5. "Those whom he predestined, he glorified."

6. Sedulius Scottus, or Sedulius the Younger, ninth-century Irish monk, author of a *Collectaneum on the Epistles of Saint Paul.*

and Saint Ambrose. That author says: "*Quos praescivit, et praedestinavit, de bonis tantum dicitur; caeteros vero non praescire, sed nescire dicitur Deus.*"[7] He then adds the reason. "It is," he says, "that everything that is evil is unworthy of the knowledge or the foreknowledge of God."

The Apostle then continues in chapter ix. For although the harshest interpretations imaginable have been offered of it, one may nonetheless say that it is merely the continuation of the same truths. He gives us an image of predestination in the example of Isaac, in the example of Jacob, both chosen by God among their brothers: "*Cum enim nondum nati essent aut aliquid boni egissent, aut mali (ut secundum electionem propositum Dei maneret), non ex operibus, sed ex vocatione dictum est ei: 'Quia major serviet minori.'*"[8] And this, "*Jacob dilexi, Esaü autem odio habui,*"[9] which the Apostle next cites, does not mean that God has reproved Esau, nor does it mean to be a symbol of the reprobation of the men who are not predestined, represented by Esau.

For there is no one, not even the most extreme Thomist, who wants to give these words a narrow construction, or to say that God has truly hated Esau, or hardened anyone. And certainly the reasoning that Saint Paul engages in next proves quite clearly that he did not mean that God could ever issue a decree of reprobation, or, if you will, has caused all those that he has not predestined to salvation to be destined to wrath, because one would be attributing false reasoning to the Apostle. "*O Homo, tu quis es qui respondeas Deo? Numquid dicit figmentum ei qui se finxit: 'Quid me fecisti sic?' Annon habet potestatem figulus luti ex eadem massa facere aliud quidem vas in honorem, aliud vero in contumeliam?*"[10] If Saint Paul were talking of a predestination without which one cannot be saved, he would be reasoning badly, for man would not complain about God having made him in a certain fashion, but about His punishing him for having emerged from His hands in that way. Blatant injustice! It must therefore be that Saint

---

7. "Those whom he foreknew and predestined, are said to be only among the good; but the others, it is said God does not foreknow them and does not know them."

8. Romans 9:11–13: "Though they were not yet born and had done nothing either good or bad, in order that God's purpose of election might continue, not because of works but because of his call, she was told, 'The elder will serve the younger.'"

9. "Jacob I loved, but Esau I hated."

10. Romans 9:20–21: "But, who are you, a man, to answer back to God? Will what is molded say to its molder, 'Why have you made me thus?' Has the potter no right over the clay, to make out of the same lump one vessel for beauty and another for menial use?"

Paul is speaking here of predestination only in the manner that I am understanding him, that is, of a predestination that God sometimes accords to man—with which, he is infallibly saved; but without which, he does not stop being able to be saved. Therefore, it remains only to see what Saint Paul was reasoning about in this chapter, the previous ones and the following ones. It is only about the calling of the Gentiles, whom he has predestined and whom he has summoned freely—a calling, however, which has not excluded the Jews from salvation. It is to silence the murmurs of the Jews, who were complaining about not being distinguished from the Gentiles. The reasons given by the Apostle correspond pretty well to Jesus Christ's parable of the workers. In chapter II of the same *Epistle,* look at where he says to the Gentiles that, just as God chose them after the Jews were rejected, they should fear that God may choose the Jews in their turn. "*Sicut enim aliquando vos non credidistis Deo, nunc enim misericordiam consecuti estis propter incredulitatem illorum; ita et isti nunc non crediderunt in vestram misericordiam, ut et ipsi misericordiam consequantur.*"[11] After which, he cries out: "*Altitudo divitiarum!*"[12] so that no one will demand a reason from God for the graces he gives. But it is not a question of punishments.

When Saint Paul says that God has predestined one to be the son of wrath, the other to be the son of mercy, he means that God has seen in a general way that there would be the damned and the saved, without sacrificing this or that one; for he saw clearly, through the arrangement of secondary causes, that there were some who would be more susceptible to the purposes than others.

As for the rest, these are ideas tossed out as they have come to my mind without scrutiny, and I have no claims to being a theologian.

Still, I will put forward a doubt at this point. One must not push the idea that the offense by a finite being against an infinite being is always infinite, for all infinities being equal, it would follow that all offenses are equal. One must pay heed to the capacity of the offending being, which has nothing infinite about it.

These are some doubts.

[1946] SOME REFLECTIONS THAT MAY SERVE AGAINST M. BAYLE'S

---

11. Romans 11:30–31: "Just as you were once disobedient to God but now have received mercy because of their disobedience, so they have now been disobedient in order that by the mercy shown to you they also may receive mercy."

12. Romans 11:33: "O the depth of the riches . . . !"

PARADOX, THAT IT IS BETTER TO BE AN ATHEIST THAN AN IDOLA-
TER, WITH SOME OTHER FRAGMENTS OF WRITINGS FROM MY YOUTH,
WHICH I HAVE TORN UP.[1]

One can judge things only by the ideas one has about them. Now the
first idea that presents itself to our minds is that of matter. Everything we
see, everything that surrounds us, is material. There is nothing up to and
including sensations that does not appear to us as an attribute of matter. It
is only by the study of philosophy that we can disabuse ourselves. I speak
of the new philosophy, for the ancient one would serve only to reinforce
prejudices. It is even certain that before M. Descartes, philosophy had
no proofs of the immateriality of the soul, for the soul can know itself in
only two ways, by idea or by feeling. Everyone agrees that we have no idea
of it; it is clear, then, that we know it only by feeling. Now philosophy
and prejudice taught the Pagans that sensations were attributes of matter.
Thus, they inevitably had to draw one of these two conclusions: either that
the soul is material, or at the very least that the body is capable of feeling.
Now if the body is capable of feeling, why deny it thought? Certainly one
is no more contradictory than the other.

{Although pagan philosophy, such as it existed, was unable to demonstrate that there were minds, I am not on that account saying that it did
not acknowledge them. What I am saying is that the first idea that presented itself to the minds of the Pagans, as to our own, was that of matter.} And when the knowledge of sensory things set their sights on their
author, it could give them only the image of a worker who had manufac-
tured the world—somewhat as an artisan puts together a machine. The
Heavens, which announce the Creator's glory, were unable to make them
know his nature. It was through the ministry of the senses that man persuaded himself of the existence of God; it was also through them that he
thought he should judge His essence. Once man had accepted this principle that God is material, he did not rest there; the imagination naturally
led him to determine His features. He figured that beauty must be one of
His principal attributes, and since man finds nothing more beautiful than
himself, he would have considered it an insult to the Divinity had he attributed to Him features other than his own. For as the Epicurean Velleius

[1946]
1. On Montesquieu's refutation of Bayle, see *pensée* 989n.

says in Cicero (book I, *De Natura Deorum*): "*Quae compositio membrorum, quae conformatio lineamentorum, quae figura, quae species humana potest esse pulchrior? . . . Quod si omnium animantium formam vincit Hominis figura, Deus autem animans est: ea profecto figura est quae pulcherrima sit omnium.*"[2]

Moreover, since reason must be one of God's main attributes, and since the senses seem to tell us that only substances that have human features are reasonable, it was easy for them to give Him a manner of being from which they thought reason was inseparable. "*Quoniam . . .* ," says Velleius, "*Deos beatissimos esse constat, beatus autem esse sine virtute nemo potest, nec virtus sine ratione consistere, nec ratio usquam inesse, nisi in Hominis figura: Hominis esse specie Deos confidentum est.*"[3] These are not the reasonings of philosophy but of nature, reasonings formed in the senses and the imagination, of which all men are dupes, and which may be called *the true fruits of childhood.*

Men, accustomed to judge what they did not see by what they did see, had no more difficulty convincing themselves that there were sex differences in the gods. All these reasonings were made carelessly; the mind became accustomed to them as the body advanced in age. Thus, one must not be surprised that the pagan religion, such as it existed, spread throughout the world and left the worshippers of the true God only a small piece of land. Each man, who was idolatrous before being reasonable, brought to it from birth a better inclination, which caused it to be regarded as a natural religion that birth itself had produced in man before education.

But to better recognize this, let us evaluate the Pagans' ideas by our ideas, and their situation by our own. What trouble do we not have, with the support of faith and philosophy, in forming the notion of an infinite Spirit that governs the universe? It is true that, with serious attention, we can defeat the resistance of our senses. But if we are on guard against them, they immediately rebel and recover their initial rights. Sometimes they

2. Cicero, *On the nature of the gods,* I.18: "what disposition of the limbs, what cast of features, what shape or outline can be more beautiful than the human form? . . . But if the human figure surpasses the form of all other living beings, and god is a living being, god must possess the shape which is the most beautiful of all."

3. Cicero, *On the nature of the gods,* I.18: "Since it is agreed that the gods are supremely happy, and no one can be happy without virtue, and virtue cannot exist without reason, and reason is only found in the human shape, it follows that the gods possess the form of man."

paint us a venerable old man; sometimes a dove. Strange weakness of man, which even the force of faith cannot defeat. (M. Arnaut)[4]

When the Pagans had fallen into this opinion that God has a body like men, they could not stop there. The multiplicity of the gods was an only too natural consequence of their principles. It was impossible for them to conceive of a simple, unique, spiritual God who is everywhere, who sees everything, who fills everything. Still, they could not resist the natural instinct to recognize a God—albeit material—who rules and governs the universe, and that awareness inevitably plunged them into the opinion of the multiplicity of the gods. For how could this massive God betake himself into all parts of the world at once? There had to be intelligent beings under him to be ministers of his will, and these intelligent beings had to have inferior Divinities under them. They thought Jupiter governed the world as a monarch governs a state. These reasonings, as I have already said, are the reasonings of instinct, and one may say that faith has not destroyed all impressions of them. In the present age, philosophers have been found who, unable to understand that God might suffice to govern the whole universe, have imagined plastic natures that govern under him, and have preferred to admit a being of which they themselves acknowledge they have no conception, than to recognize that a simple being could govern the entire universe immediately.[5]

Thus, it is seen that the Pagans fell into error only from having drawn accurate consequences from a false principle, that God has a body. But since they could reveal its falsity only through the reasonings of philosophy, etc.

I will not fail to be told that it follows from my reasoning that God is a deceiver, and that he casts men into error, without their always seeing the truth. I answer that it is not necessary for God to give us enough enlightenment to preserve our being. This ought to be enough for us. He has made us as perfect and as imperfect as he wanted; he could have made us more or less intelligent. When he reveals something to us, he graces us with a favor, but he could have hidden it from us without injustice. Is God deceiving us because the senses—those unfaithful witnesses—deceive us at every mo-

4. Probably a member of the Arnauld family, perhaps Antoine Arnauld (1612–94), leading Jansenist theologian and Pascal's friend during the Jesuit controversies.—HC

5. Ralph Cudworth (1617–88), the Cambridge Platonist philosopher, developed his theory of "plastic natures" in *True Intellectual System of the Universe* (1678).

ment? Certainly not! Perhaps God did not want us to be more certain about things so that we might be more aware of our weakness.

As for M. Bayle's atheists, the least reflection is enough for a man to cure himself of atheism. He has only to consider the Heavens, and he will find an invincible proof of the existence of God. It is inexcusable when he does not see Divinity depicted in everything that surrounds him; for as soon as he sees the effects, he must acknowledge a cause. It is not the same with idolatry, for man may indeed see and ponder the Heavenly order, yet remain stubbornly in idolatry. This disposition is not contradictory to the multiplicity of the gods, or if it is contrary, it is perhaps only by a sequence of metaphysical reasonings, often too weak without recourse to faith, that they can reveal this. I say more: perhaps the sole thing that reason teaches us about God is that there is an intelligent being that brings forth this order that we see in the world. But if one asks what is the nature of this being, one asks something that surpasses human reason. All that is known for certain is that Epicurus's hypothesis is untenable, because it attacks the existence of a being whose name is written everywhere.

The pagans would have thought they were committing a crime if they had changed religions—the more Christian their dispositions were, the more they had to remain in idolatry. (Look at the *Discourse on idolatry in general*.)

But as for the other hypotheses, which concern the particular attributes of this being, we can take the one we want, and we can even (if we want) embrace them and combat them in turn, like Cicero. For reason does not tell us if this being has a body, or if it does not; if it has all perfections; if it is infinite. All we know is that it has created us. When King Hieron had asked Simonides what God was, that philosopher asked him to give him a day to think about it. Once the day had passed and the King had posed the same question, the philosopher asked him for two days. This very idea, so dear to Father Malebranche—the idea of the Infinite—we do not have it, even though that philosopher has made it the foundation of his system. But one may say that he has built a magnificent palace in the air, which gradually disappears from view and vanishes in the clouds.

The Infinite is that to which nothing can be added, as opposed to the Indefinite, to which one is always adding. With this as a given, I take things by enumeration and say: One cannot have the idea of infinite duration, for duration is nothing other than time, whether counted by days, hours or centuries. It is clear that the idea of a thing that can be counted and that of a thing to which the mind can add nothing are two contradictory ideas, particularly since it is not possible to imagine a number so large that another cannot be added to it. I reason in the same way about extension. The idea of a thing that can be measured and that of a thing to which the mind can add nothing are contradictory, for one can never conceive of a measure so large that another cannot be added to it.

The idea of the Indefinite is the idea of a thing whose boundaries are not seen; the idea of the Infinite is the idea of a thing that is seen to have no boundaries. It is clear that this last idea cannot fit with what is counted and what is measured. It remains, then, to know whether it can be applied to a spirit, and I say that we have no concept of spirits, as everyone agrees. If we have no concept of a genus, we cannot have one of the species, or, consequently, of either the finite or the infinite spirit.

One must therefore marvel at the wondrous conduct of the one who in Scripture is named "the hidden God, *Deus absconditus.*"[6] He was content for many centuries to persuade men of his existence; then he instructed them by faith, which is one of his gifts. But its light warms the heart without illuminating the mind. It makes us ignorant of everything it teaches us, and seems to have been given us to admire, not to know; to submit, not to instruct.

God, who is a pure spirit, could not make himself known to men by an idea or by a representative image of himself. Nor could he make himself known solely by feeling, solely in the same manner by which he makes himself perceived by the Angels and the Blessed in Heaven. But since such great happiness, which is the supreme felicity, was a grace that man had to merit before obtaining it, and that he could not even acquire except by way of pain and suffering, God chose a third means of making himself known, that of faith; that way, if He did not offer him clear knowledge, He at least prevented him from lapsing into error.

[1947] [You ask me, Sir, what I think of the duration of the English government, and to predict what might be the consequences of its corruption. You . . .][1]

---

6. Isaiah 45:15.

[1947]

1. See *pensée* 1960, where Montesquieu takes up this torn and deleted text.

[1948] REFLECTIONS. Some scenes from Corneille gave me the idea for this dialogue {of Sulla}.[1] I was young, and you had to be quite young to be inspired to write by reading the great Corneille and by reading that author who is often as divine as he is.

[1949] Le D. is a petty man, without merit and birth, who has learned a type of financial jargon—instructed by Chamil——, discarded by Démare——, escaped the Chamber of Justice, introduced at the home of ——, uniquely suited to the employment he is being destined for, which is to debase a great dignity.[1] With pleasure, he has seen the seals descend and fall—from hand to hand, from wave to wave—right down to him, and as if the degradation of the post he is going to fill were the culmination of his fortune, he is charmed by the generosity of those who, in turning it down, have managed to place those seals within his grasp.

[1950] An author who writes much regards himself as a giant and views those who write little as pygmies. He thinks a man who has written only a hundred pages of good sense is a common man who has done in his whole life the work of one day.

[1951] Odd thing! It is almost never reason that makes things reasonable, and one almost never arrives at reason through reason.

When one remembers how the noble effects seen in the world have been caused, one blushes for good sense. Weren't two little Roman women, through their foolish petty vanity, the cause of that city conveying honors to Plebeians and thereby achieving that vaunted period of a perfect republic?

[1952] *Tu potes in totidem classem convertere nymphas.*[1]

I said this about England at the peace of 1748, and applied it to a mild criticism of one of my works.

[1948]
1. On the *Dialogue of Sulla and Eucratus*, see *pensée* 95 n. 1, and Allen, 98–109.

[1949]
1. D. seems to refer to Marc-René d'Argenson, lieutenant-général de police, keeper of the seals from 1718 to 1720, who was nearly prosecuted by the Chamber of Justice under the regency; the others cited are Michel Chamillart (1652–1721; see *pensée* 1306 and *Spicilège*, 431, 657, 750, and 753) and Nicolas Desmarets, marquis of Maillebois (1648–1721). The regent's edict creating a Chamber of Justice was promulgated March 14, 1716; in the ensuing crackdown on financial misconduct, a friend of Montesquie, Berthelot de Pléneuf, had to flee to Italy. For Montesquieu's views on the Chamber of Justice, see *PL,* XCVIII, 164.

[1952]
1. "Thou hast power to turn their fleet into as many nymphs." Virgil, *Aeneid,* X.83.

[1953] M. Faulques:

> *Cui pecudum fibrae, Caeli cui sidera parent.*
> (Virgil, book X.)[1]

[1954] I said of the *Journal de Trévoux* that if it were read, it would be the most dangerous work there is, in its scheme to make itself master of literature. *Ut haberent instrumenta servitutis et ephemerides.*[1]

[1955] Book X, Virgil says of Ascanius:[1]

> *Qualis gemma micat, fulvum quae dividit aurum.*[2]

I said: "Salient features should appear only on gold cloth; they are puerile when the subject is puerile."

Father Porée: "Like that precious stone that separates gold from gold."[3]

[1956] My response to the *Journal de Trévoux:* that when something has an innocent sense, one must not seek a bad sense in order to attribute it to the author; and I prove it by the *Journal de Trévoux* itself.[1]

[1957] Father Pozzi, at the Gallery of Florence—you might say he wants to occupy the entire hall and chase all those folks from it.[1]

[1953]

1. Virgil, *Aeneid*, X.176: "whom the victims' entrails obey, and the stars of heaven."

[1954]

1. "That they may have even journals as instruments of slavery." This is a play on Tacitus, *Agricola*, 14, where "journals" (*ephemerides*) replaces "kings" (*reges*), a passage Montesquieu cites in *Laws*, 10.17, 152.

[1955]

1. Ascanius, son of Aeneas.

2. Virgil, *Aeneid*, X.134: "[he] glitters like a jewel inset in yellow gold."

3. Charles Porée (1676–1742), Jesuit, Latin poet, professor of rhetoric at the Collège Louis-le-Grand in Paris.

[1956]

1. In an April 1749 letter to the Jesuit *Journal de Trévoux*, the anonymous author demands Montesquieu's elaboration on his treatment in *Laws* of suicide, polygamy, celibacy, sacrilege, his apparent praise of Julian the Apostate (Roman emperor, 361–63), his apparent fear of the social disruptions caused by Christian missions abroad. The *Journal* itself, on February 15, 1750, criticizes Montesquieu's *Défense de "l'Esprit des lois"* for focusing on a small point of interpretation of Diodorus of Sicily and thereby avoiding the larger theological problems.

[1957]

1. Fr. Simon Pozzi, Jesuit and painter; see *Voyages* (*OC*, 2:1340).

[1958] The least J—— brother had the costume of Father Le Tellier,[1] and had to be reckoned with. Didn't Barsac used to say, "We have come here from our leader"?

[1959] I said: "Those who, in order to contain the Jesuits, obliged them always to keep one of their own at Court, scarcely understood either the Court or the Jesuits, since they believed they would humble them by this."

[1960]

To Mr. Domville[1]

You ask me, Sir, what I think of the duration of the English government, and to predict what might be the consequences of its corruption.[2]

There, you offer me quite a difficult subject to treat. Perhaps my condition as foreigner makes me more capable of it than another, because I do not have either so much terror or so much hope. But I don't know if it is in the interest of your nation, I don't know if it is necessary, that these things be known with such precision. It would be good for the Prince to believe that your government is bound never to come to an end, and for the People to believe that the foundations on which it is established can be shaken. The Prince would renounce the idea of increasing his authority, and the People would give consideration to preserving their laws.

I believe, Sir, that what will preserve your government is that in essence, the People have more virtue than those who represent them. I don't know if I am mistaken, but I believe I saw this in your nation: the soldier is worth more than his officers, and the People are worth more than their magistrates and those who govern them. You have given your troops such high pay that it seems you wanted to corrupt your officers, and there are so many means of making a fortune in your government—by the government—it seems that you wanted to corrupt both your magistrates and your representatives. It is not like this with the entire body of the People, and I believe I have

[1958]
1. "The least Jesuit brother." Fr. Michel Le Tellier, S.J. (1643–1719), replaced Fr. de La Chaise as Louis XIV's confessor in February 1709. See also *pensées* 1226 and n. 7, and 2144 on him.

[1960]
1. This letter is a response to one by William Domville on June 4, 1749 (*OC*, 3:1235–37). Domville was one of the partisans of the success of *Laws* in England and was instrumental in arranging the English translation by Thomas Nugent the following year.
2. For his earlier comments on English corruption, see *Notes sur l'Angleterre* (*OC*, 3:286 and 288). See also *Laws*, 11.6, for his analysis of the English constitution.

noticed a certain spirit of liberty that is still alight and not ready to go out. And when I think about the character of that nation, it seems to me that it appears more enslaved than it is, because that which is more enslaved shows itself more out in the open, and that which is more free, less so.

I am not saying that in the elections of members of Parliament, corruption has not also slipped in. But permit me to make some observations. It is the lowest part of the nation that gets corrupted. And if, in a borough or county, there are some leading figures who are corrupting, because they are themselves corrupt, and some lower-class people who are corrupted, one may nonetheless say that the middling sort are not, and that the spirit of liberty still reigns among them. I would ask you to reflect on the particular type of corruption that is employed in these particular assemblies. There are meals, tumultuous assemblies, intoxicating liquors, factions, parties, hatreds, or feuds—means exposed to the light of day. The most dangerous corruption is the kind that is silent, that is hidden, that affects order, that seems orderly, that goes where it does not seem to be aiming to go. I would ask you to recall the corruption of Rome, and you will see that it was of an entirely different species.

1. The People formed a single body, and once the People were corrupted, the corruption unfailingly had its effect. If someone corrupts one of your boroughs, the other boroughs will not on that account be corrupted. A bad Member of Parliament has been elected; the true patriots still remain to elect a better one someday.

2. The corruption engaged in during your particular elections can operate on only a transitory matter—I mean the election of a Member of Parliament. It can concern only a clear thing—I mean the election of a Member of Parliament.

All the falsehoods, all the depths of corruption in England, therefore concern only Parliament. The Parliament may well lack integrity, but it does not lack illumination, so the corruption does not cease to be encumbered, because it is difficult to put a veil over it. True, there is scarcely a scoundrel who does not desire with all his heart to be a scoundrel—and to pass, I might add, for a good man.

I am saying, then, that among your people, the middling sort still love their laws and their liberty. I am saying more: those who betray their duty hope that the harm they do will not go so far that the people in the opposing party want to put fear into them. I am saying, then, that as long as the middling people preserve their principles, it will be difficult for your constitution to be overthrown.

It is your wealth that causes your corruption. Do not compare your wealth with that of Rome or with that of your neighbors! But compare the sources of your wealth with the sources of Rome's wealth and the sources of your neighbors' wealth. In essence, the sources of your wealth are commerce and human industry, and these sources are of such a nature that whoever draws on them cannot become rich without enriching many others. The sources of Rome's wealth were profit from the levying of taxes and profit from the pillaging of subject nations. Now these sources of bounty cannot enrich one individual without impoverishing countless others. Whence it happens that in that State, and in all those that might resemble it in this regard, there were only extremely rich people and extremely poor people. There could not be middling people, as with you, nor a spirit of liberty, as with you. There could only be a spirit of ambition, on the one side, and a spirit of despair on the other—and consequently, no more liberty.

I will make an observation here. Cicero, in speaking of the condition of the Republic, speaks of these middling people. "Who is it that forms the good party?" he says. "Is it the country people and the merchants? It is those for whom all governments are equal from the moment they are tranquil." This is not at all applicable to England's government. And although the natural spirit of these professions inclines by its nature toward tranquillity, as I said in my book in the *Laws* on the nature of the terrain, nonetheless what Cicero says here is connected only to a particular disadvantage of Rome's government, which I must discuss here.

When Rome under Sulla began to lapse into anarchy, the generals let their soldiers pillage the cities and the estates of the countryside. It was only a tranquil government that could ensure property, and as soon as civil war began to emerge, the proprietors of landed estates and the traders were bound to lapse into despair. Why did this happen? Because the natural wealth of the State had to give way to the wealth acquired by the grandees' pillaging and the tax collectors' vexations, which we were just discussing a moment ago. What will sustain your nation, then, is when the sources of great wealth are the same, and are not dried up by the larger sources of other wealth. The wisdom of your State consists, therefore, in the fact that the great fortunes are not drawn from the levy of taxes—and your laws will

be assured when the great fortunes are not drawn from military employments, and when the fortunes drawn from the civil state[3] are moderate
in scale.

[**1961**] DAGOBERT. His actions are weighed: on the one side are his
sins, which tip the scales; on the other side of the scales, a monk puts the
abbey of Saint-Denis, some quite big and heavy monks. Quite a few sins
would be needed to counter that.[1]

[**1962**] When I read Cardinal Richelieu's *Political Testament,* I regarded
it as one of the best works we have in this genre.[1] [I thought it did honor to
its author.] It seemed to me that the Cardinal's soul was there in its entirety,
and just as a painting is considered to be by Raphael because one finds that
great painter's brush in it, I likewise considered the *Political Testament* to be
by Cardinal Richelieu because I found Cardinal Richelieu's mind throughout it, and because I saw him thinking as I had seen him acting. I imagined that the Cardinal was among those very fortunate men, discussed by
a Roman author, who have received these two gifts from Heaven: to do
memorable things and to write about them. I thought Cardinal Richelieu's
Testament was an original work [which, having been greeted by the public
with applause], which, as always happens, had generated bad copies, and
that the applause with which it had been greeted induced the booksellers
to have the *Testaments* of Messrs Louvois and Colbert composed—which
are manifest forgeries.[2]

This is the reason why, in working on *The Spirit of the Laws,* I cited
that *Testament* in two or three places as a work by the one whose name
it bears. But having heard by chance from M. de Voltaire that that work
was not by Cardinal Richelieu, I deleted the passages where I had spoken
of it. But abbé Dubos, who had a great deal of knowledge on these sorts

---

3. By *état civil,* Montesquieu may also mean, in Littré's definition, "the condition of a person result-
ing from his filiation, his alliances, his family rights."—HC

[**1961**]
1. Dagobert I (ca. 603–639), Merovingian king who founded the Benedictine abbey of St. Denis
and was the first monarch to be buried there.—HC

[**1962**]
1. Montesquieu read the 1688 Amsterdam edition (*Catalogue,* 2430); Louis André, in his 1947 edition based upon a Sorbonne manuscript, concluded that the work was authentic.

2. The testaments attributed to Colbert and Louvois and published in 1693–94 were put together
by Gratien Courtilz de Sandras (1644–1712), author of historical compilations written for Dutch
booksellers.

of incidents, whom I consulted, told me that the work was by Cardinal Richelieu—that is, that it had been composed by the order of, in the sight of, and on the ideas of Cardinal Richelieu, by M. Bourzeis and another whom he named. I needed nothing more, and I put back the passages that I had removed.[3]

Today, in November 1749, there appears a pamphlet by M. de Voltaire, in which he explains the reasons that make him think the work we call Cardinal Richelieu's *Testament* is not by him.[4]

These reasons have seemed weak to me, and I have not been able to yield to them. The strongest of all are these two: that that book was published thirty years after Cardinal Richelieu's death; second, that the cardinal says they were at peace, and yet they were at war.

1. It was not in that book's nature to be published as soon as it was written; that was not its purpose. The book had been written for the King, and it had been written for the Cardinal and for the Cardinal's designs. Thus, far from publishing it, it was essential not to publish it. It was a secret document, which was bound to appear only when circumstances no longer demanded that it not appear.

2. I do not have before my eyes the terms used by Cardinal Richelieu. In all likelihood, he meant they were at peace because when he was writing, there was no civil war in France. And in fact, the normal state of war in those times was civil war. As for foreign war, there were times when Cardinal Richelieu was causing it to be waged more than waging it. There were times when we were auxiliaries rather than main parties. Moreover, as M. Bourzeis wrote concerning Cardinal Richelieu's memoirs, one cannot say that that work originates from a date, or from a particular year. They were reflections the Cardinal was writing down as they came to him. There is the date of the reflections; there is the date of the writing. It would be too gross an error on the part of whoever might have produced this testament not to know whether they were at peace or at war during the Cardinal's ministry. And the author, whoever he is, seems so informed about the

---

3. See *Laws*, 3.5, 5.10–11, and 29.16, and Brèthe, 1:253–56 nn. 18 and 18a for these changes; abbé Amable de Bourzeis (1606–72) was a diplomat, theologian, and man of letters.

4. The short work *Des mensonges imprimés et du Testament du cardinal de Richelieu* [Of published lies, and of Cardinal Richelieu's Testament] was published together with the tragedy *Semiramis* in 1749.

state of Europe during the Cardinal's ministry that he cannot have been ignorant of whether they were at peace or at war.

Another objection by M. de Voltaire is the business about the current accounts. "The Cardinal," he says, "would have been speaking against himself." I respond that the Cardinal spoke on his own behalf so much in this *Testament* that one can hardly suspect him of forgetting himself in this case. The Cardinal was not a particular minister; he was king. Far be it from him to confuse himself with someone to whom he was giving a share in the ministry.

All of M. de Voltaire's other objections weigh against the book, but determine nothing about who its author is. It is bad reasoning to say that the book is not by the Cardinal because there are passages one can criticize in it; to say that the Cardinal said *the Fargy*,[5] in speaking of a woman who was an ambassadress—she was an ambassadress for us, but for the Cardinal she was only, I believe, a lady of the bedchamber. One would have to know whether, during the time the Cardinal was writing, it showed lack of respect to say *the Fargy*. That expression may be very low or it may be very high; it may be the effect of pride, just as it may today be the effect of a bad education. Moreover, and this is what induces one to believe it, the expressions and ideas in the entire book are not low.

With regard to the term *the Queen*, instead of *the Queen-Mother*, that queen had been regent, and it was not a question of the Queen properly speaking. This is a nonchalance that was more fitting for the Cardinal than for someone else, and whoever wrote it was no more likely to lapse into it than the Cardinal, if this be regarded as a fault.

With regard to style, it can only do honor to the Cardinal. It is full of fire and motion; it is full of a certain impetuosity in the sentences, a certain natural talent, a great deal of inexactness. In short, one sees the style of a man who has always begun to write, but who has never written; one sees rather the man than the writer, and I am persuaded that the editors have put the order rather than the substance into the work.

M. de Voltaire can hardly say that the style of the *Testament* does not resemble Cardinal Richelieu's other works. It is known that he did not write his theological works, any more than our bishops have written their pastoral letters. Would we adopt the style of works he did not write as the basis for judging those he did?

5. Madeleine de Silly-Rochepot (d. 1639), wife of the duke of Fargis d'Argennes.

With regard to what is found in the *Testament* concerning the claim that the *régale*[6] extends everywhere because the Royal crown is round, this is not one of the Cardinal's ideas; he cites it (I reckon) as an idea of the jurisconsults.

Thus, I say that the *Political Testament* is by the Cardinal, because I find in it his character, his genius, his passions, his interests, his outlook, even the prejudices of his status and of the profession he had embraced. Is it M. Bourzeis, a determined Jansenist, who would have wanted to annihilate appeals of ecclesiastical verdicts to Parlementary courts?[7] Is it M. Bourzeis who would have imagined such specious things to prevent the possibility of a minister ever being displaced or convicted of bad governance? Is it M. Bourzeis who would have had such difficult, subtle, and judicious research done on the port of Marseilles, on the position of the Mediterranean, the advantages and disadvantages that the Spanish and French derive from it? It is obvious that this was the fruit of the Cardinal's successes and failures.

M. de Voltaire says that there is a contradiction between what is said in one place in this book—that the last five years of the war cost sixty million pounds—and another, where it is said that the revenues of the Royal Treasury amounted to only thirty-five million. I refer M. de Voltaire to the document provided by M. Desmarets at the beginning of the Regency.[8] He will find quite a different disproportion between revenue and expenses, and it is {not} for nothing that Louis XIV owed nearly two billion on his death. It is not for nothing that the finances were found to be ruined at the beginning of his reign—whether in his minority under M. d'Emery, or in his majority under M. Fouquet.[9]

M. de Voltaire is surprised that the manuscript has not been found in the family's possession, or indeed anywhere else. The manuscript is not found because the book is published. We know the fate of most manuscripts that

6. The *régale* was the king's right to collect the revenues from bishoprics while vacant (temporal *régale*) and to name to benefices in dependency that did not involve the cure of souls (spiritual *régale*).

7. *Appels comme d'abus*, on which, see *pensée* 1225. The Jansenists were known for supporting these appeals.—HC

8. *Mémoires de M. Desmarets sur l'administration des finances, depuis le 20 février de l'année 1708 jusqu'au 1er septembre 1715* (N.p., n.d.).

9. Michael Particelli, Lord of Emery (ca. 1595–1650), French financier of Italian origin, controller-general of finances from 1643 to 1647, and superintendent from 1647 to 1648; Nicolas Fouquet (1615–80), ambitious superintendent of finances under Mazarin, arrested for irregularities in the 1660s and spent the rest of his life in prison.

are published. We are curious about the old editions only because they take the place of the old manuscript—which the booksellers had for publication, but which has been lost or spoiled in their possession.

M. de Voltaire finds the allusions drawn from Aristotle's philosophy to be puerile. But apparently Cardinal Richelieu had not studied Cartesian philosophy! And this proves the work is by him more than by the one who published it some fifty years after his death—a time when Aristotle's philosophy was so denigrated. According to M. de Voltaire's words, then, the compiler must have been a schoolboy pedant. But no one can say that a schoolboy pedant produced this compilation.

He is surprised that a minister declared himself against the *régale*. But that minister was an ecclesiastic, and, what is more, a cardinal. Cardinal Balue was a minister, and he declared himself against the Pragmatic Sanction, which was of an entirely different importance from the honorable but useless right of the *régale*—which latter is of such petty import that even today, kings do not manage to turn it to their profit.[10]

M. de Voltaire is surprised that the Cardinal gave such petty instructions to a king who had been reigning for thirty years—for example, a king must have piety, etc. But does he not know that a minister who instructs kings has a strong incentive to give them instructions to do what they are doing? Cardinal Richelieu advises the King to be pious because he was; he advises him not to have any mistresses because he did not have any—and even, perhaps, because he had some himself.

He finds it puerile that the Cardinal tells the King that a prince should have a council. Who could better say this than the Cardinal, who cannot have forgotten his quarrel with M. de Cinq-Mars, and who had been obliged to tell the latter, in front of the King, that one does not put State affairs in the hands of children? He was telling the King what he had taken such trouble to persuade him of throughout his life: to put affairs in the hands of ministers, not favorites. These are ideas tossed around in the air and materials to straighten out, not a work.

M. de Voltaire regards what the *Political Testament* says as an absurdity: that current accounts must be limited to 6 million in gold. He asks what are 6 million in gold—whether they are millions of marks, millions of

---

10. Cardinal Jean La Balue (ca. 1421–91); Pragmatic Sanction (1438) gave substantial rights to the French king in ecclesiastical matters; see above, *pensées* 1226 n. 6 and 1302 n. 23.

louis.[11] It is easy to answer: these are six million pounds in gold. Six million in gold is stated here because the Bureau or the Royal Treasury always pays the King's current accounts in gold. Under Cardinal Mazarin, the current accounts were prodigious, surpassing 40 million. The current accounts have always been necessary, but on the other hand, it has been necessary to keep accounts in the King's Chamber so that the King could be accountable to himself. When the currency exchanges have made representations, certain limits have been put on the current accounts—and even without representations, for there are always bound to be some secret expenses. Here, Cardinal Richelieu wants the current accounts to have sufficient latitude, but elsewhere not too much, so that the administration will be prudent. The account he set up is roughly what is set up today: it is around 15 million.

[1963] Along with Lord Bath, I was at Mme d'Aiguillon's, and I said that when I had addressed an oration to the King, I was very disconcerted. Mme d'Aiguillon said: "Milord, who spoke so much at the English Parliament, was never disconcerted." "It is easier," I responded, "to speak against a king than to speak to a king."

[1964] I said: "It is known that he was bent only on having the late Duke[1] arrange the marriage of his sister with the King. By abbé Montgon's *Memoirs*,[2] it is seen that he had consented that the Spanish branch would succeed to the Crown, to the detriment of the Orleans line and therefore of the Bourbons. My goodness! He managed to do that! My goodness! He did not exactly appropriate the reputation of a magnanimous man, and because he was a fool, he appropriated the reputation of a grain merchant."

[1965] On December 20, 1749, here are the observations I have made. M. de La Ensenada is a Spanish minister of broad outlook. He has worked many operations. Here is one of them.[1]

11. A gold louis was generally worth twenty-four pounds, a gold mark between four hundred and six hundred. See "A Note on Currency," above.—HC

[1964]
1. The Duke of Bourbon. See *pensées* 912 and 2042.
2. Abbé Charles-Alexandre de Montgon (1690–1770), having entered the service of Philip V, returned to France with the secret mission of intriguing to ensure the crown to the house of Spain if the king of France died without issue. An ill-advised confidence to Cardinal Fleury caused him to be exiled to Douai. His *Memoirs* (in nine volumes) covered the years from 1725 and were published in Geneva and the Hague starting in 1745.

[1965]
1. Zeno Silva, marquis of La Ensenada (1690–1762), Spanish minister of finances under Ferdinand VI (r. 1746–59).

It is known that some piasters come back from the Indies bound for circulation in Spain, and that there are others whose extraction is permitted, and on which the merchants earn 5 percent, more or less. M. de La Ensenada has considered it appropriate to make this profit. He has denied the extraction to our merchants, sent agents into foreign countries, and made himself the banker. He has the piasters brought out and sends them to his agents, who sell them to the merchants—by means of certain bills of exchange payable on short term—and when they are paid for, he has his money remitted to Madrid, which he can do in cash, in foreign currency, or in merchandise.

In cash, this is difficult. So much the better if he does it in merchandise. But it works better to do it with the currency exchange.

Here is what would have to have been done to interrupt his operation. Assuming he had to have 10, 12, 15 million in French currency remitted to Madrid, one could have denied him his profit by making the exchange rate go down—which could easily be done by the King, by losing 100,000 or 200,000 crowns, which is an easy operation. When the Spanish minister saw that his entire operation produced little profit (for he does not cease having expenses in agents, transport of piasters, etc.), the day he received his memorandum,[2] it would only be a matter of having a petition by our merchants presented to him, and asking him for extraction in return for 2 percent profit for the King. It is certain that he would have accepted this neat, clean, and painless benefit to an operation less lucrative, more costly, and more painful—by means of which, he was abandoning his plan.

It is said that he has another one: to give Spain complete mastery of the Cadiz trade, and send merchandise directly into the Indies without the intervention of foreigners—both the items he will attract from Spanish manufactures, finished or unfinished, and those he will buy in France or Germany. And to make the Cadiz trade more independent of foreigners, he lends the Spanish the money necessary for their shipments and makes them advances. And this money, which they used to be obliged to borrow from foreigners at usurious rates, gives them the capacity to engage in their trade; foreigners, again, are deprived of this benefit, which had been very substantial. The entire trade would therefore take place directly from Spain to the Indies, all the more so in that foreigners would find themselves

2. *Mémoire*, a summary of expenses or charges (see *DAF*, 1694).—HC

deprived of primary materials—whether wool, silver. Spain would enjoy a great maritime trade, etc.

To counter all this, here is what would have to be done. There is no question of making representations by ministers or ambassadors; everyone is master on his home turf. Complain, and they will give you oracular responses; they will cite the ancient laws of Spain, other things, etc. In the past, we had a famous consul in Cadiz who always told the merchants: "Gentlemen, don't make me lodge complaints; make others lodge them to me against you. I will be strong if they complain about your smuggling, about the canings you have given out to prevent them from visiting you. But if you complain about the injustices they are doing you, I am weak."

To return to our discussion: without complaining about the {new} regulations, it would only be a matter of secretly permitting our merchants to send some well-armed vessels—half war, half merchandise—along the coasts of Spain, and to tell them to think especially about not being caught. At first, there would arise complaints in France. "We don't know what this is all about," we would say. "This must be some merchant who, no longer able to trade in Cadiz, has conceived the idea of smuggling. We'll look into that. But if you wanted to bring an end to all the obstacles you have in place against the general commerce of Europe, we would come up with something better, you and us."

It is easy to imagine that our merchants, who would send their merchandise directly from the French ports to America, would gain in: (1) the maritime trade; (2) the expenses for transporting, unloading, reloading their merchandise in Cadiz; (3) the king of Spain's tariffs; (4) the delays; (5) the formalities, both in going out and after the return; (6) the facility of selling, and of selling at will.

[1966] The English, seeing that they can no longer obtain an exclusive privilege in Spain—other than the compensation for what was left for them to enjoy from their old treaties—have turned, I reckon, elsewhere. They have negotiated with Portugal and have envisaged excluding us from that trade—and beyond that, grounding the trade we had with Spain. They have obtained sumptuary laws by which all fashions and jewelry are prohibited, and all woolen cloth is allowed except black cloth. That is, they have managed it so that Portugal gets nothing from us. Of all our woolen cloth, it was only the black cloth that we provided, and as for other merchandise, we furnished only fashions and jewelry.

This is not all. They have managed it so that Portugal has obtained permission to send vessels directly to the Indies. And since Portugal cannot by itself conduct either all the trade or all its shipping, it happens that it is the English who do it under the name and pretext of the Portuguese, and the French find themselves excluded from it without appearing to be deliberately excluded.

[1967] This year in France {1749}, we have managed a good operation: we have eliminated export tariffs on most of our manufactures. But since what are called *fashions, adornments, jewelry,* are made by countless petty workers, these petty articles—which make up a very large one—these petty articles, I say, have been left subject to the same tariffs as before, and the problem still remains in this regard.

Moreover, an important import tariff has been left on primary materials, and although this tariff is very small, it is still a big disadvantage in competition. It is nothing on a bushel; it is much on a large shipment. And the foreigner, who can send primary materials to a place where he pays nothing at all, may prefer this to sending them to a place where he pays something. In speculation, a difference in profit determines whether to ship to one place rather than another, and it is a big deal to place some obstacle, however small, in the way of shipping primary materials.

[1968] The rigidity of our customs has a crushing effect on our trade.[1] A precise declaration is required in the cargo manifests, and if the weight is found to be about 10 percent greater or less than has been declared, one is assumed to be engaging in fraud.

Here is a story I heard. A merchant sent ten quintals of licorice to a Paris banker named Le Couteux. It was found to weigh around 30 percent more than the declaration. The licorice is halted. Le Couteux writes to his correspondent on the inaccuracy of his declaration. The correspondent writes that it is in order. Le Couteux returns to the Bureau. The licorice is weighed again (this was in dry weather). It weighs 18 percent less than the declaration, so he says: "You've stolen my licorice!"

[1969] Devotion has its favorite sides. The Duchess of Brissac,[1] being at the sermon, says to the person next to her: "If they preach on Magdalene,

[1968]
1. See *Laws,* 20.13.

[1969]
1. Catherine-Madeleine Pécoil de Villedieux, Duchess of Brissac (1707–70).

you wake me up. If they preach on the necessity of salvation, you let me sleep."

[1970] To write well, one needs to skip over intermediate ideas— enough not to be boring; not too much, for fear of not being understood. It is these happy deletions that made M. Nicole say that all good books are double.[1]

[1971] One profits much in society; one profits much in one's private office. In one's office, one learns to write in an orderly way, to reason accurately, and to form one's reasonings well; the silence enables one to give coherence to what one is thinking. In society, on the other hand, one learns imagination. One runs into so many topics of conversation that one conceives of things; one sees men as pleasant and gay; one is thinking by virtue of the fact that one is not thinking—that is, that one has ideas by chance, which are often good ones.

The spirit of conversation is a particular spirit, which consists in reasonings and unreasonings that are short.

[1972] Here is a text written by a woman of sixteen; it is the late Marquise de Gontaud.[1] I have not seen the piece, which was a character portrait of the Princess of Clèves, but I have heard a report of this idea: "Hearts made for love do not commit themselves easily."

I believe this idea is true. The Prince of Clèves was lovable; it was necessary to wait for the Duke of Nemours. A heart made for love does not commit itself easily because a heart that can be touched by anything lovable is not made for love, but for a common passion. A woman who could commit herself to one of twenty lovable men that someone linked her with, and commit herself to any one of the twenty, has not a heart made for love. A heart made for love surrenders to an assemblage of lovable qualities that corresponds to the assemblage of its own qualities, which forms a particular combination not found elsewhere because it is a particular case out of countless combinations. It is then that a heart is made for love because the object that it loves could not be, cannot now be, and never can be replaced. Then, the loss of the lover is felt as the loss of love; the

[1970]
1. Pierre Nicole (1625–95), important Jansenist and author of *Essais de morale* (1671–78).

[1972]
1. Antoinette-Eustachie Crozat du Chastel (d. 1747, in her nineteenth year) had married Charles-Antoine-Armand de Gontaud in 1744.

world is no more than a man, and a man is the world. The heart that has felt nothing finds itself so surprised to feel—it is a good that it discovers in nature; it is a new being that is taken on or found. It is as big a surprise to the soul to suddenly find an order of feelings that it did not know as it would be if it suddenly discovered a new order of knowledge—except that already having knowledge means that the latter is merely an acquisition for it; but new feelings are a creation within the soul.

[**1973**] There are people whose means of preserving their health include purgatives, blood-lettings, etc. As for me, my only regimen is to diet when I have had too much, to sleep when I have stayed up late, and not to be hit with boredom by sorrows, pleasure, work, or idleness.

[**1974**] At the Battle of Bouvines, under Philip Augustus, we lost the charters of the Crown and the registers containing the service owed by each domain.[1] So we know what each Greek city paid for each domain to the Council of Amphyctions, but we do not know what each domain paid or provided in men of war to the Crown.[2]

[**1975**] I said: "Nothing is so striking to me in Paris as the enjoyable indigence of the great lords and the boring opulence of the businessmen."

[**1976**] Mme de —— said of Cardinal Fleury that he understood men enough to deceive them but not enough to choose them.[1]

[**1977**] In Paris, I hear about only two men: the one, who used to have nothing and is today very rich; the other, a man very rich in the past who today has nothing.

[**1978**] Usually, a man who does not speak is not thinking. I am talking about whoever has no reason not to speak. Everyone is quite ready to bring to light what he thinks he has thought out well; men are made like that.

[**1979**] I have said somewhere that integrity ruined Spain.[1]

[*1974*]
  1. Philip II Augustus, king of France (1180–1223); Battle of Bouvines, in Flanders, which Philip won against the English King John I Lackland and his allies—the German emperor Otto IV and Count Ferrand of Flanders—on July 27, 1214.
  2. The Council or assembly of the Amphyctions brought together representatives of twelve Greek cities and constituted a sort of tribunal designed to arbitrate or pacify conflicts between the associated cities.

[*1976*]
  1. On Louis XV's prime minister (1726–43), see *pensées* 472, 914, 1019, 1065, 1226, 1284, 1484, 1509, and 1595.—HC

[*1979*]
  1. See *pensée* 323.—HC

[1980] All princes get bored; one proof of this is that they go hunting.

[1981] I was playing badly. I abandoned a quirk that was costing me a lot of money. I want to be like those men who have quirks that cost them nothing.

[1982] Normally, those who have a large mind have a naïve one.

[1983–2003] REFLECTIONS ON THE PRINCE,[1] WHICH DID NOT MAKE IT INTO MY "ROMANS," MY "LAWS," AND "ARSACE."

[1983] The principles of dominion and obedience need to be established. Are there cases where it is permissible for a subject to disobey his prince? He should do nothing for him, and it would be quite a bizarre way of thinking to have so much respect for his prince's orders and so little for his prince's honor. It is very dangerous for a prince to have subjects who obey him blindly. If the Inca Atahualpa had not been obeyed by his people as if they were beasts, they would have prevented a hundred and sixty Spaniards from taking him. If he had been less obeyed from the time of his captivity, the Peruvian generals would have saved the Empire. If Manco Inca,[1] under Spanish control, had not on his orders prevented the uprising of his people, the Spanish would not have had time to fortify themselves against him. If Montezuma, when imprisoned, had been respected merely as a man, the Mexicans would have destroyed the Spanish. And if Guatimozin, when captured, had not with a single word ended the war, his capture would not have been the moment for the fall of the Empire, and the Spanish would have been afraid of provoking his subjects by his torture.

[1984] A perfect monarch is the one who—just toward his subjects, just also toward his neighbors, compelled sometimes to have enemies—stops being fearsome to them as soon as he has defeated them.

[1985] I cannot persuade myself that there could ever be a French prince who does not love his nation. There are indeed certain states where the princes, having to argue constantly with their subjects over their prerogatives, might be embittered by the contestation. But I cannot imagine that the same thing could happen here, where the subjects, trusting blindly

[1983–2003]

1. *Reflections on the character of some princes* (*OC,* 3:537–51).

[1983]

1. Manco-Capac, Atahualpa's brother, reigned in Peru from 1533 to 1536, under Spanish protection.

in their prince, have abandoned themselves to him almost without restriction, and have put their entire happiness in his hands.

[**1986**] If there occurs some revolt, the Prince's wisdom and prudence must regulate his clemency and justice. One might say to him: "The position you occupy can be filled by another—without its having to cost humanity rivers of blood to preserve you or to calm your fears. Your life is more precious only because it is more useful to those very men that you want to destroy. 'This people,' you say, 'is rebellious, and a great example is necessary.' As for me, I tell you that it is not up to a society to serve as example, since on the contrary, it would be on their behalf that one ought to provide it. Often when you are pardoning, you think you are engaging in an act of clemency, when you are engaging in an act of justice. Often when you are punishing, you think you are engaging in an act of justice when you are engaging in an act of cruelty.[1] Power does not belong to you; you have only its use, and you have it for only a moment. If some being could (abuse?) its power, it would be Heaven, which, being eternal, sees all creatures pass before it. But it conducts itself with as much order and regularity as if its power were dependent."

[**1987**] As for conquerors, I will tell them that it is a common trait to love war;[1] that there are many bellicose princes, just as there are many private individuals who have a violent passion for acquisition; that it is moderation, as the rarest virtue, that ought to constitute heroism; that it is not surprising that so many princes have sought to make themselves famous by their aggression against their neighbors, since nothing is so easy for them as to let themselves be led by their passions, whereas the role of a moderate and just prince is all the more laborious for being merely reasonable;[2] that these sorts of virtues cost a great deal to princes because they are real. I excuse Pompey, Caesar, and the other Roman magistrates for having loved war because it was the only means they had of escaping their mediocrity; I excuse Alexander and Charlemagne for having loved war; but I cannot understand how princes who do not leave their palaces can love it. A prince jeopardizes his condition so much by war that he can compensate for the

---

[**1986**]
1. See *pensée* 162 for a similar thought.—HC

[**1987**]
1. See *Laws*, 10.4, 142, for this theme.
2. *Raisonnable*, which may also be rendered as "equitable."—HC

risks he runs only by laurels gathered with his own hands. I can cite the example of Louis XIII, who made war for so long only for the glory of Cardinal Richelieu, and who, in the course of so much success, always saw the ministry distinguished but never the reign. A degree less of weakness would have made him the plaything of his nation, because he would have wanted to govern by himself. A degree more of weakness made him more powerful than all his predecessors, because he remained under the thumb of a minister whose genius devoured Europe, but who left him no more glory than that of the Tartar emperor who conquered China at the age of six.

[1988] By a cruel destiny, the greatest princes are those who are most discontented with their fortune. Since the latter has done much for them, they are accustomed to think it should have done everything. He who has vast possessions can no longer have anything but vast desires. Alexander, in his capacity as King of Macedonia, desired the realm of Persia; in his capacity as King of Persia, he desired all the earth he knew about; when he saw that he was going to be its master, he sent fleets to seek new peoples for himself—strange disease, which is worsened by the remedies themselves.

[1989] A king of France[1] who reflects upon his grandeur should tell the gods what Seneca used to tell an emperor: "You have heaped so many goods and so many honors upon me that nothing can be lacking in my felicity except moderation. *Tantum honorum in me cumulasti ut nihil felicitati meae desit nisi moderatio ejus.*"[2]

[1990] There have been princes who, lacking the strength or courage to distinguish themselves against their neighbors, turn all their ambition against their subjects. They have a grand idea of themselves, because they have been able to extend their authority further than their predecessors. In truth, they have good reason to congratulate themselves on having been the first ones who had the courage to violate their oath, who used forces against their subjects that had been provided to defend them, and who with good armies intimidated farmers and artisans. And since this cannot happen without corruption working its way into the State, it happens that the orders of such an adroit prince are more easily evaded, and his laws

[1989]
1. First version: "A king of Spain"
2. Tacitus, *Annals,* XIV.53.

Pensées 1991–1993

more frequently violated; so that such a prince, who knows so well how to make himself obeyed, is in reality the one who is least obeyed.

[**1991**] I will say to Princes: "Why do you exhaust yourselves so much to extend your authority? Is it to increase your power? But the experience of all countries and all times makes clear that you are weakening it. Is it to do good? But which peoples and laws are so stupid as to interfere with you when you want to do good? Thus, it is to be able to do harm.

"If you were good and just, moreover, you should not desire authority without limits. For if you are a good prince, you love your Country; if you love her, you should fear for her. But don't you have every reason to believe that not all of your successors will be as just as you?

"Even if you love your successor, you will not work to leave him unlimited authority—just as a father who loves his son does not seek to eliminate his embarrassment in the presence of a wise man who is advising him."

[**1992**] In princely courts, one usually has a highly mistaken idea of power. The king of England is actually more absolute than the Sultan. The Parliament there is far from being as inconvenient to kings and ministers as the military or the people of Constantinople are to the Seraglio or the Great Chamber.[1] Those who govern Ireland and Scotland are far from presenting a minuscule fraction of the distress there that the pashas of Anatolia and Kerch present to the Sultan. It is in Turkey that the laws of the State, that is, the customs, can be violated with less impunity than anywhere in the world. {I believe this was put in the *Romans*.}[2]

[**1993**] Since the condition of Princes emancipates them from fear of the laws, it is almost impossible for them not to be completely wicked without some system of belief.[1] This is proven by that series of successor kings to Alexander—in Egypt, in Asia, in Macedonia. It is proven by those Roman emperors who, living within a religion that had no system, were all monsters—except for five or six, who almost all owed their virtue to Stoic philosophy.

I cannot bear that a famous author[2] has maintained that a religion can-

[**1992**]
1. *Divan;* on this word, see *pensée* 1833.—HC
2. The reference has not been found.

[**1993**]
1. See *Laws,* 24.2, 460.
2. Pierre Bayle (1647–1706), on whom, see *pensées* 104, 139, 302n, 989, 1230, and especially 1946 and 2245 n. 3.

not be a restraining force. I well know that it does not always halt a man in the heat of passion. But are we always in that state? If it does not always restrain the moment, it at least restrains a life.[3]

With regard to the devotion of Princes, I advise them to be very much on their guard about it; for it is very easy for them to believe themselves better than they are in fact. Since, through a misunderstanding, devotion makes politics permissible to them, and politics in turn virtually all the vices they desire—such as avarice, pride, thirst for another's property, ambition, vengeance—it costs them almost nothing out of these vices to be devout. Whereas we who do not have reasons of State to satisfy our passions are obliged to sacrifice virtually all of them. Moreover, habit, their status, and everyone's looks demand that they compose themselves for most of their actions. Now to hold oneself up in a temple with gravity and decency is called, by most people, *being devout.*

It is asked whether a prince should place his affairs of state in the hands of a confessor.[4] There is nothing so dangerous. For those who have the worldly spirit are entirely incapable of managing his conscience, and those who do not have this spirit are incapable of managing his State. A director is set up to alert him about the misdeeds he commits. But how will he instruct him on the misdeeds that he is going to have him commit? The Prince does not discharge his duties, and he prevents the other from discharging his own.

Fear and timidity always have ruses. Superstitious princes want to negotiate with God so that he will damn their confessor in their place. "I put that," they say, "on your conscience." But God has not put it on that conscience and does not approve of these sorts of agreements.

A prince should especially not consult his director on the choice of persons he ought to elevate to honors; this would be subject to countless disadvantages. For since the choice of some inevitably entails the exclusion of others, and since no one is excluded without the reason being given, it would happen that each individual would be judged in a secret tribunal, without having any way of justifying himself.

In a word, of all those who approach the person of the Prince, the confessor is the one who should have the most credit, and the one who should have the least.

---

3. See *Laws,* 24.2, 460.
4. See *pensée* 540, where Montesquieu puts these words in the mouth of M. Zamega.

I do not even believe that the prince should get for this position a person attached to a particular monastic body. For this, there are very good reasons, among others this one: it afflicts a nation and introduces, in certain respects, a spirit of servitude. For since whoever the Prince goes and seeks in a corporate body, in order to give him his confidence, is respected at Court, those who are from the same body are likewise respected in the City and the provinces. And since the least among them is an important personage, you find yourself accosted by a thousand favorites instead of one, and all you see on all sides are masters.

[**1994**] The authority of the Sovereign must be communicated to as many people as necessary and to as few as possible. The Prince should share it with his ministers, but it must remain in their hands and not pass into others.[1]

The Prince must especially guard against private affections—a certain corporate body, certain men, certain clothes, certain opinions. Otherwise, he becomes hopelessly narrow-minded. Providence had made him for general affection; it had provided him with grand goals. This means that he should renounce not his heart—he should not, he cannot—but his whims.

The first talent of a great prince is that of knowing how to select men. For since, however he gets them, his ministers or officials will have a greater share in affairs than he, he cannot have them too skillful or too good. He therefore must get it into his head that this choice is not a matter of taste, but of reason; that a man he likes is not usually a more skillful man than a man he does not like; and that whatever time one wastes paying court to him does not make one worth more, and very often one is worth less for it.

He should be all the more guarded in his choice of ministers because it is virtually the only act of royalty that belongs to him—since the ministers, once he has chosen them, take part in all other acts.

He should not deprive his ministers of his confidence in such a way that he makes them think they are in danger, for then they no longer think of anything but maintaining themselves and combating his anxieties with their deceptions.

He should not subject them to an inner council of some favorite or

---

[1994]
1. This is a continuation of the M. Zamega dialogue on *pensée* 540.—HC

some domestics. The people love a visible authority; they cannot abide a secret government, nor being led as if by pure spirits.

He must not change ministers lightly; for it is certain that a new minister will develop new schemes, and the plan that is most contrary to what he finds established is certainly the one he will like best. Every man is as much an enemy to others' ideas as he is enamored of his own. This is seen in the buildings that a successor almost never finishes.

Furthermore, I cannot envy the condition of this third category of men, between the Sovereign and the subjects, who have only the misfortunes of the Princes' condition, and who enjoy neither the reality of sovereignty nor the advantages of private life. I advise them: not to engage in bad deeds to maintain themselves in a miserable post; to enter it with honor; to preserve themselves in it with innocence; to leave it with dignity; and when they have left it, never to return to it.

If the true meaning of the honor and glory that attend those who suffer for having done their duty were known, there is not a well-made soul who would not prefer a great downfall to the certain enjoyment of the most dazzling occupations.

[1995] As for flattery, one may warn all princes: there is a universal conspiracy formed against them to hide the truth from them. One may warn courtiers that when they are least thinking about it, they are committing great crimes—that is, those silent crimes that extort pardon because they strike so low.

But if courtiers are guilty when, by base flattery, they lull the prince's conscience to sleep, then magistrates, more obliged by their status to tell him the truth, are even guiltier. When Caracalla had had his brother Geta killed, he ordered Papinian to find excuses for that crime: "A parricide," he responded, "is not as easy to excuse as to commit."[1] One cannot help being indignant at First President de Thou who, when Charles IX went to share with the Parlement what had happened on Saint-Bartholomew's Day, wanted to justify that deed by saying that whoever did not know how to dissimulate did not know how to reign.[2] It was a greater crime for

[1995]

1. Publius Septimus Geta, Roman emperor (r. 211–12); Aemilius Papinius, Roman jurisconsult put to death by Caracalla in 212; the source seems to be Aelius Spartianus's life of Caracalla in the *Historia Augusta,* purportedly early fourth century. See also *pensée* 778.—HC

2. Christophe de Thou (1508–82), president in the Parlement of Paris; the St. Bartholomew's Day massacre of French Calvinists (Huguenots), August 23–24, 1572.

a magistrate to justify that deed with aplomb than for a violent council to decide upon it and for enraged soldiers to execute it.

Subjects' crimes are punished by torture, and they are condemned for it; these princes can be punished only by remorse and they are consoled for it. I beseech those who approach princes to compare the harm they do when they violate their duties with respect to one of their fellow citizens, with the harm they do when they violate their duties with respect to their Country. The citizens are all mortal, but the Country is eternal. After a little time, one sees an end to the harm done to them, their criticisms, and their tears; whoever is today oppressed will soon disappear, perhaps before the guilty party. But the crime that changes a state's constitution for the worse survives its author, his regret, and his remorse.

After which, he adds: "Every courtier, every minister, who, for a wretched pension or a petty increase in fortune, sacrifices the public good, is a base scoundrel who, hiding a secret key to the common treasury, filches a part of it and refuses to share legitimately what he prefers to steal completely."[3]

But why is it that in all times and all countries, favorites have been so odious? It is because, since princes have been set up to govern us, we tolerate the harm they sometimes do us out of consideration for the good they are always doing us. But favorites find themselves above others because of their unique and particular utility.

[1996] It is necessary to speak of the magnificence of Princes. They should appear with a certain external brilliance, because, since our duty is to respect them, they should for their part seek to make themselves respectable. But it is less necessary to advise them on this than on the moderation they ought to possess.

If I wanted to know a prince's power, I would not bother entering his palace, looking at the beauty of his gardens, the wealth of his retinue, the servility of his courtiers. Nothing is so ambiguous. The smallest village would teach me better what his true forces are.

Royal splendor always begins with these two points: rich citizens and well-paid soldiers.

A dilapidated palace should bring a prince less shame than four leagues of abandoned and uncultivated country.

A vainglorious king of a poor people resembles a man dressed in purple

---

3. See *Laws*, 3.5, 25–26, for Montesquieu's portrait of the courtier.

who walks proudly through the streets with his wife and children covered in rags.

[**1997**] The fundamental point of good administration is simple: it consists merely in adjusting expenses to revenues. If the latter cannot increase, the former must decrease, and until that is done, no project can be useful because there are none that do not demand more expense.

[**1998**] It may happen that the good that is done and the arrangements that are made, in respecting the laws of the State, seem less substantial and are less perceptible than certain arrangements that violate those laws under the pretext of certain needs, a certain order, a certain rule. This is because in the first case, that good is barely different from what the kings themselves do, because it can happen that the good that one does in violating the laws of the State seems greater than the first, but its effect is like a liquor given to someone with dropsy—which is doubtless a good for the present, but is an incurable ill for the future.

In a word, the good founded on the overthrow of the laws of the State cannot be compared with the harm that follows from this overthrow itself.

[**1999**] Princes who lavish honors gain nothing by it. They only encourage and even justify importunity. The more one rewards people, the more others deserve rewards. Five or six men are worthy of an honor you have granted to two or three; five or six hundred are worthy of an honor you have granted to one hundred.

[**2000**] Princely liberality should in large part be directed to men of war, who hire themselves out, so to speak, to the other citizens. But I do not advise general liberality. Soon it would be demanded by a body that feels its strength and makes its demands according to its avarice and to public fear.

Among the Romans, a similar liberality almost always weakened military discipline and overturned civil power.

[**2001**] I will here make an exhortation to all men in general, to reflect on their condition and take up some sound ideas from it. It is not impossible that they are living under a happy government without realizing it, since political happiness is such that one only knows what it is after one has lost it.

[**2002**] I had put this work under the name of M. Zamega,[1] and I had

[2002]
1. See *pensée* 540.

put it in the form of an extract of a book by M. Zamega, and I ended it this way:

"This is the work that I imagine M. Zamega would have written if he had ever come into the world; its extract I give here." {See if there might not be something there that I put in *The Spirit of the Laws*. I cut from the original everything I thought I had put there.}

[**2003**] The Prince must communicate with the people of his court, not enough to debase his dignity, but enough to make known that he lives with men. If sovereign grandeur has some delights, it also has some drawbacks, since there is nothing as sad as always being in the crowd but always living alone. This condition can be borne without boredom only in the force and vivacity of the passions. Thus, most princes become unhappy in their old age. The void in their souls is unimaginable, and it cannot be filled by an external ceremony to which they immediately become accustomed. Their lives seem entirely made for youth; nothing prepares them for that crushing age that must follow. Everyone knows what trouble it took to amuse a great monarch three or four hours a day at the end of his life.[1] To prevent this boredom, Princes have to give themselves not always courtiers, but sometimes friends. The good Roman emperors did not believe that the rights of friendship were incompatible with those of sovereign power. Early on, they should pick up a taste for reading; books are a great resource after the loss of the passions, and furthermore, the voices of the dead are the only faithful ones.

[**2004**] SOME FRAGMENTS OF A WORK I HAD WRITTEN ON PRIESTS UNDER PAGANISM, WHICH I HAVE TOSSED IN THE FIRE.[1]

Astronomy, first science, because it was the first book that was open to men.

Some priests, in order to make themselves distinguished in a more specific manner, conducted the most wretched of all operations on themselves.

Offerings should not be regarded as the causes, effects, and signs of virtue, nor should a capacity for expiating crimes be attributed to them. This would be to traffic in celestial vengeance, and as soon as the mar-

[2003]
1. Probably a reference to the entertainment regime at Versailles in the latter days of the long reign of Louis XIV (r. 1643–1715).—HC

[2004]
1. This work is thought to have been written ca. 1711; only these fragments remain.

ketplace was well-purged of a wicked man, one could declare him a good man.

Superstitious princes say within themselves: "My glory will be inseparable from my piety. It is good to do good to people who will be constantly reborn to sing of my magnificence in all times."

A superstitious prince may believe that the surest means of making himself agreeable to God is to choose as his ministers those He has chosen for His own—believing that it is extending His power as much as he can to select for the government of his State the persons who are dearest to Him.

Superstitious princes much enriched the Clergy, because the conditions of peace or of truce with Heaven were always favorable to them, and the entire advantage—strange thing!—remained with the negotiators.

"We allow as how we are wrong," the Clergy would say back then. "But it is inexcusable for you yourselves to think it. You were supposed to wait patiently for us ourselves to reform that abuse which offends you, and just because we strayed from our duty, you did not have to forget your own."

[**2005**] Did not make it into my *Défense.*[1] At the end of my response to Father Berthier on Athens,[2] I had put:

"These gentlemen like combat very much, but they are lightly armed."

[**2006–2008**] THINGS I DID NOT PUT IN MY DÉFENSE.

[**2006**] Those who produce works of the mind must consider that they will be judged by their peers. The whole advantage that a writer naturally has over his readers is that he has reflected more than they have on the matter he treats. But if the latter have reflected in their turn, they find themselves on the same footing. Self-love must learn a great secret: it speaks in the presence of self-love. What! because an author is vain, he would find readers to be modest? And because he is conceited, it could be inferred that he is not weak? A writer's candor is that charming young person's blush that would be nature's art, if nature had an art. Let us seek

---

[2005]

1. After much hesitation, Montesquieu resolved to publish, anonymously in Geneva, his *Défense de "l'Esprit des lois"* in 1750. See Derathé, 2:411–58.

2. Fr. Guillaume-François Berthier (1704–84), editor from 1745 of the Jesuit *Journal de Trévoux,* which published at least two criticisms of *Laws* (see *pensée* 1956), and said also to be a collaborator with Claude Dupin in his 1749 critique of *Laws* (see *pensées* 1572, 1643, 1877, and 2239); see also *OC,* 3:1282–86 for Fr. Castel's February 14, 1750, letter to Montesquieu detailing his efforts to assure a friendly reception for *Laws* in the Jesuit *Journal.*

to make ourselves liked if we want to make ourselves read. If it is true that a man has *esprit,* then let his *esprit* come together with other *esprits;* and if it cannot come together with them, then let it be like a precious stone that separates gold from gold.

Qualis gemma micat quae fulvum dividit aurum.[1]

Great God! how would it be possible for us always to be right? And for others always to be wrong? Good minds will therefore tremble before deciding, and the others, in compensation, will have the pleasure of affirmation.

[2007] The talent for speechifying is the most common of all. Young people who want to write always begin there—whether because their masters have found more facility in adopting this style, or because their disciples have found more in accepting it. Please look at Demosthenes. As soon as he is not thundering, he is simple. Like Heaven, he is almost always serene; he thunders only at intervals.[1]

[2008] Please observe the spirit of the Christian religion. It constantly wants you to humble yourself, and it constantly prohibits you from humbling others. It detests pride and vanity, and it prohibits you from competing with others' pride and vanity as well—or offending it, by reason of the fact that in offending others' vanity, your own finds gratifications that the religion does not approve in you. For with regard to others, the pride we want to mortify is energized by consideration of the plan we have for it; making it suffer is not a sure means of uprooting it. Pride pressed by pride would pick up strength and push against it in turn.

Would pride want to contradict pride? They would only justify each other. Modesty puts it on the defensive.

The Christian religion demands two things of us, the one charming and the other terrible: to love others and to hate ourselves.[1] God wants nothing from us but ourselves.

[2006]
1. Virgil, *Aeneid,* X.134. "[He] glitters like a jewel inset in yellow gold." Cf. *pensée* 1955.

[2007]
1. Demosthenes, Athenian orator and statesman (384–322 B.C.).

[2008]
1. See *Laws,* 24.2–8.

Insults can be evidence of the general coarseness of a nation, sometimes of its liberty and even its ingenuousness. In that case, Christian charity would be less wounded by them, because it would be undetermined whether they were the effect of the general mores or of a particular violation. But in a nation where the citizens, already bound by the laws, have become more bound by mutual consideration—and where, therefore, insults presuppose that the one against whom they are uttered is so culpable that one has been obliged to clear every obstacle—they are extremely harmful to Christian charity.

Thus, the Greeks and Romans offended less than we do, with more offensive words. In such nations, Christian charity would be less wounded by them.

Has the heart said them, or have the mores let them be said; is it the public or the private conscience that should criticize itself?

END

[2009] THIS WAS WRITTEN FOR THE BORDEAUX ACADEMY.[1] The history of Heaven interests all the world. It is composed by the astronomers of all the ages. Each records in it what he has seen or what he has calculated, and there are nations that have no other common interests but astronomical observations.

These observations make us see a simple marvel, instead of that false marvel that one is always imagining in whatever is large. They have given us sure reference points for fixing the epochs of religion; for in order to become unvarying, the history of men needs to be fixed by events that occur in Heaven.

That is how all those mythic ages—which made nonbelievers regard the Patriarchs as new men, and which established a difference between the antiquity of religion and the antiquity of the world—have been made to disappear. In that way, astronomy has become a sacred science, and we call *profane* the sciences that are useful to the human race when they do not attack the first, biggest, and strongest of its interests.

[2009]
1. Probably a fragment destined for the *Plan for a physical history of the earth, ancient and modern,* conceived by Montesquieu. Only the prospectus, published in the *Mercure* (January 1, 1719) and in the *Journal des savants* (1719): 159ff., remains. See *OC,* 3:87–88.

[**2010**] HAPPINESS. M. Maupertuis includes only pleasure and pain in his calculation—that is, everything that instructs the soul on its happiness or its unhappiness.[1] He does not include the happiness of existence and habitual felicity, which instructs about nothing because it is habitual. We call *pleasure* only what is not habitual. If we constantly had the pleasure of eating with appetite, we would not call that a pleasure; that would be *existence* and *nature*. One should not say that happiness is that moment which we would not want to exchange for another. Let us say it differently: happiness is that moment which we would not want to exchange for nonbeing.

[**2011**] I said: "I have grasped something that I already suspected: that to get along well with everyone, you must have no pretensions. If you leave the four walls of your room, you'll be shot dead. If I returned to the social world, I would want only to warm myself in the winter and take the ices in summer."

[**2012**] One must not put vinegar in one's writings; one must put salt.

[**2013**] Animals' teeth, and their facility in grinding certain things rather than others, is the sole cause of their taste for certain things rather than for others. Rats' teeth prepare them for paper; the rabbit's, tree bark; the wolves' prepare them for meat.

[**2014**] "JOURNAL DES SAVANTS," 1685, page 260.[1] Based on the *Journal d'Angleterre*, an item is reported there that has been so often treated as myth, concerning the inhabitants of Keilan on the island of Formosa, to whom nature (they say) has given a tail on their backs, like the animals.

Also spoken of there are some monkeys supposedly on the island of Java, which have a kind of bats' wings, thanks to which they fly from tree to tree.

The island of Halmahera has cats like that, if one is to believe Lord Gein, vice-governor of the neighboring island of Ternate. (Pages 260, 261.)

[2010]

1. Pierre-Louis Moreau de Maupertuis (1698–1759), geometer and astronomer, author of *Essai de philosophie morale* [Essay on moral philosophy] (1751). As president of the Berlin Academy, he had Montesquieu elected to it in 1746; cf. Montesquieu's letter of thanks to him (*OC*, 3:1071). See also *pensée* 1393.

[2014]

1. The November 12, 1685, issue contains at that page a review of Joh. Herbinio's 1678 *Dissertationes de admirandis mundi cataractis* [Essays on marvelous waterfalls of the world].

All this tends to confirm my opinion that the differences among animal species may be increasing all the time and decreasing likewise, that there were very few species in the beginning, which multiplied afterward.

[2015] I wanted to dedicate a work to the King of England,[1] and I said to him: "In traversing the different domains of your Majesty throughout Europe, one always sees the same master. Justice and mildness reign in the countries where your will is Law, as in those where your will is that of the Law.

"A great king like you, Sire, is not born solely to make the happiness of his subjects; he is born also for the felicity of the human race. This is why, with such taste for war, one has never seen such love for peace, whether because you prefer virtue to glory or because you consider that virtue is the sole glory."

[2016] If the human species perished, what difference in the other species? How could the chickens, the sheep support themselves?

[2017] SWITZERLAND.[1] Switzerland is indomitable, because there is not a man in Switzerland who is not armed and who does not know how to handle arms. And there is scarcely a State whose politics permits the arming of all its citizens. They could have their troops brought back from abroad. You would find few provisions in the country; the country would be difficult by itself.

[2018] DENMARK. At the battle that General Steinbock won against the Danish troops, there was hardly anyone {but} peasants.[1] Steinbock had four cannon, so well supplied that they were firing constantly. This was still unknown at that time, so the Danes thought the Swedes had a terrifying artillery, and the Swedes moved and attacked the Danes where they were not expecting them.

[2019] SWEDEN. Today it is the estates that govern, and that have the legislative power to themselves, for neither the King nor the Senate have any more share in the legislation than in Poland.

The government inclines toward democracy, more than in the past

[2015]
1. George II (1727–60).

[2017]
1. On Swizerland as a "federal republic," see *Laws,* 9.1–2.

[2018]
1. The Swedish general Steinbock defeated the Danes at Helsinborg, March 10, 1710.

because there were several chambers of nobility in the past. I believe it was three chambers distinguished by preeminence, and votes were cast by corps, not by head like today—which was similar to Servius Tullius's division among the Romans. The union of domains under Charles XI ruined the Nobility.[1] The operation was violent in that, not only were the domains retaken, but an account of the revenues was demanded, which caused lawsuits between families. The Nobility feels its decline and does not seem attached to that government. In the war in which Sweden lost Finland,[2] the estates did not dare entrust the government to the King; one cannot say that this constitution is really firm. The Muscovites demanded Finland because they are afraid of the spirit of conquest. What the Swedes lost of Finland was substantial, because they lost their defensive position—that is, the ridges that people were obliged to pass through to reach them—and that peace was made with intelligence on the Muscovites' part. Finland was conquered and converted in Charlemagne's manner, and one sees in a Finnish church the converter holding in his hand a whip made of iron chains; it is (I believe) Woldemar.[3]

[2020] FEBRUARY 2, 1742.[1] Our Bavarian affairs are desperate. For the Bohemian situation, we are presently in the hands of the greatest madman ever.[2] He left the dance (for he is always leaving the dance);[3] he was in Saxony, he was in Dresden, for the Elector to give him command. From there, he got in his postal coach and arrived at an inn in Prague—and all this, to ask the intendant Séchelles to furnish him bread for his troops.[4] So we're in it for 100,000 crowns a month to give bread rations to that king. If France and England had all the treasure in the world, these German beggars would siphon it away! As for me, I can't marvel enough at the lunacy that makes

[2019]

1. In 1680, King Charles XI confiscated a large part of the noble domains for the Crown's profit and redistributed it among the peasants, who thus became proprietors of a third of the soil.

2. The war occurred from 1741 to 1743.

3. Probably Valdemar II, Danish king (r. 1202–41), who forcibly baptized the defeated Estonians after the battle of Lyndanisse in June 1219.—HC

[2020]

1. Montesquieu here transcribes an extract of the letter he sent to President Barbot on February 2, 1742 (*OC,* 3:1015–16), during the War of the Austrian Succession.

2. Frederick II of Prussia (r. 1740–86).

3. *Parti du bal,* perhaps colloquial for abandoning a situation; see *DAF* (1798).—HC

4. Jean-Moreau de Séchelles (1690–1760), intendant of Hainault in Valenciennes (1727–43) and controller-general of finances (1754–56).

us send 100 million, plus 80,000 men, abroad—of whom half have virtually no more life—in order to implement the scheme that was tormenting the brain of a man who's been a worrywart ever since he's been in the world.

Adieu, Sir, I speak to you as a good Frenchman, but as a Frenchman who is not drunk.

[**2021**] Doctor Warburton treats Lord Bolingbroke in a very harsh manner.[1] Milord had complained loudly that M. Pope, out of avarice, had had the manuscript of the Patriot King, which he had entrusted to him, published.[2] "I will assume," says the doctor, "that M. Pope, out of avarice, has done this deed. For this, should you have sought to dishonor your friend? Should you not have hidden it? How do you expect posterity to believe the splendid things he has said about you?"

[**2022**] On M. Warburton's book, in which there are so many fine things and many others that are ill-founded and imaginary, I said: "It is indeed possible for a great genius to say some very fine things, mixed with others that are worthless; but it is not possible for a fool to say things that are worthless, mixed with some very fine things."

[**2023**] TO BARON STEIN. AMSTERDAM, THIS OCTOBER 20, 1729.[1]

I don't know how the folks on our Council of France can ever have a clean conscience. Our interest is in preventing the destruction of the Protestants, the Turks, and the Barbary Corsairs.

If the Emperor invaded the Turkish territory, he would set up manufactures there that would destroy our Levant trade. Without the Barbary Corsairs, the Hamburgers and other Hanseatic cities would go engage in the Levant trade. We are Catholics and Christians, but we have to support the most mortal enemies of both. We have a religion that has a visible head, but our interests are always directly opposed to his own.

It is true that under Louis XIII, we made war on the Huguenots; but I do not believe that God will ever pardon us for wanting to mislead him

---

[**2021**]

1. William Warburton (1698–1779), bishop of Gloucester; the book referred to in this entry and the next is *A Letter to . . . Viscount B. . . . Occasion'd by his Treatment of a Deceased Friend* (1749). See his letter to Montesquieu on February 9, 1754 (*OC*, 3:1492).

2. Bolingbroke's *The Idea of a Patriot King* was written in 1738 and published in 1749. The passage cited below is a paraphrase.—HC

[**2023**]

1. Johann-Friedrich, baron of Stein (1681–1735), prime minister of the duke of Brunswick. Montesquieu met him in Germany; cf. *Voyages* (*OC*, 2:1286) for a favorable account.

into thinking that we were supporting his cause out of zeal, and not for the purpose of taking La Rochelle and Montauban.[2]

If Louis XIV expelled the Huguenots from France, they are not ignorant On High that it was out of folly and court intrigue that that prince did this; for he loved money too much to do a thing like that if he thought it would ruin his manufactures.[3]

I am, Sir, . . .

[2024] The King of Prussia asked the reason why he did not love women. "You will get mad if I tell you." "No," he said. "Sire, it is because you do not love men." This is a splendid response, because it is contradictory to the expected one.

[2025–2031] THINGS THAT DID NOT MAKE IT INTO MY NOVEL ON "ARSACE" AND "ISMENIE."[1]

[2025] In drawing the character of Aspar,[1] I had put: "His mind was naturally conciliatory, and his soul seemed to approach all others." That was too long, so I eliminated "and his soul seemed to approach all others."

[2026] When I was in Medea, I was unable to have a friend, and my generous sentiments, instead of elevating souls, would have made them tremble.

[2027] I was born in Medea, and I can count illustrious ancestors . . .

At the age of fifteen, my parents set me up.[1] Two women they procured for me left me possessed of all my indifference. I knew women; I did not know love.

---

2. Huguenot strongholds in that period.—HC

3. See *pensée* 728.

[2025–2031]

1. *Arsace et Isménie: histoire orientale* (*OC*, 3:477–528), was written in 1742, according to Montesquieu's September 8 letter to Barbot (*OC*, 3:1023), a letter in which he asked his longtime friend to subject the work to close critical review. In his December 8, 1754, letter to Guasco, Montesquieu was still hesitating to send it to the printer and was looking forward to hearing Guasco's opinion (*OC*, 3:1527); the novel was only published in 1783 by Montesquieu's son, Jean-Baptiste de Secondat; the work seems to have been first translated into English anonymously in 1789, in *Fugitive Pieces* (London: Longman).

[2025]

1. See *OC*, 3:480, on the character of Aspar.

[2027]

1. See *OC*, 3:483.

I got to know this thing called *love* one day when, at a relative's house, I saw a young person of ravishing beauty.[2] My astonished soul felt itself struck forever. My lingering eyes fixed themselves on her. I do not know if I pleased her; this was a mental effort that I was in no condition to make.

She was a foreigner, and two old eunuchs were assigned her education. I went to them, and in tears I asked to have Ardaside in marriage. They made countless difficulties for me. I made them every proposal; they were incorruptible. I thought I was going to die at their knees; they were letting me die.

What was my astonishment one day when, in sadness and mortal languor, I was going to their place to make my grief and my tears speak to them, and they said to me coldly: "Ardaside is given to you. She is yours. You are virtuous, and you know how to love." What they were telling me, I was unable to believe it. I made myself repeat a hundred times that they were giving her to me. I asked to be led into Ardaside's apartment. Gods! how bewitching she was! I did not know what to say to her; I took her hand; I kissed it countless times. Her height, her air, her beauty, her gaze, her silence—everything ravished me. The acts of marriage were drawn up. I wanted to give everything; they wanted nothing. I went to the temple; I led her into my apartment, and I thought I was carrying off the world with me.

[2028] A woman who came on behalf of the Queen of the Scythians appeared. As a present for the King, she was bearing a cloth of exquisite workmanship. "King of Bactriana," she told him, "the Queen of the Scythians has woven this cloth with her beautiful hands. Look at the things she has represented on it. Here, there are some Armenians that our Scythians have pierced with their fearsome arrows; their wounds are not mortal, since they are still fighting. There, you see a heart pierced by countless nearly invisible arrows, and a child who is constantly shooting new ones; this heart is that of Isménie, and it will never heal."

[2029] I wrote her this letter:[1] "One day the Young Elm said to the

---

2. This is Ardasire; cf. *OC,* 3:483.

[2029]
1. Probably a letter from Arsace to Isménie; cf. *OC,* 3:510.

Vine: 'Be careful that I don't cover you with my shade. But join me, and we will rise together to the clouds.'"

[2030] The leader of the second band spoke to him this way: "We form with you a tree that has a fine top. You're the trunk, and we're the leaves. We'll cover you with our shade, and we'll prevent the sun from burning your roots, and we'll rise together to the clouds."

[2031] Lions have great strength; but it would be useless to them if nature had not given them eyes.[1]

[2032] APOLOGIA FOR THE "PERSIAN LETTERS." One can hardly impute to the *Persian Letters* the things that have been claimed to offend religion in them.

Those things are never found linked with the idea of examination, but with the idea of oddness; never with the idea of criticism, but with the idea of the extraordinary.

It is a Persian who was talking, and who was bound to be struck by everything he saw and everything he heard.

In this circumstance, when he talks about religion, he is bound not to appear more informed about it than about other things, like the customs and manners of the nation, which he does not regard as good or bad but as wondrous.

Just as he finds our customs bizarre, he sometimes finds strangeness in certain aspects of our dogma because he is ignorant of them, and explains them badly because he knows nothing about what holds them together and about the chain they form.

It is true that there is some indiscretion in having touched on these matters, since we are not as certain of what others may think as of what we ourselves think.

[2033] EDITOR'S PREFACE.[1] What makes up the principal merit of the *Persian Letters* is that one finds in them, without thinking about it, a sort of novel. One sees the beginning, the progression, the end. The various char-

---

[2031]
1. See *OC,* 2:513.

[2033]
1. This preface is a first draft of "Quelques réflexions sur les *Lettres persanes*" [Some reflections on the *Persian Letters*], published as a supplement to the 1754 edition. It was written shortly after Montesquieu read abbé Jean-Baptiste Gaultier's 1751 *Lettres persanes convaincues d'impiété* [Persian letters convicted of impiety]. See Vernière, 3–5.

acters are placed in a chain that binds them. As their sojourn in Europe grows longer, the mores of that part of the world assume in their heads a less wondrous and less bizarre air, and they are more or less struck by this bizarreness and this wonder according to the differences in their characters. On the other hand, the disorder in the Asian seraglio grows in proportion to the length of Usbek's absence, that is, as the fury waxes and the love wanes.

Moreover, this sort of novel usually succeeds, because we ourselves take stock of our actual situation, which does more to make us feel the passions than all the accounts of them one could offer, and this is one of the causes of the success of *Pamela* and the *Letters of a Peruvian Woman* (charming works that have appeared since).[2]

In ordinary novels, digressions can only be permitted when they themselves form a new novel. Reasonings cannot be mixed in there because, since none of the characters have been assembled for the purpose of reasoning, that would go against the design and nature of the work. But in the letter form, where the actors are not selected but forced, and where all the subjects treated are not dependent on any design or any preconceived plan, the author has given himself the advantage of being able to combine philosophy, politics, and morality with a novel, and to link everything by a secret and in some sense unknown chain.

The *Persian Letters* had such prodigious sales at the outset that the booksellers of Holland used every expedient to have sequels. They went around buttonholing everyone they ran into. "Sir," they would say, "write me some *Persian Letters.*"

But what I have just said will suffice to make clear that they are not susceptible to any sequel, still less to any mixture with letters written by another hand, however ingenious it may be.

In the first letters, there are several expressions that have been considered too bold. But please pay attention to the nature of this work. The Persians who were to play such a large role in these letters found themselves suddenly transplanted to Europe. For a time, they had to be represented as full of ignorance and prejudice. The concern was merely to reveal the generation and progress of their ideas. Their first thoughts were bound to be odd. It seemed that there was nothing to do but give them that species of oddness that can

---

2. Samuel Richardson (1689–1761), *Pamela, or virtue rewarded* (1740); Françoise d'Issembourg d'Happoncourt, Dame de Graffigny (1695–1758), *Lettres péruviennes* (1747), two best-selling novels.

be compatible with intelligence; it seems that there was nothing to do but depict the feelings they had at each thing that appeared extraordinary to them. Far from thinking of implicating some principle of religion, one did not even suspect oneself of imprudence. This justification is made out of love for the great truths, independent of respect for the human race, which it has certainly not been the intention to strike at its most delicate spot.

Please notice that these expressions are always found linked with the feeling of surprise and astonishment, never with the idea of examination, and still less {with that} of criticism.

In talking[3] about our religion, these Persians should not have appeared more informed than when they were talking about the nation's ordinary customs and practices. And if they sometimes find our dogmas odd, it will be admitted that this oddness is indelibly marked in the *Persian Letters* as never being founded on anything but their perfect ignorance of the chain that links these dogmas with our other truths. The whole charm consists solely in the contrast that exists between reality and the manner in which it is perceived. [I will even admit that I would have done just as well to have a less good book written as to touch upon these matters, since we are never as sure of the manner in which others are affected as of the manner in which we ourselves are affected.]

Out of all the editions of this book, it is only the first that was good. It did not suffer from the temerity of the booksellers. It appeared in 1721, printed in Cologne by Pierre Marteau. The one that is offered today deserves preference, because the style of the first and some errors that had slipped into the printing have been corrected in some places. These errors have been multiplied beyond number throughout the editions, because that work was abandoned by its author from its birth.[4]

END

3. First version: "If these reasons do not excuse the author, he will at least have the consolation of thinking that those who come after him will learn by his example, that the least deficiencies of this sort are irreparable."

4. Montesquieu produced three different versions of the end of this paragraph: (1) "because that work was abandoned by its author from its birth" or "from its birth by the author who took no more part in it except out of regret at having written it"; (2) "was abandoned by its author, who devoted himself to more serious things"; (3) "was abandoned by its author, who had written at a time when he was quite young, and had published his work at a time when everyone was young."

[2034]¹

[2035] ACADEMICA—FRAGMENTS OF AN ESSAY ON THE DIFFER-
ENCES BETWEEN MINDS.¹

The external resemblance of children to their fathers is not a relationship between the copy and its original, as if the father's imagination, or
some secret cause, could imprint the traits he himself has onto the children's face. That would be entirely inexplicable by science. This resemblance is founded solely on the fact that, since the child has been formed
by the father's substance, and has had a common life with the mother for
nine straight months, there is in each a correspondence in the fluids and
the solids. Thus the quality or the combination of humors that yields black
hair, white skin, nice teeth, large height, or delicate features in the father
or mother will likewise produce them in the child.² Painters know how
little it takes for a face to appear almost to resemble another, and how far
a similarity in one part is striking in the whole. A single trait dominates a
whole physiognomy.

Since human vices and virtues are usually the effect of the passions,
and the passions, the effect of a certain condition of the machinery—I
am speaking of the material side of the passions and not the formal, that
is, of that complaisance the soul feels in following the movements of its
machinery, due to the mildness it finds there—there are illnesses that can
put us in the situation we are in during the passion itself. Those illnesses
that give our blood the tendency of a bold man's blood will make us courageous; those that put us in the opposite condition will make us timid.
Doctors know that certain illnesses make a man bizarre, troubled, and
quick-tempered—deplorable state, which proves to us that we have fallen
from a more perfect state.

When doctors and moral authors are treating the passions, they are
never speaking the same language. The moralists place too much on the
soul's account; the others, too much on the body's. The former regard
man more as a spirit; the latter, more as an artisan's machine. But man is

[2034]

1. This entry, which contains merely the first lines of *pensée* 2035, was deleted.

[2035]

1. Fragments of the *Essai sur les causes qui peuvent affecter les esprits et les caractères* [Essay on the
causes that can affect minds and characters], composed in 1742 (*OC,* 3:397–430).

2. Ibid., 427, for resemblance of child to parents.

equally composed of two substances, each of which, by an ebb and flow, dominates and is dominated.

[2036] I notice that when the Barbarians poured into the Roman Empire, they engaged in no particular cruelty against ecclesiastics and revealed no religious zeal—desirous solely of booty and subsistence. But the same Barbarians, who poured into Charlemagne's Empire, engaged in strange barbarisms against ecclesiastics, the Church, monasteries.

When the Romans expelled the Barbarians and obliged them to regroup out of fear around Scandinavia, they did not talk to them about religion, but about taking on Roman mores, paying taxes, obeying. When the Franks returned to Germany, they talked to them only about baptism, churches, monasteries, priests, so that the Saxons and other peoples who pulled back withdrew enraged at the Christian religion and devoted themselves all the more to their faith for having been pressed to change it. And they established in their midst a harsh inquisition. Thus, when they left, they left with their hatred and their prejudices. Thus, the same peoples differed in the conduct and in the fury of their invasions.

It cannot be doubted that the Germans mingled with the Scandinavians. Tacitus speaks of the Suiones.[1] The ancient Swedish language and the ancient Danish language bear some resemblance to the ancient German language—whether because this was the same people that had swelled due to the above-mentioned reasons, or because in withdrawing en masse into the Northern depths, they became the major part of the Nation.

[2037] M. Forcalquier has so turned my head over the approbation that Your Excellency has given my big book that I take the liberty of thanking Y. Ex.[1] You must encourage us by Your praises; You would discourage

[2036]

1. Tacitus, *Germania*, XLIV; the eighteenth-century French translator of the *Germania*, abbé de La Bletterie, calls the Sueones the Suisons; they gave their name to Sweden or Sueonia; see *Laws*, 7.4, 99.

[2037]

1. Your Excellency. This October 24, 1749, letter (Bordeaux municipal library; ms. 1868, no. 217) is addressed to the Duke of Nivernais; cf. *OC*, 3:1261–62. Louis-Jules Barbon Mancini, duke of Nivernais, was born in 1716, the son of Philippe-Jules-François Mancini Mazarini, duke of Nevers and Donzy, and of Marie-Anne Spinóla. He was named ambassador to Rome early in 1748. He sought to prevent the condemnation of *Laws* when it came before the Congregation of the Index, corresponding with Montesquieu regularly about the affair. Louis Buffile was count and, then in 1750, marquis of Forcalquier (1710–53), lieutenant-general of Provence, whom Montesquieu refers to often in his correspondence.

us too much by Your writings. M. de Forcalquier has shown me a short account of the beauties of Rome, in a letter by Y. Ex., which made me see in a moment what I had been looking at in Rome for eight months, and gave me precise ideas on things of which I had had no more than a muddled understanding. I admit that the *Apollo* would have seduced me in Rome, if I had not had the good fortune of passing by Florence, where I swore eternal fidelity to the *Venus de' Medici,* which I regard as the best preacher the Florentines have ever had—although I do not know much about how successful it has been.[2] All this does not keep me from making a great leap to arrive at the Church of Saint Peter, and passing from the marvel that pleases to the marvel that astonishes. I greatly envy the ambassador of Malta[3] the pleasure he has of seeing You, and I would also very much like to be at a close enough distance to be able to pay You my respects. I have the honor of being, with infinite respect, of Y. Ex. the very humble and very obedient servant.[4]

[2038] A man of low birth torments himself greatly to make a fortune, that is, to be in that condition where he will blush throughout his life over his birth and over the torment of that idea.

[2039] When the late king wanted to oblige Philip V to expel the Princess of Ursins, after he had long tried and never succeeded, he assigned M. de Berwick to talk about it.[1] There was in the letter: "Tell him he owes me that, not only because he's my grandson, but also because I put the crown on his head. Tell him everything! But don't tell him I'm going to abandon him, because he would never believe it."

[2040] No one likes to be counted for nothing in company.[1]

[2041] Often we criticize our friends because we do not stop believing that we lack the perspicacity to see their faults.

2. The *Apollo* is a statue of the third century; cf. *Voyages* (*OC,* 2:1124); for the Venus, see *Voyages, OC,* 2:1318.

3. Antoine-Maurice Solar (1689–1762).

4. See *OC,* 3:1262, for a postscript to this letter.

[2039]

1. Anne-Marie de La Trémoïlle-Noirmoutier, princess of Chalais, then duchess of Vracciano, finally princess of Ursins (1642–1722), all-powerful in Spain from 1705 to 1714, exiled in 1715; the "late king" is Louis XIV. See the same anecdote in *Spicilège,* 433, and in *Ebauche de l'éloge historique du maréchal de Berwick* [Sketch for an historical eulogy of Marshal Berwick] (*OC,* 3:387).

[2040]

1. *Société,* which may also mean "society" as a whole.—HC

[2042] I said of M. the Duke[1] that he was always searching for the truth and always missing it.

[2043] We joke about everything because everything has a reverse side.

[2044] If printing had arrived in the present age, when language is so chaste and pure, we would have virtually all the works of the Ancients in mutilated form. Likewise, if it had arrived in the age of our censors.

[2045] I said: "Men who are full of themselves are always good people."

[2046] HAPPINESS. To be happy, one must not desire to be happier than others. If one had Ariosto's winged horse, or the ring that causes invisibility, would one be happier? Attach to it the shield that makes all men statues.[1]

[2047] Since the Company of the Asiento was not a lucrative thing for England, she was given a licensed ship, of 500 tons, to traffic in the American ports. All this was allocated to the South Sea Company.[1] Those who directed this business for the Company won over with large gifts those who were to measure the vessel's tonnage, so that instead of 500 tons the vessel was 800. And since a ship needs provisions, water, etc., they sent a small craft to carry all that, so there were around 1,000 tons of merchandise.

Those were the advantages. Here are the disadvantages. The Company agents were lavishly paid. Many phony expenses to corrupt the Spanish officials. The licensed ship was, so to speak, security for English conduct, and the Spanish could seize it on their first whim, as they did in the case of the *Prince-Frederick.* Moreover, it yielded only private profit. The nation was thwarted in its contraband trade with America, since it had had virtually none through Cadiz for some time. The South Sea Company's agents waged a kind of war even on the English vessels that were coming there to sell fraudulently, for fear that this might lower the price of their merchandise. Thus, England had less advantageous terms than if she had simply engaged in her contraband trade.

[2042]
1. The Duke of Bourbon. See also *pensées* 912 and 1964.

[2046]
1. See Ariosto, *Orlando Furioso,* cantos 33–35, where Astolfo flies on a hippogryph; for the durable legend of the invisibility ring, the starting point is Plato, *Republic,* bk. II (359 d ff.); the story of Perseus turning men into statues can be found in Lycophron's *Alexandra,* 844–46, of which Montesquieu owned 1596 and 1597 editions (*Catalogue,* 2084–85).—HC

[2047]
1. The Asiento Company was created in 1713 after the treaty of the Asiento between Spain and England; the South Sea Company dates to 1711.

[2048] England has just signed a treaty (1750) with Spain,[1] by which the prior treaties are referred to, and by which the coast guard no longer inspects vessels at sea. In fact, the Spanish ministry had been made to understand that this was impractical, that it was a capital offense in England to transport wool; but that as soon as the ship was at sea, there was not a single ship, foreign or national, that dared touch it, and that this was the practice everywhere.

With respect to the commerce of old Spain, it is far from being as advantageous to the English as it was at the time of the previous treaties. The Spanish have been engaging in cloth manufacture for consumption on the mainland of Spain, so they import very little English cloth. On the other hand, the English are still, and virtually alone, importing merchandise from Spanish soil: wine, oil, olives, dry fruit, etc.

[2049] The English have just given money to some electors to make the Archduke King of the Romans. It is wasted money. France does not intend to make war, and Germany had enough interest in making the Archduke King of the Romans to do so *motu proprio.*[1]

[2050] What is unfortunate at the present time in England is that the people most capable of governing her do not want to, and others cannot be ministers.

[2051] In Procopius (*War of the Goths,* book I), you see the zeal and the love with which the Jews defended Naples for the Goths against Belisarius.[1] In the *Letters* of Cassiodorus, you see with what equity Theodoric treats them. In the life of King Wamba and in the histories that concern the Narbonnaise woman (who was called *Judaeorum Prostibulum*),[2] we see how much the Jews had been esteemed by the earliest Visigoth kings.[3] All the Goths were Arians. Now by the nature of the main dogma, the Jews were bound

---

[2048]
1. The Treaty of Buen-Retiro, October 5, 1750.

[2049]
1. "Of his own accord."—HC

[2051]
1. This entry clarifies the following passage from *Laws*, 28.7, 542: "When the Saracens entered these provinces, they had been summoned; now, who could have summoned them there but the Jews or the Romans?" Belisarius, Byzantine general (ca. 500–565), defeated Witiges, king of the Ostrogoths, in Italy in 540.
2. "Strumpet of the Jews."—HC
3. Cassiodorus, *Letters,* I.37; Wamba, Visigoth king (672–80), expelled the Jews from Narbonne in 673.

not to be so alienated from the Arians as from the Catholics, and, likewise, the Arians could better tolerate the Jews than they could the Catholics.

[2052] {I have pulled this to make a chapter out of it for the end of the eighteenth book.}[1] I have always been struck, in reading the Barbarian law codes, by the lack of attention or severity in them toward parricide, so this crime is virtually mixed in with other acts of violence. And I see in Cassiodorus, book II, letter 14, that Theodoric decreed in such a case that the parricide be punished according to Roman Law.[2] As these Barbarians became more Roman, they conceived more horror for parricide. Now in some sense, I find the cause of this way of thinking on the part of the barbarian peoples—whose mores all resembled each other—I find it (I say) in Procopius (*War of the Goths,* book II), where he says, in speaking of the Herules: when someone among them was languishing or growing old, he was constrained to make a request of his intimates to have himself put to death; another would request that a relative slay him; after which, his relatives would set a fire and burn him at the stake. (See my old extract from Procopius, page 259).[3]

Look at how closely all this is related to the Germans' other mores. A request was presented to the relatives, because of their right to guarantee their relatives' lives. It seems that one could not dispose of one's life without them. It was a stranger who prepared the death, but with the relatives' consent—without which, they could have taken vengeance.

[2053] I said in an apologia: "It is the indignation of innocence."

[2054] I said: "Mediocrity is a guardrail."

[2055] Look in volume II of *Juridica,* in my extract of Vitriarius,[1] at my asterisk, which contains my reflections on the question: *Whether the dictator in Rome had sovereign power or not?*[2]

[2056] A man who has wit does not seek to show it; one does not bedeck oneself with adornments that one puts on every day.

[2052]
1. Montesquieu does not seem to have pursued this topic; book 18 of the *Laws* concerns the terrain.
2. This would probably be the *Variae epistolae,* or *Letters of Cassiodorus* (537), which contained state papers from Theodoric's reign.—HC
3. This extract is lost.

[2055]
1. This would probably be Philippus Reinhardus Vitriarius (1647–1720), author of a work inspired by Grotius, *Institutiones juris naturae et gentius* [Institutes of natural law and the law of nations] (1692 and many later editions); Montesquieu owned a 1734 edition (see *Catalogue,* 2447).—HC
2. On the Roman dictator, see *Laws,* 2.3, 16, and 11.16, 177; the *Juridica* are lost.

[2057] On abbé de Laporte, who had written against *The Spirit of the Laws* to get some pocket money from a bookseller, I said: "A man who argues to become enlightened does not embroil himself with a man who argues for a living."[1]

[2058] Men are quite extraordinary: they like their opinions more than the realities.

[2059] It is an anxious vanity that creates a bad mood. One thinks oneself inadequately treated.

[2060] The King said to the Bishop of Mirepoix, concerning a sermon:[1] "Everyone is in there. You, for example: benefices given by favor or by whimsy." "Sire," said the Bishop, "the multitude of enemies that I have here proves that it is not by favor. One might perhaps say that I give *with* whimsy, but not *by* whimsy."

[2061] I said: "A great man is he who sees fast, far and true."

[2062] People were talking about a witticism against someone. Somebody asked who had uttered it. I said, "It can only be one of his friends," and that turned out to be true.

[2063] In sending the Scottish edition of *Spirit* to Mme Dupré de Saint-Maur, I told her: "I am delighted that you will be reading me in such a splendid edition. I wish some fairy would give me a costume with which I might please you."[1]

[2064] M. Nicole has very well said that God gave self-love to man, just as he gave flavor to dishes.[1]

[2065] I compare the ladies of the Queen or of Mme the Dauphine,[1]

[2057]
1. Abbé Joseph de La Porte (1718–79), collaborator with Fréron on *L'Année littéraire* and author of *Observations sur "l'Esprit des lois,"* in 1751; see *pensée* 2092.

[2060]
1. Jean-François Boyer (1675–1755), bishop of Mirepoix (Ariège) from 1730 to 1736 and royal director of the distribution of clerical benefices after 1743.

[2063]
1. The Edinburgh edition of *Laws* appeared in 1750; see Montesquieu's September 3, 1749, letter to David Hume (*OC,* 3:1255). Marie-Marthe Allion (d. 1788), wife of Nicolas-François Dupré de Saint-Maur (1695–1774); she was closely tied with Montesquieu and was present at his deathbed.

[2064]
1. Pierre Nicole (1625–95), Jansenist and author of *Essais de morales;* see *pensée* 1970.—HC

[2065]
1. Marie-Josèphe de Saxe (1731–67) had in 1747 married the son of Louis XV, Louis, the Dauphin of France (1729–65).

who get dressed two or three times to appear before them, to those actors who play the role of guards, and who get dressed to hear each other say:[·] "Hey there![2] Guards, get going!"

[2066] When princes travel, behold the intendant who makes new outfits, joyfulness, and anything that might show opulence appear by the roadside.[1] On the road, it's a land of milk and honey; half a league away in any direction, they are dying of hunger.

[2067] People were talking about a man of letters, and were saying he was of low birth. I said: "I have always had a bad opinion of Horace, because he was the son of a freed slave."

[2068] It is said the Iroquois have eaten sixty nations, and have roasted the last Huron.[1] I do not believe it. It is said that they like the French better than the Spanish.

[2069] In Paris, the bridges are hidden like the canals.

[2070] In small cities, one has no satisfactions; in big cities, no desires.

[2071] There is normally so little difference between man and man that there is scarcely grounds for vanity.[1]

[2072] The first Christians in the Roman Empire seemed as extraordinary as the Quakers do today.

[2073] If you counted all the goods that the Irish priests have left in Ireland, you would find that it is the richest country in Europe.

[2074] One admires Your Highness, when one sees You from afar; one loves You, when one sees You from nearby; it seems that You have been created to make known the difference that exists between nobility and pride.

---

2. *Hola,* which can be an interjection toward someone of "low condition" (see Furetière).—HC

[2066]

1. For other comments on the intendant, see *pensées* 977, 1353, 1572, 1835, 1840, 1846, 1898, and 2099.—HC

[2068]

1. See *Laws,* 1.3, 8, for the Iroquois. Brèthe, 1:238 n. 10, suggests that Fr. Charlevoix's 1744 *Histoire et description générale de la nouvelle France* [History and general description of New France] or Fr. Lafitau's *Les mœurs des sauvages amériquains comparées aux mœurs des premiers temps* [The mores of the American savages compared to the mores of earliest times] (1724), which Fr. Castel had procured for Montesquieu in 1725 (*OC,* 3:809), may have been the source for his Iroquois comments.

[2071]

1. See *pensée* 612.—HC

[2075] All husbands are ugly.

[2076] The three unities of the theater assume each other. Unity of place assumes unity of time, because a lot of time is needed to transport oneself into another country. These two unities assume unity of action, because in a short time and in the same place, there can probably be only one main action; the others are secondary.

[2077] One is so accustomed to seeing rich people's country houses that one is enchanted to see those of tasteful people.

[2078] Gamblers only have surplus, never needs.

[2079] How far does the orgy of prejudice go! Haven't men managed to make men love the Inquisition![1]

[2080] I said about the people at Court: "It is impossible to enrich them or ruin them."

[2081] It is a good thing to live in France. The meals are better than in cold countries, and one has a better appetite than in hot countries.

[2082] England cannot easily dispense with thinking about land affairs. Queen Elizabeth attended to them. The aid she sent to the Dutch and the French, and her influence in the various parts of Europe, are well known. James I (through incompetence), Charles I (through impotence), Charles II (through flabbiness), James II (through religious bigotry), did not attend to them. Those four reigns were not glorious, and during them, England lost all the influence she had had under Elizabeth. To engage in maritime commerce, it is not enough to go and look for merchandise; the land and the rivers must also be open in order to transport it.

[2083] M. de Voltaire has begun his poem in two ways. First:

> *I sing this great king, who was generous and brave,*
> *Who forced the French to learn to be blessed.*[1]

And since this last line is strained, since it is pretentious, since it is in some sense sententious, he corrected it in the second edition and put:

[2079]

1. On the Inquisition, see *Laws,* 25.13 and 26.11–12, *PL,* XXIX, *Spicilège,* 459, 472, and 779.

[2083]

1. "Je chante ce grand roi, vaillant et genereux, / Qui força les Français à devenir heureux." The first edition of the *Henriade* (1723) began: "Je chante les combats et ce roi généreux" ["I sing of battles and of this generous king"]. The definitive text began: "Je chante ce héros qui regna sur la France" ["I sing of this hero who reigned over France"].

I sing this great king who ruled over France
Both by right of conquest, and by right of his birth.[2]

This is worthless, too; it seems as if a notary is talking. Here is how I would put these two lines:

I sing this great king, who was generous and wise,
Who conquered his realm and rendered it blessed.[3]

[2084] Wealth is an offense that one has to make amends for; one might say: "Excuse me if I'm so rich."

[2085] Someone criticized me for having changed toward him. I said to him: "If this is a change for you, it is a revolution for me."

[2086] I like to read a new book after the public's judgment. That is, I would rather render my inner judgment on the public than on the book.

[2087] Princesses talk a great deal because people have accustomed them to it since their childhood.

[2088] Three or four days ago, you received adoration on the part of M*** and me. The incense smoked; I don't know if it rose up to you.

[2089] I told a miser: "You are doing well to amass money during your life; we don't know what will happen after death."

[2090] EXTRACT FROM THE UTRECHT GAZETTE, MAY 5, 1750. A letter was inserted from the Baron of Spon to Chancellor d'Aguesseau on the King of Prussia's Code that is ridiculous in the servility of its flattery.[1] Among other follies, it is said there that the King has decreed that cases are to be judged not by Roman Law, but solely by his Code, and, *as a last resort,* by reason and natural equity. That's a fine last resort, and is worth quite as much as the Code, at the least.

2. "Je chante ce grand roi qui gouverna la France / Et par droit de conquête, et par droit de naissance."

3. "Je chante ce grand roi, prudent et généreux, / Qui conquit son royaume et le rendit heureux."

[2090]

1. The Baron of Spon was Austrian minister to Prussia; Henri-François d'Aguesseau (1668–1751), lawyer at the Parlement of Paris and chancellor in 1717, and then, after threats of disgrace and after being exiled by Dubois in 1727, he was again Chancellor from 1737 to 1750; the King of Prussia's Code was published in 1749 and translated into French under the title *Le code Frédéric.*

[2091] DISEASES. It is certain that sea air, heavy with saline particles, must contract the fibers, enhance their elasticity, and reduce in the vessels the faculty they have of yielding to the excessive movement of liquids. When one arrives by sea in extremely hot climates, where, upon arrival, the blood rarefies a great deal, the vessels' stiff fibers can no longer give way. That's the reason why Martinique, Santo Domingo, and the other islands of those waters are so fatal to foreigners, and why they immediately lapse into fevers caused by an extreme rarefaction of the blood, which can be cured only by jolting bloodlettings. This is proven by these circumstances: When one has had the disease, one no longer gets it; one does not have it when one has remained for a long time without getting it; people accustomed to the sea—that is, those on whose fibers the sea air has made less of an impression—are less subject to it; lastly, despite bloodlettings that seem to have exhausted all strength, they return immediately upon cure—sure sign of the fibers' elasticity; everything that increases the fibers' elasticity, like wine, is fatal; everything that increases their activity, like the venereal acts, is fatal to them. Women are less subject to this because their fibers are looser, and because through a natural restraint, they do not engage in debaucheries that might increase the contraction—and consequently, the effect of the sea air is restored sooner.

That's why islands, whose climate is normally healthy in itself, are so fatal when they are situated in warm climes. And we do not observe that those who arrive by land in warm climes contract those diseases of dissolution of the blood, like those experienced upon arrival by sea on Martinique and other Antilles Islands, on the warm American Continent, in the East Indies. That's why, when one arrives by sea in cold climes, like Canada, or the English establishments that run north along the Gulf of Mexico, this disease is not known. That's why, in the diseases of the Antilles, the air is very healthy for the residents. That's why this fever is not properly speaking epidemic. In Chardin, one can see the disease of Bandar Abbas, which is also a dissolution of the blood.[1]

[2091]
1. See Jean Chardin, *Voyages*, 9:239, for his description in 1674 of Bandar Abbas, Iranian port city on the straits of Hormuz.

I would like to begin an essay this way:

"M. Raulin, renowned doctor from Nérac,[2] in a very good essay on the ingredients of air which he has communicated to me in manuscript, has very well noted that the salts and other materials that were the ingredients of the sea air stiffened the fibers, etc. This has led me to the following reflections . . ."

[2092] When reading a book, we should be disposed to believe that the author has seen the contradictions that we imagine we are encountering there on first glance. Thus, we should begin by mistrusting our snap judgments, taking up again the passages we claim to be contradictory, comparing them together, comparing them again with what comes before and after, seeing if they are within the same system of assumptions, if the contradiction is in the content or only in our own manner of thinking. When we have properly done all this, we can pronounce with authority: "There is some contradiction."

This is not always all, however. When a work is systematic, we should still be sure we grasp the whole system. Look at a big machine made to produce an effect. You see wheels that turn in opposite directions; you would think on first glance that the machine was going to destroy itself, that the wheels were going to obstruct each other, that the machine was going to stop. It keeps going; those pieces, which at first seem to be destroying each other, combine together for the proposed purpose. (This is my response to the work of abbé de La Porte.)[1]

[2093] I said of two families—both of them stupid: one modest, the other haughty—that one represented fools as they are; the other as they ought to be.

[2094] Women, in my opinion, do very well to have as little ugliness as they can. It would be good if they could be equally ugly or equally beautiful, in order to eliminate the pride of beauty and the despair of ugliness.

---

2. Joseph Raulin (1708–84), physician from Nérac (Lot-et-Garonne), had sent the Academy of Bordeaux a memoir on this subject in 1752 (Bordeaux municipal library, ms. 828, t. 105, no. 2). In the 1754 edition of *PL,* Montesquieu added a paragraph to CXXI, 202, on diseases due to climate change that is inspired by this passage of the *Pensées.*

[2092]
1. See *pensée* 2057.

[**2095**] The existence of God was being discussed. I said: "Here's a proof in two words: there's an effect, thus there's a cause."

[**2096**] A Christian is usually someone who knows the history of his sect (a Catholic, a Calvinist, a Lutheran), but not someone who observes the precepts of his sect. It is like being Spanish or French: you are from a Country, but you are unable to prefer that Country's good to your own.

[**2097**] If a prince is ever foolish enough to make me his favorite, I will ruin him.[1]

[**2098**] To work to make one's fortune can be an entertaining thing; one is always hoping.

[**2099**] In the provinces: Paris, a North pole to attract you; the Intendant, a South pole to repel you.[1]

[**2100**] The King of Prussia wrote Gresset a letter as a poetaster would.[1] The good letters by kings are letters of exchange.[2]

[**2101**] Fine prose is like a majestic river whose waters roll on; fine verse, like a fountain that shoots forth by force—there arises something pleasing from the welter of verses.

[**2102**] On a piece of news that seemed so well tailored that it seemed to have been produced within the government's inner circle: "It's like pearls, which are fake when they are too beautiful."

[**2103**] There is more life in Cardinal de Retz's *Memoirs* than in Caesar's *Commentaries.*[1]

[**2104**] Refined people are excited by La Prévost's dance; gross people, or those who have made themselves gross, are excited by Camargo's

[2097]
1. *Ruiner* here might also mean "bankrupt."—HC

[2099]
1. For more on the intendant, see *pensées* 977, 1353, 1572, 1835, 1840, 1846, 1898, and 2066.—HC

[2100]
1. Louis Gresset (1709–77), poet and man of letters.
2. *Lettres de change,* a financial term normally translated "bills of exchange." This item is therefore a play on words.—HC

[2103]
1. Paul de Gondi, cardinal de Retz (1613–79), whose *Memoirs* were published in 1718 (*Catalogue,* 3040); see also *pensée* 1368.

dance—*irritamentum veneris languentis.*[1] She stirs up the old libertines and brings the impotent back to attention. It is our fault if we like her so much.

[2105] LA SAINT-SULPICE. She is ridiculous, but she accepts it very patiently.

[2106] I adapt to those people who like to make everyone laugh, and who attend to the public joy.

[2107] The Duchess of Berry died wounded; she had enjoyed more than the patriarchs.[1]

[2108] Perhaps the reputation of M. de La Motte's prose has harmed that of his poetry.

[2109] L. P. S. He seems to be in civil society, but he is outside it— equally incapable of rendering service and of receiving it. He is an imperturbable man.

[2110] There is a set of scales where one side is in France and the other in Holland. Despite the variation in currencies, they are still weighed.

[2111] I have seen an age when the craft of prince of the blood—which predisposed people so favorably in the past—was so disparaged that one needed more merit than another in order to seem to have any.

[2112] It is good to be inhibited; it is like being a spring that is wound up.

[2113] It is not mediciners we are lacking, it is medicine.[1]

[2114] There are some diseases that make us die more courageously than others—for example, gangrene in the blood; witness Louis XIV, Nointel and others.[1]

[2115] It is often difficult to know whether women have wit or not.

[2104]
1. "The spur of Venus." See Juvenal, *Satires,* 11.167. On La Prévost, see *Spicilège,* 774; Camargo, a famous female dancer, left the theater in 1734 to become the count of Clermont's mistress.

[2107]
1. Marie-Louise-Elisabeth d'Orléans, Mlle de Valois, duchess of Berry (1695–1719), daughter of the regent, Philippe d'Orléans, had in 1710 married Charles de France, duke of Berry.

[2113]
1. The pun is between *médecins* (doctors) and *médecine* (medicine).—HC

[2114]
1. Charles-Marie-François Olier, marquis of Angervilliers and of Nointel (1635–85), French diplomat.

They are always seducing their judges. Gaiety takes the place of wit for them. You have to wait until their youth is passed. They might then say: "I'm going to see if I have some wit."

[2116] When a man is a good geometer and is recognized as such, it still remains for him to prove that he has some wit.[1]

[2117] The Emperor's dignity is still turning heads at the Council of Vienne.[1]

[2118] Marshal Villeroy, bad joker—he was always aiming and never hitting the target; {moreover, he was vain like a silly woman}.[1]

[2119] She was a dangerous woman, Lady Stafford.[1] She didn't grace you with mockeries; she covered you in them. She inundated you, submerged you, drowned you in them. She was in the desperation of old age.

[2120] How many people abuse their reputation. A famous painter was being criticized for certain bad paintings. "Go on! Go on!" he said, "they'll never believe it was me who created them."

[2121] The English who have returned over the Channel seem as though they have returned over the river Lethe.[1] It is not that they are ungrateful, but few are in a position to host you in London, where they often have no house; they find it awkward to see you again.

[2122] I knew Ramsay.[1] He was a banal man, always the same flatteries. He was like Homer's epithets—all his heroes had light feet.

[2116]

1. In the manuscript, *pensée* 2116 seems to be an addition to *pensée* 2115 rather than a separate entry.—HC

[2117]

1. Perhaps the Church Council of Vienne in southern France (1311–12); Henry VII of Luxembourg had marched to Rome in October 1310 to claim the title of Holy Roman Emperor, which had been empty since the death of Frederick II in 1250; he was crowned June 1312.—HC

[2118]

1. On Villeroy, see also *pensées* 1167 and 1185.—HC

[2119]

1. Claude-Charlotte de Gramont, countess of Stafford (1662–1739).

[2121]

1. Lethe, the river of forgetfulness in Greek mythology.—HC

[2122]

1. Chevalier Andrew Michael Ramsay (1683–1743), Scotsman converted to Catholicism by Fénelon, leader in the Masonic movement in France; cf. *pensée* 291. His *Philosophical Principles of Natural and Revealed Religion* appeared in 1748–49.

[2123] In Vienna, I found the ministers very affable. I told them: "You are ministers in the morning and men in the evening."[1]

[2124] My friend M. Folkes, president of the Royal Society—if someone had asked me what defects he had of heart and mind, I would have had difficulty responding.[1]

[2125] It seemed to me that Chevalier Metuezen (?) never knew more than the half of things.

[2126] I have known Lord Bolingbroke, and I have unknown him. I did not care to learn morality under him.

[2127] It seems to me that we have two sorts of free-thinkers: the dandies, who deny a God they believe in, and certain preachers, who preach a God they do not believe in.

[2128] I have made the resolution to read only good books. He who reads bad ones is like a man who spends his life in bad company.

[2129] When Helvétius passed through Bordeaux, people ran to him as to the shadow of Saint Peter. "*Non inveni tantam fidem in Israël.*"[1]

[2130] In the end, the public renders justice. Here's the reason: the votes of the wise are constant, but fools' votes are various, change constantly, and cancel each other out.

[2131] I think kings are unfortunate because they cannot pay their respects, for it seems to me that the grandees' taste is to pay respects rather than receive them.

[2132] The Duke of Orleans's Regency was a splendid spectacle.

[2133] The ambassadors of France are very badly paid. The King is a giant who has himself represented by a dwarf.

[2123]
    1. Montesquieu arrived in Vienna on April 30, 1728, and left on July 8; cf. *Voyages* (*OC*, 2:967–73).

[2124]
    1. Martin Ffolkes, or Folkes (1690–1754), mathematician and antiquarian, president of the Royal Society of London, and associate member of the Bordeaux Academy (1743); Montesquieu corresponded extensively with him. In February 1730, doctor Georges-Louis Teissier, from a Protestant family in the Cévennes and then exiled in London, proposed Montesquieu as a member of the Royal Society; Ffolkes was especially supportive of his candidacy.

[2129]
    1. "Not even in Israel have I found such faith," Matthew 8:10. Claude-Adrien Helvétius (1715–71), farmer-general, Montesquieu's friend and correspondent, and later author of the controversial work *De l'Esprit* [On the mind] (1758) and the posthumously published *De l'Homme* [On man] (1771).

[2134] Count Kinski told me when I arrived in Vienna:[1] "You will find the Emperor's palace pretty rustic." I responded: "Sir, it is quite enjoyable to see the rustic palace of a prince whose subjects' houses are beautiful."[2]

[2135] Prince Eugene told me: "I have never listened to all those financial schemers, because whether you impose the tax on the shoes or on the wig, it comes to the same thing." He was quite right; it is the never-ending reforms that cause the need for reform.

[2136] The Greeks used to say: "Only in Sparta is it nice to grow old."[1] As for me, I said: "Only in Vienna is it nice to grow old." There, women of sixty had lovers. Ugly ones had lovers. One dies in Vienna, but one never grows old there.

[2137] It is a wondrous thing that the corporate body that is closest to Heaven is the most inconvenient for men . . . (the Ecclesiastics).[1]

[2138] In France, a prince of the blood is only an Epicurean God.

[2139] A liberal man is not one who buys a lot of medals because he likes them, it is a man who spends outside his tastes.

[2140] I would rather go in my coach with a harlot than with the C—— of Ch——, because I prefer people to think I have a vice rather than bad taste.

[2141] The Venetians are unsociable. When you go see them, you don't know whether you're entering by the door or by the window, whether you're bringing them pleasure or pain. There, debauchery is called *liberty.*[1]

[2142] I am building at La Brède. My building is advancing; myself, I am retreating.

[2134]
1. On Count Kinski, see *Voyages* (*OC*, 2:969).
2. See also *pensée* 1003.—HC

[2136]
1. See Plutarch, "Various Sayings of Spartans to Fame Unknown," 60 (235e). In the Loeb edition, it is *Moralia*, III.417.

[2137]
1. A reference to the Church's status as the first estate under old-regime law.—HC

[2141]
1. Cf. *Voyages* (*OC*, 2:981) for a similar thought.

[2143] Someone was saying that M. Law had had many enemies in France. "Yes," I said, "and enemies that he had never seen. One cannot be reconciled with those."[1]

[2144] I will never forgive Father Le Tellier. He is the cause of an incalculable number of our follies.[1]

[2145] Women in some parts of Italy: they have no concept of resistance.

[2146] Normally, there is not a craft easier than that of king; sometimes, there is none harder.

[2147] Molière had to have M. Diafoirus speak to make the physicians believe in the circulation of the blood. The aptly slung joke has great power.[1]

[2148] The Jewish religion is quite ancient; it is no longer à la mode.

[2149] Hearing Cardinal Polignac speak, I told him: "My lord, you do not make systems, but you speak systems."

[2150] One sees that the Germans have a desire to make something emerge from their heads, but that desire is useless.

[2151] Our lives are not like plays, which must inevitably have five acts. Some have one, others three, others five.

[2152] To make Theology clear, the theologians have made Philosophy obscure. Those people have employed many centuries muddying Philosophy.

[2153] At the Clementine College in Rome, we heard a detestable tragedy, without any admixture of bad or mediocre.[1] Nothing more is needed to ruin children's taste.

[2154] I couldn't get over my astonishment when, in reading Aristotle's *Politics,* I found all the theologians' principles on usury, word for word.

[2143]
1. On John Law, see *pensées* 530, 1017, and 1610.

[2144]
1. Fr. Michel Le Tellier, S.J., was confessor to Louis XIV from 1709 to 1715. See also *pensées* 1226 and n. 7, and 1958.

[2147]
1. The reference is to Molière, *Le malade imaginaire* [The imaginary invalid] (1673), II.5.—HC

[2153]
1. La Motte's *Romulus,* on February 21, 1729; see *Voyages* (*OC,* 2:1112).

I thought they had put them there.[1] I talked about it in *The Spirit of the Laws*.[2] But these gentlemen do not like it when their sources are revealed; their sources are unknown even to themselves, just as the source of the Nile used to be unknown. They made quite an outcry over that.

[2155] In delivering a speech to the King, the ambassadors of Siam seemed to be singing.[1] They were asked how they found our pronunciation. They said it seemed to them like singing. Look at how we judge things! In fact, anything at all removed from ordinary pronunciation seems like song.

[2156] Someone said of the Count of Boulainvilliers that he didn't know the past, the present, or the future—he was a historian, he had a young wife, and he was an astrologer![1]

[2157] Every day before their eyes, the Mohammedans[1] have examples of events so unexpected and incidents so extraordinary—from the effects of arbitrary power—that they must be naturally inclined to believe the doctrine of a rigid destiny that guides all. In our climes, where power is moderate, our acts are normally subject to the rules of prudence, and our good or bad fortune is normally the effect of our wisdom. We therefore do not have the idea of blind fate. In the novels of the Orient, you see men constantly guided by that blind fate and rigid destiny.

"The Persians," it is said in a note to the *Thousand and One Nights* (volume II, page 18), by M. Pétis de La Croix, "believe that everything that must happen until the end of the world is written on a table of light, called *louh*, with a pen of fire, called *calamazer,* and the writing above it is named *caza* or *cadar,* that is, unavoidable predestination." (Good for putting in my Preface.)

[2154]
1. See Aristotle, *Politics*, I.iii.23.
2. See *Laws*, 21.20, 387–88, on usury, as well as Derathé, 2:469–70; *OC*, 3:662–65; and Brèthe, 3:370 n. 148, for changes Montesquieu made to the passage in response to criticism by the Sorbonne censor.

[2155]
1. This would be the embassy sent to Paris by Siam in 1684.

[2156]
1. The reference is to two short works by Boulainvilliers that were circulating in manuscript (see Vernière, 286 n. 3). See *PL*, CXXXV, for a satire on astrology books.

[2157]
1. "Put in the *Novel*" (M.). This fragment was probably destined for *Arsace et Isménie.*

[**2158**] On the occasion of the disputes between the Clergy and the Parlement, and the latter's exile in 1753,[1] I said: "It is too big a blow for a dying superstition. The Clergy has lost the Nation's love. It is quite the dupe—it takes hatred for respect."[2]

[**2159**] I was saying of Lord Bolingbroke, concerning his apologia against the Pretender:[1] "It is rather against the reigning king that he ought to have written his apologia. There is no apologia to be made when all it accomplishes is to come down on an unfortunate prince." Lord Hyde said of him: "I have never left him without admiring him more and esteeming him less."[2]

[**2160**] Rules are only made to lead fools by the hand. Mothers have a thousand rules to guide their little girls. They decrease their rules as they grow up, and in the end, they reduce them to a single one.

[**2161**] THINGS THAT DID NOT MAKE IT INTO THE LYSIMACHUS DIALOGUE.[1] The laws were silent, necessity spoke, and we obeyed. My subjects are happy; but as for me, I am not. The State is tranquil, but my house is still in turmoil. Everything is alive[2] in my empire, and I have sorrow only in my palace. Who knows what miseries would have befallen me if Callisthenes had not constantly calmed my soul. Strange condition of Kings! They have only great passions. Their strength is only in action; they are always weak in self-defense. O Callisthenes! you make me fear remorse,

---

[**2158**]

1. In a long letter of July 9, 1753—addressed, no doubt, to Durey de Meinières, president of the Parlement of Paris, which at that time was in exile in Bourges (*OC*, 3:1465–69)—Montesquieu condemns the Parlement's attitude; see also Montesquieu's *Mémoire sur la Constitution Unigenitus* (*OC*, 3:469–76), written in 1753, at the time of the refusal of sacraments controversy, in which the Parlement of Paris took sides against the bull *Unigenitus* and was exiled to Bourges (May 19–October 8, 1753). For the Constitution Unigenitus, see *pensées* 273, 426, 914, 1170, 1226, and 2247.

2. See *pensée* 2164.

[**2159**]

1. James Francis Edward Stuart, the Pretender or the Knight of Saint George (1688–1766), son of James II, was recognized as king of England by Louis XIV under the name of James III. See *Voyages* (*OC*, 2:1184). The work referred to would appear to be the *Letter to Sir William Windham*, a Jacobite collaborator of Bolingbroke's; it was written in 1716 or 1717 but not published until 1753, which may help date this entry.

2. Henry Hyde (1710–53), viscount of Cornbury, then Lord Hyde, with whom Montesquieu corresponded. He was the addressee of Bolingbroke's 1735 *Letters on the study of history*, published in 1753, two years after the author's death.

[**2161**]

1. On *Lysimachus*, see also *pensées* 563 and 1666, and Allen, 76–81.

2. Alternative reading (*rit* for *vit*): "Everyone laughs" or "all is laughter."—HC

when I hardly fear the crimes. I shudder at the horrors from which you have saved me.

[**2162**] You do not need much intelligence to sow discord with everyone, but you need much to conciliate everyone. The spirit of conciliation made up three quarters of the Duke of Marlborough's heroism.[1]

[**2163**] It is easy to perceive what is ridiculous in general, but one has fine taste when one perceives what is ridiculous *there*—that is, with each group and each person.

[**2164**] ON THE QUARRELS OF 1753.[1] Shut up and listen! . . . It is your opinions that are in danger and not religion that is in danger.

You say the dying must be interrogated on the Constitution;[2] as for me, I am telling you that it is accepted, and no one should be interrogated anymore. You say it is not accepted, and it must not be accepted; as for me, I am telling you that it is accepted, and nothing more should be said about it. O Frenchmen! If you knew how splendid theology is, and what idiots theologians are! . . . Know that religion is eternal, and that it does not need your wrath to sustain itself; that it existed before the Constitution, and that it will afterward. It is the attention we pay to the combatants that creates your combat.

[**2165**] DISPARATE MATERIALS. I thought I would receive M. de Buffon at the Academy, and I wanted to put in my speech:[1]

"Talents seemed to be born under the hand and under the watchful eye of the King."

"That foreigners summon our rarest minds is our glory; their forge is here at home."

I said of Buffon, of his book:

[2162]
1. On the English military leader the Duke of Marlborough, see also *pensées* 300, 562, 635, and 767.

[2164]
1. See *pensée* 2158.
2. On the Constitution Unigenitus, see *pensées* 273, 426, 914, 1170, 1226, and 2247.—HC

[2165]
1. Georges-Louis Leclerc de Buffon (1707–88). Montesquieu was director of the French Academy when Buffon was elected to it (June 23, 1753), but not at the moment of his reception. The Revolutionary Hérault de Séchelles (1759–94) reports in his *Voyage à Montbar* (Year IX), 54–55, that Buffon had told him that Montesquieu had a foreshortened writing style that arose from the fact that Montesquieu was nearly blind, that he would forget what he had dictated, and that he was thus obliged to write in the smallest space possible.

"These grand conceptions, in this manner bold, noble and proud, which so resembles that of Michelangelo:

"*Di Migel Angel la terribil via . . .*"

"There are normally more positions than men. Nowadays, we have been having more men than positions. This is the effect of the protection that the King, etc.

"What the Academy has granted you on its own, we have all asked for, and what the public used to learn about through entreaties, it could only learn about today through our selection.

"Thus, you have been spared that embarrassment that costs so much to men of merit—of saying that they have it.

"To preserve merit's modesty is to preserve its grace; it is to leave it the advantage of pleasing a second time.

"I will presume that I am following the spirit of the Academy in abolishing the eulogies. What it has done constitutes its praise. In choosing you, Sir, it has told you everything."

[2166] During my business with the Sorbonne.[1] ". . . But I see from afar a little cloud that is growing and that looks set to produce a storm. I believe I will be obliged in the end to abandon the most tender fatherland, the most cherished king. Let us go! And in whatever place we rest our head, let us strive to place it under the laurels."

[2167] M. Queincy[1] has told me about a work of metaphysics he is writing. According to him, all our thoughts are sensations. He says he is stopping Spinoza at the first instant, where he defines substance: "that which exists necessarily." This definition is a composite of contradictory ideas: "exists necessarily" is a general notion; "that which" is a particular subject and a particular idea. No conclusion can thus be drawn from this definition.

[2168] When one has allowed a single desire to enter one's soul, one is no longer happy. That one becomes the father of countless others, especially if it is money that is desired, for money is a thing that multiplies itself. Often he who has one honor and one position knows very well that

[2166]
1. *Laws* was censured by the Sorbonne in a protracted deliberation in which Montesquieu was actively involved, from 1751 to 1754.

[2167]
1. Charles Sevin, marquis of Coincy.

he cannot have another. But he who has desired one hundred thousand francs—why would he not desire two hundred thousand?

[**2169**] What makes me like to be at La Brède is that at La Brède, it seems to me that my money is under my feet. In Paris, it seems to me I have it on my shoulders.[1] In Paris, I say: "I must spend only that much." In my countryside, I say: "I must spend all of that."

[**2170**] TO MY GRANDSON.[1] I had thought about giving you some moral precepts. But if you do not have it in your heart, you will not find it in books.

It is not our mind, it is our soul that guides us.

You can have wealth, employment, wit, knowledge, piety, charm, enlightenment; but if you do not have lofty sentiments, you will never be more than a common man.

Know, too, that nothing approximates base sentiments more than pride, and that nothing is closer to lofty sentiments than modesty.

Fortune is a condition, not a possession. It is good only in that it exposes us to view and can make us more attentive. It gives us more witnesses, and consequently more judges. It obliges us to be accountable for itself. One is in a house whose doors are always open. It puts us in crystal palaces—inconvenient because they are fragile, and inconvenient because they are transparent.

If, once you have all that nature and your present condition authorize you to desire, you let one more desire enter your soul, be forewarned: you will never be happy. That desire is always father to another. Especially if you desire things that multiply themselves, like money, what will be the end of your desires?

It remains only to ask oneself for what purpose one so desires that money. The consul Paullus sold himself for a sum to Caesar, who ruined Rome. He employed that money to have a tribunal-marketplace[2] constructed in Rome.

[**2169**]

1. The contrast rests on a play on words; "under my feet" (*sous mes pieds*) is an idiom meaning contemptible or beneath one's dignity; "on my shoulders" (*sur mes épaules*) is an idiom for carrying a burden.—HC

[**2170**]

1. Charles-Louis de Secondat (1749–1824).

2. *Basilique* (from Latin, *basilicus*), meaning a public building where justice was administered, with space on the sides for merchants to sell their wares.—HC

When you read history, look carefully at all the efforts that the leading figures have made to be great, fortunate, illustrious. Look at what part of their goal they obtained, and calculate the means on the one hand, the ends on the other. Nonetheless, the balance sheet is not precise. For the great tableaux of history are of those who have succeeded in their brilliant enterprises. Look at what part they found of that philosopher's stone they were seeking: happiness and tranquillity.

[2171] The leaves fall from the trees every winter. Five or six still cling to the tree for a few days and become the plaything of the winds.

[2172] Why is it that approbation makes so many people happy, and glory so few? It is because we live with those who approve of us, but we neither admire nor scarcely can admire except from afar.

[2173] To some folks who were saying that in Paris alone are there likable people, I said: "What are you calling *likable people?* There are a hundred thousand things to do before thinking of being likable."

[2174] Someone was saying Helvétius had given Saurin a pension of two thousand francs, and that this was quite noble.[1] "Very noble," I said, "and it will be that way for a long time, because that will not be much imitated."

[2175] Someone was recounting all of Voltaire's vices. The answer always was: "He has plenty of wit!" Impatient, someone said: "Well, that's one more vice!"

[2176] Theologians are not pacified in one dispute except on behalf of a second one. They act like the cormorants that you send fishing: they come to bring you the fish that a ring has blocked in their gullets, but you put a gudgeon in there.[1]

[2177] I thought I would produce a panegyric for the Archbishop of Sens;[1] I said:

[2174]
1. Bernard-Joseph Saurin (1706–81), lawyer at the Parlement of Paris and playwright whose subjects were borrowed from exoticism, classical antiquity, and especially English literature. In an April 1, 1767, letter to Doctor Blain, David Hume reports that Helvétius and Saurin had both counseled Montesquieu against publishing *Laws* to spare his reputation, that the public's esteem for the book had recently dwindled, validating their judgment, but that Montesquieu's friendship for them was undiminished by their candor.

[2176]
1. See *pensée* 2247 for another use of this image.—HC

[2177]
1. Jean-Joseph Languet de La Villeneuve de Gergy (1677–1753); as Archbishop of Sens in 1731, he upheld the bull *Unigenitus* against the Jansenists; he had been elected to the French Academy in 1721.

"One may say of him that at a time when most people were displaying more passion than zeal, he showed more zeal than passion.

"His sufferings, his poverty devoid of disorder, will forever prove that this zeal for religion was a love for religion.

"I cannot be in doubt: I know of people he had thought to be his adversaries; I am sure he did not take them for his enemies.

"Eloquence is relative; the variety of talents constitutes its character. The character of M. de Sens's eloquence was discussion; that of your mind is an imagination and a gaiety that never leave you. What happiness when nature has given the mind, as its character, that joy which makes only the fleeting happiness of men; that joy which flees all those who seek it; which is deaf to all those who invoke it; which follows[2] those who want to receive it; which flees those who want to communicate it; that gaiety which has for so long abandoned slavery, wealth and palaces; that gaiety which grandeur can envy, which grandeur can have, but which it certainly never imparts."

[**2178**] LITERATURE AND BELLES-LETTRES, QUINTUS CURTIUS.[1] We hardly know who the rhetorical pedant was who, lacking knowledge and judgment, drags Alexander over a land he does not know, covers him with little flowers, and writes without knowing a single one of the sources he should have drawn on. The Ancients had more sense than we do; they did not cite him anywhere. And although the purity of his style proves his antiquity, he remained in oblivion, and it seems we were waiting for Barbarism to make him emerge from it, and to put him forth as a model in the Schools—as if, in order to teach a language, it was necessary to begin by ruining the mind. Quintus Curtius will tell us that Alexander, despairing of making himself followed by the Macedonians, told them that they had only to return to Macedonia, and that he would go and conquer the world alone.[2] Arrian will tell us that the despair, sadness, and tears of the Macedonians came from the fact that Alexander had formed an army that was putting him in position to dispense with the Macedonians and complete his conquest; the cries and tears of the army, the sighs of Alexander, reconciled them.[3]

2. Alternative reading (*suit* or *fuit*), "flees."—HC

[**2178**]

1. Montesquieu owned four editions of Quintus Curtius Rufus's first-century *Historia Alexandri magni* [History of Alexander the Great] (*Catalogue,* 2772–75).

2. Quintus Curtius, *History of Alexander,* X.ii.25–30.

3. Arrian, *Anabasis,* V.28.

[2179] HOMER. The *Amadises* describe battles like Homer, but they describe them with a uniformity that is painful and distasteful.[1] Homer is so varied that nothing resembles anything else. The battles of the *Amadises* are long; those of Homer are rapid. He never stops, and he runs from event to event, while the *Amadises* linger on at ponderous length. His comparisons are funny and wonderful. Everything is cold in the *Amadises;* everything is warm in Homer. In the Greek poet, all events are born of the subject; in the *Amadises,* all are born of the writer's mind, and any other adventure would have worked as well as the one they imagined. It is not made clear why most things happen the way they do. This is because in Homer, the marvelous is in the whole, taken together; in the *Amadises,* it is only in the details.

The *Iliad* and the *Odyssey:* in the one, variety of movement; in the other, variety of stories.

Virgil, finer when he imitates the *Odyssey* in his first books than when, in the last ones, he imitates the *Iliad;* he lacked Homer's splendid fire. Without the *Iliad* and the *Odyssey,* it is likely we would not have the *Aeneid.*

Homer has been criticized because his kings cooked, which makes (it is said) a distasteful impression. I answer that it is not surprising that things were that way during heroic times. Aside from the mores being simple, it is because the kings and heads of household themselves made the sacrifices. They killed the victim, they burned a part of the fat, and since it had to be eaten, it was very easy for them to share it out in pieces, etc.

Thus, the idea of cooking in heroic times is linked with the noblest ideas of former days, such as that of sacrifice. Look at book II of the *Iliad.* Agamemnon offered Saturn's powerful son a five-year-old ox, and the most prominent heads of the army were present at that sacrifice, and Nestor, King of the Pylians, Idomeneus, etc. The victim was brought in, and after the cakes had been presented, Agamemnon said this prayer, etc. Meanwhile, the victim was presented, and they slit its throat before the altar. They cut it up, they set it on fire, and having prepared the feast, which they were supposed to do, they ate together, etc.

I observe: that the love of Country, so much expressed in the *Odyssey,*

[2179]

1. The *Amadis,* famous Spanish novel of chivalry by Garcia Rodriguez, or Ordonez, de Montalva (fifteenth–sixteenth centuries), published for the first time in 1508 and often imitated; it was the subject of Cervantes's satire in *Don Quixote* (1610).

must have made more of an impact on the Greek peoples because of their good fortune and their liberty; that most of the stories in the *Odyssey* were popular rumors, reported by travelers in those times when sailing was so difficult; that the palaces made in a supernatural manner, like that of Circe and others reported by Homer, are less filled with wonder than those of our novels, in proportion to their respective notions of luxury.

[**2180**] OVID. I will have to look at the observations I've made in my extracts from this poet.

On the affront to Lucretia, which she recounts:

> *Caetera restabant; voluit cum dicere flevit*
> *Et matronales erubuere genae.*[1]

The second line is not tedious, as some have said. When she thinks of the scale of the affront, she weeps; when she thinks of the shame that follows it, she blushes. It is her confusion that makes her weep. The feeling of her misfortune makes her weep; the perspective on her misfortune makes her blush. It is the different states in which the passions place us that Ovid expresses so well.

I said the second line was not tedious. The first line is Lucretia's feeling of misfortune and pain; the second is her feeling of modesty. Now Ovid is wonderful at depicting the passions, that is, at depicting the different feelings that arise from a passion, that precede or follow each other.

In order to grasp what length and brevity actually are, even to grasp what repetition is, three main subjects need to be distinguished: the things whose subject consists in reasoning; the things whose subject consists in depiction—such as, for example, poetry in general; those, finally, whose subject consists in expressing the agitation of the passions. In the first case, one cannot be too parsimonious: every useless word or idea is pernicious, because the mind, believing it important, gets tired or loses interest. Often, in fact, what had been clear becomes obscure, because we think that we have not understood what we have understood very well. But in the case of depiction—whether of the effects of nature, or of the effects of the passions—the mind must be in some sense a real talker, in order to express

[2180]
1. Ovid, *Fastes,* II.827–28 (see *pensée* 1680): "The rest she left unsaid, but wept and a blush o'erspread her matron cheeks."

that vast number of things that the eye sees, or the heart feels, and to make known that it has seen countless things that they have not managed to distinguish. (Make clearer)

Ovid, as I have said elsewhere, is wonderful at depicting circumstances, and what proves he is not diffuse is that he is fast-paced. In this, one may very well compare him to Ariosto.

It is said that Ovid is diffuse, and yet I don't see that anything could be cut from Ovid. Chevalier Marino is diffuse because you can cut anything you want from it—a few lines, a quarter of the work, half the work.[2] What remains will only be the better for it; that is, less unbearable.

It is said that Ovid has too much wit—that is, abandons himself too much to his wit. But if this were Ovid's flaw, it would be identified with him and would prevail in all his works, as it prevails in all of Chevalier Marino's works. Ovid did not have that mental trait, because he took on the trait that was appropriate for each subject.

[2181] M. DESPREAUX. {It is no longer permissible to write badly since the sources of the agreeable and the beautiful have become so well known. That is to say, it is very difficult to write well. In a large seraglio, it is difficult to please. We judge works of the mind with the distaste of the Sultans.}

In the preface to his last edition,[1] M. Despréaux stated (either he or his publisher) the fine witticism of Francis I and expressed it this way: "A king of France does not avenge the offenses of a duke of Orléans."[2] One should say: "The king of France does not avenge the offenses of the duke of Orléans." The one is a reflection; the other is a feeling. The one can be said of everyone; the other is striking because it can only have been said by the king of France who had that feeling. One should not make a general idea out of it. What strikes our sense of wonder is when the thing is said by the one who was feeling it and was feeling it at the moment he said it.

The two satires we have on women were written by two pedants (thus, they are not good): Despréaux and Juvenal.[3] Good God, if Horace had

---

2. Giambattista Marino (1569–1625) dedicated his *Adonis* (1623), a poem in twenty cantos and forty-five thousand lines, to Louis XIII.

[2181]

1. The 1747 edition of the *Works* of Boileau.

2. The saying is by Louis XII (r. 1498–1515), not Francis I (r. 1515–47).

3. Decimus Junius Juvenalis (ca. 55–ca. 140) (see *Catalogue*, 2076–79).

done it! But the subject is worthless, and Horace had too much wit to take on such a subject.

But fine talents have written bad works in vain; they are always inimitable from some point of view. Witness the panegyric of Mme de Maintenon in that satire on women by Despréaux.[4]

Jansenism has committed a curious offense[5] against the Muse of M. Despréaux; it has made the glory of Racine: *Esther* and *Athalie*. M. Racine has derived ideas on the grandeur of religion from it and has filled his poetry with its sentiments; M. Despréaux has derived theological discussions from it—an alien subject and inimical to poetry.

M. Despréaux's immortal works are his *Lutrin,* his *Art of Poetry,* his epistle to M. de Valincour, and others. What is painful in M. D.'s works is a rather unrefined vanity that is always manifest, an ill nature that is also manifest, and too-frequent repetition of the same satirical features, so that one sees both a heart corrupted and a mind that does not serve the heart well enough. His imitations of the Ancients have made people believe that he had more wit than talent; as for me, given the fertility of his mind, I would consider him to have more talent than wit. In fact, there is scarcely a single one of his pieces in which inventiveness is not found, in which the man of talent is not seen. His *Lutrin* is a perfect poem; it constantly holds up against the baseness and sterility of its subject by richness of invention. There is no work that was more difficult to write than that one, and perhaps we have none that is more perfect. *Nec erat quod tollere velles.*[6] The Ancients have not served him as a model. When he walks with the Ancients, he is not inferior to them, and when he walks all alone, he is not inferior to them, either. In defending the Moderns, M. Perrault was unable to cite anything better against M. Despréaux than M. Despréaux himself.[7]

[2182] MONTAIGNE. Look at what I have said about him in a small private work in the portfolio *Unpublished Works.*[1] {This is only some ideas; it has to be changed.}

---

4. Boileau, *Satire,* X.

5. Alternative reading: "furious offense."—HC

6. Horace, *Satire,* I.iv.11: "[nor was there] much that you would like to remove."

7. Charles Perrault (1628–1703), whose *Parallèle des anciens et des modernes* [Parallel between the Ancients and the Moderns] came out in 1688–92.

[2182]

1. In the catalogue of manuscripts sent by Joseph-Cyrille de Montesquieu to his cousin Charles-Louis de Montesquieu in England (March 10, 1818; cf. *OC,* 3:1575), it reads: "3rd carton entitled: unpublished work"; this text is lost.

[2183–2202] THIS DID NOT MAKE IT INTO THE "ROMANS." Nota that the beginning is at page 16.[1]

[2183] "The census, or enumeration of citizens, was in itself a very wise thing. It was the state's reconnaissance into its affairs and examination of its power. It was established by Servius Tullius. Before him, says Eutropius (book I), the census was unknown in the world."[1]

This is a note I eliminated from my *Romans.* I meant to add there: "Eutropius is hardly being judicious when he says that before that prince, the census was unknown in the world."

[2184] No longer able to possess political or military virtues, they obtained distinction only through some knowledge of the civil law, and the perfidy involved in that artistry at the bar that was able to confound innocence or give arms to crime.

[2185] PATRON. That reciprocity of duty between patron and client was quite appropriate for maintaining certain virtues among the Romans.

[2186] Those laws that gave permission to everyone to kill in crimes of blind devotion on the part of the guilty party were good for terror, but they could be dangerous. Be that as it may, we should not be surprised that the Law allowed any individual to kill a tyrant.[1] This was part of Roman mores for quite a few other crimes (pages 18 and 19). Festus and other dictionaries, *in verbo* SACER, ought to be looked at.

Such was Numa's law against whoever was eliminating or moving a boundary marker (in Dionysius Halicarnassus, page 450), and against whoever was engaging in violence against a tribune of the people (Dionysius of Halicarnassus, p. 133).[2]

[2187] Prisoners were no longer regarded as citizens; you had to vanquish or cease to be a Roman. Look at the law.

[2188] As a cause of the weakening of the Syrian empire, the succes-

[2183–2202]
1. See *pensées* 1669–74.

[2183]
1. Eutropius (Latin historian of the fourth century), *Breviarium ab urbe condita* [Digest of Roman history], I.7.

[2186]
1. See *Considerations,* XI, 110.
2. Dionysius of Halicarnassus, *Roman Antiquities,* II.84 and VI.89; Montesquieu cites the 1586 edition (*Catalogue,* 2831); legend had Numa Pompilius as the second king of Rome (ca. 715–672 B.C.).

sion of prefectures in the same family since Seleucus Nicator.[1] Because of the prefects' fraud, pirates enslaved people all over. (Look at my extract of Strabo or Strabo himself, book XIV.)[2]

[**2189**] In my Strabo extract (book XIV), look into why the Romans often preferred to entrust certain provinces to kings, who needed a certain constant deference, rather than to Roman magistrates.

[**2190**] In Athens, *murum ascendere non licebat,*[1] on pain of death. This was rather a notion of insult than of danger, for as Marcellinus says, what would be unjust about that if the Law had not prohibited it? I believe it is this way of thinking that, having passed from the Greeks to the Romans, got Remus killed.

[**2191**] In my extract on the virtues and vices of Constantine Porphyrogenitus, in the volume *Universal history,* page 309, look at the reasons that made Caracalla give the right of Roman citizenship to all the Empire's subjects. It was to augment the treasury.

[**2192**] This is a question: namely, whether the Goths came from Scandinavia to the Palus Maeotis, as Jornandes says, or if, on the contrary, they came from the Palus Maeotis to Scandinavia.[1] Some people claim that those nations that were in Mithridates' army, with which he intended to penetrate as far as Rome, were expelled by Roman arms or by fear of the Romans and took refuge in Scandinavia, and this enters into my explanation of the enormous tribal settlements of the North.

[**2193**] *Valeriano et Gallieno imperantibus, Scythae, trajecto flumine Istro, Thraciam rursum praedati, Thessalonicam, Illyriorum urbem, obsederunt.*[1] They were repulsed. *Graeci, metu perculsi, Thermopylas missa custodia tutati*

[**2188**]

1. Seleucus Nicator (ca. 355–280 B.C.), Macedonian general and founder of the Seleucid dynasty; cf. *Considerations,* V, 60.

2. The allusion is to the 1587 edition of Strabo's *Geography* (*Catalogue,* 2646); the extract is lost.

[**2190**]

1. "It was not permitted to climb the wall." "Marcel, *in Hermogen;* Michael Ephesius, in *Aristotelem, Ethica,* book V" (M.).

[**2192**]

1. The Palus Maeotis is the ancient name for the Sea of Azov; Montesquieu consulted the works of Jornandes in the 1531 edition of Zosimus's *Historiae novae* [New history] (*Catalogue,* 2732).

[**2193**]

1. "Syncellus, p. 381" (M.). "With Valerian and Gallienus in power, the Scythians, having crossed the Istrian river and pillaged Thrace again, besieged Thessalonica, an Illyrian city." On George the Monk, Syncellus, see *pensée* 142 and 1601.

*sunt. Athenienses murum a Syllae temporibus dirutum reparaverunt. Pelo-
ponesii a mari ad mare Isthmum muro constructo muniverunt. Scythae . . .
spoliis onusti domos se receperunt.*[2]

[2194] ROMANS. The Romans had a way of thinking that entirely distinguished slaves from men.[1]

They made them engage in combat against wild beasts. They used them
as gladiators and obliged them, for their pleasure, to destroy each other. At
night, they put them in pits, which they made them climb into, and then
pulled away the ladder they had used to climb down. They put them to
death at will. When the master had been killed in the house, all his slaves
were tortured, guilty or not, however many there were. When they were
sick or old, they abandoned them and had them brought to the temple of
Aesculapius. They deprived them of all the most cherished natural sentiments. They deprived them of their wives' virtue, their daughters' chastity,
their children's property.

Why degrade a part of human nature? Why give yourself natural enemies? Why reduce the number of citizens? Why have citizens who will be
restrained only by fear?

Servile war! The most just that has ever been undertaken, because
it meant to prevent the most violent abuse of human nature ever engaged in.[2]

Woe to every legislator . . . Woe to every state . . .

Multiplication of slaves, multiplication of luxury.

In a state, there must not be a body of wretched men.

Gladiators and slaves; proofs of fidelity that they gave.

The Romans were imagining they were in a position of grandeur in
which they had nothing more to hope or fear, when three unexpected
things put them in danger of ruin.

2. "The Greeks, unnerved by fear, defended Thermopylae with a dispatched guard. The Athenians
repaired the wall that had been destroyed from the time of Sulla. The Peloponnesians fortified the
Isthmus from sea to sea with a constructed wall. The Scythians . . . retreated to their homes loaded
with spoils."

[2194]

1. "Look into the different titles of the Code *De auri et argenti fodinis*" (M.). In the Codes of Theodosius and Justinian, there are no titles by this name; on Spartacus, see *pensée* 174 n. 10.

2. The three Servile wars (135–32 B.C., 104–100 B.C., and 73–71 B.C.) were slave revolts against the
Roman republic. While the reference to gladiators makes it possible that Montesquieu is referring here
specifically to the Third Servile War, sometimes called the War of the Gladiators, it seems more likely
that he is referring to all of them together without distinction. See also *Laws*, 15.2 and 15.5.—HC

The Cimbri and the Teutons, unknown enemies, suddenly appeared and, like Hannibal, came to attack Rome in Italy. They astonished by their number, their ferocity, their war cries. They came to destroy or be destroyed. Marius and Sulla had the good fortune to exterminate them and delay by several centuries the great revolution the Northern nations were to make.

Soon a war flared up—not a less dangerous one, either, because it tended to shatter the inner body of the Republic, on which all the external conquests depended. It is well known that the little republics around them gave them a share in their own government, following agreements or the encouragement they had given to colonies they had sent out.

Thus, despite the general corruption, there remained enough strength in the Republic to withstand three setbacks that came upon her one after the other: the war of the Cimbri and the Teutons, the slave war, and the war of the gladiators. She got out of those three affairs all the more fortunately for having destroyed the Teutons virtually without resistance, and escaped the other two without altering her government; whereas in the Social War and the peace that followed, she altered it completely.[3]

[2195] Enumeration of the fleets of Licinius and Constantine: those of Licinius, stronger, possessing Egypt, which had 80 triremes; Phoenicia, 80; Ionia, Dorida, 60; Cyprus, 30; Caria, 20; Bithynia, 39. (Zosimus, p. 114.)[1]

[2196] According to Aulus Gellius (XIV, 18), when the Atinian Law permitted senators to be tribunes, that office, established to keep a rein on the Senate, lost its usefulness.[1]

[2197] CORRUPTION OF ROME. To elude the laws passed to preserve matrons' dignity, Vistilia (Tacitus, book II, p. 43) declared herself a public courtesan.[1] The law of Tiberius chased Roman ladies from that unworthy redoubt.

[2198] ON THE END OF THE WESTERN EMPIRE. What a state to be in,

---

3. The Social War (91–88 B.C.), by which the Italian allies (*socii*) of Rome received rights of Roman citizenship.—HC

[2195]
1. Zosimus: *Historia nova,* II.22 (see *pensée* 871a and n. 2).

[2196]
1. Aulus Gellius, *Attic Nights,* XIV. 8.

[2197]
1. Tacitus, *Annals,* II.85.

where one part of the territories was employed in maintaining armies that were entirely independent, and the other part in maintaining other armies to contain the first.

[2199] It was the custom of the kings of Macedonia to transfer peoples from one area of their state to another; this is because that state had been formed of diverse pieces. Look at what Justin says here (book VIII, page 77) on the transfer of peoples by Philip, Alexander's father. Look also, in Titus-Livy, at those made by Philip, Perseus's father.[1] It was the same taste, same policy and design. (Extract from the *Universal History*.)

[2200] It was no longer a question of military glory. The Emperors, busy in Rome having those who were odious to them condemned, feared the least sign of eminent virtue. Along those lines, therefore, they removed as much as they could from the substance of the triumphs. Thus, one sees only defensive wars, or else they are halted as soon as they become offensive. Even the generals hardly cared anymore about military glory. That could only lead them to obtain triumphal ornaments, and that honor was so often inaptly denied and inaptly granted—it was granted to so many people, especially those unworthy of it—that people scarcely cared about it anymore. Moreover, Caesar's procurators having increased their power, they now interfered with the generals in their enterprises. I am convinced that this policy of the Emperors, from the victories of Germanicus on through many generations, was the reason why the Barbarians behind the Danube and the Rhine recovered their forces and multiplied in a big way.[1]

[2201] After defeating the Barbarians, Franks, Burgundians, and Vandals, Probus sent some of them to England,[1] who established themselves there and afterward performed good services for the Romans.[2]

Probus placed the Bastarnae in Thrace. They were a Scythian nation he had defeated, who kept faith and were always Romans. This is because he did it in the Empire's prime, and with plenty of precautions.[3]

[2199]
1. Justin, *Histories,* VIII.5; Titus-Livy, *History of Rome,* XL.3.

[2200]
1. Germanicus (15 B.C.–A.D. 19), Roman general, brother of the emperor Tiberius.

[2201]
1. Marcus Aurelius Probus, Roman emperor (276–82).
2. "Zosimus, book I, p. 390" (M.). See Zosimus, *Historia nova,* I.68.
3. "Zosimus, book I, *in fine*" (M.).

[**2202**] We are surprised that the Roman consuls, who were replaced every year, were such great men and such great heroes.[1] It was similar to our secretaries of State: good offices and good secretaries; likewise with them, good captains of the cohort and the legion, good leaders of the line.[2]

[**2203**] The usefulness of the academies is that through them, knowledge is more diffused. Whoever has made some discovery or found out some secret is led to publish it—whether to deposit it in the archives, or to reap the glory from it and even increase his fortune. Before, the learned were more secretive.

[**2204**] I have the materials ready to make a comparison between Arrian and Quintus Curtius.

[**2205**] INOCULATION FOR SMALLPOX. One scarred man will make more of an impression than a hundred successes. One needs to know how to calculate. This is what should decide most things in life.

[**2206**] My friend and protector in England, the late Duke of Montaigu—he was like those stones from which you extract fire,[1] but that remain cold.[2]

[**2207**] Politics, as it exists today, comes from the invention of the postal service.[1]

[**2208**] If I had the honor of being pope, I would send all the masters of ceremonies packing, and would prefer to be a man than a God.

[**2209**] A fine temple would be the one erected to obstinacy.

[**2210**] When one wants to talk nonsense[1] to women, one must speak not to the ear but to the imagination.

[2202]

1. See *Considerations,* I, 26, as well as *Laws,* 11.13–14, for more on the consuls.

2. See also *pensée* 2244.

[2206]

1. The reference is to the medicinal use of cauterizing stones, a use that appeared as late as the 1798 *DAF.*—HC

2. John, the duke of Montagu (1688–1749). Montesquieu had met him during his stay in London; see Robert Shackleton, *Montesquieu: A Critical Biography* (London: Oxford University Press, 1961), 123–24; see also Montesquieu's comments about him in letters to Martin Ffolkes on July 13, 1739, and November 10, 1742 (*OC,* 3:994 and 1025).

[2207]

1. Also on this theme, see *Considerations,* XXI, 198–99, and *pensées* 8 and 77.—HC

[2210]

1. *Dire des sottises* can also be colloquial for speaking lewdly or impertinently.—HC

[2211] The vices have helped countless people make their fortune. I would ask only that they be impartial.

[2212] An archbishop of Albi and of Auch, a bishop of Condom and of Comminges, are people whose exile one pays for.

[2213] I remember the King in his youth. He had no other passion but to work to death five or six horses a week, and there were complaints about it.

[2214] Of two parties, the one made up of those who do not go with the flow is normally the better one.

[2215] "Extremely amorous people," someone said, "are normally discreet."

[2216] How splendid to be an army general—at sixty, it is said of him that he is young.

[2217] I want to do a book *de Stultitia Nebulonum.*[1]

[2218] The Protestant[1] and the Catholic think in the same fashion about the Eucharist. The only thing needed is for them not to ask each other how Jesus Christ is in it.

[2219] They are quite a ridiculous sex, those women.

[2220] The Spanish and the Portuguese are still in tutelage in Europe.

[2221] In young women, beauty substitutes for wit; in old women, wit substitutes for beauty.

[2222] Nothing approaches the ignorance of French courtiers except that of Italian ecclesiastics.

[2223] Cardinal Richelieu, better subject than citizen; still a bad subject, for he sacrificed the Prince for himself when necessary.

[2224] From all the panegyrics and all the inscriptions, all that follows is the time they were made in.

[2225] An ill-placed wig normally leaves no one ill-placed with the public. Small quirks are forgiven; one is only punished for large ones.

[2226] People talk a lot about the experience of old age. Old age takes from us the follies and vices of youth, but it gives us nothing.

[2227] On the servility of Louis XIV's courtiers, I said: "A certain phi-

[2217]
1. *On the Folly of Knaves.*—HC

[2218]
1. First version: "Huguenot"—HC

losophy, widespread in our time, has it that our grandees nowadays are perhaps more knavish, but they are not as wretched."

[**2228**] I was saying that I'm not enough of a great lord to be out of cash and not know what to do about it.

[**2229**] I ask of my Country neither pensions nor honors nor distinctions. I find myself amply rewarded by the air that I breathe there; I would merely like for it not to be polluted.

[**2230**] I wrote: "I go into my forests to seek tranquillity and a calm and peaceful life; but my heart tells me you were in Paris or in Lunéville, and then my woods have nothing more to tell me."[1]

[**2231**] THE AMBITIOUS. Their ambition is like the horizon, which is always moving before them.

[**2232**] A certain M. Le Prêtre,[1] who has 500,000 pounds in annual income, won a ticket for 50,000 fr. in the Lottery. I said: "I wish that good-for-nothing had died of pleasure."

[**2233**] I said Voltaire was a general taking all his yokel army valets under his protection.

[**2234**] Lacon always makes his tasteless remarks against himself;[1] Voltaire, against others.

[**2235**] Voltaire has a plagiaristic imagination. It never sees anything if it has not been shown a side of it.

[**2236**] I cannot bear those people who win constant triumphs over others' modesty. {The insolent}

[**2237**] I will say of money what used to be said of Caligula, that there has never been such a good slave and such a wicked master.[1]

[**2238**] Money is very respectable when it is scorned.

[**2239**] Someone was talking to me about the idiotic criticism of the *Esprit des lois* by the farmer-general M. Dupin. I said, "I never argue with

[2230]
1. Montesquieu had spent time at the court of Stanislas Leczinski in Lunéville in June 1747; he sings its praises in a letter to Maupertuis at the end of that month (*OC*, 3:1089).

[2232]
1. This may be a generic reference to a priest (*prêtre*).—HC

[2234]
1. The allusion may be to Charles-Marie de La Condamine (1701–74), mathematician and fellow of London's Royal Society (1748).

[2237]
1. Suetonius, *Life of Caligula*, X.

farmers-general when it is a question of money, nor when it is a question of *esprit.*"[1]

[2240] I said: "I do not want to abandon the affairs we have for those we give ourselves."

[2241] I said: "I do not have time to get involved in my works; I have resigned them into the hands of the public."

[2242] I have only two more matters of business: one, to know how to be sick; the other, to know how to die.

[2243] I said of Voltaire: "Beware of dying your anecdotes' martyr, or your poetry's confessor."

[2244] CONTINUATION OF MATERIALS FROM THE "ROMANS." The triumphs in which the Roman People saw the images of so many unfamiliar kings pass before them were far from being as sweet to them as those in which, with the pleasure furnished by hatred, they saw the horde of Volsci passing by or the Samnites' broken weapons being carried.[1]

[2245] MATERIALS FROM ESSAYS FOR THE BORDEAUX ACADEMY, WHICH ARE NOT WORTHY OF APPEARING. I had written an essay for the Bordeaux Academy on animal gods.[1] It was worthless. Here is what I have pulled from it:

"Varro, great theologian, acknowledged three sorts of divinity: celestial gods, human gods, and animal gods.

"Labeo, often cited by Macrobius (he hardly talked about anything but the Penates gods and the human gods), had written many books about animal gods. His system was that there were certain sacrifices by means of which human souls were changed into gods called *animals,* because they had been such." (See Lilius Giraldus, page 85.)[2]

[2239]

1. Farmer-general Claude Dupin (1680–1769) had vigorously attacked Montesquieu in his *Réflexions sur quelques parties d'un livre intitulé de "l'Esprit des lois"* [Reflections on some parts of a book entitled *The Spirit of the Laws*] (Paris, 1749), of which one copy remains, in the Bibliothèque de l'Arsenal (Jur. 29 Rés). Realizing he had lacked composure and had been too personal in his attacks on Montesquieu, Dupin recalled from his friends the eight copies that he had had printed. In 1750, he published a toned-down version, with a print run of five hundred copies, of the pamphlet *Observations sur un livre intitulé de "l'Esprit des lois."* See also *pensées* 1572, 1643, and 1877 for Dupin.

[2244]

1. See *pensée* 2202; on the Roman triumphs, see *Considerations,* I, 24, 27.

[2245]

1. The essay referred to is known only by this extract.

2. Marcus Antistius Laveo (43 B.C.–A.D. 22), Roman jurisconsult; Ambrosius Macrobius Theodosius, early fifth-century Latin grammarian, *In Somnium Scipionis* [The dream of Scipio] (see *Catalogue,* 1912–13, for the 1548 and 1607 editions).

"Duris (Samian), Tzetzes, and Pausanias sully the best-established reputation that exists in Antiquity. (It's Penelope.) Mercury, who entered her palace disguised as a billy goat, made her Pan's mother.[3] He established his dominion in the forests. His subjects were shepherds who, regarding themselves as the only men and their cabins as the only cities in the world, also regarded him as the God of all nature.

"This opinion runs strongly counter to the chronology. Thus, let us not deny women a model that does them honor; great exemplars should be respected. The birth of Pan does not belong to historical time, and the gods were fully made by the time of the siege of Troy."

In my essay, I said that "all these troops of Satyrs, which the earliest men took for gods, and which the historians then took for peoples, were merely monkey-goats," and I cited Nicephorus (book IX, *Ecclesiastical History*) and Philostorgius (book III), who inform us that "there are many types of monkey in Africa and Arabia, which are related to many animals: the monkey-lion, the monkey-bear, the monkey-goat (*aegophithecus*).[4]

"The cult of Pan diminished as men lost their taste for the rustic life. He declined along with his worshippers. The Arcadians confused Jupiter with Pan. Pausanias says Lycaon dedicated the Lupercalia to Jupiter; thus, Jupiter and Pan were the same thing to them.[5]

"According to Ovid, Pan kissed Diana so brutally that from this arose the spots one perceives on the Moon.[6] The Mohammedan doctors say that the angel Gabriel, flying near the Moon, rubbed against it so roughly with one of his wings that he gave it those black marks that we see. The Indian Doctors, who emit horrible cries during a lunar eclipse in order to frighten the Dragon that is going to devour it, no doubt think these spots are scratches from that animal's claws.

3. Duris, from the isle of Samos; John Tzetzes, twelfth-century Byzantine poet and scholar (see *Catalogue*, 2724, for his *Book of histories*); Mercury, Roman god of merchants and voyagers (Hermes in Greek); Pan, god of Arcadian shepherds and of fecundity; Montesquieu may have been influenced by the article "Penelope" in Bayle's *Historical and Critical Dictionary.*

4. Nicephorus, patriarch of Constantinople from 806 to 815, author of a *History of the Greek Empire from 602 to 709* and the *Ecclesiastical History* (*Catalogue*, 245, lists the 1586 edition); Montesquieu had the *Ecclesiastical History* by Philostorgius the Arian (368–439) in a Latin 1642 edition (*Catalogue*, 254).

5. Lycaon, Arcadian king who had cut the throat of a child on Zeus's altar, or offered him as a meal to Zeus, who struck him down with his fifty children; the Lupercales were the festivals celebrated in Rome each February 15 in honor of Lupercus, the god of shepherds, in which young people went through the city lashing the crowd with a whip made of the skin of animals offered up in sacrifice. (See Plutarch's "Life of Caesar" for one description.) See *Laws*, 24.15.

6. Diana, one of the most ancient divinities, worshipped by the Latins and, as Artemis, by the Greeks.

"Evander brought the cult of Pan to Italy.[7] He was a shepherd, for he was an Arcadian. All mythologists form, as it were, two sects: some, more attached to the letter, distinguish all the divinities and multiply them; others, more subtle, relate them all and simplify them.[8] Thus, although Faunus had reigned in Latium, and his father had reigned there, and his ancestor Saturn had transferred the dominion to his descendants,[9] a certain similarity with Pan made him lose his Country, his realm, and it happened that he was annihilated in the imaginations of people who wanted to bend history to do honor to myth. Thus, although afterward the same festivals were decreed for them, I believe one was from Arcadia and the other was an Ausonian[10] prince.

"Plutarch says that Antony had himself pulled in a chariot, completely naked, by forty ladies, also completely naked.[11] These despicable ceremonies were only abolished in 496, under Theodoric in Italy, by Pope Gelasius—and even then with some difficulty, according to Onuphrius and Baronius."[12]

I began my essay this way: "Since one must not deceive anyone, I am obliged to serve notice that there may not be a word of truth in anything I am going to say.

"There is a void in the earliest times that everyone has agreed to fill. Hesiod, Homer, Virgil, Ovid—the least grave authors there are—are as valued in their domain as other writers.

"The *Penates Gods,* so called when they were good spirits, and *Lemuria* when they were bad spirits.

"Perhaps the book Aristotle wrote on animal gods, according to Servius, contained a system similar to that of Labeo.

"It was thought that these animal gods had great knowledge of the future, and this, linked with the power to do harm, constituted their entire

---

7. Evander, legendary prince of Latium, which he was said to have civilized; he introduced the festival of the Lupercales.

8. See *pensée* 2253.

9. Faunus, Roman divinity with a cult localized on the Palatine, protector of shepherds and flocks; his cult involved the procession of the Lupercales; Saturn, Italic and Roman god identified with the Greek Chronos, god of sowing and of the vine; the Saturnales were celebrated in his honor.

10. Ausonian, a poetic name for ancient Italy.—HC

11. See *Spicilège,* 66.

12. Pope Gelasius I (492–96); Onuphrius, hermit saint (d. 400) who lived near Thebes in Egypt and whose life was recounted by Saint Paphnutius; Cardinal Cesare Baronius (1538–1607), disciple of Saint Philip of Neri.

divinity—for they were not, by the way, thought to be immortal. They were subject to death, like men; they had ages; they grew old. The Satyrs, in their old age, were called *Silenuses;* it is Pausanias who informs us of this.[13]

"There is no animal more susceptible of variation than the monkey; *etenim, propter salacitatem, omnia cujusvis speciei animalia appetunt.*[14]

"By one of those points of honor much in use among the gods, there was a debate between Apollo and Pan on musical know-how. Midas was chosen as arbiter between the inventor of the flute and the inventor of the lyre."[15]

[2246] VARIOUS MATERIALS. M. Raulin had asked me to write him a dedicatory epistle for the Duke of Richelieu.[1] I did that, but since it was not respectful enough, I did not give it to him.

"I would like to dedicate my work to a great man. Not to the one who managed to assure the liberty of an allied republic; nor who at Fontenoy summoned back the Victory that was about to slip away; nor who, sent into Languedoc, was the conciliator of all minds;[2] still less to the one whom (as has been said in our provinces) a fairy, who presided over his birth, forbade to love, and commanded to please; but to the one who knows and protects the sciences and arts and who grants my own a special grace. May he cast some encouraging glance my way. I was reading in the poets that the gods sometimes descend to earth and communicate with mortals."

[2247] In France, there are three opinions on the Bull:[1] the first belongs to those who believe it to be a law of the Church and the State; the second, those who regard the Bull as a rule of faith and grant it the greatest

---

13. Satyrs were divinities of field and forest in Greek myth and were identified with the fauns by the Romans; *Silens* was a generic name for old Satyrs.

14. "[I]n fact, because of their lasciviousness, they desire all species of animals."

15. Midas, king of Phrygia in the eighth century B.C.

[2246]

1. Joseph Raulin, who dedicated his 1754 *Observations de médecine* [Observations on medicine] to Louis-François-Armand de Vignerot du Plessis, Duke of Richelieu (1696–1788) and at that time Marshal of France.

2. The "allied republic" is Genoa, which Marshal Richelieu liberated from the Austrians in August 1748—to thank him, the republic inscribed him in its golden book of Genoese nobles; the Battle of Fontenoy (1745) was won thanks to a fortunate diversion by Richelieu; as governor of Languedoc, Richelieu was able to reconcile the Protestants.

[2247]

1. *Unigenitus* (1713); cf. *pensées* 273, 426, 914, 1170, 1226, and 2158.

authority that exists on earth; the third, those who regard it as a decree that is bad in itself, which condemns things that are good in themselves. The first opinion is that of virtually all magistrates and wise, enlightened theologians. Those who hold the other two opinions are certainly not going to have a meeting of the minds. These are the people who have engaged in combat for forty years, and who are going to groan under the law of silence.

One says to the first combatants: "The Bull is not a rule of faith, because a decree cannot have more authority than the legislator himself intended to give it. It is not by a lack of power in the Legislator that it is not a rule of faith, but because the nature of the thing opposes it." One says to the second: "It is not doubted that the Church can remove from the hands of the faithful a book it deems dangerous, and it is not impossible for truths to be placed in a book with such art that they lead to errors."

These two parties have fought to the death, and what has done the harm is that there are invisible champions who have entered the lists—there are quite a few Rogers who have fought as soldiers of Leo.[2]

Today, the theologians seem to be quitting. The question is changing. What agitated people for forty years no longer agitates them. For a year, it has been only a jurisdictional question. Perhaps it is fortunate that things are turning in this direction, and perhaps it is easier to decide this dispute than the other, because this dispute concerns dogma less than it does formalities.

Theologians are like those birds one sends fishing, for which, after having the fish stopped in their gullet by a ring, one substitutes a gudgeon.[3]

[2248] It seems evident from *The Thousand and One Nights* (volume IV, *History of Ganem, son of Abou-Ajoub, surnamed "the Slave of Love,"* page 364) that in the Orient, jealousy takes little offense if a woman loves someone she has seen, and that it is offended only by the insult that a man would commit by enjoying another's wife or mistress. Here Torment is content to absolve Ganem, who had respected her and had said that whatever belongs to the master is sacred for the slave. After which, without the

---

2. Probably Roger d'Hautville, the Norman commander who began the decades-long expulsion of the Muslims from Sicily in the 1050s after defeating Pope Leo IX at the battle of Civitate in 1053. The victors professed their loyal submission while holding the Pontiff in honorable captivity; the Pope died a year later.—HC

3. See *pensée* 2176 for this image.—HC

caliph asking her to, she said she had conceived a love for Ganem, which the caliph did not disapprove, and he pardoned Ganem and told Torment he decreed that he marry her.[1]

[**2249**] PERSIAN LETTERS. When that work appeared, it was not regarded as a serious work. It was not serious. People forgave two or three rash statements for the sake of a conscience that was entirely exposed, and that was bringing criticism to bear on everything and venom on nothing. Every reader bore witness inside himself. He remembered only its gaiety. People got upset in the past as they get upset today. But in the past, they knew better when to get upset.[1]

[**2250**] TREATISE ON THE BEAUTIFUL. Vitruvius says that public and private affairs so occupy everyone in Rome that there are few individuals who have the leisure to read a book unless it is quite short.[1] I might say that in our capital, everyone is so busy with the multitude of pastimes that they do not have time to read.

[**2251**] Persecution, it's a tightly twisted rope; the force is concentrated.

APPENDIX[1]

[**2252**] Put in my *Reflections*. Other. [What I said in my last letter makes me think our mores are no longer capable of good poetry. The poetic spirit is not lacking in us, but our mores and our religion lack the poetic spirit.]

[**2248**]
1. See *pensées* 719 and 757.

[**2249**]
1. This passage was to be included in "Some reflections on the *Persian letters*," published in the posthumous edition of 1757; cf. Vernière, 3–5.

[**2250**]
1. Marcus Vitruvius Pollio (first century B.C.), author of *On Architecture* (see *Catalogue,* 1717–21, for Montesquieu's holdings).

[**Appendix**]
1. The *Pensées* proper end with *pensée* 2251. The appendix that follows is composed of fragments unedited by Montesquieu that were found in the archives of La Brède castle in 1950 by Xavier Védère and Louis Desgraves. They are included in this edition because it seems reasonable to regard them, as M. Desgraves did, as forming part of the same enterprise as the *Pensées*. For *pensées* 2252 and 2253, this edition draws also on the more recent transcription contained in *OC* Volt, 1:592–97. It should be noted that there is no reason to regard these items as dating toward the end of Montesquieu's life in the 1750s, as the last *pensées* proper do; if anything, the reverse seems to be true (see *pensées* 2255, 2256, and 2258, though also *pensée* 2266 for a later one).—HC

I called upon the copy of the last letter I wrote to a man from this country. Here is how he answered me:

"I so strongly approve of your ideas that I beg permission to add and develop the thoughts that came to me in reading your letter.

"I am persuaded that good poetry was extinguished with paganism. They were born together; they were made for each other. The former's extravagance made all the latter's digressions reasonable.

"The poetic spirit is not lacking in us, but our mores and our religion lack the poetic spirit.

"How to impart a sense of wonder to people filled with the idea of those incorporeal beings that govern the universe, and that leave nothing to the imagination—or the idea of a lone being that leaves it an amazing void?

"How to arouse people by means of those agents that always conduct themselves with wisdom and are subject to none of the passions it is claimed they stir up?

"The pagan gods, subject to the passions of men, always acted in a manner that moved the imagination. The manner in which they governed had something animated about it, something that made itself felt.

"We like to have a visible government. We like to see the connection between the gods and us men. It is flattering [and elevates human nature] to find all our weaknesses in them, and to see them distinguished from mortals only by their power.

"We like on the other hand to see men's virtue; it would appear less wondrous in the gods.

"Other. Thus, the pedant's notion that Homer gave the gods the imperfections of men and men the perfections of the gods speaks well of that great poet, since he had thereby found the only means of filling spirit with amazement and matter with wonder.

"And if it is true that Homer, merely as a theologian, adjusted his gods to poetry in this way in order to be a poet, this was great genius, since he found the sole religion that could be wedded with poetry and lend it new charms.

"In any case, I think one can say that a work of passable poetry will never be written except on the basis of Homer's ideas.

"I am certain that Milton's *Paradise Lost* succeeded only in those passages where he imitated Homer, that is, in the passions he gave his demons.[1] But even on that score, how far inferior it is to Homer.

"The divine work of this age, that *Telemachus* in which Homer seems to come alive, is irrefutable proof of the excellence of that ancient poet.[2]

"I am not among those who regard Homer as the father and master of all the sciences. That praise is ridiculous for any author, but it is absurd for a poet. Mme Dacier has done Homer harm by the ardor with which she defended him. She placed on the same side the defects of her sex and all of Homer's defects, and thus fought at a disadvantage."

[The translation by M. de La Motte does credit to Homer.[3] One reads it with pleasure. Nonetheless, Mme Dacier has quite well demonstrated that his verse could have been better at presenting the pleasing beauty of the original, which was labored in the copy.]

[2253] [Fragment of a *Persian letter.*]

USBEK

There is hardly any illumination on ancient history to be derived from Western books.[1] There is a void in the earliest times[2] that everyone has agreed to fill. The ruins themselves have perished, and yet one must build.

When history is missing, one substitutes myths. It's like in those poor countries, where one is obliged to accept the lightest currency. The poets become grave authors, and in their domain they are as valued as the most judicious historians.

This is not the history of men, but of the gods. These gods change into

[2252]
1. Montesquieu owned the 1711 and 1725 English editions of Milton's work (*Catalogue,* 2099–2100).
2. See *pensée* 115.
3. Mme Dacier's translations of the *Iliad* and the *Odyssey* came out in 1709, La Motte's of the *Iliad* in 1714 (see *Catalogue,* 2058–60).

[2253]
1. See *pensée* 2245.
2. First version: "The western histories are not more certain than ours. The truth is as modern for them as it is for us."

heroes as the times become less rude. These heroes have only men for children because children are seen at a closer distance than fathers—there you see mythic time ending and historical time beginning.

One cannot say in what chaos the historical ages found the history and generation of the gods. The mythologists formed, as it were, two different sects, as opposed in their opinions as in the spirit that guided them. Some, more attached to the letter, distinguish all the divinities, without being offended by their multiplicity. Others, more subtle, always want to simplify and mix them up together.

The poets were of the first kind, the philosophers of the second,[3] but precious little philosophy was involved in taking on the laborious task of making superstition a system and reducing to order what was constantly being scrambled by the digressions of the poets, the whims of the painters, the avarice of the priests, and the prodigious fecundity of the superstitious. But this was not the only branch of that immortal trial. The ones, being cruder, wanted to take everything literally; the others, more subtle, take everything as an allegory and relate everything to morality and natural science.

The rebel philosophers wanted to restrict that prodigious number of divinities, which had come to include abstract names of substances, but what great difference was there between those who animated all of nature and the theologians who divinized it completely?[4]

[During this time, the historians did not stop playing an equally ridiculous role. They had neither enough knowledge to evaluate the difference, nor enough good sense not to . . .]

[2254] Pufendorf was assigned by the Court of Berlin to write a book: *De rebus gestis Frederici Guillelmi electoris brandeburgensis,* Berolini, 1693, fol.[1] Many things were cut in the printing, but in that of 1695 they let slip this fact: that the Elector, miffed at several speeches by Liliehoeckus, Swedish envoy to the Senate of Poland, said these speeches would merit

---

3. First version: "There is pleasure, and even taste in seeing the immortal trial that reigns up there between the philosophers and the poets. The former reduce everything, the latter multiply without end. The former, more crude, take everything literally, the latter, more subtle, take everything as allegory and relate everything to morality and natural science."

4. Compare this passage to *pensée* 1603.

[2254]

1. *On the Achievements of Frederick William the Elector of Brandenburg.* Also known as the Great Elector, he was concurrently the duke of Prussia (r. 1640–88).—HC. The work is not in Montesquieu's *Catalogue.*

a caning; upon which, the envoy made a speech to the Senate of Poland, declaring that if the Elector had him caned, he would cane him back. The Elector wrote a long letter about it to the King of Sweden, who gave him no redress. This is on p. 1134.

[2255] [In the Paris census of 1726, they found 18,209 baptisms, 3,245 weddings, 19,252 deaths, 2,571 abandoned children.]

[2256] A book: *The reason of the Laws of England.*[1]

[2257] The remonstrances of our Estates in France are called grievances.[1] The cities of Austria also have no voice in the Estates, and go there only in the capacity of patient cities—that is to say, as bearing burdens.

[2258] 1728. The sinking fund in England can go along every year at twelve hundred thousand pounds sterling. At first, it was at four hundred thousand. By the reduction from 6 to 5 percent, it increased next by the reduction from 5 to 4 percent and by the cancellation of interest on debts paid. At present, in 1728, the government is borrowing a million sterling from the bank and five hundred thousand pounds from the Duchess of Marlborough at 3 percent interest.[1]

[2259] A falcon that is missing a feather flies half as much, especially if it is an upper feather. You fix it with an iron needle rubbed with garlic; the rust prevents the iron tip you have put in the feather's quill, as well as the quill that receives the feather, from being removed.

[2260] [Painting. The oppositions, the contrasts, the group, the whole ensemble. French painters give all their portraits a foppish air. The Flemish represent fat Venuses like fat Flemish women. French architects put in too many windows.]

[2261] [Too many ornaments make for a very bad style. This is where the gothic sins; then you cannot see the ensemble. The variety creates a uniformity in that nothing can be distinguished.]

[2256]
1. Montesquieu writes the title in English. The reference is probably to Giles Jacob (1686–1744), *The Student's Companion; or, The reason of the laws of England: Shewing, the principal reasons and motives whereon our laws and statutes are grounded, in the most essential and capital points, not only in civil but criminal cases; together with the law it self. So as to convey to all students, and others, the fundamental knowledge of the law, necessary in their studies* (London: T. Corbett, 1725).—HC

[2257]
1. On the origin of the Estates-General, see *Laws*, 28.9, 544.

[2258]
1. Sarah Jennings, duchess of Marlborough (1660–1744), favorite of Queen Anne.

[2262] If I want to have a pension, I will have it.

[2263] Voyage, representation of States—we will grab the conveniences that are there, we will dispense with the others.

[2264] Bonneval.[1] It is said that his disgrace came from many causes. For aside from his reconciliation in France, he got conned at Peterwaradin and joined the party of those who quite inopportunely thwarted Prince Eugene.[2] And when it was time to emerge from the lines, instead of building the passage directly across from the enemy as was ordered, they made their escape in a sort of diagonal, which meant that not everything happened in synch and there were some who were delayed. [This should be set straight by Bonneval's Memoir; he was not in the lines.] But victory resolved everything and restored the indulgence of the Prince who, nonetheless, had been quite angry. "They will oblige me," he would say, "to make them feel my authority." (3) Finally, the business about the Marquis of Prié,[3] Bonneval had asked him to see about having him receive the governorship of Charleroi. The marquis promised it but did just the opposite, and even represented the danger of giving a Frenchman such a fortified place in the vicinity of France. His business could have been smoothed over. He had only to avoid passing through Holland (following the order he had) and come to present himself. That Court is very mild and a sort of satisfaction would have gotten him out of the affair. He has no secret pension from the Emperor.[4] He did badly to write, as he did, to Prince Eugene. His Venetian generalship was marked by the deceptiveness of Schulembourg, who, his term expired, went off to the countryside without saying whether he intended to quit or not.[5] The nobles who were not absolutely in Bonneval's camp said: one cannot dismiss M. de Schulemburg without knowing whether he intends to quit or not. To the delegation sent to him, he said he was quite content to remain, and he likewise acquiesced in the cutback in appointments.

[2264]

1. On Bonneval and his relations with Montesquieu in Italy, see *pensée* 383n.

2. The Battle of Peterwaradin was waged by the Austrians against the Turks on August 5, 1716; cf. *Voyages* (*OC*, 2:994). In Venice, Bonneval confided his account of it to Montesquieu and wrote to him about it on October 2, 1728 (*OC*, 3:915).

3. Hercule Joseph Louis Turinetti, marquis of Prié (1660–1736), whom Montesquieu met at Vienna and at Turin; cf. *Voyages* (*OC*, 2:1036 and 1046).

4. Charles VI, emperor of Austria (r. 1711–40).

5. Johann-Matthias von Schulemburg (1661–1747), commander of Venetian land forces during the siege of Corfu by the Turks in 1716; cf. *Spicilège*, 622.

[**2265**] The difference in Talents.[1] The nature of the land contributes much to the difference in talents. Most French provinces have below the surface a kind of white chalk called marl, with which the land is covered to fertilize it. Marl is full of volatile spirits, which enter our blood both by the nourishment of the things that grow and the nutrients we feed on, and by the air that we breathe and that is mixed in with them. And this cannot be doubted, since we find iron in men's bodies and in honey. Now such volatiles, once in the air, must produce some effect there. The effect is that fickleness, inconstancy, and vivacity of the French. What helps to prove it is that Crete has a similar land, whence it has been called Crêta. Now the Cretans, somewhat like the French, are careless with the truth;[2] witness a passage from Saint Paul drawn from Epimenides, which is said to be accurate.[3]

English soil is land that is black, metallic, arsenical. The air and the food that is permeated by it have particles.

. . . the nerves and the membranes and that cause the English to be lovers of scuffles and quarrels, capricious. [Thus, in the histories, we see battles between birds rushing through the air, which scientists attribute to a particular tendency of the air that pricks their follies.]

The earth of Italy (especially the Papal State) is a *pozzuolana,* sulfurous; it is what makes the Italians bilious. There is a pozzolana[4] earth that hardens like tile and still preserves its tendencies. It is for this reason that the Italians are profound, constant in their loves and in their enmities, and never forgive, since the blood retains the tendency that it had, and the brain as well.

This must be highlighted as much as possible.

[**2266**] The Parlement is slave to the letter of the law.[1] Monarchies do

---

[2265]

1. This fragment of *La Différence des génies* [Difference in talents] is a 1717 essay that Montesquieu used in writing the *Essay on the causes that can affect minds and characters* (*OC,* 3:397–430). See also *pensées* 1191–92.

2. *Léger,* literally, light-minded, frivolous, thoughtless.—HC

3. Probably a reference to Paul's Letter to Titus, 1:12, where he cites another Cretan (Epimenides) as saying, "Cretans are always liars."—HC

4. The second usage is French (pouzolane); the first, Italian. It is a hydraulic cement used in bridge construction by the Romans and again starting in seventeenth-century France.

[2266]

1. Autograph page with a 1742 watermark.

not have an appointed day; they are the work of generations. The laws are their warp and woof, and their foundation. They are the work of each monarch, and the laws of a monarchy are the wills of all the monarchs who have reigned.[2] One will cannot destroy all the wills, but each will is the complement of all. Each monarch must add to this work because the work is never finished. Perfect today, tomorrow it is imperfect, because it is subject to time like other things in the universe, because it is subject to circumstance like all other things in the universe, because each society of men is an action, composed of the action of all minds. The intellectual world, as much in movement as the physical world, changes like the physical world.

It is the Parlement that knows all the laws made by all the monarchs, that has learned their sequence, that has known their spirit. It knows whether a new law perfects or corrupts the immense volume of other laws, and it says: things are thus, it is from there that you must begin; otherwise, you ruin the whole work. It says to the Prince, you are a legislator, but you are not all the legislators; you do indeed have all the laws executed, but you have not made all the laws. They were before you, they are with you, they will be after you. You have added your will to that of all the others, and your successors will respect your will in the same way. You will be in the body, you will make up a part of it, and you will be subject only to the Empire of time.

2. See *Laws,* 5.10, for this theme.

Thematic Table

THE FIRST PRINTED EDITION of the *Pensées,* brought out by the Genevan law professor Henri Barckhausen in two volumes from 1899 to 1901, has set the standard for the enumeration of the individual items. Although Montesquieu himself had begun the compilation by numbering the entries, he soon discontinued the practice. Since there was not always space separating the treatment of one topic from that of another, it was not always obvious where one entry was to end and another begin. With the help of a very few adjustments (see *pensées* 871 and 1631), later editors have managed to count the same number of entries as Barckhausen himself did (2,251), thereby greatly facilitating comparison between the editions.

The Genevan editor also, however, rearranged the entries completely, so instead of appearing in the order in which Montesquieu had placed them in his notebooks, they are presented under topical rubrics of Barckhausen's own devising. This practice, while adopted in the widely used Pléiade edition of Roger Callois in 1949–51, and in Daniel Oster's 1964 Intégrale edition for Seuil, has not been followed in the Desgraves editions of 1950 and 1991, in the critical edition currently in preparation by French editors, or in the present volume. One reason for Barckhausen's decision had been to help readers avoid the disorientation arising from Montesquieu's entirely nonsequential pattern of entries. In that spirit, the present volume, following Desgraves's practice in *OC* 2:1359–68 (i.e., the 1950 edition), reproduces the thematic organization contained in the original 1899–1901 edition.

Barckhausen deliberately left out a number of *pensées,* leaving his edition with 2,204 entries rather than the 2,251 that he himself had counted.[1] Although no effort is made in the present volume to situate these missing items within Barckhausen's system of topical rubrics, it will perhaps be useful to note that the omissions fall in four categories: First, the Genevan left out many of the entries that Montesquieu had deleted (see, in the present edition, *pensées* 62, 74, 91, 238, 262a, 267, 280, 418, 450, 555, 564 [in part], 565, 567, 570, 578, 601, 674, 679, 697, 732, 826, 874, 888, 964, 985, 1025, 1026, 1029, 1031 [in part], 1034, 1036, 1038, 1039, 1041, 1043–45, 1078, 1091, 1102, 1122, 1148, 1168, 1194, 1198, 1237, 1305, 1317, 1350, 1375, 1398, 1434,

---

1. For his reasoning, see *Pensées et fragments inédits de Montesquieu,* pub. Baron Gaston de Montesquieu, 2 vols. (Bordeaux: Gounouilhou, 1899–1901), 1:xxv–xxvi; for a full list of the changes, consult his Table de Concordance, 2:585–95.

1464, 1577, 1685, 1802, 1947, and 2034). Second, if Montesquieu repeated a comment in a later entry, or had included it in a longer entry earlier, Barckhausen sometimes omitted the second or the more isolated occurrence (*pensées* 770, 818, 827, 945, 1060, 1340, 1537, 1555, and 1673). Third, he omitted some of the entries consisting merely of stand-alone foreign-language quotations or bibliographical references (*pensées* 298, 302, 861, and 929–31). And finally, he excised a few entries that he found to be in questionable taste and without redeeming philosophical value (see *pensées* 448, 548, 865, 1216, and 2107). All four of these categories of omissions were restored in the Desgraves editions, as they are in the present one.[2] It should also be noted that these changes did not adversely affect the capacity of later editors to follow Barckhausen's system of enumeration.

Since Montesquieu often discussed more than one topic in a given entry, since it is not always clear what the purpose or the topic of a particular entry is, and since Barckhausen's late nineteenth-century method of categorization is not likely to be identical to that of a typical later reader, the interested reader will want to use the following table with due prudence, supplementing it perhaps with the index to the present volume.

FOREWORD

1, 2, 3.

A. MONTESQUIEU

I. His Character: 213, 350, 378, 467, 475, 595, 660, 741, 794, 804, 973, 998, 1003, 1005, 1009, 1019, 1130, 1134, 1290, 1343, 1414, 1417, 1437, 1456, 1620, 1627, 2085, 2097, 2140, 2169, 2208
II. His Life: 217, 339, 444, 632, 656, 662, 762, 763, 879, 997, 1001, 1133, 1138, 1182, 1346, 1386, 1466, 1545, 1686, 1963, 1973, 1981, 2123, 2134–36, 2142, 2153, 2228–30, 2240, 2242
III. His Family: 5, 1236, 1344, 1659, 2170
IV. His Readings: 907, 909, 963, 1249, 2086, 2128
V. His Writings: 89, 412, 609, 764, 796, 837, 932, 936, 939, 1111, 1297, 1315, 1438, 1477, 1598, 1599, 1643, 1948, 1952, 2053, 2057, 2166, 2204, 2217, 2239, 2241

2. Whether deliberately or inadvertently, there is also one entry (*pensée* 2123 in the present edition) that Barckhausen placed under two different categories (*pensées* 49 and 1685 of his edition).

B. MONTESQUIEU'S KNOWN WORKS

C. MONTESQUIEU'S UNEDITED WORKS
AND WORK FRAGMENTS

F. PSYCHOLOGY

G. HISTORY

3. See the translator's note for this term.

H. EDUCATION, POLITICS, AND POLITICAL ECONOMY

I. PHILOSOPHY

Concordance

Since many readers over the years have become familiar with Montesquieu's *Pensées* through the original enumeration of Henri Barckhausen, as followed in the Pléiade edition and in Daniel Oster's 1964 Seuil edition, it seemed useful to compile a concordance, as the 1991 Desgraves edition had also done, between the original Barckhausen edition and the present one. In what follows, the first number cited is from the Barckhausen edition; the number in parentheses from the present edition. The abbreviation *Sp.* refers to material from the *Spicilège* that Barckhausen included in his edition of the *Pensées*. The number next to it refers to the number in Desgraves's 1991 edition of the Spicilège.

1 (1)	23 (378)	45 (217)	67 (2242)	89 (1438)	111 (2032)
2 (2)	24 (1134)	46 (1001)	68 (1236)	90 (1948)	112 (2033)
3 (3)	25 (1417)	47 (2134)	69 (5)	91 (932)	113 (1609)
4 (213)	26 (2208)	48 (2135)	70 (1659)	92 (1599)	114 (1610)
5 (973)	27 (1437)	49 (2123)	71 (1344)	93 (1598)	115 (1611)
6 (1003)	28 (1456)	50 (2136)	72 (2170)	94 (1643)	116 (1612)
7 (1005)	29 (1343)	51 (339)	73 (*Sp.* 561)	95 (1952)	117 (1613)
8 (1019)	30 (2085)	52 (997)	74 (*Sp.* 562)	96 (2239)	118 (1614)
9 (1620)	31 (2097)	53 (632)	75 (*Sp.* 563)	97 (2057)	119 (1615)
10 (350)	32 (2140)	54 (2153)	76 (*Sp.* 660)	98 (2166)	120 (1616)
11 (741)	33 (998)	55 (1138)	77 (963)	99 (2053)	121 (1617)
12 (595)	34 (2169)	56 (763)	78 (1249)	100 (936)	122 (1618)
13 (660)	35 (1973)	57 (762)	79 (909)	101 (1315)	123 (1619)
14 (794)	36 (1133)	58 (662)	80 (907)	102 (2241)	124 (95)
15 (804)	37 (1182)	59 (656)	81 (2086)	103 (89)	125 (356)
16 (467)	38 (879)	60 (1466)	82 (2128)	104 (796)	126 (357)
17 (1009)	39 (1686)	61 (1386)	83 (837)	105 (1111)	127 (358)
18 (1290)	40 (1981)	62 (1545)	84 (412)	106 (939)	128 (1655)
19 (1130)	41 (2228)	63 (1963)	85 (609)	107 (2204)	129 (173)
20 (1627)	42 (2229)	64 (444)	86 (1297)	108 (2217)	130 (299)
21 (475)	43 (1346)	65 (2142)	87 (764)	109 (1519)	131 (841)
22 (1414)	44 (2240)	66 (2230)	88 (1477)	110 (2249)	132 (842)

133 (1158)	173 (2196)	213 (1698)	253 (1798)	293 (1806)	333 (1892)
134 (572)	174 (2197)	214 (1762)	254 (1913)	294 (1851)	334 (1904)
135 (573)	175 (2198)	215 (1776)	255 (1912)	295 (1910)	335 (1778)
136 (574)	176 (2199)	216 (1914)	256 (1761)	296 (1901)	336 (1694)
137 (575)	177 (2200)	217 (1758)	257 (1858)	297 (1793)	337 (1800)
138 (576)	178 (2201)	218 (1923)	258 (1890)	298 (1846)	338 (1799)
139 (577)	179 (2202)	219 (1856)	259 (1818)	299 (1848)	339 (1883)
140 (579)	180 (2244)	220 (1845)	260 (1693)	300 (1878)	340 (1884)
141 (580)	181 (1191)	221 (1728)	261 (1850)	301 (1877)	341 (1885)
142 (673)	182 (1192)	222 (1702)	262 (1837)	302 (1882)	342 (1894)
143 (675)	183 (2035)	223 (1889)	263 (1735)	303 (1796)	343 (1886)
144 (676)	184 (1433)	224 (1915)	264 (1710)	304 (1730)	344 (1801)
145 (677)	185 (1874)	225 (1720)	265 (1756)	305 (1916)	345 (1803)
146 (678)	186 (1860)	226 (1833)	266 (1815)	306 (1838)	346 (1804)
147 (713)	187 (1861)	227 (1853)	267 (1879)	307 (1782)	347 (1713)
148 (714)	188 (1723)	228 (1898)	268 (1880)	308 (1909)	348 (1887)
149 (1478)	189 (1862)	229 (1701)	269 (1757)	309 (1789)	349 (1714)
150 (1479)	190 (1707)	230 (1896)	270 (1849)	310 (1788)	350 (1745)
151 (1480)	191 (1863)	231 (1925)	271 (1774)	311 (1816)	351 (1759)
152 (1532)	192 (1866)	232 (1760)	272 (1753)	312 (1742)	352 (1888)
153 (1532a)	193 (1865)	233 (1891)	273 (1725)	313 (1743)	353 (1690)
154 (1532b)	194 (1873)	234 (1854)	274 (1746)	314 (1716)	354 (1739)
155 (1669)	195 (1870)	235 (1893)	275 (1734)	315 (1839)	355 (1738)
156 (1670)	196 (1855)	236 (1917)	276 (1902)	316 (1847)	356 (1719)
157 (1671)	197 (1926)	237 (1908)	277 (1731)	317 (1722)	357 (1750)
158 (1672)	198 (1940)	238 (1744)	278 (1708)	318 (1903)	358 (1808)
159 (1674)	199 (1871)	239 (1899)	279 (1740)	319 (1911)	359 (1766)
160 (2183)	200 (1864)	240 (1768)	280 (1790)	320 (1827)	360 (1791)
161 (2184)	201 (1868)	241 (1771)	281 (1729)	321 (1775)	361 (1895)
162 (2185)	202 (1920)	242 (1772)	282 (1737)	322 (1717)	362 (1840)
163 (2186)	203 (1872)	243 (1709)	283 (1809)	323 (1724)	363 (1792)
164 (2187)	204 (1706)	244 (1857)	284 (1703)	324 (1785)	364 (1942)
165 (2188)	205 (1705)	245 (1836)	285 (1906)	325 (1787)	365 (1817)
166 (2189)	206 (1805)	246 (1741)	286 (1852)	326 (1907)	366 (1747)
167 (2190)	207 (1786)	247 (1823)	287 (1749)	327 (1921)	367 (1748)
168 (2191)	208 (1859)	248 (1824)	288 (1712)	328 (1732)	368 (1812)
169 (2192)	209 (1763)	249 (1935)	289 (1807)	329 (1736)	369 (1752)
170 (2193)	210 (1773)	250 (1905)	290 (1819)	330 (1867)	370 (1841)
171 (2194)	211 (1755)	251 (1897)	291 (1842)	331 (1936)	371 (1813)
172 (2195)	212 (1919)	252 (1797)	292 (1781)	332 (1924)	372 (1700)

373 (1715)	413 (1767)	453 (119)	493 (1221)	533 (1283)	573 (504)
374 (1844)	414 (1769)	454 (120)	494 (1222)	534 (2165)	574 (505)
375 (1779)	415 (1780)	455 (121)	495 (1234)	535 (2177)	575 (506)
376 (1834)	416 (1727)	456 (122)	496 (1311)	536 (1820)	576 (507)
377 (1843)	417 (1691)	457 (123)	497 (1646)	537 (237)	577 (508)
378 (1699)	418 (1733)	458 (124)	498 (2063)	538 (1642)	578 (509)
379 (1777)	419 (1941)	459 (125)	499 (1024)	539 (1183)	579 (1622)
380 (1711)	420 (1697)	460 (126)	500 (1027)	540 (2015)	580 (1630)
381 (1783)	421 (1721)	461 (127)	501 (1028)	541 (2246)	581 (1726)
382 (1784)	422 (1829)	462 (128)	502 (1030)	542 (1006)	582 (2009)
383 (1751)	423 (1832)	463 (129)	503 (1031)	543 (1262)	583 (1601)
384 (1810)	424 (1695)	464 (130)	504 (1032)	544 (1292)	584 (1602)
385 (1765)	425 (1696)	465 (131)	505 (1033)	545 (510)	585 (1603)
386 (1875)	426 (1828)	466 (132)	506 (1035)	546 (511)	586 (1604)
387 (1811)	427 (1830)	467 (133)	507 (1037)	547 (512)	587 (1605)
388 (1764)	428 (1928)	468 (134)	508 (1040)	548 (513)	588 (1606)
389 (1825)	429 (1929)	469 (135)	509 (1042)	549 (30)	589 (1607)
390 (1814)	430 (1930)	470 (2025)	510 (1046)	550 (31)	590 (1608)
391 (1900)	431 (1932)	471 (2026)	511 (1047)	551 (1675)	591 (2004)
392 (1770)	432 (1704)	472 (2027)	512 (1048)	552 (483)	592 (2245)
393 (1754)	433 (1831)	473 (2028)	513 (517)	553 (484)	593 (1184)
394 (1918)	434 (2052)	474 (2029)	514 (1093)	554 (485)	594 (1962)
395 (1835)	435 (2006)	475 (2030)	515 (1144)	555 (486)	595 (1302)
396 (1821)	436 (2007)	476 (2031)	516 (1288)	556 (487)	596 (1306)
397 (1822)	437 (2008)	477 (359)	517 (1332)	557 (488)	597 (220)
398 (1794)	438 (2005)	478 (330)	518 (1333)	558 (489)	598 (221)
399 (1795)	439 (563)	479 (331)	519 (1543)	559 (490)	599 (222)
400 (1937)	440 (1666)	480 (332)	520 (2074)	560 (491)	600 (223)
401 (1938)	441 (2161)	481 (333)	521 (2088)	561 (492)	601 (224)
402 (1881)	442 (108)	482 (334)	522 (1095)	562 (493)	602 (1251)
403 (1939)	443 (109)	483 (335)	523 (1656)	563 (494)	603 (1252)
404 (1826)	444 (110)	484 (336)	524 (1658)	564 (495)	604 (1253)
405 (1927)	445 (111)	485 (337)	525 (1953)	565 (496)	605 (1254)
406 (1933)	446 (112)	486 (338)	526 (303)	566 (497)	606 (1255)
407 (1718)	447 (113)	487 (564)	527 (1284)	567 (498)	607 (1256)
408 (1876)	448 (114)	488 (640)	528 (1015)	568 (499)	608 (1257)
409 (1931)	449 (115)	489 (209)	529 (1505)	569 (500)	609 (1258)
410 (1934)	450 (116)	490 (1059)	530 (1281)	570 (501)	610 (1259)
411 (1922)	451 (117)	491 (1155)	531 (1385)	571 (502)	611 (1260)
412 (1869)	452 (118)	492 (1220)	532 (1282)	572 (503)	612 (1261)

613 (1263)	653 (1988)	693 (2014)	733 (367)	773 (1679)	813 (976)
614 (1265)	654 (1989)	694 (2013)	734 (1238)	774 (1578)	814 (1950)
615 (1266)	655 (1990)	695 (1175)	735 (2205)	775 (158)	815 (846)
616 (1267)	656 (1991)	696 (2016)	736 (1217)	776 (691)	816 (1212)
617 (1268)	657 (1992)	697 (1173)	737 (137)	777 (2155)	817 (18)
618 (1269)	658 (1993)	698 (1239)	738 (2114)	778 (415)	818 (1052)
619 (1270)	659 (1994)	699 (1240)	739 (1314)	779 (1099)	819 (1384)
620 (1271)	660 (1995)	700 (1241)	740 (1468)	780 (721)	820 (1558)
621 (1272)	661 (1996)	701 (613)	741 (1113)	781 (756)	821 (2076)
622 (1273)	662 (1997)	702 (16)	742 (216)	782 (1397)	822 (287)
623 (1274)	663 (1998)	703 (102)	743 (1196)	783 (328)	823 (817)
624 (1275)	664 (1999)	704 (788)	744 (368)	784 (685)	824 (1149)
625 (1276)	665 (2000)	705 (425)	745 (1157)	785 (704)	825 (1416)
626 (1277)	666 (2001)	706 (319)	746 (240)	786 (991)	826 (1596)
627 (1278)	667 (2003)	707 (1190)	747 (1372)	787 (39)	827 (449)
628 (1279)	668 (2002)	708 (1421)	748 (1424)	788 (790)	828 (1086)
629 (1280)	669 (1565)	709 (906)	749 (1313)	789 (664)	829 (1408)
630 (1007)	670 (1631)	710 (665)	750 (329)	790 (1654)	830 (1316)
631 (884)	671 (1692)	711 (682)	751 (992)	791 (1450)	831 (1319)
632 (934)	672 (1096)	712 (411)	752 (86)	792 (1971)	832 (996)
633 (935)	673 (1946)	713 (995)	753 (77)	793 (50)	833 (2092)
634 (524)	674 (1945)	714 (1228)	754 (899)	794 (856)	834 (1289)
635 (525)	675 (172)	715 (1309)	755 (653)	795 (599)	835 (1291)
636 (526)	676 (1115)	716 (1151)	756 (2203)	796 (2101)	836 (1541)
637 (534)	677 (720)	717 (1146)	757 (791)	797 (285)	837 (1542)
638 (535)	678 (765)	718 (322)	758 (79)	798 (520)	838 (1956)
639 (536)	679 (1022)	719 (1688)	759 (1070)	799 (1100)	839 (823)
640 (537)	680 (136)	720 (683)	760 (797)	800 (1955)	840 (1293)
641 (538)	681 (163)	721 (1076)	761 (1301)	801 (1444)	841 (2130)
642 (539)	682 (289)	722 (88)	762 (103)	802 (1970)	842 (779)
643 (540)	683 (81)	723 (672)	763 (139)	803 (554)	843 (663)
644 (541)	684 (1147)	724 (1389)	764 (806)	804 (1334)	844 (423)
645 (542)	685 (1481)	725 (2147)	765 (1189)	805 (1530)	845 (1321)
646 (543)	686 (1486)	726 (1403)	766 (1351)	806 (2012)	846 (2044)
647 (610)	687 (44)	727 (2129)	767 (*Sp.* 375)	807 (1124)	847 (171)
648 (1983)	688 (666)	728 (1121)	768 (1325)	808 (835)	848 (894)
649 (1984)	689 (820)	729 (2113)	769 (1356)	809 (105)	849 (895)
650 (1985)	690 (76)	730 (138)	770 (1359)	810 (1120)	850 (703)
651 (1986)	691 (90)	731 (2091)	771 (382)	811 (1162)	851 (251)
652 (1987)	692 (1174)	732 (366)	772 (2069)	812 (923)	852 (393)

853 (717)	893 (1215)	933 (2233)	973 (403)	1013 (1004)	1053 (1186)
854 (1097)	894 (857)	934 (2234)	974 (404)	1014 (1139)	1054 (384)
855 (855)	895 (1299)	935 (2235)	975 (405)	1015 (2211)	1055 (1075)
856 (*Sp.* 560)	896 (*Sp.* 373)	936 (2243)	976 (406)	1016 (473)	1056 (2040)
857 (1071)	897 (2103)	937 (1298)	977 (407)	1017 (1576)	1057 (27)
858 (805)	898 (667)	938 (1508)	978 (2037)	1018 (1580)	1058 (200)
859 (986)	899 (65)	939 (950)	979 (1957)	1019 (14)	1059 (612)
860 (1062)	900 (2181)	940 (*Sp.* 578)	980 (386)	1020 (708)	1060 (2071)
861 (2250)	901 (166)	941 (1137)	981 (2120)	1021 (1055)	1061 (1352)
862 (684)	902 (1054)	942 (979)	982 (882)	1022 (1211)	1062 (2172)
863 (*Sp.* 554)	903 (1335)	943 (1243)	983 (661)	1023 (1635)	1063 (733)
864 (424)	904 (1264)	944 (1647)	984 (1442)	1024 (1362)	1064 (1312)
865 (2179)	905 (141)	945 (1231)	985 (1131)	1025 (1152)	1065 (588)
866 (1681)	906 (1294)	946 (1441)	986 (2077)	1026 (1652)	1066 (1347)
867 (546)	907 (692)	947 (821)	987 (242)	1027 (2151)	1067 (2011)
868 (607)	908 (1304)	948 (1954)	988 (2104)	1028 (921)	1068 (2236)
869 (698)	909 (1600)	949 (2021)	989 (408)	1029 (547)	1069 (844)
870 (773)	910 (1295)	950 (2022)	990 (587)	1030 (390)	1070 (845)
871 (1110)	911 (2122)	951 (101)	991 (759)	1031 (1017)	1071 (309)
872 (724)	912 (872)	952 (326)	992 (1419)	1032 (2171)	1072 (768)
873 (2067)	913 (385)	953 (363)	993 (1383)	1033 (1360)	1073 (2041)
874 (928)	914 (1364)	954 (446)	994 (2010)	1034 (1590)	1074 (1105)
875 (926)	915 (795)	955 (598)	995 (658)	1035 (635)	1075 (1322)
876 (1202)	916 (143)	956 (272)	996 (58)	1036 (2064)	1076 (999)
877 (1474)	917 (1287)	957 (1449)	997 (69)	1037 (61)	1077 (1554)
878 (1680)	918 (2108)	958 (203)	998 (1166)	1038 (106)	1078 (668)
879 (2180)	919 (2174)	959 (201)	999 (696)	1039 (286)	1079 (1235)
880 (2178)	920 (68)	960 (1050)	1000 (2070)	1040 (919)	1080 (290)
881 (1475)	921 (1223)	961 (327)	1001 (897)	1041 (2045)	1081 (1012)
882 (13)	922 (709)	962 (1427)	1002 (1644)	1042 (464)	1082 (1972)
883 (1337)	923 (2083)	963 (388)	1003 (978)	1043 (2059)	1083 (631)
884 (165)	924 (641)	964 (1141)	1004 (2046)	1044 (2058)	1084 (1104)
885 (1114)	925 (896)	965 (1204)	1005 (819)	1045 (556)	1085 (2215)
886 (1533)	926 (1363)	966 (1209)	1006 (1153)	1046 (687)	1086 (1245)
887 (633)	927 (1380)	967 (397)	1007 (1201)	1047 (951)	1087 (719)
888 (585)	928 (1382)	968 (398)	1008 (33)	1048 (1101)	1088 (757)
889 (2182)	929 (1446)	969 (399)	1009 (1661)	1049 (952)	1089 (2248)
890 (1307)	930 (1460)	970 (400)	1010 (1662)	1050 (1053)	1090 (1061)
891 (1021)	931 (1589)	971 (401)	1011 (477)	1051 (1637)	1091 (532)
892 (1621)	932 (2175)	972 (402)	1012 (2168)	1052 (1653)	1092 (308)

1093 (2062)	1133 (801)	1173 (1410)	1213 (1660)	1253 (1129)	1293 (1329)
1094 (1067)	1134 (2054)	1174 (1081)	1214 (1008)	1254 (276)	1294 (2222)
1095 (880)	1135 (1387)	1175 (1376)	1215 (652)	1255 (456)	1295 (455)
1096 (28)	1136 (1106)	1176 (1426)	1216 (1126)	1256 (2210)	1296 (718)
1097 (938)	1137 (1395)	1177 (1358)	1217 (1064)	1257 (550)	1297 (159)
1098 (1181)	1138 (1400)	1178 (1066)	1218 (1177)	1258 (2145)	1298 (1330)
1099 (1023)	1139 (1625)	1179 (1193)	1219 (1188)	1259 (695)	1299 (737)
1100 (990)	1140 (2078)	1180 (686)	1220 (959)	1260 (2075)	1300 (2227)
1101 (479)	1141 (1684)	1181 (1094)	1221 (922)	1261 (284)	1301 (1465)
1102 (29)	1142 (288)	1182 (1090)	1222 (967)	1262 (716)	1302 (2216)
1103 (1056)	1143 (1632)	1183 (52)	1223 (275)	1263 (59)	1303 (1510)
1104 (634)	1144 (1116)	1184 (2163)	1224 (1083)	1264 (283)	1304 (830)
1105 (946)	1145 (878)	1185 (164)	1225 (458)	1265 (2219)	1305 (875)
1106 (451)	1146 (93)	1186 (70)	1226 (760)	1266 (2087)	1306 (1310)
1107 (2231)	1147 (4)	1187 (600)	1227 (761)	1267 (1482)	1307 (1461)
1108 (1536)	1148 (594)	1188 (807)	1228 (810)	1268 (2065)	1308 (920)
1109 (1487)	1149 (1405)	1189 (2093)	1229 (1068)	1269 (42)	1309 (983)
1110 (850)	1150 (1140)	1190 (459)	1230 (2112)	1270 (268)	1310 (307)
1111 (1404)	1151 (431)	1191 (1229)	1231 (2251)	1271 (840)	1311 (903)
1112 (1458)	1152 (1969)	1192 (1244)	1232 (2209)	1272 (1011)	1312 (1569)
1113 (2098)	1153 (727)	1193 (107)	1233 (426)	1273 (802)	1313 (1109)
1114 (304)	1154 (972)	1194 (1246)	1234 (904)	1274 (849)	1314 (1583)
1115 (2038)	1155 (1428)	1195 (1169)	1235 (949)	1275 (1413)	1315 (649)
1116 (73)	1156 (2061)	1196 (1628)	1236 (1219)	1276 (1084)	1316 (430)
1117 (2089)	1157 (1982)	1197 (47)	1237 (1197)	1277 (1213)	1317 (1366)
1118 (1200)	1158 (1597)	1198 (381)	1238 (427)	1278 (1348)	1318 (2137)
1119 (659)	1159 (2162)	1199 (1951)	1239 (71)	1279 (1069)	1319 (35)
1120 (552)	1160 (971)	1200 (1016)	1240 (1579)	1280 (1089)	1320 (2176)
1121 (593)	1161 (1088)	1201 (311)	1241 (1125)	1281 (1361)	1321 (980)
1122 (1401)	1162 (1049)	1202 (2225)	1242 (1663)	1282 (1980)	1322 (439)
1123 (636)	1163 (1443)	1203 (442)	1243 (1018)	1283 (1626)	1323 (902)
1124 (637)	1164 (937)	1204 (566)	1244 (53)	1284 (2131)	1324 (1150)
1125 (2139)	1165 (1303)	1205 (2079)	1245 (786)	1285 (2111)	1325 (11)
1126 (1117)	1166 (1160)	1206 (1459)	1246 (219)	1286 (2138)	1326 (730)
1127 (2237)	1167 (2056)	1207 (722)	1247 (1624)	1287 (858)	1327 (104)
1128 (808)	1168 (1423)	1208 (241)	1248 (2094)	1288 (15)	1328 (394)
1129 (2238)	1169 (2115)	1209 (811)	1249 (2221)	1289 (1065)	1329 (544)
1130 (2084)	1170 (2116)	1210 (2226)	1250 (893)	1290 (1369)	1330 (715)
1131 (2232)	1171 (1354)	1211 (1440)	1251 (974)	1291 (1575)	1331 (395)
1132 (518)	1172 (987)	1212 (1328)	1252 (984)	1292 (2080)	1332 (482)

1333 (581)	1373 (1406)	1413 (1975)	1453 (324)	1493 (680)	1533 (1502)
1334 (1959)	1374 (1415)	1414 (1586)	1454 (1073)	1494 (604)	1534 (1247)
1335 (453)	1375 (1425)	1415 (1587)	1455 (1462)	1495 (295)	1535 (1483)
1336 (55)	1376 (2119)	1416 (2081)	1456 (1525)	1496 (167)	1536 (605)
1337 (852)	1377 (2105)	1417 (1588)	1457 (67)	1497 (232)	1537 (707)
1338 (2073)	1378 (1331)	1418 (2173)	1458 (206)	1498 (243)	1538 (1063)
1339 (754)	1379 (1409)	1419 (2099)	1459 (208)	1499 (245)	1539 (1521)
1340 (586)	1380 (1435)	1420 (767)	1460 (12)	1500 (1390)	1540 (194)
1341 (1559)	1381 (348)	1421 (321)	1461 (41)	1501 (1503)	1541 (195)
1342 (1107)	1382 (376)	1422 (702)	1462 (2224)	1502 (1501)	1542 (961)
1343 (710)	1383 (1638)	1423 (310)	1463 (291)	1503 (36)	1543 (1517)
1344 (531)	1384 (1566)	1424 (591)	1464 (396)	1504 (1504)	1544 (1399)
1345 (571)	1385 (646)	1425 (26)	1465 (87)	1505 (705)	1545 (1515)
1346 (2156)	1386 (962)	1426 (1570)	1466 (871)	1506 (1567)	1546 (1523)
1347 (2118)	1387 (1552)	1427 (196)	1467 (1336)	1507 (49)	1547 (1518)
1348 (1232)	1388 (1013)	1428 (780)	1468 (994)	1508 (94)	1548 (24)
1349 (2149)	1389 (1296)	1429 (1161)	1469 (750)	1509 (1526)	1549 (1538)
1350 (1418)	1390 (2141)	1430 (889)	1470 (300)	1510 (212)	1550 (98)
1351 (2126)	1391 (915)	1431 (1136)	1471 (419)	1511 (1206)	1551 (699)
1352 (2159)	1392 (347)	1432 (2121)	1472 (429)	1512 (1547)	1552 (1512)
1353 (1323)	1393 (354)	1433 (1531)	1473 (731)	1513 (210)	1553 (966)
1354 (2206)	1394 (474)	1434 (781)	1474 (1568)	1514 (1324)	1554 (1156)
1355 (2124)	1395 (1164)	1435 (1286)	1475 (100)	1515 (34)	1555 (522)
1356 (1320)	1396 (97)	1436 (1326)	1476 (803)	1516 (1943)	1556 (441)
1357 (2125)	1397 (43)	1437 (1135)	1477 (545)	1517 (1944)	1557 (618)
1358 (1493)	1398 (56)	1438 (758)	1478 (650)	1518 (37)	1558 (179)
1359 (1365)	1399 (772)	1439 (2150)	1479 (789)	1519 (99)	1559 (623)
1360 (1381)	1400 (1470)	1440 (1163)	1480 (187)	1520 (1499)	1560 (1633)
1361 (1377)	1401 (988)	1441 (592)	1481 (463)	1521 (1522)	1561 (387)
1362 (1371)	1402 (1355)	1442 (916)	1482 (188)	1522 (771)	1562 (389)
1363 (1374)	1403 (1357)	1443 (149)	1483 (239)	1523 (706)	1563 (447)
1364 (1593)	1404 (1439)	1444 (782)	1484 (523)	1524 (1476)	1564 (361)
1365 (1623)	1405 (1491)	1445 (1308)	1485 (639)	1525 (1507)	1565 (1546)
1366 (2109)	1406 (993)	1446 (2102)	1486 (568)	1526 (1549)	1566 (*Sp.* 634)
1367 (1127)	1407 (1119)	1447 (409)	1487 (235)	1527 (1551)	1567 (355)
1368 (1143)	1408 (1651)	1448 (693)	1488 (433)	1528 (48)	1568 (313)
1369 (1242)	1409 (1584)	1449 (911)	1489 (234)	1529 (440)	1569 (314)
1370 (1370)	1410 (1581)	1450 (78)	1490 (192)	1530 (748)	1570 (315)
1371 (1393)	1411 (1079)	1451 (142)	1491 (1338)	1531 (1500)	1571 (1490)
1372 (1394)	1412 (1977)	1452 (1378)	1492 (292)	1532 (1498)	1572 (960)

1573 (207)	1613 (1145)	1653 (1582)	1693 (1506)	1733 (1683)	1773 (281)
1574 (611)	1614 (1218)	1654 (1447)	1694 (2024)	1734 (900)	1774 (7)
1575 (620)	1615 (745)	1655 (1452)	1695 (2100)	1735 (1103)	1775 (747)
1576 (898)	1616 (1592)	1656 (2020)	1696 (379)	1736 (228)	1776 (970)
1577 (1074)	1617 (728)	1657 (373)	1697 (340)	1737 (472)	1777 (193)
1578 (1678)	1618 (954)	1658 (583)	1698 (2017)	1738 (1014)	1778 (688)
1579 (2220)	1619 (1112)	1659 (626)	1699 (2018)	1739 (1285)	1779 (749)
1580 (927)	1620 (557)	1660 (651)	1700 (198)	1740 (1682)	1780 (318)
1581 (189)	1621 (562)	1661 (787)	1701 (140)	1741 (2106)	1781 (689)
1582 (190)	1622 (1529)	1662 (648)	1702 (734)	1742 (2043)	1782 (362)
1583 (925)	1623 (645)	1663 (75)	1703 (736)	1743 (1573)	1783 (886)
1584 (1488)	1624 (726)	1664 (1142)	1704 (744)	1744 (1629)	1784 (145)
1585 (1171)	1625 (2039)	1665 (681)	1705 (774)	1745 (1210)	1785 (247)
1586 (1172)	1626 (380)	1666 (1514)	1706 (1636)	1746 (1978)	1786 (742)
1587 (1548)	1627 (1388)	1667 (372)	1707 (2019)	1747 (1657)	1787 (743)
1588 (1250)	1628 (2144)	1668 (584)	1708 (777)	1748 (1492)	1788 (942)
1589 (1087)	1629 (1958)	1669 (1203)	1709 (250)	1749 (851)	1789 (160)
1590 (199)	1630 (800)	1670 (260)	1710 (1373)	1750 (465)	1790 (792)
1591 (1961)	1631 (*Sp.* 623)	1671 (528)	1711 (38)	1751 (1002)	1791 (1342)
1592 (2036)	1632 (1396)	1672 (151)	1712 (1159)	1752 (1057)	1792 (769)
1593 (197)	1633 (1407)	1673 (814)	1713 (2068)	1753 (1524)	1793 (831)
1594 (752)	1634 (912)	1674 (655)	1714 (6)	1754 (1379)	1794 (892)
1595 (753)	1635 (2132)	1675 (625)	1715 (2160)	1755 (1494)	1795 (918)
1596 (1051)	1636 (1949)	1676 (657)	1716 (40)	1756 (1689)	1796 (982)
1597 (627)	1637 (2143)	1677 (816)	1717 (1205)	1757 (183)	1797 (1574)
1598 (226)	1638 (2042)	1678 (1429)	1718 (1098)	1758 (218)	1798 (943)
1599 (1974)	1639 (1964)	1679 (2050)	1719 (1214)	1759 (582)	1799 (1420)
1600 (191)	1640 (1167)	1680 (2049)	1720 (1411)	1760 (8)	1800 (597)
1601 (225)	1641 (2213)	1681 (529)	1721 (1412)	1761 (2207)	1801 (828)
1602 (615)	1642 (375)	1682 (346)	1722 (461)	1762 (9)	1802 (32)
1603 (621)	1643 (391)	1683 (353)	1723 (2214)	1763 (10)	1803 (784)
1604 (622)	1644 (933)	1684 (2117)	1724 (63)	1764 (843)	1804 (370)
1605 (619)	1645 (914)	1685 (2123)	1725 (1020)	1765 (20)	1805 (751)
1606 (236)	1646 (1484)	1686 (890)	1726 (1300)	1766 (364)	1806 (940)
1607 (614)	1647 (1509)	1687 (1402)	1727 (457)	1767 (638)	1807 (776)
1608 (616)	1648 (1976)	1688 (351)	1728 (462)	1768 (957)	1808 (1367)
1609 (617)	1649 (1595)	1689 (1431)	1729 (838)	1769 (630)	1809 (887)
1610 (2223)	1650 (1511)	1690 (958)	1730 (910)	1770 (271)	1810 (968)
1611 (1368)	1651 (1463)	1691 (1591)	1731 (1585)	1771 (647)	1811 (1208)
1612 (279)	1652 (1520)	1692 (701)	1732 (1430)	1772 (901)	1812 (1230)

1813 (1550)	1853 (700)	1893 (1469)	1933 (1318)	1973 (296)	2013 (1572)
1814 (2055)	1854 (186)	1894 (1495)	1934 (1179)	1974 (343)	2014 (258)
1815 (785)	1855 (432)	1895 (1448)	1935 (174)	1975 (297)	2015 (256)
1816 (371)	1856 (533)	1896 (834)	1936 (175)	1976 (45)	2016 (1650)
1817 (369)	1857 (476)	1897 (746)	1937 (176)	1977 (793)	2017 (252)
1818 (1432)	1858 (813)	1898 (1349)	1938 (839)	1978 (1553)	2018 (255)
1819 (671)	1859 (947)	1899 (561)	1939 (2154)	1979 (1473)	2019 (17)
1820 (596)	1860 (624)	1900 (1535)	1940 (246)	1980 (832)	2020 (153)
1821 (670)	1861 (248)	1901 (383)	1941 (553)	1981 (312)	2021 (154)
1822 (809)	1862 (1072)	1902 (1345)	1942 (848)	1982 (342)	2022 (254)
1823 (885)	1863 (1327)	1903 (854)	1943 (824)	1983 (527)	2023 (257)
1824 (1563)	1864 (738)	1904 (1248)	1944 (469)	1984 (1639)	2024 (261)
1825 (466)	1865 (1451)	1905 (51)	1945 (468)	1985 (249)	2025 (1640)
1826 (1571)	1866 (253)	1906 (460)	1946 (1180)	1986 (270)	2026 (1649)
1827 (1455)	1867 (783)	1907 (2090)	1947 (*Sp.* 524)	1987 (1556)	2027 (259)
1828 (454)	1868 (739)	1908 (1560)	1948 (*Sp.* 517)	1988 (345)	2028 (277)
1829 (521)	1869 (1594)	1909 (25)	1949 (735)	1989 (244)	2029 (274)
1830 (590)	1870 (977)	1910 (85)	1950 (815)	1990 (169)	2030 (301)
1831 (944)	1871 (2066)	1911 (278)	1951 (150)	1991 (170)	2031 (341)
1832 (1467)	1872 (1353)	1912 (965)	1952 (1199)	1992 (262)	2032 (1967)
1833 (445)	1873 (812)	1913 (84)	1953 (1540)	1993 (264)	2033 (1968)
1834 (1453)	1874 (2133)	1914 (725)	1954 (643)	1994 (269)	2034 (740)
1835 (2146)	1875 (152)	1915 (1513)	1955 (1207)	1995 (323)	2035 (294)
1836 (1132)	1876 (428)	1916 (184)	1956 (1339)	1996 (1979)	2036 (320)
1837 (1634)	1877 (344)	1917 (603)	1957 (1539)	1997 (1965)	2037 (2060)
1838 (829)	1878 (2023)	1918 (941)	1958 (316)	1998 (873)	2038 (2212)
1839 (833)	1879 (352)	1919 (955)	1959 (480)	1999 (1966)	2039 (215)
1840 (569)	1880 (859)	1920 (1436)	1960 (306)	2000 (2047)	2040 (470)
1841 (766)	1881 (2082)	1921 (19)	1961 (908)	2001 (2048)	2041 (471)
1842 (1123)	1882 (155)	1922 (549)	1962 (589)	2002 (1667)	2042 (1225)
1843 (953)	1883 (1960)	1923 (608)	1963 (1645)	2003 (161)	2043 (*Sp.* 658)
1844 (755)	1884 (177)	1924 (891)	1964 (1664)	2004 (1472)	2044 (1165)
1845 (162)	1885 (1227)	1925 (147)	1965 (1665)	2005 (1489)	2045 (690)
1846 (1687)	1886 (654)	1926 (905)	1966 (185)	2006 (1485)	2046 (80)
1847 (1185)	1887 (1516)	1927 (1000)	1967 (1534)	2007 (1641)	2047 (606)
1848 (883)	1888 (1496)	1928 (205)	1968 (325)	2008 (514)	2048 (1170)
1849 (282)	1889 (1527)	1929 (1118)	1969 (180)	2009 (2110)	2049 (1226)
1850 (642)	1890 (1528)	1930 (60)	1970 (178)	2010 (530)	2050 (2164)
1851 (1422)	1891 (1391)	1931 (377)	1971 (*Sp.* 517)	2011 (317)	2051 (2247)
1852 (628)	1892 (1497)	1932 (233)	1972 (*Sp.* 517)	2012 (146)	2052 (2158)

2053 (181)	2079 (1392)	2105 (775)	2131 (1544)	2157 (1564)	2183 (519)
2054 (182)	2080 (*Sp.* 391)	2106 (436)	2132 (1561)	2158 (2051)	2184 (421)
2055 (360)	2081 (435)	2107 (1195)	2133 (*Sp.* 517)	2159 (913)	2185 (778)
2056 (273)	2082 (975)	2108 (305)	2134 (870)	2160 (266)	2186 (2157)
2057 (214)	2083 (57)	2109 (2167)	2135 (729)	2161 (2148)	2187 (948)
2058 (1128)	2084 (230)	2110 (825)	2136 (868)	2162 (92)	2188 (559)
2059 (1077)	2085 (231)	2111 (452)	2137 (365)	2163 (876)	2189 (723)
2060 (202)	2086 (349)	2112 (481)	2138 (416)	2164 (148)	2190 (83)
2061 (156)	2087 (422)	2113 (*Sp.* 632)	2139 (866)	2165 (1457)	2191 (22)
2062 (410)	2088 (82)	2114 (956)	2140 (869)	2166 (1562)	2192 (46)
2063 (1154)	2089 (1668)	2115 (981)	2141 (860)	2167 (2072)	2193 (54)
2064 (1187)	2090 (1176)	2116 (1010)	2142 (862)	2168 (204)	2194 (227)
2065 (1341)	2091 (1058)	2117 (1454)	2143 (863)	2169 (443)	2195 (694)
2066 (157)	2092 (211)	2118 (*Sp.* 374)	2144 (864)	2170 (1108)	2196 (644)
2067 (798)	2093 (799)	2119 (420)	2145 (867)	2171 (478)	2197 (516)
2068 (712)	2094 (66)	2120 (413)	2146 (871a)	2172 (551)	2198 (293)
2069 (2095)	2095 (1092)	2121 (877)	2147 (1677)	2173 (*Sp.* 509)	2199 (822)
2070 (*Sp.* 390)	2096 (1233)	2122 (23)	2148 (969)	2174 (847)	2200 (263)
2071 (1080)	2097 (853)	2123 (96)	2149 (265)	2175 (437)	2201 (836)
2072 (*Sp.* 565)	2098 (711)	2124 (434)	2150 (414)	2176 (2096)	2202 (1648)
2073 (2152)	2099 (1557)	2125 (629)	2151 (438)	2177 (2218)	2203 (1224)
2074 (989)	2100 (21)	2126 (*Sp.* 517)	2152 (392)	2178 (144)	2204 (1676)
2075 (1178)	2101 (72)	2127 (229)	2153 (168)	2179 (602)	
2076 (2127)	2102 (924)	2128 (1085)	2154 (374)	2180 (515)	
2077 (64)	2103 (1471)	2129 (1082)	2155 (560)	2181 (917)	
2078 (669)	2104 (1445)	2130 (417)	2156 (558)	2182 (881)	

Select Bibliography

To list every work that was of importance to Montesquieu would be tantamount to duplicating the contents of his personal library, one of the largest and best-preserved of the eighteenth century. The purpose here is to provide only the most elementary orientation to Montesquieu's life, his times, and his thought as manifested in *Mes Pensées*.

Primary Sources

Complete Works of Montesquieu

Œuvres complètes. Edited by Roger Caillois. 2 vols. Paris: Gallimard, Bibliothèque de la Pléiade, 1949–51.

Œuvres complètes. Edited by Daniel Oster. Paris: Seuil, 1964.

Œuvres complètes de Montesquieu. Edited by André Masson. 3 vols. Paris: Nagel, 1950–55. Cited as *OC* in the text.

Œuvres complètes de Montesquieu. Edited by Jean Ehrard, Catherine Volpilhac-Auger, et al. 22 vols. Oxford: Voltaire Foundation and Société Montesquieu, 1998–2010. The Voltaire Foundation published eleven volumes: 1–4, 8–9, 11–13, 16, and 18; the remainder are due to be published jointly by ENS of Lyon [l'Ecole Normale Supérieure de Lyon] and Classiques Garnier. Abbreviated *OCVolt* in the text.

Individual Works by Montesquieu

"Arsace et Isménie." In *Œuvres complètes de Montesquieu* (Masson), 3:477–528.

Cahiers (1716–1755). Edited by Bernard Grasset. Paris: B. Grasset, 1941.

"Considérations sur les causes de la grandeur des Romains et de leur décadence." In *Œuvres complètes de Montesquieu* (Masson), 1:349–528. Also in *Œuvres complètes de Montesquieu* (Ehrard et al.), vol. 2.

"Considérations sur les richesses de l'Espagne." In *Œuvres complètes de Montesquieu* (Masson), 3:139–55.

Défense de "l'Esprit des loix." Geneva: Barillot, 1750. Montesquieu's response to early criticisms of *The Spirit of the Laws.* Cited as *Défense* in the text.

De l'Esprit des lois. Edited by Jean Brèthe de La Gressaye. 4 vols. Paris: Belles Lettres, 1950–61. Cited as Brèthe in the text.

De l'Esprit des lois. Edited by Robert Derathé. 2 vols. Paris: Garnier Frères, 1973. A notes and variants edition. Abbreviated Derathé in the text.

"Discours sur la cause de la pesanteur des corps." In *Œuvres complètes de Montesquieu* (Masson), 3:89–93.

"Essai d'observations sur l'histoire naturelle." In *Œuvres complètes de Montesquieu* (Masson), 3:100.

"Essai sur le goût dans les choses de la nature et de l'art." In *Encyclopédie,* 7: 762–67.

"Essai sur les causes qui peuvent affecter les esprits et les caractères." In *Œuvres complètes de Montesquieu* (Masson), 3:397–430.

"Lettres de Xénocrate à Phérès." In *Œuvres complètes de Montesquieu* (Masson), 3:129–35.

Lettres persanes. Edited by Antoine Adam. Geneva: Droz, 1954. Cited as Adam in the text.

Lettres Persanes. Edited by Paul Vernière. Paris: Garnier Frères, 1960. Abbreviated Vernière in text.

"Lettre sur Gênes." In *Œuvres complètes de Montesquieu* (Masson), 2:1303–9.

"Mémoire sur la Constitution Unigenitus." In *Œuvres complètes de Montesquieu* (Masson), 3:469–76.

"Mémoire sur les dettes de l'Etat." In *Œuvres complètes de Montesquieu* (Masson), 3:23.

"Notes sur l'Angleterre." In *Œuvres complètes de Montesquieu* (Masson), 3: 283–94.

Pensées, Le Spicilège. Edited by Louis Desgraves. Paris: Robert Laffont, 1991.

Pensées et fragments inédits de Montesquieu. Edited by Henri Barckhausen. 2 vols. Published by Baron Gaston de Montesquieu. Bordeaux: Gounouilhou, 1899–1901.

"Projet d'une histoire physique de la terre ancienne et moderne." In *Œuvres complètes de Montesquieu* (Masson), 3:87–88.

Quelques réflexions sur "les Lettres persanes." A preface, published as a supplement to the 1754 edition.

"Réflexions sur la monarchie universelle en Europe." In *Œuvres complètes de Montesquieu* (Masson), 3:361–82.

"Réflexions sur la sobriété des habitants de Rome." In *Œuvres complètes de Montesquieu* (Masson), 3:357–60.

"Réflexions sur le caractère de quelques princes." In *Œuvres complètes de Montesquieu* (Masson), 3:537–52.

Translations of Montesquieu's Works

Considerations on the Causes of the Greatness of the Romans and Their Decline. Translated by David Lowenthal. 1965. Indianapolis: Hackett, 1999. Cited in the text as *Considerations* by the editor, as *Romans* by Montesquieu.

"An Essay on the Causes That May Affect Men's Minds and Characters." Translated and with an introduction by Melvin Richter. *Political Theory* 4 (1976): 132–62.

Meine Gedanken. Selected and translated, and with an afterword by Henning Ritter. Munich: Hanser, 2000. An abridged German translation of *Mes Pensées.*

Pensieri diversi. Edited and translated by Domenico Felice. Naples: Liguori Editore, 2010. An Italian translation of selections from *Mes Pensées.*

The Persian Letters. Translated by George R. Healy. 1964. Indianapolis: Hackett, 1999. Cited as *PL* in the text.

The Personal and the Political: Three Fables by Montesquieu. Translation and commentary by W. B. Allen. Lanham, Md.: University Press of America, 2008. Translations of "The Temple of Gnidus," "Lysimachus," and "Dialogue of Sulla and Eucrates." Cited as Allen in the text.

Selected Political Writings. Edited and translated by Melvin Richter. 1978. Indianapolis: Hackett, 1990.

The Spirit of Laws: A Compendium of the First English Edition . . . together with an English Translation of the "Essay on Causes Affecting Minds and Characters" (1736–1743). Edited and translated by David W. Carrithers. Berkeley: University of California Press, 1977.

The Spirit of the Laws. Translated and edited by Anne Cohler, Basia Miller, and Harold Stone. Cambridge: Cambridge University Press, 1989. Cited as *Laws* in the text.

The Spirit of the Laws. Translated by Thomas Nugent. 1750. Introduction by Franz Neumann. New York: Hafner, 1949.

Secondary Sources

Books

Acomb, Frances. *Anglophobia in France, 1763–1789.* Durham, N.C.: Duke University Press, 1950.

Actes du Congrès Montesquieu réuni à Bordeaux du 23 au 26 mai 1955 pour commémorer le deuxième centenaire de la mort de Montesquieu. Bordeaux: Delmas, 1956.

Althusser, Louis. *Politics and History: Montesquieu, Rousseau, Hegel and Marx.* Translated by Ben Brewster. London: Verso, 1972.

Aron, Raymond. *Main Currents in Sociological Thought.* Translated by Richard Howard and Helen Weaver. 2 vols. Garden City, N.Y.: Anchor Books, 1968.

Baker, Keith Michael. *Inventing the French Revolution: Essays on French Political Culture in the Eighteenth Century.* Cambridge: Cambridge University Press, 1990.

Benrekassa, Georges. *Montesquieu, la liberté et l'histoire.* Paris: Livre de poche, 1987.

Bonno, Gabriel. *La Constitution britannique devant l'opinion française de Montesquieu à Bonaparte.* Paris: Champion, 1931.

————. *La Culture et la civilisation britanniques devant l'opinion française de la paix d'Utrecht aux Lettres philosophiques (1713–1734).* Philadelphia: The American Philosophical Society, 1948.

Carcassonne, Elie. *Montesquieu et le problème de la Constitution française au XVIIIe siècle.* Paris: Presses universitaires de France, 1927.

Carrithers, David W., ed. *Charles-Louis de Secondat, Baron de Montesquieu.* International Library of Essays in the History of Social and Political Thought Series. Burlington, Vt.: Ashgate Press, 2009.

Carrithers, David W., and Patrick Coleman, eds. *Montesquieu and the Spirit of Modernity.* Studies on Voltaire and the Eighteenth Century. Oxford: Voltaire Foundation, 2002.

Carrithers, David W., Michael A. Mosher, and Paul A. Rahe, eds. *Montesquieu's Science of Politics: Essays on "The Spirit of Laws."* Lanham, Md.: Rowman and Littlefield, 2001.

Childs, Nick. *A Political Academy in Paris, 1724–1731: The Entresol and Its Members.* Oxford: Voltaire Foundation, 2000.

Courtney, Cecil. *Montesquieu and Burke.* Oxford: Basil Blackwell, 1963.

Cox, Iris. *Montesquieu and the History of French Laws.* Oxford: Voltaire Foundation, 1983.

Dedieu, Joseph. *Montesquieu et la tradition politique anglaise en France: Les sources anglaises de "l'Esprit des lois."* Paris: Gabalda, 1909.

Dodds, Muriel. *Les Récits de voyages, sources de "l'Esprit des lois" de Montesquieu.* Paris: Champion, 1929. Cited as Dodds in the text.

Durkheim, Emile. *Montesquieu and Rousseau: Forerunners of Sociology.* Translated by Ralph Manheim. Ann Arbor: University of Michigan Press, 1960.

Ehrard, Jean. *L'Esprit des mots: Montesquieu en lui-même et parmi les siens.* Geneva: Droz, 1998.

Fletcher, F. T. H. *Montesquieu and English Politics, 1750–1800.* London: Edward Arnold, 1939.

Ford, Franklin L. *Robe and Sword: The Regrouping of the French Aristocracy after Louis XIV.* Cambridge, Mass.: Harvard University Press, 1953.

Hampson, Norman. *Will and Circumstance: Montesquieu, Rousseau and the French Revolution.* London: Duckworth, 1983.

Hirschman, Albert O. *The Passions and the Interests: Political Arguments for Commerce before Its Triumph.* Princeton: Princeton University Press, 1977.

Hont, Istvan, and Michael Ignatieff, eds. *Wealth and Virtue: The Shaping of Political Economy in the Scottish Enlightenment.* Cambridge: Cambridge University Press, 1983.

Hulliung, Mark. *Montesquieu and the Old Regime.* Berkeley: University of California Press, 1976.

Keohane, Nannerl O. *Philosophy and the State in France: The Renaissance to the Enlightenment.* Princeton: Princeton University Press, 1980.

Kingston, Rebecca. *Montesquieu and the Parlement of Bordeaux.* Geneva: Droz, 1996.

Kingston, Rebecca E., ed. *Montesquieu and His Legacy.* Albany: State University of New York Press, 2009.

Krause, Sharon. *Liberalism with Honor.* Cambridge, Mass.: Harvard University Press, 2002.

Lafontant, Julien K. *Montesquieu et le problème de l'esclavage dans "l'Esprit des lois."* Sherbrooke, Québec: Naaman, 1979.

Manent, Pierre. *The City of Man.* Translated by Marc A. Le Pain. Princeton: Princeton University Press, 1998.

———. *An Intellectual History of Liberalism.* Translated by Rebecca Balinski. Princeton: Princeton University Press, 1994.

Morilhat, Claude. *Montesquieu: politique et richesses.* Paris: Presses universitaires de France, 1996.

Pangle, Thomas L. *Montesquieu's philosophy of liberalism: a commentary on "The Spirit of the Laws."* Chicago: University of Chicago Press, 1973.

———. *The Theological Basis of Liberal Modernity in Montesquieu's "Spirit of the Laws."* Chicago: University of Chicago Press, 2010.

Pocock, J. G. A. *The Machiavellian Moment: Florentine Political Thought and the Atlantic Republican Tradition.* Princeton: Princeton University Press, 1975.

———. *Virtue, Commerce, and History: Essays on Political Thought and History, Chiefly in the Eighteenth Century.* Cambridge: Cambridge University Press, 1985.

Rahe, Paul A. *Montesquieu and the Logic of Liberty: War, Religion, Commerce, Climate, Terrain, Technology, Uneasiness of Mind, the Spirit of Political Vigilance, and the Foundations of the Modern Republic.* New Haven: Yale University Press, 2009.

———. *Soft Despotism, Democracy's Drift: Montesquieu, Rousseau, Tocqueville, and the Modern Prospect.* New Haven: Yale University Press, 2009.

Rosso, Corrado. *Montesquieu moraliste: des lois au bonheur.* Bordeaux: Ducros, 1971.

Schaub, Diana Jo. *Erotic Liberalism: Women and Revolution in Montesquieu's "Persian Letters."* Lanham, Md.: Rowman and Littlefield, 1995.

Shackleton, Robert. *Montesquieu: A Critical Biography.* London: Oxford University Press, 1961.

Shackleton, Robert, David Gilson, and Martin Smith, eds. *Essays on Montesquieu and on the Enlightenment.* Oxford: Voltaire Foundation, 1988.

Shklar, Judith N. *Montesquieu.* Past Masters Series. London: Oxford University Press, 1987.

Spector, Céline. *Montesquieu, Les Lettres persanes: De l'anthropologie à la politique.* Paris: Presses universitaires de France, 1997.

———. *Montesquieu et l'émergence de l'économie politique.* Paris: Champion, 2006.

Spurlin, Paul Merrill. *Montesquieu in America, 1760–1801.* University, La.: Louisiana State University Press, 1940.

Vernière, Paul. *Montesquieu et "l'esprit des lois," ou, La raison impure.* Paris: Société d'édition d'enseignement supérieur, 1977.

Articles

Aubery, Pierre. "Montesquieu et les Juifs." Studies on Voltaire and the Eighteenth Century 87 (1972): 87–99.

Barckhausen, Henri. "L'Histoire de Louis XI." *Revue philomathique de Bordeaux et du Sud-Ouest,* 1897–98, 569–78.

Berlin, Isaiah. "Montesquieu." In *Against the Current: Essays in the History of Ideas,* edited by Henry Hardy, 130–61. Harmondsworth, U.K.: Penguin Books, 1980.

Bertière, André. "Montesquieu, lecteur de Machiavel," in *Actes du Congrès Montesquieu réuni à Bordeaux du 23 au 26 mai 1955,* 141–58. Bordeaux: Delmas, 1956.

Desgraves, Louis. "Montesquieu et Fontenelle." In *Actes du colloque Fontenelle,* edited by Alain Niderst, 307–15. Paris: Presses universitaires de France, 1989.

Galliani, Renato. "La Fortune de Montesquieu en 1789: un sondage." In *Etudes sur Montesquieu,* edited by R. Galliani and F. Loirette, 31–47. Paris: Lettres modernes, 1981.

Halévi, Ran. "The Illusion of 'Honor': Nobility and Monarchical Construction in the Eighteenth Century." In *Tocqueville and Beyond: Essays on the Old Regime in Honor of David D. Bien,* edited by Robert M. Schwartz and Robert A. Schneider. Newark: University of Delaware Press, 2003.

Kaiser, Thomas E. "The Abbé Dubos and the Historical Defence of Monarchy in Early Eighteenth-Century France." *Studies on Voltaire and the Eighteenth Century* 267 (1989): 77–102.

Koebner, R. "Despot and Despotism: Vicissitudes of a Political Term." *Journal of the Warburg and Courtauld Institute* 14, no. 3–4 (1951): 275–302.

Lutz, Donald S. "The Relative Importance of European Writers in Late Eighteenth-Century American Political Thought." *American Political Science Review* 189 (1984): 189–97.

Masson, André. "Un chinois inspirateur des *Lettres persanes.*" *Revue des Deux Mondes,* May 15, 1951, 348–54.

Rahe, Paul A. "The Book That Never Was: Montesquieu's *Considerations on the Romans* in Historical Context." *History of Political Thought* 26 (2005): 43–89.

Ranum, Orest. "Personality and Politics in the *Persian Letters.*" *Political Science Quarterly* 84 (1969): 606–27.

Rosso, Corrado. "Montesquieu et l'humanisme latin." *Cahiers de l'Association internationale des etudes françaises* 35 (1983): 235–50.

Shackleton, Robert. "Bayle and Montesquieu." In *Pierre Bayle: Le Philosophe de Rotterdam,* edited by Paul Dibon, 142–49. Amsterdam, 1959.

———. "The Evolution of Montesquieu's Theory of Climate." *Revue internationale de philosophie* 33–34 (1955): 317–29.

———. "La Genèse de *l'Esprit des lois.*" *Revue d'Histoire Littéraire de la France* 52 (1952): 425–38. Reprinted in *Essays on Montesquieu and on the Enlightenment,* edited by David Gilson and Martin Smith, 49–63. Oxford: Voltaire Foundation, 1988. Cited as Shackleton in the text.

———. "Montesquieu and Machiavelli: A Reappraisal." *Comparative Literature Studies* (1964): 1–13.

———. "Montesquieu, Bolingbroke, and the Separation of Powers." *French Studies* (1949): 25–38.

Shklar, Judith. "Montesquieu and the New Republicanism." In *Machiavelli and Republicanism,* edited by Gisela Bock, Quentin Skinner, and Maurizio Viroli, 265–80. New York: Cambridge University Press, 1990.

Solé, Jacques, "Montesquieu et la Régence." In *La Régence,* 125–30. Paris: Centre aixois d'Etudes et de Recherches sur le XVIIIe siècle, 1970.

Sullivan, Vicki. "Against the Despotism of a Republic: Montesquieu's Correction of Machiavelli in the Name of the Security of the Individual." *History of Political Thought* 27 (2006): 263–89.

Venturi, Franco. "Oriental Despotism." *Journal of the History of Ideas* 24 (1963): 133–42.

Wright, J. Kent. "A Rhetoric of Aristocratic Reaction? Nobility in *De l'esprit des lois.*" In *The French Nobility in the Eighteenth Century: Reassessments and New Approaches,* edited by Jay M. Smith, 227–51. University Park: Pennsylvania State University Press, 2006.

Reference Works and Periodicals

Benrekassa, Georges, ed. *Les Manuscrits de Montesquieu: Secrétaires, Ecritures, Datations.* Cahiers Montesquieu 8. Naples: Liguori Editore, 2004.

Cahiers Montesquieu. Collections of scholarly papers published from time to time by the Neapolitan press Liguori and by the Voltaire Foundation, spanning the years 1993 to 2005. See the individual titles elsewhere in this section.

Desgraves, Louis, ed. *Catalogue de la bibliothèque de Montesquieu.* Geneva: Droz, 1954. A detailed record of Montesquieu's extraordinary private library at the château de la Brède near Bordeaux. Abbreviated *Catalogue* in the text. There is an update by Françoise Weil (Oxford: Voltaire Foundation, 1999); it is Cahiers Montesquieu 4.

———. *Chronologie de la vie et des œuvres de Montesquieu.* Paris: Champion, 1998. A nearly day by day account of the transactions—financial, legal, personal, and literary—that Montesquieu was engaged in throughout his life.

Dictionnaire de l'Académie Française. Paris, 1694, 1762, 1798, 1835, and 1932–35. The standard dictionary of correct French. Cited as *DAF* in the text.

Dictionnaire électronique Montesquieu. http://dictionnaire-montesquieu.ens-lyon.fr/index.php. Hundreds of scholarly essays on names, places, things, and ideas featured in Montesquieu's work, brought online by the Centre National de la Recherche Scientifique and the Ecole Normale Supérieure of Lyon in 2008.

Ehrard, Jean, ed. *Montesquieu du Nord au Sud.* Cahiers Montesquieu 6. Naples: Liguori Editore, 2000.

————. *Montesquieu, l'état et la religion.* Cahiers Montesquieu. Sofia: Iztok-Zapad, 2007.

Encyclopédie, ou Dictionnaire raisonné des sciences, des arts et des métiers, par une Société des gens de lettres. Edited by Denis Diderot and Jean Le Rond d'Alembert. 17 vols. Paris: Briasson et al., 1751–67. Cited as *Encyclopédie* in the text. Montesquieu's only contribution was his essay on taste.

Féraud, Jean-François. *Dictionnaire critique de la langue française.* Marseille: Mossy, 1787–88. Often helpful for its lengthy and perceptive discussions of changes in grammatical practice over time.

Furetière, Antoine. *Dictionnaire universel contenant generalement tous les mots françois tant vieux que modernes et les termes de toutes les sciences et des arts.* 3 vols. The Hague: Leers, 1690. Contains more of the informal French usage than the French Academy dictionary.

Isambert, M., et al., *Recueil général des anciennes lois françaises.* 29 vols. Paris, 1822–33. The standard compendium of French royal laws before the Revolution of 1789.

Larrère, Catherine, ed. *Montesquieu, œuvre ouverte? (1748–1755).* Cahiers Montesquieu 9. Naples: Liguori Editore, 2005.

Lauriol, Claude, ed. *La Beaumelle et le "montesquieusisme."* Cahiers Montesquieu 3. Naples: Liguori Editore, 1996.

Littré, Emile. *Dictionnaire de la langue française.* Paris: Hachette, 1877. The standard historical dictionary of French.

Mass, Edgar, and Alberto Postigliola, eds. *Lectures de Montesquieu.* Cahiers Montesquieu 1. Naples: Liguori Editore, 1993.

Palumbo, Maria Grazia Bottaro, and Alberto Postigliola, eds. *L'Europe de Montesquieu.* Cahiers Montesquieu 2. Naples: Liguori Editore, 1995.

Porret, Michel, and Catherine Volpilhac-Auger, eds. *Le Temps de Montesquieu.* Geneva: Droz, 2002. Papers from an international colloquium held in Geneva, October 1998.

Revue Montesquieu. A publication for the Société Montesquieu by the Université-Stendhal of Grenoble 3. It began as an annual journal in 1997, moving to a biennial format in 2003. See especially no. 7 (2003–4) for the *Pensées.*

Volpilhac-Auger, Catherine, ed. *Montesquieu: Les années de formation (1689–1720)*. Cahiers Montesquieu 5. Naples: Liguori Editore, 1999.

Volpilhac-Auger, Catherine, and Claire Bustarret, eds. *L'Atelier de Montesquieu: Manuscrits inédits de La Brède*. Cahiers Montesquieu 7. Naples: Liguori Editore, 2001.

Index

Locators: Entries in the index are located by both page number, first, and then *pensée* number, in square brackets: 279[1006], for instance, refers the reader to *pensée* number 1006 on page 279. Footnotes are indicated by an "n" in the locator number. Thus 656[1280]n2 references note number 2 to *pensée* number 1280 on page 656. Page numbers in *italics* indicate illustrative material.

Names: Conventions for the indexing and alphabetization of names vary between countries and time periods, and can be confusing for readers to remember. In this index, the following rules have been applied:

French people with secular titles are indexed under their titles, not their surnames, as that is standard French practice and also how Montesquieu generally refers to them. Judith-Charlotte de Gontaud-Biron, Countess of Bonneval, for instance, will be found under Bonneval, not Gontaud-Biron. If Montesquieu refers to them by surname, however, which he sometimes does, or if the person is best known to history by his or her surname (Diane de Poitiers, Duchess of Valentinois, for instance), the person will be found under both surname and title. French princes of the blood with titles are listed by title (Bourbon, Louis-Henri, Duke of). Persons with clerical titles (e.g., Jacques-Bénigne Bossuet, bishop of Meaux) are listed as Montesquieu referred to them, and if necessary double-posted under both surname and title.

French names including *d'* and *de* are indexed at the main element; names including *Du, La,* and *Le* are indexed at those elements; and names beginning with *de La* are indexed at *La,* according to French convention and *The Chicago Manual of Style*:

A:	d'Aydie, Chevalier	L:	La Beaumelle, Laurent Angliviel de
B:	Berville, Mme de		La Borde, Vivien de
D:	Du Châtelet, Emilie		Le Moyne, Pierre

The English aristocracy are conventionally listed under both surname and title, so regardless of how Montesquieu refers to them, you will find them indexed in both places. Royal personages are generally listed by first name; Philip II (king of Spain) is in the *P*s. Persons who lived in the middle ages and who did not have proper surnames are generally listed by what we would call their first name: John Capistrano, Raoul II of Brienne. Ancient Romans are entered under the name most commonly used or the name which Montesquieu uses, with their full name in parentheses where appropriate or useful: Titus-Livy, Sulla (Lucius Cornelius Sulla), Sulpicius (Publius Sulpicius Rufus).

Montesquieu's name, in non-bibliographical entries, is abbreviated as *M* when it is not the initial word in the entry.

Barckhausen's topical rubrics: The first printed edition of the *pensées* reorganized
Montesquieu's thoughts by thematic categories, a practice adopted in some later editions
of *My Thoughts* as well. Since these terms and their subcategories are familiar to many
readers of Montesquieu, they have been retained in the index as entries, or as cross-
references to topics more in line with modern thought processes—hence the retention of
the "psychology" entry and its peculiar (to contemporary readers) subentries. The diligent
researcher can find a separate and complete listing of these topics in the "Thematic Table."

Epodes (Horace), 264[926]n1
equality: Christianity promulgating, 175[503];
through misfortune, 7[23]; women not
claiming, 511–12[1726]
Erasistratus, 307[1146]
Ercokko (Quaquen; Sudanese port), 107[270]
Erechtheus, 171[488]
escheat and shipwreck, right of, 99–100[246]
Escobar y Mendoza, Antonio de, 290–91[1059]
esprit: of ancient Greeks, 401[1354]; *bel-esprit*
versus, 411[1423]; in children, 295[1090], 411–
12[1426]; conciliation, spirit of, 649[2162]; of
conversation, 502[1682]; defined, 502[1682];
disdain in order to display wit, 444[1542];
English versus French versus Italian, 147[376];
evidence or display of, 211[686], 265[937],
634[2056]; general propositions, delight in
making, 456[1597]; general spirit of a nation,
570[1903]; in geometers, 643[2116]; humor
versus, 435–37[1530]; from insane asylums,
404[1376]; loss of taste for things requiring,
291[1062]; M's use of term, xx, 211[686]
n1, 275[987]n1; Ovid, as flaw of, 656[2180];
parental effects on, 295[1090], 411–12[1426];
princes, wit in conversation with, 319[1193];
quick-wittedness, evidence of, 288[1049];
relativity of, 310[1160]; ridiculousness,
perception of, 649[2163]; of sensible people,
273[971]; simplicity as form of, 295[1088];
of singular people, 20[52]; smart people
versus fools, 275[987], 292[1066], 294[1081],
295[1090], 295[1091], 296[1094], 401[1358],
410[1410], 414[1439], 607[1982]; talent,
defining, 412[1428]; temperament as the
passion of the mind, 387[1303]; terminology
for wit, humor, sense, and understanding,
in English versus French, 211[685]; of
thinking versus amusing people, 273[972];
vision, capacity for, 635[2061]; vivacity
versus composure in, 415[1443]; of Voltaire,
652[2175]; in women, 295[1090], 305[1129],
642–43[2115]
l'Esprit des lois (Montesquieu). See *Spirit of the
Laws*
Essais de morale (Moral Essays; Nicole, 1671–78),
234[797]n1, 605[1970]n1
*Essai sur les causes qui peuvent affecter les esprits
et les caractères* (Essay on the causes that can
affect minds and characters; Montesquieu),
39[113]n1, 98[241]n1, 138[348]n1, 317[1187]n2,
318–19[1191–1192], 629–30[2035]

Essai sur les principes du droit et de la morale
(Essay on the principles of law and morals;
d'Aube, 1743), 481[1647]n1
Essays (Montaigne, 1580), 100[247]n1
Essonne (Montlhéry), battle of (1465),
367–68[1302]
Esther (Racine, 1689), 657[2181]
d'Estrades, Godefroy, Count, 386[1302]
d'Estrades, Jean-François, Abbé of Moissac,
277[1003]
Etampes, Anne de Pisseleu, Duchess of,
372[1302]
Ethiopia, 533–34[1796–98]
Ethnica (Stephanus of Byzantium), 46[139]n1
ethnic and racial characteristics: Bohemian
leagues, 310[1164]; capital cities influencing,
454[1581]; climate, attributed to, 256[889],
356[1296]; commingling of, 30[87]; cruelties
peculiar to, 475[1638]; death for Romans
versus Christians, 203[646]; Dutch, 193[592]–
English, 7[26], 72–73[196], 130[310],
132[321], 147[376], 193[591], 214[702],
227–28[767], 231[780], 232[781], 242[827],
256[889], 275[988], 306[1135], 306[1136],
310[1161], 355[1286], 395[1326], 437–38[1531],
451[1570], 643[2121]; French, 21[56], 32[97],
138[347], 139[354], 147[376], 168[474],
225[758], 228[772], 232[781], 262[915],
276[993], 294[1079], 303[1119], 355[1286],
395[1326], 401[1355], 414–15[1439], 420[1470],
425[1491], 454[1581], 484[1651], 515[1732],
637[2081]; as genius of a nation, 138[348];
German, 72–73[196], 225[758], 646[2150];
homogenization of peoples by conquest,
535[1799]; Italian, 147[376]; Japanese,
451[1566]; Morocco, women in seraglio of
king of, 490[1661]; Negroes of West Indies,
564[1886]; physiognomy of ancients versus
moderns, 29–30[87]; Roman, 7[26], 203[646],
270[962], 283[1013], 356[1296], 447–48[1552];
Spanish, 420[1470]; suicide, attitudes toward,
7[26], 130[310], 440[1532b], 451[1570];
Venetian, 645[2141]; vices of one's own
country, importance of curing, 284[1020]
Eu, Count of (Raoul II of Brienne), 315[1184]
Eucharist, doctrine of, 664[2218]
Euclid, 20[50], 168[475], 241[820]
Eugene, Prince of Savoy (François-Eugène de
Savoie), 98[238], 126–27[300]n3, 320[1196],
541[1820]n1, 645[2135], 676[2264]
Eugenius IV (pope), 177[515]n2

This book is set in Adobe Garamond, a modern adaptation by Robert Slimbach of the typeface originally cut around 1540 by the French typographer and printer Claude Garamond. The Garamond face, with its small lowercase height and restrained contrast between thick and thin strokes, is a classic "old-style" face and has long been one of the most influential and widely used typefaces.

Printed on paper that is acid-free and meets the requirements of the American National Standard for Permanence of Paper for Printed Library Materials, z39.48-1992. ∞

Book design by Erin Kirk New, Watkinsville, Georgia
Typography by Newgen North America, Austin, Texas
Printed and bound by Worzalla Publishing Company, Stevens Point, Wisconsin